ENDKAMPF

Soldiers, Civilians, and the Death
of the Third Reich

STEPHEN G. FRITZ

THE UNIVERSITY PRESS OF KENTUCKY

Publication of this volume was made possible in part by a grant
from the National Endowment for the Humanities.

Editorial and Sales Offices: The University Press of Kentucky
663 South Limestone Street, Lexington, Kentucky 40508-4008
www.kentuckypress.com

04 05 06 07 08   5 4 3 2 1

Maps by Julia Swanson

*Every effort has been made to acquire permission to reproduce the illustrations in this book.
Any error or omission brought to the author's attention will be corrected.*

The Library of Congress Cataloging-in-Publication Data
Fritz, Stephen G., 1949-
Endkampf : soldiers, civilians, and the death of the Third Reich / Stephen G. Fritz.
p. cm.
Includes bibliographical references and index.
ISBN 0-8131-2325-9 (alk. paper)
1. World War, 1939-1945—Campaigns—Germany—Franconia.
2. World War, 1939-1945—Social aspects—Germany. 3. Franconia
(Germany)—History—20th century. I. Title.
D757.9.F68F75 2004
940.53'433—dc22
2004010763

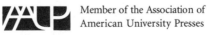

CONTENTS

LIST OF MAPS

ABBREVIATIONS
AND FOREIGN TERMS

AD	Armored Division
AIB	Armored Infantry Battalion
AJC	American Jewish Committee
Alpenfestung	Alpine Fortress (national redoubt)
Ami	American (German slang)
Armeekorps	German army corps
BaStAM	*Bayerisches Hauptstaatsarchiv München* (Bavarian State Archives, Munich)
BdM	*Bund deutscher Mädel* (League of German Girls)
Bezirksamt	local government district office
CAD	Civil Affairs Division
Cav Rcnz Sq	Cavalry Reconnaissance Squadron
CC	Combat Command
CIC	Counter Intelligence Corps
DP	displaced person
Edelweiss Piraten	Edelweiss Pirates (dissident youth gangs)
FO	Forward Observer (artillery)
Freikorps	German paramilitary groups
G-2	Intelligence section (U.S. Army)
Gauleiter	Nazi Party regional leader
Gebirgsdivision	mountain division
Gebirgsjäger	German mountain troops

Gestapo	*Geheime Staatspolizei* (Secret State Police)
GI	government issue (American infantryman)
HJ	*Hitler Jugend* (Hitler Youth)
ID	Infantry Division
IR	Infantry Regiment
Jabos	*Jagdbomber* (fighter-bombers)
JDC	(Jewish) Joint Distribution Committee
JIC	Joint Intelligence Committee (for SHAEF)
Kampfgruppe	ad hoc German battle group
Kraft durch Freude	Strength through Joy (Nazi organization)
Kreisleiter	Nazi Party district leader
Landkreis	county
Landser	German infantryman
LKA	*Landeskirchliches Archiv Nürnberg* (State Church Archives, Nuremberg)
LRA	*Landratsamt* (district administrative office)
MG	Military Government
NA	U.S. National Archives (College Park, Md.)
Nibelungentreue	blind loyalty
NSDAP	*Nationalsozialistische Deutsche Arbeiterpartei* (National Socialist German Workers Party)
OMGBY	Office of Military Government for Bavaria
OMGUS	Office of Military Government for the United States
OKW	*Oberkommando der Wehrmacht* (German Armed Forces High Command)
Organization Todt	German engineering/construction unit
Ortsgruppenleiter	Nazi Party local leader
OSS	Office of Strategic Services
Panzerfaust	one-shot antitank weapon
Panzergrenadier	armored infantry
Panzergrenadier Division	armored infantry division
Panzerkampfgruppe	armored battle group
PWD	Psychological Warfare Division, U.S. Army
Pz	*Panzer* (tank, armored)
RAD	*Reichsarbeitsdienst* (Reich Labor Service)
Regierung	government
Regierungspräsident	chief administrator of a region

ABBREVIATIONS AND FOREIGN TERMS

Reichstag	parliament
RG	Record Group
ROB	Reserve Officers Battalion
RSHA	*Reichssicherheitshauptamt* (Reich Main Security Office)
SA	*Sturmabteilung* (Storm Troopers)
SD	*Sicherheitsdienst* (Security Service, part of the RSHA)
SHAEF	Supreme Headquarters Allied Expeditionary Force
Sicherheitspolizei	security police
Spruchkammer	denazification court
SS	*Schutzstaffel* (elite Nazi troops)
StAN	*Staatsarchiv Nürnberg* (Bavarian State Archives, Nuremberg)
Tiefflieger	low-flying fighter-bombers
Tk Bn	Tank Battalion
UNRRA	United Nations Relief and Rehabilitation Agency
USFET	United States Forces European Theater
VGD	*Volksgrenadier Division*
Volk	people, nation
völkisch	national, populist
Volksgemeinschaft	national community, people's community
Volkssturm	"people's storm" (German national militia)
Waffen-SS	armed or combat SS
Wehrkraftzersetzung	undermining of the war effort
Wehrkreis	military district
Wehrmacht	German armed forces (often used to refer specifically to the army)
Werwolf	werewolf; Nazi guerrilla and resistance movement
Wolfsangel	wolf trap (a *Werwolf* symbol)

COMPARATIVE RANKS

U.S. Army	German Army	SS
General of the Army	Generalfeldmarschall (Field Marshal)	None
General	Generaloberst (Colonel General)	Oberstgruppenführer
Lieutenant General	General	Obergruppenführer
Major General	Generalleutnant	Gruppenführer
Brigadier General	Generalmajor	Brigadeführer
None	None	Oberführer
Colonel	Oberst	Standartenführer
Lieutenant Colonel	Oberstleutnant	Obersturmbannführer
Major	Major	Sturmbannführer
Captain	Hauptmann	Hauptsturmführer
First Lieutenant	Oberleutnant	Obersturmführer
Second Lieutenant	Leutnant	Untersturmführer
Master Sergeant	Stabsfeldwebel	Sturmscharführer
Technical Sergeant	Oberfeldwebel	Hauptscharführer
Staff Sergeant	Feldwebel	Oberscharführer
Sergeant	Unterfeldwebel	Scharführer
Corporal	Unteroffizier	Rottenführer
Private	Gefreiter	Sturmmann

PREFACE

In assessing the dissolution of Hitler's regime, the prominent German historian Hans Mommsen has claimed that from 1943 on, the Third Reich was in an accelerating process of internal dissolution, a situation that prompted the most radical members of the party, state, and military increasingly to assert control and assume new tasks. Further, Mommsen contends that in the last year of the war the Nazi Party embraced an "all-encompassing ideological mobilization," returning to the revolutionary ambitions of the *Kampfzeit*, the period of struggle leading to power. As part of this marshaling of support, the key goal was to cultivate "a fanatical will to hold on" and to demonstrate that the *Volksgemeinschaft* (national community) "possessed a massed will to action." To Mommsen, the breakdown of the state opened for ardent Nazis the possibility of a revival of notions of a revolutionary makeover of German society, which not only required the total mobilization of the people but also mass terror directed against any recalcitrant members of the national community.[1]

As Mommsen noted, in Adolf Hitler's last official proclamation, dated February 24, 1945, he stressed "our unshakeable will" to fight on, evoking a vision of protracted struggle on German soil, one in which the western Allies in particular would tire of fighting a desperate foe determined to defend every village and house to the last man. If defeat could not be averted, Hitler, Goebbels, and other top Nazis seemed intent on securing "the victory of the National Socialist idea" in the future. As part of this endeavor Goebbels struggled to create an effective *Werwolf* (Nazi guerrilla) movement, both to promote guerrilla war as well as guarantee the survival of Nazi ideology. Efforts to raise a people's militia, the

Volkssturm ("people's storm"), and the establishment of training camps where Hitler Youth would be indoctrinated to fight on for Nazi ideology, even after Allied occupation, were also indicative of this attempt to arouse fanatic zeal among the people. "We know that the idea lives on," Goebbels asserted, "even if all its bearers have fallen."[2]

Curt Riess, a journalist with the *New York Times,* noted that same February 1945 that this invocation of self-sacrifice, so reminiscent of Wagner, seemed to be succeeding "in making the Germans believe that even defeat and death can be—no, indeed are—something desirable and great." This *Todesverlangen* (longing for death), Riess claimed, had always played a key role in German art, literature, and music, so "what Goebbels wants is nothing but to make the Germans feel that the world's end has come with the German defeat and that their death, therefore, is a fate full of meaning." Mommsen himself conceded that the extent to which this strenuous mobilization campaign took hold among the general populace was difficult to assess, although there is little doubt that the effort succeeded in prolonging the war.[3] Despite the descending chaos, the energy and dynamism imparted by the party and its agents stabilized the Nazi system and enabled it to resist the desire of many citizens for an end to the war. Thus, in a cruel irony, the accelerating process of self-destruction actually served to create a certain coherence that aided the maintenance of the Nazi system and made it incapable of ending a lost war.

Whether intentional or not, Mommsen's claims mirror the basic ideas of chaos and catastrophe theory. Originally developed to explain phenomena in the natural world, these notions have increasingly been applied to human society. According to these hypotheses, a system in a state of turbulence and disorder is unpredictable, but out of this seeming chaos can come patterns, coherence, and a temporarily stable yet dynamic structure. Since chaos can manifest itself in either form or function, an unstable system by definition is one in the process of going from being to becoming. Catastrophe can result from this chaos, especially when a system bifurcates, or branches. Yet even in this advanced state of disarray a pattern, a coherence, stable vigorous structures, and an explosion of energy can emerge. The energy flowing through the system thus produces a self-organizing, self-maintaining, dynamic structure on the edge of chaos where, ironically, systems perform at their greatest potential. Even as it disintegrates, then, a system can organize itself to a higher level of complexity and dynamism.[4]

Finding the order in something is, of course, a necessity for historians, but order is subtle because it is context dependent. That is, the researcher must understand all the complexities of a system to gain a meaningful appreciation of it. Chaotic disorder can erupt in extreme agitation, the result of which is often randomness. Such a system would display aberrant, illogical behavior, but can also produce stability and coherence before an eventual explosion. The more complex a system is, the more numerous are the disturbances that threaten its stability, and therefore the greater the energy necessary to maintain its coherence. Complicating analysis, unstable or aperiodic systems (such as human civilizations) display complex behavior that makes predictions difficult, if not impossible. When such systems are stressed beyond certain limits, sudden outbursts of chaos take place, characterized by aberrant behavior. Human decision making, for example, has the unmistakable imprint of chaos on it. One factor that aids in decision making, though, is one's belief system. In "deep chaos" an element that helps determine a course of action is the historical dimension, a memory of a past event that took place at a critical moment and that will affect decision making, such as Hitler's determination at the end of World War II not to have another "November 1918." Order, of course, suggests symmetry, that one part of the pattern is sufficient to reconstruct the whole. Disorder also contains symmetry, in the sense that all possible transitions or movements are equally possible. Thus, it is difficult to analyze a system in decomposition, since different parts of the complex behave differently, although there is a tendency to react to disturbances by returning to a stable cycle that was active when the disturbance occurred.[5]

In the sense of a system in a state of disintegration that nonetheless continued to radiate an aura of control and seemed to have the situation in hand, chaos theory seems a good explanatory model for the Nazi regime at the end of World War II. As Herfried Münkler has emphasized, despite the continually invoked image of a *Götterdämmerung*, of a societal breakdown accompanied by catastrophic violence and disorder, the collapse of the Nazi system, coming at the end of a long and ruinous war, resembled more a slow process of deterioration than a sudden, shattering burst of light and fury.[6] Indeed, despite the evidence of defeat all around, average Germans, both military and civilian, continued obstinately to play their assigned role. The years of extreme exertion had clearly exhausted most Germans, yet hope still flickered in some that one last effort to stabilize the military fronts might result in some sort of political solution or perhaps allow time for the appearance of powerful miracle weapons. In evident confirmation of Mommsen's assertion, the energy imparted by a few managed to trump the lethargy of the many, and allowed the Nazi regime to remain a threat both to its citizens and to the enemy now on German soil. Indeed, the very uncertainty and chaotic nature of the situation at the local level aided those fanatics determined to resist, for, lacking any clear course of action, rank-and-file Germans tended to go along with directives from above.

This study owes much to the intersection of two developments: despite the persistently high levels of interest in World War II, there have been amazingly few studies of the final days and weeks of the war, especially on the western front; in addition, over the past decade or two, there has been a growing interest in investigating the impact of National Socialism at the local and regional level. As Münkler has stressed, this perspective allows one to get past the propagandistic images of grand rallies and popular adulation to the "normality and banality" of the system at the grassroots level, which, after all, was the fundament on which the Nazi regime was erected. Without the efforts of the spear carriers at the local level, who readily carried out the orders from above, the system could hardly have functioned.[7]

As with any local or regional study, there are a series of problems and questions: How did this process of disintegration play out? How much did the actions and events at the end of war owe to ideology, and how much to a mere clinging to power by Nazi officials? How much did the constantly invoked Nazi image of a Volksgemeinschaft contribute to the stubborn, persistent German resistance long after any hope for victory remained? What role did ideological fanaticism play in the *Wehrmacht* (armed forces)? What was the relationship between people, party, and army? Did the majority of civilians desire a rapid end to the war, or were they willing, however apathetically and sullenly, to do their duty and carry out Nazi decrees? Had most Germans silently rejected Nazi ideology even before the collapse of the regime? Moreover, what of the issue of victimization: to what extent could German civilians be seen as victims of their own government? To most, the war's end precipitated a sudden awareness of all that had been lost under the Nazis: lives, property, health, personal freedom and autonomy, honor, national reputation. To what extent, though, did this cause average Germans to turn away from the system?

Did the loss of so much of value disgust and disillusion ordinary citizens, or did it cause them to cling stubbornly to Nazism, because otherwise the senselessness and futility of their actions would overwhelm them?[8]

This, then, is an attempt to illustrate and understand the attitudes, expectations, actions, and motives of those at the sharp end of war in April and May 1945, and in the chaotic months that followed. The goal is not to give a complete depiction of all the events in the Franconian area of Bavaria, which in any case would be impossible, but to achieve a representative and plausible portrait of the collapse of a society, and how it affected those involved, whether soldiers or civilians, victors or losers, perpetrators or victims. Ironies abounded, not least that in April 1945, in the "most German of regions," a key question for German civilians was, were the Americans the enemy or liberator?[9] Another important issue concerned the notion of civil courage. How was it acquired? Why did some choose to resist the senseless Nazi mania for destruction at the end of the war, while others willingly obeyed the Nazis, even when they knew their actions were illegal and immoral, in addition to being pointless?

Most Germans did not experience the end of the war as liberation, at least as commonly thought by the term. But they were liberated in another sense. For them, it meant the end of the illusion of German hegemony. The end of the war witnessed a societal collapse whose consequences were a struggle for survival, a subsistence economy, occupation, and waves of refugees and displaced persons to absorb. Another important point to emerge was the limited leeway for individual decision and action: for German civilians and soldiers by the threat of flying courts-martial, for foreign forced laborers by the reality of terror directed at them, for the average American soldier by the decision of too many Germans to engage in senseless resistance.[10] Still, although their freedom of action was constrained, neither the German civilian population nor the postwar refugees consisted simply of passive victims caught between two fronts, for throughout the region people pressured local authorities to end the senseless resistance, or sought revenge for their tribulations in the "liberation" that followed. Not all the events of these terrible days can be satisfactorily explained, involving as they did a perplexing mix of military and ideological compulsion, contempt for life, self-assertion, desire for survival, fear, confusion, and anxiety, but out of the chaos perhaps some historical understanding will emerge.

In writing this book, I have benefitted greatly from the efforts of many people. I would like to extend thanks, both for their suggestions for improvement and their encouragement, to numerous colleagues with whom I have had conversations over the past few years at various historical conferences, as well as to the anonymous readers who read part of this study, which appeared as an article in *War and Society*. The late owner and editor of the *Windsheimer Zeitung*, Herr Heinrich Delp, provided a significant stimulus to this project both by opening the archives of his newspaper to me and by talking openly and honestly about the many controversial events in and around Bad Windsheim at the end of the war. I would also like to extend my gratitude to Herr Cristoph Rückert, Herr Michael Schlosser of the Stadtarchiv Bad Windsheim, and Herr Kurt Güner of the *Fränkische Landeszeitung* for their assistance and generosity. I have profited enormously from the support of my colleagues Dr. Ronnie Day and Dr. Colin Baxter, with whom I have had countless conversations concerning various aspects of World War II, from the problems of researching day-to-day military events to the question of relating local events to the larger context. I would also like to thank Nikki Lindsey, a former graduate student at East Tennessee State University (ETSU) now in the Ph.D. program at the University of Illinois, for aiding me in my research and for posing stimulating questions that forced me to think more carefully about this project. Professor Christa Hungate in the Department of Foreign Languages at ETSU has been a valued and trusted friend to me and my family; she has generously given of her time and self to aid in my research, especially in Germany. The Research Development Committee at ETSU provided grants that aided my research in Germany and at the U.S. National Archives. Finally, I owe an enormous debt of gratitude to the outstanding Interlibrary Loan Service at ETSU's Sherrod Library, and its director, Kelly Hensley, who has been a model of professional service and assistance. To all of these people, as well as those at the various archives who assisted me, I offer my sincere thanks and appreciation. Their efforts on my behalf have provided me a lesson in the meaning of professionalism and collegiality. The faults in this book are mine alone.

In "Love Song," Rainer Maria Rilke wrote of the mystical affinity between two people in love: "Everything that touches us, me and you, takes us together like a violin's bow, which draws one music out of two separate strings." This expresses far better than I ever could my feelings toward my wife, Julia, who once again gave me the support and encouragement needed to complete this project. Moreover, in addition to all of her other activities, she somehow found the time and energy to create the maps used in this book. I can truly say that without her this book could never have been completed. My wonderful daughter, Kelsey, with her lively imagination, creativity, and love of learning, has been a continual joy and inspiration to me. I have learned more from her in the past decade than I can ever hope to teach her. Both of them have enriched my life beyond measure, and to them this book is lovingly dedicated.

WAITING FOR THE END

With German forces reeling back to the *Reich* in disarray following the hammer blows of the Normandy and Southern France campaigns, the end of the war in Europe seemed tantalizingly near in autumn 1944. Readers of the *New York Times* thus might be forgiven if, on November 12, they read with skepticism two items that suggested otherwise. In an article entitled "The Nazis Still Hope for a Miracle," George Axelsson, the paper's correspondent in Stockholm, noted that the Nazi leadership understood they could no longer win the war. While Axelsson had hinted in an earlier article that the Nazis might conduct a guerrilla war from the Bavarian Alps, he now stressed their determination to prolong the fighting in order to inflict maximum casualties on their enemies, as well as in the hope of splitting the "unnatural" Allied coalition. Despite the looming chaos and massive destruction visited on Germany, it could thus be expected that the Germans would continue to fight doggedly, trusting in yet another of Hitler's miracles to save them. The other piece, "Hitler's Hideaway" by London correspondent Harry Vosser, seemed to hint at what that miracle might be. Emphasizing that the Eagle's Nest, the *Führer's* retreat near Berchtesgaden, lay in a virtually impregnable area, Vosser underscored the probability of protracted guerrilla resistance by elite *Schutzstaffel* (SS) fanatics. Not only had the area been cleared of civilian inhabitants, he claimed, but an elaborate series of tunnels and storage areas for food, water, arms, and ammunition had been carved out within the mountains. With a nicely apocalyptic touch, Vosser also alleged that the Berchtesgaden district, some fifteen miles in depth and twenty-one in length, had been wired in such a way that the push of a single button would suffice to blow up the entire area.[1]

Fantastic stuff, and likely not taken terribly seriously either by the casual reader or by any American official who happened to read the articles. Not, that is, until after the German counterattack in the Ardennes, the Battle of the Bulge, provided a shocking demonstration of their continued ability to spring nasty surprises. Yet another in a distressingly long line of intelligence oversights—stretching back through the failure to note the defensive potential of the hedgerow country in Normandy to the blunder at Kasserine Pass during the North African campaign—this latest fiasco put the Allied intelligence community on full alert. By its very nature an inexact science, intelligence assessment is a bit like trying to put a jigsaw puzzle together without seeing the original picture. Forced to process a mixture of scattered and imperfect information, some rumor, some planted by the enemy, some accurate, analysts try to take the bits and pieces and create a credible assessment based on an appraisal of enemy intentions and capabilities. Stung by the Ardennes embarrassment and fearful that they had overlooked key evidence, American and British intelligence officials in early 1945 began reexamining information, focusing on three key areas: secret weapons, guerrilla activity, and prolonged resistance in an *Alpenfestung* (Alpine Fortress, or national redoubt).[2]

Of the three fears, the latter seemed most likely and threatening. Not only did the Alpine area of southern Germany, western Austria, and northern Italy, with its massive mountain ranges, narrow valleys, and winding roads, offer an ideal defensive terrain, but German forces in Italy had already demonstrated their skill at such fighting. Furthermore, the commander of the German forces in Italy that had so stymied and frustrated the Allies, Field Marshal Albert Kesselring, had just been appointed commander of all German troops in the south. In addition, Allied advantages such as superior air power and ground mobility would to a considerable extent be neutralized by the poor weather and cramped mountainous terrain. Moreover, underground factories in southern Germany were known to be producing the latest miracle weapon, jet airplanes, which might operate from airfields hidden in the mountains.

Finally, the human factor could not be ignored, especially since Hitler had already issued any number of "stand and die" orders. Headlines in the *Völkischer Beobachter,* the Nazi Party newspaper, seemed to confirm such a determination to fight to the last, repeatedly proclaiming, "We will never capitulate," and "Relentless people's war against all oppressors." Indeed, to Churchill and others, the sustained and fanatical German resistance around Budapest and Lake Balaton in Hungary seemed pointless except as a desperate attempt to keep the eastern approaches to an Alpenfestung open for retreating German troops.[3] Worried about protracted resistance from a mountain stronghold, aware of the increasing imperatives of the Pacific war, and, not least, determined not to be caught off guard again, Allied intelligence officials set about assembling evidence to confirm their explanation for German actions.

THE ALPENFESTUNG AND REDOUBT HYSTERIA

Once begun, the search resulted in what appeared to be ample substantiation of the reality of an Alpenfestung. Ironically, the notion of a national redoubt, indeed even the name, stemmed from Swiss efforts between 1940 and 1942 to construct a mountain fortress that would serve as a deterrent to any possible German attack. By late 1943, with the tide of war turning against them, the Germans began exploring the possibility of utilizing existing World War I positions in the Dolomite Alps of Northern Italy as the basis for a defensive line running east from Bregenz on Lake Constance to Klagenfurt and then along the Yugoslav border toward Hungary. Since many of these fortifications had remained in relatively good condition, the Germans assumed they could build a strong position rather quickly. Thus, it was not until September of the following year that work began on improving the southern Alpine fortifications. That same September, the *Oberkommando der Wehrmacht* (German Armed Forces High Command, or OKW) ordered a survey of the western and northern Alpine regions with an eye toward linking these with the southern defenses. An engineering staff under Brigadier General August Marcinkiewicz was established at Innsbruck for the purpose of mapping out future defensive positions, although no actual construction began.[4]

As the Germans began initial preparations for construction of an Alpine fortress, intelligence agents just across the border in Switzerland took note. In late July 1944, Swiss intelligence agent Hans Hausamann

Map 1: Alpenfestung

sent a report to his government indicating a growing concern that fanatical Nazis would hold out in the Alps until new secret weapons or a
split in the Allied coalition produced a decisive turnaround in the war.
Swiss intelligence also informed Allen Dulles, the Office of Strategic Services (OSS) representative in Bern with whom it maintained regular contact, of the possibility of prolonged German resistance. Although himself

somewhat skeptical, Dulles conceded that the Swiss took the possibility of a redoubt seriously, so he dutifully dispatched this information to Washington, where it likely would have been relegated to the wild rumor file except for two coincidental developments in September. First, one of the many American intelligence agents working in Switzerland sent a detailed report to Washington informing of powerful German defenses in the Alps. He spoke of monstrous fortifications with underground factories, of weapons and munitions depots, of secret airfields and stockpiles of supplies. Should the Germans successfully retreat into this fortress, the agent warned, the war could be extended by six to eight months and American forces would suffer more casualties than at Normandy. Of equal concern, he predicted that the Nazis could hold out for two years in the event this last bastion was not assaulted, a situation which might encourage widespread guerrilla activity throughout occupied Germany. Then, on September 22, the Research and Analysis Branch of the OSS issued a scholarly analysis of southern Germany and its potential as a base for continuance of the war. Taken together, these reports nurtured a growing concern in Washington of the possibility of a last-ditch German defense in the south. After all, if the Swiss had created such a stronghold, it seemed only logical that the Germans could and would as well.[5]

Once conceived, the fear of an Alpine fortress exercised a strange fascination on American officials determined to avoid any further shocks like the Ardennes offensive. The Germans had certainly undertaken some type of military activity in various areas of the Alps, the idea of a Götterdämmerung struggle in a mountain aerie conformed with Hitler's personality and previous actions, and there seemed little reason to doubt that the SS would continue to obey orders and fight fanatically. Moreover, Bavaria had been the birthplace of Nazism, and many of its leaders, not least Hitler, displayed an almost mystical attraction to the mountains. Finally, because the redoubt lay in the future American zone of occupation, it would be solely an American problem if allowed to become operational. Unfortunately, despite the undeniable logic of American assumptions, much of the information on which their suppositions were based had been planted by *SS-Sturmbannführer* Hans Gontard, head of the *Sicherheitsdienst* (Security Service, or SD) office in the border town of Bregenz. Having intercepted the OSS report to Washington warning of the Alpenfestung, Gontard could only marvel at what seemed to him boundless American gullibility. In late September, in fact, Gontard showed a copy of the report to Franz Hofer, the *Gauleiter* (party leader) of Tyrol, whom the OSS regarded as a radical Nazi fanatic, in order to demonstrate the ineptitude of the American intelligence service. In a grand irony, Hofer not only perceived how American fears could be exploited by propaganda, but also that the idea of a mountain fortress made sense from a military perspective.[6]

In early November, therefore, he dispatched a memorandum to Martin Bormann, head of the Nazi Party and secretary to Hitler, that detailed the need for immediate construction of a defense line in the Alps. What had not existed, what the Americans had conceptualized, Hofer now tried to make a reality. In addition to construction of fortifications, he proposed diverting enormous quantities of supplies, munitions, machinery, and military equipment to depots within the proposed fortress area, closing the region to all civilians and refugees, transferring thirty thousand Allied POWs to the Alps for use as hostages, and withdrawing the German army in Italy, still largely intact and undefeated, to the southern defense line. To Hofer's great distress, however, no one in authority in Berlin showed interest in his suggestions, regarding them as overly pessimistic. Bormann, in fact, refused even to pass Hofer's memorandum on to Hitler for fear, at a time when great hopes were vested in the Ardennes operation, of being characterized as a defeatist.[7]

Only Propaganda Minister Joseph Goebbels recognized the value of an Alpenfestung, and then merely to exploit "redoubt hysteria" among the Americans. Convening a secret meeting of German editors and journalists in early December 1944, Goebbels ensured the dissemination of rumors about a national redoubt by expressly forbidding any mention of such a thing in German newspapers. Then, in January 1945, he organized a special propaganda section to concoct stories about Alpine defensive positions. All the stories were to stress the same themes: impregnable fortifications, vast underground storehouses loaded with supplies, subterranean factories, and elite troops willing to fight fanatically to the last. In addition, Goebbels saw to it that rumors leaked not only to neutral governments but also to German troops. Because Allied intelligence drew on POW interrogations as well as reports from neutral countries, these actions ensured the further dissemination of apparent evidence of the existence of an Alpenfestung. Finally, Goebbels enlisted the aid of the SD to produce fake blueprints, reports on construction timetables, and plans for future transfers of troops and armaments into the redoubt.[8]

Aided by the efforts of Goebbels's team, American journalists seized the tantalizing story. In late January, Austrian-born Erwin Lessner reported in a sensational article in *Collier's* on an elaborate guerrilla warfare school being run near Berchtesgaden. There, elite SS and Hitler Youth members were allegedly being instructed in partisan warfare, with the goal of harassing the conquerors and terrorizing any Germans cooperating in the occupation. Lessner emphasized that these young guerrillas, given the name Werewolves, would stage lightning raids out of an Alpine fortress, trying to inflict as much damage and as many casualties as possible before retiring back to their mountain citadel. Although confident that this guerrilla war would ultimately fail, Lessner warned that it could nonetheless cause grave difficulties if not taken seriously by the Allies. After all, he pointed out, the Nazis had the advantage of having studied all of the resistance movements that had opposed their rule, and so had a clear understanding of how to conduct an effective underground war. In Lessner's assessment, the Nazis meant guerrilla war to be another V-weapon, which, after all, in German stood for *Vergeltung* (revenge, retaliation). The goal, then, was not victory as much as it was vengeance.[9]

A few days later the Swiss added fuel to the smoldering fire. The Zurich newspaper *Weltwoche,* under the headline "Festung Berchtesgaden," reported on February 2 that "reliable reports out of Germany contained technical details of the construction of a Berchtesgaden redoubt position with the Obersalzburg as the nerve center." As the nearest neighbors to Germany, the Swiss had instant credibility, which was reinforced in the article by the accumulation of detail about the alleged mountain fortress. Running along the rugged crest of the mountains, the defensive system,

> with its installations of machine gun nests, anti-aircraft positions, radio transmitters, and secure bunkers at the passes provide evidence that the romantic dream [of sustained resistance] is taken seriously and that good German thoroughness is once again being directed at a fantastic goal. . . . In the heights around the Königssee, in the old salt mines in the area, in hollowed out mountains and along valley roads, little by little massive depots of war material, munitions, repair and maintenance shops are being established. Industrial facilities to produce war material are being built there. Airplane facto-

ries for jet fighters are being erected, huge fuel depots put in place.... Underground airfields and hangers stand ready.... Grain and potato supplies have been gathered.

"The fortress Berchtesgaden," the article emphasized, "is no legend," with its political purpose more important than its military significance. It was, the author declared, intended to keep alive "a bacterial culture of National Socialist ideology and strength" until the day when a renewed Nazism would again seize power.[10]

Little over a week after the *Weltwoche* article, a long piece in the *New York Times Magazine,* "Last Fortress of the Nazis," seemingly confirmed the Swiss assertion. The author, Victor Schiff, almost certainly had read the Swiss article, for much of his detail mirrored the information contained in the Zurich newspaper. Schiff asserted that the Nazis, having nothing to lose, would fight bitterly to the last in the hope of a reversal of fortune, and that the fight would be carried on by Hitler's fanatical elite, the SS. He went on alarmingly:

> It is noteworthy that since the beginning of the Russian offensive very little has been heard of the SS troops on the Eastern Front.... It looks as if the Wehrmacht and Volkssturm are being deliberately sacrificed in rear-guard actions.... SS formations are likely to retreat swiftly southward to a region already selected as the last theater of operations in Europe.... It will stretch from the eastern tip of Lake Constance to the approaches of Graz in Styria ... , [with] an approximate length of 280 miles and an average width of 100 miles, and a total area slightly larger than Switzerland.... It would be comparatively easy to defend this "fortress" for a very long time with some twenty divisions ... behind the formidable barrier of the gigantic chain of central and eastern Alps. ... The few gaps in the valleys ... can be sealed with more fortifications and pill-boxes dug in the rocks, and [there is] little doubt that the Todt Organization is already being used to the limit for that purpose.... We can assume that the Nazi High Command has started hoarding reserves of arms, munitions, oil, food, and textiles in a series of underground depots within the Alpine quadrangle.

Pointing to the difficulty posed by such an Alpine fortress, Schiff observed, "If they succeeded in holding out till the autumn of 1945, operations would have to come to a standstill till the spring of 1946 . . . [because of] the impossibility of any real warfare in such regions during the winter." Ending his gloomy assessment, Schiff raised the specter of "a monstrous blackmail," noting, "Since D-Day all the main political hostages from Allied countries have been moved by the *Gestapo* [German secret police] from various parts of the Reich into this Alps quadrangle."[11]

Nor could this article be dismissed as wild speculation, for Dr. Paul Schmidt, spokesman of the German Foreign Office, gave a speech on February 13 to foreign correspondents in which he boasted, "Millions of us will wage guerrilla warfare; every German before he dies will try to take five or ten enemies with him to the grave." As another journalist, Curt Riess, argued, such talk played to the element of Todesverlangen (longing for death) allegedly rampant in German culture. Just as Wagner portrayed the world's end as a "Twilight of the Gods," so Hitler and Goebbels wanted their own Götterdämmerung and hoped to convince average Germans that their death was a "fate full of meaning." By the end of the month, even the Soviets had gotten in on the action, warning in *Pravda* that the Nazis had made complete preparations for setting up "underground terrorist organizations" for the purpose of sabotage and revenge.[12]

Adding weight to these assertions, Dulles communicated his growing concern to Washington, stressing on January 22 that "The information we get here locally seems to tend more and more to the theory of a Nazi withdrawal into the Austrian and Bavarian Alps, with the idea of making a last stand there." A few weeks later, in fact, Dulles raised the possibility of not one, but several redoubts, asserting, "When organized German military resistance collapses, there will probably be more than one 'reduit' or inner fortress of Nazi resistance. . . . It seems generally accepted now that a delayed defense fortress will lie in the Bavarian and Austrian Alps. Swiss sources have information which they consider reliable that substantial amounts of foodstuffs being [*sic*] collected here, and that some underground factories are being prepared to supply arms for mountain warfare." The problem, Dulles admitted, was that "it is impossible to put your finger on the particular area where the foodstuffs are being collected, or where these underground factories are being prepared." He then closed his dispatch with a horror scenario outlined by

9

the *National Zeitung* of Basle: "The most important centers of resistance
. . . are to be in Thueringen, south of Stuttgart, and in Middle Bavaria and
Austria. There is plenty of protection there by mountains and hills, and many
fortifications have been constructed. There is already an armament industry
in operation. . . . The idea of [guerrilla warfare] existed in 1918. . . . Similar
plans are now to be carried into effect by the Nazis, with their habitual
thoroughness, and aided by their experiences with the resistance movements in occupied countries. . . . There are special schools for recruits . . .
[and] huge underground ammunition plants and tremendous stores of
ammunition and food."[13]

As influential journalists and intelligence operatives supplied seemingly detailed and knowledgeable accounts of the likelihood of endless
conflict in a mountain bastion, higher-ranking Allied intelligence officials too began to fall under its apocalyptic spell. The fear that thousands
of GIs would be killed in subduing an Alpine fortress was a nightmare
that had to be taken seriously. Increasingly, then, all military measures of
the Germans came to be viewed through the lens of the apparent reality
of an Alpenfestung. The continued fighting in Hungary now seemed to
make sense only in relation to buying time for an occupation of the redoubt. In addition, the numerous trains heading to the south (most, ironically, carrying looted art treasures to safety) were interpreted as military
supplies heading to the fortress area. Scattered rumors gleaned from POW
interrogations that referred to mysterious SS movements, bombproof
buildings in mountain regions that would serve as military headquarters
for a guerrilla war, and underground production facilities all added to
the emerging picture of a national redoubt. Even the missing SS divisions added to the weight of evidence pointing to a last-ditch resistance,
since Allied intelligence had also noticed an absence of several key SS
units before the Ardennes offensive. "Not enough weight is given the many
reports of the probable Nazi last stand in the Bavarian Alps," concluded
a counterintelligence assessment issued by the War Department on February 12. "The Nazi myth which is important . . . [to] men like Hitler
requires a Götterdämmerung." In closing, the memo urged that American commanders "down to the corps level" be alerted to the danger. A
month later, Dulles seconded this contention, noting that "present [Ger-
man] military strategy seems to be built around the idea of a reduit."[14]

Not to be outdone, the Research and Analysis Branch of the OSS
issued a long report on February 22 summarizing much of the accumu-

lating evidence from POW interrogations regarding an Alpine redoubt. Taking as a given the existence of an "inner bastion," the OSS stressed that it was an ideal gathering point for all retreating German forces. Psychological factors also pointed toward a drawn-out resistance. "Comprising as it does the Obersalzburg, the holy of holies among Nazi sanctuaries," the authors emphasized, "the [Alpine] region has a romantic appeal to potential last ditch heroes." The report then detailed the myriad activities throughout the region that supported the notion of an Alpenfestung: movement of SS troops and forced laborers, construction of fortifications, road and rail improvements, construction of barracks, warehouses, and weapons depots, installation of communication facilities, and excavation of tunnels. Taken together with evidence that the greatest efforts were in the Berchtesgaden area, the OSS could only conclude that the Nazis were concentrating their last resources for a defense of a national redoubt. Continued reports from prisoner interrogations over the next few weeks seemingly confirmed this assessment, as POWs spoke of underground barracks and armaments factories, movements of SS troops, removal of civilians from specific areas, and preparation of bridges and tunnels for demolition. Finally, Allied intelligence took particular note of the activities of Organization Todt, which had specialized in erecting defensive fortifications throughout Nazi-occupied Europe. As such, they had developed a system of standardized fabrication that allowed for the rapid construction of various types of reinforced concrete structures. Moreover, sufficient labor existed in the form of forced laborers and concentration camp prisoners to expedite any last-minute construction orders.[15]

Adding to the growing Allied fear was a mid-February report obtained by an OSS agent from neutral military attachés in Berlin that warned that the Nazis were preparing to conduct a bitter struggle from an Alpenfestung. "Military strong points are connected with each other by underground railroads," asserted the attachés. "They have sufficient supplies for many months, the best weapons, and almost the entire German stockpile of poison gas. All people engaged in the construction of these secret facilities are to be killed, including any remaining civilians, at the beginning of the battle." Since this report emanated from the heart of the crumbling Nazi empire, the OSS believed it could not be discounted, despite its sensationalist message and failure to address actual military possibilities. Nor could its claims of vast underground works be easily dismissed, for the Allies knew that the Germans had already moved many armaments factories into subterranean locations, which remained both undetected and undisturbed by Allied bombing.[16]

Peering into the unknown, worried about the possibility of yet another German surprise, Allied leaders increasingly agreed that the Alpenfestung was likely a reality. Allen Dulles noted in mid- and late March the likelihood that the fierce German resistance in the Ruhr and Berlin was aimed at gaining time to gather forces in the redoubt. He then stressed, "[Nazi leaders] now feel themselves as beyond the law. . . . We know that no fighters are more dangerous than those who fight with the energy of despair. They shrink from nothing . . . , for they have nothing more to lose." According to Major General Kenneth Strong, the head of intelligence at Supreme Headquarters Allied Expeditionary Force (SHAEF), by March 1945 his office was "receiving a continuous flow of reports that the Nazis intended to stage a final prolonged resistance" from a national redoubt. Strong admitted that the "reports of deep dugouts, secret hiding-places, underground factories, and bombproof headquarters were confusing and unconvincing. No single piece of information could be confirmed." An Alpine stronghold "might not be there," he concluded, "but . . . we nevertheless had to take steps to prevent it from being established. After the Ardennes, I was taking no more chances." Echoed Dulles from Bern:

> I have reported several times about the alleged plans of the Germans to establish a maquis or reduit. . . . On the whole I am inclined to believe in this possibility, but I must admit that a critical analysis of reliable data received so far does not indicate that the preparations have as yet progressed very far.
>
> There are a number of newspaper articles on the subject, with maps indicating the boundaries of the reduit and generalities about great hidden stores of provisions, about the preparation of underground factories, and the like. Much of this is probably fiction. . . . Some plants have been moved into the mountains. . . . Some preparations have undoubtedly been made, but not yet on the scale we have been led to believe. . . .
>
> [The Germans] have neither the supplies, the transport or the men to spare [for] any great effort to fortify and stock a vast inner fortress. And, from the practical angle, the talk of

building in the mountains great new underground factories is nonsense. It would take years. There are some tunnels . . . which can be used and adapted. But new construction on a great scale . . . has been out of the question.

Still, he hedged, "This does not mean . . . that we will not have to fight the Nazis into mountain retreats. It is likely that we will have to do so." And here he added a point important to military planners: "Nature itself, without much preparation, as the Italian campaign has shown, may make the going slow, difficult, and costly. . . . Much in the way of supplies and manpower may possibly be flung into this area at the last moment, unless our armies can cut off the Nazi retreat." In late March he returned to this theme, stressing, "Elaborate fortifications are not in themselves necessary to make a mountain area . . . a formidable fortress if defended by resolute men . . . [willing] to make a determined stand."[17]

As Allied intelligence officials struggled to gain a clear picture of German intentions, they sought to supplement their sketchy knowledge with information obtained from other channels. The SHAEF "Weekly Intelligence Summary" for the week ending March 11, for example, worried that "the main trend of German defense policy does seem directed primarily to the safeguarding of the alpine zone," and emphasized that both ground reports and limited photoreconnaissance evidence of some twenty sites indicated the likelihood of German plans for resistance in the Alps: "Defended both by nature and by the most efficient secret weapons yet invented, the powers that have hitherto guided Germany will survive to organize her resurrection. Here armaments will be manufactured in bombproof factories, food and equipment will be stored in vast underground caverns and specially selected corps of young men will be trained in guerrilla warfare, so that a whole underground army can be fitted and directed to liberate Germany from the occupying forces. . . . It thus appears that ground reports of extensive preparations for the accommodation of the German Maquis-to-be are not unfounded." In closing, the intelligence summary claimed that "considerable numbers of SS and specially chosen units are being systematically withdrawn to Austria; that a definite allocation of each day's production of food, equipment, and armaments is sent there . . . ; [and] that some of the most important ministries and personalities of the Nazi regime are already established in the Redoubt area."[18]

Immediately following the release of this report, SHAEF ordered an increase in photoreconnaissance over the suspected redoubt area. As with most of the accumulating evidence, aerial observations seemed either to confirm, or at least not to contradict, the emerging picture of an Alpine bastion. Although intelligence officials were troubled by the lack of any clear pattern to Nazi construction activity and the absence of any indication of a deliberate German move to man an Alpine fortress, aerial photographs did show a disturbing increase in the number of antiaircraft sites and weapons around Berchtesgaden. In his official postwar report, Eisenhower admitted, "Although there was no evidence of any completed system of defenses . . . air reconnaissance . . . revealed underground construction activity. . . . It was believed that some subterranean factories had been established in the area." In addition, ULTRA decrypts indicated the movement in late February and early March of German military headquarters to the south. Adding another piece to the emerging puzzle, British intelligence decoded a mid-March Japanese diplomatic message from Bern, Switzerland, that reported, "considerable stocks of war material were being accumulated in two last battlegrounds, or redoubts." Although British intelligence generally remained more skeptical about the German ability at this late stage of the war to outfit and equip an Alpine bastion, Churchill nonetheless admitted that the possibility of such a redoubt needed to be investigated.[19]

By mid-March, then, the Alpenfestung had advanced from a speculative secondary issue to one that now began to influence Allied strategy. No further confirmation of that was needed than one look at the giant map that hung in Eisenhower's headquarters bearing the legend "Reported National Redoubt." Daily, it seemed, red marks, each representing some kind of defense installation, sprouted on the map like a fever rash. Troop concentrations and jagged lines of defensive fortifications; food, ammunition, fuel, and poison gas dumps; power stations; barracks and headquarters; bombproof underground factories—each day more symbols were added, until the map was awash with red dots. Although uneasy that most were also labeled "unconfirmed," intelligence officers at SHAEF, stung by their earlier failures, now overreacted. To them, the forbidding mountain terrain of southern Germany and Austria seemed the greatest remaining threat in Europe, a nearly impregnable mountain stronghold that might prolong the war by months or even years.[20]

Despite a sober analysis by the Psychological Warfare Division

(PWD) at the end of February that regarded the whole notion of an Alpenfestung as a dubious product of Nazi propaganda, and which also emphasized German deficiencies in food, munitions, and fighting power, American intelligence officers in particular had succumbed to redoubt fever. In early March, both Bradley's Twelfth Army Group and SHAEF's Joint Intelligence Committee issued summaries that stressed the likelihood of fanatical resistance in the Alps, both to obstruct Allied occupation of south Germany and lay the basis among the young generation of a future myth that National Socialism had never capitulated. Moreover, as late as mid-April both continued to note disturbing facts, such as long lines of rail and highway traffic moving toward Berchtesgaden and the concentration of two-thirds to three-quarters of German SS and armored divisions in the south. OSS reports also seemed to confirm the assessment of the military intelligence officers. Dulles reported on April 6: "While we believe that press [sic] has somewhat exaggerated extent of German preparations and probable territorial extent of reduit, there is evidence that considerable activity has recently developed . . . and that sufficient supplies and weapons have been stored . . . to equip with light arms and feed approximately 25,000 men for period of [one] year. Work on defense of important passes into reduit and on certain underground plants . . . and hidden depots has also been pushed." In a telegram the next day, Dulles concluded, "Reduit becoming a reality. Large quantities of supplies are being accumulated. . . . Further indications are that OKW is being transferred. . . . Weissenberger [head of Wehrkreis (military district) XIII] is ardent Nazi and must be expected to fight to end."[21]

By March 21, the threat had led some American commanders, Bradley among them, to rethink operational goals. In a memorandum entitled "Reorientation of Strategy," the G-2 of Twelfth Army Group noted the continued German will to resist even after losing areas vital to military production. Further, the G-2 emphasized that "all indications suggest that the enemy's political and military directorate is already in the process of displacing to the 'redoubt' in lower Bavaria." Since Twelfth Army Group's G-2 also observed a change in German defensive tactics, giving priority to the utilization of obstacles, followed by concealment, cover, fire, and movement, all of which suggested a trend toward guerilla warfare, the inescapable conclusion seemed to be that the Germans were slowly withdrawing into a prepared fortress area. As a result, Allied strategy needed to be adjusted accordingly. Bradley now proposed that instead of thrusting toward Berlin, American forces should first split Germany in two in order to "prevent German forces from withdrawing . . . into the Redoubt," then pivot south to eliminate any remaining enemy resistance. Although based on a misassessment of Nazi intentions and capabilities, this analysis nonetheless correctly noted a variety of developments and put forward a reasonable reaction to changed circumstances.[22]

In contrast, a report issued a few days later by the G-2 of General Alexander Patch's Seventh Army, which would do the bulk of the fighting in the redoubt area, was frankly alarmist. Colonel William Quinn, who suffered from a particularly acute case of redoubt psychosis, issued an assessment on March 25 entitled "Study of the German National Redoubt," in which he expected the Germans to continue their stubborn resistance along the Seventh Army's front and slowly retire to the Alps as a last stand. Quinn concluded that the defensible nature of the Alpine region, the fact that troops from the eastern, western, and Italian fronts could all converge on the area, and the continued German resistance in the Balkans and Italy all pointed to the existence of an Alpine fortress. He also asserted that information from "fairly reliable sources" indicated that the Germans had stockpiled weapons for 200,000–300,000 elite Nazi troops, who would fight to the last under the leadership of Hitler and Himmler. Already, he claimed, "three to five very long [armament] trains" had arrived each week since early February from the Skoda works bearing new types of weapons. Further, elaborate underground munitions factories were being built, an aircraft plant capable of producing Messerschmitts was already in operation, hydroelectric plants were generating power, and giant depots containing foodstuffs had been established in the Salzburg area. Quinn proposed four scenarios for the expected German resistance: (1) an immediate retreat into the redoubt under cover of dispensable Wehrmacht units, (2) a planned retreat in stages, (3) defense of the outer reaches of the redoubt and an orderly withdrawal under pressure from Allied forces, and (4) defense of every piece of German soil to the last man. Of the possibilities, Quinn considered the third most likely, with German forces in the west holding tenaciously to the *Steigerwald,* the forested peaks along the Main River, and the Franconian Heights farther to the south, then pivoting on the Black Forest and Swabian Alps as they slowly withdrew to the south. This would allow maximum numbers of German forces to reach the Alpenfestung, which Quinn had no doubt would be defended, since the Nazi leadership still had the will to resist.[23]

Although a massive misreading of German capabilities, Quinn's report seemed to gain legitimacy from other sources. The intelligence chief of the First French Army, part of the Sixth Army Group, issued a study that confirmed Quinn's fears of the potential for an extended Alpine resistance. Recycling all the usual rumors, the French concluded that the reports of underground factories, storage depots, power plants, and synthetic fuel installations, in conjunction with the movement of prominent foreign hostages south, could only mean a Nazi intention to carry on the war from a mountain bastion. Despite the fact that his own G-2, General Eugene Harrison, doubted the veracity of the French report, General Jacob Devers, commander of the Sixth Army Group, passed it on to higher headquarters. At SHAEF, meanwhile, further ULTRA decrypts breathed more life into the redoubt. A series of Führer directives in late March, especially one ordering all units of the *Ersatz* (Replacement) Army, except those that were "pure German" units, to be placed in "rearward positions in order to support the front [in creating a] strategic zone in depth on the eastern and western fronts," seemed to substantiate fears of a transfer of elite German units to the redoubt. So, too, did intercepts which indicated that SS units were being moved to the south, along with high-level military headquarters staff and civilian ministries. From the sheer volume of ULTRA intercepts, it appeared in late March that a redoubt was prepared and the Germans were moving to occupy it.[24]

There were some in the intelligence community who, while conceding that the Germans might have theoretical plans for a mountain fortress, doubted that the enemy had the actual ability to man or defend it. Nevertheless, many of these same skeptics also admitted that, given the inconclusive and indeterminate nature of the available information, the Allies should act as though the Alpenfestung existed. Not until April 18, for example, did Dulles express forceful doubts about the reality of the redoubt. Even then he raised concern over the large number of German forces, totaling well over two hundred thousand in northern Italy alone, in addition to those fighting near Vienna and in Bavaria, which might conceivably retire into the Alps and their consequent ability to hold "this difficult mountain area for some time, assuming, as we believe to be the case, that a reasonable supply of munitions and other military supplies and food have been collected there." Three days later, though, he hedged again, saying,

"Reduit is to be taken seriously but will contain so many unreliable elements that will [sic] not hold out for long.... Military preparations within reduit feverishly but ineffectively prepared." Then, on April 25, Dulles reported cryptically, "OKW, Himmler ordered northern reduit front be held," which seemed again to provide evidence that the Alpenfestung was real. In addition, faced with stiffening German opposition along the eastern front, the Soviet leader Josef Stalin weighed in with his belief that the enemy would conduct a last-ditch resistance from a mountain stronghold in western Czechoslovakia, Austria, and Bavaria. Referring to rumors of secret negotiations in Italy, Stalin in the strongest terms also expressed his fear that the western Allies might be colluding with the Germans to halt the fighting in the west and continue it in the east, with enemy utilization of a mountain redoubt the key to the strategy.[25]

That the Allies were aware of fairly strong German mobile reserves in Czechoslovakia added to their anxiety, as did the knowledge that arduous fighting would result if even a fraction of the troops withdrawing from Italy, the Balkans, and southern Germany reached the redoubt area. Moreover, the Allies had no specially prepared troops for guerrilla warfare in the mountains, and in any case wanted to avoid any prolonged fighting, for—in the words of General Walter Bedell Smith, Eisenhower's chief of staff at SHAEF—there was "a hell of a lot of pressure" from Washington to redeploy troops to the Pacific. As General Omar Bradley remarked after the war, "This legend of the Redoubt was too ominous a threat to be ignored and in consequence it shaped our tactical thinking during the closing weeks of the war." Eisenhower, further supported in his conviction by a message from General George Marshall, now acted to prevent the specter of an Alpenfestung from becoming reality. On the chill afternoon of March 28, he composed three messages, the first of which was most significant and unprecedented. For the first time, and in order to coordinate the movements of the two powerful converging armies, Eisenhower communicated directly with Stalin. In his cable, he not only inquired of Stalin's plans, but revealed his own intention not to drive toward Berlin but to move forces to the south and southeast, "thereby preventing the consolidation of German resistance in a redoubt in southern Germany." Eisenhower then dispatched messages to Generals Marshall and Montgomery informing them of his decision and emphasizing again the "importance of forestalling the possibilities of the enemy forming organized resistance areas" either in the Alps or in Norway.[26]

British leaders reacted angrily to Eisenhower's actions, in part because they had not been consulted, partly because they thought the Americans failed to appreciate the political goals of the war, and also because British intelligence officials were less impressed by the possibility of the redoubt's existence. Despite their often caustic and acerbic remarks, though, Eisenhower's decision was not based on a whim but, as his subsequent dispatches to Marshall, Churchill, Montgomery, and the Combined Chiefs of Staff illustrate, was grounded in a sober strategic appraisal of the situation in late March 1945. Although his messages to Churchill, Montgomery, and the Combined Chiefs were terse and correct, the legendary Eisenhower temper revealed itself in the lengthy cable he sent to Marshall, in which he vented his fury at British condemnation of his action. "I am completely in the dark as to what the protests concerning 'procedure' involve," he complained to the U.S. chief of staff. "I have been instructed to deal directly with the Russians concerning military coordination." In defending his strategic decision to turn away from Berlin, Eisenhower noted irritably, "Even cursory examination of the decisive direction for this thrust . . . shows that the principal effort should under existing circumstances be toward the Leipzig region, in which area is concentrated the greater part of the remaining German industrial capacity, and to which area the German ministries are believed to be moving. . . . Merely following the principle that [British Chief of Staff] Field Marshall Brooke has always shouted to me, I am determined to concentrate on one major thrust." Eisenhower also left no doubt of his disdain for British arguments advocating a "northern thrust" toward Berlin. Not only was "Berlin itself . . . no longer a particularly important objective," but, he observed caustically, "the so-called 'good ground' in northern Germany is not really good at this time of year. That region is not only cut up with waterways, but in it the ground during this time of year is very wet and not so favorable for rapid movement. . . . Moreover, if, as we expect, the German continues the widespread destruction of bridges, experience has shown that it is better to advance across the headwaters than to be faced by the main streams." Barely containing his anger, Eisenhower then noted, "The Prime Minister and his Chiefs of Staff opposed 'ANVIL'; they opposed my idea that the German should be destroyed west of the Rhine . . . ; and they insisted that the route leading northeastward from Frankfurt would involve us merely in slow, rough-country fighting. Now they apparently want me to turn aside on operations in which would be involved many thousands of troops before the German forces are fully defeated. I submit that these things are studied daily and hourly by me and my advisors and that we are animated by one single thought which is the early winning of this war." Nor did the Supreme Commander leave any doubt as to how he believed that aim could best be realized, concluding his cable to Marshall, "I will thrust columns southeastward . . . in the Danube Valley and prevent the establishment of a Nazi fortress in southern Germany."[27]

Although unspoken at the time, years later Eisenhower acknowledged another reason for his decision to opt for a southern advance over a northern one. In an interview with Cornelius Ryan, Eisenhower stressed, "Montgomery had become so personal in his efforts to make sure that the Americans . . . got no credit, that, in fact, we hardly had anything to do with the war, that I finally stopped talking to him." Moreover, as SHAEF's deputy chief of staff, British lieutenant general Sir Frederick Morgan, put it, "At that moment Monty was the last person Ike would have chosen for a drive on Berlin—Monty would have needed at least six months to prepare." Echoing this sentiment was British major general John Whiteley, SHAEF's deputy operations chief, who noted that "the feeling was that if anything had to be done quickly, don't give it to Monty." In his March 31 cable to Montgomery, Eisenhower had underscored this final point. "My purpose," he emphasized, "is to destroy the enemy's forces and his powers to resist." Left unsaid was his belief that Montgomery could do neither quickly.[28]

That the Alpenfestung existed only as a myth, as a refuge rather than a redoubt, did not become apparent until weeks later. Although Eisenhower's decision might now seem hasty and ill-advised, given what was known at the time of both the overall military situation and Nazi tendencies, his determination to prevent a prolonged guerrilla war appears prudent. In a cable to Marshall on April 7, for example, Eisenhower noted a growing problem: "In our advance into Germany we are experiencing the same thing that always happens in an invasion of enemy territory, namely, the need to drop off fighting units to protect the rear and to preserve order among the population. This task is becoming particularly acute because of the habit of displaced persons, released by our advances, to begin rioting against their ex-masters. Because of this drain on our forces we must economize everywhere if we are to maintain the vigor and strength of our planned offensives." And maintaining vigor seemed especially important (as Eisenhower stressed in another message to Marshall later that day) in order "to disrupt any German effort to establish a fortress in the southern mountains." A week later, in a cable to the Combined Chiefs of Staff, the Supreme Commander still worried that "present evidence indicates that the Germans intend with every means in their power to prolong their resistance to the bitter end in the most inaccessible areas . . . which their troops still occupy. . . . [O]perations against certain of them . . . may involve considerable forces and also may last for some time. . . . [T]he storming of the final citadels of Nazi resistance way well call for acts of endurance and heroism on the part of the forces engaged comparable to the peak battles of the war." Significantly, Eisenhower also indicated his appreciation of "the urgent necessity for the early release of forces . . . for the prosecution of the war against Japan."[29]

With the latter in mind, Eisenhower later on April 14 dispatched another message to the Combined Chiefs in which he stressed that "to reduce the length of time for which the enemy may prolong hostilities" it was necessary to "capture . . . those areas where he might form a last stand effectively. . . . The capability of enemy forces in the south to resist will be greatly reduced by a thrust to join the Russians. . . . However, the national redoubt could even then remain in being, and it must be our aim to break into it rapidly before the enemy has an opportunity to man it and organize its defense fully." Eisenhower's greatest fear, as he noted in a cable to Marshall, also on April 14, was that "operations in the winter would be extremely difficult in the national redoubt." Nor was the Supreme Commander alone in his fears. Influential journalists, such as Drew Middleton and Hanson Baldwin of the *New York Times,* continued throughout April to warn of serious military and political problems from Nazi diehards determined to resist to the death in the national redoubt.[30] The twin ironies of Allied redoubt psychosis, as expressed in March and April 1945, were that Allied military officials were thinking more like the Nazis than the Nazis themselves, and that they mistook the logical consequences of the military attempt to split Germany in two for a deliberate Nazi decision to wage a partisan war from an Alpine fortress.

In any case, without the determined American movement to the south, German military leaders might well have sought belatedly to make a virtue of necessity and turn the redoubt into a reality. Hitler had, in fact, planned to leave Berlin for Berchtesgaden. Not until late April did he decide to stay and die in the ruins of the German capital. In driving southeastward to the Alps, the U.S. Seventh Army and the French First Army together took some six hundred thousand prisoners from mid-April to the end of the month, a total much greater than their own combined combat strengths. It thus seemed impossible that any sizeable number of German troops had reached the Alpenfestung. When asked on May 5 at the surrender ceremony the number of Germans cut off in the Alps, the German emissary for Army Group G, Lieutenant General Hermann Foertsch, astounded General Jacob Devers, commander of the Sixth Army Group, when he indicated at least 250,000 and as many as 350,000 in an assortment of remnants, with the higher figure more nearly correct. In addition, the Seventh Army bagged prominent military figures such as Field Marshals Albert Kesselring, Gerd von Rundstedt, Wilhelm List, and Wilhelm Ritter von Leeb, as well as political luminaries of the Nazi state such as Robert Ley, Julius Streicher, and Ernst Kaltenbrunner, the latter the head of the *Reichssicherheitshauptamt* (Reich Main Security Office, or RSHA), all of which seemed to add credence to the possibility of a redoubt. Moreover, SS troops under the command of General Gotlieb Berger, which included General Max Simon's Thirteenth SS-Army Corps with its remnants of the Seventeenth SS, Thirty-fifth SS, and Second *Gebirgsdivision* (mountain division), did not surrender until two days later. Although disorganized, weary, and short of food, munitions, and supplies, the total bag of more than nine hundred thousand prisoners since mid-April impressed American military officials as much for what might have been as for the absence of any redoubt.[31]

If British displeasure failed to recognize Eisenhower's reluctance to incur what he saw as needless casualties or his moral repugnance at the useless destruction produced by hopeless German resistance, they also overlooked his fear that prolonged fighting in Europe would have a negative impact on both the Pacific theater as well as the grand alliance. At this late stage of the war, Hitler could only hope to buy time, but given the prospect of new German secret weapons and the growing tensions in the allied coalition, any delay in defeating Germany raised the prospect that Hitler might be able to secure more advantageous peace terms. In the end, then, Eisenhower's aim was simple and straightforward—to destroy the German forces completely in the shortest possible time. Preventing any German retreat to the Alpenfestung had now become his primary concern.[32]

"THE GERMAN PEOPLE WILL NEVER CAPITULATE"

As a direct consequence of Eisenhower's strategic decision, powerful American forces (including the Twelfth and Fourteenth Armored Divisions, the 106th Cavalry Group, and the Third, Fourth, Forty-second, and Forty-fifth Infantry Divisions, a force of well over seventy-five thousand men and one thousand tanks) struck south and east into the heart of Middle Franconia, an area of early and extensive support for the Nazi Party. They went with the initial object of seizing the symbol-laden city of Nuremberg, then advancing rapidly to prevent any linkup of German forces in the Alpine regions south of Munich. Opposing this advance, typical of this late stage of the war, was a conglomeration of German units gathered under the overall direction of the Thirteenth SS-Army Corps, headed by SS-*Gruppenführer* Max Simon. A convinced National Socialist, Simon staunchly advocated merciless opposition, both against the American invaders as well as any war-weary members of the German civilian population inclined to avoid pointless resistance. Included in Simon's command were *Volkgrenadier* and Volkssturm units of dubious value, along with the remnants of formidable outfits such as the Second Mountain Division, the Seventeenth SS-Panzergrenadier Division *"Götz von Berlichingen"* (composed in part of ethnic Germans from Russia), and the ruins of various other once-potent divisions. In all, around eighty-five hundred men and one hundred tanks of the Thirteenth SS-Army Corps, supplemented by various units cobbled together containing perhaps ten thousand men of doubtful value, along with specialized *Kampfgruppen* (battle groups), such as SS-Kampfgruppe Dirnagel with some three thousand men and twelve 88mm antiaircraft guns, were to defend a roughly sixty-mile section of the front in rural Middle Franconia. Under the direction of tough, capable, and resolute officers schooled in the harsh atmosphere of combat on the Russian front, these units were determined to resist in the west as long as possible, in the hope of buying time for what they, and Hitler, viewed as the inevitable falling-out between the Anglo-Americans and the Soviets. Fighting both from desperation and fatalism—"enjoy the war because the peace will be terrible," ran a frequently heard refrain among German troops— they largely ignored Eisenhower's late March appeal to avoid senseless bloodshed. The first three weeks of April, then, witnessed fighting in this region of a disconcerting intensity for so late in the war, seeming to

23

validate the boast of the *Völkischer Beobachter* that "the German people will never capitulate."[33]

The geographic and administrative designation "Franconia" itself indicated less a political than a cultural area, evoking historically romantic visions and associations with the great Frankish kingdoms of the distant past. Much like Germany itself, Franconia until the nineteenth century had been splintered into a series of small territories. Some political, a few consisting of important ecclesiastical holdings centered on Bamberg and Würzburg, and others key imperial cities such as Nuremberg, Rothenburg ob der Tauber, Dinkelsbühl, and Bad Windsheim. Franconia did not become part of Bavaria until the conclusion of the Napoleonic Wars. Typical also of Germany, some almost purely Protestant areas, primarily in Middle and Upper Franconia, stood juxtaposed with equally strong Catholic regions in Lower Franconia. Notable as well was a Jewish population well above the national average. In Middle Franconia, especially, numerous villages existed in which Jews made up one-third to one-half of the population. Fürth, with a populace that was 20 percent Jewish and by containing one of only three Talmudic academies in the old Holy Roman Empire, reigned as the capital of Franconian Judaism. Because of emancipation and the process of urbanization, the Jewish population in many of these villages shrank during the course of the nineteenth century, but at the beginning of the twentieth century Middle Franconia still had one of the highest proportions of Jews in Germany.[34]

With their ancient heritage as one of the founding clans of the original German nation, and their more modern view of themselves as a bridge between Bavarian separatism and Prussian centralization, Franconians also possessed a deep-rooted sense of patriotism and nationalism. Still primarily an agricultural area dominated by small market towns and farming villages despite the burgeoning industrial region around Nuremberg, Franconia in the years before World War I displayed a not atypical electoral landscape. While the Socialist Party dominated in and around Nuremberg and the Center Party benefitted in heavily Catholic areas, the Protestant electorate grew increasingly fragmented. Added to this were persistently high levels of anti-Semitism, albeit based more on economic resentment than religious or racial hatred. Not surprisingly, then, the defeat in World War I, the humiliation of the Treaty of Versailles, the persistent social and economic crises of the early 1920s, and above all the disastrous drop in agricultural commodity prices led to increasing political polarization that left heavily Protestant Upper and Middle Franconia susceptible to National Socialist entreaties.[35]

Continuing political uncertainty, threats of communist uprisings, and a deteriorating economic situation all influenced attitudes in Franconia. In the period 1919–1923, thousands of restless young men, students, and civil servants as well as World War I veterans, gathered in locally organized paramilitary groups whose politics mixed extreme *völkisch* nationalism and anticommunism with a general dissatisfaction at postwar developments. As early as the June 1920 *Reichstag* (Parliament) elections, large sections of Franconia evidenced an extreme political polarization, as radical parties of both the right and left made considerable gains at the expense of the moderate parties of the middle. While extremists in the nascent German Communist Party hoped the postwar chaos might lead to a Soviet-style revolution, the populist nationalists on the right reacted to the shock of defeat with thoughts of revenge against the alleged "November criminals"—above all, socialists, communists, and Jews—which they held responsible for Germany's collapse. "In reality," noted one early National Socialist leader in Franconia, "the war is not yet over and therefore it is still not lost."[36]

The proliferation of völkisch paramilitary groups in Upper and Middle Franconia seemed to substantiate such a conviction, as organizations such as *Bund Oberland, Freikorps Oberland, Wiking Bund, Grenzschutz Nordbayern, Bund Frankenland,* and the *Deutschvölkische Schutz- und Trutzbund* asserted considerable political clout. Not only did these groups create a valuable personal network of populist nationalists, numbering among their members such later Nazi Party luminaries as Julius Streicher, Dietrich Eckart, Reinhard Heydrich, and Fritz Sauckel, but they also furnished much of the later political and ideological strategy used by the Nazis with such success in Franconia. The *Schutz- und Trutzbund,* for example, stressed "the pernicious and destructive influence of Jewry . . . and [considered] the removal of this influence to be necessary for the . . . salvation of German Kultur," while another early völkisch nationalist, Carl Maerz, energized a not inconsiderable following of workers in Nuremberg with his attacks on "Jewish materialism." His efforts to initiate a leftist anti-Semitism were continued after his death in 1921 by Streicher, the elementary schoolteacher and notorious Jew-baiter who in Middle Franconia sought to attract worker support through a policy of extreme nationalism and anti-Semitism.[37]

Then in his mid-thirties, Julius Streicher was a decorated war veteran, having won the Iron Cross First Class, who evidently developed an extreme hatred for Jews only after the defeat of 1918. "Through the study of books, as well as by a great many observations and experiences," Streicher related to a Nuremberg court in December 1925, he acquired "the conviction that the Jews were the originators and manipulators of the war and the Revolution and so were guilty of the distress of our people." In this, he was not unlike his later associate Adolf Hitler, who likewise sought at the time to infuse a worker-oriented nationalism and socialism with militant anti-Semitism, and who held Jews responsible for the German collapse. Streicher displayed undeniable rhetorical talents in mobilizing support throughout Middle Franconia in the early 1920s. In many villages and towns, reported the *Bezirksamt* (local government district office) Uffenheim, "almost the entire population is sworn to Streicher . . . and under the influence of the völkisch movement. . . . Even the Social Democrats support him." The central theme of his speeches, that the "international Jewish conspiracy" was responsible for the present misery and suffering in Germany, not only found popular support but was accompanied by a steady radicalization of his anti-Semitism. In large parts of Franconia, then, much of the electorate had been effectively won over to the National Socialists even before they began widespread organizational efforts in the region.[38]

Streicher's decision to join the Nazi movement in October 1922, which he viewed as a truly revolutionary group with a solution of the "Jewish question" at their crux, provided Nazism with an immediate boost in recruitment in Franconia, as he took the lead in organizing a number of new local branches of the party. His success as a propagandist, in fact, owed much to his ability to reflect and express local outrage and resentment. Just a few days before he joined the *Nationalsozialistische Deutsche Arbeiterpartei* (National Socialist German Workers Party, or NSDAP), for example, a Nuremberg court had acquitted a Jewish doctor, who had allegedly poisoned two local girls with a contraceptive, of manslaughter. Not only did the verdict outrage völkisch elements in the city, but Streicher's public reaction illustrated well his peculiar propagandistic mix of racial hatred and pornographic sensationalism. However repulsive they appear now, Streicher's tactics certainly proved successful, as he combined sentimentality, emotional intensity, violent threats, and utopian promises in an effort to gain total commitment to the Nazi movement.

Over the next year local police reports indicated a steady growth of the Nazi Party as "young people streamed into the NSDAP in especially strong numbers." Characteristically, the Nazis also agitated incessantly at the village level and generally exhibited an apparently boundless energy. In the first year of the Nuremberg branch, for example, twenty-nine restricted and twenty-six unrestricted meetings, along with forty-six mass demonstrations and one Christmas celebration, had been held. The result, as a police report of December 1922 noted, was that "the National Socialist movement was increasingly becoming the focal point of public interest." Another report registered the success of the Nazis in attracting broad support, stressing that "a good portion of the [leftist] radical element is gradually learning to think in national terms" as a result of Nazi agitation. Significantly, many reports noted not only anti-Semitic utterances at Nazi gatherings, but also remarked on the often open sympathy shown by local police authorities, many of whom participated in local meetings.[39]

Described by Max Amann, at that time the head of the Nazi Party organization, as "the first great bulwark against the Bolshevik North," Franconia generally supported direct action to strike down the unloved Weimar democracy. Numerous völkisch detachments from the region participated in the failed Nazi attempt of November 8–9, 1923, to seize power in Munich and launch a coup against the Republic. Still, the failure of the *Putsch* did little to alter the basic strength of the völkisch block in Franconia. Although the populist nationalist electorate remained in flux throughout the period 1924–1925, the Nazis encountered scant external opposition in rebuilding the movement in the area after 1925. The greatest difficulty, in fact, lay in reconciling the competing claims of leadership over the local and regional Nazi Party organization. Between 1925 and 1928 the Nazis resurrected numerous local groups throughout Middle and Upper Franconia, so that the area again became a stronghold for the party. By the Reichstag election of May 1928, the Nazis not only gained significantly higher percentages in Middle and Upper Franconia than in either Bavaria or the Reich (9.1/10.8 percent versus 6.4/2.6 percent), but among all electoral districts nationally Franconia gave the Nazis the highest percentage of votes (8.1 percent). In addition, two Nazi candidates, Ritter von Epp and Gregor Strasser, were elected to the Reichstag from Franconia, while in some small villages the Nazis captured more than 50 percent of the vote. Even before the breakthrough election of September 1930, then, the Nazis had effectively reestablished themselves in the towns and villages of Franconia, one official report noting with considerable understatement that the Nazis "appeared to have won more and more ground in the [electoral] districts." Given the onslaught of the world economic crisis, then, it came as little surprise that in the Reichstag election of September 1930 the National Socialists increased their vote in Middle and Upper Franconia considerably. From 9.1/10.8 percent of the vote, the Nazis now garnered 23.8 and 23.9 percent, almost a quarter of the electorate. In some districts, in fact, they captured anywhere from 30.5 to 47.0 percent of the vote.[40]

Between the election of 1930 and the Nazi assumption of power in January 1933, the NSDAP in Franconia experienced explosive growth, in reality becoming in many areas nothing less than a state within the existing state. Continuing their frenzied activity, mass gatherings, verbal radicalism, and swelling violence, the Nazis increasingly asserted their authority. In Neustadt an der Aisch, for example, thanks to their majority on the city council, the Nazis were able as early as 1931 to prohibit Jewish firms from securing any city business, while Nazi-influenced city councils in other towns prohibited Socialist or Communist gatherings, spent welfare funds in a "National Socialist manner," prohibited theater or musical performances deemed "cultural Bolshevism," and blocked approval of city budgets. Not surprisingly, anti-Jewish tirades, claims of Jewish corruption and economic exploitation, lurid accusations of ritual murder and sexual depravity, desecration of Jewish cemeteries, and demands for a prohibition on shopping at Jewish-owned stores also increased apace. Indeed, in many areas local authorities by 1932 had ceased trying to rein in Nazi activities, one noting that the problem consisted precisely of the fact that "60–70% of the population have a pro-Hitler attitude." The only surprise, then, was that in the various elections of 1932 the Nazis never achieved an absolute majority in Franconia, although in the presidential runoff election in April 1932 they reached 48.9 percent and in the July 1932 Reichstag election they polled 47.7 percent of the vote in Middle Franconia. In the heavily agricultural area of western Middle Franconia, however, not only did the Nazis gain a majority in the second presidential election, but in the districts of Rothenburg, Uffenheim, Neustadt an der Aisch, and Ansbach they garnered an astounding 80 percent of the vote.[41]

Now, in the sixth year of a lost war, Franconian ardor for National Socialism had waned noticeably. With the exception of the battle for

Nuremberg, historians have accorded the slugfest in Middle Franconia little mention, but it provides insight into the fierce fighting that accompanied the end of the war, while emphasizing an important yet often overlooked point: even in supposedly "uneventful" areas actions took place that affected the fate of numerous individuals, both soldiers and civilians. For them, these events often had traumatic and life-changing consequences. As Earl Ziemke has noted, "A great many Germans died in the Spring of 1945, most of them in forgotten circumstances and without many questions asked."[42] In resurrecting and reconstructing their histories, one can draw out the larger historical pattern woven into these grassroots events, as well as impart something of the nature of life in the crumbling Nazi regime. With terror directed at them by Nazi Party functionaries and SS commanders, the local population endured frightful material destruction and sundry loss of life before the war finally ground to a halt. Swept up in the internal dynamic of war, with its characteristic pattern of order and obedience, will to survive and fatalism, camaraderie and a feeling of senselessness at events, many Germans had little desire to follow their Führer into a nihilistic orgy of destruction in the spring of 1945.

The problem, though, was the very unpredictability of the last-ditch resistance. This made any sort of orderly withdrawal from the war impossible. Those who were determined to resist injected a manic dynamism and energy that could stabilize the situation just long enough to ensure widespread destruction. So the situation at the tail end of this lost war remained more complex than a simple desire to resist or not to resist. It was neither and both—and required careful individual calculations of local circumstances, a continual balancing of constantly changing forces, and a feel for how to negotiate a path through the various dangers. Those who continued the fight did so for many reasons, out of habit, from fatalism, out of fear, as a result of self-delusion, and from ideological fanaticism, but the uncertainty they produced in both GIs and German civilians resulted in a tense and unpredictable atmosphere bound to lead to tragedy. As Reinhold Maier observed in late April 1945, the path from war to peace led through the "eye of a needle."[43] It was a path strewn with danger and uncertainty, but one which everyone had to traverse.

FEARFUL ARE THE
CONVULSIONS OF DEFEAT

By the spring of 1945, Adolf Hitler's much vaunted Thousand Year Reich had become a vast battleground, a swarm of enemy tanks, jeeps, trucks, and soldiers, as Allied troops battered in from both east and west. The dead lay unburied in forests, or under the rubble of ancient cities, or in damp frontline trenches. The detritus of a disintegrating society lay remorselessly exposed: smashed boxcars, smoking locomotives, twisted rails in marshaling yards, smoldering debris in wrecked cities, long lines of forlorn refugees. The German soldier, the *Landser* (infantryman), watched fatalistically as the enemy threatened him constantly with sudden death from the air or a more mundane destruction by tank or artillery fire. The Reich's economic chain also unwound with a relentless logic, as transportation dislocations meant fewer trains, which meant infrequent deliveries of food and fuel, which meant dwindling resources for the front, farms, factories, and homes.[1]

Even the weather seemed to contribute to the Götterdämmerung-like atmosphere. A steady cold drizzle hung over southern Germany in early April 1945, the sort that chills a man's body and spirit. Nor did the dogged resistance of the German soldiers improve the mood of the average GI, for whom the thought of death or injury at this late stage, when Germany had clearly lost the war, seemed especially outrageous. Still, despite the evidence of collapse all around, few on the Allied side expected the Nazi regime to go quietly. "It is not to be expected," predicted analysts in the War Department's Intelligence Division at the end of March, "that Hitler in these last days of a national catastrophe will make an attempt to capitulate, step down, or negotiate with the Allies." Neither did the Supreme Allied Military Commander, General Dwight Eisenhower, anticipate the surrender of the Wehrmacht without the complete conquest of German territory, despite his appeal on March 31 to German soldiers to lay down their weapons and to farmers to return to their fields and not engage in resistance. As one GI put it succinctly in his diary, "Although the Krauts seem totally beaten they are still fighting. I am uneasy about this. . . . I have a strange fear that they are still fighting because they have some new technological weapon being developed to throw at us."[2]

"BETTER A HORRIBLE END
THAN HORROR WITHOUT END"

The lack of response to Eisenhower's appeal notwithstanding, no one could be under any illusions about the gravity of the German situation. Increasingly worried throughout the month about conditions in the west, for example, Joseph Goebbels noted in his diary on March 26 that "the situation in the west is more than ominous and at the moment one cannot see how or where we can stabilize our position." Still, he detected a crucial transformation the next day, remarking: "The most critical development without a doubt is in the area of the Main River and near Aschaffenburg. Here the Americans have succeeded in a surprise advance, and in fact deep into our rear, as a result of which an extraordinarily critical situation has arisen for us. . . . This could lead to the most unpleasant consequences, for such a deep break-in was completely unexpected by most of the population as well as the few available Wehrmacht contingents." By March 31 he observed gloomily, "Developments in the west naturally give rise to the greatest anxiety. . . . Looking at the map, one could well gain the impression that this is the beginning of a catastrophe . . . , and in fact the most deplorable feature of this development is that neither the civilian population nor the troops possess the necessary morale to continue the fight." As Goebbels had realized, the Nazi regime could now hope only to delay its defeat, not prevent it. In southern Germany a coherent defense barely existed, the limits of Wehrmacht resources being taxed just to cobble together a makeshift effort. The scattered and hastily assembled detachments of replacement troops, officer trainees, *Luftwaffe* ground forces, local Hitler Youth groups, and the remnants of frontline outfits that had lost most of their tanks, artillery, and heavy weapons sought to take advantage of natural barriers, such as rivers or forested ridges, as well as the numerous towns and villages in the area, in the hope of slowing down the American advance. The newly formed contingents rushed to the front suffered from inadequate training, lack of officers, and poor supply. Hampered also by lack of mobility, transportation difficulties, shortages of food, fuel, trucks, tanks, and large-caliber antitank weapons, and further constrained by the complete American dominance of the air, an effective defense seemed hardly possible.[3]

The creeping disintegration of the German war effort also made a powerful impression on the local population. Although the popular mood in Germany had stabilized following the counteroffensive in the Ardennes in December 1944, with sizable segments of the population voicing both faith in Hitler and hope for a last decisive confrontation, morale, especially in the west, began to crack in the first weeks and months of 1945 as evidence of defeat mounted. Numerous internal intelligence reports stressed how the unending stream of refugees, the unhindered penetration of Germany by waves of Allied bombers, the terror of the incessant aerial bombardment, signs of troop demoralization and disintegration, and confirmation of the tremendous material superiority of the enemy all stunned and depressed the local citizenry. Although faith in Hitler remained relatively high among virtually all segments of the populace, German society increasingly began to fragment. Internal intelligence reports at the end of February 1945 insisted that while the behavior of the working classes remained "exemplary," with almost "no grumbling in these circles," the attitude of the "so-called middle classes" was characterized by "a profound lethargy and an extensive letting go." The reports noted typical middle-class comments such as "Everything is lost, why go on working" and "In three months the war will be lost anyway." By contrast, most discontent in the working classes, according to the reports, centered not on the regime as such, but on its failure to carry out a radical restructuring of German society in order to break the power of the conservative bourgeoisie. The general proletarian attitude seemed to be that it was high time to purge these stagnant elements, and that the Führer should finally listen to the working class. In the seeming absence of viable alternatives, most workers thus clung to Hitler and increasingly demanded ruthless action against the traitors held responsible for Germany's present desperate plight.[4]

The popular mood, however, remained volatile, as Goebbels recognized. "We are already forced," he admitted on March 2, "and will soon be forced even more to make extraordinarily severe reductions in the food ration. . . . As a result it will in practice fall below the tolerable minimum subsistence level. . . . One can imagine what the effect on the public will be." A few days later, on March 8, he acknowledged, "Although our western enemies remain deeply impressed by the fantastic fighting spirit of our troops in the west . . . , one can admit that the morale of our soldiers is slowly deteriorating. . . . [T]hey have now been fighting uninterruptedly for weeks and months. Somewhere the physical strength to resist runs out. This also applies to a certain extent to the civilian population in the western German areas." Two days later, Goebbels despaired, "Letters I am now receiving indicate that German war morale has reached its nadir. The letter writers complain of the defeatist attitude of large sections of the front, but also about the massive breakdown in morale among the civilian population." Although noting with satisfaction on March 11 reports from Allied newspapers that large numbers of German POWs "still maintain the view that Germany must definitely win the war" and retained "an almost mystical faith in Hitler," Goebbels nonetheless admitted on April 1 that "the morale both of the civilian population and of the troops [in the west] has sunk extraordinarily low. People no longer shrink from criticism of the Führer. . . . They have been demoralized by the continuous enemy air-raids and are now throwing themselves into the arms of the Anglo-Americans, in some cases enthusiastically, in others at least without genuine resistance. In some cases . . . the people have even taken active steps against troops willing to resist, which naturally has had an extraordinarily depressing effect on them. . . . [T]he morale of the civilian population is extremely alarming." Goebbels's key admission, in terms of any hope of effectively continuing the war, concerned the populace's attitude toward Hitler. As he recognized a week earlier, "A fateful development seems to me the fact that now neither the Führer in person nor the National Socialist concept nor the National Socialist movement are immune from criticism."[5] Going beyond apathy and resignation, this emerging attitude represented a wholesale rejection of the social-revolutionary promise at the heart of the Nazi idea.

Reich propaganda officials, in their directives to the press, made especially strenuous efforts in the first months of 1945 to bolster morale and the spirit of sacrifice in the west. In a typical local newspaper from Middle Franconia, the *Windsheimer Zeitung,* numerous articles in January and February depicted the seriousness of the situation and the need for a willingness to sacrifice for the Fatherland. Many of these articles, however, had a "liturgical" quality to them, in that they conveyed in empty ritualistic form the substance of the message, if not always the spirit. In a lead article on January 6, for example, Hermann Delp, the editor of the paper and himself a respected World War I veteran, invoked historical examples from the Thirty Years War in his call for "resistance to the last." But having fulfilled his obligation to higher political authorities, he left the ultimate purpose of that resistance ambiguous. Indeed, Delp's examples might have suggested to careful readers that his calls for resistance aimed more at preserving the thousand-year-old imperial city of Bad Windsheim than fighting to the last against the external enemy. Although he concluded with a rousing appeal to "iron will" and the spirit of "unbroken resistance," the title he chose for his article was likely more revealing of his true intention: "Old, sturdy city, your will to live will triumph over destiny."[6]

The difficulty of measuring popular sentiment in a society in which the regime tightly controlled the flow of information, of course, lies in determining with what degree of skepticism readers perused the newspaper, and which articles had the greatest impact. Stirring poems, such as that by a local farmer that appeared on January 13, vowing defiantly, "We are Franconian farmers / always ready to die / We protect the homeland like ramparts / And don't ask after the time / . . . We are Franconian farmers / Faithful always to the Führer / And if towns and walls crumble / We'll build Germany anew!" as well as pithy slogans like "No victory without sacrifice!" seemingly conveyed a powerful message aimed at strengthening the will to resist. For every article pledging to "strike down the sons of the Steppe," others recounting the suffering of the Nuremberg populace after the aerial bombardment of January 2, and the appearance of large numbers of urban evacuees in Bad Windsheim, each with a story of misery and hardship, likely produced contrary impressions. In addition, in assessing the popular mood, the plethora of articles offering advice on how to use substitutes and manage food shortages, not to mention the almost weekly reductions in the food ration, have to be balanced against the inflamed calls of local party leaders to swear loyalty to the regime to the death.[7]

Moreover, the steady drumbeat of announcements calling elderly men, young boys, and women for military duties, as well as urging them to contribute their antiquated weapons to the final struggle, surely shook the confidence of the typical citizen. As a refrain in south Germany went, mocking the promise of new miracle weapons, "Dear Fatherland, rest secure, Granny's been drafted to the war; Could that be our new weapon?" Characteristic as well was the sardonic slogan of those overage men conscripted into the Volkssturm, "We old monkeys are the Führer's newest weapon." Yet another popular witticism had it that the Volkssturm was "the most valuable part of the *Wehrmacht*: silver hair, gold in their mouth, and lead in their bones." Finally, the regular appearance of somber death notices, peculiar to German newspapers, announcing the loss at the front of a family member must have disheartened even the stoutest advocate of resistance. Revealingly, virtually none of the death notices, even those of SS members, now proclaimed that their sons, fathers, or brothers had died a glorious death in service for the Führer. They might speak of "God's will," or a "hero's death," or "fulfillment of duty," or that the loved one died in service to the Fatherland, but in this region that had so early and consistently given its support to Hitler and the National Socialists, hardly anyone could now find solace in a death for Hitler or National Socialist Germany.[8]

In the west, where Anglo-American dominance could no longer be disguised, what was termed by the Nazi leadership a "spirit of Americanism" certainly began to spread. Intended by Nazi officials to convey the sense that individual concerns had begun to supersede concern for the nation as a whole, which lay at the core of National Socialism's glorification of the Volksgemeinschaft (indeed, a constant Nazi slogan had been *Gemeinnutz geht vor Eigennutz*, common good before individual good), this "spirit of Americanism" manifested itself most frequently as an elementary hope for personal survival. This attitude owed little to overt political or ideological considerations, but rather exemplified a general feeling of war weariness. Few wanted to lose the war, but in general the broad mass of the population remained preoccupied with simple survival, things like scrounging for food on a daily basis and hoping to avoid the terror from the skies. As the *Regierungspräsident* (chief administrator) of Middle Franconia noted in early February, "The deep penetration of the Bolshevik winter offensive . . . in connection with the increasingly troublesome lack of coal has created a deep despondency in large sections of the population. . . . This depressed mood was sharpened in Franconia by the terror attack of January 2 on Nuremberg, the city of the Reichsparteitage [Nazi Party rallies]." Nor could an article on hunger that appeared in the *Nationalsozialistische Parteikorrespondenz* (National Socialist Party Correspondence) on February 21 have lifted morale to any extent. "Medical investigations have proven," claimed the author, "that willpower also plays a considerable role in overcoming many eating problems. . . . Only those with a weak character have a panic attack when facing hunger. . . . It is an established fact that many metabolic afflictions occur only in connection with too rich a diet."[9]

As the front drew ever nearer the ancient farms and villages of Middle Franconia, even those in rural areas who had until now been spared the nightmare of aerial bombardment began to feel its impact. "It was in the first days of April 1945," remembered Lotte Gebert. "As always I rode my bike to my place of work in Bad Windsheim. About halfway there . . . I heard the hum of an airplane. I crossed the street, threw my bike in the ditch alongside the road, and cowered under a large tree with my face and body pressed to the ground. The airplane flew away and then returned. Its machine gun rattling, all the while it looked for something. . . . Suddenly all was quiet. . . . The airplane was gone. . . . It took a while before I could stand up. I leaned against the tree trunk. Tears ran down my cheeks." The sense of an intimate clash with fate, of the terror of the hunted, also resonated in other accounts of personal confrontations with *Tiefflieger* (low-flying fighter-bombers). "We had a meadow [near Obernzenn]," recalled Anni Pachtner. "I was supposed to haul manure to it in a cart pulled by two cows. . . . [One day] as I finished unloading [the manure] a large airplane came out of the west, flying rather low. It attacked me straightaway. I thought that this was the end. . . . I couldn't leave the cows alone so I stood meekly in front of them, assuming that we would now be shot. But nothing happened and the airplane flew away. . . . I went home as fast as the cows could walk, still shaking from fear. . . . I was twenty-four years old."[10]

Individuals did not always escape unharmed, however. On the morning of April 5, Robert Beining, a journalist for the *Windsheimer Zeitung*, had just gone to pick up a business letter at the local train station, where a freight train had stood for days loaded with goods meant for the airbase at nearby Illesheim. American reconnaissance planes, he remembered, had constantly been circling the area, so he thought little of their presence on this day. At about 10:00 A.M., though, Beining heard the loud chattering noise of machine guns. "We sought as much protection as we could get under desks and behind file cabinets," he recalled.

But when we heard the first bomb blasts we hurriedly scrambled into the cellar. . . . The reconnaissance planes had called in fighter-bombers, which now began to strike the entire station complex. Again and again we heard the sinister growling of the diving airplanes, then the clattering of machine guns, and finally the bomb blasts. A bomb struck so close . . . that a cellar window blew out [filling] the room with an enormous rush of air. . . . There were also a few children in the cellar who screamed and cried and called, "Mommy, I still want to live." This wailing by the children was horrible. . . .

After about thirty minutes the attack stopped and we could leave the cellar. . . . Everywhere [we saw] craters and destroyed freight cars. The locomotive, the last that the Bad Windsheim train station possessed, was burning. Tracks were twisted into coils. . . . [A] warehouse in which thousands of bushels of grain was stored was burning. . . . But the most tragic was that two young boys playing at the warehouse had lost their lives in this attack.[11]

Trapped as helpless prey in a surreal yet deadly game over which one had no control, the constant threat from the skies put an intense emphasis on self-preservation, because the body was reduced to a state of defenseless and motionless waiting. For those on the ground, these were painful moments, a murderous interlude during which the brain linked every sound with the thought of death. Caught in a narrowly circumscribed world of predator and prey, survivors recalled a feeling that the terror would suck them in, that they were slated to become the next victim of a pitiless thirst for destruction. Enfeebled and helpless when

American fighter-bombers in the first week of April twice attacked Bad Windsheim, as well as the neighboring town of Uffenheim, local authorities could respond only with public notices warning of the danger of Tiefflieger, a warning that extended to farmers tilling their fields or herding their cattle to pastures. The incessant aerial assaults forced farmers to work in their fields only very early in the morning or late at night. Indeed, local farmers in Külsheim, a small village a few miles outside of Bad Windsheim, had become so agitated and enraged that they beat one downed American pilot so brutally that when he was delivered to the nearby airbase at Illesheim for interrogation he showed no signs of life.[12]

This complete American domination of the skies also meant interruptions in the delivery of basic food items and other supplies. Although food rations had already been cut three times between March 1 and April 12, with further warnings of shortages of essential provisions, the distribution of even these scarce foodstuffs could not be guaranteed. As a result, in Middle Franconia many people, despite increasingly severe threats, had taken to hoarding, while the appearance of virtually any food item in local stores resulted in long-suffering women forming queues almost instantaneously. At times, however, this generally orderly process broke down, as civilians began "to organize" food necessities for themselves. Ironically, American fighter-bombers presented many a Franconian village with a surprise gift in the form of a partially destroyed food warehouse or a shot-up supply train caught in a local station. Given the opportunity for ready plundering, hardly anyone could resist. In mid-April a local minister witnessed a typical scene. "Around 8 a.m. began a great running about on the main street toward the center of the town," recorded the Reverend Geuder from Eibach. "After a time the people returned: they carried great quantities of shoes, linen, cloth, and the like. All came from a large police warehouse . . . that had been opened up so that it would not fall into enemy hands. The greed and the scuffling are so great that it appears that there have been wounded." Later that same day, another "inglorious scene" took place at a local depot. A freight car loaded with food for distribution had instead been plundered, with some getting large quantities and others nothing. "Is this the result of twelve years of schooling in Volksgemeinschaft?" the minister asked bitterly.[13]

Similar scenes played out in towns to the south. A twenty-year-old woman in Aichach noted in her diary on April 24, "People are acting like they're crazy. Everyone is trying to buy or grab whatever is available. Already in the early morning hours long lines stretched in front of the bakeries and grocery stores. Everyone wants bread above all because there is not supposed to be anymore in the near future. Everyone was walking and running and hurrying." Not surprisingly, this headlong tumult often degenerated into a sort of mob frenzy. "The irrational people have stormed nearly every shop . . . ," the young woman continued. "One woman was knocked down, but the people just left her lying there and stepped over her. . . . The people are all rushing about frightened and panicky. . . . In the meantime, fighter planes returned and the people all ran into each other seeking shelter." A few days later, she again witnessed similar scenes of mass tumult. Pondering the frenzied hoarding and long lines of people at food distribution spots, "I instinctively thought of the poem about Eppelein von Geilingen: 'Die ganze Stadt war toll und voll, und was an Gift und was an Groll [the whole town was crazed and drunk, some from malice and some from rage.] . . .' Everyone cursed the Nazis."[14]

Particularly after the American capture of the Rhine bridge at Remagen in early March, popular sentiment in the west turned deeply despondent, one report noting the mood was "progressively declining, fatalistic. No matter what happens, call it quits." Bitterly sardonic jokes were now directed at Hitler, in a grim parody of his earlier promises: "Give me ten years and you will have airy and sunny homes, you will not recognize your cities." Indeed, it was now impossible to recognize cities turned into piles of rubble by Allied bombing. More pointedly, numerous comments reveal that many now seemed to regard the Allied bombing raids as retribution for the Nazi treatment of the Jews. In his revealing diary of life in Nazi Germany, Victor Klemperer, always a sensitive observer of the popular mood, noted as early as January 29, 1944, that some were saying the air "attacks on Berlin and the destruction of Leipzig were retribution" for bad treatment of the Jews, while on May 9, 1944, he recorded the latest witticism: "The Führer was right when he proclaimed that Berlin would be unrecognizable in ten years." Most typical, however, was an expression of weariness so commonplace that even Goebbels repeated it in his diary: "Better a horrible end than horror without end."[15]

THE DE-GLORIFICATION OF THE WEHRMACHT

Above all, the sight of an army in complete disintegration served to dampen the illusions of even the most ardent National Socialists. With their own eyes, the German population witnessed the collapse of the Wehrmacht, as sorry groups of ragged and demoralized men trudged through the streets of their towns and villages. "It was a picture of misery," noted police official Fritz Rust of a scene near Frankfurt, "to see these exhausted, tattered, and for the most part weaponless remains of the German Army in flight. It was a picture of demoralization and dissolution." Similar scenes were recorded as remnants of this shattered army reached Franconia, just to the south. "The whole day one saw retreating German soldiers," Robert Beining noted of April 6:

> Some were bandaged, some were not. Others limped as their feet had swollen. Only a few had weapons. Some came on farm wagons, a few still on military vehicles, we saw two on unsaddled ponies. A deadly seriousness lay on all their faces, the height of despondency. . . . My wife was shocked by the misery of these German soldiers. She cried. She also asked the question that concerned all of us: "why are we still fighting when we can no longer fight?" But one could only ask this question in a soft voice, and only then to close relatives, otherwise one would inevitably be brought before a flying court-martial.[16]

Increasingly, though, the stragglers asked themselves the same question. "What is to become of me, I've lost my home and my entire family?" Reinhold Maier recorded one Landser as asking. "I don't know how I'm supposed to go on. I'll do my duty further, although I don't know why or what for." Along similar lines, Ursula von Kardorff, evacuated to a village just a few miles from Maier's, registered in her diary the bitterness of "a scruffy soldier . . . in whom the disintegration [of the army] was clearly recognizable. . . . This is like a horse race," the soldier remarked to Kardorff, "and when the race is long since over and the horse is in the stall, a little man comes along ringing a bell and announces the winner. That's where we are now." The view from the garden, noted yet another observer in April 1945, was a "scene of struggling front soldiers, irresolute . . . with the remains of their pitiful vehicles, many without leadership, waiting for something that they themselves did not know what it was: give up or flee, fight or surrender, or mutilation and death—a bleak picture of earthly confusion."[17]

In these last days of the war, a substantial portion of the Wehrmacht in the west seemed to be staggering to the rear, many retreating to their own homes, threatened with being sacrificed for something they no longer understood. To the farmers and villagers of Middle Franconia who had largely been spared the bite of war, the sight of these wretched troops filled them with a mixture of bitterness, shame, and pity. "The impression the tired and worn-out, mostly weaponless, German troops made," observed the pastor of a small village, "was in many cases shattering and gave a vivid picture of the successful breakthrough of the German defense in the west." Another observer in the same area agreed that the withdrawing troops had offered an "appalling picture," as "many could barely walk, they threw away coats, helmets, cartridge belts and blankets, with difficulty they supported themselves with gnarled canes and pushed the wretched remains of their baggage in front of them in carts or children's wagons." "The many wounded soldiers, without weapons, many without packs, were a picture of misery," confirmed yet another eyewitness. "One was painfully reminded of . . . pictures of the retreat of the Grand Army from Russia." Indeed, the scene at Edelfingen, on the Tauber River just south of Königshofen, might have been a microcosm of the human misery of an army in disintegration: "From March 27 on heavy troop traffic, but only a few intact units, they have no heavy weapons and no tanks, individual soldiers on a variety of vehicles, wounded from disbanded military hospitals on foot, even those with amputated legs."[18]

Nor was it just the sight of retreating soldiers that proved staggering. "Many German soldiers had become separated from their units," wrote one contemporary observer, "they begged at night for food and civilian clothing, they moved into the forest and left their uniforms and weapons lying in the woods." A noncommissioned officer who with a small squad of men had lost contact with their unit after a clash near Brettheim noted in a letter, "Only by the skin of our teeth did we make it through the already occupied area, around a sawmill and across a stream to a woods. . . . In the night I made a reconnaissance with four old hands in search of a case of American supplies, for we had already gone three days without getting anything to eat. I quickly determined that the Americans were there in such a large number that continuing on was pointless. Therefore we hid in the woods, then by twos and threes went off in the direction of our homes." These were not isolated incidents, as other reports recounted soldiers stealing from civilians, mailing home parts of their uniform to be dyed and remodeled for civilian use, and openly deserting. So ubiquitous were these actions, in fact, that Victor Klemperer noted in early February both the constant SS patrols looking for deserters and an order to civilians not to feed, shelter, or aid begging soldiers. Indeed, Joseph Goebbels verified both of Klemperer's observations, recording in his diary on April 4 the negative impression made by army stragglers and looters on the civilian population and the increasingly strenuous efforts to ferret out deserters.[19]

More importantly for civilian morale, reports from many areas referred to withdrawing German soldiers as "freebooters and the population as fair game," of retreating German units behaving like "wild hordes," of plundering and ransacking of local stores, of staging "drinking bouts." One account complained that the Landsers stole anything that was not tied down and unashamedly looted local food stores, while another recorded angrily that in one small village a retreating soldier had casually tossed a hand grenade through the open window of a *Gasthaus* (inn), completely destroying it. Other reports bitterly described the retreating Germans as "robbers and bandits," noting that their actions were causing "great outrage" in the local population. In February 1945, Klemperer recorded a conversation in which the talk was of "three sources of danger: the first: looting Eastern workers, the second: retreating German troops, the third: invading Russians." Writing in April from a village near Aichach in southern Germany, Klemperer made clear that civilian fear of the disintegrating Wehrmacht had now risen to the top of the list of concerns. On two separate occasions he noted emphatically the popular mood, as expressed by several women in the village: "We are now afraid *only* of the *German* soldiers."[20] If not altogether frightened of their own troops, the unexpectedly predatory nature of many retreating soldiers certainly contradicted the carefully nurtured picture of the disciplined Wehrmacht as the protector of the *Volk* (people), leaving in its place, for many, a lingering image of disrepute.

So apparent was this growing bitterness among German civilians that the Psychological Warfare Division of the U.S. Army remarked on the "thorough-going change of attitude" experienced by the local population as retreating Landsers passed through: "The Wehrmacht is an army in disintegration and in retreat, and its soldiers are going through a nasty phase . . . of demoralization. This has strongly increased the inclination of these uniformed men to mistreat the unfortunate civilian population." And the PWD noted the further consequences of this phenomenon: "If the hostility in the German population spreads, the last concrete embodiment of hope will have been lost. For the Wehrmacht was constantly . . . a symbol of German power and greatness." Nor did Nazi intelligence organizations fail to recognize the growing problem, one commenting, "The growing conscious acceptance of personal powerlessness constitutes the root of nearly all demoralizing phenomena within the troops."[21]

Although admittedly in many areas Landsers acted with discipline and self-restraint, and helped the civilian population where they could, the comment of one Nazi *Kreisleiter* (district leader) illustrated the general mood. "Very frequently," he wrote, he had heard people say, "The Russians couldn't wreak such dreadful havoc." This attitude, along with the generally correct behavior of Anglo-American troops, proved devastating to morale in the west. Goebbels, of course, used fear to stiffen the popular mood, particularly in the east, emphasizing in lurid detail the bestial atrocities perpetrated by Soviet troops on German civilians. In noting the "tremendous tenacity and repeated ingenuity" with which the Nazi regime waged war, Victor Klemperer also observed, "They do not keep the mass of people in line by tyranny alone. But above all by the ever repeated . . . : Our enemies, and in particular the Bolshevists, want to annihilate you, literally kill you. They owe everything to the bogeyman of Bolshevism." Again and again over the next few months Klemperer remarked on the "shameless" and "contemptible" use of racial hatred and fear to motivate the German public to further exertions. Goebbels's propaganda raised the specter of "the hordes from Central Asia" and warned, "The Jewish-Bolshevist mortal enemy . . . wants to exterminate us. While old men and children will be murdered, women and girls will be degraded to prostitutes. The rest will be marched off to Siberia."[22] A perverse irony lay contained in this mirror image, as Goebbels imputed to the Russians the same murderous intentions the Nazi regime had harbored, and acted upon, in the German occupation of the Soviet Union, a fact that could not have escaped the notice of many Germans.

For their part, the western allies were savaged as "air pirates." "They are murderers!" screamed the headline of an article emanating from Berlin on February 22. Not only did the writer denounce the allied "terror bombing," he also stressed the "special joy" that the "Anglo-American air gangsters" took in the murder of innocent German civilians. Nor were allied pilots alone singled out for castigation. On the same day, an accompanying report claimed to have firsthand evidence, in the form of personal statements from witnesses, of the extensive murder of wounded German soldiers in Lorraine by American GIs. The crux of both these reports, and scores like them, of course, was to show the kindred nature of the enemies in the east and west. "I am now in the process of implementing a very strongly biased anti-Anglo-American propaganda in the German press and radio," Goebbels admitted in late March:

> Up to now we have handled the Anglo-Americans much too mildly. . . . As a result morale in the west has become . . . worse. Through our atrocity campaign against Bolshevism we have succeeded in again strengthening our front in the east as well as putting the civilian population in a state of absolute readiness for defense. That we have not succeeded as well in the west primarily goes back to the fact that large parts of the population and also our troops believe the Anglo-Americans will treat them leniently. . . . Our previous propaganda, as the consequences demonstrate, has failed in its effect on the German people.

The Nazi propaganda machine also capitalized on the Morgenthau Plan, an American proposal for the postwar dismantling of German industry and reduction of living standards, to argue that Germans had nothing to hope for, in terms of better treatment, from the western Allies. Indeed, Nazi propagandists screamed insistently that the war was a struggle against western plutocrats and eastern bolsheviks, with the malignant Jew serving as the common denominator. As Klemperer recorded meticulously in his diary, Nazi propaganda increasingly stressed the threat of "the Jewish-Bolshevist plague and its Anglo-American pimps," and warned, "If we capitulate, we shall certainly die. Because not only the Bolshevists want to exterminate us, but the Anglo-Americans want to do so, too, behind both is the Jewish will to destroy." Indeed, an inflammatory article appearing in the German press in mid-March carried the headline "The Slave Traders of Yalta," and just in case the average German didn't get the message, explicitly compared the Anglo-American slave traders of the early nineteenth century with their latter day counterparts, Churchill and Roosevelt, who meant to "sell the Germans into Bolshevist slavery."[23]

Still, this shrill propaganda often backfired. As a report to the

Stuttgart SD illustrated, when it came to atrocities, many Germans instantly made the salient connection:

> Citizens are saying it is shameful to feature these [atrocities] so prominently in German newspapers. . . . What motive does the leadership have in publishing pictures like that. . . . They must surely realize that every intelligent person, upon seeing these victims, will immediately think of the atrocities we have committed on enemy soil, yes, even in Germany. Did we not slaughter the Jews by the thousands? Don't soldiers repeatedly tell of Jews who had to dig their own graves in Poland? And what did we do with the Jews who were in the concentration camps? . . . We have only shown the enemy what they can do with us, should they win.

As another remark cited in the report showed, Germans were also increasingly bitter about their own treatment by the Nazi regime: Why should the Nazis be incensed because the Soviets "had killed a few people in East Prussia? What does a life mean here in Germany?" Still others spoke not only of the "terrible and inhumane treatment meted out to the Jews by the SS," but also of the "blood guilt of the German people" and "heaven's just punishment for the deportation of the Jews."[24]

In the west, just as importantly, the generally correct treatment of civilians by American and British troops quickly undercut the apocalyptic forebodings of Nazi propaganda. Observing the entry of American troops into his village in Middle Franconia, the Protestant pastor and staunch German nationalist Adolf Rusam admitted that he immediately found these strange soldiers to be "pleasant, likable, 'Germanic' types," with a relaxed, easygoing attitude that contrasted sharply with the propagandistic image of a cruel, conquering force. "Soldiers sat and lay around the orderly room," he observed to his amazement, "smoking their cigarettes, reading, listening to the radio, and chatting about nothing in particular. It was unthinkable, according to German conceptions, that a soldier sprawled on a chair . . . would, with a casual movement of his hand and without the slightest effort to change his demeanor, pass a fountain pen to his officer so he could sign documents!" In a neighboring town, Rusam noted, the villagers appeared to be "nearly uncomprehending" that "quite a few Americans took part in the work of putting out fires." In yet another area village, Rusam recorded an episode that appeared to him characteristic of the American occupiers. Just as the GIs entered the town a local woman had given birth to a baby. As the newborn was being washed an American soldier came into the house, saw the baby, and inquired about the mother. Upon being taken to the cellar where she was being attended to, the GI immediately sought to calm the obviously apprehensive woman. "And these are the 'gangsters' and 'arsonists,'" Rusam noted disgustedly, "before whom our lying propaganda sought to instil a powerful fear!"[25]

Indeed, occupation often proved decidedly anticlimactic. When American troops entered Bad Windsheim on the morning of Sunday, April 15, no white flags were raised, no shots were fired, the Americans were simply there. A city administrator, Gustav Höhn noted in his diary, "It was eerily quiet on the morning of April 15—we all worried about the arrival of the Americans. . . . With more fear than courage I carefully left my cellar in full RAD uniform, armed with an 8mm Belgian pistol. . . . Just as I turned the corner [leading to the town hall] I saw an American tank. I immediately turned around and rushed back to the cellar, where I hurriedly changed clothes and hid the pistol in a crate of potatoes." With a number of town officials present, an American lieutenant whose parents originally came from Stuttgart read the terms of surrender: weapons, munitions, cameras, binoculars, and electrical devices were to be turned over; all men between sixteen and sixty capable of work were to start rebuilding the Aisch River bridges immediately; a curfew from 6:00 P.M. to 6:00 A.M. was to take effect immediately. After the extreme tension of the preceding days, it all seemed so commonplace. "I was already back at work at the town hall [that afternoon]," marveled Höhn, "only now taking orders from the victors, just as a few days before I took them from the now-defeated SS men . . . [One of the first orders] I received from the occupiers was to clear the *Rathaus* [city hall] of Nazi emblems. With hammer and pliers I set about removing the symbols of the Third Reich in the conference room. All the time I was watched by an MP, who immediately took the emblems for himself as souvenirs."[26]

Just to the south, in a small village near Aichach, Victor Klemperer noted with his customary meticulousness a local villager's impression of the American occupiers. "On the first day the occupation troops had taken everything out of the shops," a young woman reported, "but otherwise had been altogether decently behaved. 'The blacks too?' She almost beamed with delight. 'They're even friendlier than the others,' there's nothing to be afraid of. . . . I went back to the main square, asked two old ladies . . . for information. Again, only more emphatically, the same response to the occupiers, exactly the same beam of delight because the Negroes were especially good-natured enemies. . . . And what had been said about the cruelty of these enemies, that all had been nothing but 'slogans,' that was only 'rabble-rousing.'" Klemperer's conclusion, "How the populace is being enlightened!" could well have served as fitting commentary for other encounters with the American occupier.[27]

Although there were instances of mistreatment—one man in Bad Windsheim, for example, recalled being knocked down by a drunken GI, while another had to evacuate his home in fifteen minutes, only to return to a "total mess" a few days later—Americans were typically viewed as rather benign conquerors. "Children were playing in the street," remembered Anni Schunk of her first encounter with Americans. "The doorbell rang. . . . There stood an American officer with a carton in his hand, wonderful things, oranges, sweets. . . . I could speak no English, showed him my [wedding] ring, wanted to emphasize that I could not take these things. Just then my 3½ year old daughter Monika came running into the room. He said, 'For baby,' then I took it." Another Windsheimer, Helmut Hofmann, recalled that even as the fighting still raged in Nuremberg, GIs in Bad Windsheim, just thirty miles to the west, passed out food, chocolate, chewing gum, and cigarettes. In the small farm villages of Mittelsteinach and Abtsgreuth, a few miles north of Neustadt an der Aisch, American troops requisitioned a number of homes whose owners had to evacuate within ten minutes, and destroyed any unwelcome reminder of Nazism they encountered. Otherwise, one man remembered, "they were quite considerate in their contact with the [local] population." Even the ubiquitous American habit of seizing wristwatches as souvenirs could be brushed off with a joke: USA really stood for *Uhren stehlen's auch* (watches also stolen). To the southwest, Ursula von Kardorff, a diarist as sensitive and insightful as Klemperer, noted that "the villagers speak of nothing but the Americans. 'When the Americans come,' they say and smile without any fear. They think nothing bad will happen and imagine that justice, cigarettes, and chocolate will take the place of bombs and the Gestapo. As rational [people] they are ready as quickly as possible to raise the white flag." Similarly, just to the east, Klemperer noted the common refrain of many Bavarian villagers, "When are the Americans going to get here?" and observed, "There are too many such remarks to note down anymore."[28]

Indeed, one Nazi official admitted, despite the occasional incidents of rape or plunder, that the general assertion in many areas was that the Americans had conducted themselves "'better than our German troops.'... Based on these experiences with the Americans, the populace ... has the highest opinion of them." In his diary entries from March and April 1945, Joseph Goebbels underscored this observation, noting with bitter disappointment the relatively good reception accorded American troops and the shocking lack of resistance in some urban areas in his native Rhineland, including a white flag flying from the house in Rheydt where he was born. Informed that many German civilians in the west were aiding deserters, he remarked in disgust, "What else is to be expected of them when they receive the enemy with white flags?" Not unaware of the impact of aerial bombardment in sapping German morale in the west—"this is a war within a war," he noted, "that sometimes takes on a more gruesome form than the war at the front"—Goebbels nonetheless fumed about the failure of party leadership and the weakness displayed by people who refused to fight on. Especially repugnant, he thought, were the scenes of Germans enthusiastically waving white flags and embracing American soldiers as liberators. "Especially in the Frankfurt-Hanau area," he noted with revulsion on March 27, "the local populace are approaching the Americans with white flags; some of the women are so far demeaning themselves as to welcome and embrace the Americans. In light of this, the troops are no longer willing to fight and are either withdrawing unresistingly or surrendering to the enemy." The people of Frankfurt, Goebbels remarked with particular contempt on April 4, "seem to have been extraordinarily cowardly and servile. ... The Americans are said to have been received with large-scale demonstrations as they moved in. The Frankfurters' watchword was 'Let's kiss and make friends.' The Americans were quite prepared to kiss—particularly the Frankfurt women." Despite his further bombastic assertion that the American goal was to exterminate the German people, the Reich propaganda minister understood precisely the reason behind the positive civilian reception of the Americans. "In contrast to the Soviets," Goebbels complained on April 1, "the Anglo-Americans are not feared by the people ...; on the contrary, large sections of the populace are glad to see them come."[29]

If many German civilians eagerly awaited the arrival of American troops, the average GI displayed a complex, equivocal, and ambivalent attitude toward the German populace. By and large, American soldiers fought the Germans with little hatred or moral indignation, at least until their advance into Germany itself brought them into contact with forced labor and concentration camps. Although in postwar surveys a substantial minority of GIs admitted some animosity toward the Germans, at the time overt hatred seemed moderated by contact with the enemy. The Landser impressed GIs as a formidable opponent, efficient in combat and superbly equipped, but one whose very skill and tenacity engendered both respect and animosity, since it was this very professionalism that threatened the GI with a brutal death. Still, surveys indicated that viewing enemy prisoners, for example, made GIs realize that the Germans were "men just like us" and that it was "too bad we have to be fighting them." One infantryman suggested that the Germans had been "sold a God and Country message by his family and Führer. Or maybe he fought to protect his family from a concentration camp. Either way, he was a victim." Another GI "recognized that [German soldiers] came from families like [us] . . . and that they had loved ones and they were good guys and bad guys. . . . Personally, I had no malice at any time toward the Germans." As other Americans put it, the "average German soldier was just a young man who was drafted," "they were boys like us," "the Wehrmacht soldiers were ordinary guys," and they could be considered "decent fighting men."[30]

Perhaps Ben Tumey best summarized the prevailing mood among the average GI, noting in his diary, "I have observed that the German people as a rule are [happy] that the war is over for them. No more bombing or shelling. Some say that Hitler was and is making the poor people sacrifice and die to save his and the rich Nazis' necks. Maybe so, but it seems that regardless of what the German people say, they must have supported Hitler and his army. Maybe it was from fear, as they tell you, or just maybe it was the kind of action that the people wanted." The War Department, disturbed by these generally open-minded views, cautioned American commanders, "Many soldiers who lack vindictiveness are probably standing on the shaky ground of too much identification with the enemy as a human being. . . . These men need to be convinced that America's very survival depends upon killing the enemy with cold, impersonal determination." Despite this injunction, which easily could have been written by any of Goebbels's propagandists, two-thirds of American soldiers believed after the war that the Nazi leaders should be punished, but not the German people.[31]

Developments within combat, however, often made it difficult for GIs to maintain these views with any consistency. As Karl von Clausewitz, a nineteenth-century Prussian military philosopher, pointed out, a certain limitlessness is implicit in war, as actions on both sides lead to a continuous escalation of violence. By 1945, therefore, the danger existed that American soldiers, increasingly bitter and frustrated that the Germans continued to fight when the military verdict seemed clear, and German soldiers, desperate to protect their home territory, would set in motion an uncontrollable dynamic of brutality. Charles MacDonald, angry at the continued German resistance, which put his own life and the lives of the men in his company at risk, illustrated well this resentment. "The fifth house was a mass of flame," he noted at one of a number of interchangeable villages at the end of the war. "A grey-haired German farmer stood with his arm around his aged wife and stared at the burning house, tears streaming down both their faces. '*Alles ist kaput!* *Alles ist kaput!*' they sobbed hysterically. . . . I was not impressed; instead I was suddenly angry at them and surprised at my own anger. What right had they to stand there sobbing and blaming us for this terror? What right did they and their kind have to any emotions at all? 'Thank Adolf!' I shouted. 'Thank Hitler!' I pointed to the burning house and said, '*Der Führer!*' and laughed." Particularly as GIs stumbled unprepared upon slave labor and concentration camps, their hatred for Germans flared. "There was Germany and all it stood for," seethed Private David Webster, a Harvard student and keen observer of war, after the liberation of a labor camp. "The Germans had taken these people from their homes and sentenced them to work for life in a factory of the Third Reich. . . . Innocent people condemned to live in barracks behind barbed wire, to slave twelve hours a day. . . . With cold deliberation the Germans had enslaved the populace of Europe. The German people were guilty, every one of them." Implicit in this assessment was the conviction that all Germans were fanatics, determined to kill their enemies, a conclusion that called for one course of action. As Audie Murphy succinctly put it, "The only safe Germans are dead ones."[32]

Nor was Murphy's an isolated sentiment. "I do believe that these Germans are touched with madness," a GI wrote home after seeing a concentration camp. "It is horrible, a real Götterdämmerung, and it will take everything the world has . . . to set us to rights again. . . . One sees the Hitler Jugend [Hitler Youth] who have no conception of any other standard than force and war. . . . We must be firm with the present generations," he concluded after considering and grudgingly rejecting the idea of shooting the Germans en masse. "You people at home must remember that; you must refuse to be sucked in on reducing the severity of the life sentence which this nation must receive." Confirmed another soldier, on seeing the concentration camp survivors, "I never knew what hate was till I saw what remains of these poor devils." "In Dachau there were heaps of bodies," remembered Frank Manuel. "Hungry, typhus-infected prisoners still caged were gnawing at fresh sides of beef from the ransacked butcher shops. . . . Knee deep in flesh and blood. Enough to puke on. . . . The roads south of Dachau were crowded with victims let out from the concentration camps, still wearing the black-and-white striped cloth of the convict. . . . Their striped garments were their pride. They had endured. 'Who is to blame?' read the psychological warfare poster across a photogenic skeleton, pasted on a wall. 'Not we,' was scribbled across in answer. 'Yes, we are to blame,' was the retort scribbled across the answer." Having captured an aged guard, who inquired why they wanted him, Manuel thought bitterly, "As Wergeld [payment] for the discolored bodies, swollen thighs, broken bones, emasculated men, lacerated women, charred flesh, there was nothing but this foul old man. . . . An eye for an eye. . . . But Holy Moses . . . he has not got years enough left, this stinking old wretch. Then vengeance upon his children. . . . Justice wants fresh young maidens and bronzed youths worthy of her blows." As Manuel concluded sardonically, "Cotton Mather could do it, but we can't. . . . The sloppy romantics of the twentieth century . . . slobber over the vanquished and the near vanquished. Are you cold, my dear little Germans? Are you hungry? Take care of your calories or we shall have to."[33]

To Brendan Phibbs, a combat surgeon in the Twelfth Armored Division, the "German population didn't project any . . . praiseworthy or at least understandable attitudes. They were shameless and indefatigable," Phibbs complained,

> you had to push them to get them the hell out of the way. . . . They were a swarm; they made you want to brush them off like flies or fleas, and they went into gales of nervous laughter at the suggestion that any of them had been Nazis. . . . Them

pricks don't have no fuckin' dignity, said the soldiers, and when you considered how they transformed themselves without shame or guilt, from the mobs that howled for Jewish blood and heiled German victories with stamping boots and raised arms . . . to the whiners that capered and fawned around us, they certainly had no fucking dignity whatsoever.

With loathing and animosity dripping from his pen, Lieutenant David Olds wrote to his parents:

I would crush every vestige of military or industrial might in Germany. Let them be a pauper nation. They deserve it. . . . I would love to personally shoot all young Hitlerites. . . . You also asked about concentration camps. . . . It is hard for me to convey it all to you. You drive through the surrounding towns where there are happy little children at play, and people going about their business . . . yet within two miles of them . . . it's chimneys belching smoke from cremating ovens . . . yet the German civilians nearby either pretend not to realize them, or what is worse, see no wrong. . . . The mass graves and reburials are, for brutality, even worse. . . . [When] being re-buried in plots dug by German civilians and soldiers, Ameri-can officials and men called all the people out of the town to witness the burial, to see the bodies . . . to have that memory printed on their minds of what a horrible thing they had done. . . . They stood there, hard and sullen-faced, muttering and obstinate. . . . A shrug of the shoulders, too bad, it had to be done.

"I feel nothing when we take a town," agreed Private Charles Cavas, "and if I ever do feel the slightest sympathy you can be sure that I'll overcome it and ignore it."[34]

Despite the indignation and enmity in these personal accounts, most GIs either failed to share these sentiments, or found that their resent-ment faded rather quickly. Olds himself, while decrying the "disarming friendliness and cleverness of the Germans," admitted that the "non-fraternization policy is a farce . . . [H]ow quickly these things [concentra-tion camps] are forgotten here," he rued, and confessed, "I want to get

53

out of this country while I still hate it." The nonfraternization policy had been decided upon in 1944 both for security reasons and as a sort of "moral quarantine" of the German people in order to bring home to them the enormity of the crimes committed by their government. Thus, GIs initially approached Germany with a certain wariness and a heightened sense of suspicion, ready to see treachery and deceit in every German action. In addition, troops fresh from combat or having seen firsthand the concentration camps often transferred their hostility to the first civilians with whom they came in contact.[35]

Still, this antipathy and mistrust faded rather quickly, for the simple reason that most GIs rather quickly decided that they liked the Germans, who seemed disarmingly similar to themselves. Despite his initial hatred for the Germans and belief that they all were Nazis, Private Webster nonetheless found himself drawn to the German people. "The Germans . . . have impressed me as clean, efficient, law-abiding people," he admitted in a mid-April letter to his parents. "In Germany everybody goes out and works and, unlike the French, who do not seem inclined to lift a finger to help themselves, the Germans fill up the trenches soldiers have dug in their fields. They are cleaner, more progressive, and more ambitious than either the English or the French." Similarly, Lieutenant Jack Foley commented that "the [Germans] of their own volition, were determined to clean up and sweep out the ruins of war. Along most of the streets there were neat piles of salvageable cobble stones. Houses were worked on to remove the debris. They were still in bad shape, yet they appeared almost ready to be rebuilt. Amazing." Indeed, any number of GIs commented on the industriousness of the Germans. A *Yank* article noted with approval, "In a matter of weeks, or sometimes days, they bring order, even neatness, to cities that were twisted masses of rubble." Further eliciting praise was the fact that "somehow, despite living in cellars and bombed out buildings, the German civilians have kept clean. . . . Put them in Trenton, N.J.," concluded *Yank*, "and you wouldn't know they were German."[36]

In addition to the typical German industriousness, other Americans found the very modernism of Germany attractive and familiar. In a letter to his wife, Robert Easton, a graduate of Stanford and Harvard who had traveled extensively in Europe and America, admitted in March 1945, "The modernity of Germany, materially, is impressive. In architecture, construction, and machinery what I've seen is superior to anything else over here. There are other tokens of advanced civilization. Books . . .

and pianos and Bach, Beethoven, Mozart; tasteful etchings and paintings and marvelous photographs. There is a disciplined, thrifty quality about the neat brick homes, evidence of industry, self-respect, strength." A little over a month later, Easton noted, "We're in a rich section of small and large farms and rolling hills with patches of woods, all very beautiful. . . . I've seen enough to convince me Germany is the richest and most industrially advanced nation of Europe." A few days later, Easton could barely contain his enthusiasm for German modernism. "We've never seen anything like it," the native of southern California enthused about his first encounter with an autobahn. "We don't have such freeways in the U.S. To our eyes, it's a marvel of engineering. . . . It reminds us again of German technology, in many respects superior to ours or anybody's." Even though chastised by his wife, who reminded him of the horrors perpetrated by the Germans in the concentration camps, Easton nonetheless continued to find much in Germany praiseworthy. "I [am] so deeply impressed," he wrote in early June. "The dereliction here is ghastly: husbandless women, fatherless children, people without houses, men returning from prison camps to find both house and family gone. It is a dreadful horror . . . and yet in the streets the life of everyday goes on." Although noting some problems with former Hitler Youth members, "murderous little criminals" whose faces reflected "evil," caught stealing explosives, Easton nevertheless concluded, "The people show no hostility and considerable friendliness."[37]

As GIs began to compare Germans with other people they had encountered, their conclusions often came as a surprise. "Observations of how the Germans lived, worked, ate, and thought led the typical American soldier to make many comparisons which were adverse to the people of other European nations through which he had passed," concluded one contemporary analyst. Indeed, the comparison made most frequently was to the French and it rarely favored the latter. A poll in the fall of 1945, in fact, revealed that the average GI liked the Germans by a clear margin. "Hell," remarked one GI, summarizing the prevailing attitude, "these people are cleaner and a damn sight friendlier than the Frogs. They're our kind of people. We don't have any trouble getting along with them and they like us first rate." The common anecdote of World War II illustrating American views of foreign peoples, noted Stephen Ambrose, ran along the following lines: "The Arabs were despicable, liars, thieves, dirty . . . without a redeeming feature. The Italians were liars, thieves, dirty . . .

with many redeeming features, but never to be trusted. The rural French were sullen, slow, and ungrateful while the Parisians were rapacious, cunning, indifferent to whether they were cheating Germans or Americans. The British people were brave, resourceful, quaint, reserved, dull." The people with whom the GI identified most, however, were the Germans, who were regarded as "clean, hard-working, disciplined, educated, middle-class in their tastes and life-styles . . . just like us."[38]

Along the same lines, Private Howell Iglehart maintained (in a sentiment likely shared by many GIs) that the problem with the Germans was that they were

> just the type of folk who are content to sit back and let someone else bear the responsibility of running the government. . . . Generally speaking, these people are very much the same as many of our own people. . . . The whole condition seems to go back to one thing—indifference on the part of the citizens toward the running of the government, and the biggest crime the German people have committed is to do nothing. I do not suppose that the American people can be expected to learn a lesson from this war, but will be satisfied to say, "It can't happen here." Propaganda and indifference have certainly made it happen here in Germany.

Reflecting on the GI encounter with the German people, and the commonly expressed American sentiment that "they are just like us," Glenn Gray concluded, "The enemy could not have changed, they must reason, so quickly from a beast to a likable human being. Thus, the conclusion is nearly forced upon them that they have been previously blinded by fear and hatred and the propaganda of their own government." Although the incidence of rape increased to disturbing levels in the spring of 1945, and GIs engaged enthusiastically in commandeering and looting houses, the American soldier by and large viewed German civilians favorably. As Lee Kennett pointed out, the deep-seated desire for vengeance or to humiliate the Germans, which characterized much of Russian and French behavior, was not part of the GI's character. Defeating the Germans, one veteran noted, was "like beating a really good football team," with no need for the winners to rough up the losers.[39]

If Germans felt relieved by their treatment at the hands of the GIs, the shocking reality of the dilapidation of the German army, combined with the powerful impression made by American troops, also left many civilians aware of the complete bankruptcy of the Nazi regime. "And how did they appear?" pondered one man in late March 1945 as he sought to describe recent events:

> How excellently the American army was equipped . . . ! The soldiers looked the very picture of health, fit and well-fed, wearing uniforms of the best material. . . . At the same time their superb mechanization. We were convinced of the technical superiority of the Americans in every respect. Except for skirmishes, foot soldiers were not to be found, nowhere visible, all the soldiers were brought to the front by autos, in long columns of personal cars [jeeps]. They had everything they needed for combat as well as rest periods . . . especially food. They ate bread as white as a petal . . . , had chocolate in abundance, smoked constantly. . . . On the other hand, when one looked at our starving and emaciated soldiers retreating from the front or as prisoners of war, with their threadbare uniforms and faces made careworn by battle and suffering, it was a sight made even more shocking when next to it one saw . . . the Americans. It was clear to everyone who saw this equipment that the war had been lost the instant America had declared war, given its fresh troops and enormous reserves . . . of war material.

Heinrich Köhler, a leader of the Catholic Center Party in the Weimar Republic, admitted of his first encounter with the material might of America,

> Tears of grief, shame, and rage ran down my cheeks. . . . My God! My God! Tank after tank rolled by, one after another, really monsters with long barrels and machine guns on all sides, soldiers with grim, proud faces staring at us. . . . I began to count the monsters. At fifty-two I gave up. Still they rolled past. . . . At the end followed motorized infantry. . . . And how fresh and well-nourished they all appeared. . . . No children or old men, nothing but men between twenty and thirty years

old. . . . What powerful material rolled by us. . . . The painful surprise at the overwhelming strength of this 'tank spearhead' was general.[40]

As a postwar American analysis made clear, "The deeper reason for this feeling of being completely crushed is undoubtedly the strong psychological impression made on everyone who has seen it of the splendid equipment—an avalanche of steel—of the Allied armies." "Only now did I get an idea of the strength of the American occupation," Victor Klemperer agreed. "Vehicles of every kind were driving in all directions virtually without interruption. Huge transporters . . . , long convoys of them, ever new convoys—and we wanted to fight that . . . !" More importantly, Klemperer, himself a Jew delivered from mortal danger by the American advance, captured perfectly the humiliating sense of being smashed and overwhelmed, noting in Munich,

> Here everything is destroyed, huge piles of rubble block the road, and the crumbling ruins and the suspended and fantastically hanging beams, blocks of concrete . . . threatened to crash down with every gust of wind. . . . And the cars of the Americans were continually racing through the dust, the ruins. . . . It was these cars that made the picture of hell complete; they are the angels of judgement or the centaurs at the stream of blood. . . . They are the triumphant and cheerful victors and masters. They drive quickly and nonchalantly, and the Germans run along humbly on foot, the victors spit out the abundance of their cigarette stubs everywhere, and the Germans pick up the stubs. . . . *We,* the liberated, creep along on foot, *we* stoop down for the cigarette ends, *we,* who only yesterday were the oppressed, and who today are called the liberated, are ultimately likewise imprisoned and humiliated. Curious conflict within me: I rejoice in God's vengeance on the henchmen of the 3rd Reich . . . yet I find it dreadful now to see the victors and avengers racing through the city, which they have so hellishly wrecked.[41]

Apart from the psychological trauma, Klemperer agreed, "the Americans make neither a vindictive nor an arrogant impression. They are not soldiers in the Prussian sense at all.... The steel helmet is worn as comfortably as a hat.... I have not seen even the smallest group marching: they all drive." It was precisely this, however, that made the defeat all the more crushing, as the proud German army had succumbed, it seemed, to nothing more than a band of civilians with a limitless material superiority. Similarly, an evacuated German woman lamented at the end of April, "We saw these American troops armed to the teeth, these well-nourished faces. The contrast between them and our emaciated, pitifully equipped, fleeing, despairing soldiers was indescribable, and we were gripped by a deep revulsion against an army leadership that would ... so senselessly and irresponsibly sacrifice these honorable soldiers to an overwhelmingly superior power." As American tanks rolled through Bad Mergentheim in early April, yet another witness remarked in amazement as "tank after tank rolled through the city all day long. Giant types ... such as we had never seen before. Just then we became conscious of what a terrible superiority our troops had to fight against and that our struggle had long since become hopeless." After being taken prisoner near Munich, Karl Jering noted in his diary the endless columns of American vehicles "that even in the best period of the Third Reich I had never seen in any of our divisions. Jeeps, trucks of all sizes and types, and on each one only three or four men.... 'Look closely at that,' I told myself. 'Against that we had fought this insane war.'"[42]

More than a mere feeling of demoralization, the increasingly disorderly nature of the German retreat in the west, accompanied as it was by spiraling complaints of looting and unruly behavior on the part of the Landsers, as well as the recognition of the vast American material preponderance, produced in many civilians a special bitterness, or as Klaus-Dietmar Henke has termed it, a sort of "de-glorification of the army." Confronted with incontestable evidence of the immense lying and destructive madness of the crumbling regime, the disintegration of the Wehrmacht before their eyes eliminated the last remaining prop of German power and greatness. Hitler had repeatedly insisted that another "November 1918" would not occur, and in the most fundamental sense he proved correct, although not in the way he desired. The oft-repeated scenes of an army completely shattered by the Allies, although painful and distressing, impressed on Germans in the most trenchant and compelling way that this army had in no way been undefeated in the field. The stab-in-the-back legend that had so poisoned the political atmosphere in Germany in the 1920s would not be repeated after this war.[43]

Still, in assessing the actions of those soldiers and civilians on the firing line, this disillusionment did not necessarily, or even predominately, translate into opposition to the Nazi regime. Whether from exhaustion, resignation, lethargy, a sense of patriotic duty, or a simple desire to keep out of harm's way, the great majority of Germans, as Goebbels noted in his diary, continued, however reluctantly, to do their duty. "The mood of the German people, at home as well as at the front, sinks ever lower," Goebbels admitted on March 13. "The populace believes that our chances for victory are completely hopeless." But as he also detected, "the present state of morale should not be confused with pronounced defeatism. The people continue to do their duty and the front soldiers are also putting up a fight." Indeed, noted an American report, "one of the most striking features . . . has been the absence of uprisings even of a local character against the Nazi regime."[44] As long as this was the case, any hopes for a swift end to the war were illusory. Hitler desired a fight to the finish, and in the absence of any force within German society that could destroy his regime, his will, as so often in the past, would lead to much bloodshed and tragedy.

DEATH THROES

Pursued relentlessly through the *Odenwald,* where legend had it that the heroic Siegfried perished at the hands of a traitor, the weakened and demoralized remnants of a once formidable army straggled toward the Tauber River. Hoping for reinforcements from the last mustering of local Franconians, German commanders sought to establish a new defensive line at Königshofen that would enable them to fight a last, decisive battle. Able to summon only half the strength of their opponents, however, and unnerved by the unexpectedly rapid approach of enemy forces, leaders of the ragtag collection of German troops quickly jettisoned all plans for a resolute defense, aiming now only to delay the enemy advance as long as possible in hopes of a final reprieve that might save their cause from total defeat.

Although the season of rebirth and resurrection, no such miracle awaited the beleaguered defenders. Unwilling to risk a frontal assault across the Tauber despite its superiority in numbers and weapons, the enemy took advantage of greater mobility to cross the river both north and south of the city with the intent of outflanking and encircling the defenders. Lacking any ability to launch a counterattack, the Germans gathered in Königshofen could only fight a bitter delaying action, one certain to end in defeat. Pressed toward the *Turmberg,* an ancient fortress on the eastern side of the city atop a hill rising some 1,100 feet above the valley floor, the defenders fought furiously. Their positions finally broken by the sheer weight of their foe's material superiority, large numbers of defenders fled that evening into the woods a mile farther to the east. There a desperate denouement played out, as the assailants crushed the remnants of the German army. In all, perhaps seven thousand defenders lay dead, the last hope of a successful resistance vanished, and the key city of Würzburg fell just a few days later.[1]

This frightful battle, which marked the end of the *Bauernkrieg* (Peasants War), took place on the Friday before Pentecost, June 2, 1525. Almost exactly 420 years later, on Easter Sunday, April 1, 1945, an eerily similar series of events would unfold at precisely the same place. For the historian, the symbolism is beguiling: the Peasants War, touched off by the explosive actions of Martin Luther in challenging the established religious and social order, could be seen as a populist challenge by the "have-nots," a struggle for freedom of the oppressed in the here and now, and not in eternity. A similar populist theme was exploited four centuries later by Adolf Hitler in his rise to power and in his justification for war: following World War I, the Versailles Treaty, according to Hitler, imposed unjust and onerous demands on the German people, with the object of permanently subjecting them to the oppressive will of Great Britain and France. In the propaganda of Joseph Goebbels, World War II therefore became a self-defined war of liberation for the German Volk as it struggled to break the alleged bondage of the "plutocrats." Urged by their leaders to regard the war as a contest for the new National Socialist Germany's very existence, it thus represented a fight for freedom both in the here and now and for eternity. For Hitler and the Nazis, at least, the battle lines were clear: the forces of the old order, whether the established aristocracy or the victors of Versailles, sought once again to crush the populist, revolutionary, social, and political challenge of the people, as expressed this time in the form of the Nazi Volksgemeinschaft, or national community. And as four hundred years earlier, extinguishing the revolutionary fervor of the forces of the populist new order would result in mountains of corpses and torrents of blood, as the Nazi leadership, driven by malignant hatred and a venomous ideology, remained determined to stand up for German "rights," even to the extent of pointless bloodshed at the end of a lost war.

NIBELUNGENTREUE: LOYALTY TILL DEATH

This utter ruthlessness and uncompromising emphasis on resistance, so bewildering to the average GI, in fact owed much to the power of an even earlier and more resonant myth, one that Hitler and Goebbels looked to in order to sustain the fighting spirit of the German army—the heroic saga of Siegfried as told in the *Nibelungenlied* (Song of the Nibelungs). Designated by the writers of the Romantic movement of the early nineteenth century as the German *Iliad,* a national epic that illustrates the essence of a people, the *Nibelungenlied* became an integral part of the German search for national identity. Until the late nineteenth century, of course, "Germany" as such did not exist, and even after unification in 1871 the new nation lacked the integrating political myths of Great Britain, France, or the United States (itself a relatively new nation). In their function of imparting a common sense of community and identity, of integrating the past into contemporary events, and of transmitting key values, national myths fulfill a crucial role in guaranteeing both national identity and legitimacy.[2]

In newly unified Germany, though, genuine national myths proved stubbornly elusive. There were, to be sure, heroic and legendary figures— but they seemed either too imperial, and thus not national (such as Charlemagne), or, like Frederick the Great, too specifically Prussian to be of value. Nor did Germany possess anything like the William Tell myth of the Swiss or the frontier myth of the Americans, both of which, with their emphasis on liberation, freedom, and courageous individualism, served to emphasize key values even if they contained specific historical inaccuracies. Indeed, the only close approximation to these two myths, the *Germania* by Tacitus, merely illustrated the German deficiency when compared with other nations, for although full of praise of ancient German virtues such as loyalty, justice, generosity, and honor, it was written by a Roman not out of any great admiration for the Germans but for the express purpose of criticizing contemporary Roman society.[3] Almost by default, then, the German Romantics, in searching for a specifically German counterpart to the French influences then dominant, settled on the *Nibelungenlied,* an epic poem written around A.D.1200, as the German national epic.

In many respects this seems an odd choice, not only because it was set in a period over a millennium and a half removed from German unification, but more importantly because the tale ends not with a victory by the hero but with his total defeat and destruction.[4] Nor is the poem internally consistent, being composed of two separate tales later grafted together. The first part, made familiar through Wagner's operatic retelling, took place along the Rhine and in the Odenwald among the Franks and Burgundians, both ancient Germanic tribes. Siegfried, a valiant and heroic Franconian prince acting under a cloak of secrecy and as a vassal of Gunther, king of the Burgundians, frees Brünnhilde from an enchantment, represented by a ring of fire. Brünnhilde accepts Gunther as her husband while Siegfried marries Kriemhilde, a Burgundian princess and sister of Gunther, for whom he has developed a deep affection. The two women soon quarrel, as Brünnhilde ridicules Kriemhilde for marrying Siegfried, a mere vassal of Gunther. Kriemhilde then reveals Siegfried's and Gunther's deception; stung by this affront to her honor, Brünnhilde plots vengeance. She employs Hagen, a henchman of King Gunther and friend of Siegfried, as her instrument of revenge. Winning Kriemhilde's confidence, Hagen, who is envious of Siegfried's growing power, learns of his one vulnerable spot and treacherously strikes the fatal blow.

The second part of the legend has a historical basis: the destruction of the Burgundians by the Huns in A.D. 437. In the *Nibelungenlied* itself, the historical elements serve to illustrate the conflict between Hagen and Kriemhilde and to emphasize her vengeance against the Burgundians. In A.D. 436 the Burgundians, a Germanic tribe living on the west bank of the Rhine with their capital at Worms, rose against the Romans, a rebellion that was quickly suppressed. Determined to throw off the Roman yoke, though, the Burgundians the next year again rose in revolt. This time the Romans called on the Huns, a fierce Central Asian people already pressing hard on the German tribes from the east, to put down the uprising. Thus provided with an excuse, the Huns proved more than willing to suppress the Burgundians, killing perhaps twenty thousand of them and practically sweeping them from the face of the earth. The Burgundian King Gundahar, or Gunther, died heroically fighting the Huns, but to no avail as a whole German nation fell before the hordes of invading barbarians. In the *Nibelungenlied,* however, it is Kriemhilde who has Gunther killed and then, with Siegfried's sword, slays the bound and defenseless Hagen. In turn, Kriemhilde is then slain by a knight who is outraged at the atrocities she has committed.[5]

As the basis of an integrative national myth, the *Nibelungenlied* was riddled with problems and ambiguities, replete as it was with treachery, vengeance, and, not least, the violent death and defeat of all the main figures. As a consequence, nineteenth-century interpreters, literary critics, and nationalist writers emphasized not the events of the saga, but rather idealized the key qualities that they believed marked the ancient Teutons and thus could form the basis of the German national character: faithfulness and loyalty unto death, a willingness to carry out orders to the end with unhesitating consistency, heroic valor, stoicism in the face of death, a will to do battle, and an inextinguishable and uncompromising hatred and desire for vengeance.[6] Given the context of the long centuries of German division and weakness, a condition promoted and exacerbated by the actions of outside powers, the subtext of the *Nibelungenlied* must also have resonated powerfully in the newly unified Germany of the late nineteenth century: Germany as victim, subject to treachery and betrayal internally and browbeaten externally by those jealous of German might. Thus Siegfried, like Germany itself, although virtuous, honorable, and courageous, met his doom because of his astonishing naivete and inability to recognize the duplicity and faithlessness all around him.

Refined further in the years before World War I, and conveyed to a generation of young Germans by the public school system, the myth raised *Treue* (loyalty or faithfulness) to the level of a moral principle. In related fashion, the heroic figure, a man of the future and the embodiment of the German essence, both part of and the defining spirit of his people, one willing to sacrifice himself for the common good of the Volk, emerged as a key motif of the *Nibelungenlied*. And above all these other themes loomed the leitmotif of the saga, the terrible vengeance visited upon the slayers of Siegfried, the blood revenge exacted on those who had betrayed the guileless and virtuous hero. Interestingly, in Vienna in his late teens the young Adolf Hitler, influenced by the urgent notions of the need for a regenerative German spirit then especially in vogue among the German-speakers of the Austrian Empire, sought to complete an opera that Richard Wagner had only outlined, *Wieland der Schmiede* (Wieland the Smith). Even as a young man Hitler had fallen under Wagner's spell, being especially affected by the opera *Rienzi*. Set in mid-fourteenth-century Rome, *Rienzi* chronicled the tale of Cola di Rienzi, who rose from a humble state to become a "people's tribune," unify a splintered society, and temporarily restore the greatness of Rome. With its theme of redemption by a leader who ascended from the anonymous masses to rejuvenate a people who had sunk into degeneration, *Rienzi* appealed to Hitler's already exalted sense of his own destiny. *Wieland the Smith* emphasized a similar theme of self-liberation, with an added twist. Wieland, for Hitler, was "personified revenge, implacable and totally ruthless."[7]

Revenge was certainly a satisfying and revealing subject for a young man who thought himself cheated by the world, but it was also a dominant theme of the World War I period in Germany. Given the widespread German fear of encirclement by envious and rapacious enemies and the traumatic nature of the Great War, along with the firm belief that German defeat owed much to a "stab in the back" by internal enemies, it is perhaps not surprising that in the postwar period the *Nibelungenlied* seemed to many nationalistic Germans to have a particular relevance. Indeed, the Siegfried myth, in which Hitler performed the role of the "man of the future," along with notions of camaraderie, loyalty, life as struggle, the readiness to sacrifice, and heroic death became central elements in the Nazi vision of a Volksgemeinschaft that would restore German greatness following the multiple betrayals of World War I. The National Socialist regime, which claimed legitimacy through having breathed new life into the German nation by reaffirming the connection between state and people, thus sought to inculcate Nibelungentreue not only in the SS, where loyalty was held up as the highest virtue, but in German society as a whole by emphasizing that "idealistic German youth should cling to the [notion] of unwavering loyalty" as the central element in German heroism. In a remarkable speech given on January 30, 1943, the tenth anniversary of the Nazi "seizure of power" and on the eve of the surrender of the German Sixth Army in Stalingrad, Hermann Goering explicitly connected the impending catastrophe at Stalingrad with the final battle of the Burgundians in the *Nibelungenlied*:

> Who there fights for every block, every stone, every cellar, every trench against an overwhelming power, who fights again and again, weary, exhausted—we know a mighty, heroic tale of just such an incomparable struggle that is called "Der Kampf der Nibelungen." They also stood in a hall of fire and flame and quenched their thirst with their own blood—but fought and fought to the last. Today just such a struggle rages there

[in Stalingrad] and every German knows that in a thousand years the word Stalingrad will still have to be pronounced with solemn dread and yet remember that there Germany in the end put the stamp on final victory![8]

Goering, of course, intended his speech as an appeal to the readiness of each German to sacrifice, if necessary his life, for the greater good of Germany, but it also served to make it clear to the average German that they now had no other choice. Confronted once again by an attempt by their enemies to encircle and strangle the German nation, and again standing as a bulwark against the barbaric hordes from Asia, the average German was made to understand that the war had now become literally a struggle for the very existence of the German people, one in which there existed no place for weakness, vacillation, or half measures. Only through uncompromising hardness, an unwavering willingness to self-sacrifice, and an absolute loyalty to Hitler and the Nazi regime could Germany master this enormous and fateful struggle.[9] According to the myth, heroism lay not in any particular event or success, but in the national and racial characteristics of the participants, and Hitler was now calling these allegedly superior racial qualities into play. In a perverse irony, the cataclysmic events of the dim German past, reincarnated in mythical form, threatened once again a destruction of the German people, and the myth that had seemed so integral to the construction of a national identity in the nineteenth century, now invoked by Hitler, promised only a final Götterdämmerung of violence and bloodshed.

THE TAUBER RIVER LINE

With the burning buildings of the city of Worms serving as a fiery backdrop, forward elements of the Twelfth Armored Division crossed the Rhine River just after midnight on March 28, 1945. Tense with anticipation, chilled in the cold, damp night air, many GIs wrestled with anxious thoughts: Had the push across the Rhine finally broken the German spirit? Or would the Landsers resist further in the wooded hills to the east of the legendary river? Most worrisome, would German soldiers and civilians heed propaganda chief Joseph Goebbels's call to conduct prolonged, fanatic guerrilla warfare? Broadcasting for the first time on the evening of Easter Sunday, April 1, the *Werwolfsender* (Werwolf radio) issued a revolutionary call to the German people to take up the slogan, "Hate is our prayer. Revenge is our battle cry." Facing the unknown, yet brimming with pride at spearheading the drive into Bavaria, the men of the Twelfth Armored Division, screened by units of the 106th Cavalry Group and Fourth Infantry Division, moved cautiously to the east, advancing slowly through the Odenwald, a menacing area of steep, forested ridges unsuited for swift movement. Crisscrossed by innumerable streams and with the crest of the hills running parallel to the Rhine, the advancing American units were compelled either to follow the winding roads, thereby doubling the distance they traveled, or go cross-country and climb up over the ridges, which proved an exceedingly strenuous undertaking. To the Germans, the hills and narrow valleys formed a natural barrier that could be utilized to prevent any quick American strike to the east or south.[10]

The bulk of the German defense rested on the Seventeenth SS-Panzergrenadier Division "Götz von Berlichingen," an outfit familiar to the men of the Twelfth Armored Division, for they had confronted it repeatedly in the push to the Rhine River. Authorized by an order from Adolf Hitler on October 3, 1943, the process of forming the Seventeenth SS began hastily in November 1943. Organized in France, the division had an officer and NCO cadre from experienced *Waffen-SS* (combat) divisions, while the majority of the enlisted men consisted of draftees from Germany and *Volksdeutsche* (ethnic Germans) from central and southeastern Europe. With an initial strength of seventeen thousand men, the division suffered from a shortage of officers, although its most serious weakness stemmed from a chronic lack of transportation and anti-tank weapons. Still, it had entered combat in Normandy as early as June 8, 1944, where, despite its materiel deficiencies, it fought a stubborn defense, yielding ground only grudgingly. Over the next two months of savage fighting in the hedgerow country, the Seventeenth SS lost roughly 50 percent of its force.[11]

Reinforced in September and November 1944 with the remnants of SS-Panzergrenadier Brigades Forty-nine and Fifty-one, as well as a significant complement of Volksdeutsche from Russia, the Seventeenth SS in December spearheaded Operation Nordwind, the German counteroffensive into Alsace. Again ground down—by fierce fighting that lasted into late January 1945, as well as the steady attrition in the retreat to the Rhine—by April 1945 the roughly five thousand men left in the *"Götz,"* like their famous namesake, brandished almost as a consolation an irascible delight in their obstinacy. Named after Götz von Berlichingen, the revolutionary knight with the iron hand who had, ironically, temporarily led the peasants of these very same regions of Swabia and Franconia in their great sixteenth-century uprising against aristocratic oppression, the remnants of the Seventeenth SS had assumed a self-image of valiant defenders of justice (as they saw it), of faithful liegemen of their Führer, and of honorable fighters for an ideal. Indeed, the tenacious men of the Seventeenth SS had adopted as their unofficial slogan the legendary retort of Götz von Berlichingen to a surrender demand: "Kiss my ass!"[12] Qualities such as loyalty and constancy, holding to their convictions despite the discrepancy between ideals and reality, and struggling on in the face of the futility of their efforts lent a characteristic air of self-righteousness to the unit, which resulted both in courageous resistance and criminal actions at the end of a lost war.

Lending a further atmosphere of Götterdämmerung as the Americans advanced on March 28 through dense fog and a driving rain on roads, in the words of one GI, "meant for horse and ox carts, and not for an armored column," was the fact that the Odenwald itself was the setting for the *Nibelungenlied,* discussed above, with its evocation of a world of idealism, passion, faith, loyalty, and ultimate revenge. A myth potent enough, some GIs must have feared, for the Führer to seek to create his own legend of self-sacrificial resistance. For the most part, however, the hard-pressed German defenders in the Odenwald, although supplemented now by scattered units of the experienced forest fighters of the Sixth SS-Gebirgs (Mountain) Division *"Nord,"* lacked the antitank weapons necessary to establish an effective defense line.[13]

Over the next few days, therefore, the Germans conducted mostly a delaying action, springing ambushes out of the thickly wooded ravines, felling trees across roads, blowing bridges, and mining the major highways. Near Hüttenthal on March 29, for example, German artillery shells intermittently slammed into a key road junction as units of the Seventeenth Armored Infantry Battalion and Twenty-third Tank Battalion approached the spine of the Odenwald, forcing the GIs to run a perilous gauntlet of fire as they barreled past ruins of the *Limes,* the ancient Roman defense lines. The next day, the dangerous cat and mouse game continued, as small groups of Germans with *Panzerfäuste* surprised leading American tanks near Obersensbach and Mudau. At Ernsttal, itself sitting in the midst of the ruins of Roman watchtowers and forts, a Nazi Party warehouse crammed with thousands of bottles of French champagne and cognac offered retreating Landsers a serendipitous situation. Stuffing as much as they could in their pockets and packs, they freely imbibed the expensive French wine as they marched to the southeast. As leading tanks of Combat Command (CC) R of the Twelfth Armored Division approached Schloßau on the morning of March 30, German troops, many of them drunk, put up furious opposition. This act of bravado, fueled more by cognac than good sense, resulted only in the deaths of twelve Landsers. To the east, another American unit encountered more of the inebriated Landsers in the vicinity of the tiny village of Hornbach. Incensed by their brief resistance, the GIs not only set barns and houses afire, but crushed everything they could under the treads of their tanks. In a similar instance, GIs of the Seventeenth Armored Infantry Battalion early on the morning of March 30 caught a German unit at breakfast. With mess kits left hastily scattered around a roaring fire, the Landsers tried to escape by truck, only to be gunned down by deadly machine gun fire from American tanks and half-tracks. Perhaps two dozen Germans were killed and thirty captured in the sudden shoot-out, but more hopefully, as one GI put it, "this was the first day we had really seen lots of jerries fleeing in disorder and had a good chance to shoot at them. It made everyone feel good to think that we were paying the Germans back for our casualties."[14]

In a few places, such as Lindenfels or Eberbach, American progress slowed because of sudden, sharp firefights, but despite fears to the contrary, the Odenwald proved no particular obstacle. The fighting in both these towns did, however, provide an interesting foretaste of events to come. Just west of Lindenfels, in the early morning hours of March 29, a small troop of SS men had blown up a key section of the main road, the ominously named *Nibelungstrasse,* making it impassable, and then in a nocturnal firefight they disabled two American tanks with *Panzerfaust* (one-shot antitank weapon) fire. While German field howitzers continued sporadically to shell the road leading out of Lindenfels, GIs in the town set about collecting German soldiers retreating along the Nibelungstrasse, none of whom realized that the Americans had outpaced them. Just as revealing of the German predicament, the occupation of the town by men of the Ninety-second Cavalry Reconnaissance Squadron of the Twelfth Armored Division resulted, in the delicate phrasing of the local pastor, in "some Americans climbing immediately into bed with certain women," a German willingness to fraternize with the enemy that, whatever its other qualities, revealed the extent of war-weariness among local civilians. The other face of the Nazi regime in the last days of the war manifested itself in Eberbach, where barely more than a dozen men of the Seventeenth SS held up the American advance for nearly two days, while at the same time threatening to shoot almost two dozen forced laborers (Poles, French, Dutch, and Belgian), who they feared would plunder food stores and take revenge on local civilians.[15] Thus, in spite of the largely sporadic German resistance, it took the Americans three days to cover the roughly sixty miles to reach the Tauber River along the line Tauberbischofsheim–Königshofen–Bad Mergentheim.

Although itself hardly a major obstacle, the river lay in the *Taubergrund,* an area of steep, heavily wooded ravines and narrow defiles. By taking advantage of the natural terrain, the Germans hoped to establish a defensive line running north along the Tauber to the Main River at Würzburg, as well as south past the famous medieval city of Rothenburg to Crailsheim. This, in turn, would allow them to defend the approaches to Nuremberg as well as the main escape routes south into Bavaria and the redoubt area. Aided by the difficult terrain of the Steigerwald, a heavily forested series of heights to the east of the Tauber and south of the Main, the Germans further aimed to delay American advances by resorting to strong points centered around key towns and along the wooded areas.[16]

In the final days of March the Germans gathered together troops, primarily from Wehrkreis VII Munich, with the object of delaying the advancing GIs as long as possible west of the Tauber before withdrawing behind the river line. Along with replacement units from Augsburg and Garmisch, this hastily assembled division also included a regiment of officer training candidates from Lenggries, south of Munich, as well as artillery and *Nebelwerfer* (rocket launcher) units. Originally designated Division *"Bayern"* (Bavaria) and—on paper at least—the strongest unit in the German army, it was reconstituted as the 212th *Volksgrenadier Division* (VGD) on March 30 and placed under the command of Lieutenant Colonel Cord von Hobe. A onetime operations officer with the formidable *Grossdeutschland* Division on the Eastern front and the son-in-law of former Chief of the General Staff Franz Halder, the thirty-six-year-old Hobe came under suspicion after the unsuccessful July 20, 1944, attempt on Hitler's life. Subjected to intense interrogation by the Ge-

71

stapo, Hobe was eventually cleared of any involvement and sent to command a regiment during the Ardennes offensive of December 1944. Although destined to command the 212th VGD for only a few days, Hobe had gained a reputation as a decisive and effective officer, one who served as a skilled troubleshooter in the final weeks of the war. The 212th VGD was supported by the Thirty-eighth Regiment of the Seventeenth SS, as well as by the 88mm antiaircraft guns of the *Kampfgruppe Dirnagel*, a unit of roughly three thousand men that also included two infantry battalions. Originally a flak training unit of the SS, this battle group led by Lieutenant Colonel Oskar Dirnagel rapidly developed an astonishing level of morale and fighting power, qualities it used over the next few weeks as it continually harassed American operations throughout Middle Franconia.[17]

Because of transportation disruptions caused by incessant American air attacks, insufficient locomotives and rolling stock, and a lack of fuel for army trucks, these units arrived in the Lauda–Königshofen–Bad Mergentheim area only laboriously and piecemeal, many lacking necessary supplies, antitank weapons, artillery, munitions, and motorized vehicles. As a result, gaps inevitably occurred in the German defense line. Tank spearheads of CC-B (Task Forces Norton and Field) of the Twelfth Armored Division, for example, rapidly approached Tauberbischofsheim on March 31. At the western edge of Schweinberg, a few miles east of Hardheim, SS troopers had run their truck into a ditch by a bridge over a small stream, with the intention of using Panzerfäuste to contest the oncoming American tanks. Acting quickly, the mayor of the small village pulled the truck out with a team of horses and prevailed on the SS men to withdraw without a fight. American troops thus occupied Schweinberg unopposed, brushed aside some slight opposition at Königheim, and around 11:00 A.M. suddenly found themselves in Tauberbischofsheim on the main route toward the Tauber River bridge. As German combat engineers tried twice without success to blow the bridge, American tanks rolled across without a fight, then struck rapidly to the northeast with the objective of seizing the Main River bridge at Ochsenfurt.[18] Already by the early afternoon of March 31, then, GIs had breached the Tauber River line in the north and were swarming along the eastern bank.

This was not, however, destined to be the initial move of a rapid penetration of German defenses, but an exception to the norm in Franconia. As Gerald Linderman has noted, the rising frustration of both GIs and Landsers, the one at the continued pointless resistance and the other at his impotence in the defense of his homeland, tended to create an uncontrollable dynamic of destruction. As opposed to the war in Russia or that in the Pacific, combat in western Europe had, with some exceptions, followed "rules" commonly understood by the combatants on both sides. Americans expressed anger at what they viewed as dirty tricks by the Germans, things such as sniping, disguising their vehicles, or the counterfeit surrender, while Germans bitterly resented the GI habit of acquiring souvenirs from German corpses and prisoners, but in general, as one GI put it, "We . . . fought by rules of a sort." Although both sides proved guilty of shooting prisoners in the heat of battle during the Normandy campaign, a visible deterioration in battle comportment occurred only during and after the Battle of the Bulge in late 1944. It remained true, as William Tecumseh Sherman had noted of the Civil War, that "war is cruelty and you cannot refine it." Personal savagery increases the longer a war continues, and many participants crossed a significant threshold in early 1945. Especially apparent was the hardening in the attitude of GIs, partly from the German massacre of American prisoners at Malmedy in December 1944, but also from a rising impulse to exact vengeance on an enemy that continued to threaten their existence long after any reasonable hope of victory had vanished.[19]

In some instances, this coarsened demeanor revealed itself in a desire for personal revenge after a buddy was killed. Harold Leinbaugh witnessed a man in his company kill four Germans to avenge the death of his best friend, while a few days later he saw a tanker whose buddies had just been killed shoot down two German POWs. Howard Randall noted the actions of an American captain whose brother had just been blinded by shell fragments. In tears, he ordered his driver to take him to a wooded area, where the captain

> jumped out, walked ten paces into the woods and started shouting for any Germans . . . to come out with their hands up and surrender to him. . . . Seven Kraut soldiers stumbled out of the woods without rifles and helmets and with their hands up. . . . Then the captain backed up several paces, calmly raised his pistol higher and shot each German in the head in rapid succession. . . . The first three men died with surprised looks on their faces. . . . The next two registered horror as the gun went off in their faces. One of them clawed frantically at

his throat for a second, fell heavily to the ground, and kicked a couple of times. . . . The last three [*sic*] Germans were hit in the back of the head as they turned and started to run.

As his driver doubled over and vomited, the captain "drove like a wild man from the scene of the massacre." Nor are these accounts aberrations, the personal memoirs of most GIs revealing such episodes, especially late in the war. "Certainly it did not occur to me then," one admitted, "that to take that life [a wounded German prisoner] would be cruel and unforgivable. . . . Filled with a hate that only a man who has . . . seen his closest buddies killed can know, I raised the rifle butt to the crevice between my shoulder and collarbone and pulled the trigger. The Jerry writhed to silence."[20]

Other GIs who shot prisoners seemed motivated less by vengeance than by a desire to punish an adversary who until recently had sought to kill him, and now, if he accepted the surrender, would be sent to the rear to safety and hot food. "With the captor's emotions recently raw with fear and certain to be so again soon," Linderman observed, "he found troubling the thought that his 'victory' . . . would have no consequence for himself save to extend his personal jeopardy, while the enemy's 'defeat' would carry the captive to that personal survival so desired by the captor. Who had 'won?'" Such a motivation seemed to be at work among the men of an infantry company in southwestern Germany that was responsible for, in addition to unbridled theft and rape among the civilian population, a wholesale massacre of German prisoners. Similarly, John Toole, fighting in Middle Franconia with the Third Infantry Division, became so enraged at the sight of a preening Luftwaffe officer who had just been taken prisoner, and the thought of his captive's imminent release from danger, that he could barely suppress the desire to kill him:

A big Kraut Luftwaffe pilot comes over and has the temerity to tap me on the shoulder. He is pointing to all his medals, silver wings, and Iron Crosses and saying, arrogantly, "Ich bin offizier." He thinks he'll get better treatment if we know he's an officer and a hero. I growl at him. . . . But he just stands there and fingers his medals, repeating, "Ich bin offizier." I lose my temper, stand up and bring the butt of my pistol down on his bare head. He reels back but keeps on muttering about what an important guy he is. I holler for McTeague. He comes over and I tell him, "For Christ sake! What kind of a war is this when a goddamn enemy prisoner of war can harass a Company Commander? Get this son-of-a-bitch out of here or he's going to be a dead pilot. . . ." The "offizier" is lucky to be alive. Any other Army commander might have shot him between the eyes.

On top of the strain of combat and the death of buddies, GIs like Toole seemed particularly to resent what they saw as the arrogance of some German prisoners, now released from the constant threat of death, when they themselves had to remain vigilant during the pointless last weeks of the war. As Audie Murphy, America's most decorated soldier and a man who himself had taken personal revenge on German prisoners, noted wryly, "somebody is always forgetting the rule book."[21]

Indeed, this destructive dynamic seemed well in place at the Tauber. Seven miles to the south of Tauberbischofsheim, in the vicinity of Lauda and Königshofen, the GIs met an enemy grimly determined to inflict as much harm as possible on the invading force. On the morning of March 31, American tanks of the Ninety-second Cavalry Reconnaissance Squadron, supported by units from the Second Battalion, Twenty-second Infantry Regiment, Fourth Infantry Division, occupied without a fight the tiny village of Buch am Ahorn, about eight miles west of the Tauber, then carefully approached the *Heckfelder Wald*, a wooded ridge three miles across that sat astride the main road toward Königshofen. Young officer candidates, seventeen- and eighteen-year-old boys from the First Company of the Reserve Officers training school at Lenggries, had been hastily rushed to the front after precious little instruction, arriving at Lauda just the night before. Without direction, they now found themselves thrown into battle. The main body, having dispatched one of their number, Werner Huhn, in civilian clothes to reconnoiter the area, had time to prepare positions on the edge of Heckfeld, a small village on the eastern side of the forest. As the GIs approached the far edge of the woods, though, a small group of hastily entrenched German troops, acting as an advance guard, waited nervously. When the lead American tank came within range, about a hundred yards from his shallow foxhole, the leader of the seven-man squad, Otto Tuschwitz, carefully aimed his Panzerfaust and fired. To his amazement, the explosive projectile bounced harmlessly off the

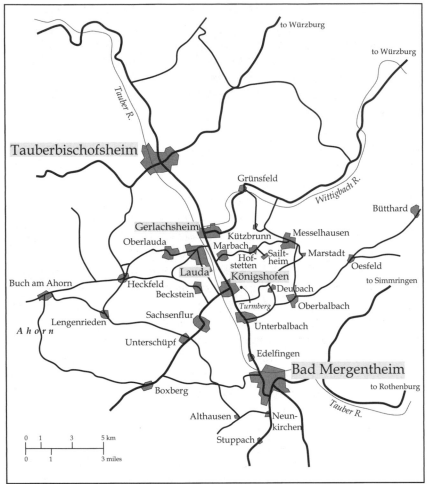

Map 2: Königshofen/Tauber River

Sherman tank. While GIs scrambled for cover and Tuschwitz cursed his weapon, the remaining Shermans quickly retreated, firing furiously from their machine guns. As the Americans regrouped, Tuschwitz, believing he had incorrectly set the detonator, hastily reset other Panzerfäuste in preparation for the next American assault. When the GIs returned and attacked both frontally and from his flanks, Tuschwitz again raised up from his concealment, took aim, and fired a second Panzerfaust, with the same result as the first. Muttering obscenities about sabotage at the factory and threatened now with complete annihilation, the German defenders, at least those who were able, quickly withdrew; three Landsers lay dead, three more were wounded, and only one escaped uninjured.[22]

A few hours later, and after the GIs had withdrawn into the woods about a mile from Heckfeld, another unit of green German troops from the Third Company, Reserve Officers Battalion (ROB) Lenggries, arrived in the village. Perhaps owing to their inexperience and lack of training, the German commanders inexplicably failed to exchange the most rudimentary of information about terrain, enemy whereabouts, or earlier firefights. Thus unaware of the situation, but jittery because of rumors of an American breakthrough, the boys pushed off from Heckfeld in the direction of Buch. Before entering the thick woods, the German commander dispatched a few soldiers, again dressed in civilian clothing, on bicycles to reconnoiter. They soon reported back falsely and likely after only the most cursory of searches that the way was clear; at that, the remainder of the outfit set off, infantry armed with Panzerfäuste. In the woods, however, the GIs had spotted the approaching enemy and, still smarting over the earlier fighting (German reports later claimed that the Americans executed some of the prisoners), prepared an ambush and quietly awaited the Germans, who marched unawares into the trap.[23]

As one Landser recalled, "We were marching on the left of the road leading to Buch am Ahorn . . . [when] we were suddenly surprised by heavy machine gun fire. Of all of them, I still had some luck. [The Americans] fired from a slight incline, so the burst of fire from the machine gun went over me." "Suddenly machine gun fire lashed out of a curve in the road," remembered another young soldier:

> Platoon leader Sergeant König ordered "take cover," [but] only four men jumped to the right of the road [and away from the firing], among them König. He screamed, "you nitwits, why did you all jump to the left?" At that, Schmid sprang up and ran toward the right side of the road, immediately drew machine gun fire, [but] managed to take cover behind a large tree. That was his good fortune, for to the left there were only small trees. . . . As Schmid ran from left to right, König screamed, "Schmid, do you absolutely want to end up in heaven!" Now tanks came rolling around the curve, stopped,

and opened a heavy fire with automatic weapons and high-explosive shells. Hardly anyone fired from our side. A Panzerfaust was fired, but didn't hit anything. The high-explosive shells worked effectively to create [deadly] splinters. . . . The tanks approached ever closer. One stood three to four meters from Schmid. Then from behind came the order to retreat. Sergeant König called, "Lads, give yourselves up!" and "Where are you?" But everything remained silent.

Schmid waved a handkerchief from behind the tree, to show that he wanted to surrender. The turret hatch opened and an Ami [GI] called out something that Schmid didn't understand. The seriously wounded Meier, shot in the stomach, begged Schmid: "Schmid, please unbuckle my belt!" As Schmid went to do this, he saw [Meier's] serious wound. The Ami yelled again, as Schmid was about a step from where Meier lay, [then the Ami] raised his machine gun and deliberately shot Meier with a salvo.[24]

As with many such cryptic and enigmatic incidents, the dilemma lies in deciphering the perpetrator's motivation. Was the GI punishing Meier for his foolish resistance, which had endangered his buddies and himself, or did he fire on the irremediably wounded man to put him out of his misery? Just as importantly, did the German defenders view this as a mercy killing or as a gruesome execution, an action that increased their enmity and willingness to resist? As became apparent over the next few weeks in Middle Franconia, personal rancor and willing violence often swelled beyond the point of control, affecting noncombatants as well as soldiers. Howard Randall, for example, related a seemingly trivial incident that had more broad and deadly consequences. Not atypically at this stage of the war, a small patrol of which he was a member found a gap in German lines and came upon a small village. Entering the mayor's office, the GIs almost fell over themselves in their lust to acquire various "souvenirs." As they left, almost as an afterthought, they warned the mayor to have white flags flown or else face the destruction of the village when the main body of American troops arrived. The GIs returned only a week later, and Randall noted with puzzlement that not a white flag was flying. That night he learned why: SS troops had gone into the village a few days after the GI raiding expedition and were infuriated at the sight of the white flags. They dragged the mayor out of his office, hung him in the town square, and then ordered all surrender flags taken down on penalty of death. "The civilians," Randall noted ruefully, "lost both ways."[25]

Less puzzling, although no less brutal for its clarity, was the result of the deadly engagement in the Heckfelder Wald. Fired upon from all sides, in a matter of minutes twenty-six Germans lay dead and four injured, while the remainder of the company scurried away in the direction of Königshofen. Although superior in numbers and firepower, the GIs followed very slowly and cautiously, occupying Heckfeld, just a few miles beyond, only at 8:00 P.M. Unwilling to go any further at night, American artillery commenced shelling Lauda, on the west bank of the Tauber perhaps two miles north of Königshofen. Unbeknownst to the Americans, however, German forces had already evacuated Lauda, which was seized the next day without a fight.[26]

Further south, in the early afternoon of March 31, units of the Seventeenth Armored Infantry Battalion passed through the *Rechenwald* and entered the village of Althausen, less than two miles southwest of the spa town of Bad Mergentheim, where they brushed aside token German resistance. As they proceeded toward Neunkirchen, another mile to the east, the GIs received heavy rifle, machine gun, and Panzerfaust fire from a small group of German defenders. The unexpected skirmish caught both sides unawares, as at 3:00 P.M. a group of local citizens had just assembled in Neunkirchen with the object of deciding whether or not to evacuate the town. The debate was quickly mooted, as American machine gun and mortar fire raked the village. "An incredible shoot-out," in the words of a German officer who observed the scene, now ensued. "The valley from Neunkirchen to Althausen appeared shrouded in a cloud of smoke out of which flashed fiery lightning. Very quickly the burning buildings turned the cloud red. After twenty minutes the shooting stopped.... Along the road sat a truck and two burning American tanks. Bodies lay unimaginably mutilated, and some inside [the tank] were still burning." The German resistance not only surprised but sobered the GIs as well, as it left at least eight Americans dead and seven wounded.[27]

As they prepared to continue the attack, however, both A and C Companies were ordered to break off and move to the northwest to help rescue other elements of the Seventeenth Armored Infantry Battalion and the Twenty-third Tank Battalion in the town of Boxberg, where Landsers of the ROB Lenggries had used fierce tank, mortar, artillery, and Panzerfaust fire to trap the Americans in a hellish house-to-house fight. The GIs had earlier brushed aside a spirited counterattack at Angeltürn, where young Germans armed with Panzerfäuste stormed out of woods to attack the enemy tanks. As the American column entered the town of Boxberg around 3:00 P.M., a Panzerfaust round slammed into a truck, which instantly burst into flames, killing at least two men and badly burning several others. Then, when the tank platoon leader stuck his head out of the hatch to get a better look, a sniper put a bullet through his helmet. That was enough for the tankers, who immediately began to hightail it out of town. Indeed, in their haste to withdraw, several tanks simply slammed into reverse, crushing the jeeps of a medic and forward artillery observer. As the Forward Observer (FO) leaped free of his jeep, he was immediately hit in the legs by a German sniper, while several other GIs suffered shrapnel wounds. In the confusing melee, which featured the disconcerting sight, at this late stage of the war, of German Me 262 jet fighters strafing the American column, one tank suffered a direct hit from a Panzerfaust and was destroyed, while three others were knocked out of action. As a demonstration of the deep changes the war had wrought, one of the units dispatched to aid the beleaguered GIs was the Third Provisional Company of the Seventeenth Armored Infantry Battalion, an African American combat unit. Still, by the time the various reinforcements arrived, the GIs on the scene had overcome the heavy enemy resistance and entered the town. As a result, both A and C Companies of the Seventeenth Armored Infantry Battalion continued a night march in preparation for an attack early the next morning toward Königshofen. Although the Americans estimated that fifty Germans had been killed in the fighting (in fact, civilians that night collected the bodies of thirty-six dead Landsers), March 31 had also proven costly for the GIs. The only consolation, perhaps, came in the form of eggs and flour liberated from a Wehrmacht storehouse in Sachsenflur; although shaken by the day's actions, a pancake and egg dinner instead of the usual steady diet of K and C rations did much to raise the GIs' spirits.[28]

These incidents, however, established a pattern that would become commonplace during the arduous fighting throughout Middle Franconia over the next three weeks: one of unexpectedly fierce resistance at key points by the Germans, and cautious, hesitant movements on the part of the Americans. Although forced by transportation difficulties and fuel shortages to mount a fragmented defense, with isolated detachments fighting a series of delaying actions with little attempt at counterattack or maneuver, the discipline of the German soldiers stayed remarkably intact. Despite the disaster engulfing them, and with no hope of winning, their soldierly instincts and tactical training remained capable—right to the end—of teaching American troops a sharp lesson if they failed to heed elemental precautions. The other typical element of later events in Middle Franconia, the harsh discipline and savage terror imposed by Nazi military and civil authorities on a war-weary local population, one that would have preferred to have seen German troops go rather than come, also surfaced over the next few days at both Königshofen and Edelfingen.

On April 1, 1945, Easter Sunday, as American troops moved to cross the Tauber River, it was the ferocity of the fighting that struck the average GI, not any German inclination to surrender without a fight. Rebuffed on March 31 in their initial efforts to cross the river and seize Königshofen, the Seventeenth Armored Infantry Battalion, supported by C Company of the Twenty-third Tank Battalion, assembled in the vicinity of Lengenrieden–Unterschüpf, two small villages a few miles west, as German units retreated into the city. With A Company of the Seventeenth Armored Infantry Battalion in the lead, the Americans, traveling in jeeps and armored half-tracks, the latter equipped with either 75mm or 105mm howitzers and a .30 or .50 caliber machine gun, moved out in the early morning hours of April 1 with the mission of forcing a crossing of the Tauber. Evidently little or no opposition was expected, for as Sergeant Carl Lyons of A Company remembered, "After getting lost once, we were soon traveling fast towards the Tauber through the darkness. Most of the men were asleep. . . . I sat down and pulled a blanket over me to get a few minutes sleep."[29]

Less than two miles from the Tauber, however, the American advance guard was ambushed by forward elements of the 316th Infantry Regiment, supported once again by the 88mm guns of Kampfgruppe Dirnagel. What followed was both brutal in its intensity and consequences. Almost immediately, three of the leading American tanks and the leading jeep were knocked out by Panzerfaust fire, and the rest of the column was raked by German small arms fire. "When the first Panzerfaust went off," Lyons recalled, "I hurled the blanket away and went over the skate mount and jumped to the ground. I moved forward to see what the trouble was. The 1st platoon immediately received orders to move out to the right flank and protect the convoy. I dismounted the men and moved to the other side of a railroad embankment to protect the column. We encountered heavy fire in all directions. The vehicles were withdrawn and the tanks moved to more protected ground."[30]

During the morning hours, as American artillery pounded Königshofen, A Company continued the attack but with little success, as three platoons were continually pinned down by small arms fire and occasional strafing runs from German Me 262s. In addition, the GIs found themselves fighting scattered German units sprinkled through the woods to their rear. At midday, a few American tanks tried a frontal assault on the Tauber bridge, which was protected by Kampfgruppe Dirnagel's 88mm guns. After the loss of two more tanks, the American forces withdrew. Hard on the heels of this withdrawal came a violent aerial attack on Königshofen, carried out by sixteen P-47s, followed by an intense artillery barrage, which left approximately three-quarters of the city in ruins. As the official history of the Twelfth Armored Division acknowledged, this was a characteristic pattern of operations at this time: "The armored columns would travel cautiously toward their objectives until the men were forced to dismount and fight for it. When heavy resistance was encountered, the tanks were brought up to soften the town or other objective. . . . If planes were needed, and they often were, the air liaison officer with each combat command would . . . direct them to the target. After a sufficient number of rounds had been poured into a town to terrify even the bravest inhabitants, the infantrymen inched their way through it, watching for snipers and strong points."[31]

Following this brutal air and artillery bombardment, C Company of the Seventeenth Armored Infantry Battalion again attacked Königshofen, even as its German defenders were emulating their brethren of four centuries earlier and were withdrawing from the burning city to more defensible positions in and around the ancient fortress of the Turmberg. As the GIs carefully worked their way into the western section of the city by early afternoon, both American artillery and German Me 262s continued their bombardment, reducing Königshofen to a sea of fire. Once across the Tauber bridge, however, they encountered fierce German resistance, as antitank fire slammed savagely into the American armored column, quickly forcing it to withdraw. As one participant later recounted, "If the experience hadn't been so serious it would have been good for a laugh. It looked as though a newsreel were being run backwards. We went into town firing every gun and two minutes later we were backing out firing faster than ever. One tank backed into a ditch and overturned while a wall from a burning building collapsed on top of it." American artillery continued to fire on the town and enemy troops and vehicles in the woods beyond, but by the evening of April 1 the Seventeenth Armored Infantry Battalion remained stalled just west of Königshofen, which had now been reduced to a heap of smoldering rubble.[32]

That same Easter Sunday, units of the Twenty-third Tank Battalion approached Edelfingen, on the east bank of the Tauber three miles south of Königshofen, with the intention of crossing the river and launching a flanking movement against the enemy to the north. Seeking to spare his village from total destruction, a German soldier on leave took it upon himself in the early afternoon to approach the advancing American troops with the idea of surrendering the town. The GIs, however, demanded that the *Ortsgruppenleiter* (local Nazi Party leader) be turned over to them. The would-be emissary of surrender thus trudged back to the village, found the local *Bonzen* (party boss), and related his activities to him. Incensed at the soldier's unauthorized action and fearful for his own life (although from what source, the enemy at his front or the Gestapo at his rear, is unclear), the party boss engaged the man in a short, heated exchange, then pulled out a pistol and shot the well-meaning Landser dead.[33]

In the meantime, the Germans had rushed a detachment of seventeen-year-old recruits from the Twelfth SS-Hitler Youth Division and infantry units from the Kampfgruppe Dirnagel into Edelfingen. Confronted with difficult terrain, subjected to repeated attacks from Me 262s, and against heavy German artillery and antitank fire, the GIs nonetheless forced a crossing of the Tauber, which resulted in the loss, according to German accounts, of at least sixteen vehicles to the stubborn defenders. Having blasted their way across the river, the GIs encountered further tenacious German resistance in the wooded ridges immediately to the east, as antitank and machine gun fire quickly halted the American advance. In the late afternoon gloom, as the boys of the Twelfth SS fought furiously, some seeking to destroy American tanks by crawling under them to plant explosive charges, they received an unexpected boost—just before 6:00 P.M. German jet fighters swooped over the column of forty American tanks, immobilized after the lead vehicle had been knocked out by one of the ubiquitous 88s. By 7:00 that evening, having lost a number of vehicles, the American advance had ground to a complete halt. Faced with this escalating opposition and fearing a strong enemy counterattack, the Americans, much to the amazement of the Germans, just before midnight withdrew to the west bank of the Tauber, seeking shelter at Unterschüpf, a few miles to the west of Edelfingen.[34]

The next day, tanks from the Twenty-third Tank Battalion moved to the north and east to join with the Twelfth and Twenty-second Regiments of the Fourth Infantry Division at Grünsfeld, on the Wittigbach River a few miles to the east of Lauda. Although advance patrols of the Twenty-second Infantry Regiment had seized Lauda unopposed on the morning of April 1, by early afternoon the Second Battalion faced increasing artillery and mortar opposition as it crossed the Tauber and advanced on Grünsfeld. By the time the Third Battalion moved through Lauda after dark, German fighter planes repeatedly struck at the column. Forced to disperse and deploy their vehicles off the road to avoid the enemy strafing, a number of GIs sought shelter in a large railroad overpass on the eastern edge of Lauda. As the men huddled silently beneath it, they could see in the distance huge flames consuming the city of Königshofen, a stark reminder of the powerful American air attack earlier in the day. As the GIs once again moved out, having beaten back a counterattack launched in the early morning hours of April 3 by troops of the Thirty-eighth Panzergrenadier Regiment of the Seventeenth SS, and having been harassed continually by German aircraft, they realized another stark fact—the easy victories of the past few days and their hopes of a quick collapse of German resistance had both proven illusory. The stiffening German resistance had shown conclusively that the stroll through the Odenwald to the Tauber had come to an end.[35]

In a coordinated pincer movement, these American units attacked to the south and east early on April 2 to clear the enemy east of the Tauber while the Seventeenth Armored Infantry Battalion attempted to seize Königshofen frontally. Against moderately heavy German small arms, antitank, Nebelwerfer, and artillery fire, harassed continually from the air, and forced to repulse at least three enemy counterattacks, the GIs struggled to advance two miles. By the end of the day, they had taken Marbach, Hofstetten, and Kützbrunn, but faced the prospect of further bitter fighting in the rugged, heavily wooded terrain. Adding to their difficulties, perhaps a thousand Polish and Russian forced laborers sought shelter behind American lines, both clogging the roads and temporarily overwhelming already jammed supply lines. More troublesome, American intelligence reports indicated the presence of a sizeable German force to the east of the Tauber and the north of Bad Mergentheim. Although the men of the Fourth Infantry had taken a couple hundred Germans prisoner, the mood by the end of the day remained sober, as a further forty-two GIs, on top of the thirty-nine from the previous day, had become casualties of the unexpectedly fierce fighting.[36]

To the south and west, the men of the Seventeenth Armored Infantry Battalion encountered similar stubborn resistance at Königshofen, where they faced a grim fight across the high ground that commanded the road and bridge leading into the city. At daybreak, American machine guns opened up a withering fire on the German defense line running along the railroad tracks just west of the Tauber. Despite heavy casualties, however, the Germans stubbornly returned fire and even forced the American units to withdraw for better protection. Early in the afternoon, the Americans launched another assault against the high ground, this time behind a rolling artillery barrage. Unfortunately, as Sergeant Lyons noted:

> My leading scouts had just reached the foot of the hill when one of our barrages landed fifty yards short, right in the middle of my platoon. It killed Bert, thirty feet in front of me, killed three men in the 3rd squad to my right and wounded several more. I was never so scared of the enemy's artillery as I was that day of our own. . . . I shouted at the men and once more we were moving against the Kraut emplacements. Ten Krauts were killed in the trenches on the hill. We gained the top of the hill and were pushing on when four enemy machine guns opened up on us. . . . It was impossible to advance and I thought it was best to withdraw the platoon to the crest of the hill.[37]

As the men of A Company continued to occupy the attention of the German defenders, C Company launched a late-afternoon attack, roaring through the startled Landsers on the backs of a platoon of tanks. Even when the GIs had pushed through the heights, seized the Tauber bridge, and entered the eastern half of Königshofen, the German defenders did not relent. "When we finally pulled over the stinking Tauber River into the burning town everyone was on edge," recalled Sherman Lans.

"Every building in town had either been burned or thoroughly wrecked by artillery.... We felt naked as our [half-tracks] were silhouetted against the sheets of flames, and we couldn't see beyond the leaping fires. ... Everybody was pretty jumpy." Catching units of C Company in a murderous ambush of small arms fire, the Germans inflicted heavy casualties, while the Third Platoon of A Company, attempting to hold the bridge across the Tauber, was subjected to a withering German artillery bombardment. Late in the afternoon of April 2, worn down by the fighting, the Seventeenth Armored Infantry Battalion was relieved and ordered to withdraw. The withdrawal proved anything but orderly, however, as German jet fighters attacked the GIs from the air, while on the ground the troops had to fight their way rearward, as isolated German units had filtered back in and reoccupied positions from which they had been cleared earlier in the day. Indeed, the fanaticism of the German resistance can be gauged from the fact that SS teams infiltrated occupied areas of the town and blew up houses that flew a white flag of surrender.[38]

THE TURMBERG REDUX

Although they had disengaged from the burning ruins of Königshofen, the men of the Seventeenth Armored Infantry Battalion found no rest, for late on April 2 they received orders to bypass the city to the north and push eastward along the route Marbach–Gerlachsheim–Grünsfeld–Butthard–Sonderhofen, with the object of cutting German routes of retreat south. The irksome chore of clearing the Tauber valley of the pockets of enemy troops bypassed by American armored units fell to the Twelfth and Twenty-second Regiments of the Fourth Infantry Division, which encountered stiff resistance in the thick woods to the east and south of Königshofen. On the morning of April 2, troops of the First Battalion, Twenty-second Infantry Regiment, seized the towns of Hofstetten and Sailtheim, then late that afternoon overcame moderately heavy artillery and Nebelwerfer fire to take Marbach. Still, as one GI admitted, "the going was plenty rugged," as shown by the forty-two casualties suffered by the First Battalion, as well as the sharply decreased number of Germans taken prisoner. With this movement to the south, it now became apparent that the American plan was to seize the commanding heights of the Turmberg by an attack from the east. Accordingly, the Germans dispatched the already battered officer candidates of ROB Lenggries to defend the position.[39]

In bitter fighting the next day, C Company of the Twenty-second Infantry Regiment succeeded early in the morning of April 3 in taking a high, wooded ridge just south of Marbach, but then found itself cut off and surrounded by a German counterattack led by troops of the ROB Lenggries and supported by Nebelwerfer fire. Amazingly, despite their desperate shortage of munitions and the fact that they had to beg local farmers for food, the young officer candidates displayed a willingness time and again to launch counterattacks against the Americans. Indeed, one survivor recalled the mounds of food, boots, rain gear, and other American supplies they captured, and noted that they had not received any official rations since the end of March. The German willingness to attack perhaps had as much to do with simple hunger as any ideological fanaticism. Not until mid-afternoon, and in further heavy combat, did other GIs reach their stranded buddies and finally secure the ridge. Even then, however, the Germans did not relent, in the early evening launching yet another assault against American positions. Caught by surprise, and taken aback by the fanaticism of the young Germans, the GIs responded not only with heavy artillery and small arms fire, but also by having tanks shoot into the tops of trees in the thick woods, showering deadly splinters down upon the infiltrating Germans. Despite their astonishing willingness to sacrifice themselves, the overwhelming American firepower ultimately proved decisive, and late that evening the Germans finally called a halt to their attacks. Of the original 150 men in the Sixth Company, ROB Lenggries, only some thirty now remained; the Americans, too, had suffered heavy casualties, losing a further forty-nine men.[40]

Nor did German resistance show any sign of abating. In fact, the next day, April 4, saw the beginning of the fiercest fighting to date. Field Marshal Albert Kesselring, Supreme Commander West, set the tone by appealing to all troops to willingly sacrifice their lives in this decisive fight for the future of Germany. Opposed again by the young officer candidates, the Twenty-second Infantry battled savagely for several days south of the Marbach–Hofstetten road in dense woods unsuitable for tanks or artillery against fanatical defenders who entrenched themselves in caves. As a regimental chaplain noted, "the ground on this ridge consisted of heavy woods with rock piles parallel to the line of advance with holes cut in them for German automatic weapons. Almost every casualty suffered was by a direct hit in the head with one bullet." On April 4, the Second

Battalion succeeded against steady German pressure and counterattacks in taking Messelhausen, advancing perhaps a mile in the face of stubborn enemy resistance, only to withdraw after numerous German assaults against both Messelhausen itself and American supply lines into the town, attacks that continued through the next day. Indeed, an incident at Löhlein, a small village outside Messelhausen, best illustrates the confused and dangerous situation. Having entered the hamlet in darkness, GIs began searching cellars with flashlights, looking for German troops. As GIs gathered at one cellar filled with civilians, an undetected German machine gunner opened up, sending some of the Americans fleeing and others down into the cellar. Another German soldier then fired a Panzerfaust round into the cellar, with predictably grisly consequences—some GIs and villagers, mostly women and children, were killed immediately, and others suffered ghastly burns and wounds. While American medics tended the wounded on both sides, a second Panzerfaust was shot through the air shaft, with even more disastrous results. The shell landed amid civilians, unleashing total pandemonium, and as flames raced through the room, shrapnel devastated women, children, and soldiers alike. Little wonder that in the house-to-house fighting over the next two days, as the struggle for Messelhausen continued, jittery GIs accidently shot both German civilians and their own comrades.[41]

To the west, the Third Battalion, now reinforced by the First Battalion, on April 5 once again encountered, in the words of the regimental after-action report, "fanatical resistance" from the young officer candidates. Indeed, one of the Germans' former unit commanders noted after the war, "They were honorable young men eager to fight, who maintained their discipline to the last and whose morale was without reproach. Admittedly, they were also better equipped than normal troops, especially with machine guns and Panzerfäusten." Chaplain Boice agreed:

> They were young, from fifteen to nineteen, but they fought with a fanaticism of which we had read but seldom met. One of these young Hitler youth had a wound in his leg which prevented his crawling away, and he was sitting under a tree. . . . The battalion medics, as usual, were going from person to person . . . administering first aid. . . . One of the medics started to approach the wounded German lad when the boy picked up a "potato masher." . . . The medic stopped and pointed to

his red cross arm band. . . . The German stared at him stonily, and as the medic again moved to approach him, he unscrewed the cap of his grenade. . . . The lad held the grenade immediately under his chin until it went off, blowing his head completely off and cleanly from his body. Such was the fanaticism of the Hitler youth.

Lieutenant Cliff Henley put it more succinctly, noting in his diary, "fighting a bunch from NCO school and are they mean. They fight to the end."[42]

Slogging through the wooded hills just east of Königshofen against this determined resistance, the GIs of the Fourth Infantry Division made agonizingly slow progress. By April 4, though, American artillery continually harassed German positions on the Turmberg, making it difficult even to supply food and water to the beleaguered defenders. Indeed, one soldier who faltered in trying to bring supplies to the besieged Germans found himself hauled before a military tribunal and charged with cowardice. Only through the sympathy of local farmers, who slaughtered livestock, did the men of the ROB Lenggries receive any food at all. In attacks throughout the day, the GIs steadily pushed the dwindling German defenders toward the crest of the hill, where they frantically dug in under fire so intense that a soldier would be hit almost as soon as he raised his head above his foxhole. Adding further misery, a steady rain forced the Landsers to use their mess kits to bail out their holes.[43]

The remaining German defenders took advantage of the darkness during the night of April 4–5 to change their positions, so that the GIs attacking early on the morning of April 5 found themselves under fire from unexpected directions, and were forced to retreat in some confusion. Nor, despite strenuous efforts throughout the day, did further American assaults succeed in dislodging the stubborn German defenders. "Heavy woods prevented the use of tanks in the attack," noted Chaplain Boice, "and intense, accurate small arms fire met every movement of the foot troops. As Captain Reid later stated, 'That was the doggondedest small arms fire Big Item Company will ever encounter.'" Their own losses mounting as a result of the pitched fighting and constant artillery bombardment, the Germans finally decided on the night of April 5–6 to evacuate the Turmberg and withdraw the exhausted remnants of the Reserve Officers Battalion. In the confusion, however, one company failed to receive the withdrawal order, so on the morning of April 6 they fought one last desperate battle, even as their comrades trudged dejectedly through Deubach in retreat. The final struggle, perhaps fittingly, centered on that historic site of slaughter on the Turmberg, where over four hundred years earlier the Peasants War had come to a bloody end. The young officer cadets fought fiercely to defend it, succumbing only when superior American forces stormed the hill. The fighting for the Turmberg had been savage, with sixty-two cadets dying in the last phase of the battle alone.[44] As a symbol of senseless loss of life and the misuse of youthful idealism, the carnage on the Turmberg, although on a much smaller scale, perhaps approximated the famous *Kindermord* (children's murder) at Ypres of World War I, although then the slaughter of innocents took place at the very beginning, rather than the end, of a ruinous war.

The GIs of the Fourth Infantry Division did not succeed in taking Deubach, little more than two miles south of Marbach (which they had seized on April 2), until the afternoon of April 6. In the face of withering American artillery and small arms fire, which left virtually all of Deubach in flames, the Germans grudgingly pulled back. Despite heavy enemy small arms fire, the men of the Third Battalion nonetheless pushed on to the south, finally succeeding in breaking the main German line of resistance and reaching the heights above Bad Mergentheim late that night. In the aftermath, the men of the Twenty-second Infantry Regiment counted over a hundred dead Germans, mostly boys of seventeen or eighteen, piled in the hotly contested woods. German civilians, too, busied themselves on April 6 in collecting the dead; in addition to the 62 on the Turmberg, they found roughly 122 more bodies of dead Landsers in the few miles between Deubach and Oesfeld. "The German dead lay piled like cord wood over every conceivable defensive terrain feature," Chaplain Boice acknowledged. "Some of the Germans had been dead for several days, and their skin was turning black and the blood clotted clothing swarmed with flies. There was the foul stench of death in the atmosphere." And not just the stench of German dead—the three days of fighting had been costly for the Americans as well, with twenty-three GIs killed, sixty-seven wounded, and three missing. In just this one week of fighting, in fact, the Twenty-second Infantry Regiment alone suffered 201 casualties, of whom 52 men, a quarter of the total casualties, were killed in action.[45]

As a further example of German fanaticism and the use (or misuse) of young boys in this futile defensive effort, on April 6 at the town of

Stuppach, a few miles south of Bad Mergentheim, a group of Hitler Youth, mostly fourteen- or fifteen-year-old boys who had been evacuated from the industrial city of Duisburg in the Ruhr, voluntarily reported for duty to an SS unit stationed in the area. Their motivations varied, some being fanatical Nazi adherents, others more interested in camaraderie or adventure, but all wanted to participate in the defense of Germany. As one survivor noted in the mid-1980s, "Making myself available for duty was my own decision—independent of the decisions of other comrades in my unit. One can only understand that with great difficulty today, but at the time we wanted to save the Fatherland. Exactly as we had been taught. We believed in it." Still, even the local SS unit commander hesitated to use these young boys until he received a decisive directive from SS headquarters: "Whoever reports voluntarily will be taken on. But the decision [to serve] is final, there is no going back." For some of the youthful fanatics, this ominous edict proved all too literal; after an hours-long battle, during which the Americans lost at least five tanks, sixty-three Germans lay dead, of whom nine were Hitler Youth. Just as portentously, a later investigation of the dead by the *Volksbundes Deutsche Kriegsgräberfürsorge* (War Graves Commission) alleged that many of the Germans had been killed after surrendering by a shot to the head or by having their skull bashed in. Surprised and incensed by the fierce resistance, some Americans, in the heat of battle, evidently exacted a harsh revenge, a tendency that would recur with disturbing frequency over the next few weeks.[46]

Similarly, in a flanking attack into the Simmringen Woods ten miles east of Königshofen, three companies of the Twelfth Infantry Regiment, Fourth Infantry Division, attacked entrenched German defenders, once again young SS officer candidates and SS-Panzer (Pz.) Grenadiers, whose professed slogan was "we fight and never give up." The Germans did not betray their self-expectations. Dug in along a three-deep defensive position between Simmringen, a village astride the R 19, a main highway running from Würzburg to the Danube at Ulm, and Stalldorf a few miles to the east, and to the distress of local villagers, the German soldiers remained determined to fight. The first and strongest defense line ran directly through the thick woods separating the two villages. Thus, even as the local priest hoisted the papal ensign and a white flag of surrender from the church tower, and as the village mayor sought to approach the Americans with a white flag, the SS commander signaled the seriousness of his intent by threatening both with execution.[47]

Having kept the Simmringen Woods under steady artillery and machine gun fire for almost two days, the GIs launched their assault into the dense forest on April 5. From the start, the GIs made only fitful progress, their advance slowed by the stubborn German defenders, an inability to maintain contact with neighboring units, and the unsuitability of the terrain for tanks. By early afternoon, in fact, not only had the American advance ground to a halt, but they had to fight off a furious German counterattack. Late that afternoon the GIs dug in for the night, preferring to keep the woods and village of Stalldorf under artillery and tank fire rather than risk a night battle in the gloomy thicket that surrounded them. Jumping off early the next morning, the Americans pushed ahead stubbornly against dogged resistance, cleared the Simmringen Woods, and began to approach Stalldorf from three sides. Faced with being cut off, and with their positions now untenable, the SS units finally retreated to the southeast, but only after the GIs of the Twelfth Infantry Regiment had expended, in the words of its assistant operations officer, "an almost unprecedented volume of small-arms fire." Even as an African American unit scoured the Simmringen Woods over the next few days for hidden Germans, some SS men obstinately resisted, to the extent that the GIs resorted to the use of flamethrowers literally to burn them out of the dense underbrush. When German civilians later searched for bodies, they found many of the SS corpses charred beyond recognition. The rather cavalier treatment accorded the crossing of the Tauber in American accounts thus lies in distinct contrast to the actual experience of many GIs, especially those who bore the brunt of the fighting in and around Königshofen. Indeed, as the postwar operational history of the U.S. Seventh Army tersely put it, in the first week of April 1945, "German air activity was greater than any . . . yet encountered," while the Germans made "economical use of tanks," artillery, and the Panzerfaust in their determined resistance.[48] Whether from ideological belief, fanatical loyalty, a sense of comradely duty, or fear of the SS, the German will to resist proved astonishingly strong at the Tauber, a dire warning of things to come as American troops pushed on to the east and south.

THROUGH THE STEIGERWALD

Having crossed the Tauber, units of the Twelfth Armored Division, primarily the Seventeenth Armored Infantry Battalion and the Twenty-third Tank Battalion, now moved rapidly eastward toward Aub, Uffenheim, and Ippesheim, hoping to skirt the ridges along the southern edge of the Steigerwald before turning south toward the Aisch River and the towns of Bad Windsheim and Neustadt, which controlled access to the *Frankenhöhe.* Subjected to constant American aerial attacks and strong artillery fire, faced with shortages of heavy weapons, artillery, food, and fuel, and deeply impressed by the overwhelming material superiority of its enemy, against which even personal bravery seemed futile, German commanders struggled to maintain the steadfastness of their troops. For the Germans, these were demoralizing days of hard fighting and heavy losses, with their only hope of delaying the Americans lying in the doggedness and courage of the Landser and the effectiveness of the remarkable Panzerfaust handheld antitank weapon.[1]

Although impressive as a tank destroyer, the Panzerfaust made deep demands on one's reservoir of personal courage, for a Landser had to lie in wait (or approach stealthily) until a tank was at point-blank range, rise suddenly to fire the one-shot weapon, then scurry to safety, all the while hoping not to be seen or hit by supporting enemy infantrymen. A veteran of the Twelfth Armored Division remembered the fanatical Germans who "hunkered in fox-holes with Panzerfäuste at the roadside, ready to die for the chance of knocking out just one tank, and they often succeeded because the Panzerfaust was a superb weapon." To combat it, GIs soon "rode on tanks, the tanks spraying the road with machine-gun fire, keeping the Germans in their holes, and the infantry tossing grenades with a looping trajectory very carefully into the holes from where they sat on top of the tanks, so that the fanatics ended with a squashy *whump*, and those who lived were really hell to take care of, all bloody scrambled. They crouched between pine-tree roadblocks until our tank guns blew them away in white flashes and splinters; they dug lines of fortifications that were target practice for our artillery. . . . Their lunatic heroism ended torn or dead." The futility of the resistance notwithstanding, in three weeks of fighting in Middle Franconia some three hundred American vehicles fell victim to Landsers wielding the Panzerfaust.[2]

Opposing the Twelfth Armored's advance were remnants of Kampfgruppe Dirnagel; the Seventy-ninth, 212th, and 352nd Volksgrenadier Divisions (severely under-strength infantry units with fewer than one thousand men each); a battle group of the Second Mountain Division with perhaps 1,500 troops; and the newly formed *Panzerkampfgruppe* XIII, more commonly referred to as *Panzerkampfgruppe Hobe*, named for its commander, Lieutenant Colonel Cord von Hobe, who took charge of the battle group on April 6. This latter outfit, although hastily cobbled together, posed particular problems for the Americans. With a mixed bag of tank destroyer units and no more than six hundred infantrymen, it included experienced officers, most with service in the east, and a highly motivated core of soldiers—military cadets, Hitler Youth adherents, and officer candidates—with an unusually high battle spirit at this late stage of the war. Despite the stiff challenge his Kampfgruppe ultimately presented, because of insufficient fuel and ammunition, poor intelligence and communication, and constant American fighter-bomber attacks, Hobe only managed to get a fraction of his available armor into action, the greater part of his tank force eventually being destroyed by their own crews. Indeed, the chronic lack of fuel and general disillusionment with the so-called wonder weapons that Hitler had promised would win the war resulted in a sardonic gibe about the latest such weapon, the one hundred-man tank: one man would sit inside while the other ninety-nine pushed.[3]

Stretched along a roughly thirty-mile line running southwest from

Iphofen in the north through Ippesheim and Herrnberchtheim to Uffenheim, Hobe aimed to force the Americans to traverse the rugged terrain of the 1,300- to 1,500-foot heights of the Steigerwald. A heavily forested region traversed by Neanderthal hunters one hundred thousand years earlier, permanently settled at least seven thousand years before the birth of Christ, overrun by Celts, Germans, and Franks, all of whom left their mark, and the scene of dreadful slaughter in both the Peasants War and the Thirty Years War, the Steigerwald once again became the focal point of invading forces. With its strategic position to the northwest of Nuremberg, and astride the main railroads and highways running from Würzburg south, any German hope of an orderly withdrawal to the Alps depended on a successful defense of the Steigerwald. Although gaps remained in his line, Hobe hoped through careful placement of his tank destroyer units and *Panzers* to fight a delaying action sufficient to allow German units to fall back in good order toward Nuremberg, Munich, and the south.[4]

"WAR AT ITS MOST VICIOUS"

Initially encountering only scattered resistance after bypassing Königshofen, the American advance grew more tentative by the early afternoon of April 3 as the GIs of the Twenty-third Tank Battalion received numerous reports from liberated French POWs and foreign laborers suggesting as many as three thousand German soldiers, mostly SS troops and including some dressed in civilian clothing, had assembled in the vicinity of Aub and Uffenheim. The first casualty of this increasing American anxiety was the village of Osthausen, just north of Aub. Amid the confusing stream of reports and rumors, the GIs decided to take no chances, bombarding Osthausen with concentrated fire from conventional and rocket-firing tanks, then carefully creeping toward the town in preparation for the final assault. Storming into the fiercely burning village at dusk, the GIs quickly rounded up the fearful inhabitants and herded them into the local cemetery. Much to their surprise, the Americans found no soldiers, indeed virtually no men, among the villagers, who watched helplessly as their town burned to the ground. After the fact, local suspicions centered on the large Polish forced labor population in the area. Perhaps incensed by mistreatment by local farmers or, more likely, burning with revenge for the August 1942 execution of one

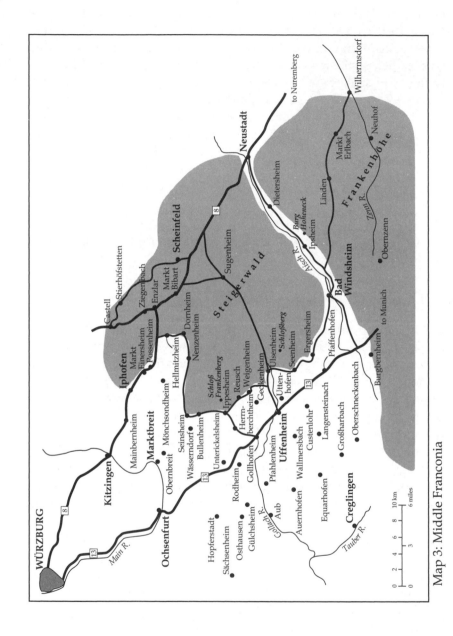

Map 3: Middle Franconia

of their own by the Gestapo (a hanging that all the Poles in the area had been forced to watch), they had, whether deliberately or not, supplied American troops with reports, incorrect as it turned out, of large concentrations of SS troops lurking in the town. As the Poles had perhaps anticipated, the ever-cautious GIs reduced Osthausen to a pile of burning rubble, demonstrating again that few emerge from war unscathed.[5]

Operating on the left flank of the Twenty-third Tank Battalion, it was the men of the Seventeenth Armored Infantry Battalion who on April 3 ran squarely into SS troops at Rodheim and on the outskirts of Herrnberchtheim. Now began a nine-day period of intense fighting, as German forces fought doggedly to prevent an American breakthrough of their defensive line. Although Rodheim fell after a short, fierce firefight, Herrnberchtheim proved much more troublesome. Ordered to take the town, at 6:00 that evening Sergeant Carl Lyons of A Company placed the trucks and attached tanks of the First Platoon in a V-formation and headed cross-country toward this village of a few hundred people. The German troops there had dug in along a railroad embankment at the western edge of town. "A group of enemy infantry [retreating from Rodheim] was seen off to the right in a thick woods," Lyons noted in his diary, "and we gave them a going-over, but we bypassed the woods and moved against the town." Then, in characteristic American fashion at this stage of the war, Lyons remarked, "We stood for awhile on the outskirts of the town machine gunning the place, allowing our artillery to set fire to parts of the town. A railroad embankment prevented a mounted attack on a broad front, so with three tanks in the lead and my half-tracks following, we advanced down the road leading under the railroad embankment and into the town." Despite Lyons's rather nonchalant account, the fight for the embankment proved particularly fierce, as it changed hands several times during the course of the evening. Indeed, as a GI from C Company noted, "Able Company was attacking [Herrnberchtheim] and it was burning fiercely. They had already lost two half-tracks to Panzerfaust fire and it was apparent the enemy was prepared to make a stand. A railroad ran . . . between our position and the main section [of town]. Cars still loaded with war materials and others crippled by our Air Force stood out starkly against the rapidly spreading flames. . . . The Krauts were taking full advantage of the cover of the disabled railroad cars and the whole embankment was strictly krautland."[6]

In any case, this "dash" into Herrnberchtheim soon faltered, for the First Platoon had "just entered the town [at 8:00 P.M.] when we were ambushed. Enemy firing broke out heavy ahead as Panzerfaust lit [*sic*] among the tanks and machine gun fire raked the men. We immediately dismounted and seized buildings to our right. The Second Platoon was rushed up, dismounted, to come abreast of us, taking the buildings on the other side of the street." As darkness fell the fighting abated somewhat, although C Company was brought in to assist in clearing the town. For the next few hours, the GIs pushed ahead through the town, in methodical, terrifying house-to-house fighting. Although the Third Platoon of A Company and an antitank platoon supported them to the rear, the GIs in Herrnberchtheim soon found themselves cut off, as the Germans forced these supporting elements to withdraw. "All night we fought Krauts who kept infiltrating," Lyons recalled. "One tank was knocked out in the center of town by a Kraut who had infiltrated through our lines. One whole enemy platoon walked right between the 1st and 2nd Platoons. . . . The enemy counter-attacked all night, and the going was fairly rough. The town was practically burning down on top of us to add to our worries. I had lost two half-tracks in the initial ambush. They had been knocked out by Panzerfausts [*sic*]. . . . Casualties had been fairly light considering the precarious position we were in. . . . Things were in a mess. We hoped daybreak would bring some relief." Confirmed Sherman Lans, of C Company, "Leaving the drivers with the tracks, the rest of the company entered the town on foot. We couldn't clean up the town at night so we set up local defenses. . . . While the drivers were alone three krauts came up on Randecker's track and set it on fire with a Panzerfaust rocket." Although given to understatement, the type of fighting Lyons and his men found themselves in tested the limits of courage of even the bravest men. As W. Y. Boyd, himself an infantryman who fought in Middle Franconia, attested in his novel *The Gentle Infantryman,* "The fighting in [a] town . . . was war at its most vicious and most merciless. No prisoners were taken by either side. . . . When they met, they fought to the death; it was that simple."[7]

Fortunately for the GIs, daybreak brought relief from their encirclement, although fighting continued to be intense. Early on the morning of April 4, the antitank platoon repelled enemy counterattacks launched from the west and north, and then cleared out a cluster of German troops in a ruined building who were attempting to knock out American positions through the use of sniper and Panzerfaust fire. By early afternoon other elements of the task force broke into Herrnberchtheim with badly needed ammunition, gasoline, and food. Still, the men of A and C Companies found themselves engaged throughout the day in firefights from all directions. Indeed, not until late that afternoon did combat patrols finally succeed in clearing the railroad embankment of Germans, in the process capturing what remained of an enemy company. Nor did the situation improve appreciably the next day. Early in the morning of April 5, as A Company moved out of Herrnberchtheim in convoy, leaving behind in the rubble the bodies of twenty-eight dead German soldiers, a flight of German Me 109s suddenly dove out of the sky and strafed the column. Completely surprised, with men running in all directions, Sergeant Lyons "pulled the machine gun [on a half-track] around and got off two shots. The gun immediately jammed. The enemy plane was spurting flame and dust was kicking up just outside the half-track. I knelt behind the shield and tried to get the gun working. Six planes went over without hardly a shot being fired at them, so complete was the surprise of their attack. . . . Only one man was killed in A Company, but it put us all on edge."[8]

Events in Obernbreit, a few miles north of Herrnberchtheim, also illustrated the tensions of war, albeit between the would-be German defenders and civilians reluctant to see their homes and villages destroyed in futile, last-ditch resistance. Already subjected to heavy American artillery fire on the morning of April 4, that evening a group of women confronted the local commander and demanded that he order the withdrawal of his troops, as well as arrange the hoisting of white flags over the town. Incensed, the lieutenant harshly rejected their plea. Not only did he order them back to their homes, but also threatened to shoot every fifth woman in town if the group did not immediately disappear. The next day, the officer's dead body was found lying on the railroad embankment; shortly thereafter, German troops withdrew from the town.[9]

Seeking to avoid another confrontation such as that at Herrnberchtheim, elements of the Seventeenth Armored Infantry Battalion on April 5 moved north a few miles before turning east in the direction of Bullenheim, a village at the foot of the high western ridges of the Steigerwald, rising in this area to over 1,500 feet. Hoping to move quickly to the east to block the German retreat along the main Würzburg–Nuremberg highway (R 8), the GIs soon found the Steigerwald to be much more conducive to defense than rapid movement. As Lans noted, "by 0930 we had pulled up on a small knoll where our observation was unlimited. A beautiful sight met our eyes. There were seven towns in view and six of them were in flames." Still, as Lans also observed, "The terrain wasn't suited for vehicles so we dismounted and started forward on foot." Forced to fight in the rugged terrain favored by the Germans in laying out their defense line, the GIs soon encountered resistance, this time at the Iff River, itself little more than a creek, just to the west of Bullenheim. "Casualties would have been too heavy if we had continued on foot," Lans noted, "so we changed our route and proceeded mounted." Attacking abreast and supported by tanks, the assault by A and C Companies nevertheless bogged down because of strong German fire from the heights beyond the creek. Quickly setting up their mortars, A Company delivered a withering fire on the German defenders while American tanks, in Lans's words, "blasted some diehards crouched in holes by the side of the road."[10]

Nor were German soldiers the only worry, for as Lans observed, "We had some trouble with the civilians. We caught one sniper who had taken a pot shot at an FO, and shot at several more who attempted to take off across an open field." A blurring of the distinction between soldiers and civilians, in fact, seemed a chronic problem in this area, as reports from the Twenty-third Tank Battalion mentioned numerous encounters with soldiers dressed in civilian clothing. Most likely, these were not SS men, as the GIs claimed, but local members of the Volkssturm, who, given the prevailing shortage of uniforms, would often wear civilian clothing with military armbands. In any case, at the sight of Germans beginning to withdraw, the tank company also opened up, resulting in at least two dozen Germans killed and an equal number taken prisoner.[11]

Still, the Germans, fortified by a tank destroyer (*Panzerjäger*) unit, continued to resist ferociously. Faced with stiff German fire that cost it several men killed and wounded, A Company called in the antitank platoon, which barreled down the road between the First and Second Platoons and soon cleared Bullenheim of its defenders. Moving across open fields toward Seinsheim, no more than a mile north of Bullenheim, the men of A Company seized the high ground overlooking the village, which was teeming with German activity. American assault guns, mortars, antitank guns, and tanks savagely bombarded the town. As First Platoon moved out to attack, Sergeant Lyons saw an amazing sight: German tanks and troops began fleeing from the town. Not only did Lyons and his men open up on them with small arms fire, but artillery continued to pound the town while P-47s knocked out several enemy tanks. Not until early evening, however, did the infantry of A and C Companies make a dismounted attack on the village, killing at least a dozen Landsers and driving out the last German defenders. Even then, the exhausted GIs found little relief, as frequent German patrols kept them on edge throughout the night. Lyons also noted, with laconic understatement, "Mail was brought up; one of the men had a discouraging letter from his wife and he went crazy."[12] This was barely a month before the war in Europe ended; as the unfortunate GI discovered, the strain of combat could take its toll at any time and place.

In the meantime, a gruesome denouement to the sharp encounters at Bullenheim and Seinsheim played out at Wässerndorf, a small village just to the west. Surprised by the rapid advance of Task Force Norton of the Twelfth Armored Division, a few SS mountain troops put up a short, furious resistance, during which an American officer was shot, allegedly by a sharpshooter firing from the local castle. Arriving on the scene, and incensed at the death of his friend, Major Norton had some eighty villagers herded into the cellar, then ordered his tanks to shoot incendiary shells into the castle and burn it down around them. Although Norton soon relented and allowed the villagers to flee, the castle, in which valuable archives from Würzburg had been stored for safekeeping, continued to burn for two weeks. In the lower village lay the bodies of twenty-three German soldiers and three civilians. Another villager, seeking to extinguish a fire in his attic, leaned out a window, shouted for help, and was promptly shot by a GI. Two American soldiers chased away yet another farmer attempting to put out a fire, and shot him on the bank of the Iff River, where his body was found that evening by a Polish laborer.[13]

The next day, April 6, the men of the Seventeenth Armored Infantry Battalion continued their attempt to cut the main German line of retreat, moving northeast in the direction of Mönchsondheim, a small town on the Breitbach River a few miles to the west of the main Würzburg–Nuremberg railroad and highway. Once again, the persistent pattern of the last few days repeated itself: strong German resistance halted the Americans as they approached the heights overlooking the town. Even as the GIs seized the high ground, they failed to generate any momentum, as carefully placed German snipers hampered movement and forced the Americans to ground. Then, before A and C Companies launched a dismounted attack just after noon, American artillery and machine gun fire from half-tracks perched on the heights above raked the village. As the men of the First and Third Platoons of A Company advanced cautiously under cover of the continuing artillery barrage, they could see Mönchsondheim burning fiercely. Entering the town, they witnessed the effects of the intense barrage—seventeen Landsers lay dead, mostly ethnic Germans from Russia, while others, dazed and frightened, stumbled out of buildings to surrender.[14]

As A Company continued its advance and seized the high ground to the east of the town, they again encountered heavy sniper fire. As they moved mortars into position to lay down advance fire, a cold rain began to fall. Quickly chilled to the bone, worn down by the steady combat of the past few days, and exhausted by lack of sleep, Sergeant Lyons worried that his men could not do much more. Despite their constant griping, however, the men of A Company continued to attack dismounted to the east, with the objective of cutting the main highway and railroad, thus preventing German troops from escaping southward to Nuremberg or the Alps. Already bombed heavily the day before by P-47s, the town of Markt Einersheim now felt the full fury of war, as American tanks and artillery unleashed a thunderous half-hour barrage. At 4:30 P.M. A Company went over to the attack and quickly broke the last line of German resistance along a railroad embankment. This last push carried them across the rail line and into Markt Einersheim astride the Nuremberg highway. Although the town's defenders offered only scattered resistance and soon withdrew to the southeast, the GIs collapsed from fatigue, allowing the Germans, "miraculously," in the words of Lieutenant Colonel Cord von Hobe, to stabilize their front by collecting the shattered remnants of units retreating from Würzburg. Still, the fighting of the last few days had seriously depleted what remained of the German defensive force, more than a thousand men being reported killed, wounded, missing, or taken prisoner. Themselves exhausted by the week of bitter fighting, the men of the Seventeenth Armored Infantry Battalion were relieved and withdrawn to the town of Unterickelsheim, three miles west of Ippesheim, for a badly needed rest.[15]

"THERE ARE TOO MANY GERMANS IN THIS COUNTRY"

Despite the efforts of the Seventeenth Armored Infantry Battalion, the breakthrough of the German defense line came to the west and south, ironically at Ippesheim, Gollhofen, and Uffenheim, precisely the area A and C Companies had been sent for rest. Although able to throw back all American attacks in this area on April 8, severe shortages of artillery, antitank weapons, and fuel, coupled with absolute American air dominance, meant that Hobe, still with sixty tanks and a Hitler Youth battalion in reserve, could not launch any effective counterattack but instead had to place his tanks in defensive positions supporting his infantry. Harassed by constant pressure from the Americans, Hobe now also faced a civilian population whose mood had grown increasingly unfriendly to their own troops. Not atypically, local inhabitants often urged German commanders to abandon their villages without resistance and proved willing to tear down antitank obstacles as soon as they were built. More seriously, Hobe also received reports of civilians interfering with supply lines and even taking random shots at German troops, a situation that made it difficult for Hobe both to communicate with and supply his forces.[16]

Still, the tension between soldiers and civilians rarely erupted into open conflict, and without the help of innumerable farm families and local villagers who took pity on the bedraggled Landsers and supplied food, drink, and shelter, the Germans would have been in no condition to continue the fight. And just to remind the GIs that they still had the will to fight, as well as to keep the Americans uncertain as to their true strength, Thirteenth SS-Army Corps ordered reinforced raiding parties sent out on April 9 and 10 on the western portion of the Gollach River line. Armed with Panzerfäuste and hand grenades, these patrols proved more an irritant than a real menace, although in some areas they did manage to shoot up a few American tanks and half-tracks. For the Germans, the American reaction to these losses must have been disheartening. At Gülchheim, for example, a Landser armed with a Panzerfaust managed to destroy an American supply truck. While the German corporal received an Iron Cross, First Class, for his "heroic" deed, the GIs merely forced local farmers to supply two hundred eggs as compensation while awaiting a new vehicle.[17]

Unsuccessful in their efforts to force a breakthrough to the north and east, the Americans now brought pressure to bear along *Reichsstraße* 13, the main north-south highway linking Würzburg and Munich. Because of the long lines of enemy convoys heading to the south, the area around Gollhofen and Uffenheim had been under virtually continuous attack by American P-47s for the past week and a half. Despite this aerial assault, the Germans had moved both tank destroyer (Panzerjäger) and infantry units into Gollhofen, determined to resist at this key point in their defense line. As a result, although American units reached the outskirts of Gollhofen as early as April 4, the GIs had made no effort to storm this stronghold, being content simply to shell the town with artillery and continue the P-47 raids. Much of Gollhofen had thus been destroyed even before the final struggle commenced. For days, fires burned out of control, dead cattle littered the fields and barnyards, and the remaining inhabitants of the village sheltered in the cellars of the church and schoolhouse. Taking advantage of the fact that the Americans had insufficient troop strength to occupy all the towns they had passed through, the Germans in Gollhofen even launched a series of nightly raids on places like Herrnberchtheim, which the GIs had seized with such difficulty in the first days of April.[18]

Now, on April 8, an incident occurred that illustrated a pattern that was becoming all too familiar in Middle Franconia. Units from both the 101st and 116th Cavalry Reconnaissance Squadrons approached the railroad crossing on the outskirts of Gollhofen, where they encountered fire from the German tank destroyer unit. That evening, in order to prevent unnecessary civilian deaths, the American commanders dispatched a young boy with the demand that the mayor and all citizens leave the town. Otherwise they would come under heavy fire. As the anxious, uncertain, and fearful civilians came out of their cellars, however, the German commander of the Panzerjägers, Lieutenant Thiel, ordered his men to drive the civilians back in and threatened to shoot any from the village who now tried to leave. Gollhofen, he said, would be held to the last man. Despite this warning, a portion of the inhabitants, led by the mayor, succeeded in slipping out of the town early on April 9 and reached American lines. The rest of the villagers remained trapped in Gollhofen with the local pastor, Reverend Stahl, who served as both a spiritual comforter and their envoy to the local German commander.[19]

The next day, April 10, as the villagers occupied themselves with burying the dead, Stahl pleaded with the German regimental commander to give up in order to avoid any further loss of civilian life and destruction to the village. The colonel in charge rejected the plea on the grounds that Gollhofen was too strategically important to surrender. Indeed, not only did the Germans intend to fight on, SS troops had been sent to Gollhofen as part of a planned counterattack against the unprotected American flank. Thus condemned to ruination, on the early afternoon of April 11, as the villagers were enjoying their first hot meal in days, American artillery bombarded the town unmercifully for about an hour, after which tank forces launched a two-pronged assault from the east and west. The attack from the east ground to a halt almost immediately, as Lieutenant Thiel and a group of Landsers armed with Panzerfäuste quickly disabled a number of American tanks. At the west entrance to the town, the Germans hurled themselves against the Americans in furious counterattacks as the GIs steadily fought their way into Gollhofen, only to be stopped in the church garden by about a dozen entrenched sixteen- and seventeen-year-old boys from a Hitler Youth unit. Armed only with a fanatical will to resist and a few Panzerfäuste, the boys threw themselves against the GIs in a suicidal undertaking, bragging that they would knock out each enemy tank for a few packs of cigarettes. With shot-up American tanks blocking the streets of the town, the attack bogged down into yet another house-to-house struggle. Toward evening, the Americans recognized that they could not seize all of Gollhofen and, not wanting to get caught in a night battle, withdrew their remaining tanks. The young Panzerjägers had won a short but sweet victory, which at least temporarily raised their spirits. Still, the Americans kept the village under heavy artillery fire all night long.[20]

That night, through an emissary, Pastor Stahl learned that the German defenders planned to withdraw from Gollhofen. Armed with this news, he made his way through the cellars, telling the beleaguered inhabitants that at daybreak they should raise white flags as quickly as possible. With the first gray light of dawn on April 12, hesitantly, cautiously, with white flags waving, Stahl and a companion, Leonhard Wagner, crept out of the church cellar to survey the situation. To their surprise, the German defenders had not left. Soldiers quickly took both men to the command post, where they were promptly arrested and sent back to regimental headquarters. Later released in a village a few miles to the south, both made their way back, white flags hoisted on walking sticks, to find Gollhofen in ruins and American forces now in occupation. An estimated 80 percent of the living quarters and 90 percent of the remaining buildings were destroyed. Such was the destruction in Gollhofen that it took weeks to uncover and bury all the animal cadavers, a task made worse by the horrendous smell of the rotting flesh. In addition, nineteen civilians and ten German soldiers lay dead, sacrificed in the futile effort to stop the American advance.[21]

To the east, GIs faced an equally stern test as they moved south along a road running parallel to the forested heights above, dominated by the menacing bulk of *Schloß Frankenberg*. The Americans aimed to seize the western end of the *Steigerwald Höhenstrasse*, the main east-west route through the woods, at Ulsenheim. Having occupied the key town of Ippesheim on April 8, elements of the 101st Cavalry Group made contact the next afternoon with troops of the Seventeenth Armored Infantry Battalion, and then struck south along the western heights of the Steigerwald. The Germans, however, had hastily reinforced the area with troops and tanks (some twenty-five in all) from the Panzer regiment Brandenburg, as well as over three hundred SS troops. Moving to occupy the village of Reusch, less than two miles south of Ippesheim, Lyons's First Platoon and the American tanks ran into a heavy barrage from German 120mm mortars and withering small arms fire from entrenched German infantry belonging to a battle group commanded by Major Günther Reinbrecht, which forced them to withdraw for the night. All that night American artillery and mortars rained constant harassing fire on Reusch, while the German defenders blew the three bridges over the Iff River.[22]

At dawn the next morning, April 10, A Company launched a dismounted attack against Reusch, whose women and young boys had for days been busily digging defensive positions for the German infantry. For Sergeant Lyons and his men, the attack on Reusch followed the now-familiar pattern. Following an artillery, tank, and mortar bombardment, First Platoon was to seize the high ground in front of the town, while Second and Third Platoons moved to enter Reusch from either flank. The barrage had the desired effect of softening the German defenders and enabling A Company to seize the town rather quickly, although German resistance resulted in the loss of three tanks. As Lyons and his men sought to turn south toward Weigenheim, however, savage German fire from an estimated three hundred SS troops dug in along the road, primarily boys from a Hitler Youth antitank battalion, halted them almost immediately. German antitank guns knocked out the two leading American tanks as they crossed the top of a hill on the edge of town, while heavy machine gun and sniper fire pinned Lyons and his men to the ground. Lyons radioed for artillery support, which helped relieve the fire on his platoon somewhat, but as another American tank moved out to the south it suffered the same fate as the earlier ones. Moreover, German Me 262 jet airplanes also assaulted the American vehicles dispersed on either side of the main road. In possession of Reusch, but unable to knock out the German antitank gun denying them exit from the village, Lyons grew increasingly frustrated by the high casualties suffered by his men, as well as the loss of another two tanks. In addition, Reusch had been heavily mined and booby-trapped by the Germans, so other GIs had been killed and wounded in the process of cleaning out the town.[23]

In the meantime, C Company waited in half-tracks, prepared to leapfrog Reusch and attack Weigenheim. Even before the assault began, a sense of apprehension began to grip the men of C Company, for as Sherman Lans observed laconically, "we were not encouraged by the frequent trips of the medic jeep carrying casualties to the rear." Nor was this concern misplaced:

> We started to press our attack mounted, and as we rumbled across an open field an enemy burp gun open up and forced us to seek defilade. The tracks deployed in a deep draw. . . . [Soon] the deep cough of a mortar warned us that sudden death was in the air. . . . The first three rounds burst, bracketing the area. . . . As the tracks maneuvered slowly in the crowded space rounds continued to fall. . . . We dismounted and started forward on foot. . . . Four hundred yards from the outskirts of Weigenheim both platoons were pinned down by fire from automatic weapons. The same mortar . . . opened up again and inflicted thirteen casualties . . . , forcing us to withdraw. . . . When the order to attack came again we had plenty of support. . . . As we jumped off a thunderous artillery barrage landed on the first row of buildings in town. . . . Two P-47's came in low and strafed just for good measure.

Only late that evening, however, did C Company succeed in taking Weigenheim, and as A Company had discovered at Reusch, they had to deactivate a number of booby traps left behind by the Germans. In the intense fighting, dozens of German and American soldiers had been killed and wounded, while both Reusch and Weigenheim sustained heavy damage. In the latter village the church and most of the buildings burned to the ground following the American fighter-bomber attacks.[24]

Fighting on April 10 had also been heavy at Uffenheim, a few miles to the south of Gollhofen and the last major obstacle along the R 13.

Seeking to avoid a direct assault on the strongly defended town of Uffenheim, troops of the 101st Cavalry Reconnaissance Squadron and the Twenty-third Tank Battalion moved over Geckenheim, midway between Uffenheim and Weigenheim, in order to attack Uffenheim from the east and south. As American and German tanks engaged in a battle on the eastern outskirts of Uffenheim, German infantry, artillery, and 88mm antitank guns opened a fierce fire on the GIs, which brought their advance to a halt. In order to get the advance rolling again, the commander of the Twenty-third Tank Battalion, Major Schrader, perched in the turret of his command tank, moved his tank forward, only to be hit by mortar shrapnel. As his tank driver quickly turned and headed back toward an aid station, the remaining American tanks maneuvered wildly to get away from the deadly German artillery fire, withdrawing toward Geckenheim. In the meantime, American P-47s launched an attack on the German artillery positions while American tanks and artillery fired on Uffenheim itself.[25]

Faced with the increasing danger of an American breakthrough along the R 13, Lieutenant Colonel Hobe on April 10 had ordered a detachment of Mark V Panthers moved from Markt Bibart on the R 8 to the west. The presence of the Panthers, along with the menacing 88s, only accentuated American difficulties when early on April 11 they launched another attack on Uffenheim. Approaching the heights to the east of the town, the two leading American tanks almost immediately fell victim to German antitank fire, while a company of African American troops came under heavy small arms fire at the *Schafhöfe*, a pasture on the outskirts of town. While fighting continued at the Schafhöfe, other GIs moved to the southeast toward the small village of Uttenhofen, probing the German line in hopes of finding a way around the forbidding enemy defenses on the eastern approaches to Uffenheim. As GIs searched houses in Uttenhofen, and generously helped themselves to a breakfast of ham and eggs, a group of P-47s, neglecting to contact the ground control officer, screamed out of the sky and launched a thunderous assault on the village. Thinking themselves under German attack, the startled GIs rushed out of houses and barns, the village of Uttenhofen a microcosm of the chaos, confusion, and destruction of war. Soon realizing that they had been bombed by their own pilots, the GIs quickly set off some recognition flares, but not before a number of them had been killed and wounded, and a few vehicles destroyed.[26]

As if to prove that neither side monopolized confusion, however, late that evening a Mark V tank and a staff car, with blackout lights burning, approached the village of Oberschneckenbach, a few miles south of Uttenhofen, unaware that advance patrols of the Seventeenth Armored Infantry Battalion had occupied the area. As the vehicles neared the American command post, a sentry waved his rifle and shouted for the drivers "to turn the damn lights out." Muttering, "What the hell's going on here," the startled GI stood dumbfounded when four German officers got out of the car and promptly raised their hands in surrender. Further adding to his astonishment, the crew of the Mark V tank did likewise. At this point, a trembling voice could be heard back in the command post calling out, "Please, I need some help. There are too many Germans in this country." Just as astounding, when searched, the tank still had a full complement of munitions.[27]

A few miles to the east, the men of the Seventeenth Armored Infantry Battalion on April 11 launched one final effort to break through the German defensive line along the western ridges of the Steigerwald. Jumping off at 5:30 A.M., the First Platoon of A Company aimed to seize hills immediately to the east of Weigenheim, where the Germans had placed infantry and tanks to block the way, in order for other elements of Combat Command R to press on toward Ulsenheim, and there continue the advance to the east in hopes of cutting off German troops in the northern Steigerwald. Securing the approaches to the *Kapellberg* with no opposition, Lyons and his men fell victim to a typical German tactic. As they approached the top of the hill, they found themselves caught in a furious burst of fire from two enemy Mark V's dug in on the reverse slope. On the radio immediately, First Platoon called for reinforcements. A squad from C Company and the Reconnaissance Platoon from Headquarters Company soon joined First Platoon, but they found their attack quickly stymied by German artillery, antitank, and machine gun fire. As other elements of the task force also approached, German antitank salvos knocked out the leading tanks and completely halted the American advance. Artillery observers called down heavy fire on the German position, but not until one of the tankers spotted the gun and let loose with a volley was it put out of action. This last obstacle surmounted, Lyons watched in relief as the task force raced forward to attack the village of Ulsenheim, four miles distant, beyond which lay the rolling countryside of the *Aischgrund*.[28]

As parts of CC-R threatened Ulsenheim, astride the key roads connecting the R 13 and R 8 through the Steigerwald, the Seventeenth Armored Infantry Battalion and Twenty-third Tank Battalion turned to the southwest with the intention of encircling the remaining German forces, most from the Seventy-ninth VGD, along the western portion of the now crumbling Gollach River line. Although briefly slowed by a local counterattack that cost two killed and two wounded, the GIs quickly moved through Großharbach, where troops of the Seventeenth Armored Infantry Battalion came across the field kitchen for a German artillery unit, then turned north through Equarhofen and Langensteinach in the direction of Aub. The speed of the American advance and the uncertain presence of German forces left many villagers in a quandary. As tanks from the Twenty-third Tank Battalion, having bypassed the mined roads and moved cross-country, suddenly appeared on the outskirts of Gehleinsmühle, just south of Pfahlenheim, the villagers reacted quickly by running up white flags. For fear of SS troops in the area, though, as soon as the GIs had passed the villagers prudently lowered the signs of surrender. Having made contact with elements of the 116th Cavalry Reconnaissance Squadron a few miles to the north, however, in less than an hour the tanks of the Twenty-third Tank Battalion suddenly reappeared moving across the open meadows. Seeing no white flags, the tankers began shooting at the village, whereupon the white flags promptly reappeared and the shelling ceased. Similarly, at both Wallmersbach and Auernhofen, German troops caught unawares refused orders to resist, preferring instead to end the pointless fighting. As demonstrated at the latter village, the biggest danger to the Americans seemed to be their own carelessness and curiosity. Wanting to disable a captured German artillery piece, GIs stuffed its barrel full of Panzerfäuste. The resulting explosion not only splintered the barrel but blew roofs off houses and shattered windows in the village. And despite being warned, the GI love of souvenir hunting also proved deadly, three men being literally blown apart in Auernhofen by hidden mines.[29]

Now surrounded on all sides, the town of Aub fell late on the afternoon of April 12, and with it the entire Gollach River line began to crumble. The same day, despite determined German resistance, American troops pushed into Uffenheim and Ulsenheim. That morning the Germans made a concerted effort to break their threatened encirclement, launching a fierce counterattack from Ulsenheim toward Uffenheim. Supported by over forty

Mustering of the *Nationalsozialistischen Kriegsopferversorgung* (National Socialist War Victims Welfare League), Bad Windsheim. (Stadtarchiv Bad Windsheim.)

Elderly *Volkssturm* men with *Panzerfäuste*. (Mahnung Gegen Rechts, Stadt Lauffen/Neckar.)

Plundering of a food shop in Lauffen/Neckar, April 1945. (Mahnung Gegen Rechts, Stadt Lauffen/Neckar.)

German POWs, February 1945. (NA, RG 111, SC 201174-S.)

Elderly POWs in Nuremberg, April 1945. (NA, RG 111, SC 203814.)

Tanks of Combat Command A, Forty-third Tank Battalion, Twelfth Armored Division, near Scheinfeld, April 16, 1945. (NA, RG 111, SC 206445.)

A tank from Troop E, Ninety-second Cavalry Reconnaissance Squadron, fires at German positions near Weschnitz (Odenwald), March 29, 1945. (NA, RG 111, 336910.)

A tank and two medics from Troop E, Ninety-second Cavalry Reconnaissance Squadron, return with a wounded platoon leader near Weschnitz (Odenwald), March 29, 1945. (NA, RG 111, SC 421379.)

Above, African American troops of the Sixty-sixth Armored Infantry Battalion, Twelfth Armored Division, in the center of the wrecked town of Erbach (Odenwald), April 1, 1945. (NA, RG 111, SC 334113.) *Below,* GIs from Second Battalion, 180th Infantry Regiment, Forty-fifth Infantry Division, routing out snipers in Königshofen, April 8, 1945. (NA, RG 111, SC 335303.)

Hitler Youth being instructed in the use of a *Panzerfäuste*. (Photo in author's possession.)

In a scene typical of the dangerous nature of street fighting even in rural areas such as Middle Franconia, soldiers of the Sixth Armored Division dodge sniper fire in Oberdorla, April 4, 1945. Note the dead GI in the foreground. (NA, RG 111, SC 203216.)

Above, After the breakthrough at Ulsenheim on April 11, 1945, soldiers of the Twelfth Armored Division enter the village of Krautostheim, five miles to the east, likely unaware of the unintentionally ironic injunction on the sign to "drive carefully." (NA, RG 111, SC 263520.) *Below,* In Franconia, GIs found that confusion often made the already chaotic situation even more dangerous. In Kronach, troops of the 101st Infantry Regiment race across the town square under fire, even as white flags fly from various buildings, April 14, 1945. (NA, RG 111, SC 206235.)

Above, To the west of Leutershausen, the town of Waldenburg illustrated the consequences of the failure to surrender. GIs from the 255th Infantry Regiment, Sixty-third Infantry Division, move through the destroyed city, April 16, 1945. (NA, RG 111, SC 205778.) *Below,* An antitank obstacle in Bad Windsheim, April 1945. (Stadtarchiv Bad Windsheim.)

fighter planes, German tanks pushed the GIs back to Uttenhofen, where they also received artillery fire from Uffenheim. Temporarily threatened with being squeezed between the two German forces, and with their supply lines cut, the GIs fought back furiously. Savage aerial assaults by P-47s soon turned the hunters into the hunted, and by late afternoon, having expended most of their ammunition and with the weather worsening, the remaining German tanks withdrew in the direction of Ulsenheim, an action that sealed the fate of Uffenheim. Now largely surrounded, and constantly battered by American artillery, the last German defenders slipped out of Uffenheim just before midnight, heading for the Aisch River and the new defensive line along the Frankenhöhe. The fighting around Ulsenheim on April 12 had been savage, as shown by the daily report of the Thirteenth SS-Army Corps, which claimed that the German counterattack had destroyed over twenty American tanks and half-tracks, along with numerous other vehicles and antitank guns.[30]

Even as American forces applied steadily mounting pressure on the German defenses along the Gollach River and on the western slopes of the Steigerwald, a new danger appeared to the north in an area known as the *Hellmitzheimer Bucht*. A broad hollow jutting into the northwestern ridges of the Steigerwald through which ran the R 8, the key highway connecting Würzburg and Nuremberg, the Germans saw it as a natural—perhaps the pivotal—strong point in their attempt to create a feasible defense line north of Nuremberg. Although GIs had cut the R 8 at Markt Einersheim on April 6, the shift of the American effort to the west had provided a temporary respite for the Germans in the area, one which allowed them to deploy new troops and begin constructing a recognizable defense line. On April 7, Lieutenant Colonel Hobe received two new infantry battalions and the Hitler Youth tank destroyer battalion *Franken,* while the next day he gained the services of a detachment from the Sixth SS-Mountain Division Nord. In addition, on April 8 Hobe secured a shipment of brand new Mark V Panther G tanks, dispatched directly from the nearby Nürberger Reichswald factory. Although Hobe now had some sixty tanks at his disposal, an acute shortage of fuel hampered their use. Hobe grouped his tanks together along with a unit of infantry under an experienced tank commander, Major Rettemeier. Given the wooded and hilly terrain, they could be expected to pose a serious menace to the American advance.[31]

Although tanks from the Ninety-second Cavalry Reconnaissance

Squadron probed the German line at Nenzenheim and Dornheim on April 8 and 9, it was not until April 10 that the fighting sharply intensified. During the night of April 9–10, American artillery steadily pounded the villages and woods along the Hellmitzheimer Bucht, even as the Germans moved in a battle group from the Seventeenth SS equipped, along with the usual complement of weapons, with an antitank rocket launcher outfitted with infrared sights for night action. Late on the morning of April 10 the two forces collided in the village of Possenheim, a few miles south of Markt Einersheim on the R 8. As Mark V's from Hobe's tank force slowed the American advance, SS troops launched a flank attack and in a series of house-to-house clashes forced the GIs to withdraw from the town. After the customary aerial assault by P-47s, the GIs renewed the attack in the early afternoon, once again pressing against heavy resistance into Possenheim, while also unleashing tank, artillery, and air bombardments against Hellmitzheim and Nenzenheim. That night in the latter village, three boys under the cover of a white flag approached American positions, informed the GIs that German troops had withdrawn, and begged the Americans to stop their artillery fire. Although promised that the shelling would cease when a white flag was visible from the church tower, no one in the village had the courage to raise it. German troops passing through the area constantly threatened to shoot anyone caught raising the white flag. Thus the destruction of Nenzenheim went on.[32]

The next day, April 11, the battering of the villages in the Hellmitzheimer Bucht continued apace, with Nenzenheim and Hellmitzheim largely reduced to ashes and rubble. Complete chaos ruled in Hellmitzheim, as the sea of flames forced villagers to flee into the surrounding fields, only to be driven back by artillery and machine gun fire. Still, American forces remained bogged down, both literally and figuratively. At Dornheim, for example, tanks of the Ninety-second Cavalry Reconnaissance Squadron got stuck in a marshy meadow, then had to rely on artillery fire to beat back an attack by troops of the Seventeenth SS. By contrast, American troops at Hellmitzheim seemed befuddled by Hobe's tactic of temporarily withdrawing from the village while it was under heavy artillery and aerial bombardment, then quickly reoccupying their positions once the firing had stopped. Time and again the ensuing tank and infantry attack was halted in close quarter fighting, with the GIs suffering disconcertingly high losses.[33]

Faced with mounting casualties and a lack of success in their frontal assaults down the R 8, American commanders now ordered Task Forces Norton and Fields of CC-B, Twelfth Armored Division, to probe a secondary road a few miles east that ran parallel to the R 8. Jumping off in the early morning hours of April 11, the GIs advanced quickly against little opposition. At Stierhöfstetten the two forces split, both heading back to the southwest toward the R 8 with the intention of trapping German forces in the Hellmitzheimer Bucht, but with Task Force Norton forming the inner ring over Ziegenbach and Enzlar, while Task Force Fields looped farther south through Scheinfeld and Markt Bibart. The latter town occupied a particularly important position, as it sat astride both the main highway and the railroad line running into Nuremberg, and had served as the off-loading terminal for German tanks and troops being rushed to the Steigerwald. The GIs had moved so quickly and from such an unexpected direction that Markt Bibart was seized by Task Force Fields in the early afternoon against almost no opposition. Similarly, Task Force Norton caught an SS unit unawares at Ziegenbach, then occupied Enzlar in the early evening.[34]

Faced now with breakthroughs on both the western and eastern portions of their defensive line, and no longer able to check the momentum of the American advance, German forces in the early hours of April 12 received orders to withdraw across the Aisch River to the heavily forested ridges of the Frankenhöhe. Unbeknownst to the GIs, they came within a hairsbreadth of bagging the German commander, Lieutenant Colonel Hobe, who with his command staff had to wend his way gingerly along timber trails over the 1,400-foot *Schloßberg* in order to get safely back to his command post. In the stiff fighting in the Hellmitzheimer Bucht, casualties on both sides had been high, Hobe alone losing a third of his tank force in just two days, losses that could no longer be made up.[35]

The early April fighting along the Gollach River and the Steigerwald proved unexpectedly fierce. In a two-week period in just a small part of the front in Middle Franconia at least 230 German soldiers had been killed, with the actual death toll certainly much higher, while the official Wehrmacht report claimed that 123 American armored vehicles had been destroyed. Still, within this picture of continued German resistance, the overwhelming superiority of the enemy had begun to erode the willingness of Landsers to continue the fight. "The feeling of inferiority and the conception that they had fulfilled their tasks," confirmed Lieutenant Colonel Hobe, "often led our troops to withdraw even when there was no immediate reason at hand." To stiffen resistance, some German officers, according to American interrogations of prisoners, had resorted to telling their men that the Americans customarily turned POWs over to the Russians. More worrisome, Hobe also noted that the local inhabitants increasingly avoided aiding the retreating German soldiers, and often showed themselves more willing to cooperate with the advancing American conquerors than with their own defenders. This tendency had already been recognized by the G-2 officer of the Twelfth Armored Division, an entry for April 1 noting that German prisoners of war complained that the civilian population was making resistance difficult. In their desire to prevent their property from being destroyed, the Landsers groused, local civilians refused to shelter German troops and hindered efforts to fortify towns for defense.[36]

Even in rural areas previously untouched physically by the destruction of war, the farmers and villagers proved just as war-weary as any bombed out city dweller. Most of these small towns and hamlets had already suffered a blood sacrifice greater than they had in World War I, so local inhabitants could see little point to any further bloodletting in an obviously lost war. Just as important, most had now lost any lingering hope in the much ballyhooed wonder weapons, or faith in Nazi officials, to alter the course of events. As the SD, the Nazi Security Service, ruefully admitted, "the hitherto reliable flicker of hope is going out," an observation seconded by American intelligence. "The enemy is completely restricted to a single capability," noted the Weekly Intelligence Summary on April 8, "to delay his defeat." As the Nazi regime would demonstrate, however, within that sole realm of action it proved willing to dispense terror in full measure on soldiers and civilians alike.[37]

RUNNING AMOK AGAINST
THE REALITY OF DEFEAT

With the American breakthrough, the Germans could no longer maintain the Steigerwald line, so now began a hasty withdrawal southeast to the next line of defense, which ran along the Frankenhöhe (Franconian heights) toward Nuremberg, itself thirty miles to the southeast. Wary of the German ability to spring nasty surprises, American troops advanced slowly and cautiously. Although German commanders, aware of their own pitiful weakness, alternately expressed amazement or a mocking contempt for this American practice, the average GI, hoping only to survive this final phase of the war, was determined to make good use of his overwhelming artillery and air superiority. As a platoon approached even a small farm village in the area, the GIs customarily dismounted their vehicles, fanned out across a field, and gingerly made for the buildings at the edge of the town. If shots rang out from the German side, the Americans responded with a shattering burst of small arms and mortar fire (supplemented with tanks and artillery if available), directed not so much at a specific target as at the town itself. Then, amidst the ragged blast of grenades and a sharp volley of rifle fire, a squad of men from one direction or another would storm the village and take control.

A few dazed and bedraggled Germans in uniforms, normally old men or young boys, would be marched off as prisoners. The GIs would then move off to the next village, hoping that white flags instead of rifle fire would greet them.

In this fluid situation, the civilian population in this predominately rural area of rolling farmland and small towns found themselves swept up in the blast of war, threatened as much by actions of their own officials as those by Americans. Under the grip of an apocalyptic aura and clinging to the hope of prolonging the war until inevitable disagreements in the Allied coalition caused it to disintegrate, Hitler, Goebbels, and others in the Nazi hierarchy viewed every town, village, and hamlet as a potential bastion from which to fight a delaying action. This, however, ran contrary to the widespread civilian desire for an immediate end to the fighting. As SD reports from Lower Franconia made clear, ordinary Germans viewed the efforts at last-ditch resistance as leading only to a catastrophe—one inspired, moreover, for reasons known only to the Nazi leadership and to promote their own self-interest. Despite Nazi propaganda, average citizens could see with their own eyes the constant retreat of German troops, the overwhelming superiority of enemy forces, and the omnipresence of Allied aircraft. Moreover, in an area that had largely been spared the ravages of war, reason and self-interest dictated that a rapid end to the fighting meant a greater chance for personal survival and avoidance of massive destruction of property. In turn, many civilians realized that the surest way to speed an end to the war was to oppose or sabotage defensive measures and seek a speedy capitulation to the oncoming enemy.[1]

By war's end, however, Hitler's Volksgemeinschaft had come full circle and now began to devour its own. It had originated as a racial-national community with the utopian promise of renewing a Germany battered and torn by World War I and the Great Depression, as well as exacting revenge on those held responsible for Germany's tribulations. Initially using violent measures to "cleanse" the German national body of "unfit" citizens, during the war it had turned to the elimination of the alleged racial enemy of Germany, the Jews. Now, in the spring of 1945, the Nazi leadership directed terror at those "healthy" Germans who no longer wished to prolong this obviously lost war. Since Hitler saw the war as being precisely for the survival of this racial Volksgemeinschaft, such an attitude was impermissible, and Germans thus had to be compelled to continue the struggle. Many in the Nazi establishment, especially Goebbels, made desperate comparisons with the Kampfzeit, the struggle for power in the early 1930s during which apparently hopeless situations were ultimately overcome through sheer persistence and effort—and faith in the Führer, who had always found a way out.[2]

Faced with the reality of a crumbling army, within which even the extraordinary bonds of camaraderie that had helped sustain its fighting ability for so long were disintegrating, the Nazi leadership had long since resorted to the harshest measures to maintain discipline. Already by mid-1944 more than twenty-six thousand death sentences had been imposed on Wehrmacht personnel for desertion or undermining of the war effort, although the exact number of those executed remains unclear. Still, as Manfred Messerschmidt has noted, the military justice system now served to sustain not only the functional capabilities of the troops, but also to guarantee the National Socialist system. Through the unrestrained use of summary courts-martial in the last months of the war, formally authorized by a Führer decree of March 9, 1945, this judicial terror exacted an ever greater toll. Between January and May 1945 the number of soldiers sentenced to death in the regular military court system has been estimated at around four thousand, while the figures for those executed by the "flying courts-martial" are likely closer to six or seven thousand.[3]

Nor were these barbarous acts restricted only to military personnel. In late 1944, harsh measures aimed at stopping deserters on the western front specifically threatened the arrest of relatives of deserters, while in early March 1945 yet another Führer decree ordered the arrest of relatives of soldiers who surrendered without fighting. With warfare now on their own territory, with domestic morale plummeting alarmingly, and with only limited means by which to mobilize the population, the Nazi regime directed its brutal actions against its own citizens in a final, frantic effort to avoid collapse. German civilians in the last months of the war thus found themselves no less threatened than their compatriots in the ranks, both from the external enemy and increasingly from their own officials. Perhaps nothing illustrates this danger better than a decree by the Reich Ministry of Justice, issued on February 15, 1945, authorizing the establishment of summary courts-martial in areas of the Reich endangered by the enemy and threatening their use against individuals deemed guilty of cowardice, shirking their duty, undermining the war effort, or acting in a self-interested fashion. Moreover, if a defendant was found guilty by these makeshift courts, the only permissible punishment was the death sentence. In the last months of the war, these drumhead courts-martial would become the instrument of choice in unleashing National Socialist terror on a demoralized and war-weary citizenry that, convinced that the war could no longer be won, had to be compelled to continue the struggle.[4]

DIE LIKE A SWINE!

In April 1945 the residents of Middle Franconia felt the full force of these measures, although the general outbreak of terror masked a complex variety of motives. Some atrocities resulted from the actions of fanatical Nazis, determined to resist to the end. Other brutalities, however, seemed more the work of nonideological, overly dutiful, and pedestrian personalities—largely decent individuals who nonetheless lacked any sense of moral or civil courage. In the German context, moreover, a sense of duty often went beyond loyalty, obedience, or acquiescence to encompass a belief that duty itself was a moral imperative, that the means were as important as the end, and that orderliness and thoroughness made up a distinctly German identity. Duty, then, meant executing the assigned task to its logical conclusion, whatever one's personal or moral objections. In addition, cowardice, confusion, or human weakness often lay behind what at first seemed merely examples of blind loyalty. As Doris Bergen has pointed out, in the profound uncertainty at the end of the war many German officials, particularly at the local level, were at a loss to determine where their best interests lay, or if they even had such a thing. Thus, many responded with frenetic action, calculated efforts to survive the war, or paralyzing inertia. Still others sought to exercise any control they could over an increasingly tumultuous situation. Significantly, however, ordinary Germans in this area seemed little motivated by any notion of political or ideological opposition to Nazism, nor did they regard the creeping administrative disintegration around them as an opportunity to throw off the Nazi system. Instead, as the front neared and the war became a frightening personal ordeal, the inhabitants of many of the towns and villages of Middle Franconia, largely women, children, and elderly men, occupied themselves with the effort to save what could be saved of their homes and villages, and with their own personal survival.[5]

As the example of Middle Franconia demonstrated, the loosening

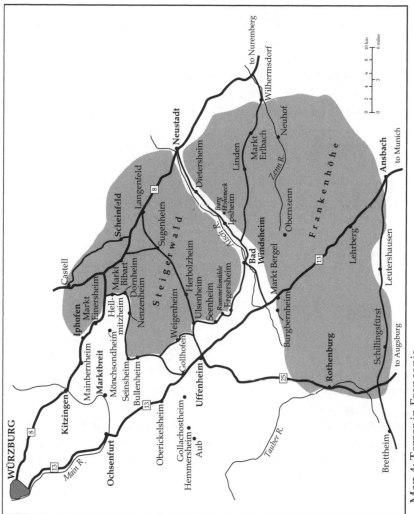

Map 4: Terror in Franconia

grip of the Nazi Party on local administration often resulted not in a lessening of danger for German civilians but in a heightened risk. The bewildering overlap of conflicting jurisdictions, combined with the flood of decrees from the top Nazi leadership threatening ever-greater punishments for those who failed to resist, led to a chaotic and uncertain situation. Many individuals, fearful for their own person or unaccustomed to wielding administrative authority, believed themselves limited in their freedom of action and constrained to carry out the harsh orders to their fullest—or abdicated responsibility in favor of the most fanatical amongst them. Finally, as events in some areas showed, contradictory orders or desires could lead to a paralyzed situation that doomed villages or individuals to destruction.[6]

In the politically tense and divided city of Ochsenfurt, for example, the local Nazi Party leadership, among them many still convinced and dedicated National Socialists determined to fight to the end, opposed civic leaders weary of war and desirous only of saving their city from unnecessary destruction. After a turbulent scene at party headquarters on March 29, where a delegation of women had gone to demand the local party leader surrender the town to the advancing Americans without a fight, a number of other women began to dismantle tank obstacles erected at the entrances to the city. The determined women drove off a group of armed Volkssturm men who sought to hinder their activity, but local Nazi officials did not concede defeat. Police placed three of the rebellious women under arrest and charged them with undermining the war effort. Given a hasty trial and sentenced to be hanged on April 1, Easter Sunday, only the timely arrival of American troops spared the women their fate. Even then, Ochsenfurt was not exempted a final bit of chaos. As GIs approached from the west, SS, Volkssturm, and Hitler Youth units, ordered to hold the town at all costs, arrived from the east. A tumult ensued, though not between American and German forces. Both German civilians and soldiers, joined by foreign forced laborers, took advantage of the collapse of local authority to plunder military warehouses. In this instance, conflicting aims resulted in much senseless destruction of foodstuffs, as, released from the rigorous constraints of the past, people engaged in a seemingly Darwinian struggle of the quick and the strong against the lame and the weak.[7]

To the south in Möckmühl, a small village in Württemberg on the edge of Franconia, the confusion of orders and objectives led to more physical devastation. Orders to evacuate the town's population contradicted the local citizenry's desire to remain in their homes and protect what they could from destruction. As a man in nearby Crailsheim said, in fatalistic yet very human terms, "it's better to die at home than to be killed on the road." At the same time, troops from the Seventeenth SS-Panzergrenadier Division "Götz von Berlichingen" received orders on April 2 to occupy the village, in which, ironically, their namesake had once been imprisoned during the Peasants War. Prodded by this legacy to resist, the determination of the Seventeenth SS to fight a battle for tradition directly clashed with the desires of the villagers to surrender without a fight and preserve their homes. The Ortsgruppenleiter (local Nazi Party leader) interceded repeatedly with the SS commander in the hope of convincing him not to defend the town. The belief that the party would have some influence on the SS proved mistaken, however, and further attempts to sway the division commander were brusquely rejected. Over the next few days, as a consequence, Möckmühl suffered considerable damage from both American and German artillery before GIs finally occupied the village on April 8.[8]

Nor was this an isolated example. Throughout the region sporadic resistance inspired by fanaticism, a misplaced sense of duty, or youthful ardor often had tragic consequences. In one representative village just north of Bad Windsheim, the Herbolzheim Volkssturm unit, with its customary composition of elderly men and young boys under the influence of a few regular army soldiers, foolishly declared the town a fortress and laid mines in the streets. As American troops approached in midmorning on April 12, shots from the village rang out. Angered, the Americans commenced a two-hour artillery barrage complemented by aerial attacks that gutted the town with incendiary and high-explosive bombs. With their village engulfed in flames, the civilian inhabitants, mostly the elderly, women, and children, fled in search of shelter to the surrounding fields, all the while under American fire. Although the German defenders departed that evening, not until the next morning did GIs enter the shattered, smoldering village. Of forty-four farmhouses, only three remained intact; sixty-eight of the one hundred large barns lay in ruins; and of eighty-six cattle stalls, sixty-three were completely destroyed and six were burnt out. Both churches fell victim to the flames, so funeral services took place at the cemetery for the seven German civilians killed, victims of a cruel and senseless decision to resist when resistance was futile. And so it went. That same day, April 12, Dornheim, Hemmersheim, Ulsenheim, Nenzenheim, and Hellmitzheim, all small farm villages virtually indistinguishable from one another, suffered the same fate as Herbolzheim. The tiny village of Langenfeld, just northwest of Neustadt an der Aisch, disappeared under a storm of American steel, the result of a single Panzerfaust shot at an approaching American tank. None of these actions affected the outcome of the war, and most would be regarded as insignificant operations, except to the twenty-four civilians who lay dead, and to their brethren who saw their ancient villages, many a millennium old, destroyed as a result of the actions of fanatic defenders of Hitler's would-be thousand-year Reich.[9]

Sometimes even determined efforts to prevent resistance backfired, as villagers found themselves overwhelmed by the vagaries of war. In Leutershausen, near Ansbach, leading citizens convinced a German commander to spare their venerable village. But as German troops withdrew just after midnight on April 18, women rushed out to clear the antitank obstacles, much to the disgust of the local Volkssturm commander, who warned, "You couldn't have done something dumber." That morning, as they anxiously awaited the arrival of American troops, villagers were instead shocked by the appearance of a small SS unit. The *Oberscharführer* (staff sergeant) in command quickly ordered all defenses replaced, threatening, "Don't even think about . . . displaying white flags, otherwise we'll open fire on the place." Nor was this an empty threat, for SS troops had already shelled a hamlet near Fürth as punishment for flying white flags. Thus intimidated, the inhabitants hastened to rebuild the tank obstacles and prepare the bridge over the Altmühl River for demolition. As the cautiously advancing GIs belatedly appeared that afternoon, the SS unit opened fire, causing the GIs to call in air support. "Between 6:00 and 7:00 that evening," a local woman recorded in her diary, "the drama began. Perhaps eight or ten bombers appeared. All of a sudden deafening noises. . . . Everything shook and trembled. . . . In a quarter-hour half of our beautiful Leutershausen ablaze. It was simply terrible." More than 120 buildings were destroyed or severely damaged, after which the SS troops meekly withdrew.[10]

Local commanders caught in unfamiliar and extraordinary circumstances often reacted with unpredictable consequences. In Aub, some ten miles south of Ochsenfurt, for example, roughly a hundred women pleaded on April 2 with the local commander, Major Rath, to surrender the town peacefully and avoid the destruction of the ancient walled village. Rath responded brusquely, telling the assembled women, "I have orders to defend Aub. A withdrawal is out of the question." As a few women shouted, "Get out or we'll burn this house down around your head," Rath simply turned his head skyward and muttered, "If only a pair of English fighters were here!" With that, the women slowly dispersed and returned to their homes.[11] A few days, a more immediately threatening military situation, and a different commander later, however, another attempt to spare Aub the destruction of war had a deadlier outcome.

By April 7, with exhausted and hungry German troops fighting desperately in a cold rain just a few miles from Aub, the mayor of the neighboring village of Baldersheim enlisted Alfred Eck, a thirty-five-year-old private who had failed to return to his unit after a short leave, to help him contact nearby GIs. Setting out early that morning in civilian clothes with a white flag, Eck and Mayor Engert quickly reached American lines, whereupon they informed the GIs of the position of German minefields and of the presence of a squad of German infantry in an adjacent cemetery. After firing a short burst of machine gun fire at the cemetery, an American officer assured Eck that Baldersheim would not be destroyed if the German soldiers withdrew and each house flew a white flag. As Eck and Engert returned to their village, Eck assured the mayor that he knew the soldiers in the cemetery and would get them to withdraw. A few minutes after Eck had departed, other villagers approached the mayor and wanted to know the situation. One went in search of Eck, only to return with the news that neither Eck nor any Landsers were to be found. Indeed, the German squad had decided to withdraw to Aub, and to take Eck, against his will, with them.[12]

In Aub, Eck encountered a situation much tenser than that a few days earlier, when he had arrived by train. American aircraft had pounded the city the day before, directing much of their fire, as did American artillery, at the *Gasthof "Zur Linde,"* an otherwise inconspicuous inn in which the German commander had established his headquarters. Enraged by the evident betrayal of his location to the enemy and the general hostility of the local populace to the German troops, deeply worried by the creeping encirclement of his force by the Americans, upset that a number of key outlying positions had been surrendered without a fight, and numb from exhaustion, the German commander, Captain August Busse, had reached the end of his emotional reserves. Born in 1914, Busse was molded by war, like others of his generation, both directly and indirectly. His father had been killed at the front in 1915, and his mother had died in the last year of World War I. Thus, Busse was raised in an orphanage. By 1933, with the Nazi rise to power, Busse was already an adherent of the Hitler Youth. From there he progressed to the Labor Service and on to an officer's training course, entering active army service in June 1935. With the outbreak of World War II, Busse served successively in the Polish, French, and Russian campaigns, where he was wounded in April 1942. For the next two years he functioned as a training officer at an infantry school. Returned to front service in May 1944, Busse suffered another wound in December of that year fighting in Kurland. Released from a military hospital in February 1945, Busse made his way to a troop training center in Grafenwöhr, near Nuremberg, and from there to command of a frontline unit at Aub.[13]

Although not a member of the Nazi Party, Busse nonetheless owed his career to the party and the army. Moreover, he commanded a unit of roughly six hundred men composed primarily of young officer-candidates and junior officers with front experience who displayed an absolute loyalty to the Nazi regime and a firm will to resist. Convinced by Nazi promises of wonder weapons that would yet turn the war in Germany's favor, these young men fought with a grim determination to buy time.[14] Busse, a brave and capable, if conventional, career officer, exhausted from days of little sleep and struggling mightily with dwindling resources to hold off the steadily encroaching Americans, was thus incapable of comprehending the motives of Alfred Eck. While the latter saw himself as attempting to save people and property from senseless destruction at the end of an obviously lost war, the former beheld a man guilty of treason, jeopardizing the safety of his men.

True to character, upon being informed on the morning of April 7 of Eck's activities, Busse flew into a rage, punched Eck violently in the face, and screamed, "That is treason and sabotage." When Eck responded with a flippant remark when asked about his party loyalties, Busse again flailed away at him. Regarding Eck's guilt as obvious, Captain Busse now stated that, according to an order received on April 5 from the Seventy-ninth Volksgrenadier Division, a court-martial had to be formed and Eck tried. Naming his adjutant and a lance corporal as members of the court-martial, with himself as its head, Busse quickly recapitulated Eck's treasonous activities. He, Eck, had not only approached American lines with the intention of surrendering the village of Baldersheim, but had also informed the enemy of the presence and location of German minefields and betrayed German defensive positions, which had then come under enemy fire. This, Busse concluded, constituted sabotage and treason, with the only possible punishment being death by hanging.[15]

Having sent for a local priest to hear Eck's confession, Busse left his headquarters to check on the military situation. Almost immediately a townsman asked Busse what was happening with the man inside, who had been seen a few days earlier in military uniform. Sent into a rage once again, Busse stormed back inside and confronted Eck, who had just finished with the priest. Demanding to know what had happened to his military papers, Eck admitted that he had buried them in his garden. Inquiring further as to why he had not returned to his unit, Eck remained silent. Even as American troops occupied neighboring villages only a few miles away, Busse reconvened the court-martial, amended the charges to include desertion, and once again pronounced the death sentence on Eck. The latter now pleaded as a soldier to be allowed to be shot, or to be sent to the front as a probationary punishment, but to no avail. Front service, Busse replied, was no longer an option, while the other members of the court-martial decided that a bullet was too good for a deserter.[16]

Around 1:00 P.M., Eck, dragged more than led by two soldiers, appeared at a hastily constructed gallows on the main square. Despite the danger of artillery fire, thirty to forty curious citizens had gathered to witness the execution. After Eck had ascended the gallows, and while the weeping priest administered the last rites in the background, Busse read the sentence. Assisted by soldiers, Eck climbed onto a chair placed on top of a table, the noose was put around his neck, and a soldier attempted to tighten it. Eck, however, instantly reached up with his right hand and grabbed the noose, so it could not be tightened. Two soldiers quickly seized Eck, bound his hands, tightened the noose, and kicked the chair out from under him. Busse then ordered that he be left hanging, as a warning, for twenty-four hours.[17]

A few days later, Busse, along with fifty men, managed to break out of the American encirclement of Aub and head to the south. After an exhausting fifteen-mile night march, with nothing to eat or drink, Busse and his men had just collapsed in a haystack when they were taken by surprise by an American attack. Wounded once more, Busse was taken prisoner and sent to a hospital, then on to a POW camp in France, where he served in a labor battalion. Ironically, while a POW, Busse wrote to a family he had come to know in Aub, expressing regret that the beautiful old town had suffered much damage during those "bitter days" because of the actions of those, like him, who were just doing their duty. As if to justify himself, Busse emphasized that at that time he simply "could not believe that everything could or should be coming to an end." Released from captivity in May 1946, Busse wandered back to Middle Franconia, on several occasions visiting friends in Aub.[18]

These visits, in fact, provoked Alfred Eck's brother to bring criminal charges of murder against Busse. After three trials, during which Busse maintained that if Eck was to be seen as a martyr of the last days of the war, then he was just as much a victim of the postwar period, Busse was eventually found guilty and sentenced to two and a half years in prison. Busse, though, was punished not so much for having ordered the execution of Alfred Eck, or of having done this for "base" motives, but for having effected it by means of an illegally constituted court-martial. Indeed, the courts took cognizance of the existence at the end of the war of various decrees requiring the use of courts-martial, of the state of physical and nervous exhaustion under which Busse labored, of his very real concerns for the safety of his men, and of Eck's problematical activities. Clearly, Busse acted not from any ideological motives, but from within a framework in which he perceived his freedom of action to be constrained. A dutiful if pedestrian career officer, Busse saw himself as a decent man who acted in the interests of his men and country, and could not conceive that he had done anything morally or legally wrong. Tormented and humiliated the rest of his life, the man who had been shaped by war remained stubbornly convinced that at some later date he would be vindicated for his actions at the end of a war that had destroyed him and his country.[19]

At roughly the same time, a similar tragedy played out in Gollachostheim, a small village a few miles east of Aub. With the unexpectedly swift approach of American armored patrols on April 1, the nervous local Volkssturm commander ordered the fifty-one-year-old Georg Gottfried to ride his bicycle to battalion headquarters in Uffenheim, six miles to the east, to receive new orders. Arriving at Gollhofen, Gottfried discovered that the Volkssturm commander had gone to Oberickelsheim, so he dutifully pedaled off toward the north. At the edge of the village, however, Gottfried was taken prisoner by GIs from the Ninety-second Cavalry Reconnaissance Squadron. Detained and interrogated that night, the Americans released Gottfried the next morning. Making his way back to Gollachostheim, the now thoroughly chilled, exhausted, and hungry Gottfried was greeted by friends and neighbors manning tank obstacles on the outskirts of the village. Telling them of his adventure, warning that the Americans would destroy everything if any resistance was offered, and noting that there were no German soldiers in the area, Gottfried went home to get some sleep.[20]

In the meantime a heated debate ensued among the Volkssturm men and the local Nazi Party leaders, during which a group of women appeared demanding that the defenses be removed. Receiving no answer, the women simply took it upon themselves to dismantle the flimsy anti-tank obstacles. There matters stood until the next evening, April 3, when retreating German soldiers, informed of the actions on the previous day, arrested Gottfried. After a short interrogation, Gottfried set off under guard toward Uffenheim. During a brief stop he was urged by a local innkeeper to flee, but Gottfried insisted that he had done nothing wrong. After a short stay in the Uffenheim jail, on April 5 Gottfried and a few other prisoners were transported to Nuremberg. During a rest stop near Emskirchen, two fellow prisoners successfully fled into nearby woods. Still convinced of his innocence, Gottfried again declined the opportunity to escape. His stubborn belief in justice proved misplaced, however, for on April 15, after a short trial in which neither witnesses nor a defense attorney were furnished, the local judge, Rudolf Oeschey, pronounced Gottfried guilty of treason for having expressed the opinion, while a member of the Volkssturm, that resistance against the Americans was senseless. Twenty minutes after the sentence was pronounced, Georg Gottfried was executed in the prison courtyard of the Ministry of Justice in Nuremberg, a site soon to gain international prominence during the postwar trials of Nazi war criminals. No such prominence attached to Gottfried, though, and not until the 1947 trial of Oeschey was his grave identified and his remains exhumed for burial in Gollachostheim.[21]

In this instance there seems little indication, at least until his case reached Oeschey's jurisdiction, that Georg Gottfried fell victim either to ideological fanaticism or an exaggerated sense of duty. Rather, at every step it appeared as if local authorities did not know what to do with Gottfried but were personally afraid, in the presence of other party, military, or Volkssturm figures whom they did not know or trust, to set him free. So instead they simply passed him along the bureaucratic chain of command until the unfortunate Gottfried ended up in the court of a Nazi loyalist. In a confused and uncertain situation, with a paralyzed sense of moral or civic courage and fearing for their own safety, these men acted in an all too human fashion. Indifference and self-interest, not ideological zeal, decided Georg Gottfried's fate.

More typical of ideological devotion and fealty to the Nazi state was the fate of a man on April 12, the fifty-five-year-old David G., who sought only to protect his mill from the wave of destruction rolling over Middle Franconia. The day before, an American patrol from Seenheim, a town about five miles to the northwest of Bad Windsheim, had searched Rummelsmühle, his farm and mill complex, and then returned to Seenheim, less than a mile away. Assuming that for himself and his family the war was now over, since his property had been formally occupied, the miller hoisted a white flag. On the morning of April 12, though, Major Erich Stentzel, a highly decorated Luftwaffe officer raised in a staunchly nationalist and conservative environment, set out from Ansbach on a reconnoitering mission with a companion, Captain B. Despite the evidence of imminent collapse all around, Stentzel nonetheless fervently believed further resistance both meaningful and a solemn duty. Charged with the task of defending the heavily forested height bisected by the main highway between Bad Windsheim and Ansbach, Stentzel was determined to hold every foot of German territory by any means necessary, in the hope of keeping the Alpine fortress viable until new miracle weapons effected a reversal of German fortunes.[22]

As the two German officers made their way north on a motorcycle, they were informed in Ergersheim of the presence of American troops in Seenheim. Hearing this, Stentzel declared that it was not too late to knock out a tank, so, armed with a pistol and with a Panzerfaust slung around his back, he and his companion raced off. As they approached Seenheim around 1:00 P.M., however, the two officers could see from a hill a German air attack on the village below. As they turned away, though, they stumbled upon the road leading to Rummelsmühle, which they now approached with no definite purpose in mind. Present at the mill and farmstead were not only the proprietor, his wife, and three daughters, but at least a dozen refugees, mostly women and children. As Stentzel neared the mill, he became enraged at the sight of the white flag, stormed inside, and reproached the ill-fated miller in the coarsest language. Although the latter responded that the Americans had already been at his place the day before and there was nothing else that he could do, the major was of another opinion: David G. had the obligation to defend his mill at all costs.[23]

As he escorted the miller into the courtyard, Stentzel informed him that, in accordance with a Himmler order of April 3 requiring that all males were to be shot in any house flying a white flag, he would now be executed and his house burned. After ordering the captain to guard the miller, Stentzel went back inside, told the wife that the house would now be burned, and rejected her plea to salvage some belongings. After driving the miller's wife, wailing daughters, and refugees away in the direction of Ergersheim, Stentzel set about torching the house. Captain B., who entertained increasing misgivings about the criminal nature of Stentzel's actions, also went inside and, in response to his inquiry as to what Stentzel actually meant to do, was told curtly to get back to the courtyard and guard the miller. As Captain B. stepped outside he noticed the miller slipping through the wood fence at the northern edge of the barn. Shouting, "Halt, halt!" B. fired a few shots in the direction of the fleeing miller as Stentzel raced out of the house. Both officers now gave chase and found David G. hiding in a hollow at the northwest corner of the barn. Without saying a word, Stentzel grabbed the pistol away from B. and fired a number of shots at the cowering miller. In a further cruel twist of fate, despite all the shots fired the miller was hit only once, but died instantly from a bullet to the brain. As the two officers walked back toward the house, with Stentzel intending now to burn the barns as well, B. noticed an American patrol approaching from Seenheim. Although the two murderers quickly fled, other GIs in the vicinity of Ergersheim opened fire on the fleeing officers, seriously wounding Captain B. Stentzel managed to fire off his Panzerfaust, hitting nothing, then ingloriously surrendered.[24]

Having been released from American captivity in November 1945, over the next ten years Stentzel held a number of managerial positions. Not until October 1955 was he formally questioned about the events at Rummelsmühle, and not until November 1958 did he come to trial. At his initial interrogation, Stentzel insisted that he had done nothing to the miller, even though the latter had insulted him, calling him a "swine and a perpetuator of the war." Only then, Stentzel claimed, did he take notice of the white flags, but merely demanded that the miller take them down.

In rejecting Stentzel's self-serving claims, the German court drily noted that "carrying out [Himmler's] flag decree was not justified from any possible military point of view," and further, that it was "completely mistaken . . . to believe that shooting the miller . . . could in any way change for the better the general political and military situation of Germany." Nor could the miller's execution serve even "as a terroristic deterrent, because in the confusion of war at that time its application in one place could not be communicated to a larger area; it was senseless." Further, the court insisted neither a staunch nationalism nor the spirit of obedience demanded the commission of crimes, for an officer such as Stentzel should have been aware of the difference between legitimate and criminal orders. Stentzel, the court concluded, could not be regarded as a completely slavish tool of the Nazi authorities, without a will or ideas of his own. Rather, he had the ability even in difficult and challenging situations to come to his own conclusions. Despite this assessment of Stentzel's guilt, it is hard to escape the conclusion that the court ordered him imprisoned for three and a half years more for his refusal to admit that he had shot a defenseless man in cold blood than for the actual crime itself. Although clever enough to dampen his earlier Nazi ardor, Stentzel, it appeared, remained unconvinced that he had done anything other than follow legitimate orders and to the fullest of his ability defend his country in the last days of a lost war.[25]

In eerily similar fashion, on April 16, just a few days after the events in Rummelsmühle, an American patrol entered the city of Burgthann, a few miles southeast of Nuremberg, and instructed the mayor on pain of total destruction of the town to order its inhabitants to fly white flags from their houses, and then they left. At the same time, a group of women angrily demanded that the mayor follow the instructions of the Americans and peacefully surrender the city. Seeking advice, the mayor returned to his office and talked with a municipal worker who, in view of the uncertain situation and the possibility of German troops reappearing, advised him to delay hoisting white flags. Under pressure from his daughter-in-law, however, the mayor notified townspeople to fly white flags. Still, some citizens remained uneasy, for they had been informed by radio and newspaper of the flag decree. The next morning a patrol from the Seventeenth SS entered the village, saw the white flags, and promptly notified their battalion commander, who thereupon decided to exact justice. Entering Burgthann, *Hauptsturmführer* (Captain) Müller challenged one resident who had white sheets hanging from his windows. Aware of the flag decree and the danger he was in, the man quickly retorted that his wife was merely airing the linens. Other citizens, though, admitted that the mayor had ordered white flags flown. Confronted by Captain Müller, the mayor defended his action by noting that the Americans had threatened to shoot him if he failed to obey their order. "Then you would have died a hero," replied Müller, "now you'll die like a swine!" Having already lost a son to the war, the mayor himself was now brutally murdered on the main street of the village. A group of women and children, observing the scene a few yards away, began screaming as the shots were fired, then scrambled for the protection of a nearby house as SS troopers shot at them as well.[26]

As with Stentzel, Müller was not brought to trial for murder until more than a decade after the events in question. Unlike Stentzel, however, Müller's initial conviction was overturned, as the appellate court found mitigating circumstances in his actions. As early as 1931, Müller, the then-fifteen-year-old son of an ardent National Socialist, had joined the Hitler Youth, moving on to what would become the Waffen-SS in 1935. In 1938 he was accepted into an officer training school of the SS, but his instruction was curtailed because of his educational and intellectual deficiencies. Almost continually in combat since 1941, the oft wounded and much decorated Müller had faced death daily and had witnessed the demise of numerous friends and comrades, which the court believed had dulled his sense of compassion and left him with a dim view of human life. Morever, the court noted, Müller had from his earliest youth been raised and indoctrinated in a National Socialist milieu, and he was thus educated to absolute obedience to the Führer and his military commanders. Having been made aware of the flag decree by his immediate superiors and determined to resist for reasons of ideology, loyalty, and duty, Müller, the appellate court reasoned, could not be held responsible for the murder of the mayor of Burgthann. In the confusing and contradictory claims of being obedient to orders, justice, and humanity at the end of the war, Müller believed himself compelled to carry out the execution of the mayor. Nor, the court concluded, did Müller possess either the rank or the education necessary to understand the criminal nature of the flag decree. Seeking to guarantee the security of his troops, Müller acted in the heat of a precarious military situation and in the hope of securing a turnaround in German fortunes.[27]

ONE FEARS THE SS LIKE THE DEVIL!

For men like Stentzel and Müller, the key questions would be: At what point does a war become senseless? And, who bears responsibility for the destruction of a village or its inhabitants in the midst of a combat situation? An incident at Brettheim, a town on the edge of Middle Franconia some nine miles southwest of Rothenburg ob der Tauber, should have served, perhaps, to put the civilian inhabitants of the region on guard. On the night of April 6–7, with tanks of the Tenth Armored Division only six miles to the west, a Volkssturm unit in Rothenburg made up of twenty-five Hitler Youth in their mid to late teens, led by a severely disabled war veteran, Corporal Bloss, was given the task of patrolling the main highway leading from Crailsheim, where American forces threatened a decisive breakthrough, to Blaufelden. Around 3:00 A.M. on April 7 the unit took up quarters at an inn in Hausen, a small village less than two miles from Brettheim. Four of the Hitler Youth, armed with rifles, hand grenades, and Panzerfäuste, then set off on a reconnaissance patrol. Since a number of the inhabitants of the hamlet were incensed at the presence of the Hitler Youth, fearing possible American reprisals, Mayor Kurz telephoned his counterpart in Brettheim, the sixty-four-year-old Leonhard Gackstatter, a respected mayor who had held the post for over thirty years, to warn him of their presence. In addition, he contacted the local Nazi Party and Volkssturm leader, the popular forty-two-year-old elementary school teacher Leonhard Wolfmeyer, who as Ortsgruppenleiter had blunted the impact of many Nazi decrees. Wolfmeyer advised Kurz not to interfere with the Hitler Youth, since they now fell under army command.[28]

That same morning, a local farmer, Friedrich Hanselmann, left his house early intending to bicycle to a neighboring village to discuss business with the butcher. Although his oldest son had been killed at Vyasma and his second son, only seventeen, was serving in an antiaircraft unit in Nuremberg, the next day was the church confirmation celebration and Hanselmann was determined to promote a festive atmosphere. On the outskirts of the village another farmer, Gottlob Krafft, had already had a run-in with the armed youth, who had threatened in coarse fashion to shoot him down. Around 7:00 A.M. the four boys passed the dairy in Brettheim, where they decided to take a rest, sullenly observed by a few dairy employees. In the meantime, a city worker, Friedrich Uhl, had hailed Hanselmann as he rode down the main street of the village and told him that "Werewolves" had just recently passed by. Hanselmann then jumped back on his bike and rode toward the edge of town, where he found the four Hitler Youth at the dairy. What happened next remains unclear, for Hanselmann's life ended a few days later under the limb of a linden tree, while the four Hitler Youth could never be found to testify at the postwar trials. Hanselmann evidently asked the boys what they were doing and was answered with talk of their assignment and duty to defend Brettheim. "We really need [the likes of] you to [defend us]!" retorted Hanselmann contemptuously. By this time, a group of local men, among them the dairy owner, Schmetzer, a fifteen-year-old apprentice named Schwarzenberger, and Uhl, had gathered. Incensed by the boys' attitude, the men confronted and disarmed them. During this action one of the men allegedly screamed that he did not want to be defended by such "snot-nosed brats," Uhl took one of the youths by the coat and shook him, and Hanselmann boxed one of the boys on the ears. Crying at the top of their lungs, the boys then fled the town, while one of the men supposedly fired a warning shot in their direction. Collecting the weapons, the men unceremoniously dumped them in a dirty farm pond. Before dispersing, one of the dairy workers nervously remarked, "Hanselmann, hopefully everything will be okay."[29]

Upon returning to the command post in Hausen, the aroused boys reported the incident in Brettheim, whereupon Corporal Bloss telephoned Rothenburg for instructions. Ordered to retrieve the weapons, Bloss and his unit headed immediately for Brettheim, where they gave the mayor an ultimatum: return the weapons by 6:00 P.M. or face the consequences. Unfortunately, the weapons lay at the bottom of a pond that would require at least a day to drain. The village dentist suggested that Mayor Gackstatter simply substitute the Panzerfäuste of the local Volkssturm unit, but those weapons were locked up and party leader Wolfmeyer had the only key—and he was nowhere to be found. Frustrated, Mayor Gackstatter could only wait helplessly while the ultimatum expired. In the meantime the commander of Thirteenth SS-Army Corps, General Max Simon, having heard of the incident, dispatched SS-Sturmbannführer (Major) Gottschalk, a longtime member of the SS and formerly with the Security Service (SD), so a person with extensive experience in such matters, to investigate and "clean up this mess in Brettheim." Accompanied by another officer and a dozen tough, battle-hardened Gebirgsjäger (mountain troops), he reached Brettheim that evening, whereupon he began his investigation. A man brutalized and desensitized by war, Gottschalk summoned the mayor and local party leader, all the men of the village, and the four Hitler Youth for interrogation, all to no avail, as the local men refused to betray one another.[30]

Enraged, Gottschalk threatened to burn the village down and shoot arbitrarily selected individuals. At that point Hanselmann came forward and admitted to being part of the group that had disarmed the Hitler Youth. Dragged out of his bed, Schwarzenberger also admitted to being involved. Another participant, Uhl, fled into the countryside. Although not formally authorized, Gottschalk, determined to dispose of the matter, decided to convene a summary court-martial. He himself undertook the role as chair, with a fellow officer (an SS major) and party leader Wolfmeyer completing the tribunal. Following a short proceeding, the two SS officers demanded the death sentence for the accused. Wolfmeyer, however, refused to sign the verdict, arguing that Hanselmann was a highly respected farmer who always helped his neighbors. Mayor Gackstatter, too, refused to endorse the verdict, declaring that he would "rather die innocent than sign." "You're only thinking of your village, Ortsgruppenleiter," Gottschalk reproached Wolfmeyer. "Here it concerns something greater." With both local officials in opposition, however, a formal pronouncement of sentence proved impossible. Nonetheless, Hanselmann and Schwarzenberger were taken into custody, and in the early morning hours of April 8 they were transported to the jail in Rothenburg.[31]

That Sunday, confirmation day, anxiety gripped Brettheim. "Is God on the side of the SS?" asked one young girl innocently, as the sound of American artillery and tank fire could be heard in the distance. Although advised to flee, Wolfmeyer instead went to the local hospital to be with his pregnant wife, who was soon to deliver their fifth child. "It is a lot when a man pleads for the life of another man," he told his wife of the events the previous evening. "I did it and the mayor after me." For his part, Mayor Gackstatter evinced more realism than Wolfmeyer, telling his wife that he would almost certainly be arrested and shot, but emphasizing again, "I would rather die innocent than have my conscience burdened by signing [a death sentence]." Sure enough, on the afternoon of April 9 the SS arrested both Wolfmeyer and Gackstatter because of their "oppositionist attitude" at the court-martial, and delivered them to the jail in Rothenburg. On that same Monday afternoon, Gottschalk convened a second court-martial at party headquarters in Rothenburg. The apprentice was released because of his age, while Hanselmann, in a one-hour hearing, was once more convicted of undermining the war effort and was sentenced to death.[32]

Not fully aware of the seriousness of his own fate, Wolfmeyer on April 9 wrote a letter to his wife from jail in which he despaired, "All of this is so stupid, so negative, arbitrary, cold, callous. At the same time, the enemy stands before the door. Or is he today already in Brettheim?" Although certainly unintentional, Wolfmeyer's question held a double meaning, for the enemy had indeed been in Brettheim—not the Americans but the SS. And ironically, only the arrival of the putative foe could save the three Brettheimers from their appointed fate. Earthly salvation was not at hand, however, as the next day, April 10, the SS transported Hanselmann, Gackstatter, and Wolfmeyer to Thirteenth SS-Army Corps headquarters at Schillingsfürst, the ancestral home of the Hohenlohes, one of the most important noble families of south Germany, where yet another court-martial condemned the three to death. Perhaps just now realizing the seriousness of his situation, Wolfmeyer offered to sign Hanselmann's execution order. Gackstatter, however—with much dignity and composure—said simply, "I am an old man. For 250 years the Gackstatter have been mayors of Brettheim. For 250 years they have led this village. . . . Never has something like this happened. I myself have been mayor for thirty-four years. . . . What, then, should I have done?" Rejecting their pleas for clemency, General Simon signed the verdict, with the hand-written addition, "hang them."[33]

As the hangman awaited, Wolfmeyer, riding in the open Wehrmacht car that was taking him to his death, requested paper and pen to write one last letter to his pregnant wife. "My darling Lore!" he wrote a half-hour before his execution, "Now my last words: because I was not hard enough last Sunday and didn't put my signature [on the death sentence], now I must die." When the three-car hangman's column reached Brettheim, Hanselmann looked around and saw his youngest son playing in the yard, to whom he gave a last wave. As Hitler Youth, transported to the village to build the gallows and view the execution, played the harmonica and slouched on the cemetery wall, the local priest noted in his diary, "Before us the enemy . . . and behind us the terror of the SS, who regard as treason and punish with hanging every attempt of the people to prevent needless destruction and loss of life." While Gottschalk read the sentences to those in attendance, Wolfmeyer muttered, "This is the thanks I get for working six years day and night [for the party]. . . . I supported the Führer and furthermore I wish him all the best." Gottschalk, having finished reading the sentences, strode over to Wolfmeyer and punched him in the chest. With American forces stalled only a few miles to the west, all three were hung on the evening of April 10 from two linden trees at the entrance to the Brettheim cemetery. Around the neck of each dead man hung a sign. One read, "I am the traitor Hanselmann," while the other two said, "I tried to protect the traitor Hanselmann." Gottschalk decreed that the bodies could not be taken down; they remained hanging for four days. After the executions, General Simon ordered public proclamations put up throughout his area of command, threatening, "The German people are determined with increasing severity to weed out such cowardly, self-serving, and irresponsible people and will not recoil from striking their families from the community of those honorably fighting German people."[34]

On the morning of April 17, a week after the executions, American tanks and artillery opened fire on Brettheim, ironically after inquiring of the local pastor, "Where is the mayor? If this village doesn't show white flags, it will be completely destroyed." As the SS in the village answered with machine gun fire, the Gebirgsjäger withdrew in the direction of Rothenburg. Advancing slowly and cautiously, the GIs halted in the woods on the edge of town, then called in an air strike. Just before noon, the village virtually disappeared under a hail of high explosive and incendiary bombs. As maddened cows ran through the streets bellowing pitiably, screaming villagers fled toward the woods, only to be caught in the crossfire between the SS and the Americans. Not until 7:30 that evening did the GIs finally occupy the town, although the next day a German Nebelwerfer fired a final salvo at Brettheim, killing six people. Not without reason had a pastor in a neighboring village confided in his diary a few days earlier, "One fears the SS like the devil!"[35]

A decade after the events in Brettheim, the German court trying Simon and Gottschalk for murder expressed its regret at the human tragedy, but nonetheless betrayed ambivalence and unease at trying "respectable" men such as Simon. The men of Brettheim, the court acknowledged, were "late victims," but of an "unfortunate chain of circumstances" during a "wretched war that could not find a timely end." To the judges, it was as if the war had taken on a life of its own and it, not mere mortals, was responsible for the senseless destruction that occurred until it chose to pass away. These remarks served as a prelude to the court's main contentions: first, that Hanselmann was guilty of undermining the war effort and so had been legitimately sentenced to death and executed; and second, that the court-martial of Wolfmeyer and Gackstatter could be regarded as valid since Simon and Gottschalk believed themselves acting against officials shirking their duty, and were motivated by military necessity and not by any desire to violate the two men's rights. General Simon in particular, the judges emphasized, still saw a purpose to the continuation of the war, namely the hope of achieving a better basis of negotiating a peace. Although using this as justification to find the defendants not guilty, the court did take note of three realities of the time: the confusing welter of increasingly harsh decrees issued both by the political and military leadership, the way in which the concept of *Wehrkraftzersetzung* (undermining the war effort) expanded in the last months of the war, and the painful experience of witnessing actions by German citizens against their own troops and thus desiring to mete out harsh punishment as an example and deterrent.[36]

At roughly the same time in Neuhof, on the Zenn River nine miles southeast of Bad Windsheim, a similar circumstance also demonstrated the willingness of Nazi military and civilian authorities to punish those deemed insufficiently zealous in their defense of the homeland. As early as April 5 the men of the local Volkssturm unit had been ordered to construct antitank defenses at the upper and lower entrances to the walled, medieval village. Declaring, "We will not build any defenses! The war is lost!" the men simply refused to obey any further orders given by their local commander. The next night women from the town sawed and distributed as firewood the logs cut previously by the Volkssturm for use as barricades. Early on the morning of April 7, police arrived from neighboring Dietenhofen and began searching houses for culprits in the mutiny. As Peter Heinlein, a participant in the events in Neuhof, recalled sardonically, "Each betrayed the other."[37]

The next day, a Sunday, two truckloads of police and SS men, along with a gallows, arrived in Neuhof. As the troops set about blocking all exits from the town, the commander of the SS unit, a lieutenant in his early twenties, ordered all residents to gather at the *Marktplatz*. There, in front of the World War I monument, with the sound of artillery thumping in the distance, he immediately launched into a tirade of abuse against "those dishonorable swine who stabbed the Wehrmacht in the back and so must die a shameful death." Against that ominous backdrop, the police and SS proceeded to arrest eight men of the Volkssturm, along with the mayor and local party leader, and brought them in handcuffs to a local inn for trial. The court-martial, presided over by SS-Major Waldeck and consisting of the local Volkssturm commander and two other non-commissioned officers, began around 8:00 P.M. and lasted well into the early morning hours of April 9.[38]

Although on trial for refusal to obey orders and for mutiny in the face of the enemy, the court-martial proved no drumhead trial, despite the presence of the gallows outside, for Major Waldeck allowed each defendant to defend himself and to give an account of the relevant events. Unable to ascertain the ringleaders, and anxious to get back to his unit, Waldeck brought the, in his words, *"Bauernkomödie"* (farce) to an end with the following verdict: no one was to be sentenced to death, the mayor and local party leader were to be released, but the eight other accused were to remain under house arrest at the inn. Obviously expecting that the incident would be lost in the rush of events, Waldeck hurriedly departed on the morning of April 9.[39]

The Nazi bureaucracy, however, stubbornly refused to drop the matter. Amazingly, with American forces nearing and the absence of virtually any military transport hampering an effective defense, toward evening on April 11 two trucks arrived in Neuhof, all twenty-eight Volkssturm men were loaded on board, and the trucks set off for Nuremberg. On arrival at police headquarters, the eight accused found themselves dumped into a single, unfurnished cell, while the other twenty were put into two common cells. Once in Nuremberg, Nazi retribution came swiftly, if not as murderously as that meted out in Brettheim. After a cursory investigation, police officials on April 13 singled out Georg Freund as the instigator of the Neuhof mutiny and sentenced him to death. Freund cheated the hangman, however, for with American forces fast approaching the outskirts of Nuremberg, the local police authorities decided on the night of April 15 to send him and the other Volkssturm men to Dachau. Chained in twos and guarded by eight policemen, in the early morning hours of April 16 the men of Neuhof set off on foot for the notorious concentration camp some one hundred miles to the south.[40]

In a surreal scenario played out all over the remnants of Hitler's Reich by political prisoners, POWs, and survivors of death camps, for the next ten days the Neuhof Volkssturm men wandered southward, living off cheese and bread supplied by farmers and sleeping in barns. Although spared the worst punishment, the men received a macabre reminder of what could have been their fate. On April 17, near the small village of Obersteinbach, twenty-five miles southwest of Nuremberg, they found a local newspaper dated April 14, 1945, with the blaring headline, "A plate of shame and humiliation; How traitors are fed!" (*gerichtet*: a play on words since '*Gericht*' can also mean justice):

> In the town of Neuhof on the Zenn the mustered Volkssturm soldiers mutinied against their Führer and removed anti-tank barriers. Today before a court-martial this monstrously traitorous act found its atonement. The ringleader Georg Freund was hanged before the assembled Volkssturm men. The remaining traitors . . . began the journey to a concentration camp.
>
> Karl Holz
> Reichs Defense Commissar

Obviously meant as a warning to others considering surrendering without resistance, this article, despite (or because of) its inaccuracies, also served as a reminder to the men of their precarious situation. Not until April 25 were they liberated, paradoxically by the American "enemy."[41]

By then, however, their homes and village had been destroyed. Cleansed of its mutinous Volkssturm men, young soldiers of the so-called children's SS took up positions in Neuhof and fiercely resisted American attempts to cross the Zenn River. As a result, on the night of April 15–16 the small market town went up in flames, destroyed in a savage artillery bombardment, one that continued long after the last Wehrmacht soldier had slunk out of town. When late that night the terrified inhabitants crept out of their cellars or returned from hiding in the surrounding woods, they found, in place of their splendid walled, medieval village, a devastated wasteland. Only the agonizing cries of the wounded, one survivor remembered, could be heard above the noise of the raging fires and collapsing buildings.[42]

THE WEIBERSTURM OF WINDSHEIM

As the previous examples illustrated, Nazi terror was not merely something inflicted from above but also something that could emanate from officials at lower levels. Even as the Nazi system was falling apart, at the grassroots level local party and Gestapo authorities often clung tenaciously to the routine of bureaucratic terror, seemingly oblivious to the circumstances around them. As events in Bad Windsheim demonstrated, such attitudes often had murderous consequences. Forced to retreat from their Steigerwald positions, German troops in mid-April withdrew to the Aisch River and beyond, hoping to delay the American advance and hold open the lines of retreat by utilizing certain key cities lying astride the major highways and bridges as fortresses. One such city was Bad Windsheim, where already on April 10 Major Günther Reinbrecht had been appointed city commandant, charged with the task of holding a bridgehead across the Aisch until the remnants of *Kampfgruppe Hobe* reached new defensive positions on the Frankenhöhe to the south. As commander of an urban "strong point," Reinbrecht fell under Führer Order number 11, issued by Hitler on March 8, 1944, and supplemented by further decrees of November 25, 1944, and April 12, 1945, as well as an OKW directive issued on the latter date, which placed any such city under military control and obligated the commander to carry out all orders "to the last." That same April 12 Heinrich Himmler appended a further proviso, ordering, "Every village and every city will be held and defended by all available means. Any German man responsible for the defense of a place who contravenes this self-evident national duty will lose his honor and life."[43]

Thus enjoined and threatened, Reinbrecht, a decorated veteran of the Polish and Russian campaigns who had lost an arm at Stalingrad, and who had recently been involved in the hard fighting along the Ippesheim–Uffenheim line, where a large number of his men had been killed, assumed command of a city whose residents were already restless and on edge. A town with a prewar population of around six thousand, Bad Windsheim had been overwhelmed in recent weeks by the arrival of as many as four thousand evacuees and refugees. The city was also a local manufacturing center whose factories churned out vehicles, munitions, and other vital war production. As such, it also housed hundreds of foreign (mostly French and Polish) forced laborers. With a Luftwaffe base boasting the new Me 262 jet fighters a few miles outside town, and sitting along an important railway line running into Nuremberg, the area had been subjected with increasing frequency over the previous months to low-level aerial attacks by American fighter-bombers. Indeed, farmers had even been strafed while working in their fields. As a result, the local inhabitants had grown increasingly jittery, so much so that one American pilot whose plane was downed a few miles outside Bad Windsheim was nearly beaten to death by outraged farmers. Even before American forces reached the Tauber River on April 1, Windsheimers had been hiding valuables, stockpiling food, and burning party uniforms.[44]

On that Easter Sunday, in fact, American planes attacked Bad Windsheim in force, seeking to destroy the Schmotzer machinery factory and the adjoining rail yards. The early morning attack, in a tragic irony, took the lives of four foreign workers employed at the factory. A few days later, on April 5, the fighter-bombers returned, this time aiming at the local food warehouse and the main rail yard, which held sixty freight cars bulging with tires, spare parts, and radio equipment destined for the airbase at Illesheim. The half-hour attack proved successful in destroying the rail yard, freight cars, and warehouse, but also resulted in the deaths of two young boys, ages seven and nine, in the heavily populated residential area adjacent to the train station. Shaken by the attack and fearful of more raids, Hans Schmotzer, the town's leading industrialist, and Hermann Delp, a wounded World War I veteran, company commander of a local Volkssturm unit, town councillor, and publisher of the local newspaper, engaged in frantic discussions about ways to save the town. As German troops, a grim seriousness on their faces, retreated through the city, there seemed little hope of preventing the destruction of Bad Windsheim.[45]

Nor did the mood in the town improve the next day, April 6, when the local Volkssturm received instructions to barricade the entrances to the city along the inner ring. The marking of houses for placement of antitank units and machine gun nests also increased the anxiety among the local populace. With beams, logs, tree trunks, carts, wagons, and farm machinery blocking all entrances to the inner city, Bad Windsheim seemed condemned to annihilation. Delp and Schmotzer, however, seemingly found a way out of the town's dilemma. On Sunday, April 8, in a tense meeting, they convinced the Nazi Kreisleiter in Neustadt that Bad Windsheim should be declared a "hospital city" and that the barricades should be taken down. As the good news spread quickly through the town, the inhabitants let out a collective sigh of relief, and the next day began the removal of the barricades, aided by foreign laborers dispatched from the Schmotzer machinery company and the Hofmann foundry.[46]

On April 10, however, Major Reinbrecht arrived with about thirty men to assume command of the city. Under threat of death if he failed to carry out his orders, Reinbrecht also faced a rebellious population willing to engage in sabotage to save their homes. (There had even been instances of stray shots being fired at German troops retreating through the city.) This stand-off intensified over the next two days. On April 11, Bad Windsheim was formally declared a "hospital city," with a large field hospital adorned with a red cross flag established in a building at the Schmotzer machinery factory. Seeking to regain control of the situation, on April 12 Reinbrecht brought the local Volkssturm and Hitler Youth units under his authority and took immediate steps to defend the city, ordering the barricades put back in place. Near panic now seized the inhabitants of Bad Windsheim. In addition to the activity of the omnipresent American aircraft, reports of the destruction of neighboring villages, and the ominous din of nearby battle, Reinbrecht's measures heightened the portentous atmosphere. Even while the local population broke into food warehouses and began hoarding vital supplies, German troops streamed toward the Frankenhöhe.[47]

The citizens of Bad Windsheim, however, refused to acquiesce in their apparent fate. "The women of the city," remembered Robert Beining, a contemporary observer, "were unwilling to sit idly and watch the war machine" devour their town. On the afternoon of April 12 a group of women met spontaneously on a downtown street and talked anxiously of ways to prevent the destruction of their town. A prominent local farmer advised them that the only way to get results was for the women, accompanied by their children, to confront the local Nazi Ortsgruppenleiter and demand that he order the Wehrmacht out of town. This advice received an enthusiastic reception, not least because somewhat similar action just a few days earlier had proven successful. The women thus decided that, accompanied by their children, they would assemble at the Marktplatz at 6:00 P.M. in order to use moral suasion in an effort to spare their homes. Fueled by word of mouth, news of the intended gathering spread rapidly. Not surprisingly, various rumors sprang up, the most suggestive being that the Schmotzers would once again take up the cause of saving the city. By 6:00 P.M. an estimated three hundred people, mostly women, children, and a few elderly men, had streamed into the main square to plead, significantly, not with the local party leader but with Major Reinbrecht to surrender the city. After waiting uncertainly for a time, during which a participant remarked, "Only a Weibersturm [women's storm] can save us," a number of women approached *Justizrat* Thekla Fischer and beseeched her to take the lead. Although other women evidently looked to Frau Christine Schmotzer for guidance, she had not yet appeared at the Marktplatz. In the meantime, Frau Babette Teufel interceded with Mayor Albert Hub, a longtime member of the Nazi Party and commander of the local Volkssturm, to help, but he replied that there was nothing more he could do for he himself had been threatened with execution. A delegation of women led by Frau Fischer finally entered Reinbrecht's command post on the ground floor of the Rathaus to plead their case, but the enraged major not only rejected their entreaty but threatened to shoot anyone who did not leave the room immediately. The delegation left, but the crowd, instead of dispersing, began to make angry noises and demand that Reinbrecht appear.[48]

The so-called *Weibersturm* of Windsheim had now turned rebellious. With young soldiers placed around the town square, Reinbrecht read the relevant OKW and Führer orders to the demonstrators and explained that he could not evacuate the town without authorization. Hardly satisfied with this, the demonstrators grew even more agitated. Some sought to storm the command post, while others shouted threats at Reinbrecht. Nervous, weary, and aware that some soldiers had earlier been fired on by the local population, Reinbrecht now sought to calm the situation by calling on a local recipient of the Knight's Cross who was home on leave, Sergeant Otto Angel, to speak to the crowd. Although credited with the destruction of thirty-eight Russian tanks, including six in one day in early March, Angel's exploits in the east meant nothing to the enraged women, who greeted him with jeers and curses. Paradoxically, the very fact that Reinbrecht and Angel were veterans of the eastern front likely upset the women more, for a large number of men from the vicinity of Bad Windsheim had perished in the Stalingrad cauldron.[49]

Mounting a wagon to talk, Angel sought to reassure the women that just because the town had been placed on defense alert did not mean that it would actually be defended. This feeble apologia only inflamed the crowd more. Some women spat on Angel, while others tried to tear the Knight's Cross from his uniform. Abuse was also hurled at Angel's wife, who had just appeared in the Marktplatz. Incensed by this, Angel drew his pistol and threatened to shoot anyone who harassed his wife. Before he could carry out his threat, however, he was pulled off the wagon by a number of demonstrators. Reinbrecht, enraged by the actions of the women as well as by an elderly man who sought to take Angel's pistol away, screamed at the crowd to disperse, while threatening to stand the offending man, Heinrich Walther, a local businessman, against the wall and shoot him. Only the intervention of a severely wounded veteran prevented Reinbrecht from executing Walther on the spot. Mayor Hub sought unsuccessfully to quiet the crowd by declaring that if Germany wanted to win the war every city could not simply be surrendered without a defense. This remarkably foolish statement threatened to unleash total chaos until Reinbrecht, resorting to a ruse, screamed "*Jabos*" (fighter-bombers) at the top of his lungs, effectively dispersing the crowd.[50]

The affair, however, was hardly over. That evening, in revenge for the demonstration, German artillery shelled Bad Windsheim, although only a few rounds actually hit the southeastern edge of the city, doing little damage. The following day, April 13, Reinbrecht, determined to avenge his humiliation and punish the ringleaders of the demonstration, ordered that Anni Schunk, who had allegedly insulted Angel, be brought to his command post in the town hall. Hauled out of her home by soldiers and brought to the Rathaus, Schunk was initially faced with a stony silence. Then, as a twelve-year-old girl was brought into the room, Reinbrecht turned to her and asked, "You are a true German girl, is that the woman?" The girl replied, "Yes," whereupon Frau Schunk insisted to Sergeant Angel, "I have done absolutely nothing to you." Incensed, Reinbrecht screamed, "You're lying, shut up!" then asked the names of the leaders of the previous night's demonstration. Refusing to answer, Schunk withstood a further tirade of abuse from the two men, after which she was placed in stocks in the town hall arcade, guarded by two soldiers with orders to shoot to kill if she attempted to escape. Reinbrecht also sought to humiliate Frau Schunk further by having her head shaved, but both incensed barbers called upon to do it refused their services. After two hours in the stocks, during which the streets of Bad Windsheim were largely deserted except for Volkssturm men, Reinbrecht once again asked for names of the leaders of the demonstration. After again declining to answer, Reinbrecht released Schunk and sent her home.[51]

As a sidelight to the events of April 13 in Bad Windsheim, a sixteen-year-old member of the Hitler Youth, in a foolhardy and risky escapade, slipped through American lines in order to report the position of enemy artillery that was menacing the German withdrawal to the Frankenhöhe at Mailheim. For his "heroic action," one in distinct contrast to the "treasonous" deed of the previous evening by the women of Bad Windsheim, Major Reinbrecht immediately awarded him the Iron Cross and had him driven around town on a motorcycle so all could see the young "hero." Ironically, for all his impetuous courage, the youth's mission proved pointless, for the Germans no longer had any artillery in place that could silence the American weapons.[52]

While the events of the Weibersturm played out in Bad Windsheim, an unknown informer (suspicion later fell on a local teacher named Vogel, although witnesses also implicated Reinbrecht and Hub) had telephoned the Gestapo in Nuremberg with news of the demonstration in Bad Windsheim, alleging that Christine Schmotzer, the wife of factory owner Hans Schmotzer, had organized and led the Weibersturm. Long under Gestapo surveillance for alleged political unreliability, both Schmotzers had been active in efforts to prevent the defense of the city, although Frau Schmotzer had not been a primary organizer of the recent protest. With German resistance crumbling all around and American troops only a few miles from Bad Windsheim, regional Gestapo headquarters in Nuremberg nonetheless dispatched *SS-Untersturmführer* (Lieutenant) Karl Schmid to exact "justice." A longtime veteran of the criminal police and Gestapo, the forty-six-year-old Schmid had been sent in August 1941 to a POW camp for Russian officers, where he later recalled that "those characterized as negative personalities" had been murdered. Dispatched to Poland in 1942, he worked in the Lublin district as commander of a unit of security police, where he participated in "clearing Poland" of Jews under the overall direction of the notorious Odilo Globocnik. Such operations routinely involved the mass shooting of Jews. Although claiming in later trial testimony that he and his comrades "had misgivings about the permissibility of these actions," and that "we often talked among ourselves that this was no work for us," Schmid admitted no personal culpability. After all, he objected, "what could we do, orders were orders." Schmid served with the security police in Poland until November 1944, when he was detailed to Army Group Center. There he did unspecified work until April 1945, when he was dispatched to Nuremberg, arriving only a few days before the unfortunate events in Bad Windsheim. Attached to the section dealing with Wehrkraftzersetzung, this, then, was the man chosen to deal with the mutinous women of Windsheim, one accustomed to direct action who would not shrink from the necessity of harsh measures.[53]

On the afternoon of April 13, Schmid met with the head of his section, Herz, who informed him of the events in Bad Windsheim and ordered him to drive there and get the names of the leaders of the demonstration. Further, he was told to shoot "a few of them," as well as to blow up their houses with hand grenades. Upon arriving in Bad Windsheim that evening, Schmid, dressed in SS uniform, and two unnamed colleagues first checked in at Reinbrecht's command post. Greeted with the words, "It's high time that you came," Schmid received the names of the women who had supposedly led the demonstration. Reinbrecht apparently labeled Frau Schmotzer as the instigator of the previous night's tumult, even though she had played little part in the demonstration. More likely, he was determined to exact retribution for the earlier activities of the Schmotzers. Given directions to the Schmotzer's house by Mayor Hub and accompanied by a local man as a guide, Schmid and his colleagues raced off in a great hurry. In the meantime, the Schmotzers, busy in the canteen building next to their house, had stepped outside along with their daughter and a few others just before 8:00 P.M. to take a break. At that moment, in the words of Hans Schmotzer, "a car came racing out of town at high speed and stopped right in front of us. An officer jumped out and shouted at me, 'Are you Herr Schmotzer?' I replied, 'Yes.'" As his wife came closer to see what was going on, recalled Schmotzer, the SS man "then asked my wife, 'Are you Frau Schmotzer?' She also answered, 'Yes,' whereupon he screamed, 'Yesterday you played a major role [in the demonstration] at the Marktplatz.' My wife replied, 'No,' but it was too late."[54]

While her horrified husband and daughter watched, Schmid drew a revolver out of his coat pocket. As her husband shouted a protest, Frau Schmotzer turned to flee but managed only a few steps before the first shot rang out. Hit in the neck, she fell face down on the sidewalk. Made aware by one of his companions that Frau Schmotzer was still alive, Schmid, shouting at Herr Schmotzer, "Be quiet or else I'll shoot you down too," then calmly walked up to the prone body of Frau Schmotzer and, in the easy, practiced manner of one who had surely performed this act many times before, shot her again in the mouth and the left eye. Schmid then placed a placard on her body that he had brought along, strong evidence that, despite his later protestations, he had come to Bad Windsheim with the intention of killing someone. Written in large red letters, it read, "A traitor has been executed."[55]

Getting back in the car, Schmid then drove off in search of Frau

Schunk, with the intention of killing her as well. Bursting into her house with pistol drawn, Schmid shouted, "Where is Frau Schunk?" Her brother-in-law replied, just as a woman entered the room, that she was not at home. As Schmid pointed his pistol at the woman, the brother-in-law screamed in horror, "That is not Frau Schunk!" With the words, "We'll be back," Schmid hurried out of the house. Not through yet, Schmid now sought out another alleged ringleader, Frau Fischer. Screaming at her that he would shoot her immediately if she did not tell the truth, Schmid demanded to know Frau Fischer's relationship with Frau Schmotzer. Frau Fischer replied that the latter had not been involved in the demonstration, whereupon Schmid bellowed that one person had already been killed, and the same would happen to her. Inexplicably, however, Schmid then muttered that he had to report back to the Rathaus, but would be back in ten minutes. Shaken but alive, Frau Fischer watched stupefied as he left her house and reported back to Reinbrecht. Informed by Reinbrecht of his suspicion that Lydia Rauch, a local actress, had been passing information to the Americans and should be arrested, Schmid, as his final act in Bad Windsheim, arrested Frau Rauch and took her with him back to Gestapo headquarters in Nuremberg, where, amazingly, she was released a few days later.[56]

Tried for murder along with Reinbrecht and Hub in August 1948 in Nuremberg, Schmid, not surprisingly, fell back on the defense of superior orders and personal compulsion, arguing: "I didn't have any other choice in my actions. I didn't know if the order came from Herz alone [the deputy head of the Nuremberg Regional Gestapo Headquarters] or if it came from the Reich Defense Commissar [for Nuremberg]. At that time I regarded myself as the head of an executive commando [and] Bad Windsheim was a combat area. If I had hesitated in my duty, then I would have—I'm absolutely convinced of this—been stood against the wall [and shot]. Just the day before Pulmer [the head of the Nuremberg Regional Gestapo Headquarters] had given a speech in which he said he would not shy away from shooting any official who did not carry out his orders. . . . I was thus worried that measures would be taken against me if I did not carry out this order. Herz as well as Pulmer both told me that I had handled the matter correctly. . . . I had an order to carry out. I couldn't risk running away because I didn't have the proper papers and Wehrmacht patrols were everywhere in the area."[57]

Seen from the present perspective, Schmid's statement clearly has the ring of rationalization and self-justification to it. Given the standing orders issued by Hitler and Himmler, and the recent events in Middle Franconia, where a number of local officials and party leaders had already been sentenced by impromptu courts-martial to prison or death, Schmid's claim perhaps can be seen in a different light. Here was a man, given his past record, who obviously would not shrink from executing people if so ordered. Still, with the war clearly at its end, both the threat of and actual implementation of summary execution tempered any inclination Schmid might have had to go easy on the accused. The tragedy here was not so much that an evil man did evil deeds, but that the murder machine the Nazi hierarchy had created and set in motion continued to function, holding both perpetrators and victims in its grip until it was itself destroyed. Time and again in Middle Franconia, amid transportation dislocations, the breakdown of normal civilian services, and with American forces literally at the gate, the system of SS and Gestapo terror persisted in meting out violence to those Germans who sought to end the now utterly futile and senseless resistance.

Despite his plea of personal compulsion and fear for his own life, Schmid was found guilty of manslaughter and sentenced to ten years in prison. Justifying their sentence, the trial judges claimed that Schmid's action did not constitute murder, for he had not acted out of base motives, nor was the shooting of Frau Schmotzer malicious or cruel. Since the impulse had come from his superiors and not from Schmid himself, who only doggedly carried out orders, the court ruled that he could not be held liable for the crime of murder. Although they found that he betrayed a "contemptible weakness of character," the judges determined that Schmid did not possess ultimate guilt in the sense of the law, because he acted as the executor and not the originator of the evil deed. Nor, the court concluded, could his action be seen as malicious or cruel, since Schmid had not tried to disguise his intent or deceive Frau Schmotzer, but acted with dispatch to shoot her, and then had not allowed her to suffer. Still, the judges acknowledged that Schmid, in police service since October 1919, was familiar with the foundation of the law and judicial procedure and thus had to know that the order issued him in Nuremberg was criminal in its nature, and that therefore he was under no obligation to carry it out. A personal assessment of guilt and responsibility should, therefore, have overruled blind obedience. The plea of military necessity also fell short, the court ruled, because his superiors in

Nuremberg could not immediately threaten Schmid, who in any case could have bought time by the simple expedient of seeming to conduct a formal investigation. Still, the confusion at the end of the war, the judges decided, could not under the circumstances allow Schmid to be characterized as "a brutal Gestapo official." The cold-blooded shooting of a thirty-nine-year-old women had to be atoned, though, so with a distinct impression of reluctance, the court felt compelled to imprison Schmid.[58]

In convoluted fashion, then, the court held Schmid guilty of a crime, castigated him for obeying an illegal order, and denied his claim of acting under fear for his own life, despite the fact that his superiors threatened to kill anyone not obeying orders to the last, and that just such atrocities had already occurred in Middle Franconia. On the other hand, the judges tilted toward leniency in their sentencing, since Schmid, despite his murderous actions in both the POW camp and Poland between August 1942 and March 1945, where he had certainly killed innocent Jews as a result of criminal and illegal orders, somehow appeared now to be respectable. Nor, they decided, could this cold-blooded murderer be regarded as a vicious Gestapo man. In similar fashion, in rejecting his plea for leniency, a German appeals court nonetheless asserted that his activities outside regular police procedures, where he had participated in the "special treatment" [*Sonderbehandlung*], or murder, of POWs and civilians had made him an "obedient, if also in part an anxious, tool of mass murder." As the appeals court noted, Schmid admitted "with shocking candor" that he had no particular reservations about being chosen as an expert for such duty.[59]

Schmid's earlier participation in mass murder thus now served as a mitigating factor, as if he was seen by the court as a victim as much as a perpetrator. More troubling was the seeming ease with which Schmid, and others like him, made the transition from ordinary policeman to mass murderer. Schmid, like many in his situation, did not appear to be motivated as much by ideology or inner conviction as by the pursuit of his own self-interest. Already an experienced murderer, he would have killed anyone designated by his superiors. As Dirk de Mildt concluded of ordinary operatives in the euthanasia program, an assessment that could equally apply to Schmid, "Selecting the victims was not their job, slaughtering them was."[60] Taken together, the events in Bad Windsheim demonstrated the courage of some civilians, especially women, at the local level and the dangers they faced in trying to protect their homes. In addi-

tion, they demonstrated the extent to which the terror apparatus continued to operate in a steadily disintegrating Germany, and the willingness
of individual members of this apparatus to carry out orders they knew to
be murderous and senseless.

THE BANALITY OF TERROR:
ROBERT LIMPERT IN ANSBACH

The affair in Bad Windsheim was also illustrative of the fact that a system
in a state of turbulence and disintegration is not only unpredictable, but
that out of this seeming chaos a temporarily stable yet dynamic structure
can emerge. The energy imparted by a fanatical ideologue, a careerist, or
even a functionary simply keeping the routine flowing often enabled the
terror system to maintain itself or to lash out in illogical ways at those in
opposition. As events in Ansbach confirmed, this uneasy stability often
collapsed in catastrophe. There, just a few days after the tragic incident in
the town fifteen miles to the north, a nineteen-year-old student, Robert
Limpert, convicted by a summary court-martial of undermining the war
effort through the distribution of leaflets urging the residents of the city
not to resist, was hung in tragicomic fashion even as American tanks
approached a few blocks away.

The son of a retired railroad inspector, Limpert had long since attracted notice in Ansbach both for his academic brilliance and his openly
antagonistic attitude toward the National Socialist regime, for which he
was expelled from the local *Gymnasium* (college-prep high school). Spared
extensive military service because of a severe heart condition, Limpert
enrolled for the winter semester at the University of Würzburg, where he
experienced the devastating March 1945 air raid that left most of the
splendid former archbishopric in ruins. Traumatized by the extent of the
destruction in Würzburg, Limpert returned to Ansbach, the seat of government of Middle Franconia and itself a marvelous example of baroque
and rococo architecture, determined to prevent such a calamity in his
native city. Limpert, his father later recalled, spoke often of the tragic and
senseless destruction of Würzburg, all because it had been declared a
"fortress," to be held at all costs. In a city now consisting mostly of anxious women, children, and the elderly, Limpert resolved to act to spare
Ansbach the same fate, a decision that put his life on a collision course
with that of another academically oriented German.[61]

On March 27, 1945, forty-nine-year-old Colonel Ernst Meyer, a Luftwaffe training officer at the nearby airbase in Katterbach, received orders to take over as *Kampfkommandant* and organize the defense of Ansbach. The son of a distinguished professor of physics at the University of Freiburg, Meyer himself, after four years of service in the army during World War I, earned a doctorate in physics in 1924, then worked as an assistant in the Physics Institute at the University of Leipzig. A member of the National Socialist Party since May 1933, he also belonged to the National Socialist Welfare Organization, the Nazi professors association, the Labor Front, and was an officer in the *Sturmabteilung* (Storm Troopers, or SA). A highly intelligent, well-educated individual, Meyer nonetheless had earned a reputation as a hard-boiled, merciless officer and blindly loyal follower of Hitler—a man whose extreme sense of duty to the Führer outweighed all notions of morality or compassion. Until the final capitulation, as he later claimed, he believed firmly in ultimate victory.[62] Educated and socialized in a pre-Nazi era, Meyer stood as proof that not only the young could be fanatical believers. Having been entrusted with the defense of Ansbach, he vowed to fight until the last bullet.

Already on the night of April 7, Limpert, at considerable personal danger, had plastered flyers on walls, doors, shop windows, and party bulletin boards. In inflammatory language Limpert castigated the "*Nazibonzen,*" the party big shots, for continuing "the senseless resistance only because they did not want any ordinary German to survive their own downfall." In another flyer Limpert warned that any town that offered opposition would be destroyed by American forces, so he urged his fellow citizens to fly white flags and save Ansbach from senseless destruction. Closing with the cry, "Death to the Nazi hangmen," Limpert demanded that his compatriots take action to decide their own fate. His last flyer, distributed on the night of April 17, once again insisted that defense of Ansbach meant its complete destruction, and it urged residents to dismantle antitank obstacles and thwart Nazi plans. Despite Limpert's passionate efforts, these open calls to sabotage the military defense of the city shocked most Ansbachers and elicited little response except a determination by criminal police authorities to apprehend those responsible for the flyers.[63] Clinging doggedly to routine procedure even as the state they served collapsed around them, police officials undertook the investigation of the source of the rabble-rousing flyers.

Since by mid-April 1945 the fighting front had neared to just a few miles, most governmental offices, including the criminal police, had evacuated the city, leaving behind only a skeletal administration. This reality thrust the sixty-three-year-old head of the local constabulary (*Schutzpolizei*), Captain Hauenstein, and his assistant Zippold, celebrating his sixty-first birthday on April 18, into the vortex. Both police officials had served well over thirty years in Ansbach and typified a certain bureaucratic attitude in their obeisance and reluctance to assume responsibility. Nor did their inclination to act independently increase on April 12, when not only were the police brought under the control of the Wehrmacht, meaning the personal command of Kampfkommandant Meyer, but Ansbach officials were made aware of the decree from SS-General Simon, based on the recent events in Brettheim, demanding toughness toward local populations and strict adherence to orders. Meyer also received the OKW directive holding commanders personally responsible, on threat of death, for the execution of all orders. Prompted by the OKW order, Meyer on April 14 issued instructions to all of his subordinates ordering them to shoot everyone in a house flying the white flag and to burn the house. "The Werwolf," he threatened sinisterly, "battles the enemy and executes traitors."[64]

Hauenstein was in many respects not unwilling to surrender Ansbach without a fight, but his reservations were overwhelmed by two events between April 14 and April 18. First, on April 15, he was ordered by Meyer to execute a Pole sentenced to death by a court-martial, but initially refused on the grounds that the court-martial had been illegally constituted. Only when Meyer threatened to bring Hauenstein himself before a tribunal did the police commander withdraw his objections and allow the Pole to be executed by one of his officials. Then, on April 17, Hauenstein had the regrettable task of reporting to a local military commander, Major Schwegler, that it would be impossible to build all of the required tank obstacles. Schwegler first dressed down Hauenstein, then remarked pointedly, "I don't want to hear any reports about difficulties. . . . Don't forget, you'll lose your head if the anti-tank obstacles are not ready." For Hauenstein, essentially a decent man left abandoned by other city officials, unwilling or unable to stand up to military authorities, and lacking civil courage, this proved too much. As he confessed later, "That was the second death threat within two days. . . . Rational reasons no longer counted."[65]

Indeed, as American forces crept ever closer, the tension in the city became acute, an unbearable pressure that had to burst forth. That same April 17, as Hauenstein's nerves snapped, Colonel Meyer raced around the city as a veritable one-man alarm brigade, rounding up stray soldiers, insisting that antitank obstacles be completed, and demanding complete obedience to the Führer to the bitter end. Despite his superhuman exertions, however, the signs of disintegration and imminent collapse lay all about. That night, scores of pictures of Hitler could be seen floating in the Fränkische Rezat, while brown uniform jackets, the discarded skin of once proud and powerful local party officials, suddenly appeared in dark corners and ditches throughout the city. The next morning, April 18, Ansbachers awoke to warm, early summer temperatures, trees blooming in all their splendor, and the sound of artillery fire in their immediate vicinity. Remembered one man:

> The people acted as if they were crazy. . . . I drove a wagon into Oberhäuserstraße. . . . As I came into the Endresstraße [I saw] people force their carts and wagons through a barely six feet wide opening in an anti-tank obstacle made from fallen trees. . . . As I came to the Bachmann factory I could barely believe my eyes: at least a hundred women, children, and grandfathers scrambled about. . . . With my wagon I drove into the warehouse. . . . There, a good half of the storehouse was stacked to the ceiling with cases. Some young lads sat on top of the mountain of cases like baroque angels and threw the goods down. . . . In a few minutes I had my wagon loaded to half a man's height. . . . My haul was at least 200 cans, each weighing around a kilo: lard, sausage, beef, liverwurst, and pork.

Outside the warehouse the man found a frenzied mob, with people cursing, screaming, and pushing desperately to get at the spoils. In the meantime, a few German soldiers, armed with rifles and Panzerfäuste, crouched in doorways or lay in gardens, awaiting the GIs now on the edge of the city.[66]

Robert Limpert also had a mission: the time had come to save his city from destruction. Although early that Wednesday morning a delegation of women had already unsuccessfully urged the mayor to order the surrender of Ansbach, fortune evidently smiled on Limpert, for Mayor Böhm declared himself in sympathy with the young man's efforts. Limpert now hurried off to inform some of his like-minded colleagues of his triumph, stopping on the way to tell crowds of people of the mayor's decision and urging them to hang sheets out of all windows. As one participant noted, "People who spoke out in favor of further resistance were almost beaten by the excited crowds." In the process, Limpert overheard rumors to the effect that Colonel Meyer meant to defend Ansbach "to the last." Determined to prevent this, he decided to cut the cable between Meyer's command post and the troops fighting at the front, which ran through the northern and eastern edges of Ansbach. As Limpert cut the cable around 11:00 A.M. he was observed by a pair of thirteen- to fourteen-year-old Hitler Youth who knew him personally. Informing a couple of men in the area, one of whom happened to be one of the boys' uncle and an old party member, they then raced off to police headquarters to report what had just transpired.[67]

Although Meyer had abandoned the command post early that morning, Zippold and a police colleague felt compelled to investigate the charges. Having confirmed the sabotage of the cable, Zippold then gave a full report to Hauenstein. The latter declared that this was certainly a matter for the criminal police, but because they had already left Ansbach the Schutzpolizei would have to take up the matter and investigate. Clinging grimly to bureaucratic routine even with the enemy only a few miles away, Hauenstein now authorized another policeman, Döhla, to go to Limpert's house and look for incriminating evidence. Not only did Döhla find evidence, but Limpert had in the meantime returned home and was arrested as well. Events now began to spin out of control. In the chaos, nothing would have been easier than to drop the matter quietly and let Limpert go. As a later American investigator concluded, though, Zippold in particular possessed a typical bureaucratic temperament in that he wanted to have a successful conclusion to a case. As a result, Zippold and Hauenstein continued with this macabre ritual, contacting *Regierungsvizepräsident* (deputy regional administrator) Bernreuther, the highest ranking government official left in Ansbach, for his advice. Bernreuther proved adept at slipping responsibility and expressing misgivings but also clearly worried that any hint of failure to perform his duties might in the turbulent circumstances endanger his own life. Bernreuther, the American investigator decided, as an experienced jurist and administrator, who was aware that the conquest of Ansbach was only hours away, could have been expected to act humanely to prevent a pointless death. Instead, he clung to the letter of the law and the lethal mentality of a dying system.[68]

Thus, the case of Robert Limpert seemed to have assumed a life of its own, independent of military reality and the imminent collapse of Nazi control. At roughly the same time as the events concerning Limpert unfolded, Colonel Meyer confronted a group of enraged women in Eyb, a small village on the northeast edge of Ansbach, who had attempted to sabotage defense measures in the area. The resolute women had evidently intimidated the local mayor, but the appearance of Meyer at 10:30 A.M. produced a dramatic scene, as the Kampfkommandant threatened to burn the village and shoot the mayor if it was not defended. Already in an agitated state, seeing traitors, defeatists, and shirkers all around him, Meyer exploded with rage when informed of Limpert's actions and hurried back to police headquarters. Meyer, as Elke Fröhlich has noted, like many other devout Nazis, seemed at the moment of impending disintegration to be "running amok against the reality of defeat." Meanwhile, Hauenstein, likely in an attempt to buy time and avoid an ultimate decision, had instructed Zippold to write a report on the Limpert case. Time ran out, though, a little after 1:00 P.M., when Meyer stormed into Hauenstein's office demanding to see "the fellow who cut the cable." When Limpert was brought into the room, Meyer seemed especially irate at the youth and apparent health of the accused, an initial impression that might well have doomed him. Asking Limpert about the telephone cable, the youth answered evasively, a reply that momentarily left Meyer unsure of what to do. Hauenstein quickly interjected that more evidence had been gathered, whereupon he took Meyer into Zippold's office for a look.[69]

Meyer's reaction was swift and unambiguous. "For me," he said later, "there was no doubt that I had found the man who had already engaged in treason for the past eight days. . . . While forward in the front lines . . . brave soldiers risked their lives to defend the homeland[,] a coward attacked them in the back. I now had to act. I said, 'Gentlemen, we'll now immediately form a court-martial . . .' Silence everywhere. I had the impression of a certain helplessness. I now asked each individual their opinion." Silence still reigned. Hauenstein, knowing a response was expected of him, finally said, cautiously and indirectly, "From the investigation and accompanying evidence Limpert appears to be strongly suspected of having engaged in activities hostile to the state." Evidently picking up on his boss's hesitation, Zippold suggested that Limpert had not acted alone and noted that "further investigation would clear up the matter." If the two policeman hoped thereby to delay any final judgment, they had completely misjudged Meyer's mood. Barely had Zippold finished before Meyer brusquely announced, "I sentence Limpert to death by hanging; the sentence will be carried out immediately." According to Zippold, Meyer also declared that the entire Limpert family would be executed, whereupon both policeman rushed to their defense. Unwilling to press the issue, Meyer said curtly, "We don't have any time, let's get going."[70]

Less than fours hours from the town's capture, or in the case of Robert Limpert, the town's liberation, one final miscarriage of justice thus played out at the entrance to the Ansbach Rathaus. Informed by Hauenstein that he had no one available to carry out the execution, Meyer replied, "Then I'll do it myself." He ordered Hauenstein and Zippold, both visibly upset by the sentence, to serve as witnesses. Limpert then was dragged out through the arched entranceway, where he asked for a pastor, a request summarily rejected by Meyer. Now began a chain of blunders that would have been farcical if not for the tragic end. Planning to hang Limpert from a hook embedded in the Rathaus wall about seven feet from the ground, Meyer discovered that he had no rope. While a policeman ran off to find a line, the Kampfkommandant blustered about screaming, "Where's the rope?" Finally receiving it, Meyer set about making a noose while an assistant scrambled to secure the other end to the hook. As Meyer went to put the noose around Limpert's neck, however, the condemned youth ducked, tore away from Meyer's grasp, and ran for his life. Meyer and a few police officers sprang after him, catching him some seventy-five yards from the Rathaus. Although kicked and punched by the policemen and screaming for help, none of the passersby came to his aid or spoke out for him.[71]

Once more dragged to the execution site, Meyer put the noose around the neck of the ill-fated Limpert, ordered him to stand on some stones, then pulled a stone from under his feet. The sudden weight, however, broke the rope and Limpert, already unconscious, fell motionless to the ground. Meyer quickly formed a new noose, placed it around the neck of the lifeless Limpert, and with the help of a policeman hauled the body up until it hung free. Meyer then read some of Limpert's offending flyers, fixed a note that read, "I am the author" to Limpert's body, and ordered that the corpse remain hanging for three days, or "until it stank." Turning to address a small crowd of people gathered to witness the execution, Meyer then explained that the hanged man was a traitor and deserved to die, that the Americans had lost five tanks in the vicinity of Ansbach, that the general military situation was not unfavorable, and that the city would likely not fall to the enemy. According to witnesses, Meyer then jumped on a requisitioned bicycle and pedaled out of town. Around 5:30 P.M., advancing GIs discovered and cut down Limpert's body. Going inside the Rathaus, they found Hauenstein waiting patiently at his desk to surrender. The GIs were so deeply affected by the tragedy surrounding Robert Limpert that in the official history of the Seventh Army his is the only example cited of the terror directed at German civilians by their own authorities at the end of this lost war.[72]

Reflecting in mid-May 1945 on events in his area, a pastor in a village near Brettheim concluded that they had shown that "the gulf between the mood of local officials and the feeling of the people had become unbridgeable." Indeed, as Klaus-Dietmar Henke has remarked, the fact that a few local officials, party members, or soldiers sought to act responsibly at the end of the war does not obviate the fact that others, through indifference, human error, cowardice, revenge, or fanaticism committed or acquiesced in criminal actions against their own citizens. Just as Nazi rule in occupied Europe resulted in steadily increasing violence, now the terror turned inward, so that many Germans began to perceive that not until occupation by the putative enemy could a minimal level of security be expected. For many, occupation brought a sense of liberation, a release from the constant fear. As American intelligence reports from late April 1945 noted, Germans felt generally liberated from the horror of war, but specifically from the fear of the Gestapo. "The inhabitants of all villages," a rural Middle Franconian pastor wrote pointedly in June 1945, "had, in view of our own false propaganda, a great deal of anxiety about occupation. . . . Still more feared, however, were our own troops, especially SS units." What Henke has termed "the instrument of terror of the Volksgemeinschaft," the SS, and their tool of destruction, the flying courts-martial, not only cast a wide net of terror but also harvested a growing bitterness. The Berlin journalist Ursula von Kardorff, having evacuated to southwest Germany, noted in her diary the "destructive madness" of the SS and voiced an opinion many others shared. "The SS," she despaired, "is now the worst enemy, more menacing than the Americans who are conquering us. . . . I simply cannot understand the Germans who in the last minute murder each other and by their own hand destroy their country."[73]

157

The intensification of the terroristic measures against their own people did not result in a stiffening of resistance that allowed a dramatic turnaround in the fortunes of war; nor did it culminate in a glorious Götterdämmerung. Rather, as Herfried Münkler has noted, disintegration of the command structure, the very confusion of orders as well as the competitive and often contradictory desires of different layers of Nazi officialdom, allowed some possibility of autonomous action on the part of individuals. And these "initiatives of ordinary people," as an Allied intelligence report termed them, even if they emanated from a relatively small proportion of the population, nonetheless represented a meaningful current of opposition to the continuation of a senseless war. Determined to make use of whatever freedom of action they possessed, these courageous citizens, for the most part women, respected farmers or businessmen, religious or community leaders, and even a few local party officials seized the initiative in order to save their homes and villages. In virtually none of the examples from Middle Franconia, perhaps only in the case of Robert Limpert, did ideological opposition to National Socialism play a key role. More often, people with a healthy dose of common sense simply came to the realization that, however much they might have wished for a German victory, any continuation of the war would result only in further useless sacrifices and suffering.[74]

Did they mean to begin the creation of a new order, as Henke and Münkler suggest? Probably not. But for a large part of the civilian population, threatened by brutal Nazi measures at the end of the war, trust in the Nazi regime at last came to an end. In addition, Henke is surely correct in noting that even before the final collapse of government German society was moving toward "self-determination." Although the local protests against the continuation of the war were not, for the most part, the result of any political or ideological opposition to Nazism, they nevertheless marked a final casting off of a regime that in the end had brought only hardship and privation. In essence, at considerable risk to themselves, they had already begun thinking of the future and of the task of reconstruction.[75]

ACROSS THE FRANKENHÖHE

Having broken the Steigerwald defense line at both its eastern and western ends, American troops noted a steady withdrawal of scattered German units under cover of the rain-soaked darkness during the night of April 12–13. As GIs of the Twenty-third Tank Battalion and 101st Cavalry Reconnaissance Squadron set out in pursuit on the morning of April 13, however, two German infantry companies, supported by eight Mark V Panther tanks, launched a furious counterattack at Buchheim, a few miles west of the strategically important city of Bad Windsheim. The German tanks had hardly left their concealment, remembered Emil Gabriel, a gunner on one of the Mark V's, when they ran into defensive fire from roughly forty American tanks. Racing across open fields toward Buchheim, a Sherman scored a direct hit on Gabriel's tank, setting it afire. As the tank commander scrambled to escape through the turret, machine gun fire killed him, his mangled corpse blocking the exit. Gabriel crawled quickly through the burning tank toward the loading bay, struggled out, and dropped to the ground at the rear of the blazing Mark V. Although himself suffering from second- and third-degree burns on his face, hands, and legs, Gabriel attempted to get away from the immediate area, since antitank rounds were still slamming into the burning hulk. As he sprang from cover, though, machine gun fire caught him across both legs. Badly wounded and crying for help, Gabriel lay unattended in the field for hours. That evening, using the clock chimes from the Buchheim church for orientation, he crawled forward, in excruciating pain from his burns, until he collapsed in a ditch, totally exhausted. Only after eighteen hours had passed did a local farmer find Gabriel, barely alive, and take him to an American aid station.[1]

What locals remembered as the "tank battle of Buchheim" barely registered in the larger consciousness of the war, Panzerkampfgruppe Hobe drily reporting that two Shermans and two Mark V's had been lost, while American sources claim the destruction of three enemy tanks and approximately fifty German casualties. To Gabriel, though, who suffered through an agonizing train journey to a hospital and then a POW camp, the action represented an "irresponsible, suicidal undertaking." The fighting in Middle Franconia largely ended as it had begun, with pitched battles at fiercely contested road junctions and river crossings, along with a continued senseless loss of life. As the Third, Forty-second, and Forty-fifth Infantry Divisions approached the outskirts of Nuremberg, units of the Twelfth Armored and Fourth Infantry Divisions turned on April 14 in a southerly direction with the objective of blocking any large-scale German retreat by seizing Danube River bridges as quickly as possible. Although a continuous line of German resistance had largely ceased to exist, hastily assembled ad hoc battle groups nonetheless fought a skillful rearguard action. Stoutly defending roadblocks with cleverly hidden 88mm antitank guns and well-placed small arms fire, they inflicted casualties out of proportion to their strength. Large numbers of displaced persons and liberated foreign laborers also clogged the roads and hampered movement, as did the ubiquitous passive defense measures of the Germans, such as trees felled across roads, mines, and blown bridges. Indeed, the Germans so effectively utilized these obstacles that some American units found themselves working all day to remove or bypass the impediments. On one occasion, an American unit reached a roadblock and began removing it, only to find the felled trees stretching into the distance. A reconnaissance patrol sent down the road to discover the length of the block reported back, amazed, that German troops were busily chopping down trees and extending the barricade even as the GIs tried to clear it.[2]

As a result, American units advanced slowly over the next few days, in a grinding combat routine that frazzled the nerves of the average

American soldier. Armored columns normally would start their operations around 8:00 A.M., advance cautiously because of the numerous mines laid at crossroads and at the entrances and exits to towns, seize farm villages along the main line of march, and then cease operations by 5:00 P.M. Defensive positions would be established in the last town taken in anticipation of local counterattacks, and prisoners would be put in temporary "stockades" (usually barns), while individual GIs would avidly search hen houses for fresh eggs and butcher shops for meat to "liberate." The next morning, supply trucks unloaded in the night would return to their depots with the POWs, while the GIs again moved out to the south.[3]

THE AISCHGRUND AND BURG HOHENECK

As German troops withdrew from their now indefensible positions in the Steigerwald and crossed the Aisch River at key cities, such as Bad Windsheim and Neustadt, they sought to establish a new defensive position in the Frankenhöhe, a line of steep, heavily wooded ridges running parallel to the Aisch from Burgbernheim in the west to Neustadt in the east. Bounded on the north and south by the Aisch and Zenn rivers, and traversed by strategic north-south highways and railroads, the thick forests of the Frankenhöhe offered the last possibility of checking the American advance before Nuremberg and the rolling farmland leading to the Danube. Perhaps fittingly, the dominating presence in the Aischgrund, Burg Hoheneck, a twelfth-century fortress perched menacingly some 1,300 feet above the Aisch River, had long cast the shadow of the swastika over the region, serving since the mid-1920s as a training facility for the National Socialist Party in Bavaria.

First mentioned in documents in 1132, the property variously of Hohenlohes, Hohenzollerns, Senckendorffs, and the Counts of Nuremberg, a shelter for robber barons, ransacked and destroyed over the centuries in the Städtekrieg (1381), the Peasants War (1524–1525), the Second Markgrafenkrieg (1553), the Thirty Years War (1618–1648), and the Napoleonic Wars (1798–1815), Burg Hoheneck fell into disrepair in the nineteenth century. Its massive stone blocks hauled off by local villagers as building material, the once formidable fortress lay half-destroyed, its ruins used both by local nationalist and Christian groups for special celebrations. Largely unnoticed in the turbulent events of

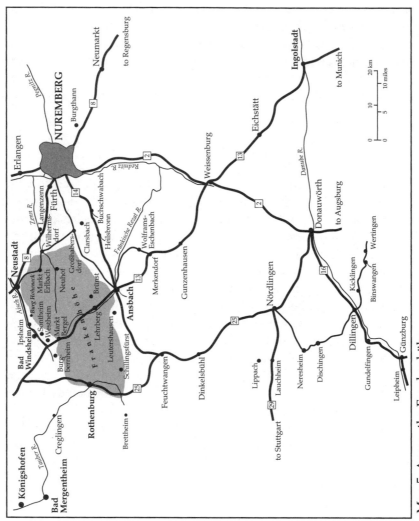

Map 5: Across the Frankenhöhe

1919, Julius Friedrich Lehmann, a Munich publisher, a fervent nationalist, and a future member of the National Socialist Party, purchased Burg Hoheneck. His son-in-law, the veterinarian Dr. Friedrich Weber, headed the Bund Oberland, originally formed after World War I as the Freikorps Oberland, one of the many paramilitary bands composed of fiercely nationalistic and anticommunist war veterans. Staunchly antidemocratic, contemptuous of the new Weimar Republic, and with an abiding hatred for the Versailles Treaty, Dr. Weber in the early 1920s transformed this group of mercenaries into a political movement of some importance in Middle Franconia. Although not part of the rapidly growing National Socialist movement, Dr. Weber and other members of the Bund Oberland in the tumultuous inflation year of 1923 supported Adolf Hitler's attacks on the democratic regime in Berlin and participated with the Nazis in the ill-fated Beer Hall Putsch of November 1923.[4]

Sentenced along with Hitler to prison, Dr. Weber after 1925 maintained a certain personal distance from the National Socialists. Although the NSDAP had been banned following the Putsch attempt, the local party organization in Middle Franconia simply transformed itself into the "German Work Community" (*Deutsche Werkgemeinschaft*), which under the leadership of the notorious Julius Streicher promoted a völkisch, nationalist, and virulently anti-Semitic program. Streicher, in fact, often visited Burg Hoheneck and the village of Ipsheim, finding willing adherents in the farming areas of the Aischgrund, a local report noting as early as April 1922 the extensive support for Streicher in the region around Burg Hoheneck. Indeed, despite the cooling of relations between Dr. Weber and Hitler, from 1925 on, Burg Hoheneck served as a key center for rallies and ceremonies of the reconstituted Nazi Party in Middle Franconia. For example, the seventieth birthday of the racist philosopher and Hitler favorite Houston Stewart Chamberlain was celebrated in 1925, sports competitions and musical festivals were organized, and a large demonstration was held in honor of Gregor Strasser, a prominent Nazi leader from nearby Bad Windsheim, in Burg Hoheneck. Hitler himself, accompanied by Rudolf Hess and Joseph Goebbels, even attended one such solemn ceremony, the burial at Burg Hoheneck of the staunchly anticommunist former police chief of Munich, Dr. Ernst Pöhner, in the autumn of 1927. More importantly, Burg Hoheneck became a key conference center, particularly favored by the SA (Storm

Troopers), the Nazi paramilitary force, for training its leaders from across southern Germany.[5]

Concerned also by the alleged swamping of German culture by foreign—and especially Jewish—influences, the Nazis sought to counter this trend toward "cultural bolshevism" with a healthy dose of völkisch tradition. To that end, Josef Stolzing, the main editor of the *Völkischer Beobachter,* the Nazi Party newspaper, composed an anti-Semitic and nationalist drama, *Arnold von Hoheneck,* to reclaim the German heritage. Ostensibly a medieval saga featuring period costumes and weapons, the pageant, first performed in June 1925, briefly made Burg Hoheneck and Ipsheim a focal point for thousands of cultural nationalists. A festival hall seating seven hundred people was constructed, special trains brought visitors to the small village of Ipsheim, and professional actors performed the play. Not much on subtlety, the drama left little to the imagination as far as the intended message. "The gigantic shame of Germany . . . after a struggle so full of heroic courage," began one stanza. It went on, bemoaning:

> Our proud, victorious Army so cowardly stabbed in the back. . . .
> Today we have become a slave people,
> We must toil in feudal labor for the entire world,
> for there on the Rhine stands our ancient enemy. . . .
> In his pay a mongrel pack of curs . . . ,
> and with it the sneering grin of the grotesque Jew. . . .
> So Burg Hoheneck has become the gathering point
> Of men throughout the broad Fatherland. . . .
> The colors are black-white-red
> But within blazes the holy swastika!
> Germany awaken from your disgrace and shame!
> And does not this house in which we stay today,
> this simple building that consecrates noble art,
> that avers nothing of the new spirit,
> does not this Hoheneck radiate far and wide throughout Franconia?

As if to demonstrate conclusively that Germany had indeed awakened and swept aside the recent humiliations, in 1934 *Arnold von Hoheneck* was performed at the dedication of a "Heroes Grove" at Burg Hoheneck attended by a number of prominent political and military figures, among them some generals and admirals of the old imperial armed forces. Throughout the 1930s, in fact, Burg Hoheneck remained a favorite of Nazi authorities. In July and August 1936 trains of the Nazi *Kraft durch Freude* (Strength through Joy) organization brought people to special performances of *Arnold von Hoheneck,* while the thick forests around the castle proved particularly appealing to prominent hunters, such as Hermann Goering, himself a native of Middle Franconia.[6]

Once the war began, not only did Ipsheim and the area around Burg Hoheneck send many young men to the armed forces, but foreign workers began to arrive almost immediately. Eventually as many as seventeen French POWs and fifteen *Ostarbeiter,* forced laborers from eastern Europe, toiled in mostly agricultural work in the area. In addition, Ipsheim hosted a large *Reichsarbeitsdienst* (Reich Labor Service, or RAD) camp, originally housing young men and then after 1942 young women engaged in agricultural service. Moreover, during the course of the war the village received a constant inflow of refugees, perhaps three hundred in all, from the bomb-ravaged industrial areas of Germany. Tellingly, Burg Hoheneck served as a safe-storage area for many of the priceless treasures from the German National Museum in Nuremberg. Finally, Ipsheim and the surrounding area had been especially shaken by the disaster at Stalingrad in the winter of 1942–1943. Not only had many of the ill-fated soldiers of the Sixth Army come from south Germany, but a number stemmed from Ipsheim and other towns in the Aischgrund. Although the male population of the village in early 1945 consisted only of those over sixty-five, young boys, and the invalid, Ipsheim still furnished its requisite Volkssturm unit of elderly SA men and Hitler Youth members. In all, Ipsheim would lose 103 men out of a prewar population of under 2,000 inhabitants (118 if men from the refugee and evacuee families are included), or 53 percent of those who went to war. In stark terms, every second Ipsheimer failed to return from the war, a price made high both by the losses at Stalingrad and by the enthusiasm with which local people had early on embraced Nazism.[7]

American troops coming from the north and west reached the Aisch River at Ipsheim by mid-afternoon on April 14, where they found a village drained of its earlier Nazi ardor. Antitank obstacles having already been cleared by local residents, the GIs entered the village without a fight. Still, facing the heavily forested heights south of the Aisch dominated by Burg Hoheneck, the men of Task Force Norton (Fifty-sixth Armored Infantry Battalion) preferred simply to fire across the river at the RAD camp rather than press ahead, a decision made easier by a brief German counterattack that evening from the woods surrounding Burg Hoheneck. Although Ipsheim was spared any deaths or destruction, the American artillery fire did result—in dreadful irony—in the death of a Polish forced laborer in the village of Eichelberg, nestled just beneath Burg Hoheneck. As Lieutenant Colonel Hobe later remarked with some pride, "It appeared that they had considerable respect for us." With further action temporarily in abeyance, that Saturday evening the local villagers of Ipsheim flocked to a church service to give thanks for the deliverance of the village without destruction; in the overflowing church sat a number of American soldiers. Despite the fact that just a few days earlier seventeen young RAD men from the local camp had been killed when an American fighter-bomber had attacked their train, Ipsheimers seemed less upset by the presence of GIs in their midst than relieved that this catastrophic period of German history was, for them, now over.[8]

The next day, hoping to avoid a fight on the steep approaches to Burg Hoheneck, the Americans concentrated on forcing the Aisch at Dietersheim, just to the east of Ipsheim. Although reinforced by units from the Ninety-second Cavalry Reconnaissance Squadron, by the evening of April 15, Task Force Norton, delayed by persistent sniper fire as well as occasional Panzerfaust shots from units of the Hitler Youth tank destroyer battalion Franken, had advanced only another five miles. Stopping for the night in the tiny village of Kotzenaurach, Task Force Norton was perched less than three miles from the next objective, the vital bridges over the Zenn River at Neuhof and Wilhermsdorf. To the left of Task Force Norton, in the vicinity of Oberroßbach, Task Force Fields on the late morning of April 15 stumbled on a number of heavy Panther tanks maneuvering with some difficulty over narrow, twisting forest paths. After a brief but surprisingly intense fight in which a number of vehicles on both sides were damaged and destroyed, Task Force Fields, crossing behind the line of advance of Task Force Norton, continued a gingerly advance toward Linden, a village bursting with retreating enemy troops. Kept abreast of German strength and movements by liberated Polish forced laborers, the GIs nonetheless suffered nagging casualties as German rearguard troops caught them unawares with sudden fusillades from artillery, mortars, and the ever-present Panzerfaust. Aware of his own extreme weakness, with too few exhausted, undersupplied troops desperately trying to build a defensive line, and only eight operational tanks at his disposal, Hobe in his postwar report "once again had to marvel at the hesitant advance of the Americans. They appeared to have considerable respect for these tired, but also courageous, German soldiers." American hesitation was also due, one might add, to the fact that none of the GIs wanted to be the last soldier killed in a war that would clearly be over soon.[9]

If American forces seemed to be approaching in a leisurely fashion, the situation in Wilhermsdorf, on the Zenn River, was literally heating up. On April 15, American fighter-bombers swooped in low over the rail yards, setting afire several tank cars. As the flaming fuel flowed out of the ruptured containers, ditches on either side of the main road leading from the station blazed fiercely. That same evening, as the first shells fell in the vicinity of the town, German engineers prepared the bridges over the Zenn and Ulsenbach for demolition, then stood guard as hundreds of German troops streamed across during the night. The sinister stillness of the long night disappeared early on the morning of April 16 when residents in the vicinity of the road and railroad bridges over the Ulsenbach were rudely awakened by shouts of "Alarm!" Given but a few minutes to evacuate their houses, most fled with only the clothes hastily thrown on their backs. Hardly had they left, in fact, when powerful detonations shook the area. Chunks of stone from the demolished bridges flew through the air, while doors and windows in the neighboring houses shattered from the impact of the detonations. With the sounds of battle now uncomfortably close, most residents of the town sought shelter in cellars or air-raid bunkers.[10]

As advance elements of Task Force Norton reached the outskirts of Wilhermsdorf at 10:30 A.M. on April 16, Liselotte Lutter and her brother snuck into the attic of their house. Frau Lutter later remembered that the view from the window "shocked us, American tanks were in the *Heuleite* [woods to the west of the town]. . . . The [German] soldiers who had lingered at our house wanted to use the attic in order to bring the enemy under fire. It took all our persuasiveness to deflect them from this undertaking, which certainly would have resulted in the destruction of our house." A few houses away Ludwig Götz and his father observed the same American advance and hurried into their cellar. "Arriving there," Götz recalled, "we listened tensely to the ever-approaching drone of the tank engines. The sound of the tanks came nearer and nearer, but then we didn't hear any tanks going along the road outside. As we crept out to see what was going on we saw that the tanks had changed direction right at the edge of town and were withdrawing. It had the appearance as if the American troops knew of the mines laid on the main road into town by German soldiers."[11]

Nonetheless, around 11:00 A.M. the three tanks reappeared and began climbing the road into Wilhermsdorf. The first American tank struck one of the mines, which blew off its right track, and thereafter it could only turn in a circle. The two other tanks quickly withdrew, taking up defensive positions behind a six-foot-high wall surrounding a field to the west of town. Immediately the tanks and accompanying American infantry began to fire on German troops in the woods and open fields along the Zenn River, some of whom in desperation sought shelter in a large manure pile. Content not to press the attack but to use their superior firepower to good effect, the Americans over the next few hours poured artillery and small arms fire into the contested area. "This resulted in great losses among the German troops caught in the fields," remembered Götz, "for the accompanying American infantry could shoot them down like rabbits." Frau Lutter recalled seeing one of the German soldiers who was "already wounded, jump up with his hands raised and wave a white handkerchief . . . and then suddenly he collapsed, probably wounded again. He screamed loudly for help. The whole time he cried, 'Mother help me! Mother help me!' Nobody could help him, however, for anybody who tried would have been killed. As the time passed his cries became fainter and fainter, and then everything was quiet." While this individual drama played out, German artillery across the river went into action against the American tanks, with no appreciable results except massive material destruction of houses in Wilhermsdorf.[12]

Although the defense of a roughly ten-mile stretch of the Zenn River running from Neuhof through Wilhermsdorf to Langenzenn stretched Kampfgruppe Hobe perilously thin, its resistance at Wilhermsdorf caused the forward elements of the Fifty-sixth Armored Infantry Battalion to await the remainder of the force. As American troops appeared in strength around 3:00 that afternoon, they began, from the German perspective, a rather leisurely attack on the main bridge across the Zenn, over which German troops were fleeing in the direction of Nuremberg. From the American point of view, however, the bridge represented a choke point, which served as a perfect killing ground. As the fighting raged over the next two hours, German losses mounted steadily, for the defenders of the bridge stubbornly refused to give ground or surrender. Not until 5:00 P.M. did the fighting sputter to a halt.

As the sounds of shots died away, to be replaced by the cries of the wounded, the inhabitants of Wilhermsdorf came out of their cellars to a numbing picture of destruction. Dead and wounded Landsers were strewn in heaps around the bridge, while buildings and houses in the immediate vicinity lay in ruins. Although their stubborn resistance had delayed the American advance for seven hours, at least twenty-nine German soldiers had been killed and another sixty wounded, many of them in hideous fashion, with limbs torn away and intestines spilling out of ruptured bellies. As Veronika Martinetz helped in the dreadful task of tending the wounded, she came upon a horribly mangled soldier, his face sweat-covered and chalky white, with most of his lower body blown away. An older woman noticed him as well, Martinetz later remembered, and mumbled, "God willing, he's already dead," whereupon the Landser answered in a barely audible whisper, "Not yet."[13]

As a number of German civilians began the gruesome chore of collecting the dead for burial in a mass grave, the often confusing and conflicting emotions of war were on full display. While the local Lutheran minister deplored the "un-German" actions of some who joyously welcomed the American arrival, other citizens provided civilian clothing to hidden German soldiers so that they might escape captivity. Furious at such fanatic resistance and spooked by the large number of Landsers hiding in houses and cellars, some GIs reacted with considerable vindictiveness. "On the way to my house," recalled Gottlieb Freund, "I watched as an American killed a young German soldier despite his having his hands raised." That was not the only incident. "As I left my cellar after the long exchange of fire to see what was happening," Frieda Stroh remembered, "I unfortunately saw two soldiers, with their hands up, being shot by the enemy." Although other inhabitants of Wilhermsdorf recalled that most American troops had acted in an exemplary fashion, the risk of death this late in the war prompted some GIs, in a rage induced by anger, fear, and anxiety, to exact a harsh revenge.[14]

A few miles upriver at Neuhof, the scene of an earlier drama in which the police and SS had arrested a number of local Volkssturm men and then sent them to Nuremberg to stand trial for disobeying orders and mutiny, the Ninety-second Cavalry Reconnaissance Squadron also encountered furious German resistance, which halted its advance for two days. Slogging south from Linden on April 15, the GIs had already run across numerous roadblocks and had lost a few tanks to the ubiquitous Panzerfaust when they were halted by strong resistance from a battle group of young SS soldiers just a few miles north of Neuhof. While German troops repulsed an attack launched around 5:00 that afternoon, the remainder of the American force rolled into Neuziegenrück, perhaps two miles to the north. Having pounded Neuhof with artillery fire continually through the night, heavy fog forced the GIs to delay their assault until 10:00 the next morning. Blanketing Neuhof with phosphorus shells, strong fires erupted throughout the town, forcing inhabitants and defenders alike to seek shelter in cellars or flee outside. An infantry and tank attack launched at noon was repulsed by fierce German resistance, which resulted only in an increase in the intensity of American artillery and tank fire. Although bombarded constantly throughout the afternoon, American patrols only succeeded in capturing the Zenn bridge around 5:00 P.M. By that time, only a few buildings still stood intact in Neuhof, most of the ancient village having been reduced to a glowing pile of ash and shattered stones. Cries from the wounded, strewn about with a dozen or so dead, intermingled with shouts for help from those still fighting fires and the occasional shots from American tanks to create a Dantesque atmosphere.[15]

Following the daylong struggle at Wilhermsdorf, American forces moved quickly in the late afternoon to cross the Zenn, the GIs pushing a few miles to the south on the evening of April 16 before halting for the night at Meiersberg. The next morning, moving out earlier than usual, Task Forces Fields and Norton advanced swiftly against disintegrating German opposition, seeking to cut the R 14 between Nuremberg and Ansbach. With Task Force Fields slowed by resistance at Schwaighausen, Task Force Norton fought one last sharp battle at Großhabersdorf, less than fifteen miles east of Ansbach. There, parts of the Hitler Youth tank destroyer battalion Franken, fragments of a reserve battalion of infantry from Fürth, remnants of a unit of *Panzergrenadiers,* a few tanks, and a battery of 88mm guns had established a thin defensive line along the Bibart River that blocked access to the main Ansbach–Nuremberg railroad and highway. Around mid-morning, the onrushing Americans smacked up against this hurriedly assembled, hodgepodge German resistance. The result was a short yet disconcertingly violent and intense engagement, one in which two German Mark V's and a number of American tanks were disabled or destroyed in close combat. Task Force Norton nonetheless brushed aside this opposition, crossed the Bibart, rejoined Task Force Fields, reached Fernabrunst and Clarsbach on either side of the main rail line to Nuremberg, and pushed a few miles further south to the R 14, occupying Heilsbronn that evening against little resistance. Moving out at 11:00 the next morning, the task forces then struck southwest toward Ansbach, the administrative center of Middle Franconia, with the intention of cutting off retreating German forces. The GIs encountered little resistance until they reached Katterbach, just east of Ansbach. After a brief firefight, which resulted in several Germans killed and fifteen taken prisoner, the highway was cleared of mines and the American tank column proceeded west into Ansbach, arriving in that city by 4:30 on the afternoon of April 18 against virtually no enemy resistance.[16]

At the same time that the men of the Fifty-sixth Armored Infantry Battalion approached Ansbach from the northeast, Sergeant Lyons and the troopers of the Seventeenth Armored Infantry Battalion continued their push on the city from the north, advancing down the main Würzburg–Ansbach–Munich highway. After the fierce fighting on the Steigerwald, Lyons and his men on the afternoon of April 11 had been ordered southwest toward Oberschneckenbach, some fifteen miles west of Bad Windsheim, in order to mop up an area of enemy resistance that had been bypassed. As Lyons soon discovered, being bypassed did not make the Germans any less willing to fight fiercely. Over the next few days the men of A and C Companies engaged in a confusing series of operations, from rooting Germans out of forests, bagging more than five hundred prisoners and destroying huge stores of captured equipment, to withstanding desperate German counterattacks and nearly continuous sniper fire. The chronic American sport of souvenir hunting also proved deadly, one incident alone costing Lyons three men when, against orders, they went into a local village, stepped on a mine, and were killed.[17]

After crossing the Aisch and rejoining the rest of the Seventeenth Armored Infantry Battalion on April 14, Lyons and his men encountered a very fluid but dangerous situation. The Germans had moved parts of the Second Mountain Division, perhaps 1,500 men along with tanks and self-propelled guns, into the Frankenhöhe, the heavily forested heights which the divisional commander, Generalleutnant (Major General) Willibald Utz, deemed highly advantageous for defense by his experienced troops. Unable to establish a continuous line of defense, the Germans hoped instead to harass and delay the American advance by blowing up key rail and highway bridges and by using intermittent small arms and antitank fire, as well as heavy artillery and mortar barrages, to force the GIs into slow and careful movements. At any number of places along the fifteen miles separating Bad Windsheim and Ansbach, this pattern recurred. Harassed all day by small arms fire, both A and C Companies of the Seventeenth Armored Infantry Battalion, for example, had just entered Burgbernheim late in the afternoon of April 14 when the Gebirgsjäger in the hills opened up with light artillery and mortar fire on the GIs in the town below. With one man killed and a number of others wounded, the enraged Americans confronted the village mayor, who had assured the GIs that no Germans were in Burgbernheim, and accused him of giving false information. Finally able to persuade the Americans that he knew nothing of the presence of the Gebirgsjäger, the fortunate mayor escaped with his life, even as an artillery duel raged between the opposing sides. Nor was this an isolated incident. Advancing a few miles to the east, GIs cautiously approached Markt Bergel. Warned by Polish forced laborers of the presence of a strong German force in the wooded heights above, as well as an extensive tunnel complex housing both an ammunition and airplane factory, the Americans had just begun searching the town when a terrific mortar barrage rained down on them from out of the hills to either side, which resulted in a number of casualties.[18]

The next day, April 15, offered much of the same. With the R 13 totally blocked by debris from the German detonation of a massive stone railroad bridge, the axis of advance shifted from the main highway a few miles to the east toward the village of Westheim. To reach this objective, however, the GIs had to traverse a high wooded ridge held by two battalions of the 137th *Gebirgsjägerregiment* (mountain infantry), a force of approximately six hundred troops armed with 81mm mortars and 75mm and 105mm howitzers, that subjected every American movement to an intense and accurate barrage. Ordered that morning to seize the heights surrounding Westheim, American tanks encountered a hail of antitank and machine gun fire that stalled their advance in Sontheim, a few miles north of Westheim. By mid-morning A Company of the Seventeenth Armored Infantry Battalion had struggled the three miles between Markt Bergel and Westheim under constant mortar and artillery fire from the Petersburg heights and had fought their way into Westheim. While a vicious artillery duel raged, the GIs attempted to clear the village of German troops, only to be caught unawares by a sudden headlong counterattack launched by the Gebirgsjäger from the hills above. Once recovered from their surprise, however, the GIs brought their superior firepower to bear and quickly drove the Germans back into the wooded heights. When they then attempted to seize the high ground to the southeast, a savage German artillery and mortar attack threw the advancing column into considerable disarray. With the bulk of their tanks pinned down in Sontheim, GIs of the Seventeenth Armored Infantry Battalion and the Eighth Infantry Regiment (Fourth Infantry Division) launched a mid-afternoon assault against German positions on the heavily forested ridges to the south, a clearing operation that lasted well into the evening before the Germans were finally driven away and the GIs from the Fourth Infantry Regiment occupied the town of Obernzenn. Still, while the GIs out-posted the towns of Markt Bergel, Sontheim, and Westheim for the evening, the mood was grim, as the realization took hold that despite the crumbling German defense lines the Americans had sustained heavy casualties from the unseen enemy lurking in the hills of the Frankenhöhe.[19]

On April 16, the Americans, seeing no possibility of a direct assault down the R 13 toward Ansbach, sought to bypass enemy strong points by wending a tortuous route to the north and east before again turning south. Notwithstanding the weakening German resistance, the GIs' advance through the forested heights north of Ansbach proved hazardous and nerve wracking. Harassed by blocked and mined roads and subjected to sudden bursts of mortar and Panzerfaust fire, the GIs pressed steadily south, that night occupying Neustetten, midway between Bad Windsheim and Ansbach. The following day witnessed a repetition of this cautious, grinding advance. Although slowed in the morning near Rügland by a large roadblock of downed trees and halted for a time in mid-afternoon by antitank and artillery fire near Birkenfels, that evening the advancing Americans reached the village of Brünst, no more than five miles from Ansbach.[20]

As the GIs moved to secure the village for the night, they experienced firsthand the disintegrating nature of German resistance. All night Sergeant Lyons and the men of A Company could hear German troops pouring down the country lanes around Brünst, in a desperate attempt to escape the tightening American noose, as German artillery and mortars kept up a steady drumbeat not far away. Moving now to trap as many Germans as possible, during the morning of April 18 troops of the Seventeenth Armored Infantry Battalion, operating just north of Ansbach, bagged well over a thousand prisoners. As the men of A and C Companies, along with units of the Twenty-third Tank Battalion, finally entered Ansbach late in the afternoon of April 18, they linked up with the Fifty-sixth Armored Infantry Battalion and took considerable satisfaction in the long lines of German prisoners streaming to the rear, a cheering sign that enemy resistance had, they thought, at long last begun to crumble. To any Germans still inclined to resist, the fate of the thousand-year-old village of Leutershausen, seven miles west of Ansbach, would soon stand as a stark warning; in response to shots fired by SS troops in the village on April 19, Leutershausen was completely destroyed by American fighter-bombers.[21]

THE HOLY GRAIL LOST

With the capture of Ansbach on April 18, the focus of battle in Middle Franconia shifted thirty miles to the northeast to the shrine of Nazism, Nuremberg, which Hitler had ordered defended to the last man. Symbolically enough, on April 20, Hitler's fifty-sixth birthday, soldiers of the Third Infantry Division breached the medieval wall in the vicinity of the ancient fortress, once the center of power in the Holy Roman Empire, and entered the old city. Shortly before noon, the commander of the Second Battalion, Seventh Infantry Regiment, reported to headquarters, "I am now standing in the *Adolf-Hitler-Platz*," the central square where in years past at the *Reichparteitag* the Führer had proudly reviewed endless marching units. The significance of this event could not be greater, and was not lost on the Americans. The next day, in the presence of Seventh Army commander Lieutenant General Alexander Patch, Fifteenth Corps commander Major General Wade Haislip, and the commanders of the Third and Forty-fifth Divisions, Major Generals John O'Daniel and Robert Frederick, American combat units, with fighter-bombers flying overhead, made a triumphal victory march through the heart of the wrecked

Nazi citadel. To complete the symbolism, on April 22, following a victory parade by the Third Infantry Division through the *Zeppelinfeld,* American engineers blew up the huge stone laurel wreath and swastika perched above the speaker's tribunal at the Nazi Party congress grounds. As the guns fell silent, more than 90 percent of the buildings in Nuremberg lay in ruins, shattered by the combined effects of aerial bombing and ground combat.[22]

Perhaps fittingly, however, the Germans had another surprise in store for the Americans. One local Wehrmacht commander had already warned German civilians that "houses that show a white flag will be set on fire [and] those guilty shot. The Werwolf battles the enemy and executes traitors." Just as they intended to punish their own who proved unwilling to fight to the last, the Germans also lashed out one last time against the American invader. As CC-A of the Twelfth Armored Division, supported by the 232nd Infantry Regiment, Forty-second Infantry Division, moved south across the R 14 between Heilsbronn and Buchschwabach on the morning of April 18, they crashed headlong into a German defensive position fortified by five concealed Tiger tanks, each with a 128mm cannon capable of piercing armor at a distance of over two miles. At the same time, near Clarsbach, other GIs met a similarly rude reception as they tried to penetrate German defenses along the R 14. Stalled by the 88mm guns of Kampfgruppe Dirnagel, an adversary familiar to them from the Tauber River fighting at Königshofen earlier in the month, the GIs found themselves pushed back by a counterattack from a Hitler Youth unit, supported by a few tanks, across the main highway to the railroad line at Raitersaich. To the west, though, units of the Ninety-second Cavalry Reconnaissance Squadron and Troops A and C of the 116th Cavalry Reconnaissance Squadron pushed across the R 14 against determined enemy resistance, seized the bridge over the Fränkische Rezat at Schlauersbach, and moved rapidly south.[23]

Nine miles southeast of Ansbach, at the symbol-laden village of Wolframs-Eschenbach, named after Wolfram von Eschenbach, the legendary author of the medieval saga *Parsifal,* Troop A, 116th Cavalry Reconnaissance Squadron, encountered fierce German resistance from elements of the Seventeenth SS-Panzergrenadier Division "Götz von Berlichingen." In an ironic twist, it now seemed as if life was to imitate art. At its core, the *Parsifal* legend told of redemption through suffering, but after Richard Wagner's reworking, additional themes attractive to

Hitler emerged, not least the myth of blood. Hitler, like Wagner, was tormented by the belief that western and German civilization were threatened by progressive degeneration as a result of miscegenation, a process that could only be halted by a regeneration of the Volk through pure blood. As the future Führer remarked to Hermann Rauschning,

> What is celebrated [in Wagner's *Parsifal*] is not the Christian . . . religion of compassion, but pure and noble blood, blood whose purity the brotherhood of initiates has come together to guard. The king then suffers an incurable sickness, caused by his tainted blood. Then the unknowing but pure human being is led into temptation, either to submit . . . to a corrupt civilization . . . or to join the select band of knights who guard the secret of life, which is pure blood itself. All of us suffer the sickness of miscegenated, corrupted blood. How can we purify ourselves and atone . . . ? This compassion admits of only one outcome, to allow the sick to die. . . . Only a new nobility can bring about the new culture. . . . The man who sees the meaning of life in conflict will gradually mount the stairs of a new aristocracy. . . . But the mass is prey to decay and self-disintegration. At this turning-point in the world's revolution the mass is the sum of declining culture and its moribund representatives. They should be left to die.[24]

In addition to an obsession with racialism, one can also detect in the above passage a tension in Hitler's thinking between notions of redemption (healing) and revenge (conflict). Humanity is in need of salvation, but this deliverance can only be attained through relentless struggle against a sick and corrupt world. Renewal is thus possible, if one chooses to join the struggle, but once begun, it is a fight to the death. If unable to heal the decaying world, the task of vengeance requires the destruction of that world.

In the last days of his failed effort at a "regeneration" of mankind, then, the urgent necessity was destruction, as if the achievement of a heroic death caused all else to fade into insignificance. And in another symbolic display, the last act of this apocalyptic drama in Middle Franconia was to be played out in conjunction with Hitler's birthday. As Troop A of the 116th Cavalry Reconnaissance Squadron engaged the enemy in Wolframs-Eschenbach on the afternoon of April 18, Troop C bypassed to the west, then three miles south, after a brief, bitter fight, they occupied Merkendorf, an ancient village on the Nesselbach River protected by a five hundred-year-old city wall. In yet another indication of the ordeal German civilians faced, caught as they were between the onrushing Americans and the terror of their own authorities, just the day before the local Nazi Kreisleiter descended on Merkendorf in order to inspect the local defenses. At an antitank obstacle on the R 13 blocking the main entrance into the village, itself one of only three portals offering access, a crowd of around 150 women, supported by the village mayor, remonstrated angrily with the Kreisleiter for a removal of the defenses and a peaceful surrender of the town. As at Bad Windsheim a few days earlier, not only did this protest prove unsuccessful, but Gestapo officials arrived in the middle of the night to arrest a number of the women. In contrast with the town to the north, however, local authorities prevented the Gestapo from taking its desired revenge in Merkendorf.[25] Any relief on the part of the village inhabitants that they had been spared the blast of war, however, proved premature.

The same day that the GIs occupied Merkendorf, April 18, the SS-Battalion *"Deggingen II,"* nominally part of the *Kampfverband SS-Nord* but now subordinated to the Second Mountain Division, received orders to attack the Americans, who threatened a breakthrough on the R 13, and drive them out of Merkendorf. Reconnaissance quickly revealed that the GIs had assembled a force of forty to fifty tanks in the town, so that evening the Germans took up positions on the edge of a forest less than two miles away. They now decided to send two reinforced companies, armed with the alarmingly effective Panzerfaust, into the town under cover of darkness with the goal of destroying as many American tanks as possible. Striking from the north and east at 3:00 A.M. on April 19, the Third Company celebrated Hitler's birthday a day early by catching the dozing GIs completely by surprise. Before the startled Americans could recover from their initial shock, the SS men stormed through the streets of the village shooting up tanks and half-tracks. After a pitched battle lasting over an hour, Third Company withdrew, having destroyed at least six tanks and a half-track at the loss of only two men wounded.[26]

Attacking from the south and west at the same time, First Company had not been so fortunate. Having put a heavy tank that blocked their approach out of service, these men now found themselves involved in a savage firefight. The company commander had been killed immediately at the beginning of the action, and within a few minutes all platoon leaders fell wounded or killed. Leaderless, the Germans nonetheless fought on, at one point reaching the American command post, where four Germans attempting to enter through the windows were shot. For over two hours, a bloody series of hand-to-hand battles raged throughout the village, as the GIs repulsed the German attack with small arms, knives, and even furniture thrown from windows. A fierce counterattack by the enraged Americans led to more savage fighting, but despite their overwhelming superiority in men and firepower, the GIs proved unable to subdue the battered survivors of First Company. Observing the battle from a distance, Lieutenant Colonel Cord von Hobe noted with astonishment that light German reconnaissance planes outfitted with the ever-present Panzerfaust swooped in to attack American armored vehicles. By 9:00 A.M., however, the appearance of twelve heavy tanks and a battalion of motorized infantry from Wolframs-Eschenbach convinced the dwindling German force finally to withdraw from the ruins of Merkendorf. Although First Company destroyed three medium and three light tanks, they had suffered fearsome casualties. Just how dreadful the toll was, however, remains open to question. While German sources admit to the loss of 11 dead, 24 wounded, and 29 missing, the Americans claimed that of the 150 attackers, 80 were killed and 16 were captured, while there were an unknown number of wounded. The GIs losses were 2 killed, 11 wounded, and 4 missing. As for material losses, the Germans destroyed six medium tanks, six light tanks, three jeeps, two howitzers, and a half-track, in addition to a number of damaged vehicles that could be salvaged.[27]

Late that afternoon, to their astonishment, the Germans observed signs of movement on the part of the Americans, not to the south to attack them but to the north. Having received orders to rejoin the Twelfth Armored Division at Ansbach and then push southwest to the Danube, the men of Troop C reluctantly pulled out of the ruins of Merkendorf. The next morning, April 20, as German patrols reported the area empty of the enemy, SS men reoccupied the town. Around 9:00 A.M., at the cemetery north of the village, they discovered two mass graves. In one they found eleven bodies, in the other fourteen, all presumably executed by the enraged Americans in the aftermath of this disconcertingly ferocious combat. The battle for Middle Franconia was thus ending as it had begun, with senseless yet fanatical resistance, all to no purpose, and with the now thoroughly frustrated Americans determined to break that resistance one way or the other.[28]

A SPRINT TO THE DANUBE

With the end of the fighting in Middle Franconia, an operation that had lasted three weeks, the Americans had now largely overcome the last major organized German resistance, as, in the words of SS-*Obersturmbannführer* (Lieutenant Colonel) Ekkehard Albert, the chief of staff of the German Thirteenth SS-Army Corps, "in view of our own inferiority and the complete exhaustion of our troops hardly any serious opposition could be offered. . . . In an increasingly vocal way the question was being asked, what did we hope to achieve with this senseless fighting? Again and again the concerns and inner reservations of the troops and their leaders regarding the continued struggle were calmed [only] by the hope of a 'wonder weapon.'" Perhaps this chimera alone can explain the performance of the battered German units, for over the next few days, in a series of running defensive engagements, the Landsers demonstrated an amazing skill and perseverance, despite poor or nonexistent communications, in retreating largely intact across the Danube. Indeed, for all the excitement of the race to the Danube, American forces proved unable to cut off sizeable numbers of the Germans north of the river. As Colonel Charles Graydon of the 101st Cavalry Group admitted, "we had been witnessing the disintegration of not only the Wehrmacht but of an entire nation. . . . Hitler's divisions, with few exceptions, were down to less than one-third strength. Added to their ranks had been thousands of school-age young boys and old men unfit for battle. . . . [Still] many of us held a grudging respect for the way they continued to resist with as much skill as they did. It was apparent, however, that they were losing their will to resist, with the exception of . . . [the] SS troops, who continued to fight fanatically." Still, the GIs found this mad dash to the Danube and beyond into the Alpine redoubt all the more exhilarating because of the absence of the dogged, wearing resistance encountered in Middle Franconia.[29]

Advance elements of the Twelfth Armored Division had already on April 19 begun moving west from Ansbach toward Leutershausen and

Schillingsfürst before turning south in the direction of Feuchtwangen. Encountering little opposition, practically all units of the Twelfth Armored Division had passed through Feuchtwangen by the early afternoon of April 20, so they continued south another ten miles along the R 25 until they reached Dinkelsbühl, CC-A entering the town by early evening. Faced with increasing enemy resistance and a blown bridge over the Wörnitz River, the GIs settled in for a night's rest in the picturesque medieval village as combat engineers set about repairing the damaged bridge. The Americans found little respite, however, for during the night German patrols attempted to infiltrate into Dinkelsbühl, while the engineers found themselves fired on by enemy artillery and shot at by snipers, the latter mostly women and young boys from the local Hitler Youth.[30]

This harassing activity continued on April 21, when at 6:30 in the morning, on a miserably cold and rainy day, GIs from the Seventeenth Armored Infantry Battalion found themselves rudely awakened by an aerial attack by light training planes outfitted with Panzerfäuste under their wings and fuselage. That and other such enemy activities seemingly did little except put the GIs into a foul mood that carried over the rest of the day and into the next. Advancing on the right flank of the Twelfth Armored Division's line of march, for example, troopers of the Twenty-third Tank Battalion on the morning of April 22 ran into some three hundred young SS recruits in the village of Lippach, about twenty miles south of Dinkelsbühl. Attacking just before noon, the tankers soon found themselves embroiled in a nasty situation, as the Germans responded with heavy small arms, Panzerfaust, artillery, and Nebelwerfer fire. Not until 4:00 that afternoon did the GIs manage to crack the German resistance and enter Lippach. As most of the tankers hurried on to Lauchheim, the Third Provisional Company, a unit of African Americans, searched the town for hidden enemy soldiers. What they found, however, proved to be as explosive as any German booby trap, for in the late afternoon the black GIs stumbled upon an alcohol warehouse. Perhaps stressed by the recent shoot-out in the streets of Lippach, some of the GIs sought solace in the bottled spirits. According to German reports, approximately twenty-five drunken GIs drove a group of POWs through the village streets, beating them as they proceeded toward the cemetery. Investigators later found six Germans with their skulls bashed in at the entrance to the cemetery, another ten, most shot through the head, were found in a meadow at the

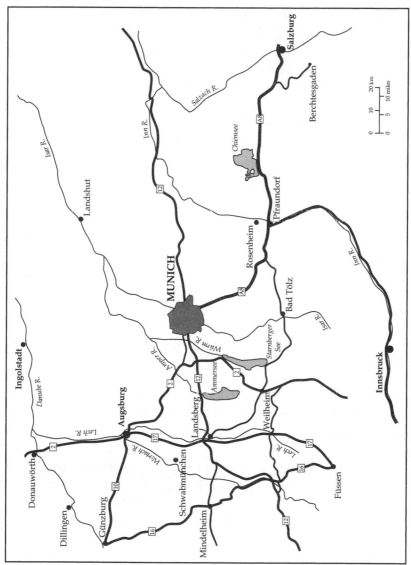

Map 6: Across the Danube

edge of town, and others were found who had been shot in the back or crushed by tank treads. In all, thirty-six SS men lost their lives in Lippach, roughly two-thirds of them after the battle had ended. Evidently not satisfied with just disposing of the German POWs, the black GIs now turned on the defenseless civilians of Lippach. Some twenty women between the ages of seventeen and forty were allegedly raped before the rampage came to an end.[31]

While the next day the Seventeenth Armored Infantry Battalion and Twenty-third Tank Battalion attacked some one thousand Germans entrenched along the Eger River at Lauchheim, to the east other elements of the Twelfth Armored Division had raced almost unnoticed to the Danube at Dillingen, a pattern that demonstrated conclusively the German's were no longer able to conduct coordinated defensive operations. At Lauchheim, moreover, where the Germans had managed to establish a defense line, enemy resistance proved more confused than orchestrated. Amid a hail of small arms and Panzerfaust fire from all directions, the GIs quickly broke the brief German opposition, crossed the Eger, and raced on to the Danube at Lauingen. Indeed, so surrealistic was this brief encounter that most American casualties resulted from shelling by their own artillery. As another example of the strange scene, Sergeant Carl Lyons of A Company, Seventeenth Armored Infantry Battalion, established his command post in a local beer hall, where he enjoyed a freshly cooked wiener schnitzel even as German artillery shells landed in the general vicinity.[32]

If the situation in Lauchheim was odd, the events in Dillingen the day before could reasonably be described as extraordinary. Karl Baumann, a resident of Dillingen, remembered that Sunday morning, April 22, another raw, damp day, as notable only for its seeming ordinariness:

> To be sure, vehicles and troops moved through the streets more or less in great haste . . . [but] in Königsstrasse as on any Sunday there was little traffic, and not until the Hitler Youth finished their customary Sunday morning roll call . . . did some life appear [in the street]. . . . Then suddenly a powerful blast shook the entire town. . . . Outside on the church square people shouted that the bridge in Lauingen [three miles to the west] had been detonated. . . . Almost immediately came the first rifle shots. At the same time we heard the rattle of machine

guns. The Americans were here . . . , for most of the inhabitants certainly somewhat of a surprise.

Surprised would be an understatement; indeed, most residents of
Dillingen were shocked by the sudden appearance of the GIs. After all,
not only had a special detachment guarded this vital bridge over the
Danube since 1943, but six 250-kilogram aerial bombs had long since
been placed under the bridge and wired for detonation. Moreover, the
commander of the guard unit checked the connections three or four times
each day to ensure that they were in working order.[33]

The speed and daring of the American advance, however, had simply caught everyone on the German side unawares. Baumann, in amazement, recalled that the Americans came from the north, then raced

> through the Kapuzinerstrasse, down the [hill], and attempted
> without stopping to get to the Danube bridge, which they ob-
> viously hoped in a surprise strike to seize intact. Only one
> tank halted on the heights [above the bridge], turned its tur-
> ret, and fired a salvo as the Hitler Youth . . . took up defensive
> positions. . . . We expected the explosion of the bridge at any
> moment, which for many of us meant a serious danger to our
> lives. . . . But very shortly we could all breathe easier. The tank
> spearhead had quickly overwhelmed the roadblock, met very
> little resistance at the Danube, and within a few minutes seized
> control of the bridge.

Although again understated, Baumann's memory was remarkably accurate. The American units, A Company of the Sixty-sixth Tank Battalion
led by Lieutenant Charles Ippolito and C Company of the Forty-third
Tank Battalion under the command of Captain William Riddell, comprising Task Force Two of CC-A, had moved out early on April 22. At
Neresheim, some fifteen miles to the north of the Danube, Captain Riddell,
in telephoning the mayor of Dillingen, discovered to his amazement that
the Danube bridge there was still intact. Having encountered little German resistance along their route that morning, the astonished Americans found themselves confronted with a unique opportunity to pull off
a second "Remagen." With guns blazing, the GIs dashed into Dillingen
and surged onto the bridge before the startled Germans could react. Even

as the desperate defenders belatedly undertook to detonate the explosive charges, Captain Riddell and three GIs ran along the side of the bridge cutting the detonator wires. With tanks providing covering fire, a squad of infantry then raced across the bridge in a half-track and quickly dug in on the other side. At 11:45 A.M. Task Force Two reported by radio to Twelfth Armored Division the electrifying news that they had successfully seized a bridge across the Danube.[34] Despite all their efforts at an orderly retreat, then, before they had time to establish even a minimal defensive line behind the river, the German position had been rendered untenable.

Even as the bulk of Lieutenant Colonel Clayton Well's Sixty-sixth Armored Infantry Battalion swept into Dillingen, Germans on the other side of the river seemed blissfully unaware of what had happened. Approaching German vehicles therefore proved easy targets for American tanks. One German, however, realized all too well what had happened. A lieutenant by the name of Schneider, an officer in a Nebelwerfer battery and by all accounts a fanatical believer in "final victory," for whom resistance to the last was a sacred obligation, jumped in full uniform into the rapidly flowing waters of the Danube. Evidently attempting to reach the southern end of the bridge, where he hoped to detonate the explosive charges by hand, Schneider made little headway against the powerful current and drowned before reaching his goal. Other hastily organized German counterattacks also met a similarly disastrous fate. Neither poorly equipped units of convalescent troops nor fainthearted Volkssturm men had any success in dislodging the American bridgehead. Even the normally fanatic and reliable Hitler Youth proved unequal to the task, the young soldiers, seeing the hopelessness of their mission, throwing their weapons away and surrendering en masse to the GIs. In fact, CC-A reported taking over four thousand POWs during the day. Equally fruitless were attempts by Me 262 jet fighters and a battery of 88mm artillery to destroy the bridge. The only determined German assault against the bridge failed, ironically, when a column of trucks filled with Landers approaching from the south ran over a minefield hurriedly laid out under orders of the frenetic, but now drowned, Lieutenant Schneider. The young zealot, it seems, expected American troops to stumble across the minefield and blow themselves to bits; in the event, it was only German soldiers who fell victim to the mines. By the end of the day, CC-A had carved out a bridgehead some five miles wide and three miles deep;

the last obstacle before the Alpine redoubt had now been decisively breached.[35]

A report by a lieutenant in the Gebirgsjäger, given a special assignment to take action against the American bridgehead, accurately described the German dilemma on the night of April 22–23. "I drove with my motorcycle in the direction of Dillingen. . . . The Americans had already penetrated into Kicklingen with tanks. A few hundred yards behind Binswangen lay two [German] machine gun positions," recalled the lieutenant, his tone resonant with scorn at the completely inadequate armament, "two whole machine guns. The defense for a bridgehead that the enemy was steadily expanding! A young lieutenant approached with his company. I shouted at him: 'Why don't you remain here, what is your assignment?'—'I have to clear off.'—'From whom did you get this order?'—'Ah, there's no longer anyone giving sensible orders!'" Returning to Wertingen, the Gebirgsjäger lieutenant could only scrape up ten Hitler Youth boys from Sonthofen for a counterattack. Armed with only ten Panzerfäuste, which none of the boys knew how to use, fourteen hand grenades, and a carbine, the lieutenant and his ragtag band set out in a fierce rainstorm to assault the American bridgehead. Near Binswangen, the group discovered that even the two German machine guns had now disappeared. Undaunted, they advanced within five hundred yards of Binswangen, when American artillery opened up. "In the darkness, I saw the boys give a frightened start . . . [but] then their performance and stance was quite good. Their baptism of fire. Then the rain stopped and a bright moonlight poured over the open meadow between the woods and the village. I went alone on ahead, but without machine gun protection there was nothing we could do. With only ten Panzerfäuste you can't do anything against tanks and armored vehicles. . . . I had no desire to let these ten fine young boys be shot to death at night." Still, the lieutenant marveled, "They were so disappointed that they had not gotten into action."[36]

In desperation, the German command on the afternoon of April 22 ordered a squadron of FW 190 fighter-bombers to attack and destroy the bridge as quickly as possible. The planes, loaded with special 250-kilogram amphibious bombs equipped with optical and thermal fuses, were to swoop in low over the river and release their load just before the bridge. At this point, the current would carry the bombs down river to the target, where either shadows from the bridge or the colder temperature of the water would detonate the explosives. Even as German reconnaissance planes reported that the Americans already had a strong concentration of flak guns at the bridge, a bomb specialist was flown in from Prague to supervise the setting of the fuses and the loading of the bombs. Working feverishly into the night, the pilots struggled with their nerves as they constantly went over the details of their suicidal mission. Because of technical difficulties, however, the attack could not be carried out until April 24.[37]

A thin layer of fog covered the airfield at Neubiberg as the eleven FW 190s, escorted by thirteen Me 109s took off early that morning. The skies were remarkably quiet as the Germans, observing absolute radio silence, flew toward the Dillingen bridge. Heartened by the unexpected advantage of complete surprise, the pilots, on reaching the Danube, dropped down to no more than thirty feet above the river as they started their bomb run. Even as the GI flak crews went into action, the pilots of the FW 190s, almost as in an exercise, swooped in on the bridge, let loose their bomb load, and headed for home unharmed. Fearful of an American counterstrike, the pilots actually landed on the autobahn some six miles from their airfield, confidently expecting to hear news of the destruction of the bridge when they arrived back at base. Dismay soon replaced elation, however, as reconnaissance aircraft reported that the bridge remained intact. To their consternation, the pilots learned that the bombs had indeed worked, but had exploded against a pontoon bridge that American combat engineers had hurriedly constructed just in front of the main bridge. The next day, with the advantage of surprise lost, ten FW 190s, accompanied by sixteen Me 109s, once again embarked on what now seemed certainly to be a *Himmelfahrtskommando* (mission to heaven). This time the tranquility of the skies seemed more sinister than comforting, and as they approached the bridge at Dillingen a deafening barrage from the American antiaircraft guns confirmed the pilots' worst fears. Menaced by a thick wall of flak and pounced on from above by American fighter planes, in desperation the Germans released their bombs too early. Although detonations peppered the ground in front of the bridge, the structure itself remained untouched. Their nightmares realized, only half the pilots returned to their bases, and although a third strike resulted in the north pier of the bridge being hit, it remained fully open to traffic.[38]

All of this frenzied activity, however, served no purpose. Even as the

Germans continued their stubborn efforts to destroy the bridge at Dillingen (on April 24 five Fi 156 Storch landed a ten-man special commando unit that unsuccessfully tried to reach the bridge), to the west other units of the Twelfth Armored Division and the Third and Fourth Infantry Divisions swarmed across the Danube. By now, only at isolated spots did the Germans offer any effective opposition. While CC-B and CC-R mopped up bypassed areas of resistance near Bopfingen and Lauchheim, the 101st Cavalry Group occupied Lauingen. Still, the Germans proved capable of inflicting not insignificant casualties at those points where they had an organized defense. In the vicinity of Leipheim, roughly fifteen miles to the west of Dillingen, the Seventeenth Armored Infantry Battalion and units of the Fourth Infantry Division on April 25 sought to seize the autobahn bridge over the Danube. Although the bridge was blown just before noon, for over an hour that afternoon the GIs withstood a savage artillery bombardment which left a number of men killed and wounded. Similarly, GIs moving against Binswangen and Wertingen on April 24 and 25 encountered surprisingly stiff resistance. At Offingen, ten miles upriver from Dillingen, elements of the Fifty-sixth Armored Infantry Battalion and 714th Tank Battalion on the afternoon of April 25 found themselves caught in furious street fighting with young SS officer candidates. Battling house to house, the GIs were forced to withdraw under heavy mortar and Nebelwerfer fire. They attacked again, once more withdrew, then leveled the town in an intense artillery barrage. That evening, in a final assault, two companies of the Fifty-sixth Armored Infantry Battalion overcame intense small arms fire while pushing into the town, securing it only at 10:00 that evening. The next day, the Sixty-third Infantry Division received the brunt of German attention, as they fought off a desperate counterattack by SS troops in the vicinity of Günzburg, twelve miles west of Dillingen. Nonetheless, by late afternoon on April 26, units of the Twelfth Armored Division, now over thirty miles south of Dillingen, overran a German column southeast of the small village of Immelstetten and, supported by savage artillery fire, inflicted well over a thousand casualties on the disorganized Germans. Facing little further resistance, the GIs then crossed the Wertach River near Hiltenfingen and drove on toward Munich, less than thirty miles to the east.[39]

Aiming to block the northern approaches to the Alpine redoubt, the Twelfth Armored Division and the 101st Cavalry Group moved to skirt Munich to the south, on April 27 reaching Landsberg on the Lech River, an ancient garrison city made famous by one Adolf Hitler, who wrote *Mein Kampf* while imprisoned in the local fortress. At Landsberg, the GIs also had a sickening encounter with the gruesome consequences of Hitler's racialist ideology. Overrunning a forced labor camp that the Germans had hastily tried to destroy, the GIs observed a revolting scene: almost two thousand corpses lay strewn around the facility, some burned, others rotting, while hollow-eyed, emaciated skeletons wandered aimlessly along the roads and through the fields. The contrast with their first clear view of the majestic Alps in the distance could not have been more jarring.[40]

Despite the efforts of isolated commanders to form some semblance of a defense, the situation from the German perspective had deteriorated into pure chaos. "Daily the German soldier stood before a choice," noted SS-Obersturmbannführer (Lieutenant Colonel) Ekkehard Albert, chief of staff of the Thirteenth SS-Army Corps, "death, captivity, desertion, or fight on, only to be confronted with the same decision the next day." Signs of complete disintegration were everywhere. As Lieutenant Colonel Cord von Hobe worked frantically to cobble together any sort of resistance, moving frenetically from village to village, he observed with disgust, "Again and again in these villages I found baggage trains, supply troops, and Luftwaffe personnel laying around in peace and luxury awaiting the end of the war. . . . I left this baggage to the Americans. Better they burden the Americans. For the Americans, taking prisoners meant not only jammed roads but also loss of time, which would spare us blood and energy." Still, even Hobe realized that such scenes meant the end was near. "The attitude of the civilian population became ever more threatening . . . [and] we no longer bothered to demand their support," he admitted, noting bitterly that "plundering [by civilians] was the surest sign of the imminent arrival of the enemy."[41]

From April 28, then, American forces struck eastward virtually at will, while most German troops hoped merely to make it to the mountains, where they might slip away unnoticed and be spared captivity. As the Twelfth Armored Division followed the 101st Cavalry Group across the Lech River, German resistance now consisted mostly of a few hastily thrown up roadblocks. Weilheim fell on April 29, and as the month ended GIs found themselves deep into the northern section of the feared Alpine redoubt, relieved that the expected fanatical last-ditch resistance had failed to materialize. With the end of the war now clearly only days away, GIs reacted paradoxically, alternately acting with extreme caution and seeming complete abandon. On May 2, for example, the Seventeenth Armored Infantry Battalion raced eastward on the Munich–Salzburg autobahn, traveling an astonishing sixty miles in eight hours and arriving at Pfraundorf on the Inn River by mid-afternoon. As one GI confessed, the pure exhilaration of the moment swept aside all hesitation. "After we hit the highway those old tin boxes shook out of low gear, dusted the cobwebs from fourth gear and raced down the beautiful four-lane road at full speed," noted Sherman Lans.

> A leap-frog play was quickly perfected. Two half-tracks would roar down the highway, one of the tracks would stop at a bridge or underpass while a few men dismounted and checked the structure for mines and cut any wires leading to demolition charges. The other track would then speed to the next bridge. This was really a May heyday. All the tracks were pouring lead on surprised Krauts who tried to hide in brush piles, foxholes, or took to the woods. . . . In that drive we surprised too many enemy vehicles to count, passed up many pieces of usable enemy equipment, bypassed thousands of the enemy, and we were only stopped twice.[42]

The dogged German resistance finally broken, the accumulated frustration of days spent creeping in fear at a snail's pace now released, Lans's account captures the pure exuberance, the intoxication, the giddiness felt by many GIs at the realization that they were in the final days. "There was only one hitch in the whole drive," Lans admitted ruefully, almost as an afterthought, but quite a hitch it was:

> We crossed over a large bridge which was set to blow, but we managed to cut the wires to the explosives before any damage was done. The whole of CC-R was to pass over the bridge but the 23rd Tank Battalion was so far behind by this time that the squad left to guard the bridge, for fear of being left, followed the rest of the column before the 23rd appeared. When the 23rd got there some SS men had rewired the explosives and as the third vehicle started across they blew the bridge. In

consequence we were in Pfraundorf 24 hours without so much as radio contact with friendly forces and it was 72 hours before our supply line was restored.

German resistance had been so shattered and the average Landser so demoralized, though, that during the time the Seventeenth Armored Infantry Battalion was cut off, they threatened only to overwhelm the GIs in their rush to surrender. Still, reminders of what could have happened were never far removed. On May 3, while advancing toward Innsbruck in a blinding snowstorm, the Seventeenth Armored Infantry Battalion lost two vehicles and all their occupants to a sudden burst of German artillery. The ambush also cost the lives of five men of the 495th Armored Field Artillery, traveling in the same convoy.[43]

After traversing the sixty miles from the Rhine to the Tauber in just a few days, to cover the next fifty miles from Königshofen to Ansbach, pressing through the Steigerwald and Frankenhöhe against a German blocking force considerably inferior in strength, had taken American troops three weeks and a heavy expenditure of tanks, half-tracks, ammunition, and artillery shells. The cost in lives proved sobering as well. Of the units that bore the brunt of the hard fighting in the Tauber–Steigerwald–Frankenhöhe region, the Seventeenth Armored Infantry Battalion lost 20 men killed in action, with another 118 wounded and 9 missing, 147 battle casualties compared to 7 killed among 59 battle casualties for the preceding month (in which it had fought to and crossed the Rhine), while the Fifty-sixth Armored Infantry Battalion lost 43 killed, 206 wounded, and 9 missing, for a total of 258 battle casualties. Not only were total Seventh Army losses in April 1945 higher than in any other month of action (and it entered combat in August 1944), but of all Seventh Army units in the month of April 1945, the Twelfth Armored Division suffered casualties second only to the Sixty-third Infantry Division. That outfit found itself engaged in furious fighting along the Jagst and Kocher Rivers in the vicinity of Crailsheim for much of the month, a bloody standoff that resulted in 479 American deaths and over 1,700 total casualties. In roughly a three-week period, 232 men of the "Hellcats" had been killed, 800 wounded, and 122 reported missing in action, over 1,000 men lost in an operation that fails to rate even a sentence in most official histories of the war. Amazingly, in April 1945, the Twelfth Armored Division sustained losses that represented, respectively, 45, 35, and

34 percent of its total killed in action, wounded, and battle casualties—this in an outfit that had entered combat in early December 1944 and had faced the brunt of the fierce "Northwind" German offensive into Alsace in early 1945. Nor was it a marginal unit. Based on interrogations, German POWs cited the Twelfth Armored as one of the two most feared divisions on the western front, the Fourth Armored Division being the other. In a unit-by-unit comparison, the Twelfth Armored Division, operating in rural Middle Franconia, suffered more casualties than any of the three American units (Third, Forty-second, or Forty-fifth Infantry Divisions) incurred in the capture of Nuremberg. In addition, the Fourth Infantry Division, fighting in conjunction with the Twelfth Armored Division, suffered losses of 146 men killed and 489 wounded in action.[44]

For a variety of reasons, German personnel losses are hard to determine with any precision. Few of these cobbled-together units kept any records of losses, German graves registration had largely ceased to exist, and sympathetic civilians buried some of those killed. To gain a sense of the intensity of the fighting in the *Endphase* (final stage), though, it is worth noting the latest calculations of German military deaths by Rüdiger Overmans. Through his careful and exhaustive research, Overmans has concluded that approximately 1.23 million German military personnel (including Volkssturm men, who suffered more than 50 percent of the entire losses) died in the final four months of the war. This average of roughly three hundred thousand killed monthly (compared with "only" one hundred thousand per month on the eastern front in 1944) represented the highest such German losses in the entire war. Even if one accepts his further estimate that two-thirds of the casualties in the Endphase occurred on the eastern front, that still leaves over four hundred thousand deaths during the hard fighting in the west. In the triangle of terror and destruction marked by Aschaffenburg, Ansbach, and Heilbronn, estimates of civilian deaths alone number over two thousand, with an equal number of soldiers sent to their deaths just in the region bounded by the Main and Neckar Rivers. A unit history prepared by the Ninety-second Cavalry Reconnaissance Squadron claimed that in April 1945 in Middle Franconia it had killed 1,650 German soldiers and wounded over 2,500, but American estimates tended to be inflated. The five-day battle for Nuremberg likely cost the lives of over 1,000 German soldiers and civilians (with fewer than 150 GIs killed), while German sources persist in the claim that well over 500 SS men were shot in the Nuremberg and Dachau areas under suspicious circumstances in the last days of the war. American sources give some credence to this claim, one report from the Forty-fifth Infantry Division noting cryptically on April 20, 1945 (Hitler's birthday) that two hundred Germans had been "liquidated" in Nuremberg. By the end of the month, the Twelfth Armored Division reported capturing thirty-two thousand prisoners, with more than ten thousand being taken on April 28 alone. Of the roughly seventy thousand total POWs credited to the division, nearly half were taken in the last days of April 1945.[45]

By throwing a mixed bag of men into battle, many with little training and all with insufficient weapons, supplies, and equipment, German commanders had sent their troops to the slaughter, in a futile attempt to offset iron with blood. No rationality or military purpose attended to this decision, for Germany was going to lose the war in any case. Rather, it illustrated the destructive will of Nazi political and military leaders, both against the enemy and their own population. In directing terror at all, Nazi authorities took little notice of the military situation and betrayed no regard for the well-being of the local civilian population. All villages and hamlets were to be used as obstacles and defensive positions, with the result that many heretofore untouched by war fell victim to the wave of destruction unleashed in the last days of the conflict. To the average citizen this meant only unnecessary and pointless terror and devastation. But to the Nazi leadership, having created a system that reveled in terror and unwilling to bring the destruction to an end, there existed another goal, yet realizable. For Hitler, the end of the Nazi regime and the end of the German people and nation were to be synonymous.

As war had assumed a life of its own, independent of the will of the people, many Germans ironically saw their own soldiers as a greater danger than the Americans. While Nazi propaganda continued to portray Volk and army, citizen and soldier, forged together and fighting side by side, civilians for the most part just wanted the war to end, while Landers numbly fought on, exhausted from their exertions, ground down by overwhelming enemy superiority, and suffering from lack of supplies. The hesitancy of the American advance, in a further paradox, ensured that more Germans, both soldiers and civilians, would be killed—by both sides—and more villages destroyed. For the civilian population, threatened by brutal Nazi measures at the end of war, trust in the regime finally came to an end. People could now see with their own eyes the senselessness of continuation of the war, for there no longer existed any possibility of winning or even defending against the enemy. At the end of this war most Germans wanted only to preserve and salvage what could be preserved and salvaged. They had already begun thinking of the future and of the task of reconstruction. An advertisement in the *Windsheimer Zeitung* for a local bank put it succinctly, "save in war, build in peace!"[46]

STRUGGLE UNTIL FIVE
AFTER TWELVE

During the Thirty Years War, that disastrous period of chaos and
calamity between 1618 and 1648, German peasants grew increasingly weary of having their farms plundered and burned, their wives
and daughters raped, and their sons taken away by the various marauding bands who fought in the service of one or another of the Great
Powers of Europe. To the long-suffering peasant, it seemed irrelevant
whether Catholic or Protestant laid waste in order to save his soul, or
whether French, Austrian, or Swedish troops ultimately gained ascen-
dancy. Driven to despair, a number of farmers on the Lüneberg Heath
gathered in secret, swore sacred oaths of unity, and formed themselves
into a vigilante force for mutual protection of their homes and communities. Farmers by day, at night they struck at isolated mercenaries,
raided enemy encampments, and exacted vengeance on those who had
wrought havoc on their lands. Using the sign of the *Wolfsangel* (wolf
trap) as both a menacing warning and proud acknowledgment of its
actions, this first Werwolf group hoped to deter further destruction by
playing on primal anxieties of the savage and relentless ferocity of the
wolf. The term was likely meant as well to draw on ancient fears of lycan-

thropy, a fear of people who appeared ordinary by day but were driven by a powerful blood-lust at night.[1]

Popularized in 1910 in a hugely successful novel by Hermann Löns, *Der Wehrwolf,* the Werwolf legend took on overtones of völkisch romanticism in the pre–World War I period. The compelling adventure story emphasized the struggle for survival of individuals caught in the grip of powerful forces, and Löns also suggested that only in the Volk, the close-knit racial community, could one find the necessary qualities of heroism and steadfastness needed to surmount a great crisis. In order to protect their homes and communities, moreover, Löns's simple peasants demonstrated a willingness, when required, to go to the limits of brutality and terror, actions one of his characters described as "terrible but beautiful." This image of a united, resolute racial community struck responsive chords among Nazi officialdom, who fantasized howls of vengeance rising from a chorus of Werewolves as enemy forces violated the sacred soil of Germany.[2]

None was more smitten than propaganda chief Joseph Goebbels. Disappointed with the initial Nazi incarnation as a group of SS partisans whose task was to harass enemy lines of supply and communication, Goebbels dreamed of a Werwolf movement issuing from diehard Nazi fanatics among the populace, true revolutionaries who would exact revenge on the enemy as well as insufficiently zealous Germans. Moreover, as the journalist Curt Riess noted in late April, the Nazi propaganda minister hoped further to create chaos in postwar Germany. "The worse things become," Riess emphasized, "the greater is the chance that the Germans will forget how bad it was under Hitler. Future generations will believe that things were wonderful under Hitler." Calling Goebbels's propaganda a "hidden time bomb," Riess continued,

> Conditions will be quite terrible in defeated Germany. . . . Hitler may look wonderful to many Germans in retrospect. For this reason Dr. Goebbels must wish for desperate conditions in post-Hitler Germany. . . . People who starve long for the times when they did not starve. . . . The Nazis . . . definitely want those Germans who survive this war to go hungry next winter and many winters to come. . . . They want chaos in Germany, in Europe.
>
> For, the more things get out of hand the greater the loss

in prestige of those who are more or less responsible for this postwar world, the Allies. And the greater will be the prestige of those who warned against this post-war world, the Nazis. . . . The unhappy Germans must be made not only to believe that the Nazis were right . . . , but also that they were infinitely better off under the Nazis; they must think of the Third Reich as the lost paradise. Goebbels is trying to bring about just that.[3]

As Riess realized, even at this late hour, March and April 1945, Goebbels acted with enormous energy to realize his vision of continued fanatic resistance coupled with future chaos. Significantly, little more than six months after the end of the war, Riess's fears seemed to be unfolding. "Conditions under the Nazis are being glorified in comparison with present day conditions," warned an American intelligence report. "Alleged injustices and other internal faults of Military Government administration are constantly harped upon. . . . The Americans are accused of hypocrisy in persecuting the war criminals at Nuremberg: if the German leaders are guilty of 'crimes against humanity,' then so are the Russians." More pointedly, a report a few weeks later noted the latest rumblings of disgruntled Germans: "In the Third Reich nobody had to freeze, as we do today, not to mention hunger. If only we had the Nazis again, we should be better off."[4] If chaotic conditions had enabled the most fanatic Nazis to impose their will on a crumbling Germany, so even in defeat chaos in the immediate postwar months might, ironically, serve the same purpose.

THE HOUR OF THE WERWOLF?

On the first day of April 1945, Easter Sunday, *Deutschlandsender* (German radio) in a national broadcast announced in ominous fashion the formation of a German resistance movement. "Hate is our prayer. Revenge is our battle cry," the announcer exulted in apocalyptic terms:

> Those towns in the west of our country which have been destroyed by Allied terror raids . . . have taught us to hate the enemy. The blood and tears of our brutally murdered men, of our despoiled women and of our children . . . cry out for revenge. Those who have banded together in the Werwolf proclaim their determined, irrevocable oath, never to bow to the

enemy's will but rather . . . to offer resistance . . . and to go out facing death proudly and defiantly to wreak revenge by killing the enemy. . . . Every means is justified to strike a blow to damage the enemy.

The Werwolf . . . will decide the life and death of our enemies, as well as of those traitors to our own people. . . . [T]he enemy . . . should know that in those areas of Germany which he occupies he will meet an opponent . . . more dangerous because he is not tied by limitations of bourgeois methods of warfare."

Moreover, the Nazi broadcaster warned, "From now on every Bolshevik, every Brit, every American on German soil is fair game." In no uncertain terms, it seemed, the Nazis had defiantly expressed their intention of fighting a partisan war, of continuing the struggle even after military defeat on the battlefield, a prospect meant to strike fear among both the occupied and the occupiers, who quickly took note of the speech. Not only did Goebbels, who authored the speech, exult in his "extraordinarily revolutionary appeal," but he noted jubilantly that the western Allies saw "in the Werwolf an exceptionally dangerous instrument of the German will to resist at any price. . . . Nothing frightens London more than the certain development of chaos in Germany."[5]

"There is evidence of design," warned an American intelligence report just four days after the radio broadcast, "particularly among the young of Germany, to conduct guerrilla warfare . . . against American forces." Indeed, *Time* magazine reported in mid-April on the howl of vengeance emanating from a young German female broadcaster, who boasted:

> I am so savage, I am filled with rage . . .
> Lily the Werewolf is my name.
> I bite, I eat, I am not tame . . .
> My Werewolf teeth bite the enemy.
> And then he's done and then he's gone.

However silly such a refrain might sound today, American authorities took the threat seriously, especially since organized Werewolves had just a few weeks earlier assassinated the Allied-appointed mayors of Aachen and Meschede and killed three U.S. officers in Frankfurt. Indeed, another intelligence report from early May 1945, after recounting the arrest of a number of armed Hitler Youth, stressed, "The Werewolf organization is not a myth. . . . In every important city, the Werewolf organization is directed by an officer of the SD. . . . The membership of the Werewolves is made up of persons of all ages and of both sexes, with a high proportion of under twenty years of age. . . . The present cadres of the Werewolves are estimated to number more than 2,000." There thus seemed reason to fear that this shadowy and fanatic Nazi resistance group might become the war's "epilogue of hate."[6]

Despite the sinister tones of Goebbels's proclamation, with the end of formal hostilities in early May 1945 an uneasy calm settled on Germany after six years of the most violent warfare. Even as American troops settled into a peacetime routine, however, reminders of their ambivalent status abounded. In some areas the GIs were greeted with relief as liberators, but in others the German population regarded them with hostility and resentment. Although generally correct in their behavior, the occasional theft and rape, and more so the requisitioning of homes and apartments for billets, produced a constant tension in the relationship between occupier and occupied. For their part, Americans at all levels displayed a keen wariness and anxiety amidst the defeated population, being especially fearful of anything smacking of Werwolf activities.

This sensitivity stemmed partly from indoctrination, partly from experience. GIs had been instructed that, in general, Germans were all Nazi adherents and had enthusiastically supported Hitler's bloody war of conquest, so they should remain alert even after the fighting had ended. American troops headed for occupation duty received *Pocket Guide No. 10*, a booklet ostensibly issued to inform the soldiers about the country they were to occupy. The Germans, GIs were informed, knew nothing of the principle of "fair play," had no compunctions about breaking their word, and generally were not to be trusted. Indeed, the *Pocket Guide* reminded GIs not to "forget that you are ordered into Germany now partly because your fathers forgot so soon what the war was about last time. They took it for granted that the friendly reception the Germans gave them after the Armistice in 1918 proved that Germany meant well after all. Our whole country let down its guard too easily last time." Along with language tips, the *Pocket Guide* contained pithy reminders such as "Keep Your Distance," "Keep Your Eyes Open," and "Keep Your Guard

Up," in addition to the following: "You are in enemy country! These people are not our allies or our friends. . . . However friendly and repentant, however sick of the Nazi Party, the Germans have sinned against the laws of humanity and cannot come back into the civilized fold by merely sticking out their hands and saying, 'I'm sorry . . .' Don't forget that eleven years ago, a majority [*sic*] of the German people voted the Nazi Party into power."[7]

In addition, articles in publications aimed at soldiers, such as *Army Talks*, advised GIs to be mistrustful of every German, to report any suspicious activity immediately, and to "never forget that you are here as a conqueror and not as a liberator. . . . All Germans are guilty of war. Do not believe and say, 'forgive and forget.'" Blurbs on Armed Forces Radio bombarded GIs with reminders to be on guard, often couched in terms that inadvertently mimicked Nazi racial ideology and propaganda: "Every friendly German civilian is a disguised soldier of hate. Armed with the inner conviction that the Germans are still superior . . . , [they believe] that one day it will be their destiny to destroy you. Their hatred and their anger . . . are deeply buried in their blood. A smile is their weapon by which to disarm you. . . . In heart, body, and spirit . . . every German is Hitler. Hitler is the one man who stands for the beliefs of Germans. Don't make friends with Hitler. Don't fraternize!" Indeed, the "Special Orders for American-German Relations," from which sprang the famous nonfraternization edict, explicitly instructed GIs that "The Germans have a lesson to learn. They must learn the lesson well. Each of us must teach them."[8]

Moreover, young Germans, and especially young German women, were to be regarded as the greatest potential threat. An intelligence report in early June 1945, for example, stressed that "the staunchest supporters of the Nazi were the women, who were more fanatical than the men." Not only this, but the young fräuleins were showing themselves cleverer and more cunning than their male counterparts, the report also indicating, "In some localities the women palled with the American soldiers who gave them chocolate etc. which the women used to feed hidden SS-men and Werwolf. . . . The [local] population . . . feel insecure and are afraid of an increase in this terrorism." Nor was this fanaticism to be regarded as merely a regional or local aberration. As the *Pocket Guide* put it, German youth had been thoroughly indoctrinated, the "victims of the greatest educational crime in world history." From February 1945, every

GI bound for the European theater had to see a documentary film, *Your Job in Germany*, which described the younger generation in Germany as "the most dangerous. . . . They know no other system than the one that poisoned their minds. They are soaked in it. . . . [T]hey have been trained to hate and destroy." Further, the film informed GIs that their mission in Germany was not education, but to guard an entire nation, so that while respecting German rights and property, they were not to fraternize or befriend Germans. "Every German is a potential source of trouble," the film concluded, "therefore there must be no fraternization. . . . The German people are *not* our friends."[9]

Once in occupied Germany, both *Stars and Stripes*, in articles and editorial cartoons, and American Forces Network (AFN), in radio broadcasts, sought actively, often with a crude bluntness, to remind GIs of the ban on fraternization and to avoid association with "Fraternazis." "A pretty girl is like a melody," AFN blared throughout 1945. "But the melody of a pretty German girl is your death march. She hates you, just like her brother who fought against you. . . . Don't fraternize!" One radio spot stressed, "Pretty German girls can sabotage an Allied victory. . . . Don't fraternize!" while yet another warned, "If, in a German town, you bow to a pretty girl . . . you bow to Hitler and his reign of blood. You caress the ideology that means death and persecution. Don't fraternize!" A contemporary observer, Tania Long, also stressed this theme of hate and contempt in a December 1945 article that took a harsh view of German women. Although admitting that women suffered most from the hardships of life in postwar Germany, Long also asserted, based on opinion polls taken in the city of Darmstadt, that German women were more completely Nazified than men and that it would be harder to eradicate the Nazi toxin from their minds. Furthermore, Long claimed that German women had only contempt for the GIs with whom they consorted, seeing such relations merely as an opportunity to gain material advantages. At the same time, Long feared that such alluring and devious creatures would poison the minds of gullible GIs, thus creating sympathy for the downtrodden Germans and causing them to forget the tasks of re-education and the eradication of Nazism.[10]

As a result of the hard fighting of April 1945, many GIs had taken these lessons to heart. Moreover, troops of the Seventh Army had already had to deal with the reality of Werwolf activities. In the vicinity of Hockenheim in the Odenwald, Werwolf organizers had stockpiled explosives and local civilians had taken shots at the American occupiers. On April 2, a group suspected of Werwolf connections managed to push a locomotive and some rail cars over a damaged overpass onto a passing American armored column on the autobahn below, killing several GIs and destroying a number of vehicles. Two weeks later, a German unit deliberately left behind American lines ambushed and murdered the occupants of a staff car who had lost their way and were wandering aimlessly through the forest. A Military Government official had been killed in the initial blast of gunfire, but the other officer, Captain Peter Cummins of the Counter Intelligence Corps (CIC), had been only lightly wounded. Taken back to the partisan group's headquarters for interrogation, Cummins later was returned to the spot of the ambush and murdered by order of the German commander. Perhaps in response to the numerous incidents of sniping already encountered by GIs, Military Government intelligence authorities had warned in early April of guerrilla warfare in scattered localities against American forces. Indeed, the report noted, a group of fourteen-year-old boys apprehended with pistols and hand grenades stated bluntly that "they were part of a group of 200 similar youths whose purpose was to kill American soldiers."[11]

Nor did events in the "spiritual center" of Nazism, Nuremberg and surrounding Middle Franconia, lessen the apprehensions of many GIs. Encounters with Hitler Youth boys and, in a few cases, *Bund deutscher Mädel* (League of German Girls, or BdM) girls armed with Panzerfäuste and determined to destroy American tanks had already put GIs on guard, so much so that they instinctively regarded even innocent actions as potential Werwolf activities. In Aub, for example, retreating German troops had left behind a few rifles in the house of the Grimm family. Under American instructions to turn in all weapons, the mother on the morning of April 14 instructed her fourteen-year-old son, Hans, to collect the rifles and take them to American headquarters at the Rathaus. Putting on a military overcoat that had also been abandoned, the young Hans, with carbines slung from his shoulders, dutifully trudged off toward city hall. As he made his way through an only partially cleared tank trap, however, Hans startled an American sentry. Looking up, the GI saw a blond haired boy in a military coat carrying a number of rifles, so immediately took him for a member of a Werwolf group. Screaming at him in English, which Hans could not understand, the GI prepared to shoot the teenage "saboteur" when at that moment a young woman who knew some English carefully approached the American and explained the situation. Seizing the rifles from Hans, the GI summarily smashed them against the tank obstacle and, for good measure, confiscated the military overcoat as a souvenir. Similarly, a local farmer collecting the detritus of battle—abandoned German rifles, hand grenades, and Panzerfäuste, all of which posed a threat to the civilian population—made the mistake of not taking these collected weapons immediately to the American military headquarters. Arrested and subjected to intense CIC interrogation, the man was eventually released when it was determined that he acted under authorization of the mayor of Aub. In these cases, potential tragedy had been averted, but both illustrate how strongly the specter of the Werwolf was lodged in the minds of the average GI.[12]

Thus, the malevolent vow of Gauleiter Karl Holz that "Nuremberg will be defended. Even if we have no weapons, we'll spring at the Americans and tear their throats open," seemed hardly an empty threat. Although some GIs could scornfully dismiss young *Hitler Jugend* (HJ, Hitler Youth) soldiers in baggy uniforms too big for them with the taunt, "Go home to your mother," interrogation of numerous teenage boys and girls not only confirmed this group as having the greatest potential for making trouble, but often left the questioners astounded with the youths' outspoken fanaticism. One twelve-year-old Hitler Youth leader shocked his CIC examiner by declaring, "I hate you Americans. I wish I had a pistol to kill all of you. I shall never betray my Führer as long as I live.... I shall continue my fight for Hitler and Nazi Germany. Do not hope ever to eradicate our National Socialist ideals or ideas. There are enough of us left to continue the fight as long as we live." As if to confirm this mindset, in mid-April G-2 intelligence issued an alert that warned of likely Werwolf attacks on Hitler's birthday (April 20), a warning reemphasized in another study circulated a few days later. On April 23 a young German, Erich B., was sentenced to death and executed by American authorities for sabotage and the attempted murder of a GI. Following the execution, American commanders received orders to post flyers in occupied areas informing Germans of this action and warning them of the consequences of resistance. In an implicit threat to the civilian population, potential saboteurs were put on notice that occupation authorities would keep a sharp eye on suspicious activities. Still, as one American intelligence official confessed, the fanaticism of the Hitler Youth constituted the most formidable obstacle to a successful occupation.[13]

In Franconia, where local party and military officials generally supported the organization of Werwolf units, only the unexpectedly rapid arrival of American forces prevented resistance activities on a larger scale. The Werwolf as a fully organized and operational force thus remained—as a June 1945 U.S. intelligence report made clear—a hallucination of the Germans and still more of the Americans. A Seventh Army report in May nonetheless emphasized that although large bands of saboteurs had not materialized, small groups and individuals still constituted a danger. These activities, at the level of petty harassment, could range from smearing the so-called Wolfsangel on walls in an act of defiance to cutting telephone lines to placing mines and decapitation wires on roads. Intended by the Nazis, as Roderick Watt has observed, as "a menacing symbol of intimidation representing the savage and relentless ferocity of the wolf," the sign also served as a deterrent, warning of the summary justice the Werwolf would enact on its enemies. "The sign of the Werewolf kept reappearing on white walls," noted Frank Manuel, an American intelligence officer in Franconia, "a vertical line, traversed in the middle by a horizontal line that at one end had a vertical line perpendicular to it, pointing upward. Most members of the Counter Intelligence Corps were of the opinion that it was merely a hastily drawn swastika. . . . One folklorist maintained that it represented an iron prong thrust into a tree and baited with meat to ensnare wolves. The wolf would jump for the meat, catch his snout on the prong, and hang there." The ominous threats, as Manuel realized, were meant to remind GIs that the Werwolf lurked, ready "to strike down the isolated soldier in his jeep, the MP on patrol, the fool who goes a-courting after dark, the Yankee braggart who takes a back road."[14]

Nor were these mere empty boasts. Already in early April American intelligence reported instances of GIs in vehicles being killed by trip wires suspended across local roads that detonated antipersonnel mines. In confirmation of such activities, Swiss newspapers reported in late May 1945 that young Nazi partisans continued to snipe at Allied troops, string decapitation wires across isolated country roads, and mine stretches of highways. On occupation duty in late May near Berchtesgaden, John Toole, who had fought through Nuremberg with the Third Infantry Division, noted in his diary an encounter with a young man wounded in the thigh. On being questioned, the youth merely pointed to a meadow in the high mountains and said he was shot there. After a firefight the next morning involving an American patrol and fifteen Germans, Toole led a platoon into the area, where he spotted about twenty armed Germans moving away. As the GIs approached a farmhouse at the end of the meadow, they saw a woman carrying a suitcase running out of the door and up the mountainside. After a short distance she dropped the bag but continued her flight. When Toole opened it, he found a Schmeisser machine pistol and ammunition. Puzzled by all of this, Toole reported the incident to battalion headquarters, where the S-2 informed him that they were part of a local Werwolf group. Toole's comment, "Werewolves, whatever that is."[15]

Also in late May, two HJ boys in Bamberg blew up an abandoned German ammunition train, while in Ansbach a band of former Hitler Youth led by the twenty-one-year-old Kurt Hoesch stockpiled explosives and harassed German women who fraternized with GIs. The situation in Ansbach was so tense, in fact, that members of the Military Government detachment were warned to sleep not in their quarters but with loaded pistols in their offices. In late April Military Government authorities arrested a band of former SA men and seized a small stock of firearms hidden in woods near Neustadt an der Aisch, while in May CIC agents attached to the Twelfth Armored Division broke up the nucleus of a well-organized Werwolf organization near Dinkelsbühl and uncovered a Werwolf cell near Heidenheim, complete with secreted arms and ammunition, made up of former SS and Hitler Youth leaders. That June, other CIC investigators uncovered a cache including motorcycles, pistols, rifles, machine guns, Panzerfäuste, hand grenades, a mortar, explosives, and great quantities of ammunition in a forest near Dinkelsbühl. They belonged to a Werwolf group made up of a number of seventeen-year-old Hitler Youth led by a former SS-Sturmbannführer (Major). The next month a young former SS man suspected by the CIC of Werwolf activities committed suicide in Bad Windsheim, while farther south the CIC stumbled upon a stockpile near Füssen of some thirty rifles, four machine guns, five hundred hand grenades, supplies of ammunition, tents, canned food, and seven thousand liters of gasoline. Meanwhile, near Schwäbisch Gmund, investigators seized a group of youth between fourteen and seventeen along with numerous rifles, a few machine guns, and more than ten thousand rounds of ammunition. Not surprisingly, in July 1945 the Twelfth Army Group issued a memo warning of Werwolf activities and instructing military personnel to be alert for Germans working within American installations who might be possible saboteurs.[16]

By that fall, American authorities regarded the various Werwolf bands as "one of the greatest threats to security in both the American and Allied Zones of Occupation," stressing that young Germans had attacked GIs in the company of German girls, cut communication wires, murdered American soldiers by use of decapitation wires, committed acts of arson, and continued to plan subversive activities. In late October, in his third report as military governor of the American zone, General Dwight Eisenhower noted increasingly violent reactions by young German men to the fraternization of German women with GIs and warned of the possibility of organized resistance or a popular uprising if such discontent persisted. As if to confirm his fears, following an increasing number of attacks on GIs, American troops in late November arrested three thousand Germans and seized large stores of ammunition in a series of raids aimed at forestalling the formation of a German resistance movement. Further arrests in the foothills of the Bavarian Alps in April 1946 netted not only nine young men suspected of Werwolf activities, but also led to the discovery of a list of people to be "wiped out." Just as worrisome, interrogators concluded that large numbers of former Wehrmacht and SS officers, supported by black market activities and the local population, still roamed the mountains hoping to foment opposition to the U.S. occupation. Indeed, in January 1946 three U.S. Military Government officers investigating Werwolf connections with the black market were brutally murdered in Passau, first beaten to death and then doused with gasoline and burned. As a precaution, GIs in the Passau area were ordered to carry arms with them at all times. Not only did reports of diehard SS holding out in the mountains persist until well into 1946, but American authorities took seriously rumors that some former Hitler Youth had organized an "88" movement bent on fomenting political disorder through acts of sabotage. Since the letter H was the eighth in the alphabet, CIC understood the organization's name, and its alleged greeting, "*achtundachtzig*" (eighty-eight), to mean *Heil Hitler.* By the spring of 1946, in fact, a new trend had Military Government (MG) officials worried, as "youth . . . [were] indulging in a hero worship spree for the 'heroes' of the Third Reich." Months after the utter German collapse, then, American soldiers and officials displayed a great anxiety concerning Werewolves, and their ability to undermine an orderly occupation.[17]

An example from June 1945 best illustrates this overheated climate of fear. Obsessed with ferreting out possible Werewolves among Germans working for American occupation authorities, the Civil Affairs

Division(CAD), which had administrative control of the Military Government detachments, came to the conclusion that a secret message was imbedded in the identity cards of all German employees of the Military Government. The experts at CAD had somehow determined that in Germany the left ear had to be shown on all identity cards. Moreover, they claimed in a bulletin issued in June, many adherents of the Werwolf had received incorrectly photographed German identity cards, in which the right ear was visible. Therefore, the bulletin stressed, "the right ear is the Werewolf ear," so any German with an identity card revealing a right ear must ipso facto be a member of this subversive group![18] Despite the temptation to use silliness like this to diminish the actual impact of the Werwolf in postwar Germany, the fact of the matter was that the threat of such a guerrilla movement early on put American authorities in a high state of alert, so that any large-scale, organized emanations of Werwolf activities were spotted and broken up very quickly. At the local level, however, small-scale and individual acts of intimidation, violence, and terror clearly flourished through 1947, claiming many victims. For them, the absence of a comprehensive insurgent movement likely proved little comfort.

"THE GERMAN SOLDIER FOUGHT FOR SIX YEARS, THE GERMAN WOMAN FOR ONLY FIVE MINUTES"

At the local level a pattern of increasing harassment emerged in the winter of 1945–1946, continuing into that spring, which centered on the growing resentment at fraternization between GIs and German women. Emotionally deprived and left lonely by the absence of men during the war and through the immediate postwar months and years, many suffering the trauma of homelessness, virtually all struggling to survive on the meager official rations, it was little wonder that to many the young, friendly, attentive, untroubled, and carefree GIs seemed to offer the chance to live again. "They were so healthy, clean, well-fed," remarked Anneliese Uhlig, who also noted pointedly that it had been a long time since she "had seen a man who wasn't crippled in some way." Similarly, for love- and sex-starved American soldiers, warned in the crudest terms that all Germans were Nazi beasts, the reality that the German fraülein was attractive, accommodating, and accessible came as a welcome revelation. Writing for *Newsweek* in December 1945, James P. O'Donnell noted wryly, "American soldiers pay no attention to German men. To German women they do." Rather revealingly, GIs quickly replaced the term nonfraternization with nonfertilization. "Fraternization is strictly a matter of sex," claimed Julian Bach Jr., a roving correspondent for *Army Talks*, in 1946. "An American with a German woman is with her because she is a woman, not because she is a German." Indeed, as early as July 1945 Percy Knauth noted obliquely in *Life* magazine that "fraternization had taken on a brand-new meaning," one a careful reader understood to be sexual in nature.[19]

If many GIs sought the company of German women for sexual reasons, without doubt many *Ami-liebchens* (GI sweethearts) pursued a relationship for material gain, as expressed in a popular song in the summer of 1945. "Do you live only on (ration) card 3, baby," it asked,

> or do you have something else on the side, baby,
> a Jack, a Jim from overseas,
> with chocolate and coffee
> and a large wallet with proceeds?
> Don't be so serious about love, baby,
> for a G.I. has so much more, baby,
> if he says 'I love you,' don't say no, baby,
> just move to the land of the calories.

Given the chronic shortage of food in immediate postwar Germany, and the fact that GIs provided the fraüleins with desperately needed commodities that often saved themselves and their families from starvation, it was hardly surprising that many "foreign affairs," the subject of a critical 1947 Billy Wilder movie, blurred the line between love and prostitution. For others, GIs offered the chance to be young and enjoy life, to experience something new, to be temporarily freed from the daily burdens of a strenuous and wearisome existence. And for some, perhaps as a surprise on both sides, the relationships blossomed into genuine love. Despite the complex motives behind fraternization, one thing remained clear: neither American authorities nor many Germans liked it. Along with political fears of the sly "Nazi Gretchen" ("Fraternazis" in GI slang), U.S. officials also worried about the spread of venereal disease, euphemistically termed *Veronika Dankeschön* among occupation troops. For their part, many Germans, especially former soldiers returning from POW camps, regarded such liaisons as shameful collaboration with the enemy.[20]

As early as September 1945, reports from southern Bavaria indicated that roving bands of former SS soldiers periodically sought to intimidate women, especially in small towns, and the first signs of widespread anti-fraternization actions in Franconia surfaced only a few months later. Leaflets appeared in early November in some towns containing verses berating German women in general, and a few by name, for socializing with American soldiers. Near Dinkelsbühl, the small town of Wassertrudingen was rife with gossip that once U.S. troops left the area wholesale hair-cuttings of girls who had gone out with GIs would commence. Dispensing with rumor, one missive chided a woman by name, "You are a very filthy creature. An American whore," and concluded menacingly, "You should not wonder yourself if one of these days you should find your head shorn." More ominously, in a few of these villages bands of young men and former German soldiers patrolled the streets nightly in search of German girls in the company of GIs, in some cases assaulting the women. In one small village, for example, a group of teenage boys attacked a girl who had a GI boyfriend, shaved her head, and then forced her to run through the town naked. Still, she was lucky compared to an unfortunate woman in Bayreuth who had her hair set on fire.[21]

Nor were such incidents confined to more traditional rural areas. In Fürth, for example, where young women with American friends, so-called chocolate broads, had already been threatened with incarceration in stocks, menacing leaflets appeared in early December 1945 directed at German women and the "comical chewing-gum soldiers" with whom they were consorting. Although briefly mentioning the problems caused by the serious shortage of food and fuel, the leaflets clearly focused anger and resentment at the growing sexual relations between fräuleins and GIs. Significantly, this male-female, soldier-civilian (and often black-white) tension materialized precisely at the time increasing numbers of former Landsers returned from POW camps, a theme illustrated well in the Fürth leaflets. In self-pitying fashion, they bemoaned the fact that German civilians ignored the "treatment . . . being inflicted on our POW's who bravely fought for six years. They have no roofs over their heads; day and night they are in the open air; this is how the German people returns thanks to them." True anger, though, was directed at German women:

> And what is the attitude of the German woman? She does
> not deign to look at the soldier coming home from the war,

but she flings herself to the breast (if there is any) of those comical "chewing gum soldiers." And all this for a bar of chocolate or a couple of cigarettes. Is this behavior of the German women not shameful? . . . She is shameless enough to have intercourse with Negroes. . . . Is it for this that millions of brave Germans have given their lives? . . . And what about [those] who lost their lives through the ruthless methods of air warfare? Have you already forgotten . . . ? Many of you have stooped to become informants. . . . Does this not rouse a feeling of shame in you? Pull yourselves together and face the enemy. Avenge your fathers and brothers. . . . They shall not have fallen in vain. Long live the ideas of Adolf Hitler.

"The time has come," the author(s) threatened in a second leaflet, "to show what it means to be a German. But unfortunately most of our . . . women have no correct notice of the meaning of that word . . . *To be a German is to have a faithful heart.* Now vindicate your honor."[22]

Similar remarks, such as "The German soldier fought for six years, the German woman for only five minutes," "For six years the German soldier offered brave resistance, the German woman cannot resist one bar of chocolate," and "He fell for the fatherland, she for cigarettes," appeared throughout the American zone of occupation, an indication of the widespread resentment at incidences of fraternization, as well as of the high levels of male-female tension within the German community. In his travels throughout the American zone, Julian Bach Jr. noted the constant appearance of the following poem:

GERMAN WOMEN!
What German women and girls do,
Makes a man weep . . . ,
One bar of chocolate only or one piece of gum
Gives her the name German whore.
How many soldiers gave their lives for those women!
. . . No God, no confessing and no prayer
Can help, because the shame will last.
We will give no pardon.
. . . Dirt belongs to dirt.

Eventually some forty Germans were arrested in connection with post-ing the poem, among them the originator of the verse, a seventeen-year-old former Hitler Youth member who admitted anger at being ignored by German girls in favor of GIs. In a similar expression of rage, a young German, just released from captivity and standing in a railroad station, became furious at the sight of two fräuleins talking with a GI. As soon as the American left, the ex-Landser rushed over, grabbed one of the women, and began to cut off her hair with nail scissors, stopping only when an MP summoned by the other girl arrived and arrested him.[23]

As GI-German female relations continued to flourish into 1946, so the hostility of German men grew apace. Anger at the *"Ami-Schicksen"* (GI-whore) dalliances remained at high levels in the Fürth area. In one hate-filled pamphlet from 1946, an author put his disapproval into verse:

> The German woman carries on in shameless
> fashion with foreigners!
> Do you have no shame, you German lass?
> Yet you know that you are dragging us all in the dirt
> and besmirching the honor of the German woman to boot.
> It took six years to beat the German soldier,
> but only five minutes to get the German woman to come around.
> We have no cigarettes and no butter,
> the foreigners have coffee and sugar.
> You don't care about skin color,
> as long as he offers you a chocolate bar.
> Still, we hope that soon you fall into the hands of the Russian.
> Then, you see, you'll get a real lesson
> and no German man will look at you again.

Nor did German men necessarily wait for the Russians to teach their women a lesson, as the numerous examples of hair cuttings demonstrated. Indeed, these relationships often generated considerable animosity in local communities, especially when prominent women were involved. A local schoolteacher in Amberg, for example, faced discrimination because of her engagement to a Jewish displaced person (DP). In Ansbach, the daughter of the onetime mayor and district party leader, her father now incarcerated in an internment camp, elicited much disapproval, verbal and otherwise, by her open fraternization with an American officer. Even greater disapproval was directed at the wife of a former SS-Obersturm-bannführer, an "Old Fighter" and participant in the burning of the synagogue in Ansbach during the *Kristallnacht* violence in November 1938, for which action he now sat in an internment camp in Hammelburg. Although desirous of marrying an American judge, a Jew no less, she hastened to assure her neighbors in the community that her husband-to-be was seeing to the release of her old husband! "It is too bad," lamented one woman concerned with the "degradation" of the German people, "[that] the race theory did not sink deep enough into the minds of these German girls."[24]

Even in early 1947 a young woman working for the U.S. military as a translator, after announcing in a local newspaper her engagement to a GI, could receive the following, written on an old piece of *Feldpostpapier* (army stationery):

Exhausted to death, after long weeks
the Landser creeps home,
with feet sore and a question in his ear:
How will he find our homeland?
. . . The German woman lives happily today,
but in the worst way. . . .
You German women, aren't you ashamed?
The German soldier, without an arm, without a leg,
you now feel indifferent to him.
For admittedly he lacks coffee and butter,
but the foreigners have everything, even sugar.
And they bring you chocolate,
so even their skin color doesn't matter.
Five years it took for them to defeat us,
they got you, however, in only five minutes.
. . . Still, the day will come when you will pay.
Each of you knows precisely how you have disfigured the homeland:
. . . how you sullied the honor of the German woman.
. . . Then before all the world you will be taught,
that the German man respects you not.

Without doubt, much of the bitterness and hate in these anonymous missives stemmed from self-pity or even self-loathing on the part of re-

turning German soldiers. "It is not only that the German man is returning home in defeat," complained Walther von Hollander churlishly in
1946. "The victor has moved in with him and he has to realize that a
small, not particularly valuable section of women has fallen prey to them."
Despite Hollander's dismissive assessment of the "worth" of those women
who fraternized, it is difficult not to see in his complaint rage at the di-
minished status of German men. Much to their discomfort, chocolate
and cigarettes conferred power and represented a vigor and attractive-
ness they no longer had. Once the masters of the continent, ex-Landsers
were now reduced to such impotent objections that some German women
not only seemed to prefer enemy soldiers, but not infrequently prefer
those of "inferior" race. After years of schooling in Nazi racial ideas, this
may have come as the hardest blow of all.[25]

   Although often crude and simplistic, the many bitter pamphlets
and caustic observations also expressed another overriding truth: after
six years of war, destruction, and now utter defeat, German men and
women often had considerably different perceptions of postwar reality.
In the long years of war, with large numbers of men away at the front, the
traditional balance of power between the sexes had shifted, as women
had assumed key roles in factories, on farms, and in offices. In addition,
the massive uprooting of families and the pervasive destruction of normal life by the war undoubtedly contributed to a change in traditional
notions of morality. Moreover, this more assertive, self-confident German
woman contrasted noticeably in 1945 with the listless, apathetic, emaciated, and disoriented men who returned from POW camps. "Oh great God!
How miserable can it get?" despaired the journalist Ruth Andreas-Friedrich
in July 1945 on seeing the first returning German soldiers:

> Among the smart American uniforms, the well-fed figures in
> the occupying forces, the first German soldiers appear ragged
> and haggard, sheepishly looking around like caught offend-
> ers. . . . They drag themselves through the streets. Seeing them
> one wants to look away because one feels so ashamed of their
> shame, of their wretched, pitiful looks. Are these the glorious
> victors whom Adolf Hitler years ago had sent into the war so
> well-equipped? They shamble around like walking ruins.
> Limbless, invalid, ill, deserted, and lost. A gray-bearded man
> in a tattered uniform leans against a wall. With his arms around

his head he is quietly weeping. . . . It is terrible to see gray-bearded men cry, unable to stop crying. . . . "Heil Hitler!" one feels like cursing out of angry compassion when one sees them.

Confused, desolate, taciturn, in a bewildered and psychologically remote state, many men found it difficult to accommodate themselves to the new conditions created by the war. As one ex-soldier lamented, "We men come home and find that so much is different from what we had imagined." But as Andreas-Friedrich observed insightfully, many women found it impossible to empathize. Women often viewed these men not as returning heroes but, as Dagmar Barnouw has remarked, "as demoralizing remnants, reminders of the bad past."[26]

Once they shook off the lethargy induced by defeat and demoralization, German men began to take exception both to their American occupiers as well as the new assertiveness and confidence of German women. Already angry at having to compete for German women with soldiers from the richest nation on earth, former Landsers also resented the attitude of many women that it was their duty to overhaul the abortive society created by the men. Implicit in this outlook was a dual reproach: not only had the men lost, but it had been a shameful and dishonorable war in any case. Moreover, both fraternization and the wave of rapes that swept Germany in the first months of occupation signaled the absolute defeat of Nazi Germany, and with it the complete impotence of its male agents. In the battle for control and power, German men lost in both the public and private spheres, unable either to protect their women from sexual violence or to control them within the family. As a result, many men retreated into a mythic world that contrasted soldierly steadfastness with female collaboration, loyalty versus treachery to Germany. As early as August 1945 the Information Control Division concluded that "the G.I. and the German Fraülein is Germany's primary social problem." With the return of the POWs and the "remasculinization" of German society, unmistakable tensions emerged among the triad of GIs, "Fräuleins," and "Krauts." Julian Bach astutely noted that "the extent to which German men accept 'fratting' is the thermometer which registers the degree to which they accept defeat, contain their national pride, and look forward to a new and more congenial way of life." Only by accepting sexual relations between GIs and German women, in other words, could German men shed their Nazi past and assume a new identity.[27]

Occasionally, reports from rural areas indicated that the return of POWs had resulted in a reduction in tensions between German men and GIs, but more often this resentment flared into violence against American soldiers. In Passau a former Hitler Youth who had fought at the front stumbled on a neighbor having sex in the woods with a GI. In a rage—"she was on top, her bare butt was showing"—the boy quickly took a slingshot and some rocks out of his pocket and, in intimations of the Old Testament, avenged German honor from a distance of twenty yards. By the autumn of 1945 Military Government authorities noted increasing violence directed at GIs in the company of German women. Most of the incidents involved physical assaults or beatings, but in some rare instances Germans shot GIs, which, as one report noted laconically, "made walking at night with German female companions . . . a dangerous occupation." Dangerous, indeed, as three GIs discovered in the spring of 1946, as they were wholly or partially castrated by German assailants in retaliation for fraternization with German women. By April, in fact, an upsurge of violence, primarily physical assaults, against GIs and fraternizing fräuleins seemed to indicate a new level of German resentment. In July, a nineteen-year-old GI in Munich also discovered the perils of fraternization. As he and his German girlfriend sat on a park bench a German crept up behind them and shot both, the American fatally. Since a rash of similar incidents had erupted a few months earlier in Berlin, authorities concluded they constituted part of a pattern of increasing German resistance. In a near-miss from 1947, two tires came off the jeep of a GI and his German girlfriend traveling from Neukirchen to Mannheim. On investigation, it was found that not only had the tire bolts been loosened, but the battery had been sabotaged so that a fire would have soon started. Suspicion quickly fell on the son of the woman's neighbors, who had just been released from a POW camp.[28]

As the number of these incidents multiplied, and increasingly took on the character of political resistance, American authorities took notice. A Third Army report that same spring emphasized "the substantial number of attacks on United States military personnel in the company of German girls is the only phase of fraternization that assumes any importance since . . . [t]hese assaults were carried on . . . by individuals or small groups of German male civilians as an expression of their dislike for the association of German girls with United States soldiers." Perhaps not surprisingly, American authorities at the same time also noted a disturbing breakdown in the behavior and discipline of GIs. Given the virtual absolute freedom and power of being "the conqueror," many American soldiers seemed to exhibit no self-control, with much of this outlandish behavior consisting of sexual harassment of German women. Military Government officials quickly took steps to bring the behavior of GIs under control, but fraternization itself continued, and with it escalating German contempt and disapproval. "The [German] attitude," noted an American report on public opinion in July 1946, "is that neither the food, clothing, nor other fraternization advantages can outweigh the shame of wholesale collaboration." Terms that emerged in the popular vernacular such as *Schokoladensau* (chocolate bitch), *Schokoladenhure* (chocolate whore), or the more polite but no less censorious *Schokoladenmädchen* (chocolate girl) all asserted the connection in the popular mind between fraternization and prostitution.[29]

More worrisome from the American point of view, anti-fraternization activities, whether directed at American soldiers or the German women who accompanied them, seemed increasingly to be acts of resistance and political defiance. In Frankfurt, for example, a former female Werwolf admitted in March 1946 to taking part in hair cuttings of German women fraternizing with GIs. By late spring, MG officials worried about "an increase of resentment against girls who fraternize with American soldiers" and noted that "active anti-fraternization organizations are in the process of being formed. Printed poems threatening German women who fraternize have been found." Indeed, the report warned, "among many German youths there exists a basic feeling of resentment which might lead to the development of subversive organizations. . . . [T]here is talk among German youths of the need for forming 'vigilante' committees." Nor did they have any doubts as to the reason behind this activism. "Smear sheets and threats continue to be made against girls who fraternize with American soldiers," another report emphasized, "and CIC reports . . . mention this growing resentment against girls who 'fraternize.'" The deeper problem with this simmering resentment, as the head of a local detachment near Nuremberg noted, was its larger impact: "As a whole, there is ample evidence that the attitude of the German people towards the Americans is growing steadily worse. This growing hostility and hate would be understandable if it came exclusively from Nazi circles, but the fact that it can be found in all walks of life, even among people who are anti-Nazi, is significant."[30]

Furthermore, some intelligence reports indicated that numerous instances of especially egregious examples of fraternization seemed designed deliberately to provoke racial violence and conflict among American soldiers as a means of undermining the occupation. Groups of young Germans in both Mannheim and Stuttgart, for example, worked to incite black and white GIs against each other by flaunting taboo sexual relations. In January 1946 the CIC took notice of "an especially intense flare-up of anti-Negro sentiment" in the small towns around Würzburg, where a number of German women were beaten or subjected to head shavings. The tension led to a rash of serious brawls between black GIs and German males who objected to interracial fraternization. In one telling incident a white CIC agent who intervened on behalf of a German was threatened with a beating himself by the black troops. In strikingly similar episodes half a year apart, the first in Herzogenaurach near Nuremberg, the other in Munich, black soldiers used armed intimidation to secure the release of German women, often prostitutes, arrested in raids conducted by German police and U.S. Constabulary forces. Nor were these incidents aberrations, as American reports listed numerous other similar episodes throughout Bavaria. By August 1946 Military Government officials openly worried that "the increase of troubles between white and colored soldiers" would undermine the occupation. Making the situation even more explosive, in virtually all of these incidents American occupation authorities sympathized not with their own black troops, who they blamed for improper behavior, but with the occupied Germans. "Negro soldiers," admitted one confidential report, "feel themselves persecuted by white MP's as well as by German police." This inevitably resulted in bitter feelings that invariably ran along racial lines.[31]

U.S. occupation authorities took very seriously evidence that antifraternization activities represented a form of political resistance. As the counterintelligence service of the Seventh Army noted, such actions seemed dangerously "similar to the situation which developed in so many other countries formerly occupied by the Germans—in other words, [it is] a form of expression of opposition to the occupying powers." Throughout the chain of command, military government officials fretted that antifraternization activities could mushroom into opposition against all Germans who cooperated with the Americans, and thus undermine the occupation. Intelligence reports that indicated local "clergy is becoming more active in denouncing openly German girls who associate with American military personnel" were viewed as especially alarming because it seemed to indicate a growing institutional opposition to the occupation and a German refusal to reconcile themselves to defeat. At universities in Erlangen and Munich, for example, a noticeable anti-American attitude among students and professors concerned American officials, as did an informal ban on allowing anyone who had cooperated with "the enemy" from joining the faculty. Not only did the content of many courses remain unchanged from the Nazi period, such as one at Munich on racial theories, but Military Government authorities worried about the reappearance of another antidemocratic legacy of the past, the ultranationalist paramilitary groups of the Weimar period. With a third or more of the Munich student body made up of former Wehrmacht veterans, and the existence of several underground murder squads confirmed by CIC, American fears of mushrooming radicalization seemed not unwarranted. In March 1946, in fact, General Joseph McNarney, the commander of American forces in Germany, put U.S. troops on alert and warned of the possibility of an uprising of young Germans.[32]

As if to confirm these worries, in early 1946 intelligence reports flooded in of Germans hiding firearms and ammunition, while in both January and March CIC investigated renewed incidents of decapitation wires strung across roads in the vicinity of Scheinfeld, Neustadt, and Ansbach. In early April 1946, occupation officials in Ansbach, Neustadt an der Aisch, and Neuhof reported that groups of young German men had taken to marching through the towns singing Nazi and German military songs, as well as holding poetry readings denouncing fraternization between German women and GIs, especially blacks. Intelligence officials also took note of resistance activities by young people who had appropriated the name of an anti-Nazi youth group, the *Edelweiss Piraten* (Edelweiss Pirates). Comprised of former members and officers of Hitler Youth units, as well as young people left adrift by the collapse of Nazism, the loosely organized group was best described in one intelligence report as a "sentimental, adventurous, and romantically anti-social [movement]." Precisely because it attracted so many youth and ex-soldiers without work or families desperately searching for something to believe, U.S. officials regarded it with a seriousness second only to the Werwolf. Throughout 1946, CIC, MP, and Constabulary forces, as well as German police, engaged in incessant efforts to ferret out members of this amorphous organization. One raid in late March nabbed eighty former German officers, members of the Edelweiss Piraten, who had a list of four hundred persons slated for liquidation, among them Dr. Wilhelm Hoegner, the minister-president of Bavaria. Intelligence reports from Nuremberg estimated that nearly seven thousand people belonged to various groups loosely associated with the Edelweiss Piraten. Bands of former SS men, HJ boys, and BdM girls had organized, CIC concluded, for the purpose of liberating imprisoned SS men, carrying out acts of terror against Polish and Jewish DPs, blowing up bridges and rail lines, attacking freight trains, harassing German women who fraternized with Americans, and sabotaging the war crimes trial. Some suspected members of these groups had been seized in rural hideouts, along with stashes of ammunition and antitank rockets. More worrisome, in late March American and British authorities seized more than a thousand people, many after gun battles erupted, in connection with "the first major attempt to revive Nazi ideologies." Among those arrested were Arthur Axmann, last head of the Hitler Youth, along with five other prominent former youth leaders, all with the long-term goal of building the foundation of a new Nazi state.[33]

Following threats against Military Government officials in various areas, as well as reprisals against anyone working for or associating with Americans, especially German women, U.S. occupation authorities responded vigorously. With increased numbers of patrols and search operations by U.S. Constabulary troops, as well as the creation and arming of a German gendarmerie, Edelweiss Piraten activities decreased in the summer of 1946. After another outburst that fall, most spectacularly in a series of bomb attacks perpetrated by a former SS major on denazification courts in the Stuttgart area, reports of such activities declined markedly. Still, clear signs of lingering anti-American resentment remained, as revealed by rhymes popular among young Germans that autumn. "The Jew pushes [profiteers], the Pole stabs / But the Ami doesn't notice that," ran one, while another asserted, "Whether a Nazi or not / The Ami robs and spares you not." The most offensive couplet, though, redolent with anti-Semitism and racial arrogance claimed, "The Ami brings the Jews in / For he himself is a Jewish pig." By the end of the year, a bitter anti-occupation poster appeared that denounced Americans as criminals against humanity. "Germans remain united," it thundered, "do not let yourself be split! Sabotage the denazification. . . . Do they not have greater crimes on their conscience than we? Has a criminal the right to try another criminal?"[34]

This relative lull shattered in a burst of violence in early 1947, presaged by the spate of bombings in Stuttgart in late 1946. On the night of January 7 an explosion damaged the *Spruchkammer* (denazification court) in Nuremberg in which Michael Härtl, the former head of the local Gestapo jail, had just been tried and had his case sent on to a regular court for further proceedings. Large-scale raids quickly brought the arrest of two suspects and uncovered a group of well-organized former Nazis engaged in the theft of munitions and explosives from American depots. Despite this swift reaction, a second bombing rocked Nuremberg on the night of February 1 when a bomb exploded in the office of Camille Sachs, the president of the denazification court trying Franz von Papen, a politician instrumental in bringing Hitler to power and only recently acquitted by the International Military Tribunal. Although the explosion blew out the windows and doors of Sachs's office, no one was injured. Despite a massive search for the perpetrators, which centered on Alfred Zitzmann, a former functionary of the Hitler Youth, member of the Waffen-SS, and leader of a Werwolf unit, resentment at denazification continued to fester. On February 26, U.S. intelligence officials, in a series of raids, arrested hundreds of suspected members of a Nazi underground movement. Noting that the Germans had encountered scores of resistance movements in the areas they had occupied during the war, and thus had learned something of how to organize and run such operations, U.S. officials warned of the likelihood that scattered opposition groups would continue to pop up, as well as of "threats of retaliation against Spruchkammern and Military Government employees." More ominously, one of the arrested resistance leaders had threatened the use of bacteriological weapons, a threat given credence by the simultaneous seizure of Hans Georg Eidmann, a former officer in the bacteriological section of the German High Command. Further, an intelligence report of March 12 called attention to a series of bombing actions against denazification courts throughout Bavaria as a sign that "the illegal Nazi organization thinks the time ripe for direct action."[35]

Hard on these bombings followed a further outrage in Nuremberg on March 26, when a German grenade tossed through a window of the local Jewish Welfare Building, used as a transient home for Jewish DPs, caused considerable damage. Creating further insecurity, four former SA

men were arrested in late March and were charged with having organized in a number of cities resistance cells aiming at the "liberation" of
SS prisoners in American captivity. Violent incidents also persisted
throughout the remainder of 1947, ranging from incidents of shots fired
at GIs in April to a series of explosions in October that rocked American
facilities in neighboring Württemberg. In the latter episode, the CIC arrested a former SA commander and a number of ex-Hitler Youth leaders.
Just as worrisome, in a number of areas public brawls broke out between
Germans and Jewish DPs, as resentment at the perceived high levels of
DP criminality and Jewish black market activities boiled over. Even as
American authorities noted a striking increase in anti-Semitism and pro-
Nazism, an anti-Nazi German scientist claimed that "the Germans are at
present more ardently pro-Nazi and anti-Semitic in their outlook than
they were during the Third Reich. I am always taken aback when people
with whom I got along fairly well until 1945 . . . now defend the Nazis and
wish only for one thing—to have Hitler back." As a Würzburg University
professor noted wryly, "an occasional 'Heil Hitler' still works wonders."
Yet another German academic concluded morosely, "If things continue
like this, we shall have terrorism in a year."[36]

Yet despite these gloomy prognostications, the violent events of early
1947 represented not the commencement of a prolonged period of terrorist activity, but the last flurry of a dying movement. As Perry
Biddiscombe has noted, despite a not inconsiderable degree of resistance
activity, which resulted in between three thousand and five thousand
deaths, the Werwolf attempt to create a self-sustaining guerrilla movement ultimately failed. Lack of strong leadership and organization, the
utter physical and psychological exhaustion of the German people, fear
of reprisals by occupation forces, and an absence of any possibility of
long-term success all combined to mitigate against any effective resistance. Moreover, the threat of an extensive Werwolf movement operating out of Alpine sanctuaries had in the waning months of the war caused
the American military to alter its operations. With the turn to the south
to achieve a swift conquest of the Alpenfestung, the fighting in Franconia
and Bavaria assumed a mixed character of normal combat interspersed
with guerrilla warfare, a situation that resulted in a higher level of violence, destruction, and repression than otherwise warranted. As a result,
would-be guerrillas found little rest and were unable to effectively melt
into the local population. Although U.S. policy had always been to enter

Germany as conquerors, not as liberators, the Werwolf threat, Biddiscombe emphasized, strengthened this intention, so that enforcing and maintaining security became the immediate, overriding American goal.[37] Given such an atmosphere, those initially inclined to resist quickly found the scope of any such actions narrowly circumscribed. Ironically, then, although American military authorities feared a chaotic period of postwar terror directed at them by fanatical SS and Werewolves operating out of the Alpenfestung, the total collapse of the Nazi system resulted in an upsurge of violence directed at Germans themselves by former forced laborers and Jewish survivors of the Holocaust seeking revenge for the millions of their murdered compatriots.

THERE CAN BE NO RETURN
TO NORMALITY

Speaking with a Military Government official in the peaceful town of Heidelberg in mid-May 1945, a correspondent for the *New York Times,* skeptical of the many reports of looting and violence by former displaced persons, suddenly heard a woman's scream. Going outside, he saw a middle-aged woman "running down the tree-lined street with blood pouring from a gash in her arm. . . . She had been halted by a former Russian slave [laborer] who demanded her bicycle and who whipped out a stolen bayonet and slashed her when she refused to surrender it." Although the specter of the Werwolf and a prolonged guerrilla resistance most alarmed Military Government officials, local detachment and intelligence reports indicated that the greatest actual violence and disorder emanated from the "wandering hordes" of DPs, especially noticeable in the countryside, at the end of the war. Since the Allied High Command estimated a total of six to eight million DPs in the western zones of occupation, with the largest concentration in the U.S. zone, American officials feared that they would sharpen the existing chaos, thus undermining the order and stability vital for a successful occupation.[1]

This was not a misplaced concern. Because of the continued Nazi re-

sistance to the very end of the war, the destruction of facilities and disloca-
tion of civilian life was far greater than anticipated. Although in the first
weeks and months of the occupation the German civilian populace had generally remained obedient, the unexpectedly vast DP population and their
impromptu migrations within Germany threatened to disrupt this fragile
equilibrium. Military Government officials worried that these "swarms of
migrant liberated foreigners who have only their bundles ... [would], unless
they receive some systematic care, aggravate the disorder by seizing what
they need." Indeed, American authorities openly conceded that

> the most difficult immediate problem was not control of the
> native population ... but the rounding up and caring for the
> foreign slaves impressed into service of the Germans. . . . The
> sudden liberation of millions of half-starved, half-crazed pe-
> diculous [lice-infested] inmates of hundreds of labor camps
> threatened to swamp the machinery of the Military Govern-
> ment. . . . Thousands of displaced persons are roaming the
> highways, hiding in woods and on farms, and reports of loot-
> ing and violence by these recently freed victims of German
> oppression are common. . . .
>
> Suddenly set free after months and years of back-break-
> ing toil, near starvation, cruel and inhuman treatment, with
> the fear of death always in their hearts, these hapless, helpless
> humans' first thought was revenge, and their first act was to
> set forth upon the highways, bound they knew not where.

As much as they represented a human tragedy, though, a crucial fear of
the Military Government centered on the consequences of their understandable desires for revenge. Allied military records for May and June
1945 made this worry starkly evident: charges of robbery, theft, and rape
against Soviet and Polish DPs "exceeded by several hundred per cent the
complaints against all other groups."[2] Given this reality, American officials fretted that the criminal actions of DPs might provoke the very chaos
that lingering Nazi diehards desired.

THOSE DAMNED POLES!

In the chaos and breakdown of services that characterized the final days of Nazi Germany, much of the theft and plundering committed by foreign workers aimed merely at securing the food necessary for survival. Nevertheless, to a considerable degree such actions also represented acts of revenge, some spontaneous, others planned, against both the Nazi regime in general and specific individual Germans. Although there existed a pent-up resentment at the years of mistreatment to which they had been subjected, many forced laborers reacted as well to the murderous frenzy of Nazi authorities at the end of the war. Their very existence an intolerable provocation racially, the instances of plundering by the dispossessed foreign (mostly eastern European) workers seemed to substantiate National Socialist ideology, and thus justify harsh police measures. Moreover, the occasional shoot-outs between German police and marauding bands of forced laborers confirmed the most frightening of Nazi racial anxieties: the eastern European "bandits" were now despoiling Germany itself. In those last days, the Gestapo and Security Police reacted with predictable harshness, often executing foreign workers immediately after arrest, sometimes shooting them even in the absence of plundering as a form of preventive action.[3]

Tensions between the German civilian population and the large numbers of foreign agricultural laborers existed in Franconia well before the end of the war. Although vital as a source of manpower in the countryside, foreign workers from eastern Europe were regarded by the Nazi regime as particularly dangerous from a racial perspective. Indeed, fears that the closer working relationships and less stringent police controls in rural areas would lead to sexual activities between Poles and Germans, which from the Nazi racial point of view would inevitably "defile" the allegedly superior Aryan blood, increased steadily during the war. Nor were these anxieties necessarily misplaced. As Jill Stephenson has pointed out, rural and small town Germans generally reacted to the foreign workers with a mix of self-interest, pragmatism, and human feeling. Still, although rural foreign workers were undoubtedly better off than their industrial comrades, the persistent denunciation of such workers during the war years for various "crimes" illustrated very real tensions. Even though the majority of such denunciations involved sexual matters, the growing dependence of farmers on foreign laborers meant increased room for autonomy on the latter's part, which some Germans viewed as unacceptable.[4]

During the course of the war, then, Nazi reactions to transgressions by rural foreign workers grew steadily more radical. In July 1941 and

Map 7: Bavaria

again in mid-1942 in the Nuremberg area, for example, Polish men had been executed for having sexual relations with German women, after which all Poles in the area were forced to view the bodies. Similarly, the Fürth Gestapo executed the Polish farm worker Andrzey Koba on August 12, 1942, because his farmer-master deemed him insubordinate and unruly. The hanging, carried out in a meadow near Oellingen, just a few miles north of Aub, was intended as a pointed warning to other forced laborers who might seek to take advantage of the increasing German difficulty in supervision and control, for this time all Poles in the area were required to be present for the actual execution. Throughout the remainder of the war, the Gestapo continued to carry out public hangings of Polish agricultural workers in Franconia, although increasingly the spectacle was only for Poles, as Germans were discouraged from viewing the executions.[5]

Not surprisingly, then, the sudden collapse of Nazi authority removed any remaining inhibitions that Polish and eastern European forced laborers might have had at seeking retribution on their former masters. Liberated from former restrictions, many threw themselves with relish into a pandemonium of rape, thieving, and looting, often tolerated by the Allied liberators, which created a genuine mood of terror among the German population. Shortly after their liberation in Nuremberg, in a particularly gruesome example, a band of Russian forced laborers from the Langwasser camp set off in the direction of the city center. Their attitude angry and hostile, the Russians certainly meant to take revenge on their former tormentors. Along the way, however, they ran across a cask of wine, which they consumed in a rush of euphoria. Now a drunken mob, they wandered off aimlessly, finally ending at the city zoo, where they unleashed a massacre on the animals. Bears were strangled, lions killed, and flamingoes roasted like grill hens. "These barbarians have butchered [almost three hundred] innocent creatures," an elderly man observed indignantly, while another bystander remarked pointedly, "You should instead be happy that their hate was not directed at you."[6]

In the first weeks and months following the end of the war, it often seemed as if occupation authorities, in their inability to control the countryside, condoned the widespread criminality, as bands of Poles terrorized rural areas, staging break-ins where they stole food, money, clothes, and bicycles. Still, toleration had its limits. "Those damned Poles!" came to be a constant complaint of American Military Government officers, remembered a UN Relief and Rehabilitation Agency (UNRRA) official. "It's no wonder that the Germans treated them the way they did." Defeated, angry, resentful of the fact that they but not foreign workers were subject to a curfew, which allowed the DPs to roam around at night, German villagers could do little but voice complaints to local authorities. Unprepared for the unexpected euphoria of liberation and the thirst for revenge exhibited by many foreign workers, U.S. Military Government officials, for their part, struggled to come to terms with the actions of people they quickly came to regard either as inherently uncontrollable or mean-spirited and ungrateful.[7]

Much of the irritation in U.S. Army–DP relations stemmed from the fact that the large numbers of DPs overwhelmed available facilities. Not only did military authorities have to care for the millions of DPs overrun by the Allied advance, but between July 1945 and July 1946 an average of ten thousand arrived in the American zone of occupation per month. As a consequence, DPs often found themselves housed in barns, former concentration camps, or rough barracks built for the German Labor Service, living on basic rations, and denied the special consideration they thought their due. A commission of inquiry undertaken in the summer of 1945 by Earl G. Harrison found as well the "almost unanimous feeling" among army officials that "we have to get along with the Germans," but that the DPs were "only temporary," and that uncooperative and criminal elements in DP camps undermined the larger goal of good relations with the Germans. A letter signed by fifty GIs sent in early 1946 to a number of publications as well as to all members of Congress noted the bleak conditions under which DPs lived and worked at a camp at Illesheim, near Bad Windsheim, and concluded, "DPs are living almost as bad as they ever did. . . . As surely as we won the war, we will lose the peace unless every officer . . . in a position of authority knows the difference between a DP and a POW, between the liberated and the conquered." An Army Information Branch publication also noted the all-too-human revulsion of GIs who "found it difficult to understand and like people who pushed, screamed, clawed for food, smelled bad, who couldn't and didn't want to obey orders." As a lieutenant in Augsburg complained, "We feed and house these refugees, yet instead of showing their gratitude, many of them treat us as if we were their jailers."[8]

American authorities, of course, had not witnessed the earlier German mistreatment of foreign laborers, so they displayed little sympathy for retaliatory actions that the average DP regarded as justified. Moreover, the criminality and black market activities of many DPs alienated American occupation officials, one of whom, Harold Zink, stressed: "Military Government started out with a very sympathetic attitude toward displaced persons and a distinctly stern attitude toward the Germans. As time went on, though . . . , it became increasingly difficult to maintain the ideal warm relations with [the DPs]. On the other hand, considerable sympathy was aroused for the German populace by widespread looting and violence on the part of the displaced persons." Richard C. Raymond, an UNRRA district director, admitted in April 1946 that whereas GIs had earlier seen DPs as unfortunate victims of Nazism, now they viewed them as "black marketeers, criminals, or bums." Within a few months of the war's end, in fact, surveys showed that the GI's attitude toward Germans had become markedly more favorable. Warned by U.S. Army propaganda to expect a bestial horde of man-eaters, most GIs found instead "friendly old people and sweet young girls." Not surprisingly, American soldiers quickly came to prefer the company of Germans to the "dirty, destitute, and argumentative . . . DP's who were always making demands upon them." As a contemporary observer, David Bernstein, noted:

> The paradox is this: that, for Americans especially, the individual German is an attractive person. These children were charming little people; they were pathetic in their need . . . yet they did not whine or pester; they stood there quietly, with trust in their eyes. And the American heart went out to them.
>
> As for the adults, they strike most Americans in Germany as decent, pleasant, rather kindly people, who respect their parents, love children, and lavish affection on pets; they are admirably clean and orderly, and have all the solid qualities favored by Ben Franklin.
>
> For most Americans, it is increasingly difficult to associate such individuals with the crimes and bestiality of Germans as a group. This is the paradox of the individual German vs. the collective German. A child, a pretty girl, a wise old lady, is friendly to him, and the American cannot remember what he has been told about the German record. The contrast is too great to be believed.

Already nurturing a strong sense of their own victimization, many DPs thus regarded the ever closer relations between GIs and Germans as detestable, one observing that "the hardest thing is to look outside the camps and see the German so much better off than we are, even the ones who used to be our guards and tormenters."[9] Inevitably, this led to a tense and explosive situation.

The riotous activities of former forced laborers, and the lack of control exercised by American authorities, produced an overwrought atmosphere of fear and trepidation, especially in the small farm villages and isolated farmsteads dotting rural Middle Franconia. In the area around Aub, for instance, armed bands of Poles, using both Wehrmacht and U.S. Army vehicles they had "organized," roamed virtually unchecked, plundering and terrorizing the countryside, and not infrequently engaging in clashes with American MPs. More worrisome to U.S. authorities, a band of eastern European DPs supplemented by American deserters set up shop in the ruins of the castle in Aub and began widespread looting and drunken rampages throughout the region. Targeting local inns and farmsteads, the marauders typically stole food, wine, and liquor, often forcing the terrified victims to cook a feast to be consumed immediately. On the morning of April 28, for example, a band of Ukrainians plundered the village of Gollhofen, which had already suffered extensive combat damage just a few weeks earlier, seizing food, clothing, and shoes. That night, drunken GIs and Polish DPs returned, with guns blazing, demanding schnaps and young women. To the east, in Emskirchen, MPs assembled over two hundred GIs in the local train station under armed guard, most arrested on charges of rape and looting.[10]

Although many thefts in the days and weeks immediately after the end of fighting related to survival, others were inextricably connected with vengeance, the former forced laborers often targeting specific individuals or families for the purpose of exacting revenge for earlier mistreatment. In rural Middle Franconia, particularly in the farming areas around Bad Windsheim, Neustadt an der Aisch, Scheinfeld, Rothenburg, and Dinkelsbühl, thousands of eastern European forced laborers supplemented by the steady arrival of new DPs found themselves adrift with few provisions for their daily sustenance. With some DPs housed in numerous camps scattered throughout the area, but many more living outside the camp structure, most initial complaints of DP lawlessness centered on the petty theft of food, clothing, and bicycles. Very quickly, however, the basic nature of this malfeasance changed significantly: roving bands of organized and armed DPs began on a widespread basis to systematically loot rural areas. In virtually all such attacks, the pattern was the same. After cutting telephone lines to isolated farmsteads or villages, DPs brandishing weapons would burst through the door, brusquely order any inhabitants to lie on the floor or lock them in the cellar, then proceed to ransack and plunder the house. Any resistance on the part of the Germans would be met with a flurry of gunshots, most often into the air but occasionally striking a farmer dead.[11]

In Middle Franconia, judging from Military Government reports, the Poles were the worst offenders, likely because they formed the largest single national group and found themselves adrift since they generally opposed repatriation to their newly communized homeland. In a few instances justice came as a result of institutional investigation of complaints. A team of the War Crimes Commission spent the month of August 1945 probing Polish claims of mistreatment by a firm in Neustadt an der Aisch. As a result, eight Germans were arrested and held for trial. More often in the first months after the war, however, retribution came swiftly and personally. Near Nuremberg former slave laborers on June 1 shot three men, five women (after they had been raped), and a six-year-old child who were gathering wood in a forest. The area around Markt Bergel, where large numbers of Polish forced laborers had been employed, suffered from frequent and repeated attacks by armed gangs, who destroyed what they could not take with them. In the Rothenburg area, a former Polish agricultural laborer methodically organized a series of thefts targeting the tiny farming settlement in which he had worked.[12]

Similarly, during the fall of 1945 well-organized, armed bands of Polish DPs in *Landkreis* (county) Scheinfeld continually raided and looted the rural villages of Hellmitzheim, Altenspeckfeld, and Neubauhof, creating an "extremely tense and apprehensive" atmosphere among the local populace. More disturbing, a wave of violence, seemingly targeted at specific farmers, swept Landkreis Dinkelsbühl in the summer of 1945, culminating in the brutal murder in August of a seventy-year-old farmer and his wife while they slept. That November, U.S. Army authorities acknowledged that thousands of DPs had been responsible for numerous instances of looting, rape, and murder. A *New York Times* reporter was told of "repeated instances where the displaced persons were roving from the camps and, moved by understandable vengeance, tried to extort large sums of back wages from German farmers for whom they had had to work under threats of death, which sometimes were carried out." As confirmation, American officials cited the example of the murder of "eight persons, comprising three generations of a German family." In a rural area near Marktheidenfeld, moreover, the correspondent found a situation in which a band of some thirty Polish DPs "for months had been terrorizing the countryside, robbing farmhouses, and eluding patrols. . . . The desperadoes . . . have a hideout in the neighboring extensive forests and are equipped with pistols and rifles as well as vehicles." During these early postwar months, in fact, it often seemed as if the DPs were uncontrollable. Conscious of the injustice and mistreatment they had suffered, some DPs felt justified in retaliating against their former German oppressors. In July 1945 in neighboring Württemberg, for instance, Soviet DPs shot two Germans and excused their action with the claim that they believed they had acted legally.[13]

As these assaults continued through the winter months, local officials formed security committees in their towns and villages to combat the roving bands of DPs, but to little avail. Not only had German civilians been forced to turn in all their firearms to Military Government authorities, but, for the most part, the rural German police were also unarmed. Moreover, those who did have weapons had little impact, for they operated under instructions not to use their arms against DPs under any circumstances. Because the marauding DPs not infrequently wore American army uniforms and drove in jeeps or other military vehicles, the impotent rage of German civilians often turned to resentment against the occupation, as rumors quickly spread that American authorities deliberately permitted DP lawlessness as a form of retribution. One rumor, rife among both Germans and DPs, claimed that on November 8 and 9, the overlapping anniversaries of the failed Beer Hall Putsch of 1923 and the Kristallnacht anti-Jewish pogrom of 1938, all DPs would have the right to loot and plunder without fear of arrest. Although this rumor proved to be just idle chatter, the underlying apprehension had potentially serious consequences. "The German attitude toward the American occupation has become a bitter, hostile one," noted a late November 1945 intelligence report from Nuremberg. "Before Germany was entirely defeated the masses were looking forward to the coming of the Americans. . . . They felt indeed that the Americans would 'liberate' them. Now, after seven months of occupation, they feel that the Americans not only did not liberate them, but have become the severest of all occupying forces." Noted another report, "The Bavarian people do not understand why the Allies still maintain friendly relations with the Polish Displaced Persons . . . [who], they claim, have shown themselves to be 'undemocratic, dirty animals' by their robbing and looting of the poor 'defenseless German.'"[14] Left out of the report was any comment on this rather glaring example of lingering Nazi racialism, as well as extremely selective popular memory.

This upsurge in crime and looming anarchy in the countryside, along with an alarming deterioration in GI discipline, forced the U.S.

Army hurriedly to create a police force to restore order. This Constabulary, made operational on July 1, 1946, arrived none too soon. By the summer of 1946, in fact, DP crime had resulted in a virtual "reign of terror" in the rural areas of Middle Franconia. Judging from the reports of American Military Government officials, physical assaults and murder were beginning to rival theft as the major offenses in the region. Indeed, as one report noted, "while the [DP] population remains at about 3% of the total Bavarian population they . . . are known to commit 18% of the serious crimes." In the area around Bad Windsheim, for example, roving bands of "well-organized . . . , armed, and vicious Poles" terrorized isolated farming communities in June 1946. Attacking entire villages, the marauders, dressed in U.S. uniforms, carrying army weapons, and driving American vehicles, customarily assaulted German civilians before stealing money, jewelry, and other valuables, in addition to looting food and clothing. Although the local MG detachment suspected Polish guard units and other DPs from nearby camps as the culprits, "the protection afforded the perpetrators by numerous agencies [i.e., UNRRA] sponsored and backed by the Army made the stamping out of all such activity a gross impossibility." This lawless rampage in Landkreis Uffenheim climaxed in July with the abduction and rape of a five-year-old girl by a DP from the UNRRA camp at Obernzenn. This crime caused particular resentment among both Germans and GIs not only for its heinous nature, but because, as the Bad Windsheim MG officer noted bitterly, "The guilty man is known but is sheltered in the UNRRA lager." The newly operational Constabulary, however, acted swiftly to bring the situation under control. In a vigorous show of force and series of raids known as Operation Tally Ho, the situation quickly stabilized, one local report noting laconically, "The growing tendency to defy American authority has been checked by the snappy, roving U.S. Constabulary patrols which whip through every little town and village throughout the countryside, reminding many . . . that the U.S. is still occupying [the area]."[15]

American security forces, in fact, seemed to devote a disproportionate share of time and effort to combating DP criminality, a favorite tool being the so-called target or shake-down raid. In September 1945 American troops raided a number of DP camps, among them one housing Polish DPs in Ansbach, in order to disrupt black market activities. These raids continued over the next few months despite increasing bitterness and resistance from the DPs, culminating in November and December 1946 in massive actions against DP camps in Bamberg and Wildflecken. Although most Germans and many American officials tended to view crime and DPs as synonymous, the reality was far more complex. The long years of war, as well as the twelve-year education in amorality provided by the Nazis, had resulted in a general collapse of notions of law, decency, and morality. In the chaotic situation following the war, therefore, the crime rate for both DPs and Germans soared, as if the collapse of the Nazi order meant that all rules had now been abrogated. Moreover, the illegalities of the black market implicated GIs, DPs, and Germans in an unholy triangle of suppliers, brokers, and buyers, all involved in criminal activities to a greater or lesser degree and for varying motives. To an enterprising GI, for example, a situation marked by great demand and limited supply of basic commodities brought opportunities to make money to finance postwar projects. Many GIs openly declared that they intended "to continue selling in Germany until they have enough dollars to be able to take it easier when they return to the U.S.A." For a package of American cigarettes, the "currency" of most black market transactions, purchased for less than a dollar in the PX, a GI might conservatively receive eight hundred reichsmarks in return. With little effort, therefore, a GI could buy an expensive piece of gold jewelry or other valuables costing 7,000 RM on the black market for less than ten dollars. Such opportunities proved irresistible to thousands of GIs who happily supplied desperately scarce commodities.[16]

For DPs, given considerable leeway because of their special status, brokering deals on the black market meant improving their miserable existence or, especially for Jewish DPs, securing the funds necessary for emigration. Nor were the Jewish DPs worried about the illegality or possible damage done by black market activities. As a MG official from Bamberg admitted, "The most difficult task is to control the Displaced Persons Camps. UNRRA has to be notified every time one wishes to enter a camp. In many cases UNRRA officers themselves are the biggest suppliers of the black market." With the crimes recently perpetrated against them by the Germans seared in their consciousness, most Jews either could see little harm in what they were doing, or could care less. Finally, for the Germans, living on official daily rations that varied from 900 to 1,500 calories a day, trading on the black market was the only alternative to a slow death by starvation. Not surprisingly, given these circumstances, DPs, Germans, and GIs all exhibited higher than normal rates of criminality, with the peak of DP crime in the summer and fall of 1946, after which only negligible differences in the rates of criminality existed among the three groups.[17] Still, given the fluctuating food rations and the ever-present specter of hunger that characterized the first postwar months and years, the problem of the black market and associated criminality remained one of the most pressing facing Military Government. As virtually all MG officials realized, fear of starvation not only nourished the most basic anxieties but also threatened to undermine occupation rule by encouraging lawlessness and doubt in the efficacy of the Military Government.

"IT IS BETTER TODAY TO BE A CONQUERED GERMAN THAN A 'LIBERATED' JEW"

If the Military Government struggled with the contentious issue of treatment of displaced persons in general, and specifically of bringing DP criminality under control, a far more explosive situation concerned the handling of Jewish DPs. Although relatively small in number compared with their fellow DPs, the overwhelming majority of Jews, some 145,000 by the spring of 1946, were crowded into the American zone of occupation, above all in Bavaria. In addition, another wave of Jewish refugees, numbering perhaps one hundred thousand, streamed into Bavaria in the late summer of 1946 following the pogroms in Kielce, Poland. Forced to seek shelter in the land of those who had just perpetrated massive crimes against them, anxious, insecure, restless, and facing an uncertain future, Jews of the "surviving remnant" found themselves in an awkward position. On the one hand, Zionist activists sought to focus all Jewish energy on the creation of an independent Jewish state in Palestine. To this end, they acted to steer as many Jewish DPs as possible into the American zone of occupation, aiming to create a mass problem that would support the arguments of pressure groups in the United States that the only solution lay in the creation of the state of Israel. Balancing this, however, were understandable desires for justice and revenge. One DP summarized the dilemma perfectly, remarking, "Yes, you must forgive your enemies, but not before they have been hanged."[18]

Moreover, the absence of a clear American policy toward the Jewish DPs allowed the development of dangerous tensions among the tri-

angle of GIs, Germans, and DPs. Initially, the army blundered in not placing Jews in a distinct category, and instead segregated Jewish DPs according to nationality. German, Austrian, Hungarian, Rumanian, or Bulgarian
Jewish survivors of the Holocaust thus found themselves regarded as
former "enemy nationals" and denied the special care accorded to DPs
regarded as victims of German aggression. As a result, concentration camp
survivors not infrequently found themselves placed back in their former
camps alongside ex-camp guards, often wearing their hated striped camp
uniforms and subsisting on a monotonous diet of watery soup and moldy
black bread. The outcry over the abysmal living conditions of the Jewish
DPs led to the creation of the Harrison Commission, led by Earl G.
Harrison, dean of the University of Pennsylvania Law School and American representative on the Inter-Governmental Committee on Refugees,
in the summer of 1945. Finding it intolerable that Jews were housed behind barbed wire fences in former concentration and forced labor camps,
while living in crowded, unsanitary, and "generally grim conditions,"
Harrison remarked in one particularly scathing paragraph of his final
report, "As matters now stand, we appear to be treating the Jews as the
Nazis treated them except that we do not exterminate them. They are in
concentration camps in large numbers under our military guard instead
of S.S. troops. One is led to wonder whether the German people, seeing
this, are not supposing that we are following or at least condoning Nazi
policy." Outraged by the report, President Harry Truman responded
swiftly—in a letter dated August 31—ordering General Eisenhower to
improve conditions in the DP camps "in order to make clear to the German people that we thoroughly abhor the Nazi policies of hatred and
persecution." One way to do this, he suggested, was to "intensify our
efforts to get these people out of camps and into decent houses until they
can be repatriated. . . . These houses should be requisitioned from the
German civilian population. . . . [They] cannot escape responsibility for
what they have brought upon themselves."[19]

Stung by Truman's apparent criticism of his handling of the situation, Eisenhower immediately swung into action, directing that the daily
caloric ration for Jewish DPs be increased to 2,500, twice that of German
civilians, and that improvements in their living conditions be made. Even
as American authorities acted quickly in the late summer of 1945 to
ameliorate the situation of Jewish DPs, they thus laid the groundwork
for escalating tensions between DPs on the one side and GIs and Ger-

mans on the other. American officials now undertook the creation of a number of specifically Jewish DP camps, in some cases housing Jews in former military barracks, while in others resettling them in homes and apartment buildings from which Germans had been summarily evicted. With the possible exception of the desperate food situation in the first years of occupation, nothing angered Germans as much as this arbitrary expropriation of their homes and property. What Military Government officials referred to as "painful friction" provoked numerous complaints, considerable unrest, ill-concealed resentment, protest movements led by women, and a special bitterness. Nor did the Americans achieve much understanding by pointing out that Nazi authorities had acted considerably more harshly in German-occupied Europe, and that those now being given consideration had been targeted for extermination by the Hitler regime, for whom "special handling" had meant something quite different.[20]

Perhaps nothing embittered the DPs, both Jewish and non-Jewish, as much as the seeming German civilian incomprehension of the brutal methods used by their own regime in occupied areas, or the sheer hypocrisy with which they bemoaned the requisitions, practiced on a much smaller scale, now being used against themselves. The situation deteriorated further in the spring and summer of 1946 with the arrival in the American zone of large numbers of Polish Jews fleeing anti-Semitic violence in their native country. Not only did they further tax already overburdened services, but they exacerbated German-Jewish tensions by raising anew the German prejudice against the Ostjuden (eastern European Jews), who seemed so alien in their customs, behaviors, and attitudes.[21]

Even the most common German complaints about Jewish DPs, their allegedly rampant and open black market activities, charges seemingly substantiated by Military Government reports, intensified the negative stereotype of Jews as sharp traders and profiteers from the misery of others. "We have in camp a number of professional criminals," the head of the Windsheim DP camp admitted. "We are, however, determined to drive them out of camp. The CIC is aware of their existence and has promised to help us." Moreover, the extensive trading in scarce items underscored the Jews' unique position and ability to obtain such items, the German handicaps in this regard, and the ultimate German responsibility for both their plights, which neither relished. In a time of desperate shortages, not only were many Germans envious of Jewish goods, but the German-Jewish relationship of the previous years was reversed—the Jews now seemingly had considerable leverage in the face of German impotence. Quite simply, food was power, and those without food chafed at their weakness. One American relief worker admitted that to the Germans the DP camps must have seemed a paradise of "sugar and spam, margarine and jam, plus cigarettes and vitamized chocolate bars." In addition, the frequent anti–black market raids conducted by the U.S. Constabulary gave a distorted picture of the extent of Jewish involvement in the black market. "If you only read the newspapers to learn about occupation affairs," admitted the same aid worker, "you gained the impression that [Jews] were the whole of the DP problem." American "search and seizure" operations tended to garner wide attention while similar raids conducted by German police on German communities or non-Jewish DP camps received little notice. In truth, as noted above, virtually everyone in the Germany of 1945–1948 was involved in the black market, for the simple reason that to live on the official rations was impossible. As Irving Heymont, head of the Landsberg Jewish DP camp, noted, "If we were to imprison everyone who barters, we would have to convert Germany into one big jail."[22]

If Jews participated in illegal black market activities at rates roughly similar to Germans or non-Jewish DPs, one major difference that highlighted the seemingly greater Jewish criminality was the very openness with which they conducted their business. Abraham Hyman, who between 1946 and 1949 served as both assistant to the Adviser on Jewish Affairs and as Acting Adviser, admitted that the sheer brazenness of Jewish DPs involved in the black market, openly using "their camps as their bases of operation . . . , gave the impression that the Jewish DP's dominated the black market." A mid-July 1946 incident provided a good example of this impudence. In Bad Windsheim, where a Jewish DP camp had just been established a few weeks earlier, MPs on the night of July 12 arrested three Jewish DPs for stealing a cow. When asked where the cow was stolen, the DPs replied, "What cow?" even though one of them still had hold of the rope attached to the animal, which was grazing contentedly a few feet away. Significantly, though, Hyman also noted that "they were more brazen because, having been stripped of their possessions and left orphaned by the Germans, they felt no obligation to consider the harm the black market might be causing the German economy." Indeed, given the enormity of the crimes committed against them and their bitterness and hostility toward Germans, the overwhelming majority of Jew-

Adolf Hitler, flanked by Rudolf Hess and Joseph Goebbels, at Burg Hoheneck for the burial of Ernst Pöhner, November 23, 1927. In the background between Hess and Hitler is Hitler's driver, Julius Schreck. (Reprinted by permission from the book *Ipsheim: Die Chronik eines Fränkischen Dorfes* by Christoph Rückert [Ipsheim: Marktgemeinde Ipsheim, 1989], photographer unknown.)

GIs from Combat Command B, Twelfth Armored Division, on an attack mission wait while a treadway bridge is installed near Dietersheim, April 14, 1945. (NA, RG 111, SC 260368-1.)

Above, A bridge is installed under fire near Dietersheim by combat engineers from the Twelfth Armored Division, April 14, 1945. (NA, RG 111, SC 326747.) *Below,* A GI from Combat Command A, Twelfth Armored Division, looks for more Germans after his unit has just killed several fleeing from the burning vehicle in the background. Near Emskirchen, north of Wilhermsdorf, April 16, 1945. (NA, RG 111, SC 206446.)

GIs from the Eleventh Armored Division experience the perils of street fighting east of Nuremberg in the town of Wernberg, April 22, 1945. (NA, RG 111, SC 205298.)

Antiaircraft gunners from the Twelfth Armored Division hit this German plane, one of ten shot down over a three-day period, as it attempted to bomb the Danube River bridge at Dillingen, April 25, 1945. (NA, RG 111, SC 135582.)

Soldiers from the Ninety-second Cavalry Reconnaissance Squadron locate a camouflaged Werwolf hut near Dischingen used by Hitler Youth and SS fanatics, May 30, 1945. (NA, RG 111, SC 334152.)

Die Wolfsangel (wolf trap), sign of the Werwolf.

Above, Two GIs in Nuremberg chat with German women, April 1946. (NA, RG 111, SC 234642.) *Below,* Former slave laborers, now displaced persons, set up a makeshift camp near Nuremberg, May 1945. (NA, RG 111, SC 303606-1.)

Above, German women are forced to evacuate their homes to make room for Jewish displaced persons, Landsberg, January 1946. (U.S. Holocaust Memorial Museum, courtesy of Irving Heymont. Photographer: George Kadish/Zvi Kadushin. Photograph #61095.) *Below,* Contraband goods seized by U.S. Constabulary troops during a raid on the DP camp at Bad Windsheim, May 4, 1948. (NA, RG 111, SC 300439.)

Above, American military police cordon off the area outside the courthouse where the trial of the Landsberg rioters is in session, July–August 1946. (U.S. Holocaust Memorial Museum, courtesy of Herbert Friedman. Photographer: Unknown. Photograph #82290.) *Below,* Konsum bakery, Nuremberg, April 1946. (NA, RG 111, SC 235807.)

Above, American and German investigators found four full bottles and two empty bottles of arsenic under the floor of the Konsum bakery, Nuremberg, April 22, 1946. (NA, RG 111, SC 235808.) *Below,* Georg Kerling, a member of the German criminal police, is shown inside a hole in the floor of the bakery where bottles of arsenic were located, Nuremberg, April 22, 1946. (NA, RG 111, SC 235809.)

ish DPs agreed on one thing—they would do nothing to contribute to the restoration of the German economy. "We slaved for the Germans long enough," went a customary refrain, "let them slave for us now."[23]

If not exactly an attitude marked by an explicit desire for revenge, it nonetheless betrayed a sentiment common among Jewish DPs that, having survived the horrors of the Holocaust, they had earned certain privileges, among them the right not to contribute to the recovery of the nation responsible for the mass slaughter of Jews. Further, disappointment at their failure to be resettled quickly in Palestine and the depressing realization that they were stuck in dreary DP camps for the foreseeable future produced mounting frustration and anger. "We don't mind overcrowding itself," a Jewish DP in Landsberg Camp remarked to an American observer. "But while we are crowded into barracks, twenty or thirty to a room, the Germans and even Nazi party members in town are living in their own homes. Why can't we be assigned the houses in town until we leave . . . ?" As another observed bitterly, "It is better today to be a conquered German than a 'liberated' Jew." A deep psychological chasm thus separated Jews and Germans. "How to behave with a German citizen . . . is a daily dilemma," remembered Simon Shochet, "which is resolved according to the specific situation." Even though they developed rudimentary day-to-day relationships, and some men out of a deep psychological need to gain revenge even had sexual liaisons with local women, the Jewish DPs, as Rabbi Philip Bernstein noted at the time, "hated them with an unforgiving hate. They were unwilling to accept any plan that involved some concession to the Germans."[24]

Not surprisingly, this anger was often discharged on local civilians and GIs, both of whom frequently displayed an astonishing insensitivity or outright anti-Semitism. As occupation failed to produce instant improvement in German living conditions and the influx of millions of German refugees expelled from the east sharpened the hardships of daily life, and as desperate food shortages persisted into 1947, many Germans reacted bitterly, at times blaming Americans, at other times the Jewish DPs, and sometimes both. Although a Third Army intelligence report of November 1945 warned that "the general attitude of the civilians is gradually changing from obviously genuine friendliness . . . to a definitely reserved and cold attitude," in general Germans directed their discontent toward the Jewish DPs, not the American conquerors. Various polls tracking anti-Semitism all showed high or rising levels among Germans between 1945 and 1947, although in truth similar levels of resentment were registered against German refugees resettled in their midst. In a December 1946 survey released in March 1947, the American Military Government found that in its zone of occupation, 22 percent of the people could be classified as racists, another 21 percent as anti-Semites, and 18 percent as extreme anti-Semites, a result consistent with the findings of a poll released in May 1947 by the Munich-based Information Control Division. According to this sampling, anti-Semitic tendencies had increased during the preceding eight months. Of those responding, 19 percent declared themselves to be Nazis, a further 22 percent supported Nazi ideas, and another 20 percent admitted to being convinced anti-Semites. Nor did this represent the peak of postwar anti-Semitism. Yet another Office of Military Government, United States (OMGUS), survey released in May 1948 indicated that racial hatred had actually increased from the 1947 levels. As late as August 1949, in a survey done by German pollsters, over half the respondents agreed that anti-Semitism was largely the result of uniquely Jewish characteristics. Perhaps not surprisingly, a wave of desecrations of Jewish cemeteries erupted in Franconia in early 1948 and swept through much of Bavaria. "No one can work in Germany for even a brief period," noted a member of the American Displaced Persons Commission, "without being conscious of the deep, underlying hatred and hostility against the Jews." Another American lamented, "anti-Semitism is now more deep-seated than in Hitler's day."[25]

Some analysts ascribed the resiliency of German anti-Semitism to a moral torpor, others to a lack of any sense of responsibility for what had happened to the Jews. A Military Government report noted with great insight that Germans "remain unconvinced that they acted as criminals, but they have become aware that they must have been great fools," a realization that now produced an attitude of sullen apathy. Still others attributed the backlash against Jews to the fact of a guilty conscience, that the Jewish DPs in their midst amounted to a constant reproach, a silent accusation they could not rebut. Conscious of having committed a massive crime, yet at the same time unwilling or unable to make amends, the German people came to fear Jewish retribution, with the result that this very anxiety fueled the growth of a new round of anti-Semitism. More to the point, in the context of the tribulations of the occupation, many Germans deeply resented the preferential treatment Jewish DPs received with respect to food, the requisitioning of homes, and certain freedoms and immunities they enjoyed that were denied to themselves. In addition, over and above general occupation costs, Germans had to pay substantial sums specifically to finance the DPs. For many Germans, this mound of difficulties represented a deliberate effort on the part of the Military Government, egged on by the Jews, to humiliate them. An intelligence report from January 1946 aptly summarized the German attitude: "The crimes committed by a small group of usurpers in the name of the German people weigh heavily on the individual citizen. The people consider themselves as victims rather than as co-conspirators in these crimes. Therefore, on the whole, they do not consider themselves inferior, guilty, or second-rate in comparison with other people." Preoccupied with their own misery, largely convinced that they were the injured party, the Germans persuaded themselves, as Abraham Hyman noted, "that they owed nothing to the remnants of European Jewry on their soil."[26]

To a dismaying extent, then, Germans tended to blame Jewish DPs for the hardships of postwar life, for the food and housing shortages, and for the excesses of the black market that allegedly hampered their own economic recovery. Their privations thus came to be seen by many as the vengeance of international Jewry. While some Germans bemoaned the "Jewish hate propaganda" allegedly directed against them, others, "outspoken in their claim that Jewish elements are responsible for the majority of black market activities," came to see this as part of a diabolic plan on the part of the Jews, abetted by American officials, to "destroy the German people." One incident quoted by Dr. Phillipp Auerbach, the Bavarian state commissioner for Victims of Political and Racial Persecution, perhaps best illustrated the attitude of many Germans. On a train a German woman, engaged in a conversation about Auschwitz with a Jewish woman, was upbraided by a fellow passenger: "What do you care about the Jewish sow? What the Allies are doing to the Germans today is much worse than anything that ever happened in Auschwitz." In essence, far too many Germans sought to stifle a sense of guilt by convincing themselves that they too had been victims of Nazism, and continued to suffer even after it had been destroyed.[27]

Neither did Jewish DPs necessarily find the support and understanding they sought from the U.S. Army or its soldiers. Not only did the Jewish DPs, overwhelmingly eastern European in background, have little in common with most GIs, but the average American soldier seemed completely unprepared either emotionally or intellectually to deal with the daily problems of the residents of DP camps. Instead of grateful survivors, GIs encountered people who were disgruntled, demanding, suspicious to the point of hostility, and mistrustful of all authority. Moreover, as Rabbi Bernstein noted at the time, most GIs had "contacts with [Jewish] DP's only at the point of trouble. Because these soldiers were usually young and lacking in background for the understanding of so alien and complex a problem, it was hard for them to have a sympathetic or just evaluation of these uprooted Jews. Increasingly . . . as German girls influenced American men, the Americans were affected by German attitudes." This latter point, although seemingly trivial, appeared often in contemporary assessments of the problem of GI attitudes toward Jews, one local Jewish leader charging that American troops acted more harshly toward Jewish DPs because "the U.S. soldiers are subjected to the influence of their German girlfriends." The real irritant was perhaps not so much GI fraternization with German women, but what it represented. Jewish DPs complained that American soldiers had become far too friendly with the former enemy and were too quick to forgive them their misdeeds of the recent war; indeed, many GIs seemed not to realize that there had even been any such crimes. So ill-informed were American soldiers, for example, that a counterintelligence officer, presumably in a position to know, when ordered to release the chaplains among German POWs, remarked in astonishment, "There is something strange about the composition of the German chaplaincy corps. I find among them chaplains of all faiths but no Jews."[28]

Just as disturbing as this basic ignorance of recent events, numerous surveys found high levels of anti-Semitism among GIs in Germany. One such study, prohibited from being released but leaked to an observer with the American Jewish Committee (AJC), indicated a shocking level of anti-Semitism among GIs. "A very high proportion believe . . . that Hitler was *partly right* in his treatment of Jews," noted the AJC representative, obviously taken aback by the results. In another study conducted in 1946, over half the GI respondents said that Hitler had done good things for the Germans, while nearly a quarter believed that Hitler had "good reason" to treat Jews as he had. Nor were these attitudes confined merely to rank-and-file soldiers. A member of the Military Government responsible for the administration of DP camps, Colonel Harry S. Messec, wrote in December 1945 that his "general impression" of the Jews in the DP camps was that they were "born psychopathic liars," and that the Polish Jews had fled westward because in Poland they no longer would be permitted the opportunity to engage in their "money-lending" activities.[29]

If this repulsive anti-Semitic stereotyping was not crude enough, General George S. Patton went even further, remarking in September 1945 with regard to the problem of DP camps, "There remains much to do . . . because the typical representative of Jewish DP's is a type of sub-human, without any of the cultural and social education of our age. I have never seen a group of people that possess less intelligence and character. Practically all have expressionless, brown-gray eyes . . . that is proof in my opinion of their low intelligence." As if to confirm that this observation, which even the notorious Jew-baiting Nazi Julius Streicher would have approved, was not a mere slip of the tongue, Patton later noted that the Jewish DPs stood "lower than animals." Little wonder, then, that Jewish DPs believed they were singled out for searches and black market raids. Indeed, the nature of the American raids on Jewish DP camps, in which armed MPs or Constabulary troops, usually supported by tanks or half-tracks, surrounded a camp before dawn then descended on it, waking the people and ordering them out into the streets, seemed almost deliberately designed to evoke horrifying memories of Nazi *Aktionen* in the ghettos of occupied Poland. Startled, upset, and incensed, Jewish DPs not infrequently responded in a verbal rage, shouting epithets such as "American SS" and "American Gestapo" at the GIs.[30]

Not surprisingly, these confrontations stirred antagonisms between Jewish DPs and GIs that, after a period of multiplying irritations, erupted in open hostilities in the spring and summer of 1946. While Jewish DPs saw themselves as marked for especially harsh treatment in the fight against black market activity, American officials often had an opposite perception. "Black Market activity remained at a very low level until recent weeks," ran a not atypical local Military Government report, the writer's disgust barely contained, "when the coming of large numbers of Jewish DPs and persecutees to Windsheim brought all control of such operations to an abrupt halt. Orders sent down by higher headquarters completely handcuffed a highly efficient police set-up as to any ability to even investigate those who quite openly carry on operations. . . . Among the German population a deep resentment is evident."[31] Indignant and frustrated at their perceived impotence in the face of open black marketeering, while at the same time unsympathetic and uncomprehending of the attitude and feelings of the Jewish DPs, American security of-

243

ficials and their German police associates struggled to control a barely concealed anger at the "special treatment" (and how ironic and pregnant with meaning that phrase was) accorded the Jews.

As German police began searches in DP camps and accosted individual Jews in an effort to dampen black market activity, scuffles and confrontations resulted that raised tensions considerably. Already in the first few months of 1946—as shown by an incident between Jewish DPs and German police in Mannheim, by the murder of two Jews in and around Munich, as well as by confrontations at camps in Fürth, Oberammergau, and Lampertheim—passions had risen to an alarming level. In March 1946, however, an incident in Stuttgart resulted in the first widespread violence. Around 6:00 A.M. on March 29, approximately two hundred armed German police, accompanied by police dogs and supervised by eight American MPs, pulled up outside the DP "camp," which was really just a row of requisitioned apartment buildings on Reinsburgstrasse in the southwestern part of the city, that housed a little over 1,300 Polish Jews. Hoping to break up an alleged black market ring that operated from the camp, the police, using loud speakers and banging on doors to rouse those still asleep, ordered all camp inhabitants into the street. Although some black market activity might well have been occurring, the method used to combat it showed an incredible insensitivity to recent events. Terrified at the sight of the German police, transported in their own minds back to the horrors of the ghetto-clearing Aktionen in Poland, the Jews reacted instinctively by hurling at the police whatever was at hand.[32]

Fearing the situation was getting out of control, the MPs left for reinforcements, evidently not realizing the potential danger of a clash between the DPs and the German police. Around 7:00 A.M., as the Germans dragged a handcuffed boy into the street, enraged Jews began cursing and striking policemen, which, according to eyewitnesses, led the Germans to begin beating the refugees with rubber truncheons. One such refugee was the thirty-five-year-old Samuel Danziger, an Auschwitz survivor just recently reunited with his wife and two young children, who was struck down by a blow to the head just as he turned to leave. As he got up, a policeman, later identified by a bystander as a former camp guard at Auschwitz, fired without warning into the crowd and killed Danziger with a bullet through the head. In all, the police fired about twelve shots, wounding another four people, while twenty-eight German police suffered injuries. "It was," one DP remarked bitterly, "the day of the ghetto all over again."[33]

Although the raid had been approved by a local American public safety officer, neither the UNRRA camp director nor senior American officials seem to have been notified beforehand of the operation. Moreover, the incident seemed part of a troubling pattern. Admitted a Military Government official at the time, "Anti-Semitism . . . has risen to the surface again. . . . The Stuttgart killing was not an isolated incident. Police Chief Karl Weber of Stuttgart, when asked if he did not think the job of raiding DP camps had better be left to Americans, said 'the German police knew better than Americans what they were looking for and how to find it.'" As the MG official noted in disgust, "For thirteen years and longer [sic] the German police 'knew what to look for' in their raids against the Jewish people." As a result of the brutality of the raid and the subsequent outrage, General Joseph T. McNarney, commander of U.S. forces in the European theater, banned German police from making raids into any Jewish DP camp. American troops were to conduct any such future operations, although given GI-DP tensions, this likely seemed little comfort to the DPs. Indeed, in the same report, the MG official had gone on to emphasize, "Too much stress cannot be laid on the terrific disillusionment which exists in the minds of all people who were liberated from Nazism. DP's . . . still in Germany say that the 'Brown Terror' has been substituted by one of a different color. . . . The atmosphere and conditions of the average DP camp are little better than the work camps of the Nazis. . . . The problem grows in intensity and is one which must be met with a realistic and humane policy on the part of the Army to prevent further bloodshed."[34]

Nor was this particular official guilty of hyperbole. In sight of the famous prison in Landsberg where Adolf Hitler had written *Mein Kampf*, anger and frustration between Jewish DPs on the one side and Germans and GIs on the other spilled over into large-scale violence. In mid-February, five German civilians had been attacked and severely beaten near the DP camp, one of the largest in the American zone, while particularly egregious black market activities had further inflamed emotions. A March 23 report from the Landsberg MG detachment asserted, "The Landsberg Jewish DP Camp has become a haven for criminals. The local German Police are not permitted to enter the camp and American Troops entering the camp are given no cooperation by the DP Police. Numerous cases of

German civilians, including men, women and children, passing by the Jewish DP Camp at night, have been severely beaten to the extent that they must be hospitalized." Nor did matters improve. In order to give a special significance to Purim, the joyous festival of the deliverance of the Jews from threatened destruction by Hamann, DPs in the camp at Landsberg turned the late March event into a rejuvenating celebration and denunciation of Nazism: Hamann's defeat was transmuted into Hitler's defeat. Insulting slogans and caricatures of Hitler appeared throughout the camp, the festival culminating in a ceremonial burning of a copy of *Mein Kampf* that night. The ghosts of the past could not be exorcized that easily, however, as the April 6 detachment report noted two troubling incidents. In the first, four young Jewish DPs on March 29 were ordered by two German policemen "to leave the premises of a German firm where they were trying to illegally appropriate an engine belonging to the firm. The DP's refused to obey and as a result were struck on the back and rear . . . by the Policemen's clubs." The report's author added, with some obvious distaste, that the "UNRRA has officially described this incident as an Anti-Semitic act." This was followed on April 4 by three separate incidents in which Jewish DPs attacked and beat up German civilians. Significantly, in one episode "eight to ten Jews stopped a German on a bicycle and asked him, 'Are you German?' He said 'Yes, I am.' The Jews then asked if he had heard what happened at Stuttgart and, giving him no time to reply, attacked him from all sides."[35]

As tensions continued growing that spring, the Landsberg MG detachment identified the key problem in its April 13 report, commenting:

> There is a definite and growing resentment evidenced by the German population towards the Jewish DP's because of these incidents of beatings by gangs of Jewish DP's.
>
> The Jewish DP's on the other hand naturally enough hate the Germans and feel that they are still being discriminated against because German people have houses and some of the DP's must live in a camp. . . . They also complain of other things of similar nature, clothing, inability to work, food, and to earn money.

The DPs, one is tempted to scream, complained not only because they found themselves stuck in the land of the perpetrators, but also because those "other things of similar nature" so dismissively listed by the report's author constituted precisely those attributes of normal life that they longed for but were denied. The attitude of local MG could already be inferred from phrases such as "gangs of Jewish DP's," but the general sympathies of the average GI became clearer in the April 27 report. In reciting numerous incidents, two stood out. In the first, three Jewish girls walking down a street near the newly opened enlisted men's club were insulted and one knocked down by an American soldier, while in the second a GI beat a Jewish DP with an iron bar, seriously injuring him. In commenting on the past month of escalating tensions, the relevant official at MG headquarters in Munich stressed only the positive behavior of Germans, indirectly contrasting it with that of Jews: "It will be noted that no instances were reported of German civilians physically attacking Jewish DP's. This situation is general. Since the end of the Third Reich . . . there have been very few reports of attacks upon Jews by German civilians. . . . It is also noteworthy that there exists in Landsberg a situation of non-cooperation between the UNRRA staff and the MG staff."[36]

The highly charged situation at Landsberg exploded at the end of the month. On April 27, Germans in the town of Dießen, on the Ammersee a little more than ten miles from Landsberg, celebrated with beer and song the return of a group of local men from Allied POW camps. That same evening in a somber ceremony the five thousand Jewish DPs in the Landsberg camp marked the third anniversary of the Warsaw ghetto uprising. Early the next morning word reached the DP camp that two Jewish DPs guarding a kibbutz at Dießen had disappeared. In the overwrought atmosphere that lingered from the previous evening, a rumor spread quickly through the camp that the two Jewish men had either been kidnapped or murdered by Germans. At once around seven hundred of the camp's residents, angry and upset at what they thought was yet another outrage perpetrated by Germans against Jews, spilled onto the main road that dissected the camp. As Germans passed by, some fifty of the DPs attacked them and destroyed several vehicles. American MPs who were rushed to the camp to control the situation found it in a complete uproar, the Jews demanding local Germans as hostages to guarantee the return of the missing DPs. Only after several hours of heated protest did the Jews calm down and begin to return to the camp. In all eighteen Germans, most dragged from a bus that was then set afire, had been injured, three seriously, although no one had been killed.[37]

Around noon, however, another brawl erupted on a nearby field when MPs went to seize two young Jewish DPs who were assaulting some Germans. As the MPs began marching the youths away, approximately twenty of their friends rushed over to protest the arrest, angry at what they believed to be American concern for Germans and failure to protect Jews. Strong words followed, then some of the DPs began pelting the GIs with rocks, while others screamed "American SS" and "American Gestapo." After a short struggle, the MPs brought the situation under control and marched the twenty young DPs off to detention. That night, just as the armored cars that had briefly patrolled the camp were being withdrawn, the two missing Jewish guards reappeared. Far from having been kidnapped, the two had simply gone absent without leave, taking a train to Munich for the day. In a horrifying demonstration of the anger, rage, and bitterness produced by the growing tensions between Germans and DPs, as well as by the increasing sense of Jewish hopelessness at being stuck in the land of those who had perpetrated the Holocaust, an erroneous rumor had sparked a violent riot.[38]

Nor did any resolution come from this event, the Jewish DPs believing themselves unjustly arrested and imprisoned (a painful reminder of their concentration camp days), the Germans apparently reaffirmed in their conviction of DP criminality, and the Americans, caught in the middle, upset at being compared to Nazis and angry at perceived Jewish ingratitude. As the Military Government admitted,

> what happened at Landsberg is only part of a larger picture—a picture of hatred, frustration and humiliation. Most of these Jews have been confined in concentration camps for the past seven years or longer. Their intelligentsia has been deliberately killed off. They have not been exposed to the refining influences of education or decent society; but on the other hand have had before their eyes . . . examples of terrible atrocity and barbarism committed by SS and Wehrmacht troops. To this is added the frustration and humiliation of the fact that more than a year after their liberation they are still herded together in camps.

American officials also recognized that "within this larger picture outbreaks similar to that which occurred at Landsberg might conceivably take place at any of the DP camps." Then, quoting a Bavarian official involved in Jewish welfare activities, the MG predicted bleakly, "further outbreaks of violence will occur because 'the future looks so hopeless and black for [the DPs].'"[39]

Indeed, the most important repercussion appeared to be a further deterioration in relations between GIs and Jewish DPs, a development that added to the already strong Jewish sense of being isolated in hostile surroundings. In June, Jews at the DP Camp in Leipheim launched a hunger strike and work stoppage to protest alleged mistreatment by GIs, a claim echoed by Jewish DPs in Bamberg. More worrisome, on successive days in July incidents at Bad Windsheim and Wolfratshausen revealed the gulf of misunderstanding, suspicion, and enmity that separated all sides. In the former town, at about 10:00 P.M. on the night of July 25, 1946, an American soldier, Private First Class Robert Reed, was returning to his billet on Kulsheimerstrasse, accompanied by two German boys and four German girls. As he approached a water tank designated for use by American troops only, a facility that he was in charge of, Reed noticed two members of the Jewish Internal Police Force from the neighboring DP camp lying on top of the tank. Fearing a problem at his point of responsibility, Reed confronted the two men, telling them they had no right to be there. In an apparent misunderstanding caused by language difficulties, one of the Jews, Israel Moszkowicz, evidently approached Reed in a threatening manner and was struck in the chest by the private. Seeing a large number of DPs advancing from the camp screaming "Nazi-Americans," Reed rushed to his billet to get a carbine. When he came out, though, he was intercepted by an UNRRA camp administrator, who managed to disperse the crowd of DPs, while Reed left for the Military Police station.[40]

In the meantime, the local public safety officer, Lieutenant Robert Gooch, notified of the disturbance while playing cards with three members of the UNRRA administration in a hotel across from the police station, had just begun to question Reed about the incident when at roughly 10:20 P.M. he received a telephone call informing him that an angry crowd of DPs had assembled outside the enlisted men's quarters. Gooch jumped in his car, accompanied by Sergeant Lester Lowery, Private Reed, and Mr. E. M. West, the deputy director of the UNRRA team, and sped off for the billets. As Gooch drove into the yard of the enlisted men's quarters, his headlights illuminated a scene of roughly fifty DPs milling about restlessly. Gooch instructed the GIs to get out of the car with him but not to

249

fire unless so ordered, then in a loud voice shouted "*Raus*" to the assembled crowd of eastern European Jews, who paid no attention to him since few of them knew German. Gooch, in his own words, then yelled, "*Gehe weg* (go away), God damn it," but when no one moved he began to fire into the air, as did Reed and Lowery. As the DPs began to scatter wildly, Gooch, through the twilight gloom, saw a man holding a cigarette running back toward the house. Aiming at the cigarette, Gooch fired and saw it suddenly disappear. Hehl Lustgarten, a Jewish DP, fell wounded in the thigh. Although the DPs had now dispersed, Gooch and the two GIs hurried back to the police station for more weapons and ammunition. Returning to the enlisted men's quarters and seeing all was calm, they drove to the water tank, the site of the original disturbance, where they were confronted by a highly agitated Dominic Capilongo, who had just that morning been removed as camp director. According to Gooch, Capilongo immediately began berating Reed and demanded that Gooch inform the private who he was. Betraying the high level of tension between army and UNRRA personnel that had developed in the weeks since the camp had opened earlier that summer, Gooch responded angrily, "This is Mr. Capilongo, Director of UNRRA Team 621 Windsheim, a U.S. civilian who to the best of my knowledge and belief has absolutely no right to command any member of the U.S. Army to do anything." With that the MPs left.[41]

Again indicative of the deteriorating state of GI-DP relations, the intelligence report sent to the G-2 of the Third Army for the week of July 31 claimed that "a mob of 150 Jewish Displaced Persons" had actually "attacked an enlisted men's billets," this after a GI had been assaulted by two Jewish DPs! In that same report, intelligence analysts noted an incident on July 24 at Türkheim near Stuttgart in which a "crowd of about 250 persons . . . , mostly Jews," had to be broken up by Constabulary troops, and another on July 27 in which "about ten Jews beat two women, one 80 years old, who were trying to prevent the Jews from looting an orchard." As local civilians detained the youths, the report noted, "about 100 Jews stormed the village," before being dispersed by Constabulary forces and German Rural Police. These incidents, in fact, proved ancillary to the major episode of that explosive week—the "riot" near Wolfratshausen on July 24 when "Jewish Displaced Persons attacked German police," an assault that "resulted in the death of one Displaced Person and the wounding of another." The report also noted that "Eight German civilians taken as hostages by the Displaced Persons were later released by Military Police." In addition, in a resumption of the mayhem the next day, a confrontation between DPs and MPs left a number of the former wounded.[42]

As with the report on the "Jewish incident" at Bad Windsheim, the statement describing the affair at Wolfratshausen was notable for sins of both commission and omission, engaging in hyperbole while at the same time neglecting certain key details. The camp at Föhrenwald, near the town of Wolfratshausen some fifteen miles south of Munich, had originally been built in 1939 by I. G. Farben to house workers at a local munitions plant. Following the war, former forced laborers had been given temporary shelter, but in September 1945 American authorities decided to convert it into a purely Jewish DP camp. Almost immediately, MG officials noted a high state of tension between DPs and local German civilians fearful of DP looting and "rampages." By the following summer, Föhrenwald housed more than five thousand DPs in a facility meant for half that number, and as in similar camps in the area, inadequate living conditions and the failure to be quickly resettled in Palestine left many DPs frustrated, restless, and irritable. In addition, although the U.S. Army supplied sufficient food, it was mostly a monotonous diet of canned and dehydrated C rations. As elsewhere, German claims that local black market activities centered on the camp aggravated tensions, the origins of which lay in the desperate shortages of food and other basic commodities. In order to secure supplies of meat and fresh food, camp inhabitants indeed engaged in the black market, which greatly strained relations with army authorities, who had a very limited tolerance for such activity. Moreover, the American guarantee of a minimum of 2,500 calories a day for Jewish DPs versus the provision of roughly 1,300 calories to the German population left the latter angry and envious, a circumstance that easily led to wild rumors and misunderstandings. Furthermore, as UNRRA officials admitted, in view of their recent history, the Jewish DPs had little respect for German property.[43]

Neither did local American military commanders necessarily have much empathy for the Jews under their control. An April 1946 report by the Ninth Infantry Division, which had jurisdiction over Föhrenwald, emphasized that the "most troublesome problems" related to "Jewish groups," and that they were guilty of "lack of cooperation" and "outright disobedience." "These people," the report stressed, "spend much of their time in black market dealings and openly flaunt this fact . . .

knowing full well the [German] police could not bother them. . . . Because of their conduct they have renewed the feelings of anti-Semitism in the civilian population. . . . They are permitted to escape from situations in which other DP's are summarily handled. . . . This, in turn, has a definitely bad effect on the German population, who, when conscious of such situations, rather incline toward the belief that Hitler was not such a bad judge of the Jew, after all."[44] Striking in this assessment, of course, were the complete absence of any sympathy for the plight of the surviving Jews, as well as the slightest comprehension of recent history or just how the Jews had come to be DPs in the first place. Preoccupied with law and order and obsessed with rooting out the black market, local military authorities saw their task as ensuring security; if as a result elemental notions of justice suffered, so be it.

Tensions in Föhrenwald first erupted in late May 1946, an outburst sparked by American actions. On the evening of May 22 two drunken GIs entered a house in Wolfratshausen, planning to visit some German girls who lived on the third floor. A Jewish family resided on the second floor, and on the night in question they had visitors from the nearby DP camp. For whatever reason, as the drunken soldiers climbed the stairs, they stopped at the Jewish apartment. With pistols drawn, the GIs ordered the Jews to stand at attention while another Jew was told to play a harmonica. One of the soldiers drew a knife and demanded identification papers and money, striking one of the DPs in the face with a pistol butt when he refused to hand over his papers. The GI then repeatedly asked if they were all Jewish, and when one of the group replied affirmatively, the soldier muttered, "Son of a bitch Jew" and hit the man on the head with his gun. Some of the Jews managed to get out of the apartment and fled back to the DP camp, where they informed the DP police of what had happened. The wildest rumors now circulated rapidly through the camp. As hundreds of people sat in the camp theater watching a movie, for example, a man burst in shrieking, "Massacre! They're killing Jews in Wolfratshausen!" With that, hundreds of DPs streamed out of the camp, heading for Wolfratshausen, a few miles distant. Having been notified, UNRRA authorities hurriedly sought to prevent a disaster. Margaret Gerber, the assistant director, later recalled seeing

> a mob of DP's milling around and shouting angrily. We drove
> the jeep to the edge of the crowd and got out. . . . I realized

that the DP's were beating up on a German who was bleeding about the head and protesting loudly that he hadn't done anything. I fought my way through the crowd and tried to get them to leave the man alone. The German clung to me for dear life. . . . However, the crowd was violent and we were both thrown into the ditch. The German was torn away, beaten again, thrown to the ground and kicked. . . . His life was in jeopardy. . . . I succeeded in getting him piled into an UNRRA truck. I climbed in with him, and we drove off to the camp police station.

In the meantime, several hundred DPs had started north on the road to Wolfratshausen, determined to avenge what they believed to be a renewed murder of Jews by Germans.[45]

While Gerber was involved in saving a German civilian, Henry Cohen, the camp director, had gone to German police headquarters, where, with local and U.S. Army officials, he sought to coordinate a response. Army authorities agreed to allow Cohen the opportunity to regain control of the situation, at the same time establishing a roadblock roughly a mile north of the camp in case he failed. Fortunately for all concerned, Cohen and the DP police succeeded in containing the surge of people and persuading them to return to camp. Still, the army report on the incident, released in July, ironically the day before the larger riot, reflected the tensions, the underlying anti-Semitism, and the military preoccupation with order in an occupied land. To the army investigator, all was clear-cut: "On 22 May 1946 between the hours of 1930 and 2230 Jewish DP residents in the Föhrenwald assembly center created a disturbance in the vicinity of the camp that resulted in injury to three or more civilians and an attempt to detain an officer of the United States Army. An estimated 300 of the camp residents were involved in the disturbance. Although various rumors of shooting, kidnaping and otherwise maltreating Jews were current, evidence indicated that the activity of the DPs was probably the result of agitation by and on behalf of Mr. Cohen, UNRRA Camp Director." Apparently, Cohen had fallen afoul of army officials a few weeks earlier when, worried about the progressive demoralization of the DPs, he had dispatched telegrams, little realizing that they would likely be intercepted by military intelligence, to influential friends in the United States urging them to assert political pressure to rectify conditions at

Föhrenwald. Amazingly, the army report made no reference to the actions of the drunken American soldiers that had sparked the disturbance, preferring instead to blame the Jewish UNRRA director of a Jewish DP camp for deliberately inciting his charges to riot.[46]

Collective anger, frustrations, and misunderstandings thus marred relations between Jewish DPs, German civilians, and American military authorities even before the late July outburst, which once again was sparked by black market tensions. Responding to a rash of cattle thefts and suspecting black marketeers operating out of Föhrenwald, local German police, barred from entering a Jewish DP camp since the events in Stuttgart a few months earlier, set up a roadblock a few hundred yards from the entrance to the camp on the evening of July 24. At about 9:30 P.M., as several hundred camp inhabitants were taking their nightly stroll along the road in front of the camp, two German policeman on motorcycles ran down a truck with three Jews and a German driver that had failed to halt at the checkpoint. Allegedly seeing money changing hands, the policemen brusquely demanded that the Jews get out of the truck. They then ordered one back to the camp while questioning the other two. As the first man headed for the entrance, he heard a cry for help, but as he started back the elder of the two policemen fired a shot over his head. This, however, had the opposite effect of that desired, as large numbers of DPs began gathering around the truck. The Germans maintained that the Jews tried to disarm them, a charge hotly denied by the DPs. In any event, the older policeman completely lost his composure and fired four or five shots into the crowd. Isac Feldberg, one of the strollers, was shot in the back and killed, and another Jew was wounded. In the confusion, one German policemen jumped on the motorcycle and the other climbed into the truck and both sped from the scene. According to one report, fifty to a hundred Jews now came out of the camp, went into nearby Wolfratshausen, and engaged in brawls with local Germans, during which another six people were injured and eight Germans forced into the camp as hostages. The DP police eventually managed to calm the crowd and herd them back to Föhrenwald, although MPs and Constabulary troops threw a cordon around the camp as a precaution. Not until 1:00 A.M., though, were the eight Germans who had been forced into the camp escorted out.[47]

The next day, camp authorities obtained permission for a truck with a hearse and sixteen mourners to leave the camp at 5:00 P.M. for the Jewish cemetery in Gauting, ten miles away. At the last minute, someone supposedly got permission from the MPs, but apparently not from the Constabulary troops, for other DPs to line the road leading from the camp. As several hundred Jews began to emerge from the camp, the UNRRA director hurried out and, evidently fearing a recurrence of the melee of the night before, asked the troops to push the crowd back into the camp. The troops, alarmed by the large number of Jews approaching them, reacted more harshly than necessary by forming a cordon and roughly forcing the DPs back toward the camp. The Jews, confused by the actions of the GIs, quickly became angry and began shouting "American Gestapo" at the Constabulary troops. Whether unintentionally or as a result of overzealousness, and one would have to think the latter, some of the GIs wounded a number of Jews in the back and thighs with their bayonets. The incidents at Wolfratshausen, of course, were symptomatic of the whole series of disturbances throughout Bavaria in the summer of 1946 that heightened tensions, which persisted well into 1947, between Germans and GIs on one side and DPs on the other. Forced to live for an extended period in difficult conditions among the very people responsible for the murder of their families and destruction of their communities, many DPs not surprisingly became embittered by their unwelcome interlude in postwar Germany, while Germans remained resentful that the Jewish DPs were fed and cared for from the local German economy. As Zalman Grinberg, first president of the Central Committee of Liberated Jews in the American Occupation Zone, noted in October 1945, "Here [in Germany] is gathered the remnant of [Europe's] Jews and here is our waiting room. It is a bad waiting room but we hope that the day will come in which the Jews will be led to their place."[48]

NO MOURNING AND NO WEEPING: REVENGE!

Most Jewish DPs in these episodes acted impetuously, out of frustration and the immediate stress of events, flare-ups that continued until the DP camps themselves were finally closed. In May 1947, for example, riots again broke out at Landsberg DP camp, while in late July an angry crowd of Jews from the Bleidorn DP camp at Ansbach attacked American soldiers and kidnapped two before their fellow GIs rescued them. The abduction, the Jews claimed, amounted to "a retaliatory measure for an earlier alleged assault by American soldiers on two members of the camp's population." The Jews involved in these actions thus were not actively seeking revenge, but responded to what they perceived as immediate provocations. Amazingly, despite (or perhaps because of) the enormity of the crime committed against them, most Jewish DPs evinced little desire for retribution. Certainly, as a number pointed out, they felt a deep hate, but this did not necessarily translate into a wish for revenge. In part, many survivors saw a return to traditions of law, justice, and morality as imperative for the renewal of Jewish life. Some simply felt alienated from the past and present and focused all attention on the future. For still others, revenge was pointless. As one woman noted, revenge could not restore the blood of the lost Jews. "No," she concluded, "we want no revenge, only understanding." In addition, the sheer scale of the Nazi murder of Jews mitigated notions of revenge. Noted one DP, the Jews "cannot repay with the same currency. . . . Bloody revenge appears worthless to us when measured against the magnitude of our sacrifices." Commented another, when pondering the theme of an eye for an eye: "The enormity of the crime makes this impossible." For most survivors, then, it was vital to look to the future and to keep in mind the difference between justice and revenge.[49]

Some, however, gave vent to a primal emotion expressed powerfully by an anonymous poet in *Haaretz* in November 1942, "No mourning and no weeping: revenge!" To many survivors, it was vital that the murderers should know that "revenge will come, as is written: 'an eye for an eye, a tooth for a tooth.'" As Joseph Harmatz, one of the avengers, asserted, "We had to do something so that people would realize that atrocities would be punished." Leipke Distel agreed, insisting, "We wanted to prove to the world that we were not ready to accept silently all the murders and deaths." The head of the principal vengeance group, *Nakam* (Hebrew for revenge), Abba Kovner, perhaps best expressed the emotions felt by many young survivors at the time. A man with a charismatic personality, the leader of a band of Jewish partisans that fought the Nazis from the forests of Lithuania, a poet who radiated spiritual and moral power, Kovner admitted that at the end of the war the idea of revenge possessed him. Seeing the small group that had gathered around him as "messengers of fate," Kovner, in trying to delineate their mental state at that time, later explained, "The destruction was not around us. It was within us. . . . We did not imagine that we could return to life, or that we had the right to do so." To Kovner, true revenge had to be precisely proportional. From the beginning, therefore, he thought in terms of killing 6 million Germans: "The act should be shocking. The Germans should know that after Auschwitz there can be no return to normality." Less eloquently, but expressing well the visceral hatred they felt, another member of the group noted bitterly, "We're here for revenge. . . . Why should it just be us remembering Auschwitz? Let them remember the one city that we'll destroy."[50]

One such reckoning supposedly came in mid-1945, according to interviews with the alleged perpetrators conducted by BBC journalist Michael Elkins. While fishing, a group of boys from a *Hachsharot* camp near Ulm that trained young Jews in farming and commercial fishing practices discovered a cache of weapons hidden in a small stream that fed into the Danube River. After informing a local leader of the *Bricha,* the underground network that directed Jews to Palestine, one of the twelve waterproof chests was retrieved and opened. Inside, the DPs found automatic weapons and ammunition. After replacing the chest, the young men from the nearby *Hachsharot* camp formed teams in order to observe the cache surreptitiously. A few nights later the observers, sitting in trees and watching through binoculars, were startled by the appearance of a Werwolf company that had come to drill. The local Bricha commander now notified Kovner, whose vengeance squads operated out of Munich and Nuremberg. Kovner, Elkins alleged, quickly dispatched eleven men to the area. Not until after another two weeks of anxious waiting, however, did the Werwolf unit again assemble under cover of darkness in the woods near the cache. As the predominantly young Werewolves exulted in the hate-filled speeches of their leaders, eleven men armed with submachine guns and hand grenades suddenly emerged from the evening gloom. In a hail of bullets and shrapnel all 140 of the young fanatics fell dead, as did the deputy commander of the unit, Erwin Weinmann, once a member of the Security Police, now gunned down in his former SS uniform. But the story did not end here. An investigation into the killings supposedly conducted by German and American occupation authorities produced no evidence but, according to Elkins, led members of the vengeance squad to former SS-*Obersturmführer* (Lieutenant) Hubert Schwartz, late of Auschwitz, and Dr. Ernst Wetzel, a top Nazi official in the Race and Resettlement Office, both of whom disappeared shortly thereafter under mysterious circumstances.[51]

Unfortunately, no corroborating evidence has yet come to light to support Elkins's account, so except for his supposed interviews the dramatic incident in the woods outside Ulm remains as shadowy as the circumstances in which it allegedly occurred. There can be no doubt, however, that Kovner and the members of his group dreamed of just such retaliatory actions, albeit on a much grander scale. Charged with raw emotion in the days following the end of the war, and distraught at the massive scale of the Nazi crime against the Jews, Kovner's group originally intended to poison the water supply of a number of German cities, foremost among them Hamburg and Nuremberg. To that end, the largest of the vengeance squads made their way to Nuremberg, the very symbol of Nazi tyranny, which, as team leader Joseph Harmatz noted, "was precisely why we wanted to begin our revenge actions there." In the late summer of 1945, remembered Harmatz, not without some satisfaction, "The proud city of the Reichsparteitage [Nazi Party rallies] lay in ruins," reduced to a field of rubble. Using false papers that identified him as a former Polish forced laborer and DP by the name of Maim Mendele, Harmatz quickly secured a room in the neighboring city of Fürth, although not without being made rudely aware of lingering anti-Semitism. Noticing the odd name, Maim, his landlady in Fürth, known locally as the Jerusalem of Franconia for its formerly large Jewish population, remarked, "That sounds almost like the Jewish 'Chaim.' But fortunately almost none of the Jewish rabble has survived."[52]

Putting aside this crude reminder of recent events, Harmatz set about finding secure rooms for the remainder of his group, no easy task given the desperate shortage of housing caused by the vast destruction. Using alcohol, cigarettes, chocolate, and other goods obtained from American sources, however, Harmatz succeeded not only in finding lodgings, but also in placing a member of his group, a skilled engineer from Cracow who spoke good German named Willek Schwerzreich, inside the municipal water company. Within a relatively short period of time, moreover, Schwerzreich managed to ascertain how the water system operated, which lines ran toward American residential areas, the alternate supply systems, and at precisely what points to put poison into the system to kill the largest possible number of Germans. "Everything was prepared," Harmatz recalled, "we only needed the 'material.'" Ready to act, anxious to begin the desired revenge, Harmatz and his team now suffered a harsh blow—headquarters in Paris ordered them to freeze the project temporarily.[53]

Unbeknownst to Harmatz, Abba Kovner had met with disaster in trying to secure the necessary quantities of poison, the "material" that the Nuremberg group needed to set its revenge in motion. In order to gain support for the project, Kovner had traveled to Palestine in July 1945. There he met with leading officials of the Jewish Agency, the Jewish Brigade, and *Haganah*, the Jewish defense force, both to inform them of the plans for revenge and to gain their backing for this and future actions. Kovner soon discovered, however, that an enormous gulf existed between Jewish leaders in Palestine and the onetime partisans. The former had a completely different set of priorities, one centered on getting as many survivors as possible to Palestine and securing the creation of an independent Jewish state. Spectacular acts of vengeance might be emotionally satisfying in the short term, but almost certainly would hinder the larger goal of a Jewish homeland. In an August letter to his deputy in charge of the Paris headquarters, Pasha Reichman, Kovner acknowledged that Jewish officials in Palestine would never agree to the plan to poison drinking water. They might, however, support a Plan B, an action against some twelve thousand former SS officers and high-ranking Nazis interned in a former POW camp at Langwasser, a part of the city of Nuremberg located, ironically, adjacent to the facilities used for the Nazi Party rallies. Still, there remained the problem of acquiring material to poison the internees. Kovner later claimed to have overcome this difficulty through the intervention of Chaim Weizmann, leader of the Zionist Organization, the future first president of the state of Israel, and a chemist by training. In a private meeting, Kovner maintained that the seventy-one-year-old Weizmann listened sympathetically to his plan, agreed that revenge was legitimate, and remarked, "Were I younger and in your place, I might do the same thing." Weizmann then, according to Kovner, wrote the name of a chemist and a letter of introduction and indicated that the man would help in preparation of the necessary poison. In testimony recorded for Israeli archives, Kovner further asserted that it was Ernst David Bergman, later a leading nuclear scientist in Israel, who prepared the poison for him, which was packed for travel in two canisters. Weizmann also evidently put Kovner in touch with Hans Moller, the owner of a large textile concern, who allegedly furnished the money needed to execute Plan B.[54] Although Kovner's account cannot be confirmed by sources other than his oral testimony and that of some of his former associates, the fact remains that Kovner did acquire both poison and money in Palestine.

Thus, although the Jewish leadership in Palestine had uniformly rejected Kovner's plan for massive revenge, he nonetheless left in mid-December 1945 for the return trip to Europe with the means to carry out Plan B. Armed with false papers supplied by Haganah, traveling with one of its soldiers as an escort, and wearing the uniform of the Jewish Brigade, Kovner made his way to Alexandria, Egypt, where he boarded a British ship bound for Toulon, France. In his rucksack he carried, in addition to the usual items, such as cigarettes and notebooks, two canisters of poison and gold dust hidden in toothpaste tubes. On the fourth day of the voyage, as the ship entered the port of Toulon, Kovner heard his assumed name being called over the loudspeaker, with orders to report to the ship's captain. Startled, and assuming that someone had betrayed him, Kovner immediately took one of the canisters of poison and poured its contents into the sea. He was about to do the same with the second canister, but decided instead to give it to his escort. Informing him of the contents, Kovner told the soldier to deliver it to the Paris address he had written on a piece of paper. Kovner then went up on deck, reported to the captain, and was immediately arrested, even though the British authorities seemingly had no idea why. Although jailed in military prisons in Cairo and Jerusalem for four months, the British never asked Kovner about the poison or his revenge plans. Evidently tipped off by high-ranking officers in the Haganah who wanted to foil Kovner's revenge plans but not have him punished, the British had simply been informed in vague terms that he was a threat. Although the gold made it to Paris, his escort, fearful of being implicated, dumped the second canister of poison into the sea as well. At the same time Nachum Schadmi, head of the Haganah in Europe, dispatched a courier to Munich, Dov Shenkal, ostensibly to support Kovner's group but also to control it. To the Jewish leadership in Palestine, revenge remained problematical. Jewish concerns, they believed, should not be dominated by vengeance but by the creation of a Jewish state. To them, as the Israeli historian Benny Morris has noted, "foreign friends were more important than dead Germans."[55]

In the meantime, the avengers of Kovner's group continued to live in almost unendurable tension amid a German society they detested and plotted to destroy. "The Germans here were getting food rations," Harmatz recalled bitterly, "we had been dying of hunger under Nazi occupation. The Germans here were taking their children out in little prams, they had milk to feed them and still they complained that the level of fat in the milk was not high enough. They, on the other hand, grabbed our children and babies by the legs or by the hair and threw them against telephone poles and into the furnaces." Frustrated, at times near despair, Harmatz admitted that "many of us became nihilistic. Life was not important, neither your own nor anyone else's." Suffering from terrible migraines caused by the stress, he and the Nuremberg team nonetheless struggled on. At one point, in fact, the group considered a daring operation of their own. Since November 1945 the trial of the major Nazi war criminals had been taking place at the Palace of Justice in central Nuremberg. Closely following the events in the local newspaper, Harmatz and the others found the tedious day-to-day process of introducing evidence to prove guilt both incomprehensible and outrageous. "It made us sick to watch this," Harmatz recalled. "The facts were well known, our people had been murdered." To him and his men one thing was clear: the accused had earned a death sentence, which they meant to deliver. Armed with submachine guns and hand grenades, some of the group intended to storm the courtroom and "make an end to the great heroes."[56]

The plan unraveled, however, because of the extremely tight security maintained at the Palace of Justice. Not only did armed GIs guard the courtroom, but American tanks sealed off the area around the Justice building. Moreover, in response to rumors of possible Werwolf activities and the discovery in Fürth of a hidden cache of weapons and explosives, American authorities in February 1946 drastically tightened security at the trial. Unable to secure visitors' passes and unlikely to breach the security cordon, Harmatz and his men reluctantly dropped the idea of storming the war crimes trial. An interesting sidelight remains to this episode, however, although neither Harmatz nor anyone else connected with his group has ever claimed responsibility. In late December 1945 a band of men armed with submachine guns broke into the office of Julius Streicher's defense lawyer, forced the occupants into the cellar, and then ransacked the house. Although making off with some valuables, of more interest was the fact that they took the great majority of the files concerning Streicher's defense.[57]

In any case, in the late winter of 1946, the vengeance group now turned all their attention to Plan B. Harmatz relied on the help of Yitzak Ratner, a chemist from Vilna and close friend and partisan colleague of Abba Kovner, to supply the poison. Ratner had relocated in Paris and in October 1945 established a laboratory in the city's Nakam headquarters, where he began experimenting with different materials. By early 1946 he had established that bread brushed with arsenic would be most suitable for the attack on the SS internees at Langwasser. Tests conducted on cats proved conclusive: the substance was extremely deadly. At Langwasser itself, a camp used originally for Russian POWs and forced laborers in sight of the *Reichsparteigelände,* between twelve thousand and fifteen thousand internees, most former SS officers or prominent Nazis, were jammed into primitive barracks. "It was teeming with Field Marshals and Reich Ministers," wrote Ernst von Salomon, himself a prominent former Freikorps man and Nazi enthusiast, in his postwar autobiographical novel, *Der Fragebogen* (The Questionnaire). Ratner concluded that for such a large population at least twenty kilograms (forty-four pounds) of arsenic would be necessary.[58]

Serious planning for the operation began in January 1946. Harmatz selected a young woman named Dobka Debeltov, who had joined the group just a short time earlier, to find out which bakery prepared the bread for the camp. She soon discovered that the camp's bread was supplied by the Konsum-Genossenschaftsbäckerei, one of the few large Nuremberg bakeries that had survived the war relatively intact. The twenty-four-year-old Leipke (Arie) Distel, a native of Vilna, a member of the ghetto underground from 1941 to 1943, and a former saboteur, now assumed the key role in the drama. Posing as a Polish DP awaiting a visa to Canada, where he would work in an uncle's bakery, Distel gained an interview with the manager of the Konsum bakery and explained that he wanted to obtain whatever experience he could—even if he had to work without pay. Initially rebuffed, Distel soon returned loaded with supplies of cigarettes, alcohol, and chocolate, and secured work in the storeroom, an important and strategic position. Over the next few months, working a variety of duties, Distel carefully noted the system in the bakery, while other group members studied the routine for transportation and distribution of the bread in Stalag 13. Every evening the avengers met in their rooms in Fürth to discuss and refine their plan. Most crucially, they sought to determine who ate the bread, since large numbers of American guards were also present. The key breakthrough came when Harmatz managed to place two of his group inside the camp as administrative assistants. As a result, they learned that on Sundays the Germans ate the regular ration of black bread, while the GIs received a special order of white bread. That meant, therefore, that the plan would have to be carried out on a Saturday night.[59]

With everything ready, the group set the date of the operation for Saturday night, April 13, 1946. Originally, a similar attack on the same day was set for Dachau, the former concentration camp near Munich that housed some thirty thousand former SS members. On April 11, though, fearing that the Americans had uncovered information about the planned attack, Pasha Reichmann canceled the Dachau operation. In Nuremberg, however, the venture proceeded according to plan. A few days earlier, Dov Shenkal, strapping seven rubber hot water bottles around his body, delivered the arsenic to Harmatz, and then collapsed, exhausted from the weight of the material. Over the next few days, Distel sneaked the bottles into the bakery and concealed them in a cache under the wooden floorboards. A hiding place had also been prepared in case the avengers were discovered. After months in the bakery, having to listen to his fellow workers complain of the "lazy and parasitic" Jewish DPs in the area, wondering if those he worked with had participated in the mass murders of Jews, fearing the answer if he asked, having to walk by the empty, ghostly ruins of the stadium where the Nazis had held their rallies and pronounced the infamous racial laws, Distel waited impatiently for the crucial day to arrive. Exhausted emotionally from the strain of living among the enemy, he simply wanted to get out of Germany and on with his life.[60]

Under a brilliant, cloudless blue sky, great excitement prevailed on April 13 among both the bakery employees and the avengers. Since that Saturday was a holiday, the workers not only had a shortened day but there would be no second shift operation. Having already smuggled two accomplices in unnoticed that morning, when work let out for the day at noon Distel made his way toward a warehouse, where he planned to hide until everyone was gone. With horror, however, he saw his supervisor hurriedly approaching. Smiling broadly, the latter remarked, "It's good that you're still here. Do me a favor and lock the outside doors, I'm in a hurry. You can drop off the keys with the guard." Cursing silently, Distel took the keys, although this could disrupt the entire plan. Not turning the keys over to the watchman would be too dangerous, but after he did so, he would be locked out with his fellow conspirators inside. At a nearby park Distel conferred with Harmatz, who had also intended to sneak into the bakery that afternoon. They decided Distel would somehow have to slip back inside. Fortunately for Distel, the guard was neither especially diligent nor observant. When the guard went to a grocery around the corner to buy a couple bottles of beer, Distel managed to get back inside.[61]

Hiding in the storage area, Distel and the other two men waited until dark to begin their deadly work. After having retrieved the hot water bottles, they poured the arsenic mixture into a large metal bowl. Then, in assembly line fashion, one stirred the liquid continuously while Distel handed the loaves of bread to the third conspirator, who brushed the poison onto the bread. After two hours of furious work the men had painted some three thousand loaves. In their intense concentration, however, they failed to notice that outside a storm had come up. As the wind began howling the men suddenly heard a loud banging noise—a gust had torn a shutter loose, which now rattled loudly against the building. The three avengers scrambled madly, knowing that the watchman would soon come to investigate. Luckily for them, they had a contingency plan. Since bread was desperately scarce in Germany, the men made it look as if there had been an attempted robbery. Quickly, they tossed a few loaves into a bag and set it next to an open window. As one of the conspirators made his way out the window and down a drainpipe, the second hid in an empty drum, while Distel took the remaining arsenic and slipped it into the hiding place under the floorboards. As expected, the night watchman assumed he had interrupted an attempted robbery. Still, he called for a local policeman, who on arrival confirmed his assessment of an abortive break-in. When the Germans finally left, Distel and his accomplice emerged from hiding. As the stormy night gave way to the light gray of dawn, the two conspirators quickly climbed out a window, scampered across the roof, and scrambled down a drainpipe. With delivery trucks idling nearby, they scurried off into the street and, according to plan, made for the Czech border. Distel, in fact, took a taxi to the border, although not before assuring the startled driver that he had money to pay for the trip.[62]

Despite all their efforts, however, the attempt to kill large numbers of SS men proved no more successful than the thwarted plan to poison German water supplies. Although some claimed at the time that anywhere from seven hundred to a thousand died, the truth was more prosaic. Although Harmatz in his memoirs defiantly maintained, "we know that some died," official reports suggest that even though large numbers of men became sick, none died. On April 20 the *New York Times* reported that more than 1,900 German prisoners at Langwasser had been sickened by poisoned bread, while three days later they raised the total to over 2,200, among them were over two hundred seriously ill who had been sent to local hospitals. Similarly, on April 22 the *St. Louis Post-Dispatch* put the total poisoned at 2,283, while noting that a search was on for a "Polish DP." The Munich-based *Süddeutsche Zeitung* on April 24 quoted high-ranking American officials as saying that no prisoners had died and none were expected to, while the *Nürnberger Nachrichten* assured its readers that the civilian bread supply had not been affected by the incident. "Some were blinded for a time," remembered a former SS prisoner at the camp, Franz-Josef Scherzer, "but to my knowledge no one died. . . . Each of us received 300 grams of bread. . . . It tasted terrible. We noticed that right away. Then it was as if we had an attack of fever. We had diarrhea, some for eight or ten days, and everything swam before our eyes. At first we didn't know what was happening. The Americans didn't tell us anything, but they reacted immediately and sent the seriously ill to hospitals. . . . But if any had died I would have known about it." American and German investigators quickly discovered the hiding place under the floorboards, where they also found the remaining arsenic, rubber gloves covered with arsenic residue, and the brushes used to paint the bread. Although toxicological reports indicated sufficient levels of arsenic to be deadly, the investigators concluded that by brushing the arsenic mixture only on the underside of the loaves, and not on the entire loaf, the conspirators had unknowingly diluted the poison. Moreover, the arsenic courier, Dov Shenkal, later claimed that the Haganah leadership had also taken steps to assure that the poison would not be deadly.[63]

Abba Kovner and his followers had dreamed of a "shocking deed" to quench their desire for destruction, but ultimately they had to settle for a less satisfying action, the results of which remain unclear to this day. Far from the hoped for six million dead, or even tens of thousands, the avengers of Nakam had to seek solace in the grim conviction that American authorities had engaged in a self-serving coverup and that at least some SS men had been killed at Langwasser. Finally out of Germany after months of tense, conspiratorial activity, the avengers increasingly turned their attention to Palestine, some willingly, others reluctantly, still loathe to discard thoughts of revenge entirely. To Distel, in fact, it was not a question of vengeance, but of simple justice. "We acted morally," he claimed. "Jews had a right to revenge themselves on the Germans." But the time for large-scale actions had passed, the order of the day now being individual acts of retribution. In the end, as Shenkal admitted, "our revenge was tiny and almost unimportant in the shadow of the industrial mass murder" of the Nazis. As Tom Segev has noted, however understandable the visions of revenge of the Nakam group, they belonged to another world. A former Jewish Brigade soldier and member of the Israeli Knesset perhaps put it most fittingly when he remarked that the ultimate vengeance on Hitler was the sight of the Israeli flag flying in Bonn.[64]

AFTERWORD

Attempting to come to grips with the demon of National Socialism, Thomas Mann in his anguished novel from exile, *Doctor Faustus* (1947), reflected once again on a theme that haunted him his entire life, the dangerous German fascination with the darkly creative. Mann interspersed his tale of the composer Adrian Leverkühn with contemporary accounts of the spreading destruction of the great German cities, the physical representation of that magnificent German culture to which he clung and which the Nazis had reduced to rubble. Much of the power of his writing in this work sprang from a profound moral outrage, made more pronounced by his overweening sense of disappointment that Germany had allowed itself to be taken over by the enemies of reason and humanity. Mann felt, as his brother Heinrich recognized, betrayed by Germany. His Germany, the "good" European Germany of arts and letters, of culture, of music, of thought had gone fatally astray and had been replaced by a terrifying German Europe willed by the "bearers of a barbarism . . . wallowing in ruthlessness." "How strange that lament for culture," Mann noted with irony, "raised now against crimes that we called down upon ourselves."[1]

This indignant disgust that the German culture of which he was so proud had been hijacked by a gang of criminals persisted throughout the book. "Our propaganda," thundered his protagonist, "has a curious way of warning the foe against incursion on our soil, our sacred German soil, as if that would be some grisly atrocity. . . . Our sacred German soil! As if anything were still sacred about it, as if it had not long ago been desecrated again and again by the immensity of our rape of justice and did not lie naked, both morally and in fact, before the power of divine judgement. Let it come! There is nothing else to hope for, to want, to wish." A German patriot in the best sense of the word—"the ineluctable recognition of hopeless doom is not synonymous with a denial of love"—Mann fervently desired that this regime responsible for a national catastrophe of unprecedented proportions "must vanish, laden with the curse of having made itself intolerable to the world—no, of having made us, Germany, the Reich, let me go farther and say Germanness, everything German, intolerable to the world." In chronicling the "convulsions of our day . . . this earth-shaking, plummeting havoc" that enveloped Germany in the spring of 1945, Mann confronted a bitter truth, "Everything is pushing and plummeting toward the end, the world stands in the sign of the end, at least . . . for us Germans, whose thousand-year history—confounded, carried to absurdity, proven by its outcome to have gone fatally amiss . . . —is rushing into the void, into despair, into unparalleled bankruptcy, is descending into hell amid the dance of thundering flames."[2]

By the end of the novel, and the war, Mann, in wrestling with themes of apocalypse and retribution, worried for "our unhappy nation, sapped by misery and dread . . . , weary with old sadness, old horror," then agonized over

reports of a "freedom movement" christened with the name "Werwolf," a unit of berserk boys who, by hiding in the forests to burst forth at night, have already rendered the fatherland a meritorious service by . . . murdering many an intruder. . . . And so, to the bitter end, the crudest fairy tale, that grim substratum of saga deep in the soul of the nation, is still invoked—not without finding a familiar echo.

Meanwhile a transatlantic general has the inhabitants of Weimar file past the crematoria of their local concentration camp and declares (should one say, unjustly?) that they, citizens who went about their business in seeming honesty and tried to know nothing, though at times the wind blew the stench of burned human flesh up their noses—declares that they share in the guilt for these horrors that are now laid bare and to which he forces them to direct their eyes. . . . Our thick-walled torture chamber, into which Germany was transformed . . . , has been burst open, and our ignominy lies naked before the eyes of the world. . . . I repeat, our ignominy. For is it mere hypochondria to tell oneself that all that is German—even German intellect, German thought, the German word—shares in the disgrace of these revelations and is plunged into profoundest doubt? Is it morbid contrition to ask oneself the question: How can "Germany" . . . open its mouth again to speak of mankind's concerns?

One can call what came to light here the dark possibilities within human nature in general—but it was in fact tens of thousands, hundreds of thousands of Germans who committed the acts before which humanity shudders, and whatever lived as German stands now as an abomination and the epitome of evil. What will it be like to belong to a nation whose history bore this gruesome fiasco within it, a nation that has driven itself mad, gone psychologically bankrupt, that admittedly despairs of governing itself and thinks it best that it become a colony of foreign powers . . . because the dreadfully swollen hatred all around it will not permit it to step outside its borders—a nation that cannot show its face?

As Mann understood, and many other Germans have since come to realize, "this defeated nation now stands wild-eyed before the abyss" because Hitler not only brought this devastation and shame on them, but actually willed it, preferring German immolation in a thunderous Götterdämmerung to a meek surrender that would have spared the last, unnecessary destruction.[3]

The events of April and May 1945, and those that followed in postwar Germany, were to a large extent determined by the memories on both sides of an earlier date, November 1918. Adolf Hitler had long vowed that another "November 1918," by which he meant the loss of a war because of internal betrayal and collapse of civilian morale, would never be repeated. Upon coming to power in January 1933, he had set about constructing a society, the much touted Volksgemeinschaft, that would produce the national unity and cohesive sense of purpose necessary to wage a war for *Lebensraum* and to construct the racial "New Order" in Europe. For their part the western Allies, and in particular American leaders, were convinced that in order to prevent the emergence of another "stab in the back" myth the German people would need a conclusive demonstration of their absolute defeat. The complete destruction and occupation of Germany followed as a logical and inevitable consequence of these parallel determinations to fight a total war fully to the end.

Although it has become fashionable in some circles in present-day Germany to refer to the Allied "liberation" of the German people from the Nazi tyranny—before his death, Heinrich Böll had predicted that one would be able to tell everything about another German just by whether they referred to April 1945 as the defeat or the liberation—the Americans did not come as liberators, nor did the bulk of the German people regard them as such. From the start, the American intention was to conquer and defeat, then occupy Germany. By the same token, despite a general war weariness and desire to end the war, the majority of Germans nonetheless continued to follow the Nazi regime's orders and to do their duty. Whether from ideological fanaticism, belief in new "wonder weapons," faith in Hitler, desire for benefits provided by Nazi policies, or a general attitude of "muddling through," the dominant theme of these last weeks of the war was one of steadfast fulfillment of duty. In addition, otherwise positive notions such as loyalty, courage, discipline, patriotism, and camaraderie also contributed to this "hold-out effect." The result of this perseverance, ironically, was the creation of sufficient order within the larger chaos to permit the Nazi hierarchy to continue to direct and control events within Germany.

This process of holding on, however, was more nuanced and differentiated than mere fanatical Nibelungentreue. Bitter resistance did not suddenly give way to complete collapse; rather, energetic efforts at defense coexisted with attempts at peaceful surrender, while fierce fighting gradually gave way to ever more isolated instances of opposition by smaller bands of soldiers. The complicated and often hostile relations between army, party, SS, and civilians further muddled and distorted the situation. As a result, the conquest and defeat of Germany, as well as the occupation that evolved into a "liberation," unfolded in a gradual process over a number of months. In the first phase, roughly from the abortive attempt on Hitler's life in July 1944 through the remainder of the year, the Nazi regime made energetic and surprisingly successful efforts to mobilize the last resources of the German people and economy. With the failure of the V-weapons, as well as the inability of the counteroffensives in the Ardennes and Alsace to blunt the western Allied onslaught and turn the tide, even the most fanatic Nazi loyalist had to recognize the grim reality.

As a result, in the second stage, from roughly mid-January through April 1945, Hitler sought to stem the accelerating disintegration of his regime through ever-harsher terror measures directed at his own people and army. Reduced now to the desperate hope of a political miracle that would split the enemy coalition, the Nazi hierarchy nonetheless, through their own renewed fanaticism, injected a manic energy into the crumbling system that sustained it over the final months of the war. Vital to this continued resistance were the terrorist actions and threats of actions of the SS and the Gestapo. The situation in Franconia contradicts, to a certain extent, the emerging research in Germany that has demonstrated greater Wehrmacht complicity than previously supposed in atrocities against civilians on the eastern front. Most of the terror in Franconia emanated from SS, Gestapo, and Nazi Party authorities, which all displayed a greater disposition to perpetrate atrocities against their own citizens than did the Wehrmacht. Moreover, this willingness to use violence against German soldiers and civilians contributed both to the often fierce resistance and to the general confusion of war in Franconia. Although largely thrown into battle as a desperate attempt to stem the American advance, the ad hoc battle groups of SS and Hitler Youth units, sprinkled with contingents of officer cadets, often mounted an astonishingly effective defense. These men had been more thoroughly socialized and indoctrinated into the Nazi system, so they displayed both higher morale and a more determined commitment to Nazi ideology than did other soldiers. Perhaps, as well, they were more eager to prove themselves in battle.

This was a difficult and ambiguous time for ordinary Germans, most of whom, as German patriots, hoped for the best but in their own rational self-interest also sought to save what they could from the creeping destruction all around them. As the front drew ever nearer, the increasing lack of any clear line of authority, accompanied by the breakdown of law, allowed for some personal initiative and autonomy. However, civil courage and attempts at self-determination often came with a high price, as the path from war to peace was strewn with potentially fatal obstacles from all sides. Not only did Germans have to contend with the indeterminate actions of their own authorities, but they also faced the often unpredictable conduct of the enemy. On a number of occasions documented in this study, surrendering German soldiers fell victim to the rage of GIs who, angry and resentful at the nonsensical resistance, lashed out by shooting those they held responsible for endangering their lives at the end of a soon-to-be-over war.

A recurring phenomenon of note in Franconia was the large-scale involvement of women in pressuring local authorities to surrender without a fight, a circumstance that likely had much to do with the specific nature of women's experience and perception of war. By the end of the war, after all, German women had also suffered the trauma of war, from the shattering experience of constant aerial bombardment of German industrial cities to the harrowing flight from the invading enemy armies. In addition, though, women suffered the added strain of struggling to keep what was left of their homes and families together, as well as from the pervasive fear of rape and violence by the occupying enemy soldiers. Not surprisingly, then, many women evidenced a compelling desire to end the war quickly and thus to seize as much control over their fate as possible.

The final phase, the evolution from occupation to liberation, began in the final days and weeks of the war and extended over the first two years of the postwar period. Important in this process was not so much the directives issued by American occupation authorities as the conduct, attitude, and relations between GIs, Germans, and the large number of displaced persons in the American zone of occupation. The visual contrast between the dispirited, ragged bands of retreating German soldiers and the material might of the American conquerors contributed to a deglorification of the German military and growing enmity toward the regime that had misused and destroyed the fruit of German youth. Just as significant, however, were the nonmaterial attributes of the average GI, who displayed a rapidly changing attitude toward Germans. Initially rather indifferent, the experience of liberating labor and concentration camps produced a smoldering hatred for Germans among many American soldiers. In addition, the anxieties for their own lives raised by the unpredictable nature of German resistance led to sporadic atrocities against German soldiers and civilians.

Very quickly, however, this mood gave way to a generally benign view of German civilians. After the initial fears of German resistance and guerrilla warfare had waned, and as German criticism of fraternization ebbed, personal contact and observation between GIs and Germans, which contradicted the mutually unflattering propaganda, as well as growing problems with the large DP population in the American zone, led Americans and Germans to move closer to one another. Although fraterniza-tion produced immediate tensions, the ease with which some young women embraced GIs seeming to mock the sacrifices of German sol-diers, these strains tended to evaporate rather quickly and never pro-duced any insurmountable barriers to good relations. Moreover, in their attitude toward army life, which was largely nonchalant, and in their be-havior toward the occupied enemy, which was generally fair and benevo-lent, the ordinary GI displayed a democratic attitude in action that did more to promote re-education among Germans than any initiative from above ever accomplished.

Given the enormity of what had been done to them, the end of the war brought surprisingly few attempts at large-scale revenge against the Germans by the former forced laborers and Jewish survivors of the Ho-locaust, and the few big efforts at retribution that were made failed. Al-though the numerous small-scale acts of retaliation and the daily tensions of life in the DP camps led to an unfortunate emotional distancing be-tween GIs and DPs, this had relatively few negative long-term conse-quences. The end of the war, for victors and vanquished, victims and perpetrators, displaced persons and Germans, signaled the close of an era. Most survivors wanted to get on with the task of building the future, which represented a "liberation" in the most fundamental sense, one from the self-defeating and destructive hatreds of the past. Hitler thus suffered a double defeat. In smashing his Third Reich, the Allies not only defeated him physically, but those who survived, both German and non-German, in their determination to build anew, thoroughly repudiated his basic aims. Bent but not broken by the horrors of the epoch through which they had lived, neither Germans nor the millions of displaced persons within Germany's borders descended into the final hopelessness that Thomas Mann had feared, for in the midst of death, life continued.

NOTES

PREFACE

1. Hans Mommsen, "The Dissolution of the Third Reich: Crisis Management and Collapse, 1943–1945," *Bulletin of the German Historical Institute* 27 (fall 2000): pp. 9–23; See also: Doris Bergen, "Death Throes and Killing Frenzies: A Response to Hans Mommsen's 'The Dissolution of the Third Reich: Crisis Management and Collapse, 1943–1945,'" *Bulletin of the German Historical Institute* 27 (fall 2000): pp. 25–37.

2. Mommsen, "Dissolution of the Third Reich," pp. 17–19.

3. Curt Riess, "Will Goebbels Win His Goetterdaemmerung?" *New York Times Magazine*, February 25, 1945, pp. 35–36; Mommsen, "Dissolution of the Third Reich," pp. 17–19.

4. Stephen Kellert, *In the Wake of Chaos: Unpredictable Order in Synamical Systems* (Chicago: Univ. of Chicago Press, 1993), p. 3; Ilya Prigogine and Isabele Stengers, *Order Out of Chaos: Man's New Dialogue with Nature* (New York: Bantam Books, 1984), passim; Mitchell Waldrop, *Complexity: The Emerging Science at the Edge of Order and Chaos* (New York: Simon and Schuster, 1992), passim; A. B. Cambel, *Applied Chaos Theory: A Paradigm for Complexity* (San Diego: Academic Press, 1993), pp. 3–4, 15; Friedrich Cramer, *Chaos and Order: The Complex Structure of Living Systems,* trans. David I. Loewus (New York: VCH Publishers, 1993), pp. 6–7; Judy Petree, "History of Chaos Theory," http://www.wfu.edu/~petrejh4/HISTORYchaos.htm. Accessed and material gathered on November 2, 2001. "History of Chaos Theory," "Order and Sustainability in Chaos," "Deep Chaos," and "Complexity: Self-Organization in Chaos" all in author's possession.

5. Kellert, *In the Wake of Chaos,* pp. 3–8; Prigogine and Stengers, *Order Out of Chaos,* pp. xxvii, 189; Cambel, *Applied Chaos Theory,* pp. 3–4, 15; Uri Merry, *Coping with Uncertainty: Insights from the New Sciences of Chaos, Self-Organization and Complexity* (Westport, Conn.: Praeger Publishers, 1995), p. 65; Ilya Prigogine and

Gregoire Nicolis, *Exploring Complexity: An Introduction* (New York: W.H. Freeman, 1998), p. 218; Judy Petree, "Order and Instability in Chaos," http://www.wfu.edu/~petrejh4/Instability.htm; Judy Petree, "Complexity: Self-Organization in Chaos," http://www.wfu.edu/~petrejh4/selforg.htm. Accessed November 2, 2001.

6. Herfried Münkler, *Machtzerfall: Die letzten Tage des Dritten Reiches dargestellt am Beispiel der hessischen Kreisstadt Friedberg* (Berlin: Siedler Verlag, 1985), p. 7.

7. Ibid.

8. Ibid., pp. 8–10; Karl Kunze, *Kriegsende in Franken und der Kampf um Nürnberg im April 1945* (Nuremberg: Selbstverlag des Vereins für Geschichte der Stadt Nürnbergs, 1995), p. 1.

9. Elke Fröhlich, "Ein junger Märtyer," in Martin Broszat and Elke Fröhlich, ed., *Bayern in der NS-Zeit*, vol. 6, *Die Herausforderung des Einzelnen. Geschichten über Widerstand und Verfolgung* (Munich: R. Oldenbourg Verlag, 1983), p. 232.

10. Kunze, *Kriegsende in Franken*, p. 3.

1. WAITING FOR THE END

1. George Axelsson, "German Turmoil Is Reflected in Many Rumors," *New York Times Magazine*, September 10, 1944, p. 3; George Axelsson, "The Nazis Still Hope for a Miracle," *New York Times Magazine*, November 12, 1944, pp. 8, 44; Harry Vosser, "Hitler's Hideaway," *New York Times Magazine*, November 12, 1944, p. 36.

2. Marvin L. Meek, "Ultra and the Myth of the German 'National Redoubt,'" (M.A. thesis, U.S. Army Command and General Staff College, 1999), ch. 3; Stephen Ambrose, *The Supreme Commander* (New York: Doubleday, 1970), p. 649.

3. Meek, "Ultra," ch. 1, 3; *Völkischer Beobachter*, February 3, 1945, February 13, 1945, March 13, 1945, April 3, 1945, April 28, 1945; Rodney Minott, *The Fortress That Never Was: The Myth of Hitler's Bavarian Stronghold* (New York: Holt, Rinehart, and Winston, 1964), pp. 12, 38, 48–55, 72, 74, 141–45; Dwight D. Eisenhower, *Crusade in Europe* (New York: Doubleday, 1948), p. 397; Stephen Ambrose, *Eisenhower and Berlin, 1945* (New York: Norton, 1967), pp. 73–76; Charles B. MacDonald, *The Last Offensive* (Washington, D.C.: Office of the Chief of Military History, U.S. Army, 1973), p. 407; Winston Churchill, *The Second World War*, vol. 6, *Triumph and Tragedy* (Boston: Houghton Mifflin, 1953), pp. 452, 457; Kenneth Strong, *Intelligence at the Top: The Recollections of an Intelligence Officer* (London: Cassell, 1968), pp. 187–88; F. Harry Hinsley, *British Intelligence in the Second World War* (New York: Cambridge Univ. Press, 1988), pp. 713–16.

4. Minott, *Fortress That Never Was*, pp. 10–14; Generalmajor August Marcinkiewicz, "Report on the Alpenfestung," Foreign Military Study B-187, pp. 1–5, U.S. National Archives (NA), Record Group (RG) 319; General der Pionier Alfred Jacob, "Report Concerning the German Alpine Redoubt," Foreign Military Study B-

188, pp. 1–2, NA, RG 319; General der Gebirgstruppen Georg Ritter von Hengl, "Report on the Alpine Fortress," Foreign Military Study B-459, pp. 4–6, NA, RG 319.

5. Janusz Piekalkiewicz, *Spione, Agenten, Soldaten: Geheime Kommandos im Zweiten Weltkrieg* (Munich: Herbig, 1969), p. 509; Karl Stuhlpfarrer, *Die Operationszonen "Alpenvorland" und "Adriatisches Küstenland" 1943–1945*, Publikationen des österreichischen Instituts für Zeitgeschichte und des Instituts für Zeitgeschichte der Universität Wien, vol. 7 (Vienna: Hollinek, 1969), p. 160; Franz W. Seidler, *Phantom Alpenfestung? Die geheimen Baupläne der Organisation Todt* (Berchtesgaden: Verlag Plenk, 2000), pp. 9–10; Allen Dulles, Document 4-11, Radiotelephone Transmission No. 173, July 10, 1944 (extract), and Document 4-60, Telegram 4471-73, August 12, 1944, in Neal H. Petersen, ed., *From Hitler's Doorstep: The Wartime Intelligence Reports of Allen Dulles, 1942–1945* (University Park: Pennsylvania State Univ. Press, 1996), pp. 327–29, 366; Franz Hofer, "The Alpine Fortification and Defense Line: A Report on German and U.S. Views of the 'Alpine Redoubt' in 1944, Annex #1," Foreign Military Study B-457, pp. 1–4, NA, RG 319; Minott, *Fortress That Never Was*, pp. 14–19; Office of Strategic Services, Research and Analysis Branch, Report No. 232, *South Germany: An Analysis of the Political and Social Organization, the Communications, Economic Controls, Agriculture and Food Supply, Mineral Resources, Manufacturing and Transportation Facilities of South Germany* (Washington, D.C.: GPO, 1944).

6. Minott, *Fortress That Never Was*, pp. 16–20; Allen Dulles, Document 5-10, Radiotelephone Transmission No. 267, January 18, 1945, Document 5-15, Radiotelephone Transmission No. 270, January 22, 1945, and Document 5-107, Telegram 9099, April 21, 1945, in Petersen, *From Hitler's Doorstep*, pp. 429–30, 433, 506–8; Seidler, *Phantom Alpenfestung*, pp. 27–28; Ambrose, *Supreme Commander*, p. 649; Stuhlpfarrer, *Operationszonen*, pp. 159–62; Heinz Weibel-Altmeyer, *Alpenfestung: Ein Dokumentarbericht* (Vienna: Cura Verlag, 1966), pp. 16–17; Hofer, "Alpine Fortification, Annex #3," pp. 1–8; Franz Hofer, "The National Redoubt," Foreign Military Study B-458, pp. 9–12, NA, RG 319.

7. Hofer, "Alpine Fortification, Annex #3," pp. 1–8; Seidler, *Phantom Alpenfestung*, pp. 28–29.

8. Seidler, *Phantom Alpenfestung*, pp. 28–29; Minott, *Fortress That Never Was*, pp. 21–27; Walter Hagen, *Unternehmen Bernhard. Ein historischer Tatsachenbericht über die größte Geldfälschungsaktion aller Zeiten* (Wels: Verlag Welsermühl, 1955), pp. 231–32; Wilhelm Hoettl, *Hitler's Paper Weapon* (London: Rupert Hart-Davis, 1955), pp. 148–49; Reuben E. Jenkins, "The Battle of the German National Redoubt—Planning Phase," *Military Review* 26, no. 9 (December 1946): p. 6; Lyman B. Kirkpatrick Jr., *Captains without Eyes* (Boulder, Colo.: Westview Press, 1987), pp. 148–49; Petersen, *From Hitler's Doorstep*, pp. 14–15.

9. Erwin Lessner, "Hitler's Final V Weapon," *Collier's*, January 27, 1945, pp. 14, 47–48.

10. "Festung Berchtesgaden?" *Weltwoche,* February 2, 1945; Seidler, *Phantom Alpenfestung,* pp. 11–12.

11. Victor Schiff, "Last Fortress of the Nazis," *New York Times Magazine,* February 11, 1945, pp. 9, 46–47; Raymond Daniell, "Nazis Fight for Time and Political Miracle," *New York Times,* February 11, 1945.

12. "Nazis See Project for Mass Murder," *New York Times,* February 14, 1945; Curt Riess, "Will Goebbels Win His Goetterdaemmerung?" *New York Times Magazine,* February 25, 1945, pp. 8, 35–36; "Pravda Says Nazis Dig In for New War," *New York Times,* February 27, 1945.

13. Allen Dulles, Document 5-15, Radiotelephone Transmission No. 270, January 22, 1945, and Document 5-33, Radiotelephone Transmission No. 276, February 13, 1945, in Petersen, *From Hitler's Doorstep,* pp. 433, 447–49.

14. Minott, *Fortress That Never Was,* p. 39; Cornelius Ryan, *The Last Battle* (New York: Pocket Books, 1966), pp. 208–9; Jenkins, "Battle of the German National Redoubt—Planning Phase," pp. 3–8; Kirkpatrick, *Captains without Eyes,* pp. 252, 256–59; Donald E. Shepardson, "The Fall of Berlin and the Rise of a Myth," *Journal of Military History* 62, no. 1 (January 1998): pp. 135–53; Office of Strategic Services, NA, RG 226, L 50257, 122509, XL 8027, quoted in Seidler, *Phantom Alpenfestung,* p. 16; Allen Dulles, Document 5-67, Radiotelephone Transmission No. 288, March 16, 1945, in Petersen, *From Hitler's Doorstep,* pp. 475–77.

15. Office of Strategic Services, NA, RG 226, XL 8027, L 45276, 124057, quoted in Seidler, *Phantom Alpenfestung,* pp. 16–18.

16. Report of military attaches quoted in Wilhelm von Schramm, *Geheimdienst im Zweiten Weltkrieg. Organisationen, Methoden, Erfolge* (Munich: Langen, 1979), p. 359; Seidler, *Phantom Alpenfestung,* pp. 18–19.

17. Ambrose, *Eisenhower and Berlin,* pp. 74–75; Allen Dulles, Document 5-67, Radiotelephone Transmission No. 288, March 16, 1945, and Document 5-76, Radiotelephone Transmission No. 290, March 27, 1945, in Petersen, *From Hitler's Doorstep,* pp. 475–77, 484–85; Strong, *Intelligence at the Top,* pp. 187–88; Allen Dulles, Document 5-49, Radiotelephone Transmission No. 283, March 3, 1945, and Document 5-76, Radiotelephone Transmission No. 290, March 27, 1945, in Petersen, *From Hitler's Doorstep,* pp. 461–62, 484–85.

18. SHAEF, "Weekly Intelligence Summary No. 51 for the Week Ending 11 March 1945," quoted in Meek, "Ultra," ch. 3.

19. General Dwight D. Eisenhower, *Report by the Supreme Commander to the Combined Chiefs of Staff on the Operations in Europe of the Allied Expeditionary Force 6 June 1944 to 8 May 1945* (London: His Majesty's Stationery Office, 1946), pp. 135–38; Ambrose, *Eisenhower and Berlin,* pp. 75–76; Meek, "Ultra," ch. 4; ULTRA message BT 5959, DTG (Date/Time Group) 282110Z February 1945 (28 February 1945, 2110 hours), BT 6180, DTG 031833Z March 1945, BT 7796, DTG 201817Z March 1945, BT 8465, DTG 262124Z March 1945, BT 8569, DTG 271531Z March 1945, BT

9458, DTG 042221Z April 1945, in British Public Records Office, *ULTRA Documents* (New York: Clearwater Publishing Company, 1978); Hinsley, *British Intelligence*, pp. 713–16; Seidler, *Phantom Alpenfestung*, pp. 18–19; Churchill, *Triumph and Tragedy*, p. 457; Ralph Bennett, *Ultra in the West* (New York: Charles Scribner's Sons, 1979), p. 260.

20. Ryan, *The Last Battle*, pp. 207–8.

21. "Weekly Intelligence Summary for Psychological Warfare No. 22 for the Week Ending 24 February 1945," SHAEF Psychological Warfare Division, Executive Section, NA, RG 331, Decimal File 1944–1945, Entry 87; "The Inner Zone and the Redoubt," 10 March 1945, SHAEF, Joint Intelligence Committee, NA, RG 260, AGTS 14-3; Klaus-Dietmar Henke, *Die amerikanische Besetzung Deutschlands* (Munich: R. Oldenbourg Verlag, 1995), pp. 939–40; 12th Army Group, "Weekly Intelligence Summary No. 35 for the Week Ending 11 April 1945," and SHAEF, Joint Intelligence Committee, "Disposition of German Forces after the Junction of the Allied and Russian Armies," April 20, 1945, quoted in Jeff Korte, "Eisenhower, Berlin, and the National Redoubt," *Gateway: An Academic Journal on the Web*, issue no. 6, http://grad.usask.ca/gateway, p. 14; Allen Dulles, Document 5-87, Telegram 8349, April 6, 1945, and Document 5-89, Telegram 8759 to Paris, April 7, 1945, in Petersen, *From Hitler's Doorstep*, pp. 492–95. Most of the not inconsiderable road and rail traffic to the south consisted, in fact, of Nazi ministries or looted art treasures being relocated.

22. Headquarters, 12th Army Group, "Reorientation of Strategy, Appendix A: G-2 Report on German Plans for Continued Resistance, The National Redoubt," March 21, 1945, quoted in Minott, *Fortress That Never Was*, pp. 50–54; Ryan, *The Last Battle*, p. 209.

23. Seventh U.S. Army, *The Seventh United States Army in France and Germany, 1944–1945* (Heidelberg: Aloys Gräf, 1946), 3:pp. 761–62; Minott, *Fortress That Never Was*, pp. 54–55; Ryan, *The Last Battle*, pp. 209–10; Seidler, *Phantom Alpenfestung*, pp. 18–19.

24. Seidler, *Phantom Alpenfestung*, pp. 19–22; BT 8059, DTG 230638Z March 1945, BT 8308, DTG 251937Z March 1945, BT 8465, DTG 262124Z March 1945, BT 8569, Part 3, DTG 271531Z March 1945, BT 8569, Part 2, DTG 271531Z March 1945, BT 8788, DTG 291530Z March 1945, in *ULTRA Documents*.

25. Hinsley, *British Intelligence*, pp. 716–17; Meek, "Ultra," ch. 4; Seidler, *Phantom Alpenfestung*, p. 25; Schramm, *Geheimdienst im Zweiten Weltkrieg*, p. 367; Allen Dulles, Document 5-104, Radiotelephone Transmission No. 293, April 18, 1945, Document 5-107, Telegram 9099, April 21, 1945, and Document 5-114, Telegram 10137 to Paris, April 25, 1945, in Petersen, *From Hitler's Doorstep*, pp. 504–8, 513; Minott, *Fortress That Never Was*, pp. 79–80; Ryan, *The Last Battle*, pp. 210–11.

26. Jenkins, "Battle of the German National Redoubt—Planning Phase," pp. 6–7; Seidler, *Phantom Alpenfestung*, p. 24; Minott, *Fortress That Never Was*, pp. 106–7; Harry C. Butcher, *My Three Years with Eisenhower: The Personal Diary of Captain*

Harry C. Butcher, U.S.N.R., Naval Aide to General Eisenhower, 1942–1945 (New York: Simon and Schuster, 1946), pp. 809–15; Omar N. Bradley, *A Soldier's Story* (New York: Holt, Rinehart, and Winston, 1951), pp. 536–37; Ryan, *The Last Battle,* pp. 210–13; Eisenhower to Military Mission to Moscow, March 28, 1945, Eisenhower to Bernard Law Montgomery, March 28, 1945, Eisenhower to George Catlett Marshall, March 28, 1945, in Alfred D. Chandler Jr., ed., *The Papers of Dwight David Eisenhower. The War Years: IV* (Baltimore: Johns Hopkins Univ. Press, 1970), pp. 2551–53.

27. Churchill, *Triumph and Tragedy,* pp. 458–70; Ryan, *The Last Battle,* pp. 226–30; Seidler, *Phantom Alpenfestung,* p. 25; Henke, *amerikanische Besetzung,* pp. 942–43; Stephen Ambrose, *Eisenhower,* vol. 1, *Soldier, General of the Army, President-Elect, 1890–1954* (New York: Simon and Schuster, 1983), pp. 391–97; Carlo D'Este, *Eisenhower: A Soldier's Life* (New York: Henry Holt, 2002), pp. 696–98; Eisenhower to George Catlett Marshall, Cable FWD 18345, March 30, 1945, Eisenhower to Winston Spencer Churchill, Cable FWD 18334, March 30, 1945, Eisenhower to Bernard Law Montgomery, Cable FWD 18389, March 31, 1945, Eisenhower to Combined Chiefs of Staff, Cable FWD 18403, March 31, 1945, in Chandler, *Papers of Dwight David Eisenhower,* 4:pp. 2560–63, 2567–71.

28. Ryan, *The Last Battle,* pp. 234–35; Eisenhower to Montgomery, Cable FWD 18389, March 31, 1945, in Chandler, *Papers of Dwight David Eisenhower,* 4:p. 2568.

29. Eisenhower to Marshall, Cable FWD 18697, April 7, 1945, Eisenhower to Marshall, Cable FWD 18710, April 7, 1945, Eisenhower to Combined Chiefs of Staff, Cable FWD 19189, April 14, 1945, in Chandler, *Papers of Dwight David Eisenhower,* 4:pp. 2589, 2592, 2604–5.

30. Eisenhower to Combined Chiefs of Staff, Cable FWD 19190, April 14, 1945, in Chandler, *Papers of Dwight David Eisenhower,* 4:p. 2609; Eisenhower to Marshall, April 14, 1945, quoted in Ryan, *The Last Battle,* p. 314; Drew Middleton, "Nazi Die-Hards Man Their 'National Redoubt,'" *New York Times,* April 8, 1945; Hanson W. Baldwin, "'Battle of Pockets' Ahead," *New York Times,* April 19, 1945; Curt Reiss, "Planned Chaos—The Nazi Goal," *New York Times Magazine,* April 22, 1945, p. 10; Gene Currivan, "3rd Set to Attack Redoubt Borders," *New York Times,* April 25, 1945, pp. 1, 4; Drew Middleton, "3rd Army 15 Miles from Austrian Line," *New York Times,* April 26, 1945, pp. 1, 10.

31. Reuben E. Jenkins, "The Battle of the German National Redoubt—Operational Phase," *Military Review* 26, no. 10 (January 1947): pp. 24–26; Seventh U.S. Army, *The Seventh United States Army,* 3:pp. 856–61; Minott, *Fortress That Never Was,* pp. 125–27.

32. Ambrose, *Eisenhower and Berlin,* pp. 69–71; Eisenhower to Combined Chiefs of Staff, Cable FWD 19189, April 14, 1945, in Chandler, *Papers of Dwight David Eisenhower,* 4:p. 2605; Minott, *Fortress That Never Was,* pp. 65–74.

33. Henke, *amerikanische Besetzung,* pp. 777–83; Karl Kunze, *Kriegsende in Franken und der Kampf um Nürnberg im April 1945* (Nuremberg: Selbstverlag des

Vereins für Geschichte der Stadt Nürnberg, 1995), pp. 140, 192, 425; Erich Spiwoks and Hans Stöber, *Endkampf zwischen Mosel und Inn: XIII. SS-Armeekorps* (Osnabrück: Munin Verlag, 1976), pp. 180–81; Lieutenant Colonel Cord von Hobe, "Einsatz der Panzer-Kampfgruppe XIII vom 06.04–05.05 1945," Foreign Military Study B-772, quoted in Spiwoks and Stöber, *Endkampf,* pp. 184–85; SS-Obersturmbannführer Ekkehard Albert (Chief of the General Staff of XIII. SS-Army Corps), "Einsatz des XIII. SS-A.K. zwischen Rhein und Alpen vom 26.03.–06.05.1945," Foreign Military Study B-737, quoted in Spiwoks and Stöber, *Endkampf,* pp. 212–17; Generalmajor (Brigadier General) Erich Schmidt (Commander, 352. Volksgrenadier Division), "Mitteldeutschland," Foreign Military Study B-604, quoted in Spiwoks and Stöber, *Endkampf,* pp. 234–36; "Beurteilung der Lage," 30.3.45 and 1.4.45, in M. Wind and H. Günther, ed., *Kriegstagebuch. 17. SS-Panzer-Grenadier-Division "Götz von Berlichingen": 30. Oktober 1943 bis 6. Mai 1945* (Munich: Schild Verlag, 1993), n.p.; *Völkischer Beobachter,* February 3, 1945.

34. Rainer Hambrecht, *Der Aufstieg der NSDAP in Mittel- und Oberfranken 1925–1933* (Nuremberg: Schriftenreihe des Stadtarchivs Nürnberg, 1976), pp. 1–4; Josef Dünninger, "Franken und Bayern. Die Begegnung zweier Stämme im neuen Staatsverband," *Schönere Heimat* 23 (1964), p. 245; Hanns Hubert Hofmann, "Ländliches Judentum in Franken," *Tribüne. Zeitschrift zum Verständnis des Judentums* 7 (1968), pp. 2894–2900.

35. Hambrecht, *Aufstieg der NSDAP,* pp. 4–11; Karl Bosl, "Franken in Bayern, Bayern und Franken. 150 Jahre Zugehörigkeit zu Bayern," *Schönere Heimat* 23 (1964), p. 206; Uwe Lohalm, *Völkischer Radikalismus. Die Geschichte des Deutschvölkischen Schutz- und Trutzbundes 1919–1923* (Hamburg: Leibniz Verlag, 1970), p. 119; Hofmann, "Ländliches Judentum in Franken," p. 2894; Zdenek Zofka, "Wahlen in Bayern 1848–1994," *Der Staatsbürger* 11 (November 11, 1994): pp. 5, 7–8, 10–11.

36. Hambrecht, *Aufstieg der NSDAP,* pp. 13–15; Hans Fenske, *Konservativismus und Rechtsradikalismus in Bayern nach 1918* (Berlin/Zurich: Gehlen, 1969), p. 53; Werner Maser, *Die Frühgeschichte der NSDAP. Hitlers Weg bis 1924* (Frankfurt: Athenäum Verlag, 1965), pp. 212–19; Wolfgang Benz, *Süddeutschland in der Weimarer Republik. Ein Beitrag zur deutschen Innenpolitik 1918–1923* (Berlin: Duncker and Humblot, 1970), pp. 271–72.

37. Hambrecht, *Aufstieg der NSDAP,* pp. 16–33; Harold Gordon, *Hitler and the Beer Hall Putsch* (Princeton: Princeton Univ. Press, 1972), pp. 88–119; Robert G. L. Waite, *Vanguard of Nazism: The Free Corps Movement in Postwar Germany, 1918–1923* (New York: Norton, 1952), pp. 206–7; Geoffrey Pridham, *Hitler's Rise to Power: The Nazi Movement in Bavaria, 1923–1933* (New York: Harper Torchbooks, 1973), pp. 23–25; Lohalm, *Völkischer Radikalismus,* pp. 113–14, 157, 261–62, 289, 307–11; Klaus-Dieter Schwarz, *Weltkrieg und Revolution in Nürnberg* (Stuttgart: Klett, 1971), p. 327.

38. Robin Lenman, "Julius Streicher and the Origins of the NSDAP in

Nuremberg, 1918–1923," in Anthony Nicholls and Erich Matthias, ed., *German Democracy and the Triumph of Hitler* (New York: St. Martin's Press, 1971), pp. 130–37; Hambrecht, *Aufstieg der NSDAP,* pp. 16–33; Pridham, *Hitler's Rise to Power,* pp. 23–25; Bezirksamt Neustadt an der Aisch to Regierung von Mittelfranken, March 14, 1922, Staatsarchiv Nürnberg (StAN), Kammer des Innern XIII, 5686a; Bezirksamt Uffenheim to Regierung von Mittelfranken, April 25, 1922, StAN, Kammer des Innern II, 714.

39. Lenman, "Julius Streicher," pp. 138–43; Hambrecht, *Aufstieg der NSDAP,* pp. 34–45; Lagebericht der Polizeidirektion Nürnberg-Fürth, December 12, 1922, StAN, Polizei 339; Lagebericht der Polizeidirektion Nürnberg-Fürth, November 25, 1922, StAN, Polizei 339; Geschichte der NS-Ortsgruppe Scheinfeld, StAN, Rep. 503 IV, p. 96; Gordon, *Beer Hall Putsch,* pp. 74–87; Pridham, *Hitler's Rise to Power,* pp. 45, 52.

40. Lenman, "Julius Streicher," pp. 150; Christoph Rückert, *Ipsheim: Die Chronik eines fränkischen Dorfes* (Ipsheim: Marktgemeinde Ipsheim, 1989), pp. 84, 92 n 13; Hambrecht, *Aufstieg der NSDAP,* pp. 48–98, 133–35, 190–93; *Statistisches Jahrbuch für den Freistaat Bayern* 16 (1924): pp. 468–73; *Statistisches Jahrbuch für den Freistaat Bayern* 17 (1926): pp. 600–609, 640–45; *Statistisches Jahrbuch für den Freistaat Bayern* 18 (1928): pp. 598–603, 606–7, 618–21; Halbmonatsbericht der Regierung von Mittelfranken, July 19, 1929, quoted in Hambrecht, *Aufstieg der NSDAP,* p. 170; *Statistisches Jahrbuch für den Freistaat Bayern* 19 (1930): pp. 576–77.

41. Hambrecht, *Aufstieg der NSDAP,* pp. 201–3, 206–24, 230–33, 238–54, 266–67, 270–77, 338–46, 360–61; Bezirksamt Neustadt an der Aisch to Ministerium des Innern, May 13, 1930, StAN, Kammer des Innern II, 689; Lagebericht der Polizeidirektion Nürnberg-Fürth, March 6, 1931, StAN, Polizei 354; Bezirksamt Rothenburg to Regierung von Mittelfranken, January 29, 1931, StAN, Kammer des Innern II, 690; Bezirksamt Uffenheim to Regierung von Mittelfranken, January 20, 1931, StAN, Kammer des Innern II, 692; Bezirksamt Feuchtwangen to Regierung von Mittelfranken, December 29, 1931, StAN, Kammer des Innern II, 692; Polizeidirektion Nürnberg-Fürth to Ministerium des Innern, August 18, 1932, StAN, Kammer des Innern II, 225; *Fränkische Tagespost,* May 23, October 27, November 2, 1932, January 13, 1933; Bezirksamt Uffenheim to Ministerium des Innern, August 16, 1931, StAN, Kammer des Innern II, 695; Bezirksamt Uffenheim to Regierung von Mittelfranken, September 18, 1931, StAN, Kammer des Innern II, 691; Bezirksamt Erlangen to Regierung von Mittelfranken, March 14, 1932, StAN, Kammer des Innern II, 692; Bezirksamt Uffenheim to Regierung von Mittelfranken, July 23, 1932, StAN, Kammer des Innern II, 693; Bezirksamt Neustadt an der Aisch to Regierung von Mittelfranken, July 23, 1932, StAN, Kammer des Innern II, 693; *Zeitschrift des Bayerischen Statistischen Landesamts* 64 (1932): pp. 396–98, 462–69.

42. Earl Ziemke, *The U.S. Army in the Occupation of Germany* (Washington, D.C.: Center for Military History, U.S. Army, 1975), p. 184.

43. Reinhold Maier, *Ende und Wende: Das Schwäbische Schicksal, 1944–1946. Briefe und Tagebuchaufzeichnungen* (Stuttgart: Rainer Wunderlich Verlag, 1948), p. 231.

2. FEARFUL ARE THE CONVULSIONS OF DEFEAT

1. For a good description of the chaotic conditions in Germany in early 1945, see Frank E. Manuel, *Scenes from the End: The Last Days of World War II in Europe* (South Royalton, Vt.: Steerforth Press, 2000), pp. 17–45. For a personal account from the German perspective of the difficulties in travel, see Reinhold Maier, *Ende und Wende: Das Schwäbische Schicksal, 1944–1946. Briefe und Tagebuchaufzeichnungen* (Stuttgart: Rainer Wunderlich Verlag, 1948), pp. 121–252.

2. War Department, Military Intelligence Division, G-2, "Expected Developments of April 1945 in the German Reich," NA, RG 165, Civil Affairs Division (CAD) 014; Klaus-Dietmar Henke, *Die amerikanische Besetzung Deutschlands* (Munich: R. Oldenbourg Verlag, 1995), p. 777; Alfred D. Chandler, ed., *The Papers of Dwight David Eisenhower*, vol. 4, *The War Years* (Baltimore: Johns Hopkins Univ. Press, 1970), pp. 2566–68; Eisenhower's appeal to German soldiers quoted in Erich Spiwoks and Hans Stöber, *Endkampf zwischen Mosel und Inn: XIII. SS-Armeekorps* (Osnabrück: Munin Verlag, 1976), p. 419; John H. Toole, *Battle Diary* (Missoula, Mont.: Vigilante Press, 1978), p. 105.

3. Diary entries of March 26, March 27, and March 31, 1945, in Joseph Goebbels, *Tagebücher 1945: Die letzten Aufzeichnungen* (Hamburg: Hoffmann und Campe, 1977), pp. 384, 390–91, 465–66 (Diary entries refer to events of the previous day. In the English translation of these final entries, however, the dates have been altered, so what appears in the German original on April 2, for example, appears as an entry for April 1 in the English version.); Henke, *amerikanische Besetzung*, pp. 779–81; Karl Kunze, *Kriegsende in Franken und der Kampf um Nürnberg im April 1945* (Nuremberg: Verein für Geschichte der Stadt Nürnberg, 1995), pp. 26–31.

For the general military situation in southern Germany, see: SS-Obergruppenführer and General der Waffen-SS Paul Hauser, "Kämpfe der Heeresgruppe G vom 22.03.–.04.04.1945," Foreign Military Study D-703; General Karl Weisenberger, Commander of Wehrkreis XIII, "Der Wehrkreis XIII in den letzten Kriegsmonaten," Foreign Military Study B-818; General Karl Weisenberger, Commander of Wehrkreis XIII, "Der Wehrkreis XIII im Einsatz gegen die amerikanischen Armeen," Foreign Military Study B-228a.

4. Marlis G. Steinert, *Hitler's War and the Germans: Public Mood and Attitude during the Second World War*, ed. and trans. Thomas E. J. de Witt (Athens, Ohio: Ohio Univ. Press, 1977), pp. 290–306; Ian Kershaw, *Popular Opinion and Political Dissent in the Third Reich: Bavaria, 1933–1945* (Oxford: Clarendon Press, 1983), pp. 296–330.

5. Diary entries of March 2, March 8, March 10, March 11, April 1, and March 24, 1945, in Goebbels, *Tagebücher 1945*, pp. 77–78, 146–47, 178, 185–86, 482–83, 368.

6. Hermann Delp, "Alte, feste Stadt, dein Wille zum Leben siegte über das Schicksal," *Windsheimer Zeitung*, January 6, 1945, p. 4.

7. *Windsheimer Zeitung*, January 10, 11, 13, 16, 17, 19, 30, and February 1, 5, 7, 1945, but see it generally for January–April 1945.

8. Manuel, *Scenes from the End*, pp. 37–38 (In German, the ditty ran, *Lieb Vaterland machst ruhig sein / Mann zieht schon jetzt die Oma ein / Kann das die neue Waffen sein?*); Kunze, *Kriegsende in Franken*, p. 55; SHAEF, G-5 Information Branch, "G-5 Weekly Intelligence Summary, No. 2, 28 February 1945," NA, RG 331, Entry 54; Henke, *amerikanische Besetzung*, p. 135; *Windsheimer Zeitung*, January 10, 11, 13, 16, 17, 19, 30, and February 1, 5, 7, 1945, but see it generally for January–April 1945. Of over seventy military-related death notices that appeared in the paper between January and April 1945, only two mentioned dying for the Führer.

9. Steinert, *Hitler's War*, pp. 306–9; "Bericht des Regierungspräsident von Mittelfranken (Ansbach)," February 8, 1945, quoted in Kunze, *Kriegsende in Franken*, p. 51; "Essensschwierigkeiten," *Nationalsozialistische Parteikorrespondenz*, February 21, 1945, quoted in Erich Kuby, *Das Ende des Schreckens: Januar bis Mai 1945* (Munich: Deutscher Taschenbuch Verlag, 1986), p. 61. See also, Kershaw, *Popular Opinion*, p. 291.

10. Personal accounts of Lotte Gebert and Anni Pachtner, in *Windsheimer Zeitung*, April 4 and 8, 1995.

11. Personal account of Robert Beining, in *Windsheimer Zeitung*, April 5, 1995.

12. *Windsheimer Zeitung*, March 23, 31, April 5, 7, 10, 12, 1945; Ulrich Herz, ed., "Windsheim im Frühjahr 1945" (Bad Windsheim: Steller-Gymnasium, 1995), n.p.

13. *Windsheimer Zeitung*, March 1, 15, 24, 29, April 5, 12, 1945; Herz, "Windsheim im Frühjahr 1945," n.p.; "Kriegschronik des Pfarrers Geuder: Die Evangelisch-Lutherische Kirchengemeinde Nürnberg-Eibach 1939–1946 im Kirchenkampf and Weltkrieg," Pfarrarchiv der Evangelisch-Lutherische Gemeinde Eibach, quoted in Kunze, *Kriegsende in Franken*, p. 186.

14. "Tagebuch einer Zwanzigjährigen," in Kuby, *Ende des Schreckens*, pp. 162–63. The poem, "Eppelein von Geilingen," was written by Ernst Weber. The full stanza in question reads:

Die ganze Stadt war toll und voll,
und was an Gift und was an Groll
man schon seit Jahr und Tagen
geheim in sich getragen,
das machte sich gewaltsam Luft.

the whole town was crazed and drunk,
some from malice and some from rage
that for days and years now
they had carried inside them,
that made for an explosive atmosphere.

15. Steinert, *Hitler's War*, pp. 306–9; Kershaw, *Popular Opinion*, pp. 368–69; Victor Klemperer, *I Will Bear Witness: A Diary of the Nazi Years*, vol. 2, *1942–1945*, trans. Martin Chalmers (New York: Random House, 1999), pp. 294, 314, 396, 399, 437; diary entry of March 27, 1945, in Goebbels, *Tagebücher 1945*, p. 392.

16. Henke, *amerikanische Besetzung*, pp. 960–61; Fritz Rust, "Nachtrag zu meinem Kriegstagebuch 1939 bis 1945. Ereignisse vor und nach dem 28.3.1945, die für die Nachwelt erhalten bleiben sollen," quoted in Herfried Münkler, *Machtzerfall. Die letzten Tage des Dritten Reiches dargestellt am Beispiel der hessischen Kreisstadt Friedberg* (Berlin: Siedler Verlag, 1985), p. 93; personal account of Robert Beining, in *Windsheimer Zeitung*, April 6, 1995.

17. Maier, *Ende und Wende*, p. 224; Ursula von Kardorff, *Berliner Aufzeichnungen: Aus den Jahren 1942–1945* (Munich: Nymphenburger Verlagshandlung, 1976), p. 249; diary entry of E. Barth, April 17, 1945, in Kuby, *Ende des Schreckens*, p. 177.

18. Manuel, *Scenes from the End*, pp. 25–26; "Lagebericht des evangelischen Pfarrers von Oberampfrach an das Dekanat Feuchtwangen von 24.5.1945," in Landeskirchliches Archiv Nürnberg (LKA), Aktenbestand des Landeskirchenrates München, Berichte über Vorgänge bei der militärischen Besetzung; "Bericht der Gemeinden Aschhausen, Frankenbach, und Edelfingen," quoted in Friedrich Blumenstock, *Der Einmarsch der Amerikaner und Franzosen im Nördlichen Württemberg im April 1945* (Stuttgart: W. Kohlhammer Verlag, 1957), pp. 25–26.

19. Letters from Neusaß bei Schöntal and Brettheim, quoted in Blumenstock, *Einmarsch*, pp. 26–27; Steinert, *Hitler's War*, p. 299; Herz, "Windsheim im Frühjahr 1945," n.p.; Klemperer, *I Will Bear Witness*, 2:pp. 400–402; diary entry of April 4, 1945, in Goebbels, *Tagebücher 1945*, pp. 508–9. See also: diary entries for March 13, 14, 25, 27, April 8, 1945, pp. 213, 247, 379, 390, 393, 525–29.

20. Henke, *amerikanische Besetzung*, pp. 959–60; Steinert, *Hitler's War*, p. 307; Klemperer, *I Will Bear Witness*, 2:pp. 403, 422, 462–63 (emphasis in the original).

21. "Weekly Intelligence Summary, No. 10, 2 December 1944," Psychological Warfare Division, NA, RG 331, SHAEF, Special Staff, Executive Section, Entry No. 87; Henke, *amerikanische Besetzung*, p. 959; Steinert, *Hitler's War*, p. 300.

22. Henke, *amerikanische Besetzung*, p. 960; Klemperer, *I Will Bear Witness*, 2:pp. 389, 425, 438, 465.

23. *Windsheimer Zeitung*, January 15, 1945, p. 4, and February 22, 1945, p. 1; diary entry of March 28, 1945, in Goebbels, *Tagebücher 1945*, p. 402; Steinert, *Hitler's War*, pp. 285, 297; Klemperer, *I Will Bear Witness*, 2:pp. 425, 435, 438.

24. Steinert, *Hitler's War,* pp. 288; Kershaw, *Popular Opinion,* p. 366; Klemperer, *I Will Bear Witness,* 2:p. 399.

25. Henke, *amerikanische Besetzung,* p. 960; Adolf Rusam, "Aus meinem Leben als Dorfpfarrer in der Kriegszeit. Tagebuch über die ereignisse der letzten Kriegswochen, die militärische Besetzung und den politischen Umschwung in Oberampfrach, 26. März–10. Mai 1945," LKA Nuremberg, Aktenbestand des Landeskirchenrats München, Berichte über Vorgänge bei der militärischen Besetzung.

26. *Windsheimer Zeitung,* April 15, 16, 1995; diary entry of Gustav Höhn, April 15–16, 1945, in Ulrich Herz, ed., "Und das Leben geht weiter: Windsheim, 1945–1949" (Bad Windsheim: Steller-Gymnasium, 1996), n.p.

27. Klemperer, *I Will Bear Witness,* 2:pp. 470–71.

28. Statements by Gustav Höhn, Anni Schunk, Heinrich Hoffmann, and Heinrich Büttner, in Herz, "Und das Leben geht weiter," n.p.; "Ortsteil Abtsgreuth Geschichte: Nachkriegszeit und Gegenwart," http:www.muenchsteinach.de/abtsgreuth/geschichte/histabti.htm; Hans Woller, *Gesellschaft und Politik in der amerikanischen Besatzungszone. Die Region Ansbach und Fürth* (Munich: R. Oldenbourg Verlag, 1986), p. 59; Kardorff, *Berliner Aufzeichnungen,* p. 247; Klemperer, *I Will Bear Witness,* 2:p. 448. Steinert, *Hitler's War,* p. 304.

29. Steinert, *Hitler's War,* p. 304; diary entries of March 6, 9, 22, 27, April 4, and 1, 1945, in Goebbels, *Tagebücher 1945,* pp. 121, 162, 337, 397, 507–8, 482–83; Earl R. Beck, *Under the Bombs: The German Home Front, 1942–1945* (Lexington: Univ. Press of Kentucky, 1986), pp. 188–89.

30. Gerald F. Linderman, *The World within War: America's Combat Experience in World War II* (Cambridge: Harvard Univ. Press, 1997), pp. 96, 115; Peter Schrijvers, *The Crash of Ruin: American Combat Soldiers in Europe during World War II* (New York: New York Univ. Press, 1998), pp. 57, 62–73; Annette Tapert, ed., *Lines of Battle: Letters from American Servicemen, 1941–1945* (New York: Pocket Books, 1987), pp. 77, 79, 215–16; Toole, *Battle Diary,* pp. 10, 91; Henry E. Giles, *The G.I. Journal of Sergeant Giles,* comp. and ed. Janet Holt Giles (Boston: Houghton Mifflin, 1965), pp. 39, 53, 318; Robert Easton, *Love and War: Pearl Harbor through V-J Day. World War II Letters and Later Reflections by Robert and Jane Easton* (Norman: Univ. of Oklahoma Press, 1991), pp. 4, 285; Leon Standifer, *Not in Vain: A Rifleman Remembers World War II* (Baton Rouge: Louisiana State Univ. Press, 1992), pp. 165–66; Stephen F. Ambrose, *Band of Brothers: E Company, 506th Regiment, 101st Airborne from Normandy to Hitler's Eagle's Nest* (New York: Simon and Schuster, 1992), pp. 99, 248; Studs Terkel, "'The Good War': An Oral History of World War II* (New York: Pantheon Books, 1984), pp. 5, 259, 380; Michael D. Doubler, *Closing with the Enemy: How GIs Fought the War in Europe, 1944–1945* (Lawrence: Univ. Press of Kansas, 1994), p. 258.

31. Ben Tumey, *G.I.'s View of World War II: The Diary of a Combat Private* (New York: Exposition Press, 1959), p. 18; Morale Services Division, Army Services

Forces, *What the Soldier Thinks: A Monthly Digest of War Department Studies on the Attitudes of American Troops* (Washington, D.C.: Army Services Forces, War Department, December 1943–September 1945), no. 7, p. 9; Samuel Stouffer, et al., *The American Soldier: Combat and Its Aftermath* (Princeton: Princeton Univ. Press, 1949), 2:pp. 158, 162, 232–34.

32. Linderman, *World within War,* pp. 138–39, 142; Schrijvers, *Crash of Ruin,* pp. 72–84; J. Glenn Gray, *The Warriors: Reflections on Men in Battle* (New York: Harper and Row, 1959), p. 146; Charles MacDonald, *Company Commander* (Washington, D.C.: Infantry Journal Press, 1947), p. 189; Ambrose, *Band of Brothers,* p. 264; Audie Murphy, *To Hell and Back* (New York: Henry Holt, 1949), p. 39.

33. Harold P. Leinbaugh and John D. Campbell, *The Men of Company K: The Autobiography of a World War II Rifle Company* (New York: Morrow, 1985), pp. 160–61; Manuel, *Scenes from the End,* pp. 79–83. In early medieval Anglo-Saxon and Germanic law, *Wergeld* was the value upon the life of a man in accordance with his rank that was paid as compensation to the relative of a slain person.

34. Brendan Phibbs, *The Other Side of Time: A Combat Surgeon in World War II* (Boston: Little, Brown, 1987), pp. 248–49; Tapert, *Lines of Battle,* pp. 284–86, 245; Schrijvers, *Crash of Ruin,* pp. 137–40, 143–46.

35. Tapert, *Lines of Battle,* pp. 284,286; Lee Kennett, *G.I.: The American Soldier in World War II* (New York: Warner Books, 1987), pp. 212–13.

36. Ambrose, *Band of Brothers,* pp. 257, 265; Kennett, *G.I.,* pp. 216–17.

37. Easton, *Love and War,* pp. 19, 298–99, 305–6, 344–45; Schrijvers, *Crash of Ruin,* pp. 140–42.

38. Joseph R. Starr, *Fraternization with the Germans in World War II* (Frankfurt: Office of Chief Historian, European Command, 1947), p. 28; Kennett, *G.I.,* p. 217; Petra Goedde, *GIs and Germans: Culture, Gender, and Foreign Relations, 1945–1949* (New Haven: Yale Univ. Press, 2003), p. 59; Ambrose, *Band of Brothers,* p. 255.

39. Tapert, *Lines of Battle,* pp. 269–70; Gray, *The Warriors,* p. 152; Kennett, *G.I.,* pp. 217–18.

40. Henke, *amerikanische Besetzung,* pp. 961–62; diary entry of March 30, 1945, in Heinrich Köhler, *Lebenserinnerungen des Politikers und Staatsmannes, 1878–1949,* ed. Josef Becker (Stuttgart: Kohlhammer, 1964), pp. 342–43.

41. SHAEF, G-5 Information Branch, "G-5 Weekly Journal of Information, No. 12, 11 May 1945," NA, RG 331, Entry 54; Henke, *amerikanische Besetzung,* p. 961; Klemperer, *I Will Bear Witness,* 2:pp. 484, 488.

42. Klemperer, *I Will Bear Witness,* 2:p. 488; Henke, *amerikanische Besetzung,* pp. 961–63; diary entry of May 1, 1945, in Karl Jering, *Überleben und Neubeginn. Tagebuchaufzeichnungen eines Deutschen 1945–1946* (Munich: Günter Olzog Verlag, 1979), p. 16.

43. Henke, *amerikanische Besetzung,* pp. 958–59.

44. Diary entry of March 13, 1945, in Goebbels, *Tagebücher 1945,* p. 211; Head-

quarters, European Civil Affairs Division, "General Intelligence Bulletin No. 44, 5 May 1945," NA, RG 260/390/47/19/1.

3. DEATH THROES

1. Jürgen Wohlfahrt, "Die Bauernkriegs-Schlacht von Königshofen. Ein Versuch, Einige Historische Rätsel zu Lösen," *Hierzuland* 19, no. 1 (1995): pp. 18–31; Carlheinz Gräter, "Der Königshofer Turmberg im Bauernkrieg," *Badische Heimat* 78 (1998): pp. 233–38; Carlheinz Gräter, *Der Bauernkrieg in Franken* (Würzburg: Stürtz Verlag, 1975), pp. 125–32.

2. Martin Zurwehme, "'. . . aber die Treue ist gehalten bis in den Tod.' Der Nibelungenmythos im 19. und 20. Jahrhundert," *Geschichte lernen* 52 (1996): p. 34; Herfried Münkler, "Das Nibelungenschicksal und die deutsche Nation. Zur Funktion von Mythen in der Politik," *Forschung Frankfurt: Wissenschaftsmagazin der Johann Wolfgang Goethe-Universität Frankfurt* 1, no. 1 (1989): p. 5.

3. Klaus von See, "Das Nibelungenlied—ein Nationalepos?" in Joachim Heinzle and Annelise Waldschmidt, ed., *Die Nibelungen. Ein deutscher Wahn, Ein deutscher Alptraum* (Frankfurt: Suhrkamp, 1991), pp. 43–57.

4. See, "Das Nibelungenlied," p. 58.

5. "The Nibelungenlied," Online Medieval and Classical Library Release #31, University of California-Berkeley, http://sunsite.berkeley.edu/OMACL/Nibelungenlied.

6. Ibid.; See, "Das Nibelungenlied," pp. 66–67; Zurwehme, "Treue," p. 35

7. See, "Das Nibelungenlied," pp. 68–77; Werner Wunderlich, "'Ein Hauptbuch bey der Erziehung der deutschen Jugend . . .' Zur pädagogischen Indienstnahme des *Nibelungenliedes* für Schule und Unterricht im 19. und 20. Jahrhundert," in Heinzle and Waldschmidt, ed., *Die Nibelungen*, pp. 119–34; Brigitte Hamann, *Hitler's Vienna: A Dictator's Apprenticeship* (New York: Oxford Univ. Press, 1999), pp. 23–24, 66; Edward Gaines, "From Bayreuth to Nuremberg: Richard Wagner and the German National Socialist *Weltanschauung*," *USM History Review*, http://www.usm.maine.edu/~history/.

8. See, "Das Nibelungenlied," p. 92; Peter Krüger, "Etzels Halle und Stalingrad: Die Rede Görings vom 30. 1. 1943," in Heinzle and Waldschmidt, ed., *Die Nibelungen*, p. 153.

9. Krüger, "Etzels Halle," pp. 153–69.

10. Text of radio broadcast of April 1, 1945, in James Lucas, *Experiences of War: The Third Reich* (London: Arms and Armour Press, 1990), pp. 168–69; *New York Times*, April 2, 1945; Helmut Veeh, *Die Kriegsfurie über Franken 1945 und das Ende in den Alpen*, 3rd ed. (Bad Windsheim: Verlagsdrückerei Heinrich Delp, 1998), p. 32; Twelfth Armored Division, *A History of the United States Twelfth Armored Division, 15 September 1942–17 December 1945: The Hellcats in World War II* (1947; reprint, Nashville, Tenn.: Battery Press, 1978), p. 59; Special Operations Report, "Task

Force Rodwell, Interview with Major John Swink, Acting Assistant S-3 (Operations Officer) 12th Infantry Regiment, 4th Infantry Division," NA, RG 407, Entry 427.

11. Georg Tessin, *Verbände und Truppen der deutschen Wehrmacht und Waffen-SS* (Frankfurt: E.S. Mittler und Sohn, 1965–1980), passim; Bundesarchiv/Militärarchiv Freiburg (BA/MA) RH 10/112 and 10/324; Gliederung des 17. SS-Pz.Gren.Div. "Götz von Berlichingen," Stand 15.9.44, BA/MA RS 3-17/13; Hans Stöber, *Die Sturmflut und das Ende. Geschichte der 17. SS-Pz.Gren.Division "Götz von Berlichingen"* (Osnabrück: Munin Verlag, 1976), 1:pp. 48–52, 64, 243–60, 501–2; "17. SS-Panzer Grenadier Division 'Götz von Berlichingen,'" http://home.swipnet.se/normandy/gerob/pzdiv/17sspgdiv.html.

12. Gliederung des 17. SS-Pz.Gren.Div. "Götz von Berlichingen," Stand 15.9.44, BA/MA RS 3-17/13; "The 17th SS-Panzer-Grenadier Division," http://www.100thww2.org/gerunit2/17.html; Helmut Günther, *Die Sturmflut und das Ende. Geschichte der 17. SS-Pz.Gren.Division "Götz von Berlichingen,"* vol. 3, *Mit dem Rücken zur Wand* (Munich: Schild Verlag, 1991), pp. 503–5.

13. Friedrich Blumenstock, *Der Einmarsch der Amerikaner und Franzosen im Nördlichen Württemberg im April 1945* (Stuttgart: W. Kohlhammer Verlag, 1957), p. 37; Veeh, *Kriegsfurie,* p. 80; Sergeant Carl J. Lyons, "Personal Account, Company A, 17th Armored Infantry Battalion, 12th Armored Division," http://www.acu.edu/academics/history/12ad/17aibx/lyons6.htm.

14. Veeh, *Kriegsfurie,* pp. 84–87; Lyons, "Company A"; Sherman B. Lans, "Mount Up! The History of Company C, 17th Armored Infantry Battalion, 12th Armored Division," University of Tennessee Special Collections, MS-2012, Box 8, Folder 12, pp. 39–41; "After Action Report," 23rd Tank Battalion (Tk Bn), 12th Armored Division (AD), NA, RG 407/612-TK-(23)-0.3; "History of the 495th Armored Field Artillery Battalion, 12th AD," http://www.acu.edu/academics/history/12ad/495afax/howlong.htm.

15. Veeh, *Kriegsfurie,* p. 82; Günther, *Sturmflut,* 3:pp. 215–20.

16. Twelfth Armored Division, *Twelfth Armored Division,* p. 59.

17. Veeh, *Kriegsfurie,* pp. 98–99, 109–10, 261; Erich Spiwoks and Hans Stöber, *Endkampf zwischen Mosel und Inn* (Osnabrück: Munin Verlag, 1976), pp. 180–81; Lieutenant Colonel Cord von Hobe, "Einsatz der Panzer-Kampfgruppe XIII vom 06.04–05.05 1945," Foreign Military Study B-772, in Spiwoks and Stöber, *Endkampf,* pp. 184–85; Karl Kunze, *Kriegsende in Franken und der Kampf um Nürnberg im April 1945* (Nuremberg: Selbstverlag des Vereins für die Geschichte der Stadt Nürnbergs, 1995), pp. 140, 192; "Beurteilung der Lage," 30.3.45 and 1.4.45, in M. Wind and H. Günther, ed., *Kriegstagebuch. 17. SS-Panzer-Grenadier-Division "Götz von Berlichingen": 30. Oktober 1943 bis 6. Mai 1945* (Munich: Schild Verlag, 1993), n.p.; SS-Obersturmbannführer Ekkehard Albert, "Einsatz des XIII. SS-A.K. zwischen Rhein und Alpen vom 26.03.–06.05.1945," Foreign Military Study B-737, in Spiwoks and Stöber, *Endkampf,* pp. 216–17.

18. Veeh, *Kriegsfurie*, pp. 100–102; "G-3 Periodic Report," CC-B, 12th AD, NA, RG 407/612-CCB-1.8-3.17.

19. Gerald R. Linderman, *The World within War: America's Combat Experience in World War II* (Cambridge: Harvard Univ. Press, 1997), pp. 90–142; Harold P. Leinbaugh and John D. Campbell, *The Men of Company K: The Autobiography of a World War II Rifle Company* (New York: Morrow, 1985), p. 134.

20. Leinbaugh and Campbell, *The Men of Company K*, p. 148; Howard M. Randall, *Dirt and Doughfeet: Combat Experiences of a Rifle-Platoon Leader* (New York: Exposition Press, 1955), pp. 104–5; Grady P. Arrington, *Infantryman at the Front* (New York: Vantage Press, 1959), pp. 165–66; Linderman, *World within War*, pp. 124–25.

21. Linderman, *World within War*, pp. 113–14, 123–24, 130–32; Lester Atwell, *Private* (New York: Simon and Schuster, 1958), pp. 392–93, 428–29, 493–96; John H. Toole, *Battle Diary* (Missoula, Mont.: Vigilante Press, 1978), pp. 138–39; Audie Murphy, *To Hell and Back* (New York: Henry Holt, 1949), pp. 100, 176–77.

22. Hermann Kriegl, *Sinnlos in den Krieg gejagt: Das Schicksal von Reserve-Offiziers-Bewerbern 1945. Zeitzeugen und Dokumente* (Diessen: Grafische Kunstanstalt und Verlag Jos. C. Huber, 1995), pp. 85–89; Spiwoks and Stöber, *Endkampf*, pp. 207–8; Veeh, *Kriegsfurie*, pp. 104–6, 140.

23. Kriegl, *Sinnlos*, pp. 89–93, 127; Spiwoks and Stöber, *Endkampf*, pp. 207–8; Veeh, *Kriegsfurie*, pp. 104–6, 140; Dr. William S. Boice, "History of the Twenty-second United States Infantry in World War II," University of Tennessee Special Collections, MS-1259, Box 1, Folder 4, p. 141.

24. Kriegl, *Sinnlos*, pp. 90–93, 127.

25. Linderman, *World within War*, pp. 107–8; Randall, *Dirt and Doughfeet*, pp. 88–90.

26. Kriegl, *Sinnlos*, pp. 90–93, 127; Spiwoks and Stöber, *Endkampf*, pp. 207–8; Veeh, *Kriegsfurie*, pp. 104–6, 140; Boice, "History of the Twenty-second United States Infantry," p. 141.

27. "Unit History," 17th Armored Infantry Battalion (AIB), 12th AD, NA, RG 407/612-INF-(17)-0.2; "G-2 Periodic Reports," 12th AD, NA, RG 407/612-2.1; "Periodic Reports," CC-R, 12th AD, NA, RG 407/612-CCR-0.9; Blumenstock, *Einmarsch*, pp. 41–43.

28. "Unit History," 17th AIB, 12th AD, NA, RG 407/612-INF-(17)-0.2; "G-2 Periodic Reports," 12th AD, NA, RG 407/612-2.1; "After Action Report," 23rd Tk Bn, 12th AD, NA, RG 407/612-TK-(23)-0.3; Lans, "Mount Up!" pp. 41–42; Lyons, "Company A"; "History of the 495th Armored Field Artillery Battalion"; Kriegl, *Sinnlos*, pp. 59–62, 73–78; Veeh, *Kriegsfurie*, pp. 108–9.

29. Lyons, "Company A"; "History of the 17th Armored Infantry Battalion, 12th Armored Division," http://www.acu.edu/academics/history/12ad/17aibx/hist17.htm; Charles B. MacDonald, *The Last Offensive* (Washington, D.C.: Office of the Chief of Military History, 1973), p. 413. The Seventeenth Armored Infantry Battalion itself numbered about one thousand men.

30. Lyons, "Company A"; MacDonald, *Last Offensive*, p. 413.

31. "After Action Report," 17th AIB, 12th AD, NA, RG 407/612-INF-(17)-0.3; "S-3 Journal," 17th AIB, 12th AD, NA, RG 407/612-INF-(17)-0.7; "History of the 495th Armored Field Artillery Battalion"; Lans, "Mount Up!" p. 43; Veeh, *Kriegsfurie*, pp. 142–43; Twelfth Armored Division, *Twelfth Armored Division,* pp. 62–64.

32. "After Action Report," 17th AIB, NA, RG 407/612-INF-(17)-0.3; "S-3 Journal," 17th AIB, NA, RG 407/612-INF-(17)-0.7; "History of the 495th Armored Field Artillery Battalion"; Lans, "Mount Up!" p. 43; Veeh, *Kriegsfurie,* pp. 143–44.

33. Blumenstock, *Einmarsch,* p. 33.

34. "After Action Report," 23rd Tk Bn, 12th AD, NA, RG 407/612-TK-(23)-0.3; "History of the 495th Armored Field Artillery Battalion"; Spiwoks and Stöber, *Endkampf,* pp. 209–10; Veeh, *Kriegsfurie,* pp. 144–46.

35. Boice, "History of the Twenty-second United States Infantry," p. 141; "Combat and Infantry Journal," 22nd Infantry Regiment (IR), 4th Infantry Division (ID), NA, RG 407/304-INF (22)-0.7; "After Action Report," 22nd IR, 4th ID, NA, RG 407/304-INF (22)-0.3; "History of the 22nd Infantry Regiment," NA, RG 407/304-INF (22)-0; Veeh, *Kriegsfurie,* p. 148. Indicative of what was to come, the 22nd Infantry Journal recorded thirty-nine battle casualties for April 1. See "Combat and Infantry Journal," 22nd IR, 4th ID, NA, RG 407/304-INF (22)-0.7.

36. "Combat and Infantry Journal," 22nd IR, 4th ID, NA, RG 407/304-INF (22)-0.7; "After Action Report," 22nd IR, 4th ID, NA, RG 407/304-INF (22)-0.3; "After Action Report," 12th IR, 4th ID, NA, RG 407/304-INF (12)-0.3.

37. "After Action Report," 17th AIB, NA, RG 407/612-INF-(17)-0.3; "S-3 Journal," 17th AIB, NA, RG 407/612-INF-(17)-0.7; Lyons, "Company A."

38. "After Action Report," 17th AIB, NA, RG 407/612-INF-(17)-0.3; "S-3 Journal," 17th AIB, NA, RG 407/612-INF-(17)-0.7; Lyons, "Company A"; Lans, "Mount Up!" p. 43; Veeh, *Kriegsfurie,* p. 144; Werner Haupt, *Das Ende im Westen 1945* (Dorheim: Podzun, 1972), pp. 161–62; Perry Biddiscombe, *Werwolf! The History of the National Socialist Guerrilla Movement, 1944–1946* (Toronto: Univ. of Toronto Press, 1998), p. 105.

39. "After Action Report," 17th AIB, NA, RG 407/612-INF-(17)-0.3; "S-3 Journal," 17th AIB, NA, RG 407/612-INF-(17)-0.7; "Combat and Infantry Journal," 22nd IR, 4th ID, NA, RG 407/304-INF (22)-0.7; "After Action Report," 22nd IR, 4th ID, NA, RG 407/304-INF (22)-0.3; Veeh, *Kriegsfurie,* pp. 148–49, 151.

40. "Combat and Infantry Journal," 22nd IR, 4th ID, NA, RG 407/304-INF (22)-0.7; "After Action Report," 22nd IR, 4th ID, NA, RG 407/304-INF (22)-0.3; "History of the 22nd Infantry Regiment, 1 January 1944 to 1 January 1946," NA, RG 407/304-INF (22)-0, p. 87; Veeh, *Kriegsfurie,* pp. 151–53; Kriegl, *Sinnlos,* pp. 111–16; Blumenstock, *Einmarsch,* p. 46.

41. "Aufruf des Oberbefehlshaber West," 4.4.45, in Wind and Günther, *Kriegstagebuch;* "Combat and Infantry Journal," 22nd IR, 4th ID, NA, RG 407/304-INF (22)-0.7; "After Action Report," 22nd IR, 4th ID, NA, RG 407/304-INF (22)-

0.3; Boice, "History of the Twenty-second United States Infantry," pp. 143–44; Veeh, *Kriegsfurie*, pp. 157–58; Kriegl, *Sinnlos*, pp. 118–20.

42. "Combat and Infantry Journal," 22nd IR, 4th ID, NA, RG 407/304-INF (22)-0.7; "After Action Report," 22nd IR, 4th ID, NA, RG 407/304-INF (22)-0.3; Boice, "History of the Twenty-second United States Infantry," pp. 143–44; Blumenstock, *Einmarsch*, p. 27; "Swede's Diary," Historical Account of the 22nd IR, 4th ID, University of Tennessee Special Collections, MS-1764, Box 5, Folder 1, p. 31.

43. "Combat and Infantry Journal," 22nd IR, 4th ID, NA, RG 407/304-INF (22)-0.7; "After Action Report," 22nd IR, 4th ID, NA, RG 407/304-INF (22)-0.3; Blumenstock, *Einmarsch*, p. 46; Boice, "History of the Twenty-second United States Infantry," p. 144; Veeh, *Kriegsfurie*, pp. 153–54.

44. "Combat and Infantry Journal," 22nd IR, 4th ID, NA, RG 407/304-INF (22)-0.7; "After Action Report," 22nd IR, 4th ID, NA, RG 407/304-INF (22)-0.3; Boice, "History of the Twenty-second United States Infantry," p. 143; Veeh, *Kriegsfurie*, pp. 155–56; Spiwoks and Stöber, *Endkampf*, pp. 208–9; MacDonald, *Last Offensive*, p. 413; Seventh U.S. Army, *The Seventh United States Army in France and Germany, 1944–1945* (Heidelberg: Aloys Graf, 1946), 3:p. 773.

45. "Combat and Infantry Journal," 22nd IR, 4th ID, NA, RG 407/304-INF (22)-0.7; "After Action Report," 22nd IR, 4th ID, NA, RG 407/304-INF (22)-0.3; Veeh, *Kriegsfurie*, pp. 155–60; Blumenstock, *Einmarsch*, p. 46; Boice, "History of the Twenty-second United States Infantry," p. 144; "Losses in Action," 22nd Infantry Regiment, NA, RG 407/304-INF (22)-0.3.

46. Günther, *Sturmflut*, 3:pp. 233–35.

47. Veeh, *Kriegsfurie*, pp. 270–72; "After Action Report," 12th IR, 4th ID, NA, RG 407/304-INF (12)-0.3; "Unit Report," 12th IR, 4th ID, NA, RG 407/304-INF (12)-0.9; Swink Interview, NA, RG 407, Entry 427.

48. Veeh, *Kriegsfurie*, pp. 271–72; "After Action Report," 12th IR, 4th ID, NA, RG 407/304-INF (12)-0.3; "Unit Report," 12th IR, 4th ID, NA, RG 407/304-INF (12)-0.9; Swink Interview, NA, RG 407, Entry 427; Seventh U.S. Army, *Seventh United States Army*, 3:p. 777.

4. THROUGH THE STEIGERWALD

1. Erich Spiwoks and Hans Stöber, *Endkampf zwischen Mosel und Inn* (Osnabrück: Munin Verlag, 1976), p. 233; SS-Obersturmbannführer Ekkehard Albert, "Einsatz des XIII. SS-A.K. zwischen Rhein und Alpen vom 26.03.–06.05.1945," Foreign Military Study B-737, in Spiwoks and Stöber, *Endkampf*, pp. 212–17.

2. Brendan Phibbs, *The Other Side of Time. A Combat Surgeon in World War II* (Boston: Little, Brown, 1987), p. 247; Albert, "Einsatz des XIII. SS-Armee Korps," in Spiwoks and Stöber, *Endkampf*, pp. 231, 233.

3. Lieutenant Colonel Cord von Hobe, "Einsatz der Panzer-Kampfgruppe XIII von 06.04–05.05.1945," Foreign Military Study B-772, in Spiwoks and Stöber, *Endkampf*, pp. 238–

40; Albert, "Einsatz des XIII. SS-A.K.," in Spiwoks and Stöber, *Endkampf,* pp. 250–53; Karl Kunze, *Kriegsende in Franken und der Kampf um Nürnberg im April 1945* (Nuremberg: Selbstverlag des Vereins für die Geschichte der Stadt Nürnbergs, 1995), pp. 126, 173, 425.

4. Hobe, "Panzer-Kampfgruppe XIII," in Spiwoks and Stöber, *Endkampf,* pp. 238–40; Albert, "Einsatz des XIII. SS-A.K.," in Spiwoks and Stöber, *Endkampf,* pp. 250–53; Kunze, *Kriegsende in Franken,* pp. 173, 425; http://www.schwanberg.de/schwanberg/geschichte.html.

5. "After Action Report," 23rd Tk Bn, 12th AD, NA, RG 407/612-TK-(23)-0.3; Helmut Veeh, *Die Kriegsfurie über Franken 1945 und das Ende in den Alpen,* 3rd ed. (Bad Windsheim: Verlagsdrückerei Heinrich Delp, 1998), pp. 161–66.

6. Sergeant Carl J. Lyons, "Personal Account, Company A, 17th Armored Infantry Battalion, 12th Armored Division," http://www.acu.edu/academics/history/12ad/17aibx/lyons6.htm; Werner Franz, "Die Geschichte des Marktes Ippesheim," http://www.ippesheim.de; Sherman B. Lans, "Mount Up! The History of Company C, 17th Armored Infantry Battalion, 12th Armored Division," University of Tennessee Special Collections, MS-2012, Box 8, Folder 12, pp. 44–45.

7. "After Action Report," 17th AIB, 12th AD, NA, RG 407/612-INF-(17)-0.3; Lyons, "Company A"; Lans, "Mount Up!" p. 45; W. Y. Boyd, *The Gentle Infantryman* (Los Angeles: Burning Gate Press, 1985), p. 48.

8. "After Action Report," 17th AIB, 12th AD, NA, RG 407/612-INF-(17)-0.3; "S-2 Journal" and "S-3 Journal," 17th AIB, 12th AD, NA, RG 407/612-INF-(17)-0.7; Lyons, "Company A"; Lans, "Mount Up!" p. 45; Veeh, *Kriegsfurie,* p. 265.

9. Veeh, *Kriegsfurie,* p. 172.

10. "After Action Report," 17th AIB, 12th AD, NA, RG 407/612-INF-(17)-0.3; "S-2 Journal" and "S-3 Journal," 17th AIB, 12th AD, NA, RG 407/612-INF-(17)-0.7; Lyons, "Company A"; Lans, "Mount Up!" p. 45; Veeh, *Kriegsfurie,* pp. 172–73.

11. Lans, "Mount Up!" p. 45; "After Action Report," 23rd Tk Bn, 12th AD, NA, RG 407/612-TK (23)-0.3.

12. "After Action Report," 17th AIB, 12th AD, NA, RG 407/612-INF-(17)-0.3; "S-2 Journal" and "S-3 Journal," 17th AIB, 12th AD, NA, RG 407/612-INF-(17)-0.7; Veeh, *Kriegsfurie,* pp. 172–75; Lyons, "Company A"; Lans, "Mount Up!" p. 46.

13. Veeh, *Kriegsfurie,* p. 173; "After Action Report," 56th AIB, 12th AD, NA, RG 407/612-INF-(56)-0.3; "Narrative of Operations, April 1945," Headquarters, CC-R, 12th AD, NA, RG 407/612-CCR-0.9.

14. "After Action Report," 17th AIB, 12th AD, NA, RG 407/612-INF-(17)-0.3; "S-2 Journal" and "S-3 Journal," 17th AIB, 12th AD, NA, RG 407/612-INF-(17)-0.7; Lyons, "Company A"; Lans, "Mount Up!" p. 46; Veeh, *Kriegsfurie,* p. 178.

15. Lyons, "Company A"; Hobe, "Panzer-Kampfgruppe XIII," in Spiwoks and Stöber, *Endkampf,* p. 239; Veeh, *Kriegsfurie,* p. 182.

16. Hobe, "Panzer-Kampfgruppe XIII," in Spiwok, *Endkampf,* p. 240; see also, Veeh, *Kriegsfurie,* pp. 121, 127, 172, 262–63, 295–303, 438–39, 460, 496, and passim.

17. Veeh, *Kriegsfurie*, pp. 318–21.

18. Ibid., pp. 321–25.

19. "After Action Report," 116th Cavalry Reconnaissance Squadron (Cav Rcnz Sq), NA, RG 407/304-CAV-101-0.3; *Windsheimer Zeitung*, April 9, 10, 11, 12, 13, 1995; Veeh, *Kriegsfurie*, pp. 321–25; Hobe, "Panzer-Kampfgruppe XIII," in Spiwoks and Stöber, *Endkampf*, pp. 240–41.

20. Veeh, *Kriegsfurie*, pp. 325, 375–76; "After Action Report," 116th Cav Rcnz Sq, NA, RG 407/304-CAV-101-0.3; *Windsheimer Zeitung*, April 9, 10, 11, 12, 13, 1995; Hobe, "Panzer-Kampfgruppe XIII," in Spiwoks and Stöber, *Endkampf*, pp. 240–41.

21. Veeh, *Kriegsfurie*, pp. 376–77; *Windsheimer Zeitung*, April 9, 10, 11, 12, 13, 1995; Hobe, "Panzer-Kampfgruppe XIII," in Spiwoks and Stöber, *Endkampf*, pp. 240–41.

22. "S-2 Journal," 8th IR, 4th ID, NA, RG 407/304-INF-(8)-0.7; "After Action Report," 17th AIB, 12th AD, NA, RG 407/612-INF-(17)-0.3; "S-2 Journal" and "S-3 Journal," 17th AIB, 12th AD, NA, RG 407/612-INF-(17)-0.7; Lyons, "Company A"; Veeh, *Kriegsfurie*, pp. 326, 328, 330.

23. Lyons, "Company A"; "S-2 Journal" and "S-3 Journal," 17th AIB, 12th AD, NA, RG 407/612-INF-(17)-0.7; "After Action Report," 116th Cav Rcnz Sq, NA, RG 407/304-CAV-101-0.3; Hobe, "Panzer-Kampfgruppe XIII," in Spiwoks and Stöber, *Endkampf*, p. 240; Veeh, *Kriegsfurie*, pp. 328, 330–32.

24. Lans, "Mount Up!" p. 49; "After Action Report," 17th AIB, 12th AD, NA, RG 407/612-INF-(17)-0.3; "S-2 Journal" and "S-3 Journal," 17th AIB, 12th AD, NA, RG 407/612-INF-(17)-0.7; "Narrative of Operations, April 1945," CC-R, 12th AD, NA, RG 407/612-CCR-0.9; "After Action Report," 116th Cav Rcnz Sq, NA, RG 407/ 304-CAV-101-0.3; *Windsheimer Zeitung*, April 10, 1995.

25. "S-3 Journal," 23rd Tk Bn, 12th AD, NA, RG 407/612-TK-(23)-0.7; Veeh, *Kriegsfurie*, pp. 333, 336.

26. Veeh, *Kriegsfurie*, pp. 338–40, 344; "S-3 Journal," 23rd Tk Bn, 12th AD, NA, RG 407/612-TK-(23)-0.7.

27. "After Action Report," 17th AIB, 12th AD, NA, RG 407/612-INF-(17)-0.3.

28. Lyons, "Company A"; Veeh, *Kriegsfurie*, p. 342.

29. "After Action Report," 17th AIB, 12th AD, NA, RG 407/612-INF-(17)-0.3; "S-2 Journal" and "S-3 Journal," 17th AIB, 12th AD, NA, RG 407/612-INF-(17)-0.7; Lyons, "Company A"; Veeh, *Kriegsfurie*, pp. 350–57.

30. Veeh, *Kriegsfurie*, pp. 378–82; "Narrative of Operations, April 1945," CC-R, 12th AD, NA, RG 407/612-CCR-0.9.

31. Veeh, *Kriegsfurie*, pp. 384–86; Hobe, "Panzer-Kampfgruppe XIII," in Spiwoks and Stöber, *Endkampf*, pp. 240–41.

32. Veeh, *Kriegsfurie*, pp. 388–90; Helmut Günther, *Die Sturmflut und das Ende. Geschichte der 17. SS-Pz-Gren.-Division "Götz von Berlichingen,"* vol. 3, *Mit dem Rücken zur Wand* (Munich: Schild Verlag, 1991), pp. 354–55; "After Action Report: Operations in Germany, April 1945," 92nd Cav Rcnz Sq, 12th AD, NA, RG 407/612-

CAV-0.3; "Operations in Germany, April 1945," Division Artillery, 12th AD, NA, RG 407/612-ART-0.7.

33. Veeh, *Kriegsfurie,* pp. 392–93; Günther, *Sturmflut,* 3:p. 355; "After Action Report," 92nd Cav Rcnz Sq, 12th AD, NA, RG 407/612-CAV-0.3; "Operations in Germany, April 1945," Division Artillery, 12th AD, NA, RG 407/612-ART-0.7.

34. Veeh, *Kriegsfurie,* pp. 394–95, 402–5; Günther, *Sturmflut,* 3:p. 355; "After Action Report: Operations in Germany, April 1945," 56th AIB, 12th AD, NA, RG 407/612-INF(56)-0.3; "After Action Report: Operations in Germany, April 1945," 714th Tk Bn, 12th AD, NA, RG 407/612-TK(714)-0.3; "G-3 Periodic Report," CC-B, 12th AD, NA, RG 407/612-CCB-1.8-3.17; "Operations in Germany, April 1945," Division Artillery, 12th AD, NA, RG 407/612-ART-0.7.

35. Veeh, *Kriegsfurie,* pp. 394–95, 407–9; Günther, *Sturmflut,* 3:p. 355; Hobe, "Panzer-Kampfgruppe XIII," in Spiwoks and Stöber, *Endkampf,* pp. 241–42; "After Action Report," 56th AIB, 12th AD, NA, RG 407/612-INF-(56)-0.3; *Windsheimer Zeitung,* April 12, 13, 14, 1995.

36. *Windsheimer Zeitung,* April 12, 13, 14, 1995; *Oberkommando des Wehrmachts, Bericht von 14.4.1945,* in Ulrich Herz, ed., "Windsheim im Früjahr 1945" (Bad Windsheim: Steller-Gymnasium, 1995), n.p.; Hobe, "Panzer-Kampfgruppe XIII," in Spiwoks and Stöber, *Endkampf,* pp. 243–44; "G-2 Journal," 12th AD, NA, RG 407/612-2.2.

37. Report of Pastor Dannheimer, Rothenburg ob der Tauber, "Kriegsfackel über den Dörfern," in *Rothenburg o. d. Tauber: Schicksal einer deutschen Landschaft* (Rothenburg ob der Tauber: Verlag J.P. Peter, 1950), quoted in Spiwoks and Stöber, *Endkampf,* pp. 256–57; SD report, end of March 1945, in Marlis G. Steinert, *Hitler's War and the German: Public Mood and Attitude during the Second World War,* ed. and trans. Thomas E. J. de Witt (Athens, Ohio: Ohio Univ. Press, 1977), p. 309; Sixth Army Group, "G-2 Weekly Intelligence Summary of April 8, 1945," in Sixth Army Group History, sec. 1, ch. 9, p. 254, NA, RG 332, ETO, Historical Division Program Files; Klaus-Dietmar Henke, *Die amerikanische Besetzung Deutschlands* (Munich: R. Oldenbourg Verlag, 1995), pp. 777, 844–45.

5. RUNNING AMOK AGAINST THE REALITY OF DEFEAT

1. Klaus-Dietmar Henke, *Die amerikanische Besetzung Deutschlands* (Munich: R. Oldenbourg Verlag, 1995), pp. 797–99; Ian Kershaw, *The Führer Myth: Image and Reality in the Third Reich* (Oxford: Oxford Univ. Press, 1987), pp. 206, 214; Hildebrand Troll, "Aktionen zur Kriegsbeendigung im Frühjahr 1945," in Martin Broszat, Elke Fröhlich, and Anton Großmann, ed., *Bayern in der NS-Zeit,* vol. 4, *Herrschaft und Gesellschaft im Konflikt,* Part C (Munich: R. Oldenbourg Verlag, 1981), p. 647.

2. See, for example, the diary entry of April 2, 1945, in Joseph Goebbels, *Tagebücher 1945: Die letzten Aufzeichnungen* (Hamburg: Hoffmann und Campe, 1977), p. 498.

3. Henke, *amerikanische Besetzung,* pp. 804–11; Manfred Messerschmidt and Fritz Wüllner, *Die Wehrmachtjustiz im Dienste des Nationalsozialismus. Zerstörung eine Legende* (Baden-Baden: Nomos Verlagsgesellschaft, 1987), pp. 77–81, 305–14; Manfred Messerschmidt, "Deutsche Militärgerichtsbarkeit im Zweiten Weltkrieg," in Hans-Jochen Vogel, Helmut Simon, Adalbert Podlech, eds., *Die Freiheit des Andern* (Baden-Baden: Nomos Verlagsgesellschaft, 1981), p. 117.

4. OKW Directive of November 19, 1944, in Rudolf Absolon, ed., *Das Wehrmachtsstrafrecht im 2. Weltkrieg. Sammlung der grundlegenden Gesetze, Verordnungen und Erlasse* (Kornelimünster: Bundesarchiv, Abt. Zentralnachweisstelle, 1958), pp. 97–98; Führer Decrees of March 5, 9, 1945, in Rolf-Dieter Müller and Gerd R. Ueberschar, *Kriegsende 1945: Die Zerstörung des Deutschen Reiches* (Frankfurt: Fischer Taschenbuch Verlag, 1994), pp. 163–64; Troll, "Aktionen zur Kriegsbeendigung," pp. 647–48; Decree by Reichs Justice Minister Thierack of February 15, 1945, in Müller and Ueberschar, *Kriegsende 1945,* pp. 161–62. For the popular mood in Middle Franconia, see "Lagebericht des Gendarmeriepostens Gunzenhausen," March 27, 1945, and "Lagebericht des Gendarmeriepostens Markt Berolzheim," March 27, 1945, Staatsarchiv Nuremberg (StAN Nuremberg), Bestand Landratsamt (LRA) Gunzenhausen Abgabe 61, number 4346; "Lagebericht für Monat März 1945 des Gendarmeriepostens Eichstätt," March 25, 1945, StAN Nuremberg, Bestand NSDAP, number 40, quoted in Henke, *amerikanische Besetzung,* pp. 813–16.

5. On the German sense of duty, see Wilhelm Heinrich Riehl, *Die deutsche Arbeit* (Stuttgart: J.G. Cotta'scher Verlag, 1861), and Joan Campbell, *Joy in Work, German Work: The National Debate, 1800–1945* (Princeton: Princeton Univ. Press, 1989); Doris Bergen, "Death Throes and Killing Frenzies: A Response to Hans Mommsen's 'The Dissolution of the Third Reich: Crisis Management and Collapse, 1943–1945,'" *Bulletin of the German Historical Institute* (Washington, D.C.) 27 (fall 2000): pp. 27–29; Henke, *amerikanische Besetzung,* pp. 820–21; Elke Fröhlich, "Ein junger Märtyrer," in Martin Broszat and Elke Fröhlich, ed., *Bayern in der NS-Zeit,* vol. 6, *Die Herausforderung des Einzelnen. Geschichten über Widerstand und Verfolgung* (Munich: R. Oldenbourg Verlag, 1983), p. 231; report of Pastor Dannheimer, Rothenburg ob der Tauber, cited in Erich Spiwoks and Hans Stöber, *Endkampf zwischen Mosel und Inn. XIII. SS-Armeekorps* (Osnabrück: Munin Verlag, 1976), pp. 256–58; *Stadtchronik* (Bad Windsheim), cited in Spiwoks and Stöber, *Endkampf,* pp. 258–60. For a sense of the popular attitude and everyday life, see *Windsheimer Zeitung,* February–April 1945, passim.

6. Bergen, "Death Throes and Killing Frenzies," pp. 27–29; Henke, *amerikanische Besetzung,* pp. 820–21; Fröhlich, "Ein junger Märtyrer," p. 18; Henke, *amerikanische Besetzung,* p. 824.

7. Helmut Veeh, *Die Kriegsfurie über Franken 1945 und das Ende in den Alpen* (Bad Windsheim: Verlagsdruckerei Heinrich Delp, 1998), pp. 120–21.

8. Henke, *amerikanische Besetzung,* pp. 821–22, 836; Helmut Günther, *Die Sturmflut und das Ende. Geschichte der 17. SS-Pz.Gren.Division "Götz von Berlichingen,"* vol. 3, *Mit dem Rücken zur Wand* (Munich: Schild Verlag, 1991), pp. 277–80.

9. *Windsheimer Zeitung,* April 11, 12, 13, 14, 1995.

10. Hans Woller, *Gesellschaft und Politik in der amerikanischen Besatzungszone. Die Region Ansbach und Fürth* (Munich: R. Oldenbourg Verlag, 1986), pp. 55–57; eyewitness accounts from Stadtarchiv Leutershausen, quoted in Woller, *Gesellschaft und Politik,* p. 55; "Oberkirchenrat Schieder an Evangelisch-Lutherischen Landeskirchenrat," May 11, 1945, Landeskirchliches Archiv (LKA) Nuremberg, Bestand: Kreisdekan Nürnberg, Nr. 14-502.

11. "Lfd. Nr. 180, Verbrechen der Endphase: Aub (Bayern), 7. April 1945. LG Würzburg vom 14. 11. 1949, Ks 2/49; LG Würzburg vom 11. 12. 1948, Kls 59/48; OLG Bamberg vom 16. 3. 1949, Ss 26/49," in Adelheid Rüter-Ehlermann and C. F. Rüter, eds., *Justiz und NS-Verbrechen. Sammlung Deutscher Strafurteile Wegen Nationalsozialistischer Tötungsverbrechen 1945–1966* (Amsterdam: Univ. Press Amsterdam, 1969), 5:pp. 571–72, 579; Veeh, *Kriegsfurie,* p. 127.

12. "Lfd. Nr. 180, Verbrechen der Endphase: Aub," in Rüter-Ehlermann and Rüter, *Justiz und NS-Verbrechen,* 5: pp. 577, 582–83; Veeh, *Kriegsfurie,* p. 297.

13. "Lfd. Nr. 180, Verbrechen der Endphase: Aub," in Rüter-Ehlermann and Rüter, *Justiz und NS-Verbrechen,* 5:pp. 575–76.

14. Ibid., 5:p. 578.

15. Ibid., 5:pp. 583–85; Veeh, *Kriegsfurie,* p. 298.

16. "Lfd. Nr. 180, Verbrechen der Endphase: Aub," in Rüter-Ehlermann and Rüter, *Justiz und NS-Verbrechen,* 5:pp. 585–86; Veeh, *Kriegsfurie,* pp. 298–99.

17. "Lfd. Nr. 180, Verbrechen der Endphase: Aub," in Rüter-Ehlermann and Rüter, *Justiz und NS-Verbrechen,* 5:pp. 587–91; Veeh, *Kriegsfurie,* pp. 299–300.

18. Veeh, *Kriegsfurie,* pp. 575–76.

19. "Lfd. Nr. 180, Verbrechen der Endphase: Aub," in Rüter-Ehlermann and Rüter, *Justiz und NS-Verbrechen,* 5:pp. 587–91; Veeh, *Kriegsfurie,* pp. 577–81.

20. Veeh, *Kriegsfurie,* p. 262.

21. Ibid., pp. 262–63.

22. "Lfd. Nr. 472, Verbrechen der Endphase: Rummelsmühle bei Seenheim (Bayern), 12. April 1945. LG Ansbach vom 2. 1. 1959, Ks 3/58," in Irene Sagel-Grande, et al., eds., *Justiz und NS-Verbrechen. Sammlung Deutscher Strafurteile Wegen Nationalsozialistischer Tötungsverbrechen 1945–1966* (Amsterdam: Univ. Press Amsterdam, 1976), 15:pp. 373–77.

23. Ibid., 15:pp. 375–77.

24. Ibid., 15:pp. 377–80; Henke, *amerikanische Besetzung,* pp. 853–54; "Bericht über die Besetzung von Ergersheim durch die Amerikaner," Evangelisch-Lutherische Pfarramtes Ergersheim an den Landeskirchenrat in Ansbach von 2 June 1945, LKA

Nuremberg, Bestand Landeskirchenrat München; Troll, "Aktionen zur Kriegsbeendigung," pp. 657–58; Ulrich Herz, ed., "Windsheim im Frühjahr 1945" (Bad Windsheim: Steller-Gymnasium, 1995), n.p.; Fröhlich, "Ein junger Märtyrer," p. 257.

25. "Lfd. Nr. 472, Verbrechen der Endphase: Rummelsmühle," in Sagel-Grande, *Justiz und NS-Verbrechen*, 15:pp. 374, 380–81, 391–92.

26. "Lfd. Nr. 466, Verbrechen der Endphase: Burgthann (bei Nürnberg), 17. April 1945. LG Nürnberg-Fürth vom 1. 10. 1958, 638 Ks 5/56 and BGH vom 22. 10. 1957, 1 StR 116/57," in Sagel-Grande, *Justiz und NS-Verbrechen*, 15:pp. 277–81; Troll, "Aktion zur Kriegsbeendigung," pp. 655–56.

27. "Lfd. Nr. 466, Verbrechen der Endphase: Burgthann," in Sagel-Grande, *Justiz und NS-Verbrechen*, 15:pp. 281–93.

28. "Lfd. Nr. 421, Justizverbrechen: Rothenburg o. T., Schillingsfürst, und Brettheim, 5., 9., und 10. April 1945. LG Ansbach vom 19. 10. 1955, Ks 1/52, Ks 1–2/54, and BGH vom 7. 12. 1956, 1 StR 56/56," in Sagel-Grande, *Justiz und NS-Verbrechen*, 13:pp. 365–66; Otto Ströbel, *Die Männer von Brettheim*, 2nd ed. (Kirchberg an der Jagst: Wettin Verlag, 1988), pp. 6–9.

29. "Lfd. Nr. 421, Justizverbrechen: Rothenburg o. T., Schillingsfürst, und Brettheim," in Sagel-Grande, *Justiz und NS-Verbrechen*, 13:pp. 366–67; Ströbel, *Brettheim*, pp. 9–10; See also: Fröhlich, "Ein junger Märtyrer," pp. 236–39; Spiwoks and Stöber, *Endkampf*, pp. 390–94.

30. "Lfd. Nr. 421, Justizverbrechen: Rothenburg o. T., Schillingsfürst, und Brettheim," in Sagel-Grande, *Justiz und NS-Verbrechen*, 13:pp. 362, 367–68; Ströbel, *Brettheim*, pp. 11–17.

31. "Lfd. Nr. 421, Justizverbrechen: Rothenburg o. T., Schillingsfürst, und Brettheim," in Sagel-Grande, *Justiz und NS-Verbrechen*, 13:pp. 367–68; Ströbel, *Brettheim*, pp. 18–21.

32. "Lfd. Nr. 421, Justizverbrechen: Rothenburg o. T., Schillingsfürst, und Brettheim," in Sagel-Grande, *Justiz und NS-Verbrechen*, 13:pp. 368–69; Ströbel, *Brettheim*, pp. 20–23.

33. "Lfd. Nr. 421, Justizverbrechen: Rothenburg o. T., Schillingsfürst, und Brettheim," in Sagel-Grande, *Justiz und NS-Verbrechen*, 13:pp. 369–71; Ströbel, *Brettheim*, pp. 24–27; Fröhlich, "Ein junger Märtyrer," p. 238.

34. "Lfd. Nr. 421, Justizverbrechen: Rothenburg o. T., Schillingsfürst, und Brettheim," in Sagel-Grande, *Justiz und NS-Verbrechen*, 13:pp. 369–72; Ströbel, *Brettheim*, pp. 28–35; Fröhlich, "Ein junger Märtyrer," pp. 239–40; Spiwoks and Stöber, *Endkampf*, pp. 390–94; Henke, *amerikanische Besetzung*, pp. 787, 837, 840.

35. Ströbel, *Brettheim*, pp. 36–37; Adolf Rusam, "Aus meinem Leben als Dorfpfarrer in der Kriegszeit. Tagebuch über die letzten Kriegswochen, die militärische Besetzung und den politischen Umschwung in Oberampfrach 26. Marz-10. Mai 1945," Anhang zu Ahnen-Liste Rusam-Kaeppel, Ergänzungsband, bearbeitet

von Kirchenrat Adolf Rusam, LKA Nuremberg, Berichte über Vorgänge bei der militärische Besetzung.

Interestingly enough, despite his fear of the SS in the last days of the war, Pastor Rusam on May 2 expressed surprise at the jubilant reaction of the people of his village to the news of Hitler's death. "Really shocking!" he wrote in his diary, "The Führer, for twelve years the leader of the state, dead—and now this outbreak of joy! And that among the children, who since their earliest youth had to greet each other with 'Heil Hitler!' With that one can gauge just what a terrible burden in the end this man meant to his poor people."

36. "Lfd. Nr. 421, Justizverbrechen: Rothenburg o. T., Schillingsfürst, und Brettheim," in Sagel-Grande, *Justiz und NS-Verbrechen*, 13:pp. 372–80. The sentence in question ran: *Sie wurden späte Opfer jenes unglückseligen Krieges, der nicht einmal rechtzeitig sein Ende finden konnte.*

37. Theodor Georg Richert, "Neuhof an der Zenn im April 1945," *Fürther Heimatblätter* 17, no. 5 (1967): pp. 160–67; report of Peter Heinlein, in Spiwoks and Stöber, *Endkampf*, pp. 266–68; Troll, "Aktionen zur Kriegsbeendigung," p. 649.

38. Richert, "Neuhof an der Zenn im April 1945," pp. 160–67; report of Auguste Paul in Spiwoks and Stöber, *Endkampf*, pp. 268–71; Troll, "Aktionen zur Kriegsbeendigung," p. 649.

39. Richert, "Neuhof an der Zenn im April 1945," pp. 160–67; report of Auguste Paul in Spiwoks and Stöber, *Endkampf*, pp. 271–72; Troll, "Aktionen zur Kriegsbeendigung," p. 649.

40. Richert, "Neuhof an der Zenn im April 1945," pp. 160–67; report of Peter Heinlein, in Spiwoks and Stöber, *Endkampf*, pp. 272–74; Troll, "Aktionen zur Kriegsbeendigung," p. 649.

41. Report of Peter Heinlein, in Spiwoks and Stöber, *Endkampf*, pp. 272–74.

42. Report of Fränzi Reuter in Richert, "Neuhof an der Zenn im April 1945," p. 167; *Windsheimer Zeitung*, April 9, 11, 13, 15, 1995; "After Action Report," 101st Cavalry Group, NA, RG 407, Entry 427; Henke, *amerikanische Besetzung*, p. 793.

Ironically, just a few days later, a column of American POWs, including men of Company A of the Seventeenth Armored Infantry Battalion, Twelfth Armored Division, found themselves on the same walking tour of Germany. Having survived the ill-fated breakout of the Hammelburg POW camp and a savage American air raid on Nuremberg on April 21, the men, under the watchful eyes of Army Air Corps P-51s, spent the remainder of the war walking the country roads of southern Franconia, eating potatoes from the fields, and sleeping in barns. See accounts of Carl Helton and Marvin Drum, "Company A, 17th Armored Infantry Battalion," http://www.acu.edu/academics/history12ad/17aibx/.

43. "Führerbefehl Nr. 11 vom 8. März 1944, Kommandanten der festen Plätze und Kampfkommandanten," in Herz, "Windsheim im Frühjahr 1945," n.p.; "Führerbefehl vom 25. November 1944 & 12. April 1945, Übergabe von Festungen

und Städten," in Müller and Ueberschär, *Kriegsende 1945*, pp. 169–70; "Aufgaben der Kampfkommandanten: Gemeinsame Bekanntmachung des Chefs des Oberkommandos der Wehrmacht, des Reichsführers-SS und des Leiters der Parteikanzlei vom 12. April 1945," in C. F. Rüter and D. W. De Mildt, eds., *Justiz und NS-Verbrechen. Sammlung Deutscher Strafurteile Wegen Nationalsozialistischer Tötungsverbrechen 1945–1966. Register zu den Bänden I-XXII* (Amsterdam: Holland Univ. Press, 1998), p. 199; "Verteidigung von Städten: Fernschreiben des Reichsführers-SS vom 12. April 1945," in ibid., p. 200.

44. Herz, "Windsheim im Frühjahr 1945," n.p.; *Windsheimer Zeitung*, March 10, 22, 23, April 10, 12, 1945.

45. *Windsheimer Zeitung*, April 12, 1945, April 1, 5, 6, 1995.

46. *Stadtchronik* (Bad Windsheim), in Spiwoks and Stöber, *Endkampf*, p. 259; *Windsheimer Zeitung*, April 8, 9, 1995; Herz, "Windsheim im Frühjahr 1945," n.p.

47. *Stadtchronik* (Bad Windsheim), in Spiwoks and Stöber, *Endkampf*, p. 260–61; "Verbrechen der Endphase: Bad Windsheim (Bayern), 13. April 1945. LG Nürnberg-Fürth vom 20.8.1948, KLs 152/48 and OLG Nürnberg vom 11.11.1948, Ss 191/48," in Rüter-Ehlermann and Rüter, *Justiz und NS-Verbrechen*, 3:p. 173; *Windsheimer Zeitung*, April 10, 11, 1995; Herz, "Windsheim im Frühjahr 1945," n.p.; Troll, "Aktionen zur Kriegsbeendigung," p. 650; Karl Kunze, *Kriegsende in Franken und der Kampf um Nürnberg im April 1945* (Nuremberg: Selbstverlag des Vereins fur Geschichte der Stadt Nürnbergs, 1995), p. 174.

48. *Stadtchronik* (Bad Windsheim), in Spiwoks and Stöber, *Endkampf*, p. 261–63; *Windsheimer Zeitung*, April 12, 1995; Kurt Güner, "Sie wollte Leben retten und wurde von Nazis ermordet," *Fränkische Landeszeitung* (Ansbach), March 31, 1995; Herz, "Windsheim im Frühjahr 1945," n.p.; Troll, "Aktionen zur Kriegsbeendigung," pp. 651–52; Kunze, *Kriegsende in Franken*, pp. 174–75; statements of Thekla Fischer, August 18, 1948, and Babette Teufel, August 18, 1948, Staatsanwaltschaft b. Landgericht Nürnberg-Fürth, Nr. 2792. Interestingly, the term *Weibersturm* had long been a part of Bad Windsheim's history. In May 1525, during the Peasants War, the women of the at-that-time imperial city rebelled and stormed an important public building in their search for relief from miserable economic circumstances. See Alfred Estermann, *Bad Windsheim: Geschichte und Gegenwart einer fränkischen Stadt* (Bad Windsheim: Verlagsdruckerei Heinrich Delp, 1989), p. 79.

49. *Stadtchronik* (Bad Windsheim), in Spiwoks and Stöber, *Endkampf*, p. 261–63; *Windsheimer Zeitung*, March 20, 1945, April 12, 1995; Herz, "Windsheim im Frühjahr 1945," n.p.; Troll, "Aktionen zur Kriegsbeendigung," pp. 651–52; Kunze, *Kriegsende in Franken*, pp. 174–75.

50. *Stadtchronik* (Bad Windsheim), in Spiwoks and Stöber, *Endkampf*, p. 261–63; Herz, "Windsheim im Frühjahr 1945," n.p.; Troll, "Aktionen zur Kriegsbeendigung," pp. 651–52; Kunze, *Kriegsende in Franken*, pp. 174–75.

51. *Stadtchronik* (Bad Windsheim), in Spiwoks and Stöber, *Endkampf*, p. 261–

63; *Windsheimer Zeitung,* March 20, 1945, April 12, 1995; statement of Anni Schunk, March 29, 1995, in Herz, "Windsheim im Frühjahr 1945," n.p.; Troll, "Aktionen zur Kriegsbeendigung," pp. 651–52; Güner, "Sie wollte Leben retten"; Kunze, *Kriegsende in Franken,* pp. 174–75.

52. Herz, "Windsheim im Frühjahr 1945," n.p.

53. "Hans Schmotzer an den Herrn Oberstaatsanwalt beim Landgericht Nürnberg-Fürth, 4 Dezember 1946, Betrifft: Ermordung der Frau Christine Schmotzer," "Beschuldigtenvernehmung (Schmid, Karl) in der Voruntersuchung gegen Reinbrecht, Günther wegen Totschlags," "Erklärung des Angeklagten Schmid vor dem Landgericht Nürnberg-Fürth vom 18.8.1948," all in: Staatsanwaltschaft beim Landgericht Nürnberg-Fürth, Nr. 2792; "Verbrechen der Endphase: Bad Windsheim," in Rüter-Ehlermann and Rüter, *Justiz und NS-Verbrechen,* 3:pp. 173–75, 177; Henke, *amerikanische Besetzung,* p. 854; Troll, "Aktion zur Kriegsbeendigung," p. 652.

54. "Verbrechen der Endphase: Bad Windsheim," in Rüter-Ehlermann and Rüter, *Justiz und NS-Verbrechen,* 3:pp. 174–77; "Beschuldigtenvernehmung (Schmid, Karl) in der Voruntersuchung gegen Reinbrecht, Günther wegen Totschlags," "Erklärung des Angeklagten Schmid vor dem Landgericht Nürnberg-Fürth vom 18.8.1948," "Hans Schmotzer an den Herrn Oberstaatsanwalt beim Landgericht Nürnberg-Fürth, 4 Dezember 1946, Betrifft: Ermordung der Frau Christine Schmotzer," "Aussage Hedwig D. vom 19.8.1948," "Zeugenaussage Rolf V. vom 19.8.1948," "Aussage von Emmi J. vom 19.8.1948," "Erklärung des Zeugenaussage Johann Friedrich Dasch," "Erklärung des Zeugenaussage Irmgard Schmotzer," "Anklageschrift der Staatsanwaltschaft beim Landgericht Nürnberg-Fürth vom 23.5.1948," all in: Staatsanwaltschaft beim Landgericht Nürnberg-Fürth Nr. 2792; Güner, "Sie wollte Leben retten"; Kurt Güner, "Gegen Mörder ohne Chance," *Fränkische Landeszeitung* (Ansbach), March 31, 1995.

55. "Verbrechen der Endphase: Bad Windsheim," in Rüter-Ehlermann and Rüter, *Justiz und NS-Verbrechen,* 3:pp. 174–77; "Aussage Hedwig D. vom 19.8.1948," "Zeugenaussage Rolf V. vom 19.8.1948," "Aussage von Emmi J. vom 19.8.1948," "Erklärung des Zeugenaussage Johann Friedrich Dasch," "Erklärung des Zeugenaussage Irmgard Schmotzer," "Anklageschrift der Staatsanwaltschaft beim Landgericht Nürnberg-Fürth vom 23.5.1948," all in: Staatsanwaltschaft beim Landgericht Nürnberg-Fürth Nr. 2792; *Windsheimer Zeitung,* April 13, 1995; Güner, "Gegen Mörder"; *Fränkische Landeszeitung* (Ansbach), August 21, 1948, March 31, 1995; Herz, "Windsheim im Frühjahr 1945," n.p.; *Stadtchronik* (Bad Windsheim), in Spiwoks and Stöber, *Endkampf,* p. 261–63; *Windsheimer Zeitung,* April 12, 1995; Troll, "Aktionen zur Kriegsbeendigung," p. 652.

56. Herz, "Windsheim im Frühjahr 1945," n.p.; "Verbrechen der Endphase: Bad Windsheim," in Rüter-Ehlermann and Rüter, *Justiz und NS-Verbrechen,* 3:pp. 174–75.

57. "Erklärung des Angeklagten Schmid vor dem Landgericht Nürnberg-Fürth vom 18.8.1948," Staatsanwaltschaft beim Landgericht Nürnberg-Fürth Nr. 2792, Niederschrift der Sitzung, p. 3; "Verbrechen der Endphase: Bad Windsheim," in Rüter-Ehlermann and Rüter, *Justiz und NS-Verbrechen*, 3:pp. 179–80.

58. Verbrechen der Endphase: Bad Windsheim," in Rüter-Ehlermann and Rüter, *Justiz und NS-Verbrechen*, 3:pp. 178–81; *Fränkische Landeszeitung* (Ansbach), August 21, 1948.

59. "Beschluss in der Strafsache gegen Reinbrecht, Günter; Schmid, Karl; Hub, Albert, 20.8.1948," Staatsanwaltschaft beim Landgericht Nürnberg-Fürth, Nr. 2192; "Revisionsbegründung in der Strafsache gegen Reinbrecht, Günter; Schmid, Karl; Hub, Albert," Oberlandesgericht Nürnberg vom 11.11.1948, Ss 191/48; "Verbrechen der Endphase: Bad Windsheim," in Rüter-Ehlermann and Rüter, *Justiz und NS-Verbrechen*, 3:pp. 183–86; Herz, "Windsheim im Frühjahr 1945," n.p.

60. Dirk de Mildt, *In the Name of the People: Perpetrators of Genocide in the Reflection of their Post-War Prosecution in West Germany. The "Euthanasia" and "Aktion Reinhard" Trial Cases* (The Hague, London, and Boston: Martinus Nijhoff Publishers, 1996), pp. 304, 310.

61. "Verbrechen der Endphase: Ansbach, 18. April 1945. LG Ansbach vom 14.12.1946, KLs 24/46 and OLG Nürnberg vom 20.5.1947, Ss 35/47," in Adelheid Rüter-Ehlermann and C. F. Rüter, ed., *Justiz und NS-Verbrechen. Sammlung deutscher Strafurteile wegen nationalsozialistischer Tötungsverbrechen 1945–1966* (Amsterdam: Univ. Press Amsterdam, 1968), 1:p. 117; Fröhlich, "Ein junger Märtyrer," pp. 228–31.

62. "Verbrechen der Endphase: Ansbach," in Rüter-Ehlermann and Rüter, *Justiz und NS-Verbrechen*, 1:p.116; Fröhlich, "Ein junger Märtyrer," p. 232.

63. Fröhlich, "Ein junger Märtyrer," pp. 233–34.

64. Ibid., pp. 235, 240–41.

65. Ibid., pp. 240–41; "Verbrechen der Endphase: Ansbach," in Rüter-Ehlermann and Rüter, *Justiz und NS-Verbrechen*, 1:p. 123.

66. Fröhlich, "Ein junger Märtyrer," pp. 242–43; *Fränkische Landeszeitung* (Ansbach), July 4, 1970.

67. "Verbrechen der Endphase: Ansbach," in Rüter-Ehlermann and Rüter, *Justiz und NS-Verbrechen*, 1:p. 118; Fröhlich, "Ein junger Märtyrer," pp. 244–46; *Fränkische Landeszeitung* (Ansbach), April 24, 1946, April 18, 1955, July 15, 1969, July 4, 1970, April 18, 1980.

68. "Verbrechen der Endphase: Ansbach," in Rüter-Ehlermann and Rüter, *Justiz und NS-Verbrechen*, 1:p. 118; Fröhlich, "Ein junger Märtyrer," pp. 246–49; *Fränkische Landeszeitung* (Ansbach), April 24, 1946, April 18, 1955, July 15, 1969, July 4, 1970, April 18, 1980; Seventh U.S. Army, *The Seventh United States Army in France and Germany 1944–1945* (Heidelberg: Aloys Gräf, 1946), 3:p. 778.

69. "Verbrechen der Endphase: Ansbach," in Rüter-Ehlermann and Rüter, *Justiz und NS-Verbrechen*, 1:p. 119; Fröhlich, "Ein junger Märtyrer," pp. 245, 249–50.

70. "Verbrechen der Endphase: Ansbach," in Rüter-Ehlermann and Rüter, *Justiz und NS-Verbrechen*, 1:p. 119; Fröhlich, "Ein junger Märtyrer," p. 250.

71. "Verbrechen der Endphase: Ansbach," in Rüter-Ehlermann and Rüter, *Justiz und NS-Verbrechen*, 1:pp. 119, 127; Fröhlich, "Ein junger Märtyrer," pp. 250–52.

72. "Verbrechen der Endphase: Ansbach," in Rüter-Ehlermann and Rüter, *Justiz und NS-Verbrechen*, 1:pp. 119–20; Fröhlich, "Ein junger Märtyrer," pp. 251–52.

73. Henke, *amerikanische Besetzung*, pp. 838–44; SHAEF, "Political Intelligence Report, 30 April 1945," NA, RG 331, Decimal File, May 1943–August 1945, Entry 1; SHAEF, G-5, "Weekly Journal of Information," no. 12, May 11, 1945, NA, RG 331, 131.11; SHAEF Information Branch, "Weekly Intelligence Summary for Psychological Warfare," no. 31, May 2, 1945, NA, RG 331, Entry 54; SHAEF, Psychological Warfare Division, "General Intelligence Bulletin," no. 41, March 31, 1945, NA, RG 331, Decimal File 1944–1945, Entry 87; "Bericht über die Feindbesetzung der Kirchengemeinde bezw. über vorausgehende Kampfhandlungen," Pfarramtes Obermichelbach über Wassertrüdingen an das Evangelisch-Lutherische Dekanat Dinkelsbühl, June 1, 1945, LKA Nuremberg, Dekanat Dinkelsbühl; Ursula von Kardorff, *Berliner Aufzeichnungen, 1942–1945*, 2nd ed. (Munich: Deutscher Taschenbuch Verlag, 1976), pp. 253–54; Woller, *Gesellschaft und Politik*, pp. 57–58.

74. Henke, *amerikanische Besetzung*, pp. 821, 843–45; Herfried Münkler, *Machtzerfall Die letzten Tage des Dritten Reiches dargestellt am Beispiel der hessischen Kreisstadt Friedberg* (Berlin: Siedler Verlag, 1985), pp. 32–33; Troll, "Aktionen zur Kriegsbeendigung," pp. 647, 689.

75. Henke, *amerikanische Besetzung*, pp. 821, 843–45; Münkler, *Machtzerfall*, pp. 98–99; Troll, "Aktionen zur Kriegsbeendigung," pp. 647, 689.

6. ACROSS THE FRANKENHÖHE

1. "After Action Report," 101st Cav Rcnz Sq, NA, RG 407/304-CAV-101-0.3; *Windsheimer Zeitung*, April 13, 14, 1991; Helmut Veeh, *Die Kriegsfurie über Franken 1945 und das Ende in den Alpen*, 3rd ed. (Bad Windsheim: Verlagsdrückerei Heinrich Delp, 1998), pp. 431, 434; Karl Kunze, *Kriegsende in Franken und der Kampf um Nürnberg im April 1945* (Nuremberg: Selbstverlag des Vereins für die Geschichte der Stadt Nürnbergs, 1995), pp. 173–74.

2. "After Action Report," 101st Cav Rcnz Sq, NA, RG 407/304-CAV-101-0.3; *Windsheimer Zeitung*, April 13, 14, 1991; Veeh, *Kriegsfurie*, p. 434; Kunze, *Kriegsende in Franken*, pp. 173–74; Special Operations Report, "Task Force Rodwell, Interview with Major John Swink, Acting Assistant S-3 (Operations Officer) 12th Infantry Regiment, 4th Infantry Division," NA, RG 407, Entry 427.

3. Twelfth Armored Division, *A History of the United States Twelfth Armored Division, 15 September 1942–17 December 1945: The Hellcats in World War II* (1947;

reprint, Nashville, Tenn.: Battery Press, 1978), pp. 68–69; "Combat and Infantry Journal," 8th IR, 4th ID, NA, RG 407/304-INF-(8)-0.7.

4. Christoph Rückert, *Ipsheim: Die Chronik eines fränkischen Dorfes* (Ipsheim: Marktgemeinde Ipsheim, 1989), pp. 14, 18–19, 26–27, 33–34, 37, 47–51, 63–64, 83–86; Rainer Hambrecht, *Der Aufstieg der NSDAP in Mittel-und Oberfranken, 1925–1933* (Nuremberg: Schriftenreihe des Stadtarchivs Nürnberg, 1976), pp. 17, 101.

5. Bezirksamt (BA) Uffenheim to Regierung von Mittelfranken, April 25, 1922, Staatsarchiv Nuremberg (StAN), Kammer des Innern II, 714; Halbsmonatsbericht der Regierung von Mittelfranken, April 20, 1925, *Bayerisches Hauptstaatsarchiv München*, Abteilung II (BaStAM), Ministerium des Äußern, 102153; Gendarmerie Ipsheim to BA Uffenheim, January 8, 1927, BaStAM, Sonderabgabe I, 1548; Lagebericht der Polizeidirektion Nürnberg-Fürth, November 22, 1927, StAN, Polizeidirektion Nürnberg-Fürth, 347; Halbsmonatsbericht der Regierung von Mittelfranken, November 18, 1927, BaStAM, Ministerium des Äußern, 102153; Hambrecht, *Aufstieg der NSDAP,* pp. 28–29, 101–2, 199, 323, 458; Rückert, *Ipsheim,* pp. 83–86.

6. Lagebericht der Polizeidirektion Nürnberg-Fürth, July 31, 1925, StAN, Polizeidirektion Nürnberg-Fürth, 342; Josef Stolzing, *Arnold von Hoheneck,* quoted in Hambrecht, *Aufstieg der NSDAP,* pp. 514–15; Rückert, *Ipsheim,* pp. 84–88.

7. "Französische Kriegsgefangene in Ipsheim," *Windsheimer Zeitung,* September 8, 9, and 10, 1984; Gemeinde Archiv Ipsheim, Document Numbers 101, 139, 141, and unnumbered file from 1946; Rückert, *Ipsheim,* pp. 89–91. Neighboring Bad Windsheim, which had also been an early bastion of pro-Nazi sentiment, lost 283 men killed or missing out of a prewar population of roughly 6,000. Another 43 residents of the town perished in the Holocaust. See Albrecht Vornberger, ed. *Keiner wußte, was geschah—Windsheim in der Nazi-Zeit* (Ansbach: DGB-Bildungswerk Westmittelfranken, n.d.), pp. 100, 123.

8. "After Action Report," 56th AIB, 12th AD, NA, RG 407/612-INF-(56)-0.3; "After Action Report," 92nd Cav Rcnz Sq, 12th AD, NA, RG 407/612-CAV-0.3; "After Action Report," 714th Tk Bn, 12th AD, NA, RG 407/612-TK(714)-0.3; Veeh, *Kriegsfurie,* p. 439; Lieutenant Colonel Cord von Hobe, "Einsatz der Panzer-Kampfgruppe XIII vom 06.04–05.05 1945," Foreign Military Study B-772, in Erich Spiwoks and Hans Stöber, *Endkampf zwischen Mosel und Inn. XIII. SS-Armeekorps* (Osnabrück: Munin Verlag, 1976), p. 243; Rückert, *Ipsheim,* p. 91.

9. "After Action Report," 56th AIB, 12th AD, NA, RG 407/612-INF-(56)-0.3; Owsley C. Costlow, ed., "Division Operations for the Month of April 1945," in *Combat Highlights of the United States Twelfth Armored Division in the European Theater of Operations, 1 December 1944–30 May 1945* (Prepared by G-3 Information and Education Section, 1954), p. 4; Veeh, *Kriegsfurie,* p. 443–44; Hobe, "Panzer-Kampfgruppe XIII," in Spiwoks and Stöber, *Endkampf,* pp. 244–45.

10. Personal reports of Ludwig Götz, Paul Schemm, Babette Haßler, Lisabeth Pfeffer, Frieda Stroh, and Babette Roder, in Spiwoks and Stöber, *Endkampf,* pp. 278–

79; Theodor Georg Richert, "Die letzten Tage des Zweiten Weltkrieges im Gebiet des Schulverbandes Wilhermsdorf," StAN, Bestand: Die letzten Tage des 2. Weltkrieges in Wilhermsdorf, Nr. 2454/4.

11. Personal reports of Liselotte Lutter and Ludwig Götz, in Spiwoks and Stöber, *Endkampf,* pp. 279–80.

12. Personal reports of Ludwig Götz and Liselotte Lutter, in Spiwoks and Stöber, *Endkampf,* pp. 280–83; Richert, "letzten Tage."

13. Richert, "letzten Tage"; personal reports of Dr. Friedrich Nitsche and Veronika Martinetz, in Spiwoks and Stöber, *Endkampf,* pp. 286–87.

14. Entry in the "Pfarrbuches der Evangelisch-Lutherische Kirchengemeinde Wilhermsdorf" and personal reports of Gottlieb Freund, Frieda Stroh, Dr. Friedrich Nitsche, Liselotte Lutter, Marie Torka, Ludwig Götz, and Paul Schemm, in Spiwoks and Stöber, *Endkampf,* pp. 283–88; Richert, "letzten Tage"; Klaus-Dietmar Henke, *Die amerikanische Besetzung Deutschlands* (Munich: R. Oldenbourg Verlag, 1995), p. 793; "After Action Report," 56th AIB, 12th AD, NA, RG 407/612-INF-(56)-0.3.

15. "After Action Report," 92nd Cav Rcnz Sq, 12th AD, NA, RG 407/612-CAV-0.3; Vech, *Kriegsfurie,* p. 451; Henke, *amerikanische Besetzung,* p. 793.

16. "After Action Report," 56th AIB, 12th AD, NA, RG 407/612-INF (56)-0.3; "After Action Report," 101st Cav Rcnz Sq, NA, RG 407/304-CAV-101-0.3; Costlow, "Division Operations," p. 4; Veeh, *Kriegsfurie,* pp. 456–57; Spiwoks and Stöber, *Endkampf,* p. 246.

17. "After Action Report," 17th AIB, 12th AD, NA, RG 407/612-INF-(17)-0.3; "S-2 Journal" and "S-3 Journal," 17th AIB, 12th AD, NA, RG 407/612-INF-(17)-0.7; Sergeant Carl J. Lyons, "Personal Account, Company A 17th Armored Infantry Battalion, 12th Armored Division," http://www.acu.edu/academics/history/12ad/17aibx/lyonsb.htm; Twelfth Armored Division, *Twelfth Armored Division,* p. 66.

18. Lyons, "Company A"; "After Action Report," 17th AIB, 12th AD, NA, RG 407/612-INF-(17)-0.3; "S-2 Journal" and "S-3 Journal," 17th AIB, 12th AD, NA, RG 407/612-INF-(17)-0.7; "Combat and Infantry Journal," 8th IR, 4th ID, NA, RG 407/304-INF-(8)-0.7; "After Action Report," 8th IR, 4th ID, NA, RG 407/304-INF-(8)-0.3; "Unit Report," 8th IR, 4th ID, NA, RG 407/304-INF-(8)-0.9; SS-Obersturmbannführer Ekkehard Albert, Chief of Staff, XIII SS-Army Corps, "Einsatz des XIII. SS-A.K. zwischen Rhein und Alpen vom 26.03–06.05.1945," Foreign Military Study B-737, in Spiwoks and Stöber, *Endkampf,* p. 252; *Windsheimer Zeitung,* April 13, 1995; Veeh, *Kriegsfurie,* pp. 435–36.

19. Lyons, "Company A"; "After Action Report," 17th AIB, 12th AD, NA, RG 407/612-INF-(17)-0.3; "S-2 Journal" and "S-3 Journal," 17th AIB, 12th AD, NA, RG 407/612-INF-(17)-0.7; "S-3 Journal," 23rd Tk Bn, 12th AD, NA, RG 407/612-TK-(23)-0.7; "Combat and Infantry Journal," 8th IR, 4th ID, NA, RG 407/304-INF-(8)-0.7; "After Action Report," 8th IR, 4th ID, NA, RG 407/304-INF-(8)-0.3; "Unit Report," 8th IR, 4th ID, NA, RG 407/304-INF-(8)-0.9; Veeh, *Kriegsfurie,* pp. 441–42.

20. Lyons, "Company A"; "After Action Report," 17th AIB, 12th AD, NA, RG 407/612-INF-(17)-0.3; "S-2 Journal" and "S-3 Journal," 17th AIB, 12th AD, NA, RG 407/612-INF-(17)-0.7; "S-3 Journal," 23rd Tk Bn, 12th AD, NA, RG 407/612-TK-(23)-0.7; "Combat and Infantry Journal," 8th IR, 4th ID, NA, RG 407/304-INF-(8)-0.7; "After Action Report," 8th IR, 4th ID, NA, RG 407/304-INF-(8)-0.3; "Unit Report," 8th IR, 4th ID, NA, RG 407/304-INF-(8)-0.9; Veeh, *Kriegsfurie,* pp. 452, 457–61.

21. Lyons, "Company A"; "After Action Report," 17th AIB, 12th AD, NA, RG 407/612-INF-(17)-0.3; "S-2 Journal" and "S-3 Journal," 17th AIB, 12th AD, NA, RG 407/612-INF-(17)-0.7; "S-3 Journal," 23rd Tk Bn, 12th AD, NA, RG 407/612-TK-(23)-0.7; "Combat and Infantry Journal," 8th IR, 4th ID, NA, RG 407/304-INF-(8)-0.7; "After Action Report," 8th IR, 4th ID, NA, RG 407/304-INF-(8)-0.3; "Unit Report," 8th IR, 4th ID, NA, RG 407/304-INF-(8)-0.9; Veeh, *Kriegsfurie,* pp. 452, 457–61; Hans Woller, *Gesellschaft und Politik in der amerikanischen Besatzungzone: Die Region Ansbach und Fürth* (Munich: R. Oldenbourg Verlag, 1986), pp. 55–56.

22. "Operations Report," 7th IR, 3rd ID, April 20, 1945, NA, RG 407/Entry 427; Kunze, *Kriegsende in Franken,* pp. 274–78 and passim; Veeh, *Kriegsfurie,* pp. 464–82; Henke, *amerikanische Besetzung,* pp. 794–95; *Stars and Stripes,* April 21, 1945; Seventh U.S. Army, *The Seventh United States Army in France and Germany 1944–1945* (Heidelberg: Aloys Graf, 1946), 3:pp. 796.

23. Veeh, *Kriegsfurie,* pp. 459, 474, 491, 496; "After Action Report," 101st Cav Rcnz Sq, NA, RG 407/304-CAV-101-0.3; "After Action Report," 92nd Cav Rcnz Sq, 12th AD, NA, RG 407/612-CAV-0.3; "After Action Report," CC-A, 12th AD, NA, RG 407/612-CCA-0.3; "Unit Histories," Headquarters, 12th AD, NA, RG 407/612-0.2; Colonel Charles K. Graydon, "With the 101st Cavalry in World War II, 1940–1945," http://members.tripod.com/1-101cav/ww2.html.

24. "After Action Report," 101st Cav Rcnz Sq, NA, RG 407/304-CAV-101-0.3; Graydon, "101st Cavalry"; Hermann Rauschning, *Gespräche mit Hitler* (Zurich and New York: Europa Verlag, 1940), pp. 216–17.

25. Veeh, *Kriegsfurie,* p. 496; Hildebrand Troll, "Aktionen zur Kriegsbeendigung im Frühjahr 1945," in Martin Broszat, Elke Fröhlick, and Anton Großmann, eds., *Bayern in der NS-Zeit,* vol. 4, *Herrschaft und Gesellschaft im Konflikt,* Part C (Munich: R. Oldenbourg Verlag, 1981), p. 654. (Troll mistakenly dates the demonstration as occurring on April 13.)

26. "After Action Report," 101st Cav Rcnz Sq, NA, RG 407/304-CAV-101-0.3; "After Action Report," Captain Louis Bossert, C Troop, 116th Cav Rcnz Sq; Graydon, "101st Cavalry"; description of battle by SS trooper W. Vopersal, quoted in Veeh, *Kriegsfurie,* pp. 496–97; Spiwoks and Stöber, *Endkampf,* pp. 321–24. Although Veeh and Spiwoks quote the same eyewitness account, they provide differing dates for the attack on Merkendorf, Veeh citing April 19 while Spiwoks claims it occurred on April 20. A careful check of a number of American reports all lend credence to April 19 as the day of the battle. All available American units had been reassembled on April 20 to exploit a

breakthrough southwest of Ansbach along the axis Feuchtwangen–Dinkelsbühl. See "G-1 After Action Report," Headquarters, 12th AD, NA, RG 407/612-1.0; "Unit Histories," Headquarters, 12th AD, NA, RG 407/612-0.2; "Periodic Reports," Headquarters, CC-R, 12th AD, RG 407/612-CCR-0.9; "G-3 Periodic Report," CC-B, 12th AD, RG 407/612-CCB-1.8-3.17; "After Action Report," CC-A, 12th AD, NA, RG 407/612-CCA-0.3; "After Action Report," 92nd Cav Rcnz Sq, 12th AD, NA, RG 407/612-CAV-0.3; "After Action Report," 101st Cav Rcnz Sq, NA, RG 407/304-CAV-101-0.3; "After Action Report," 8th IR, 4th ID, NA, RG 407/304-INF-(8)-0.3; "Unit Report," 8th IR, 4th ID, NA, RG 407/304-INF-(8)-0.9; Graydon, "101st Cavalry."

27. "After Action Report," 101st Cav Rcnz Sq, NA, RG 407/304-CAV-101-0.3; "After Action Report," Captain Louis Bossert, C Troop, 116th Cav Rcnz Sq; Graydon, "101st Cavalry"; Vopersal, in Veeh, *Kriegsfurie*, pp. 496–97; Hobe, "Panzer-Kampfgruppe XIII," in Spiwoks and Stöber, *Endkampf*, p. 318; Spiwoks and Stöber, *Endkampf*, pp. 321–24.

28. "After Action Report," 101st Cav Rcnz Sq, NA, RG 407/304-CAV-101-0.3; Graydon, "101st Cavalry"; Veeh, *Kriegsfurie*, pp. 497–98; Spiwoks and Stöber, *Endkampf*, pp. 321–24.

29. Albert, "Einsatz des XIII. SS-A.K. in Spiwoks and Stöber, *Endkampf*, p. 309; Graydon, "101st Cavalry."

30. "After Action Report," Headquarters, CC-A, 12th AD, NA, RG 407/612-CCA-0.3; Twelfth Armored Division, *Twelfth Armored Division*, p. 69; "After Action Report," 17th AIB, 12th AD, NA, RG 407/612-INF-(17)-0.3; "S-3 Journal," 23rd Tk Bn, 12th AD, NA, RG 407/612-TK-(23)-0.7; "Periodic Reports," CC-R, 12th AD, NA, RG 407/612-CCR-0.9; Albert, "Einsatz des XIII. SS-A.K.," in Spiwoks and Stöber, *Endkampf*, pp. 310–11; Veeh, *Kriegsfurie*, pp. 505–6.

31. "After Action Report," 17th AIB, 12th AD, NA, RG 407/612-INF-(17)-0.3; Sherman B. Lans, "Mount Up! The History of Company C, 17th Armored Infantry Battalion, 12th Armored Division," University of Tennessee Special Collections, MS-2012, Box 8, Folder 12, p. 55; "S-3 Journal," 23rd Tk Bn, 12th AD, NA, RG 407/612-TK-(23)-0.7; Veeh, *Kriegsfurie*, pp. 513–14.

32. "After Action Report," 17th AIB, 12th AD, NA, RG 407/612-INF-(17)-0.3; "S-3 Journal," 23rd Tk Bn, 12th AD, NA, RG 407/612-TK-(23)-0.7; Lyons, "Company A"; Veeh, *Kriegsfurie*, p. 515.

33. Veeh, *Kriegsfurie*, pp. 517–18.

34. Joachim Brückner, *Kriegsende in Bayern 1945. Der Wehrkreis VII und die Kämpfe zwischen Donau und Alpen* (Freiburg: Verlag Rombach, 1987), pp. 99–101; Veeh, *Kriegsfurie*, pp. 517–18; "After Action Report," Headquarters, CC-A, 12th AD, NA, RG 407/612-CCA-0.3; Twelfth Armored Division, *Twelfth Armored Division*, pp. 69–70; "Speed Is the Password: The Story of the 12th Armored Division," http://nicanor.acu.edu/academics/history/12ad/speed2.htm.

35. Twelfth Armored Division, *Twelfth Armored Division*, pp. 69–70; "After

Action Report," Headquarters, CC-A, 12th AD, NA, RG 407/612-CCA-0.3; "Operations in Germany, April 1945," Division Artillery, 12th AD, NA, RG 407/612-ART-0.7; Veeh, *Kriegsfurie,* pp. 518–19.

36. Report of Gebirgsjäger lieutenant in Brückner, *Kriegsende in Bayern,* pp. 103–4.

37. Colonel Walter Dahl, quoted in Veeh, *Kriegsfurie,* p. 520; Brückner, *Kriegsende in Bayern,* p. 106; Dr. Arnold Schromm, "Kriegsende 1945—'Stunde Null' in Lauingen und im Landkreis Dillingen," http://www.bndlg.de/~albertus/geschichte/FertigeSachen/kriegsende1945.htm.

38. Dahl in Veeh, *Kriegsfurie,* pp. 520–21; "Kriegstagebuch Luftflotte 6," Bundesarchiv-Militärarchiv Freiburg (BA-MA), RL 7/617, fol. 236, in Brückner, *Kriegsende in Bayern,* p. 108; Walther Dahl, *Rammjäger. Das letzte Aufgebot* (Heusenstamm bei Offenbach: Orion-Heimreiter Verlag, 1961), pp. 215–18; Schromm, "Kriegsende 1945"; Twelfth Armored Division, *Twelfth Armored Division,* p. 70; "After Action Report," Headquarters, CC-A, 12th AD, NA, RG 407/612-CCA-0.3; "Operations in Germany, April 1945," Division Artillery, 12th AD, NA, RG 407/612-ART-0.7; "Combat and Infantry Journal," 8th IR, 4th ID, NA, RG 407/304-INF-(8)-0.7.

39. Veeh, *Kriegsfurie,* pp. 521–26; "Kriegstagebuch Luftflotte 6," BA-MA, RL 7/617, fol. 236, in Brückner, *Kriegsende in Bayern,* p. 108; Twelfth Armored Division, *Twelfth Armored Division,* p. 70; "S-3 Journal," 17th AIB, 12th AD, NA, RG 407/612-INF-(17)-0.9; "Periodic Reports," Headquarters, CC-R, 12th AD, NA, RG 407/612-CCR-0.9; Lyons, "Company A"; "After Action Report," 714th Tk Bn, 12th AD, NA, RG 407/612-TK(714)-0.3; "After Action Report," 56th AIB, 12th AD, NA, RG 407/612-INF-(56)-0.3; "Operations in Germany, April 1945," Division Artillery, 12th AD, NA, RG 407/612-ART-0.7; "Combat and Infantry Journal," 8th IR, 4th ID, NA, RG 407/304-INF-(8)-0.7; Graydon, "101st Cavalry."

40. "Operations in Germany, April 1945," Division Artillery, 12th AD, NA, RG 407/612-ART-0.7; Graydon, "101st Cavalry"; Lyons, "Company A"; Twelfth Armored Division, *Twelfth Armored Division,* p. 71; "Speed Is the Password."

41. Albert, "Einsatz des XIII. SS-A.K.," in Spiwoks and Stöber, *Endkampf,* p. 333; Hobe, "Panzer-Kampfgruppe XIII," in Spiwoks and Stöber, *Endkampf,* pp. 341–42.

42. Twelfth Armored Division, *Twelfth Armored Division,* p. 76; Lans, "Mount Up!" pp. 57–58. See also Lyons, "Company A"; "How Long, How Long in Infinite Pursuit: History of the 495th Armored Field Artillery Battalion," http://www.acu.edu/academics/history/12ad/495afax/howlong.htm; "Speed Is the Password"; "S-3 Journal," 17th AIB, 12th AD, NA, RG 407/612-INF-(17)-0.7; "S-3 Journal," 23rd Tk Bn, 12th AD, NA, RG 407/612-TK-(23)-0.7.

43. Lans, "Mount Up!" p. 58; Lyons, "Company A"; "How Long."

44. Seventh U.S. Army, *Seventh United States Army,* 3:pp. 893, 895; "Casualty Report, April 1945," 17th AIB, 12th AD, NA, RG 407/612-INF-(17)-1.16; "After Action Report, April 1945," 56th AIB, 12th AD, NA, RG 407/612-INF-(56)-0.3; "After

Action Report, April 1945," 12th IR, 4th ID, NA, RG 407/304-INF (12)-0.3; "After Action Report, April 1945," 22nd IR, 4th ID, NA, RG 407/304-INF (22)-0.3. For overall casualty figures, see Seventh U.S. Army, *Seventh United States Army,* 3:pp. 1037–38; "12th Armored Division, Casualties," http://www.army.mil/cmh-pg/documents/eto-ob/12AD-ETO.htm. For casualty figures for other individual units of the 12th Armored Division, see "Casualty Report, April 1945," 92nd Cav Rcnz Sq, 12th AD, NA, RG 407/612-CAV-1.16; "After Action Report, April 1945," 714th Tk Bn, 12th AD, NA, RG 407/612-TK (714)-0.3; "History of the 714th Armored Tank Battalion," http://www.acu.edu/academics/history/12ad/714atbx/contestp.htm; "After Action Report, April 1945," Division Artillery, 12th AD, NA, RG 407/612-ART-0.7; "Casualty Report, April 1945," 66th AIB, 12th AD, NA, RG 407/612-INF-(66)-0.2; "After Action Report," 101st Cav Rcnz Sq, NA, RG 407/304-CAV-101-0.3; "After Action Report," 8th IR, 4th ID, NA, RG 407/304-INF-(8)-0.3; "Unit Report," 8th IR, 4th ID, NA, RG 407/304-INF-(8)-0.9.

45. Rüdiger Overmans, *Deutsche militärische Verluste im Zweiten Weltkrieg* (Munich: R. Oldenbourg Verlag, 1999), pp. 265–76; Friedrich Blumenstock, *Der Einmarsch der Amerikaner und Franzosen im Nördlichen Württemberg im April 1945* (Stuttgart: W. Kohlhammer Verlag, 1957), p. 221; Henke, *amerikanische Besetzung,* pp. 789–90; "Operations in Germany, April 1945," 92nd Cav Rcnz Sq, 12th AD, NA, RG 407/612-CAV-0.3; Kunze, *Kriegsende in Franken,* p. 304–7; Spiwoks and Stöber, *Endkampf,* pp. 395–406; Helmut Günter, *Die Sturmflut und das Ende. Geschichte der 17. SS-Pz.Gren.Division "Götz von Berlichingen,"* vol. 3, *Mit dem Rücken zur Wand* (Munich: Schild Verlag, 1991), p. 442 fn. 30; Historical Board, ed., *The Fighting Forty-Fifth: The Combat Report of an Infantry Division* (Baton Rouge, La.: Army and Navy Publishing Company, 1946), p. 180; Costlow, "Division Operations," pp. 1–2; Twelfth Armored Division, *Twelfth Armored Division,* p. 78. On May 1, 1945, the Seventh Army reported over 150,000 German POWs in its stockades: Seventh U.S. Army, *Seventh United States Army,* 3:p. 893.

46. Henke, *amerikanische Besetzung,* pp. 821–44, 958–65; Troll, "Aktionen zur Kriegsbeendigung," p. 689; *Windsheimer Zeitung,* January 19, March 26, 1945.

7. STRUGGLE UNTIL FIVE AFTER TWELVE

1. Roderick Watt, "*Wehrwolf* or *Werwolf?* Literature, Legend, or Lexical Error into Nazi Propaganda?" *Modern Language Review* 87, no. 4 (October 1992): pp. 879–82; Perry Biddiscombe, *Werwolf! The History of the National Socialist Guerrilla Movement, 1944–1946* (Toronto: Univ. of Toronto Press, 1998), p. 13; Frank E. Manuel, *Scenes from the End: The Last Days of World War II in Europe* (South Royalton, Vt.: Steerforth Press, 2000), pp. 55–56.

2. Hermann Löns, *Der Wehrwolf* (Düsseldorf: Diederichs, 1958), passim; Löns quoted in Gordon Craig, *The Germans* (New York: G.P. Putnam's Sons, 1982), p.

205; Watt, "*Wehrwolf* or *Werwolf?*" pp. 884–90; Biddiscombe, *Werwolf,* p. 12–19; Manuel, *Scenes from the End,* pp. 56–57; *Völkischer Beobachter,* April 3, 1945.

3. Diary entries of March 27, 29, 30, April 1, 2, 4, 8, 1945, in Joseph Goebbels, *Tagebücher 1945. Die letzten Aufzeichnungen* (Hamburg: Hoffmann und Campe, 1977), pp. 393–94, 442, 457, 487, 495, 498, 508, 520–21; Curt Riess, "Planned Chaos—The Nazi Goal," *New York Times Magazine,* April 22, 1945, p. 10.

4. "Weekly Intelligence Report No. 5 for Week Ending 3 January 1946," "Weekly Intelligence Report No. 7 for Week Ending 17 January 1946," Office of Military Government for Bavaria (OMGBY), Intelligence Branch, NA, RG 260/390/47/19/1.

5. Text of *Deutschlandsender* broadcast of April 1, 1945, in James Lucas, *Experiences of War: The Third Reich* (London: Arms and Armour Press, 1990), pp. 168–69; *New York Times,* April 2, 1945; Klaus-Dietmar Henke, *Die amerikanische Besetzung Deutschlands* (Munich: R. Oldenbourg Verlag, 1995), p. 943; report of German radio broadcast of April 1, 1945, "G-2 Journal," 12th AD, NA, RG 407/612-2.2; diary entries of April 2, 8, 1945, in Goebbels, *Tagebücher 1945,* pp. 498, 520–21.

6. "Weekly Civil Affairs/Military Government Summary for Week Ending 5 April 1945," Headquarters, 6th Army Group, G-5 Section, Records of Intelligence Division, Weekly Intelligence Reports, NA, RG 260/390/47/19/1; *Time,* April 9, 1945, p. 40, and April 16, 1945, p. 40; "General Intelligence Bulletin No. 44 for Week Ending 5 May 1945," Headquarters, European Civil Affairs Division, NA, RG 260/390/47/19/1. For reactions to the broadcast and Werewolves, both negative and positive, see Victor Klemperer, *I Will Bear Witness: A Diary of the Nazi Years, 1942–1945* (New York: Random House, 1999), 2:pp. 439–42, 464–67.

7. Army Services Forces, ed., *Pocket Guide No. 10, Germany* (Washington, D.C.: Information Branch, U.S. Army, [1944]), pp. 4–10.

8. *Army Talks* 3, no. 7 (February 17, 1945); *Army Talks,* quoted in diary entry of December 27, 1945, in Karl Jering, *Überleben und Neubeginn. Tagebuchaufzeichnungen eines Deutschen 1945–1946* (Munich: Günter Olzog Verlag, 1979), pp. 81–82; Petra Goedde, *GIs and Germans: Culture, Gender, and Foreign Relations, 1945–1949* (New Haven: Yale Univ. Press, 2003), pp. 46–48; Marita Krauss, "'Vee GAYT ess ee-nen.' Lebenssplitter aus dem Umgang mit Besatzern," in Friedrich Prinz and Marita Krauss, ed., *Trümmerleben* (Munich: Deutscher Taschenbuch Verlag, 1985), pp. 180–81; Joseph R. Starr, *Fraternization with the Germans in World War II* (Frankfurt: Office of Chief Historian, European Command, 1947), p. 22; "Special Orders for American-German Relations" quoted in Henke, *amerikanische Besetzung,* p. 188.

9. "Weekly Military Government Report No. 4 for Week Ending 11 June 1945," Headquarters, Detachment E1 F3 for Land Bayern, NA, RG 260/390/47/19/1; transcript of Army documentary film, *Your Job in Germany* by Frank Capra, quoted by David Culbert, "American Film Policy in the Re-Education of Germany after 1945," in Nicholas Pronay and Keith Wilson, ed., *The Political Re-Education of Germany and Her Allies after World War II* (London: Croom Helm, 1985), p. 201; *Pocket Guide;*

Harald Leder, "Changing People's Minds? American Reorientation in Germany after World War II," http://home.t-online.de/home/RIJONUE/leder.htm, p. 4. See also Harald Leder, "Americans and German Youth in Nuremberg, 1945–1956: A Study in Politics and Culture" (Ph.D. diss., Louisiana State University, 1977).

10. "Don't Get Chummy with Jerry," *Stars and Stripes*, October 10, 1944; Henke, *amerikanische Besetzung*, pp. 188–91; Tamara Domentat, *"'Hallo Fräulein.' Deutsche Frauen und amerikanische Soldaten* (Berlin: Aufbau-Verlag, 1998), p. 34; Starr, *Fraternization with the Germans*, p. 22; Tania Long, "They Long for a New Fuehrer," *New York Times Magazine*, December 9, 1945, pp. 8, 44.

11. *New York Times*, April 3, 1945; Biddiscombe, *Werwolf*, p. 158; Ian Sayer and Douglas Botting, *America's Secret Army. The Untold Story of the Counter Intelligence Corps* (New York: Franklin Watts, 1989), p. 234; U.S. Army Intelligence Center, *History of the Counter Intelligence Corps* (Baltimore: U.S. Army Intelligence Center, 1959), 20:pp. 110–11, 116; "Weekly Civil Affairs/Military Government Summary for Week Ending 5 April 1945," Headquarters, 6th Army Group, G-5 Section, Records of Intelligence Division, Weekly Intelligence Reports, NA, RG 260/390/47/19/1.

12. Helmut Veeh, *Die Kriegsfurie über Franken 1945 und das Ende in den Alpen,* 3rd ed. (Bad Windsheim: Verlagsdruckerei Heinrich Delp, 1998), pp. 564, 567. For reports of BdM girls wielding Panzerfäuste during combat in Nuremberg, see "Tagebuch einer Zwanzigjährigen," in Erich Kuby, *Das Ende des Schreckens, Januar bis Mai 1945* (Munich: Deutscher Taschenbuch Verlag, 1986), p. 163.

13. Hans Holzträger, *Die Wehrertüchtigungslager der Hitler-Jugend, 1942–1945: Ein Dokumentarbericht* (Ippesheim: Verlag des Arbeitskreises für Geschichte und Kultur der deutschen Siedlungsgebiete im Südosten Europas e.V., 1991), p. 101; "G-2 Journals," 12th AD, NA, RG 407/612-2.2; report of April 20, 1945, in U.S. Army Intelligence Center, *History of the Counter Intelligence Corps,* 20:pp. 138–39; proclamation of April 24, 1945, in "Monthly Counter Intelligence Report No. 14 for Week Ending 25 April 1945," 7th U.S. Army, NA, RG 407, Box 2633; "Periodic Report for Week Ending 22 April 1945," 90th Infantry Division, NA, RG 407, Box 13298; Henke, *amerikanische Besetzung*, p. 948; Sayer and Botting, *America's Secret Army*, p. 234.

14. Biddiscombe, *Werwolf,* p. 75; Watt, "*Wehrwolf* or *Werwolf?*" pp. 881–82; Manuel, *Scenes from the End*, pp. 56–58. The Werwolf insignia was also prominently displayed in other areas. For an illustration of its prevalence, and the anxiety it aroused in the German population, see the report of an OSS officer for the Stuttgart area: Fritz Eberhard, "Stuttgart im Mai 1945," in Ulrich Borsdorf and Lutz Niethammer, eds., *Zwischen Befreiung und Besatzung. Analysen des US-Geheimdienstes über Positionen und Strukturen deutscher Politik 1945* (Wuppertal: Peter Hammer Verlag, 1976), pp. 58–59.

15. "General Intelligence Bulletin No. 44 for Week Ending 5 May 1945," Headquarters, European Civil Affairs Division, NA, RG 260/390/47/19/1; Biddiscombe, *Werwolf,* p. 75; *Neue Zürcher Zeitung,* May 29, 1945; *Stars and Stripes,* May 27, 1945; U.S. Army Intelligence Center, *History of the Counter Intelligence Corps,*

26:pp. 87–88; John H. Toole, *Battle Diary* (Missoula, Mont.: Vigilante Press, 1978), pp. 151–53.

16. Hans Woller, *Gesellschaft und Politik in der amerikanischen Besatzungszone. Die Region Ansbach und Fürth* (Munich: R. Oldenbourg Verlag, 1986), p. 66; "War Diary," Detachment H3A3 (Neustadt an der Aisch), entry for April 29, 1945, NA, RG 260/390/41/13/3; "Historical Report," June 25, 1946, Military Government Liaison and Security Office, Landkreis Dinkelsbühl, OMGBY, NA, RG 260/390/47/5/1; "G-2 Monthly Histories, Operations in Germany, 24 May–31 May 1945," 12th AD, NA, RG 407/612-2; "Historical Report," Military Government Detachment I6H2 (Bad Windsheim), Entry for August 29, 1945, NA, RG 260/390/41/13/3; Henke, *amerikanische Besetzung*, pp. 950–52; "G-2 Periodic Report No. 137 for Week Ending 17 July 1945" and "G-2 Periodic Report No. 138 for Week Ending 18 July 1945," Headquarters, 12th AD, NA, RG 407/612-2; "Historical Report for May and June 1945," G-5, 3rd U.S. Army, NA, RG 331, SHAEF, G-5, Information Branch, Entry 54; "Military Government Activities 29 April–5 May 1945," "Report of 8 May 1945," G-5, 7th U.S. Army, NA, RG 407, Box 2673; "Weekly G-2 Report No. 291 for Week Ending 11 July 1945," 7th U.S. Army, NA, RG 338, Files 1944–1946, Box 18; "Extracts from 12th Army Group Counter-Sabotage Bulletin No. 7 for Week Ending 2 July 1945," Headquarters, 12th AD, NA, RG 407/612-2.

17. Major James M. Snyder, "The Establishment and Operations of the United States Constabulary, 3 October 1945–30 June 1947," (Headquarters, U.S. Constabulary: Historical Sub-Section C-3, 1947), U.S. Army Military History Institute, Carlisle Barracks, Pa., p. 210; Biddiscombe, *Werwolf,* p. 75; "Weekly Military Government Report No. 4 for Week Ending 11 June 1945," Headquarters, Detachment E1 F3 for Land Bayern, NA, RG 260/390/47/19/1; "G-2 Weekly Intelligence Summary No. 14 for Week Ending 18 October 1945," United States Forces European Theater (USFET), State Department Decimal File 1945–1949, 740.00119 Control (Germany), NA, RG 59; "Weekly Intelligence Report No. 1 for Week Ending 6 December 1945," "Weekly Intelligence Report No. 2 for Week Ending 13 December 1945," "Weekly Intelligence Report No. 3 for Week Ending 20 December 1945," "Weekly Intelligence Report No. 7 for Week Ending 17 January 1946," "Weekly Intelligence Report No. 9 for Week Ending 31 January 1946," OMGBY, Intelligence Branch, NA, RG 260/390/47/19/1; "Periodic Report for Week Ending 11 April 1946," "Periodic Report for Week Ending 17 April 1946," "Periodic Report for Week Ending 8 May 1946," "Periodic Report for Week Ending 30 May 1946," "Periodic Report for Week Ending 7 August 1946," Office of Military Government for Land Bavaria, NA, RG 260/390/47/19/1; Henke, *amerikanische Besetzung*, p. 952; *New York Times*, November 1, 24, 1945, January 12, 13, 14, 15, 17, 1946; *Nürnberger Nachrichten*, April 18, 1946.

18. "General Bulletin No. 47 for Week Ending 11 June 1945," European Civil Affairs Division, NA, RG 331, SHAEF, G-5, Information Branch, Entry 54; Henke, *amerikanische Besetzung*, p. 952.

19. Anneliese Uhlig quoted in Elfrieda Bethiaume Shukert and Barbara Smith Scibetta, *War Brides of World War II* (New York: Penguin, 1988), p. 130; Goedde, *GIs and Germans*, pp. 106–8; Domentat, *Hallo Fräulein*, pp. 39–44, 51–57; Henke, *amerikanische Besetzung*, pp. 193–98; James P. O'Donnell, "Do the Fraüleins Change Our Joe?" *Newsweek*, December 24, 1945, p. 50; Julian Bach Jr., *America's Germany: An Account of the Occupation* (New York: Random House, 1946), pp. 71–72, 76–78; Percy Knauth, "Fraternization: The Word Takes on a Brand-New Meaning in Germany," *Life*, July 2, 1945, p. 26.

20. Domentat, *Hallo Fräulein*, pp. 161–82; Goedde, *GIs and Germans*, pp. 90–93; A. Steinhoff, "Jugend hinter Gittern," *Der Regenbogen* 2, nos. 11–12 (1947); Judy Barden, "Candy Bar Romance—Women of Germany," in Arthur Settel, ed., *This Is Germany* (1950; reprint, Freeport, N.Y.: Books for Libraries Press, 1971), p. 165; *New York Times*, January 27, 1946, October 26, 1947; Barbara Supp, "Trümmerfrauen: Protokoll eines gescheiterten Aufbruchs," in Spiegel Special, *Die Deutschen nach der Stunde Null, 1945–1948* 4 (1995), pp. 84–89; William L. White, *Report on the Germans* (New York: Harcourt, Brace, 1947), p. 149; Hermann-Josef Rupieper, "Bringing Democracy to the Frauleins: Frauen als Zielgruppe der amerikanischen Demokratisierungspolitik in Deutschland, 1945–1952," *Geschichte und Gesellschaft* 17 (1991): pp. 65, 84, 90–91; David Rodnick, *Postwar Germans: An Anthropologist's Account* (New Haven: Yale Univ. Press, 1948), p. 107; Gabriele Jenk, *Steine gegen Brot. Trümmerfrauen schildern den Wiederaufbau in der Nachkriegszeit* (Bergisch-Gladbach: Bastei Lübbe, 1988), pp. 31–32; Marc Hillel, *Die Invasion der Be-Freier. Die GIs in Europa, 1942–1947* (Hamburg: Ernst Kabel Verlag, 1981), pp. 167–93; Louise Drasdo, "Keinen Dank für Veronika Dankeschön," *Sozial extra* 4 (1986): p. 36; Starr, *Fraternization with the Germans*, pp. 76–77; "Disabilities and VD," *Newsweek*, July 22, 1946, p. 28; "The G.I. and VD," *Newsweek*, September 2, 1946, p. 50; diary entries of June 13, August 5, October 31, November 11, 16, 21, December 19, 25, 1945, January 5, 22, 1946, in Jering, *Überleben und Neubeginn*, pp. 27, 40, 57, 61, 62–63, 64, 72, 78, 94, 104; Christian Koch, Rainer Büschel, and Uli Kuhnle, *Trümmerjahre: Nürnberg, 1945–1955* (Munich: Hugendubel, 1989), p. 25; *Nürnberger Nachrichten*, February 9, 1946, January 4, March 8, 1947.

The German version of the song went:

Lebst Du etwa nur auf Karte 3, Baby,
oder hast Du noch was nebenbei, Baby,
einen Jack, einen Jim aus Übersee,
mit Schokolade und Kaffee
und einem großen Portemonnaie?
Nimm es mit der Liebe nich so schwer, Baby,
so ein Ami hat ja soviel mehr, Baby,
wenn er sagt 'I love you,' sag nicht nein, Baby,
zieh ins Land der Kalorien ein.

21. "Intelligence Annex to Weekly Report of the Office of Military Government for Bavaria for the Period 8–15 November1945," OMGBY, Intelligence Branch, Weekly Intelligence Reports 1945–1947, NA, RG 260/390/47/19/1; "Intelligence Annex to the Weekly Detachment Report," December 22, 1945, Office of Military Government for Kreis Scheinfeld, Detachment H-270, NA, RG 260/390/41/13/3; "Intelligence Annex to Weekly Report of the Office of Military Government for Bavaria for the Period 22–29 November 1945," OMGBY, Intelligence Branch, Weekly Intelligence Reports 1945–1947, NA, RG 260/390/47/19/1; Snyder, "United States Constabulary," p. 211; "U.S. Survey Discloses Returning German Soldiers' Views," *New York Times,* August 23, 1945; "SS Remnants Warn German Women: Bavaria Underground Placards Threaten Reprisals for Any Fraternizing with the Yanks," *New York Times,* September 30, 1945; Domentat, *Hallo Fräulein,* p. 189; "Subversive Incidents Related to Fraternization," in Starr, *Fraternization with the Germans,* pp. 73–76.

22. Bericht des Landjägerbezirks Fürth an das Landratsamt, September 21, 1945, Staatsarchiv Nürnberg (StAN), Bestand Landratsamt Fürth, Nr. 40/1; report from Stadtkreis-Landkreis Fürth, "Weekly Intelligence Report No. 1 for Week Ending 6 December 1945," "Weekly Intelligence Report No. 2 for Week Ending 13 December 1945," OMGBY, Intelligence Branch, NA, RG 260/390/47/19/1. Emphasis in the original.

23. Perry Biddiscombe, "Dangerous Liaisons: The Anti-Fraternization Movement in the U.S. Occupation Zones of Germany and Austria, 1945–1948," *Journal of Social History* 34 (spring 2001): pp. 615, 620–21; Bach, *America's Germany,* pp. 79–83.

24. Woller, *Gesellschaft und Politik,* pp. 71–72; "Weekly Intelligence Report No. 5 for Week Ending 3 January 1946," OMGBY, Intelligence Branch, NA, RG 260/390/47/19/1; "Periodic Report for Week Ending 30 May 1946," "Periodic Report for Week Ending 11 September 1946," Office of Military Government for Land Bavaria, NA, RG 260/390/47/19/1. The German version ran as follows:

Die deutsche Frau treibt's in schamloser
Weise mit Ausländern!
Schämst Du Dich nicht, Du Deutsche Frau?
Du weißt doch, daß Du uns alle in den
Schmutz hinabziehst und zugleich die Ehre
der Deutschen Frau befleckst.
Es dauerte sechs Jahre, um die deutschen
Soldaten zu schlagen, aber es dauerte nur
fünf Minuten, um eine Deutsche Frau rumzukriegen!
Wir haben keine Zigaretten und keine Butter,
der Ausländer hat Kaffee und Zucker.
Du scherst Dich nicht um seine Hautfarbe,

solange er Dir eine Tafel Schokolade anbietet.
Dennoch hoffen wir, daß Du bald den Russen in die Hände fällst.
Dann nämlich wirst Du wirklich Deine Lektion bekommen
und kein deutscher Mann wird Dich mehr ansehen.

25. Domentat, *Hallo Fräulein*, pp. 183–88; Walther von Hollander, "Über Ehezerrüttung, Ehetrennung, Ehescheidung," cited in Klaus-Jörg Ruhl, ed., *Frauen in der Nachkriegszeit, 1945–1963* (Munich: Deutscher Taschenbuch Verlag, 1988), pp. 35–37; "Periodic Report for Week Ending 3 April 1946," "Periodic Report for Week Ending 11 April 1946," Office of Military Government for Land Bavaria, NA, RG 260/390/47/19/1. In German, the poem went:

> *Zu Tode erschöpft, nach langen Wochen*
> *kommen die Landser nach Hause gekrochen,*
> *die Füße wund und die Frage im Ohr:*
> *Wie finden wir unsere Heimat vor?*
> *. . . In Freuden lebt heute die deutsche Frau,*
> *aber auf schlimmste Art, wir wissen's genau.*
> *. . . ihr deutschen Frauen, schämt ihr euch nicht?*
> *Die deutschen Soldaten, ohne Arm, ohne Bein,*
> *die können euch jetzt wohl gleichgültig sein.*
> *Denen fehlt es freilich an Kaffee und Butter,*
> *aber die Fremden haben alles and dazu noch Zucker.*
> *Und bringt einer sogar noch Schokolade herbei,*
> *dann ist die Hautfarbe auch einerlei.*
> *Fünf Jahre brauchten sie, um uns zu besiegen,*
> *euch können sie jedoch in fünf minuten kriegen.*
> *. . . doch einst kommt der Tag, da werdet ihr büßen.*
> *Das merkt euch genau, die ihr die Heimat entstellt:*
> *. . . in den Schmutz die Ehre der deutschen Frau.*
> *. . . Dann seid ihr vor aller Welt belehrt,*
> *daß euch ein deutscher Mann nicht ehrt.*

26. Ruth Andreas-Friedrich, *Battleground Berlin: Diaries, 1945–1948*, trans. Anna Boerresen (New York: Paragon House Publishers, 1990), pp. 77–78; Biddiscombe, "Dangerous Liaisons," pp. 613–14, 619; Dagmar Barnouw, *Germany 1945: Views of War and Violence* (Bloomington: Indiana Univ. Press, 1996), pp. 172–73.

27. Barnouw, *Germany 1945*, pp. 173, 176; Biddiscombe, "Dangerous Liaisons," pp. 611–15; Gabriele Strecker, *Überleben ist nicht genug: Frauen 1945–1950* (Freiburg im Breisgau: Herder, 1981), pp. 16, 55–56; Atina Grossmann, "Eine Frage des Schweigens? Die Vergewaltigung deutscher Frauen durch Besatzungssoldaten,"

Sozialwissenschaftliche Informationen 24, no. 2 (1995): pp. 111, 118; ICD survey cited in "U.S. Survey Discloses Returning German Soldiers' Views," *New York Times,* August 23, 1945; "Periodic Report for Week Ending 11 April 1946," "Periodic Report for Week Ending 30 May 1946," "Periodic Report for Week Ending 17 July 1946," "Periodic Report for Week Ending 7 August 1946," Office of Military Government for Land Bavaria, NA, RG 260/390/47/19/1; Bach, *America's Germany,* p. 110.

28. Peter Seewald, "'Grüß Gott, ihr seid frei.' Passau 1945," in Wolfgang Malanowski, ed., *1945. Deutschland in der Stunde Null* (Reinbek bei Hamburg: Rowohlt Taschenbuch Verlag, 1985), p. 105; diary entry of December 21, 1945, in Jering, *Überleben und Neubeginn,* p. 75; "Periodic Report for Week Ending 17 April 1946," "Periodic Report for Week Ending 30 May 1946," "Periodic Report for Week Ending 5 June 1946," "Periodic Report for Week Ending 19 June 1946," "Periodic Report for Week Ending 17 July 1946," "Periodic Report for Week Ending 7 August 1946," Office of Military Government for Land Bavaria, NA, RG 260/390/47/19/1; "Annual Historical Report," July 6, 1946, Military Government Liaison and Security Office, Landkreis Neustadt an der Aisch, Detachment B-273, NA, RG 260/390/47/5/1; Biddiscombe, "Dangerous Liaisons," pp. 622–23; *New York Times,* January 5, 10, July 12, 1946; Domentat, *Hallo Fräulein,* pp. 188–89.

29. "Report of Operations for the Quarterly Period 1 April–30 June 1946," Headquarters, 3rd U.S. Army, NA, RG 338/17, Box 80; Snyder, "United States Constabulary," pp. 217–21; "Weekly Intelligence Report No. 15 for Week Ending 14 March 1946," OMGBY, Intelligence Branch, NA, RG 260/390/47/19/1; "Periodic Report for Week Ending 3 July 1946," "Periodic Report for Week Ending 17 July 1946," "Periodic Report for Week Ending 24 July 1946," "Periodic Report for Week Ending 7 August 1946," "Periodic Report for Week Ending 14 August 1946," Office of Military Government for Land Bavaria, NA, RG 260/390/47/19/1; John Willoughby, "The Sexual Behavior of American G.I.'s during the Early Years of the Occupation of Germany," *Journal of Military History* 62 (January 1998): pp. 166–68, 172–74; Biddiscombe, "Dangerous Liaisons," pp. 623–27; USFET G-2 "Weekly Intelligence Summary," no. 52, July 11, 1946, quoted in Biddiscombe, "Dangerous Liaisons," pp. 626–27; Harold Zink, *The United States in Germany, 1944–1955* (Princeton, N.J.: Van Nostrand, 1957), pp. 136–40, 143–44; Franklin Davis Jr., *Came as a Conqueror: The United States Army's Occupation of Germany, 1945–1949* (New York: Macmillan, 1967), p. 145.

30. Biddiscombe, "Dangerous Liaisons," pp. 622, 626–31; "Periodic Report for Week Ending 30 May 1946," "Periodic Report for Week Ending 5 June 1946," "Periodic Report for Week Ending 12 June 1945," Office of Military Government for Land Bavaria, NA, RG 260/390/47/19/1.

31. Biddiscombe, "Dangerous Liaisons," pp. 622, 626–31; USFET G-2 "Weekly Intelligence Summary," no. 67, October 24, 1946, USFET G-2 "Weekly Intelligence Summary," no. 68, October 31, 1946, and USFET G-2 "Weekly Intelligence Sum-

mary," no. 29, January 31, 1946, all quoted in Biddiscombe, "Dangerous Liaisons," pp. 629–30; Headquarters, U.S. Constabulary, "Weekly Intelligence Summary," October 31, 1946, June 10, 1947, quoted in Snyder, "United States Constabulary," pp. 218–19; diary entry of December 26, 1945, in Jering, *Überleben und Neubeginn,* p. 79; Goedde, *GIs and Germans,* pp. 109–11; "Periodic Report for Week Ending 17 April 1946," "Periodic Report for Week Ending 30 May 1946," "Periodic Report for Week Ending 5 June 1946," "Periodic Report for Week Ending 24 July 1946," "Periodic Report for Week Ending 31 July 1946," "Periodic Report for Week Ending 14 August 1946," "Periodic Report for Week Ending 28 August 1946," "Periodic Report for Week Ending 4 September 1946," "Periodic Report for Week Ending 11 September 1946," Office of Military Government for Land Bavaria, NA, RG 260/390/47/19/ 1. For a personal account from a distinguished historian, then a young member of the Constabulary, of the manner in which racial tensions often flared, see David Brion Davis, "World War II and Memory," *Journal of American History* 77, no. 2 (September 1990): pp. 580–87.

32. USFET G-2 "Weekly Intelligence Summary No. 13 for Week Ending 11 October 1945," quoted in Biddiscombe, "Dangerous Liaisons," p. 631; "Weekly Intelligence Report No. 11 for Week Ending 14 February 1946," OMGBY, Intelligence Branch, NA, RG 260/390/47/19/1; "Periodic Report for Week Ending 11 April 1946," "Periodic Report for Week Ending 24 July 1946," "Periodic Report for Week Ending 28 August 1946," Office of Military Government for Land Bavaria, NA, RG 260/390/ 47/19/1; *New York Times,* April 23, 1946; J. Glenn Gray, "Munich University: Class of '50. A Case Study in German Re-Education," *Commentary* 5, no. 5 (May 1948): pp. 440–48; *New York Times,* March 23, 1946.

33. USFET G-2 "Weekly Intelligence Summary No. 33 for Week Ending 28 February 1946," quoted in Biddiscombe, "Dangerous Liaisons," p. 626; Perry Biddiscombe, "'The Enemy of Our Enemy': A View of the *Edelweiss Piraten* from the British and American Archives," *Journal of Contemporary History* 30 (1995), pp. 45–55; "Weekly Intelligence Report for Week Ending 26 January 1946," Office of Military Government for Kreis Scheinfeld, Detachment H-270, NA, RG 260/390/41/13/ 3; "Weekly Intelligence Report No. 11 for Week Ending 14 February 1946," "Weekly Intelligence Report No. 12 for Week Ending 21 February 1946," "Weekly Intelligence Report No. 14 for Week Ending 7 March 1946," "Weekly Intelligence Report No. 15 for Week Ending 14 March 1946," OMGBY, Intelligence Branch, NA, RG 260/390/47/19/1; "Periodic Report for Week Ending 3 April 1946," "Periodic Report for Week Ending 11 April 1946," "Periodic Report for Week Ending 17 April 1946," "Periodic Report for Week Ending 24 April 1946," "Periodic Report for Week Ending 1 May 1946," "Periodic Report for Week Ending 8 May 1946," "Periodic Report for Week Ending 5 June 1946," "Periodic Report for Week Ending 26 June 1946," "Periodic Report for Week Ending 3 July 1946," "Periodic Report for Week Ending 24 July 1946," "Periodic Report for Week Ending 31 July 1946," "Periodic Report for

Week Ending 21 August 1946," "Periodic Report for Week Ending 11 September 1946," "Periodic Report for Week Ending 2 October 1946," "Periodic Report for Week Ending 16 October 1946," Office of Military Government for Land Bavaria, NA, RG 260/390/47/19/1; *New York Times,* March 31, April 24, 1946.

34. "Periodic Report for Week Ending 24 July 1946," "Periodic Report for Week Ending 14 August 1946," "Periodic Report for Week Ending 21 August 1946," "Periodic Report for Week Ending 11 September 1946," Office of Military Government for Land Bavaria, NA, RG 260/390/47/19/1; "Establishment of Road Blocks" and "Check and Search Operation," in Snyder, "United States Constabulary," Appendix; "50 Jahre Polizei in Mittelfranken," http://www.polizei.bayern.de/ppmfr/wir/hist.htm; *Nürnberger Nachrichten,* November 1, 23, 1946, January 8, 11, 18, 22, 1947; "Periodic Report for Week Ending 30 October 1946," "Periodic Report for Week Ending 25 December 1946," Office of Military Government for Land Bavaria, NA, RG 260/390/47/19/1. In German, the rhymes went: *"Der Jude schiebt, der Pole sticht / Der Ami aber sieht es nicht." "Warst du Nazi oder nicht / Der Ami raubt und schont dich nicht." "Der Ami holt die Juden 'rein / Er ist ja selbst ein Judenschwein."*

35. *Nürnberger Nachrichten,* November 1, 1946, January 8, 11, 15, 18, February 5, 8, 26, March 8, 1947; *New York Times,* February 2, 3, March 28, 1947; *Süddeutsche Zeitung,* February 4, 1947; Kurt P. Tauber, *Beyond Eagle and Swastika: German Nationalism since 1945* (Middletown, Conn.: Wesleyan Univ. Press, 1967), 1:p. 405; Snyder, "United States Constabulary," p. 212; "Stimmungsbericht des Ansbacher Oberbürgermeisters an die Militärregierung," February 12, 1947, in Hans Woller, "Zur Demokratiebereitschaft in der Provinz des Amerikanischen Besatzungsgebiets," *Vierteljahrshefte für Zeitgeschichte* 31 (1983): p. 352; "Intelligence Report for Week Ending 8 January 1947," "Intelligence Report for Week Ending 15 January 1947," "Intelligence Report for Week Ending 5 February 1947," "Intelligence Report for Week Ending 12 February 1947," "Intelligence Report for Week Ending 19 February 1947," "Intelligence Report for Week Ending 26 February 1947," "Intelligence Report for Week Ending 12 March 1947," OMGBY, Intelligence Branch, NA, RG 260/390/47/19/1.

36. *Nürnberger Nachrichten,* March 29, 1947; Robert R. Rogers, "Four SA Men to Face Trial for Nazi Plot," *Stars and Stripes,* March 27, 1947, pp. 1, 12; "Nazi Officers Caught in Underground Plot," *Stars and Stripes,* March 29, 1947, p. 4; "4 SA Officers to Go on Trial Tomorrow," *Stars and Stripes,* April 7, 1947, p. 4; "7 Germans Sentenced in Resistance Moves," *Stars and Stripes,* April 26, 1947, p. 4; Major General E. N. Harmon, *Combat Commander: Autobiography of a Soldier,* with Milton MacKaye and William Ross MacKaye (Englewood Cliffs, N.J.: Prentice-Hall, 1970), pp. 289–90; Wolfgang Jacobmeyer, "Jüdische Überlebende als 'Displaced Persons.' Untersuchungen zur besatzungspolitik in den deutschen Westzonen und zur Zuwanderung osteuropäischer Juden 1945–1947," *Geschichte und Gesellschaft* 9 (1983): pp. 439–40; "Intelligence Report for Week Ending 8 January 1947," "Intelli-

gence Report for Week Ending 15 January 1947," "Intelligence Report for Week Ending 22 January 1947," "Intelligence Report for Week Ending 29 January 1947," "Intelligence Report for Week Ending 5 February 1947," "Intelligence Report for Week Ending 5 March 1947," "Intelligence Report for Week Ending 19 March 1947," "Intelligence Report for Week Ending 26 March 1947," "Intelligence Report for Week Ending 16 April 1947," OMGBY, Intelligence Branch, NA, RG 260/390/47/19/1; "Weekly Intelligence Summary No. 11 for the Period Ending 22 March 1947," "Weekly Intelligence Summary No. 15 for the Period Ending 19 April 1947," "Weekly Intelligence Summary No. 16 for the Period Ending 26 April 1947," Headquarters, First Military District, NA, RG 260/390/47/19/1.

37. "Weekly Intelligence Summary No. 31 for the Period Ending 9 August 1947," Headquarters, First Military District, NA, RG 260/390/47/19/1; "Intelligence Report for Week Ending 13 August 1947," "Intelligence Report for Week Ending 20 August 1947," OMGBY, Intelligence Branch, NA, RG 260/390/47/19/1; Biddiscombe, *Werwolf,* pp. 276–85; Snyder, "United States Constabulary," pp. 129–32, 153–54, 206–7, 221–23, 230–35.

8. THERE CAN BE NO RETURN TO NORMALITY

1. *New York Times,* April 7, 10, May 18, 1945.

2. John MacCormac, "Wandering Hordes in Reich Alarming," *New York Times,* April 7, 1945; Gladwin Hill, "Big Job for U.S. in Reich," *New York Times,* April 29, 1945; Raymond Daniell, "Released 'Slaves' Troubling Allies," *New York Times,* May 18, 1945; "Tide of 'DP's' Ebbs," *New York Times,* August 30, 1945.

3. See, for example, Intelligence Annex to Weekly Reports and Weekly Intelligence Reports for the period May 1945–December 1947, OMGBY, Intelligence Branch, NA, RG 260/390/47/19/1, Boxes 168–71; Lieutenant Daniel Lerner (Psychological Warfare Division, SHAEF), "Notizen von einer Reise durch das besetzte Deutschland (Anfang April 1945)," in Ulrich Borsdorf and Lutz Niethammer, eds., *Zwischen Befreiung und Besatzung. Analysen des US-Geheimdienstes über Positionen und Strukturen deutscher Politik 1945* (Wuppertal: Peter Hammer Verlag, 1976), pp. 29–33; Wolfgang Jacobmeyer, *Vom Zwangsarbeiter zum Heimatlosen Ausländer. Die Displaced Persons in Westdeutschland 1945–1951* (Göttingen: Vandenhoeck und Ruprecht, 1985), p. 27; Ulrich Herbert, *Fremdarbeiter: Politik und Praxis des "Ausländer-Einsatzes" in der Kriegswirtschaft des Dritten Reiches* (Bonn: J.H.W. Dietz Nachf., 1985), pp. 327–32, 341–42; Ulrich Herbert, *A History of Foreign Labor in Germany, 1880–1980: Seasonal Workers, Forced Laborers, Guest Workers,* trans. William Templer (Ann Arbor: Univ. of Michigan Press, 1990), pp. 184–85; Jill Stephenson, "Triangle: Foreign Workers, German Civilians, and the Nazi Regime. War and Society in Württemberg, 1939–1945," *German Studies Review* 15, no. 2 (May 1992): p. 353; Robert Gellately, *The Gestapo and German Society: Enforcing Racial Policy, 1933–*

1945 (Oxford: Clarendon Press, 1990), pp. 245–50; Robert Gellately, *Backing Hitler: Consent and Coercion in Nazi Germany* (Oxford: Oxford Univ. Press, 2001), pp. 236–41. For examples of the shooting of foreign workers because of their alleged danger to the German population, see: "Lfd. Nr. 129, Verbrechen der Endphase: Nürnberg, Februar 1945. LG Nürnberg-Fürth, KLs 299/48, OLG Nürnberg, Ss 83/49," in Adelheid Rüter-Ehlermann and C. F. Rüter, eds., *Justiz und NS-Verbrechen. Sammlung Deutscher Strafurteile Wegen Nationalsozialistischer Tötungsverbrechen 1945–1966* (Amsterdam: Univ. Press Amsterdam, 1969), 4:pp. 343–54; "Lfd. Nr. 252, Verbrechen der Endphase: Pforzheim-Brötzingen, 2. Februar 1945. LG Karlsruhe, KLs 9/48, OLG Stuttgart, 2Ss 82/49," in Rüter-Ehlermann and Rüter, *Justiz und NS-Verbrechen*, 7:pp. 625–46; "Lfd. Nr. 255, Verbrechen der Endphase: Ochsenfurt, März 1945. LG Würzburg, Ks 12/50," Rüter-Ehlermann and Rüter, *Justiz und NS-Verbrechen*, 7:pp. 705–16; "Lfd. Nr. 412, Verbrechen der Endphase: Schweinfurt, 21. März 1945. LG Würzburg, Ks 4/53, BGH 1StR353/52, BGH 1StR357/53," in Irene Sagel-Grande, et al., eds., *Justiz und NS-Verbrechen. Sammlung Deutscher Strafurteile Wegen Nationalsozialistischer Tötungsverbrechen 1945–1966* (Amsterdam: Univ. Press Amsterdam, 1975), 13:pp. 21–68; "Lfd. Nr. 458, Verbrechen der Endphase: Langenbachtal, März 1945. LG Arnsberg, 3Ks 1/57," in Sagel-Grande, *Justiz und NS-Verbrechen*, 14:pp. 563–628; "Lfd. Nr. 486, Verbrechen der Endphase: Langenbachtal, 20. März 1945/21. März 1945. LG Hagen, 3Ks 1/57, BGH 4StR438/58, BGH 4StR242/60," in Sagel-Grande, *Justiz und NS-Verbrechen*, 16:pp. 169–252; "Lfd. Nr. 508, Verbrechen der Endphase: Eversberg, März 1945. LG Hagen, 3Ks 1/57, BGH 4StR417/61," in Sagel-Grande, *Justiz und NS-Verbrechen*, 17:pp. 281–314; "Lfd. Nr. 893, Verbrechen der Endphase: Lörrach, April 1945. LG Waldshut, 850426, BGH 860122," publication in preparation.

4. Stephenson, "Triangle," pp. 339–59; Gellately, *Gestapo and German Society,* pp. 232–50; Gellately, *Backing Hitler,* pp. 155–60, 175–82.

5. Gellately, *Gestapo and German Society,* pp. 232–44; Gellately, *Backing Hitler,* pp. 155–60, 173–79; Helmut Veeh, *Die Kriegsfurie über Franken 1945 und das Ende in den Alpen,* 3rd ed. (Bad Windsheim: Verlagsdrückerei Heinrich Delp, 1988), p. 166.

6. Stephenson, "Triangle," pp. 353–54; Frank E. Manuel, *Scenes from the End: The Last Days of World War II in Europe* (South Royalton, Vt. : Steerforth Press, 2000), pp. 63–72; Jim G. Tobias and Peter Zinke, *Nakam. Jüdische Rache an NS-Tätern* (Hamburg: Konkret Literatur Verlag, 2000), p. 19.

7. Stephenson, "Triangle," pp. 353–54; Frank E. Manuel, *Scenes from the End: The Last Days of World War II in Europe* (South Royalton, Vt.: Steerforth Press, 2000), pp. 63–72; UNRRA official quoted in Herbert, *Fremdarbeiter,* pp. 343–44; Jacobmeyer, *Zwangsarbeiter,* pp. 46–50; diary entries of December 18, 20, 24, 27, 1945, January 1, 15, 24, 1946, in Karl Jering, *Überleben und Neubeginn. Tagebuchaufzeichnungen eines Deutschen 1945–1946* (Munich: Günter Olzog Verlag, 1979), pp. 71, 73–74, 77, 80–81, 87, 101, 105; "Weekly Military Government Report No. 2 for Week Ending 28

May 1945," "Weekly Military Government Report No. 4 for Week Ending 11 June 1945," Headquarters, Detachment E1 F3 for Land Bayern, NA, RG 260/390/47/19/1; "Intelligence Annex to Weekly Report of the Office of Military Government for Bavaria for the Period 8–15 November 1945," "Intelligence Annex to Weekly Report of the Office of Military Government for Bavaria for the Period 22–29 November 1945," OMGBY, Records of Intelligence Division, Weekly Intelligence Reports 1945–1947, NA, RG 260/390/47/19/1; "Weekly Intelligence Report No. 1 for Week Ending 6 December 1945," "Weekly Intelligence Report No. 3 for Week Ending 20 December 1945," "Weekly Intelligence Report No. 4 for Week Ending 27 December 1945," "Weekly Intelligence Report No. 5 for Week Ending 3 January 1946," "Weekly Intelligence Report No. 6 for Week Ending 10 January 1946," "Weekly Intelligence Report No. 7 for Week Ending 17 January 1946," OMGBY, Intelligence Branch, NA, RG 260/390/47/19/1.

8. Leonard Dinnerstein, "The U.S. Army and the Jews: Policies toward the Displaced Persons after World War II," *American Jewish History* 8, no. 3 (1979): pp. 357–63; "Periodic Report for Week Ending 3 April 1946," "Periodic Report for Week Ending 25 September 1946," "Periodic Report for Week Ending 11 December 1946," Office of Military Government for Land Bavaria, NA, RG 260/390/47/19/1; Office of the Chief Historian, European Command, *The First Year of the Occupation,* Occupation Forces in Europe Series, 1945–1946 (Frankfurt: Office of the Chief Historian, European Command, 1947), Table I: "Status of Displaced Persons as of 31 July 1945"; report of Earl G. Harrison, July 28, 1945, in Albert A. Hutler, *Agony of Survival* (Macomb, Ill.: Glenbridge Publishing, 1989), pp. 206–29; *New York Times,* September 30, 1945; "Displaced Persons," *Commonweal* 43 (March 1, 1946): pp. 502–4; *Army Talk* 151 (November 30, 1946); Army lieutenant quoted in Samuel Lubell, "The Second Exodus of the Jews," *Saturday Evening Post* 219 (October 5, 1946), p. 86.

9. Zink quoted in Dinnerstein, "U.S. Army and the Jews," p. 363; Jacobmeyer, *Zwangsarbeiter,* p. 208; Samuel A. Stouffer, et al., *The American Soldier: Combat and Its Aftermath* (Princeton: Princeton Univ. Press, 1949), 2:pp. 564–73; *New York Times,* January 25, 1946; Julius Posener, *In Deutschland 1945–1946* (Jerusalem: Siedler, 1947), p. 13; Leonard Dinnerstein, "German Attitudes toward the Jewish Displaced Persons (1945–50)," in Hans L. Trefousse, ed., *Germany and America: Essays on Problems of International Relations and Immigration* (New York: Brooklyn College Press, 1980), p. 243; David Bernstein, "Europe's Jews: Summer, 1947. A Firsthand Report by an American Observer," *Commentary* 4, no. 2 (August 1947): p. 105; Earl G. Harrison, "The Last Hundred Thousand," *Survey Graphic* 34 (December 1945): pp. 470–72. Virtually every intelligence report from the end of the war through 1947 contains references to DP black market activity and criminality, as well as tensions between GIs/Germans and DPs. See "Weekly Intelligence Reports" for May 1945–December 1947, OMGBY, Intelligence Branch, NA, RG 260/390/47/19/1.

10. "Intelligence Annex to Weekly Report of the Office of Military Government for Bavaria for the Period 22–29 November 1945," OMGBY, Records of Intel-

ligence Division, Weekly Intelligence Reports 1945–1947, NA, RG 260/390/47/19/1; Veeh, *Kriegsfurie,* pp. 568–69.

11. "War Diary," September 1944–July 1945, Detachment H3A3 (Neustadt an der Aisch), NA, RG 260/390/41/13/3; "Monthly Historical Report," November 1945, "Monthly Historical Report," December 1945, Office of Military Government for Kreis Uffenheim, Detachment I6H2 (Bad Windsheim), NA, RG 260/390/41/13/3-3; "Report for Month of July 1945," "Report for Month of November 1945," "Military Government Monthly Historical Report for Month of March 1946," "Military Government Monthly Historical Report for Month of May 1946," Military Government Liaison and Security Office, Landkreis Rothenburg ob der Tauber, Detachment B-268, NA, RG 260/390/47/5/1; "Weekly Summary," 24 November 1945, Office of Military Government for Kreis Scheinfeld, Detachment H-270, NA, RG 260/390/41/13/3; "Intelligence Annex to Weekly Report of the Office of Military Government for Bavaria for the Period 8–15 November 1945," "Intelligence Annex to Weekly Report of the Office of Military Government for Bavaria for the Period 22–29 November 1945," OMGBY, Records of Intelligence Division, Weekly Intelligence Reports 1945–1947, NA, RG 260/390/47/19/1; "Weekly Intelligence Report No. 1 for Week Ending 6 December 1945," "Weekly Intelligence Report No. 3 for Week Ending 20 December 1945," "Weekly Intelligence Report No. 4 for Week Ending 27 December 1945," "Weekly Intelligence Report No. 5 for Week Ending 3 January 1946," "Weekly Intelligence Report No. 6 for Week Ending 10 January 1946," "Weekly Intelligence Report No. 7 for Week Ending 17 January 1946," "Weekly Intelligence Report No. 10 for the Week Ending 7 February 1946," OMGBY, Intelligence Branch, NA, RG 260/390/47/19/1; "Periodic Report for Week Ending 11 April 1946," "Periodic Report for Week Ending 17 April 1946," "Periodic Report for Week Ending 1 May 1946," "Periodic Report for Week Ending 17 July 1946," "Periodic Report for Week Ending 24 July 1946," "Periodic Report for Week Ending 31 July 1946," "Periodic Report for Week Ending 28 August 1946," "Periodic Report for Week Ending 4 September 1946," "Periodic Report for Week Ending 11 September 1946," "Periodic Report for Week Ending 7 November 1946," Office of Military Government for Land Bavaria, NA, RG 260/390/47/19/1.

12. "Monthly Historical Report," September 11, 1945, Military Government Detachment H-273 (Neustadt an der Aisch), NA, RG 260/390/41/13/3; "Weekly Intelligence Report No. 1 for Week Ending 6 December 1945," "Weekly Intelligence Report No. 3 for Week Ending 20 December 1945," "Weekly Intelligence Report No. 4 for Week Ending 27 December 1945," "Weekly Intelligence Report No. 5 for Week Ending 3 January 1946," "Weekly Intelligence Report No. 7 for Week Ending 17 January 1946," "Weekly Intelligence Report No. 9 for Week Ending 31 January 1946," "Weekly Intelligence Report No. 11 for Week Ending 14 February 1946," OMGBY, Intelligence Branch, NA, RG 260/390/47/19/1; "Intelligence Annex to Weekly Report of the Office of Military Government for Bavaria for the Period 8–15 Novem-

ber 1945," "Intelligence Annex to Weekly Report of the Office of Military Government for Bavaria for the Period 22–29 November 1945," OMGBY, Records of Intelligence Division, Weekly Intelligence Reports 1945–1947, NA, RG 260/390/47/19/1; "Periodic Report for Week Ending 3 April 1946," "Periodic Report for Week Ending 11 April 1946," "Periodic Report for Week Ending 24 July 1946," "Periodic Report for Week Ending 11 September 1946," "Periodic Report for Week Ending 25 September 1946," "Periodic Report for Week Ending 7 November 1946," Office of Military Government for Land Bavaria, NA, RG 260/390/47/19/1; "Intelligence Report for Week Ending 29 January 1947," OMGBY, Intelligence Branch, NA, RG 260/390/47/19/1; "Weekly Intelligence Summary No. 11 for the Period Ending 22 March 1947," "Weekly Intelligence Summary No. 15 for the Period Ending 19 April 1947," "Weekly Intelligence Summary No. 16 for the Period Ending 26 April 1947," "Weekly Intelligence Summary No. 24 for the Period Ending 21 June 1947," "Weekly Intelligence Summary No. 25 for the Period Ending 28 June 1947," "Weekly Intelligence Summary No. 27 for the Period Ending 12 July 1947," "Weekly Intelligence Summary No. 28 for the Period Ending 19 July 1947," "Weekly Intelligence Summary No. 31 for the Period Ending 9 August 1947," Headquarters, First Military District, NA, RG 260/390/47/19/1; Hermann Glaser, *1945: Ein Lesebuch* (Frankfurt: Fischer Taschenbuch Verlag, 1995), p. 190; *Nürnberger Nachrichten,* June 27, 1994; Veeh, *Kriegsfurie,* pp. 568–69; "Report for Month of July 1945," Annual Historical Reports, Military Government Liaison and Security Office, Landkreis Rothenburg ob der Tauber, Detachment B-268, NA, RG 260/390/47/5/1.

13. "Weekly Summary," November 24, 1945, Office of Military Government for Kreis Scheinfeld, Detachment H-270, NA, RG 260/390/41/13/3; "Intelligence Annex to Weekly Report of the Office of Military Government for Bavaria for the Period 22–29 November 1945," OMGBY, Records of Intelligence Division, Weekly Intelligence Reports 1945–1947, NA, RG 260/390/47/19/1; "Historical Report," June 25, 1946, Military Government Liaison and Security Office, Landkreis Dinkelsbühl, Detachment B-261, NA, RG 260/390/47/5/1; "Periodic Report for Week Ending 24 July 1946," Office of Military Government for Land Bavaria, NA, RG 260/390/47/19/1; *New York Times,* November 27, 1945; Jacobmeyer, *Zwangsarbeiter,* pp. 47–48.

14. "Intelligence Annex to Weekly Report of the Office of Military Government for Bavaria for the Period 8–15 November 1945," "Intelligence Annex to Weekly Report of the Office of Military Government for Bavaria for the Period 22–29 November 1945," OMGBY, Records of Intelligence Division, Weekly Intelligence Reports 1945–1947, NA, RG 260/390/47/19/1; "Weekly Intelligence Report No. 1 for Week Ending 6 December 1945," "Weekly Intelligence Report No. 7 for Week Ending 17 January 1946," "Weekly Intelligence Report No. 8 for Week Ending 24 January 1946," "Weekly Intelligence Report No. 10 for Week Ending 7 February 1946," OMGBY, Intelligence Branch, NA, RG 260/390/47/19/1.

15. Major James M. Snyder, "The Establishment and Operations of the United

States Constabulary, 3 October 1945–30 June 1947," (Headquarters, U.S. Constabulary: Historical Sub-Section C-3, 1947), U.S. Army Military History Institute, Carlisle Barracks, Pa., pp. 1–78; Major General E. N. Harmon, *Combat Commander: Autobiography of a Soldier*, with Milton MacKaye and William Ross MacKaye (Englewood Cliffs, N.J.: Prentice-Hall, 1970), pp. 279–84; D. Steinmeier, "The Constabulary Moves Fast," *Army Information Digest* 2, no. 11 (November 1947): pp. 10–11; "Intelligence Annex to the Weekly Detachment Report," December 22, 1945, Office of Military Government for Kreis Scheinfeld, Detachment H-270, NA, RG 260/390/41/13/3; "Annual Report for Military Government of Bavaria," June 25, 1946, Military Government Liaison and Security Office, Landkreis Uffenheim, Detachment B-271, NA, RG 260/390/47/5/1; "Historical Report," June 25, 1946, Military Government Liaison and Security Office, Landkreis Dinkelsbühl, Detachment B-261, NA, RG 260/390/47/5/1; "Annual Historical Report," July 6, 1946, Military Government Liaison and Security Office, Landkreis Neustadt an der Aisch, Detachment B-273, NA, RG 260/390/47/5/1; "Wochenbericht an die Militärregierung für die Woche 29 August bis 4 September 1946," Military Government Liaison and Security Office, Landkreis Uffenheim, Detachment B-271, NA, RG 260/390/41/13/3-3; "Periodic Report for Week Ending 24 July 1946," Office of Military Government for Land Bavaria, NA, RG 260/390/47/19/1.

16. Snyder, "United States Constabulary," pp. 207–10 and Appendix 8: "Crimes, Offenses, and Serious Incidents," n.p.; Harmon, *Combat Commander*, pp. 290–91; Harold Zink, *The United States in Germany, 1944–1955* (1957; reprint, Westport, Conn.: Greenwood Press, 1974), pp. 138–40; "Stimmungsbericht des Ansbacher Oberbürgermeisters an die Militärregierung," September 6, 1946, in Hans Woller, "Zur Demokratiebereitschaft in der Provinz des Amerikanischen Besatzungsgebiets," *Vierteljahrshefte* für *Zeitgeschichte* 31 (1983): p. 349; Jacobmeyer, *Zwangsarbeiter*, pp. 46–50, 192–94, 210–16; Philip S. Bernstein, "Displaced Persons," *American Jewish Yearbook* 49 (1947–1948): pp. 526–27; Dieter Franck, *Jahre unseres Lebens 1945–1949* (Munich: Piper, 1980), pp. 122–37; "Weekly Intelligence Report No. 1 for Week Ending 6 December 1945," "Weekly Intelligence Report No. 10 for Week Ending 7 February 1946," "Weekly Intelligence Report No. 11 for Week Ending 14 February 1946," OMGBY, Intelligence Branch, NA, RG 260/390/47/19/1; "Periodic Report for Week Ending 11 April 1946," "Periodic Report for Week Ending 24 July 1946," Office of Military Government for Land Bavaria, NA, RG 260/390/47/19/1; Norbert Ehrenfreund, "Constab Seizes 46 in Dawn Raid on DP Camp," *Stars and Stripes*, April 26, 1947, pp. 1, 12; Ernest Reed, "DP Train Raid Nets $500,000 Illegal Cargo," *Stars and Stripes*, May 6, 1947, p. 4.

17. "Periodic Report for Week Ending 24 July 1946," Office of Military Government for Land Bavaria, NA, RG 260/390/47/19/1; Juliane Wetzel, "'Mir szeinen doh.' München und Umgebung als Zuflucht von Überlebenden des Holocaust, 1945–1948," in Martin Broszat, Klaus-Dietmar Henke, and Hans Woller, eds., *Von Stalingrad*

zur Währungsreform. Zur Sozialgeschichte des Umbruchs in Deutschland (Munich: R. Oldenbourg, 1988), pp. 354–55; Angelika Königsseder and Juliane Wetzel, *Lebensmut im Wartesaal. Die jüdischen DPs (Displaced Persons) im Nachkriegsdeutschland* (Frankfurt: Fischer Taschenbuch Verlag, 1994), pp. 136–37; Constantin Goschler, "The Attitude towards Jews in Bavaria after the Second World War," *Leo Baeck Institute Yearbook* 36 (1991): p. 449.

18. Wolfgang Jacobmeyer, "Jüdische Überlebende als 'Displaced Persons.' Untersuchungen zur Besatzungspolitik in den deutschen Westzonen und zur Zuwanderung osteuropäischer Juden 1945–1947," *Geschichte und Gesellschaft* 9 (1983): pp. 421–35; Juliane Wetzel, "'Displaced Persons.' Ein vergessenes Kapitel der deutschen Nachkriegsgeschichte," *Aus Politik und Zeitgeschichte*, B 7-8/95, pp. 35–36; Jael Geis, "'Ja, man muß seinen Feinden verzeihen, aber nicht früher, als bis sie gehenkt werden.' Gedanken zur Rache für die Vernichtung der europäischen Juden im unmittelbaren Nachkriegsdeutschland," in *Menora: Jahrbuch für deutsch-jüdische Geschichte* (Munich: Piper Verlag, 1998), 9:pp. 155, 164–68; Königsseder and Wetzel, *Lebensmut im Wartesaal*, pp. 47–57. Figures for the number of Jewish DPs in the American zone of occupation in 1946 are bewilderingly contradictory, ranging from a low of 145,000 to a recent claim of some 330,000. For a good discussion of this issue, see Atina Grossmann, "Victims, Villains, and Survivors: Gendered Perceptions and Self-Perceptions of Jewish Displaced Persons in Occupied Postwar Germany," *Journal of the History of Sexuality* 11, nos. 1–2 (January/April 2002): pp. 295–96.

19. Dinnerstein, "U.S. Army and the Jews," pp. 355–58; Leonard Dinnerstein, *America and the Survivors of the Holocaust: The Evolution of a United States Displaced Persons Policy, 1945–1950* (New York: Columbia Univ. Press, 1982), pp. 291–93; Königsseder and Wetzel, *Lebensmut im Wartesaal*, pp. 35–46; report of Earl G. Harrison, August 24, 1945, in Hutler, *Agony of Survival*, pp. 208, 221–22; text of Truman's letter to Eisenhower in the *New York Times*, September 30, 1945.

20. Dinnerstein, "U.S. Army and the Jews," pp. 358–64; Dinnerstein, *America and the Survivors*, pp. 9–46; Königsseder and Wetzel, *Lebensmut im Wartesaal*, pp. 24–57; Mark Wyman, *DP's: Europe's Displaced Persons, 1945–1951* (Ithaca: Cornell Univ. Press, 1989), pp. 131–56; Yehuda Bauer, *Out of the Ashes: The Impact of American Jews on Post-Holocaust European Jewry* (Oxford: Oxford Univ. Press, 1989), pp. 40–42, 87–88; Samuel Gringauz, "Our New German Policy and the DP's: Why Immediate Resettlement Is Imperative," *Commentary* 5, no. 6 (June 1948): pp. 509–10; Jacobmeyer, "Jüdische Überlebende," pp. 436–39; Koppel S. Pinson, "Jewish Life in Liberated Germany: A Study of the Jewish DP's," *Jewish Social Studies* 9, no. 1 (1947): pp. 101–8; Goschler, "Attitude towards Jews in Bavaria," pp. 445–51; Moses Moskowitz, "The Germans and the Jews: Postwar Report. The Enigma of German Irresponsibility," *Commentary* 2, no. 1 (July 1946): p. 13; Bernstein, "Europe's Jews," pp. 106–7; "Weekly Intelligence Report No. 5 for Week Ending 3 January 1946," "Weekly Intelligence Report No. 6 for Week Ending 10 January 1946," "Weekly In-

telligence Report No. 7 for Week Ending 17 January 1946," "Weekly Intelligence Report No. 9 for Week Ending 31 January 1946," OMGBY, Intelligence Branch, NA, RG 260/390/47/19/1; "Periodic Report for Week Ending 3 April 1946," "Periodic Report for Week Ending 11 April 1946," "Periodic Report for Week Ending 24 April 1946," "Periodic Report for Week Ending 17 July 1946," "Periodic Report for Week Ending 31 July 1946," "Periodic Report for Week Ending 25 September 1946," "Periodic Report for Week Ending 11 December 1946," Office of Military Government for Land Bavaria, NA, RG 260/390/47/19/1.

21. Pinson, "Jewish Life," pp. 101–8; Goschler, "Attitude towards Jews in Bavaria," pp. 445–51; Moskowitz, "Germans and Jews," p. 13; Bernstein, "Europe's Jews," pp. 106–7.

22. "Weekly Intelligence Report No. 10 for Week Ending 7 February 1946," "Weekly Intelligence Report No. 14 for Week Ending 7 March 1946," OMGBY, Intelligence Branch, NA, RG 260/390/47/19/1; "Periodic Report for Week Ending 24 July 1946," "Periodic Report for Week Ending 31 July 1946," "Periodic Report for Week Ending 25 September 1946," "Periodic Report for Week Ending 16 October 1946," "Periodic Report for Week Ending 30 October 1946," "Periodic Report for Week Ending 7 November 1946," Office of Military Government for Land Bavaria, NA, RG 260/390/47/19/1; "Intelligence Report for Week Ending 26 February 1947," "Intelligence Report for Week Ending 12 March 1947," "Intelligence Report for Week Ending 26 March 1947," "Intelligence Report for Week Ending 16 April 1947," OMGBY, Intelligence Branch, NA, RG 260/390/47/19/1; "Weekly Intelligence Summary No. 31 for the Period Ending 9 August 1947," Headquarters, First Military District, NA, RG 260/390/47/19/1; "Intelligence Report for Week Ending 22 August 1947," OMGBY, Intelligence Branch, NA, RG 260/390/47/19/1; S. Abramowicz (A.J.D.C. Representative, Team 621), "Report on Windsheim DP Camp," 5 August 1946, in *Testaments to the Holocaust. Series Three: The Henriques Archive from the Wiener Library, London* (Woodbridge, Conn.: Primary Source Microfilm, 2000), Reel 19; Ehrenfreund, "Constab Seizes 46 in Dawn Raid," *Stars and Stripes*, April 26, 1947, pp. 1, 12; Reed, "DP Train Raid," *Stars and Stripes*, May 6, 1947, p. 4; Kathryn Hulme, *The Wild Place* (Boston: Little, Brown, 1953), pp. 124, 211–12; Königsseder and Wetzel, *Lebensmut im Wartesaal*, pp. 135–38; Wetzel, "Mir szeinen doh," pp. 354–55; Goschler, "Attitude towards Jews in Bavaria," pp. 449–50; Jacobmeyer, "Jüdische Überlebende," pp. 441–42; Bauer, *Out of the Ashes*, p. 268; Abraham S. Hyman, *The Undefeated* (Jerusalem: Geffen Publishing House, 1993), pp. 290–94; Irving Heymont, *Among the Survivors of the Holocaust: The Landsberg DP Camp Letters of Major Irving Heymont, United States Army* (1982; reprint, Cincinnati: Hebrew Union College Press, 1992), p. 63.

23. Hyman, *The Undefeated*, pp. 294, 345; "Periodic Report for Week Ending 24 July 1946," Office of Military Government for Land Bavaria, NA, RG 260/390/47/19/1; "Weekly Intelligence Report No. 7 for Week Ending 17 January 1946," OMGBY, Intelligence Branch, NA, RG 260/390/47/19/1; Pinson, "Jewish Life," pp. 111–13;

Königsseder and Wetzel, *Lebensmut im Wartesaal,* pp. 137–38; Moskowitz, "Germans and Jews," pp. 12–13.

24. "Survey of Attitudes among Jewish Displaced Persons Circles," 8 January 1947, Counter Intelligence Corps, USFET, Region VI (Bamberg), in Wolfgang Jacobmeyer, "Polnische Juden in der amerikanischen Besatzungszone Deutschlands 1946/1947," *Vierteljahrshefte für Zeitgeshichte* 25, no. 2 (April 1977): pp. 129–30, 133; Leo Srole, "Why the DP's Can't Wait: Proposing an International Plan of Rescue," *Commentary* 3, no. 1 (January 1947): pp. 13–16; Bartley C. Crum, *Behind the Silken Curtain. A Personal Account of Anglo-American Diplomacy in Palestine and the Middle East* (New York: Simon and Schuster, 1947), p. 83; Simon Shochet, *Feldafing* (Vancouver: November House, 1983), pp. 160–62; Zeev W. Mankowitz, *Life between Memory and Hope: The Survivors of the Holocaust in Occupied Germany* (New York: Cambridge Univ. Press, 2002), pp. 243–44; Bernstein, "Displaced Persons," pp. 528–29.

25. Third Army Intelligence Report, November 1945, quoted in Edward N. Peterson, *The American Occupation of Germany: Retreat to Victory* (Detroit: Wayne State Univ. Press, 1977), p. 225; "Intelligence Annex to Weekly Report of the Office of Military Government for Bavaria for the Period 22–29 November 1945," OMGBY, Records of Intelligence Division, Weekly Intelligence Reports 1945–1947, NA, RG 260/390/47/19/1; "Weekly Intelligence Report No. 7 for Week Ending 17 January 1946," OMGBY, Intelligence Branch, NA, RG 260/390/47/19/1; "Periodic Report for Week Ending 11 April 1946," "Periodic Report for Week Ending 25 September 1946," Office of Military Government for Land Bavaria, NA, RG 260/390/47/19/1; "German Attitudes toward the Expulsion of German Nationals from Neighboring Countries," Report No. 14A, July 8, 1946, "An Investigation to Determine Any Changes in Attitudes of Native Germans toward the Expellees in Wuerttemberg-Baden," Report No. 28, November 14, 1946, "Opinions on the Expellee Problem," Report No. 47, February 20, 1947, "Anti-Semitism in the American Zone," Report No. 49, March 3, 1947, "German Reactions to Expellees and DP's," Report No. 81, December 3, 1947, "Prejudice and Anti-Semitism," Report No. 122, May 22, 1948, in Anna Merritt and Richard Merritt, eds., *Public Opinion in Occupied Germany. The OMGUS Surveys, 1945–1949* (Urbana, Chicago, and London: Univ. of Illinois Press, 1970), pp. 90–92, 112–14, 144–45, 146–48, 186–87, 239–40; *Neue Zeit,* May 4, 5, 1947; Joe Flemming, "Anti-Semitism Still Exists in Zone, Survey Shows," *Stars and Stripes,* May 5, 1947, p. 7; Gringauz, "German Policy and the DP's," p. 511; Elisabeth Noelle and Erich Peter Neumann, *Jahrbuch der Öffentlichen Meinung 1947–1955* (Allensbach am Bodensee: Verlag für Demoskopie, 1956), p. 129; Goschler, "Attitude towards Jews in Bavaria," pp. 443–44, 451; Dinnerstein, "German Attitudes," p. 242.

26. Moskowitz, "Germans and Jews," pp. 10–13; Institut für Besatzungsfragen, *Das DP-Problem. Eine Studie über die ausländischen Flüchtlinge in Deutschland* (Tübingen: Mohr, 1950), pp. 87–91; "Annual Report for Military Government of Bavaria," June 25, 1946, Military Government Liaison and Security Office, Landkreis

Uffenheim, Detachment B-271, NA, RG 260/390/47/5/1; "Weekly Intelligence Report No. 7 for Week Ending 17 January 1946," "Weekly Intelligence Report No. 9 for Week Ending 31 January 1946," "Weekly Intelligence Report No. 11 for Week Ending 14 February 1946," OMGBY, Intelligence Branch, NA, RG 260/390/47/19/1; "Periodic Report for Week Ending 11 April 1946," "Periodic Report for Week Ending 8 May 1946," "Periodic Report for Week Ending 12 June 1946," "Periodic Report for Week Ending 17 July 1946," "Periodic Report for Week Ending 31 July 1946," "Periodic Report for Week Ending 25 September 1946," Office of Military Government for Land Bavaria, NA, RG 260/390/47/19/1; Goschler, "Attitude towards Jews in Bavaria," p. 449–51; Peterson, *American Occupation,* pp. 295–97; Earl F. Ziemke, *The U.S. Army in the Occupation of Germany, 1944–1946* (Washington, D.C.: Center for Military History, U.S. Army, 1975), p. 285; Hulme, *The Wild Place,* pp. 125–26; Zink, *United States in Germany,* pp. 296–98; *New York Times,* March 21, 23, 1946; Wyman, *DP's,* pp. 167–68; Hyman, *The Undefeated,* pp. 343, 348–50.

27. "Weekly Intelligence Report No. 5 for Week Ending 3 January 1946," "Weekly Intelligence Report No. 6 for Week Ending 10 January 1946," "Weekly Intelligence Report No. 7 for Week Ending 17 January 1946," OMGBY, Intelligence Branch, NA, RG 260/390/47/19/1; "Periodic Report for Week Ending 3 April 1946," "Periodic Report for Week Ending 1 May 1946," Office of Military Government for Land Bavaria, NA, RG 260/390/47/19/1; Dinnerstein, "German Attitudes," pp. 241–42; Dr. Phillipp Auerbach, "Anti-Semitism in Bavaria," quoted in Gringauz, "German Policy and the DP's," p. 512.

28. Hyman, *The Undefeated,* pp. 296–301; Lubell, "Second Exodus," p. 86; Jacobmeyer, "Jüdische Überlebende," pp. 440–41; Dinnerstein, "U.S. Army and the Jews," p. 366; Crum, *Silken Curtain,* pp. 84, 90–91; Samuel H. Flowerman and Marie Jahoda, "Polls on Anti-Semitism: How Much Do They Tell Us?" *Commentary* 1, no. 6 (April 1946): p. 83; Wyman, *DP's,* pp. 173–74; Bernstein, "Displaced Persons," p. 531; "Survey of Attitudes among Jewish Displaced Persons," in Jacobmeyer, "Polnische Juden," p. 131; Bertram S. Korn, "Last Barrier to Jewish Equality," *Jewish Digest* 7, no. 7 (April 1962): pp. 11–17.

29. Dinnerstein, "U.S. Army and the Jews, p. 362; Hyman, *The Undefeated,* pp. 43–44, 299–300; *New York Times,* January 25, 1946; *Newsweek,* February 4, 1946, p. 57; Colonel H. S. Messec (OMGUS POW and DP Division) to General Stanley R. Mickelsen (USFET, G-5 Division), December 19, 1945, in Jacobmeyer, "Jüdische Überlebende," pp. 432–33.

30. General George S. Patton quoted in Königsseder and Wetzel, *Lebensmut im Wartesaal,* p. 30; "Survey of Attitudes among Jewish Displaced Persons," in Jacobmeyer, "Polnische Juden," p. 132; Hyman, *The Undefeated,* pp. 25, 290–91, 293.

31. "Annual Report for Military Government of Bavaria," June 25, 1946, Military Government Liaison and Security Office, Landkreis Uffenheim, Detachment B-271, NA, RG 260/390/47/5/1.

32. "Periodic Report for Week Ending 3 April 1946," Office of Military Government for Land Bavaria, NA, RG 260/390/47/19/1; Leo W. Schwarz, *The Redeemers: A Saga of the Years 1945–1952* (New York: Farrar, Straus and Young, 1953), pp. 104–10; Mankowitz, *Life between Memory and Hope,* pp. 257–58; *New York Times,* March 29, 30, and 31, 1946; Hyman, *The Undefeated,* pp. 289–90; Dinnerstein, *America and the Survivors,* pp. 49–50; Königsseder and Wetzel, *Lebensmut im Wartesaal,* p. 138.

33. Schwarz, *The Redeemers,* pp. 104–10; Mankowitz, *Life between Memory and Hope,* pp. 257–58; *New York Times,* March 29, 30, and 31, 1946; Hyman, *The Undefeated,* pp. 289–90; Dinnerstein, *America and the Survivors,* pp. 49–50; Königsseder and Wetzel, *Lebensmut im Wartesaal,* p. 138.

34. Schwarz, *The Redeemers,* pp. 104–10; Mankowitz, *Life between Memory and Hope,* pp. 257–58; *New York Times,* March 29, 30, and 31, 1946; Hyman, *The Undefeated,* pp. 289–90; Dinnerstein, *America and the Survivors,* pp. 49–50; Königsseder and Wetzel, *Lebensmut im Wartesaal,* p. 138; "Periodic Report for Week Ending 3 April 1946," Office of Military Government for Land Bavaria, NA, RG 260/390/47/19/1.

35. "Periodic Report for Week Ending 1 May 1946," Office of Military Government for Land Bavaria, NA, RG 260/390/47/19/1; Wyman, *DP's,* pp. 153–54; Hyman, *The Undefeated,* pp. 23–25; Schwarz, *The Redeemers,* pp. 111–17; Mankowitz, *Life between Memory and Hope,* pp. 258–59.

36. "Periodic Report for Week Ending 1 May 1946," Office of Military Government for Land Bavaria, NA, RG 260/390/47/19/1.

37. Wyman, *DP's,* pp. 153–54; Hyman, *The Undefeated,* pp. 23–25; Schwarz, *The Redeemers,* pp. 111–17; Mankowitz, *Life between Memory and Hope,* pp. 258–59; *New York Times,* April 30, 1946.

38. Hyman, *The Undefeated,* pp. 25–28; Mankowitz, *Life between Memory and Hope,* p. 260; *New York Times,* April 30, 1946.

39. "Periodic Report for Week Ending 1 May 1946," Office of Military Government for Land Bavaria, NA, RG 260/390/47/19/1.

40. Jacobmeyer, "Jüdische Überlebende," pp. 439–40; "Narrative Report of Displaced Persons Incident, Windsheim, July 25, 1946," OMGBY, Public Safety Office for Regierungsbezirk Oberfranken und Mittelfranken, Ansbach, July 31, 1946, "Report of Incidents Involving Jewish Displaced Persons at Windsheim," Headquarters, USFET, G-5 Division, August 14, 1946, "Statement of Pfc. Robert Reed, 26 July 1946" and "Statement of Israel Moszkowicz, 25 July 1946," in "Reporting of Crimes, Offenses and Serious Incidents," July 26, 1946, Military Government Liaison and Security Office, Landkreis Uffenheim, Detachment B-271, all in NA, RG 260/390/ 42/31/2.

41. "Narrative Report of Displaced Persons Incident, Windsheim, 25 July 1946," OMGBY, Public Safety Office for Regierungsbezirk Oberfranken und Mittelfranken, Ansbach, July 31, 1946, "Report of Incidents Involving Jewish Displaced Persons at

Windsheim," Headquarters, USFET, G-5 Division, August 14, 1946, "Statement of 2nd Lt. Robert T. Gooch, 26 July 1946," "Statement of Sgt. Lester Lowery, 26 July 1946," and "Statement of Pfc. Robert Reed, 26 July 1946" in "Reporting of Crimes, Offenses and Serious Incidents," July 26, 1946, Military Government Liaison and Security Office, Landkreis Uffenheim, Detachment B-271, all in NA, RG 260/390/42/31/2.

42. "Periodic Report for Week Ending 31 July 1946," OMGBY, Intelligence Division, Weekly Intelligence Reports, NA, RG 260/390/47/19/1.

43. Angelika Schardt, "'Der Rest der Geretteten.' Jüdische Überlebende im DP-Lager Föhrenwald 1945–1947," in Wolfgang Benz, ed., *Dachauer Hefte 8: Überleben und Spätfolgen* (Munich: Deutscher Taschenbuch Verlag, 1996), pp. 53–68; "Weekly Intelligence Report No. 1 for Week Ending 6 December 1945," OMGBY, Intelligence Branch, NA, RG 260/390/47/19/1; Königsseder and Wetzel, *Lebensmut im Wartesaal*, pp. 99–172; Henry Cohen, "The Anguish of the Holocaust Survivors," Public Lecture, April 13, 1996, http://www.remember.org/witness/cohen.html, pp. 1–6; Wetzel, "Displaced Persons," p. 38.

44. Cohen, "Anguish of the Holocaust Survivors," pp. 2–3.

45. Ibid., pp. 6–7.

46. "Operations Report," Assistant Chief of Staff, G-3, 9th Division, July 23, 1946, quoted in Cohen, "Anguish of the Holocaust Survivors," pp. 7–8.

47. *New York Times,* July 26, 30, 1946.

48. Ibid.; "Intelligence Report for Week Ending 8 January 1947," "Intelligence Report for Week Ending 22 January 1947," "Intelligence Report for Week Ending 29 January 1947," "Intelligence Report for Week Ending 5 February 1947," "Intelligence Report for Week Ending 12 February 1947," "Intelligence Report for Week Ending 5 March 1947," OMGBY, Intelligence Branch, NA, RG 260/390/47/19/1; "Weekly Intelligence Summary No. 11 for the Period Ending 22 March 1947," "Weekly Intelligence Summary No. 15 for the Period Ending 19 April 1947," "Weekly Intelligence Summary No. 16 for the Period Ending 26 April 1947," "Weekly Intelligence Summary No. 24 for the Period Ending 21 June 1947," "Weekly Intelligence Summary No. 25 for the Period Ending 28 June 1947," "Weekly Intelligence Summary No. 27 for the Period Ending 12 July 1947," "Weekly Intelligence Summary No. 28 for the Period Ending 19 July 1947," "Weekly Intelligence Summary No. 30 for the Period Ending 2 August 1947," "Weekly Intelligence Summary No. 31 for the Period Ending 9 August 1947," Headquarters, First Military District, NA, RG 260/390/47/19/1; Wetzel, "Displaced Persons," p. 35.

49. "Officials, Jews Term Munich Row 'Closed,'" *Stars and Stripes,* May 2, 1947, p. 4; "Troopers Subdue Polish DP Riot in Altstadt Camp," *Stars and Stripes,* May 12, 1947, p. 4; "Constab Runs Pole DP Camp after Quelling New Riots," *Stars and Stripes,* May 13, 1947, p. 4; "Weekly Intelligence Summary No. 30 for the Period Ending 2 August 1947," Headquarters, First Military District, NA, RG 260/390/47/19/1; *New*

York Times, August 5, 1947; Wyman, *DP's,* pp. 173–74; Mankowitz, *Life between Memory and Hope,* pp. 239–42; Jael Geis, "'Ja, man muß seinen Feinden verzeihen, aber nicht früher, als bis sie gehenkt werden.' Gedanken zur Rache für die Vernichtung der europäischen Juden im unmittelbaren Nachkriegsdeutschland," in *Menora: Jahrbuch für deutsch-jüdische Geschichte* (Munich: Piper Verlag, 1998), 9:pp. 155–68; Cilly Kugelmann, "Identität und Ideologie der Displaced Persons: Zwei historische Texte aus den DP-Lagern," *Babylon* 5 (1989): pp. 70–72.

50. Unsigned poem, *Haaretz,* November 30, 1942, and Natan Gurdus, "Let the World Cry Out!" *Haaretz,* November 26, 1942, quoted in Tom Segev, *The Seventh Million: The Israelis and the Holocaust,* trans. Haim Watzman (New York: Hill and Wang, 1993), p. 150; Jim Tobias, "Die Juden hatten ein Recht, sich zu rächen," *Aufbau: deutsch-jüdische Zeitung,* October 1, 1999; "Vorschriften sind Vorschriften," *taz,* February 2, 2000; John Kantara, "Der Krieg war aus, Dov Shenkal und seine Freunde hatten nur ein Ziel: Vergeltung für den Massenmord an den Juden," *Die Zeit,* no. 50 (1997); Segev, *The Seventh Million,* pp. 142, 147.

51. Michael Elkins, *Forged in Fury* (New York: Ballantine Books, 1971), pp. 200–204.

52. Tobias, "Die Juden hatten ein Recht"; Tobias and Zinke, *Nakam,* pp. 38–39; Joseph Harmatz, *From the Wings* (Lewes, Sussex, England: Book Guild, 1998), pp. 130–31.

53. Harmatz, *From the Wings,* pp. 131–33; Tobias and Zinke, *Nakam,* pp. 39–41.

54. Tobias and Zinke, *Nakam,* pp. 33–35; Kantara, "Der Krieg war aus"; Elkins, *Forged in Fury,* pp. 230–37; Segev, *The Seventh Million,* pp. 142–43.

55. Segev, *The Seventh Million,* pp. 144–45; Rich Cohen, *The Avengers* (New York: Alfred A. Knopf, 2000), pp. 202–3; Tobias and Zinke, *Nakam,* pp. 36–37; Harmatz, *From the Wings,* pp. 138–39; Kantara, "Der Krieg war aus."

56. Harmatz, *From the Wings,* pp. 132–37; Tobias, "Die Juden hatten ein Recht"; Tobias and Zinke, *Nakam,* pp. 43–44.

57. Harmatz, *From the Wings,* pp. 132–37; Tobias, "Die Juden hatten ein Recht"; Tobias and Zinke, *Nakam,* pp. 43–44; *Nürnberger Nachrichten,* January 5, February 6, 1946; Sonderdruck der *Nürnberger Nachrichten, Trümmerjahre 1945–1950* (Nuremberg: Nürnberger Nachrichten, 1985), p. 35.

58. Tobias and Zinke, *Nakam,* pp. 43–44; Harmatz, *From the Wings,* p. 139; Ernst von Salomon, *Der Fragebogen* (Hamburg: Rowohlt, 1961), pp. 664–66.

59. Harmatz, *From the Wings,* pp. 134–35; Tobias and Zinke, *Nakam,* pp. 13–15, 45–46; Tobias, "Die Juden hatten ein Recht."

60. Harmatz, *From the Wings,* pp. 139–40; Kantara, "Der Krieg war aus"; Tobias, "Die Juden hatten ein Recht"; Tobias and Zinke, *Nakam,* pp. 11–12, 17–19, 46.

61. Tobias and Zinke, *Nakam,* pp. 12–13, 47; Tobias, "Die Juden hatten ein Recht"; Harmatz, *From the Wings,* p. 140.

62. Tobias and Zinke, *Nakam*, p. 47; Tobias, "Die Juden hatten ein Recht"; Harmatz, *From the Wings*, p. 140; Cohen, *The Avengers*, pp. 209–10; Michael Bar-Zohar, *The Avengers*, trans. Len Ortzen (New York: Hawthorn Books, 1969), pp. 49–50.

63. Tobias and Zinke, *Nakam*, pp. 47–51; Tobias, "Die Juden hatten ein Recht"; Mankowitz, *Life between Memory and Hope*, pp. 237–38; Harmatz, *From the Wings*, p. 140; Cohen, *The Avengers*, pp. 211–12; Bar-Zohar, *The Avengers*, pp. 50–51; *New York Times*, April 20, 23, 1946; *St. Louis Post-Dispatch*, April 22, 28, 1946; *Süddeutsche Zeitung*, April 23, 1946; *Nürnberger Nachrichten*, April 27, 1946; "Toxikologischer Untersuchungsbericht," in "Monatsbericht des Oberbürgermeisters Nürnberg, 19. April 1946 bis 20. Mai 1946," Stadtarchiv Nürnberg, C29, Nr. 425; "Vorschriften sind Vorschriften," *taz*; Kantara, "Der Krieg war aus."

64. Segev, *The Seventh Million*, pp. 146, 151–52; Tobias, "Die Juden hatten ein Recht"; Kantara, "Der Krieg war aus."

AFTERWORD

1. Hans Wysling, ed., *Letters of Heinrich and Thomas Mann, 1900–1949*, trans. Don Reneau, with additional translations by Richard and Clara Winston (Berkeley: Univ. of California Press, 1998), pp. 256–57, 300–301; Thomas Mann, *Doctor Faustus: The Life of the German Composer Adrian Leverkühn as Told by a Friend*, trans. John E. Woods (New York: Vintage Books, 1997), pp. 183–84.

2. Mann, *Doctor Faustus*, pp. 356, 184, 474.

3. Ibid., pp. 504–6; Christopher Hitchens, "The Wartime Toll on Germany," *Atlantic Monthly*, January/February 2003, pp. 182–89.

BIBLIOGRAPHY

PRIMARY SOURCES

U.S. HOLOCAUST MEMORIAL MUSEUM, WASHINGTON, D.C.

Photo Archives

U.S. NATIONAL ARCHIVES (NA), COLLEGE PARK, MD., RECORD GROUP (RG)

59: General Records of the Department of State.
111: Records of the Office of the Chief Signal Officer.
165: Records of the War Department General and Special Staffs.
242: Captured German and Related Records on Microform in the National Archives.
    T-77: German Armed Forces High Command (OKW).
    T-78: German Army High Command.
    T-79: German Army Areas (Wehrkreise).
    T-312: German Army Field Commands (Armies).
    T-314: German Army Field Commands (Corps).
    T-315: German Army Field Commands (Divisions).
260: Records of U.S. Occupation Headquarters, World War II.
319: Records of the Army Staff, Counter Intelligence Corps Collection.
319.20.8: Records of the Foreign Military Studies Program.
    B-132, Fritz Hickl, "National Redoubt and RAD Austria."
    B-133, Josef Punzert, "The National Alpine Redoubt."
    B-136, Friederick Karl von Eberstein, "National Redoubt (Battle Sector VII SS and Police)."

B-140, Otto Hoffmann, "National Redoubt."

B-159, Karl Kriebel, "The Alpine Redoubt (Wehrkreis VII)."

B-187, Generalmajor (Brigadier General) August Marcinkiewicz, "Report on the Alpenfestung."

B-188, General der Pionier Alfred Jacob, "Report Concerning the German Alpine Redoubt."

B-211, Anton Glasl, "Wehrkreis XVIII (October 1944–May 1945)."

B-225, Gottlob Berger, The Alpine Redoubt."

B-228a, General Karl Weisenberger, Commander of Wehrkreis XIII, "Der Wehrkreis XIII im Einsatz gegen die amerikanischen Armeen."

B-457, Franz Hofer, "The Alpine Fortification and Defense Line: A Report on German and U.S. Views of the 'Alpine Redoubt' in 1944, Annex #1."

B-458, Franz Hofer, "The National Redoubt."

B-459, General der Gebirgstruppen Georg Ritter von Hengl, "Report on the Alpine Fortress."

B-460, General der Gebirgstruppen Georg Ritter von Hengl, "Evaluation of Manuscripts Concerning National Redoubt."

B-461, General der Gebirgstruppen Georg Ritter von Hengl, "The Alpine Redoubt."

B-583, General der Infanterie Friedrich Schulz, "Bericht über Lage, Auftrag, und Maßnahmen (im großen) der Heeresgruppe G im April 1945."

B-604, Generalmajor (Brigadier General) Erich Schmidt (Commander, 352. Volksgrenadier Division), "Mitteldeutschland."

B-703, SS-Obergruppenführer and General der Waffen-SS Paul Hauser, "Kämpfe der Heeresgruppe G vom 22.03.–04.04.1945."

B-737, SS-Obersturmbannführer (Lieutenant Colonel) Ekkehard Albert (Chief of the General Staff of XIII. SS-Army Corps), "Einsatz des XIII. SS-A.K. zwischen Rhein und Alpen vom 26.03.–06.05.1945."

B-772, Lieutenant Colonel Cord von Hobe, "Einsatz der Panzer-Kampfgruppe XIII vom 06.04–05.05.1945."

B-818, General Karl Weisenberger, Commander of Wehrkreis XIII, "Der Wehrkreis XIII in den letzten Kriegsmonaten."

331: Records of Allied Operational and Occupation Headquarters, World War II.

332: Records of U.S. Theaters of War, World War II.

338: Records of United States Army Commands, 1942– .

407.3: Reports Relating to World War II and Korean War Combat Operations and to Activities in Occupied Areas 1940–54.

GOVERNMENT PUBLICATIONS

Army Services Forces, ed. *Pocket Guide No. 10, Germany.* Washington, D.C.: Information Branch, U.S. Army, [1944].

BIBLIOGRAPHY

Bennett, Linda, and Marcus W. Floyd. *Displaced Persons.* Frankfurt: Office of Chief Historian, European Command, 1947.

Costlow, Owsley C., ed. *Combat Highlights of the United States Twelfth Armored Division in the European Theater of Operations. 1 December 1944–30 May 1945.* Washington, D.C.: G-3 Information and Education Section, 1954.

Frederiksen, Oliver J. *The American Military Occupation of Germany, 1945–1953.* Frankfurt: Historical Division, U.S. Army, Europe, 1953.

Geis, Margaret L., and George J. Gray. "The Relations of Occupation Personnel with the Civil Population, 1946–1948." In Office of the Chief Historian, European Command, ed. *Occupation in Europe Series.* Karlsruhe, 1951.

Historical Board, ed. *The Fighting Forty-Fifth: The Combat Report of an Infantry Division.* Baton Rouge, La.: Army and Navy Publishing Company, 1946.

Morale Services Division, Army Services Forces. *What the Soldier Thinks: A Monthly Digest of War Department Studies on the Attitudes of American Troops.* Washington, D.C.: Army Service Forces, War Department, December 1943–September 1945, no. 7.

106th Cavalry Group. *The 106th Cavalry Group in Europe.* Augsburg: J.P. Himmer K.G., 1945.

Office of the Chief Historian, European Command. *The First Year of the Occupation.* Occupation Forces in Europe Series, 1945–1946. Frankfurt: Office of the Chief Historian, European Command, 1947.

———. *The Second Year of the Occupation.* Occupation Forces in Europe Series, 1945–1946. Frankfurt: Office of the Chief Historian, European Command, 1947.

———. *The Third Year of the Occupation: First through Fourth Quarter, 1 July 1947–30 June 1948.* Occupation Forces in Europe Series, 1947–1948. Frankfurt: Office of the Chief Historian, European Command, 1948.

———. *The Fourth Year of the Occupation, 1 July–31 December 1948.* Occupation Forces in Europe Series, 1948. Karlsruhe: Office of the Chief Historian, European Command, 1949.

———. *Morale and Discipline in the European Command, 1945–1949.* Occupation Forces in Europe Series, 1945–1949. Karlsruhe: Office of the Chief Historian, European Command, 1951.

———. *History of the U.S. Constabulary, 10 Jan 46–31 Dec 47.* Frankfurt: Office of the Chief Historian, European Command, 1947.

Office of Strategic Services, Research and Analysis Branch. Report No. 232. *South Germany: An Analysis of the Political and Social Organization, the Communications, Economic Controls, Agriculture and Food Supply, Mineral Resources, Manufacturing and Transportation Facilities of South Germany.* Washington, D.C.: GPO, 1944.

Seventh U.S. Army. *The Seventh United States Army in France and Germany, 1944–1945.* Heidelberg: Aloys Gräf, 1946.

BIBLIOGRAPHY

Snyder, Major James M. "The Establishment and Operations of the United States Constabulary, 3 October 1945–30 June 1947." Headquarters, U.S. Constabulary: Historical Sub-Section C-3, 1947, U.S. Army Military History Institute, Carlisle Barracks, Pa.

Starr, Joseph R. *Fraternization with the Germans in World War II.* Frankfurt: Office of Chief Historian, European Command, 1947.

Twelfth Armored Division. *A History of the United States Twelfth Armored Division, 15 September 1942–17 December 1945: The Hellcats in World War II.* 1947. Reprint, Nashville, Tenn.: Battery Press, 1978.

U.S. Army Intelligence Center. *History of the Counter Intelligence Corps.* Baltimore: U.S. Army Intelligence Center, 1959.

U.S. Army, Twelfth Army Group. *Don't Be a Sucker in Germany.* Washington, D.C., May 1945.

UNIVERSITY OF TENNESSEE SPECIAL COLLECTIONS

Avery, Arthur C. "European Theater. 12th Armored Division. Memoirs." University of Tennessee Special Collections, MS-1881, Box 1, Folder 7.

Boice, Dr. William S. "History of the Twenty-second United States Infantry in World War II." University of Tennessee Special Collections, MS-1259, Box 1, Folder 4.

———. "Historical Accounts of 4th Infantry Division, 22nd Infantry Regiment." University of Tennessee Special Collections, MS-1259, Box 5, Folder 1.

Broadhead, Phillip (Military Government Officer). University of Tennessee Special Collections, MS-2012, Box 3, Folders 19, 21–22, 25, 32, 34; Box 4, Folders 2, 6, 17.

Curry, Gene A. "European Theater. 12th Armored Division. Memoirs." University of Tennessee Special Collections, MS-1608, Box 1, Folder 17.

Hamlin, John W., Jr. Photographs. University of Tennessee Special Collections, MS-2012, Box 6, Folders 66–67.

Hansen, John A. Photographs. University of Tennessee Special Collections, MS-1608, Box 3, Folders 1–2.

Lans, Sherman B. "Mount Up! The History of Company C, 17th Armored Infantry Battalion, 12th Armored Division." University of Tennessee Special Collections, MS-2012, Box 8, Folder 12.

Laughlin, Edward. "The Labor Camp." University of Tennessee Special Collections, MS-2012, Box 8, Folder 24.

———. "Contacts with German Prisoners of War." University of Tennessee Special Collections, MS-2012, Box 8, Folder 25

———. "Village Street Fighting." University of Tennessee Special Collections, MS-2012, Box 8, Folder 26

BIBLIOGRAPHY

————. "The Village, Female German Soldiers, The Bank, April 1945." University of Tennessee Special Collections, MS-2012, Box 8, Folder 32.

Lesemann, William, Jr. "Displaced Persons (DP's), Europe." University of Tennessee Special Collections, MS-2012, Box 8, Folder 57.

Loth, Don. "European Theater. 12th Armored Division. Journal." University of Tennessee Special Collections, MS-1881, Box 15, Folder 19.

Mackenson, John C. Photographs. University of Tennessee Special Collections, MS-2012, Box 9, Folder 5.

Pearson, Alton. "European Theater. 4th Infantry Division, 12th Infantry Regiment. Memoirs." University of Tennessee Special Collections, MS-1764, Box 17, Folder 5.

"Swede's Diary," Historical Account of the 22nd Infantry Regiment, 4th Infantry Division. University of Tennessee Special Collections, MS-1764, Box 5, Folder 1.

Vickery, Dorothy S. "Memoirs of Europe after World War II, 1945–1947." University of Tennessee Special Collections, MS-2012, Box 14, Folder 34.

Walker, Laurence C. "Through the Schwarzwald to Berchtesgaden." University of Tennessee Special Collections, MS-2012, Box 14, Folder 35.

BAYERISCHES HAUPTSTAATSARCHIV MÜNCHEN, ABTEILUNG II (BASTAM)

Ministerium des Äußern, 102153.
Sonderabgabe I, 1548.

GEMEINDE ARCHIV IPSHEIM

Document Numbers 101, 139, 141; non-numbered file from 1946.

STAATSARCHIV NÜRNBERG (STAN)

Bestand: Die letzten Tage des 2. Weltkrieges in Wilhermsdorf, Nr. 2454/4.
Bestand: Landratsamt Fürth, Lfd. Nr. 40–41.
Bestand: Landratsamt Gunzenhausen, Abgabe 61, Lfd. Nr. 4346.
Bestand: Landratsamt Uffenheim, Abg. 1956, Rep. 212/18 VIII, Lfd. Nr. 214–15; 1888; 1994; 2003.
    Abg. 1970/71, Rep. 212/18, Lfd. Nr. 102; 117; 248; 254; 1608; 1612–14.
Bestand: NSDAP.
    Geschichte der NS-Ortsgruppe Scheinfeld, Rep. 503 IV.
Kammer des Innern II, 225; 689–93; 695; 714.

BIBLIOGRAPHY

Kammer des Innern XIII, 5686a.
Polizeidirektion Nürnberg-Fürth, 339; 347; 354.

STADTARCHIV BAD WINDSHEIM

Photographs.
Stadtchronik.

STADTARCHIV NÜRNBERG

"Toxikologischer Untersuchungsbericht." In "Monatsbericht des Oberbürgermeisters Nürnberg, 19. April 1946 bis 20. Mai 1946," C29, Nr. 425.

LANDESKIRCHLICHES ARCHIV (LKA) NÜRNBERG

"Bericht über die Besetzung von Ergersheim durch die Amerikaner," Evangelisch-Lutherische Pfarramtes Ergersheim an den Landeskirchenrat in Ansbach von 2 June 1945, Bestand Landeskirchenrat München.

"Bericht über die Feindbesetzung der Kirchengemeinde bezw. über vorausgehende Kampfhandlungen," Pfarramtes Obermichelbach über Wassertrüdingen an das Evangelisch-Lutherische Dekanat Dinkelsbühl, 1 June 1945, Dekanat Dinkelsbühl.

"Lagebericht des evangelischen Pfarrers von Oberampfrach an das Dekanat Feuchtwangen von 24.5.1945." In Aktenbestand des Landeskirchenrates München, Berichte über Vorgänge bei der militärischen Besetzung.

"Oberkirchenrat Schieder an Evangelisch-Lutherischen Landeskirchenrat," May 11, 1945, Bestand: Kreisdekanat Nürnberg, Nr. 14-502.

Rusam, Adolf. "Aus meinem Leben als Dorfpfarrer in der Kriegszeit. Tagebuch über die ereignisse der letzten Kriegswochen, die militärische Besetzung und den politischen Umschwung in Oberampfrach, 26. März-10. Mai 1945," Anhang zu Ahnen-Liste Rusam-Kaeppel, Ergänzungsband, bearbeitet von Kirchenrat Adolf Rusam, Aktenbestand des Landeskirchenrats München, Berichte über Vorgänge bei der militärischen Besetzung.

JUSTIZ UND NS-VERBRECHEN

"Lfd. Nr. 010, Verbrechen der Endphase: Ansbach, 18. April 1945. LG Ansbach vom 14.12.1946, KLs 24/46." In Adelheid Rüter-Ehlermann and C. F. Rüter, eds., *Justiz und NS-Verbrechen. Sammlung Deutscher Strafurteile Wegen Nationalsozialistischer Tötungsverbrechen 1945–1966.* Amsterdam: Univ. Press Amsterdam, 1968, 1:pp. 113–28.

BIBLIOGRAPHY

"Lfd. Nr. 029, Verbrechen der Endphase: Ansbach, 18. April 1945. LG Ansbach vom 28.8.1947, KLs 24/46 and OLG Nürnberg vom 20.5.1947, Ss 35/47." In Adelheid Rüter-Ehlermann and C. F. Rüter, eds., *Justiz und NS-Verbrechen. Sammlung Deutscher Strafurteile Wegen Nationalsozialistischer Tötungsverbrechen 1945–1966.* Amsterdam: Univ. Press Amsterdam, 1968, 1:pp. 643–58.

"Lfd. Nr. 083, Verbrechen der Endphase: Bad Windsheim (Bayern), 13. April 1945. LG Nürnberg-Fürth vom 20.8.1948, KLs 152/48 and OLG Nürnberg vom 11.11.1948, Ss 191/48." In Adelheid Rüter-Ehlermann and C. F. Rüter, eds., *Justiz und NS-Verbrechen. Sammlung Deutscher Strafurteile Wegen Nationalsozialistischer Tötungsverbrechen 1945–1966.* Amsterdam: Univ. Press Amsterdam, 1969, 3:pp. 171–86.

"Lfd. Nr. 129, Verbrechen der Endphase: Nürnberg, Februar 1945. LG Nürnberg-Fürth, Kls 299/48, OLG Nürnberg, Ss 83/49." In Adelheid Rüter-Ehlermann and C. F. Rüter, eds., *Justiz und NS-Verbrechen. Sammlung Deutscher Strafurteile Wegen Nationalsozialistischer Tötungsverbrechen 1945–1966.* Amsterdam: Univ. Press Amsterdam, 1969, 4:pp. 343–54.

"Lfd. Nr. 179, NS-Gewaltverbrechen in Lagern: Langenzenn (Bayern), 1943–1944. LG Nürnberg-Fürth vom 14. 11. 1949, Ks 8/49." In Adelheid Rüter-Ehlermann and C. F. Rüter, eds., *Justiz und NS-Verbrechen. Sammlung Deutscher Strafurteile Wegen Nationalsozialistischer Tötungsverbrechen 1945–1966.* Amsterdam: Univ. Press Amsterdam, 1969, 5:pp. 563–68.

"Lfd. Nr. 180, Verbrechen der Endphase: Aub (Bayern), 7. April 1945. LG Würzburg vom 14. 11. 1949, Ks 2/49; LG Würzburg vom 11. 12. 1948, Kls 59/48; OLG Bamberg vom 16. 3. 1949, Ss 26/49." In Adelheid Rüter-Ehlermann and C. F. Rüter, eds., *Justiz und NS-Verbrechen. Sammlung Deutscher Strafurteile Wegen Nationalsozialistischer Tötungsverbrechen 1945–1966.* Amsterdam: Univ. Press Amsterdam, 1969, 5:pp. 569–600.

"Lfd. Nr. 252, Verbrechen der Endphase: Pforzheim-Brötzingen, 2. Februar 1945. LG Karlsruhe, KLs 9/48, OLG Stuttgart, 2Ss 82/49." In Adelheid Rüter-Ehlermann and C. F. Rüter, eds., *Justiz und NS-Verbrechen. Sammlung Deutscher Strafurteile Wegen Nationalsozialistischer Tötungsverbrechen 1945–1966.* Amsterdam: Univ. Press Amsterdam, 1969, 7:pp. 625–46.

"Lfd. Nr. 255, Verbrechen der Endphase: Ochsenfurt, März 1945. LG Würzburg, Ks 12/50." In Adelheid Rüter-Ehlermann and C. F. Rüter, eds., *Justiz und NS-Verbrechen. Sammlung Deutscher Strafurteile Wegen Nationalsozialistischer Tötungsverbrechen 1945–1966.* Amsterdam: Univ. Press Amsterdam, 1969, 7:pp. 705–16.

"Lfd. Nr. 412, Verbrechen der Endphase: Schweinfurt, 21. März 1945. LG Würzburg, Ks 4/53, BGH 1StR353/52, BGH 1StR357/53." In Irene Sagel-Grande, et al., eds., *Justiz und NS-Verbrechen. Sammlung Deutscher Strafurteile Wegen Nationalsozialistischer Tötungsverbrechen 1945–1966.* Amsterdam: Univ. Press Amsterdam, 1975, 13:pp. 21–68.

BIBLIOGRAPHY

"Lfd. Nr. 421, Justizverbrechen: Rothenburg o. T., Schillingsfürst, und Brettheim, 5., 9., und 10. April 1945. LG Ansbach vom 19. 10. 1955, Ks 1/52, Ks 1–2/54, and BGH vom 7. 12. 1956, 1 StR 56/56." In Irene Sagel-Grande, et al., eds., *Justiz und NS-Verbrechen. Sammlung Deutscher Strafurteile Wegen Nationalsozialistischer Tötungsverbrechen 1945–1966.* Amsterdam: Univ. Press Amsterdam, 1975, 13:pp. 360–404.

"Lfd. Nr. 458, Verbrechen der Endphase: Langenbachtal, März 1945. LG Arnsberg, 3Ks 1/57." In Irene Sagel-Grande, et al., eds., *Justiz und NS-Verbrechen. Sammlung Deutscher Strafurteile Wegen Nationalsozialistischer Tötungsverbrechen 1945–1966.* Amsterdam: Univ. Press Amsterdam, 1975, 14:pp. 563–628.

"Lfd. Nr. 466, Verbrechen der Endphase: Burgthann (bei Nürnberg), 17. April 1945. LG Nürnberg-Fürth vom 1. 10. 1958, 638 Ks 5/56 and BGH vom 22. 10. 1957, 1 StR 116/57." In Irene Sagel-Grande, et al., eds., *Justiz und NS-Verbrechen. Sammlung Deutscher Strafurteile Wegen Nationalsozialistischer Tötungsverbrechen 1945–1966.* Amsterdam: Univ. Press Amsterdam, 1975, 15:pp. 275–97.

"Lfd. Nr. 472, Verbrechen der Endphase: Rummelsmühle bei Seenheim (Bayern), 12. April 1945. LG Ansbach vom 2. 1. 1959, Ks 3/58." In Irene Sagel-Grande, et al., eds., *Justiz und NS-Verbrechen. Sammlung Deutscher Strafurteile Wegen Nationalsozialistischer Tötungsverbrechen 1945–1966* Amsterdam: Univ. Press Amsterdam, 1976, 15:pp. 371–97.

"Lfd. Nr. 486, Verbrechen der Endphase: Langenbachtal, 20. März 1945/21. März 1945. LG Hagen, 3Ks 1/57, BGH 4StR438/58, BGH 4StR242/60." In Irene Sagel-Grande, et al., eds., *Justiz und NS-Verbrechen. Sammlung Deutscher Strafurteile Wegen Nationalsozialistischer Tötungsverbrechen 1945–1966.* Amsterdam: Univ. Press Amsterdam, 1977, 16:pp. 169–252.

"Lfd. Nr. 508, Verbrechen der Endphase: Eversberg, März 1945. LG Hagen, 3Ks 1/57, BGH 4StR417/61." In Irene Sagel-Grande, et al., eds., *Justiz und NS-Verbrechen. Sammlung Deutscher Strafurteile Wegen Nationalsozialistischer Tötungsverbrechen 1945–1966.* Amsterdam: Univ. Press Amsterdam, 1975, 17:pp. 281–314.

"Lfd. Nr. 893, Verbrechen der Endphase: Lörrach, April 1945. LG Waldshut, 850426, BGH 860122," publication in preparation.

Rüter, C. F., and D. W. De Mildt, eds., *Justiz und NS-Verbrechen. Sammlung Deutscher Strafurteile Wegen Nationalsozialistischer Tötungsverbrechen 1945–1966. Register zu den Bänden I–XXII.* Amsterdam: Holland Univ. Press, 1998.

OTHER DOCUMENTS

Abramowicz, S. (A.J.D.C. Representative, Team 621). "Report on Windsheim DP Camp," August 5, 1946, in *Testaments to the Holocaust. Series Three: The Henriques Archive from the Wiener Library, London.* Woodbridge, Conn.: Primary Source Microfilm, 2000, Reel 19.

BIBLIOGRAPHY

"An Investigation to Determine Any Changes in Attitudes of Native Germans toward the Expellees in Wuerttemberg-Baden," Report No. 28, November 14, 1946. In Anna Merritt and Richard Merritt, eds., *Public Opinion in Occupied Germany. The OMGUS Surveys, 1945–1949.* Urbana, Chicago, and London: Univ. of Illinois Press, 1970, pp. 112–14.

"Anti-Semitism in the American Zone," Report No. 49, March 3, 1947. In Anna Merritt and Richard Merritt, eds., *Public Opinion in Occupied Germany. The OMGUS Surveys, 1945–1949.* Urbana, Chicago, and London: Univ. of Illinois Press, 1970, pp. 146–48.

British Public Records Office. *ULTRA Documents.* New York: Clearwater Publishing Company, 1978.

Eberhard, Fritz. "Stuttgart im Mai 1945." In Ulrich Borsdorf and Lutz Niethammer, eds., *Zwischen Befreiung und Besatzung. Analysen des US-Geheimdienstes über Positionen und Strukturen deutscher Politik 1945.* Wuppertal: Peter Hammer Verlag, 1976, pp. 58–78.

Eisenhower, Dwight D. *Report by the Supreme Commander to the Combined Chiefs of Staff on the Operations in Europe of the Allied Expeditionary Force 6 June 1944 to 8 May 1945.* London: His Majesty's Stationery Office, 1946.

"German Attitudes toward the Expulsion of German Nationals from Neighboring Countries," Report No. 14A, July 8, 1946. In Anna Merritt and Richard Merritt, eds., *Public Opinion in Occupied Germany. The OMGUS Surveys, 1945–1949.* Urbana, Chicago, and London: Univ. of Illinois Press, 1970, pp. 90–92.

"German Reactions to Expellees and DP's," Report No. 81, December 3, 1947. In Anna Merritt and Richard Merritt, eds., *Public Opinion in Occupied Germany. The OMGUS Surveys, 1945–1949.* Urbana, Chicago, and London: Univ. of Illinois Press, 1970, pp. 186–87.

Lerner, Lt. Daniel (Psychological Warfare Division, SHAEF). "Notizen von einer Reise durch das besetzte Deutschland (Anfang April 1945)." In Ulrich Borsdorf and Lutz Niethammer, eds., *Zwischen Befreiung und Besatzung. Analysen des US-Geheimdienstes über Positionen und Strukturen deutscher Politik 1945.* Wuppertal: Peter Hammer Verlag, 1976, pp. 27–40.

"Opinions on the Expellee Problem," Report No. 47, February 20, 1947. In Anna Merritt and Richard Merritt, eds., *Public Opinion in Occupied Germany. The OMGUS Surveys, 1945–1949.* Urbana, Chicago, and London: Univ. of Illinois Press, 1970, pp. 144–45.

"Prejudice and Anti-Semitism," Report No. 122, May 22, 1948. In Anna Merritt and Richard Merritt, eds., *Public Opinion in Occupied Germany. The OMGUS Surveys, 1945–1949.* Urbana, Chicago, and London: Univ. of Illinois Press, 1970, pp. 239–40.

"Survey of Attitudes among Jewish Displaced Persons Circles," January 8, 1947, Counter Intelligence Corps, United States Forces European Theater (USFET),

Region VI (Bamberg). In Wolfgang Jacobmeyer, "Polnische Juden in der amerikanischen Besatzungszone Deutschlands 1946/1947," *Vierteljahrshefte für Zeitgeshichte* 25, no. 2 (April 1977): pp. 127–35.

Statistisches Jahrbuch für den Freistaat Bayern, vol. 16 (1924); vol. 17 (1926); vol. 18 (1928); vol. 19 (1930).

Staatsanwaltschaft b. Landgericht Nürnberg-Fürth, Nr. 2792:

Anklageschrift der Staatsanwaltschaft beim Landgericht Nürnberg-Fürth vom 23.5.1948.

Aussage von Thekla Fischer vom 18.8.1948.

Aussage von Babette Teufel vom 18.8.1948.

Aussage von Emmi J. vom 19.8.1948.

Aussage von Hedwig D. vom 19.8.1948.

Beschluss in der Strafsache gegen Reinbrecht, Günter; Schmid, Karl; Hub, Albert, 20.8.1948.

Beschuldigtenvernehmung (Schmid, Karl) in der Voruntersuchung gegen Reinbrecht, Günther wegen Totschlags.

Erklärung des Angeklagten Schmid vor dem Landgericht Nürnberg-Fürth vom 18.8.1948.

Erklärung des Zeugenaussage Johann Friedrich Dasch.

Erklärung des Zeugenaussage Irmgard Schmotzer.

Hans Schmotzer an den Herrn Oberstaatsanwalt beim Landgericht Nürnberg-Fürth, 4 Dezember 1946, Betrifft: Ermordung der Frau Christine Schmotzer.

Zeugenaussage von Rolf V. vom 19.8.1948.

Oberlandesgericht Nürnberg vom 11.11.1948, Ss 191/48.

Revisionsbegründung in der Strafsache gegen Reinbrecht, Günter; Schmid, Karl; Hub, Albert.

Zeitschrift des Bayerischen Statistischen Landesamts, vol. 64 (1932).

CONTEMPORARY NEWSPAPER AND MAGAZINE ARTICLES

Axelsson, George. "German Turmoil Is Reflected in Many Rumors." *New York Times Magazine,* September 10, 1944, p. 3.

———. "The Nazis Still Hope for a Miracle." *New York Times Magazine,* November 12, 1944, pp. 8, 44.

———. "Confusion Inside Germany." *New York Times,* April 15, 1945.

Baldwin, Hanson W. "The Nazis' Last Stand." *New York Times,* April 16, 1945.

———. "'Battle of Pockets' Ahead." *New York Times,* April 19, 1945.

Bernstein, David. "Europe's Jews: Summer, 1947. A Firsthand Report by an American Observer." *Commentary* 4, no. 2 (August 1947): pp. 101–9.

Bernstein, Philip S. "Displaced Persons." *American Jewish Yearbook* 49 (1947–1948): pp. 526–27.

BIBLIOGRAPHY

"Constab Runs Pole DP Camp after Quelling New Riots." *Stars and Stripes*, May 13, 1947, p. 4.

Currivan, Gene. "3rd Set to Attack Redoubt Borders." *New York Times*, April 25, 1945.

Daniell, Raymond. "Nazis Fight for Time and Political Miracle." *New York Times*, February 11, 1945.

———. "Disintegration of Germany Proceeds Rapidly." *New York Times*, April 15, 1945.

———. "The Defeat of Germany Is Only the Start." *New York Times Magazine*, April 15, 1945, pp. 5, 44.

———. "Released 'Slaves' Troubling Allies." *New York Times*, May 18, 1945.

———. "Organized Risings Possible in Reich, Eisenhower Warns." *New York Times*, November 1, 1945.

———. "Rebirth of Nazism Called Possibility." *New York Times*, January 14, 1946.

Delp, Hermann. "Alte, feste Stadt, dein Wille zum Leben siegte über das Schicksal." *Windsheimer Zeitung*, January 6, 1945.

"Disabilities and VD." *Newsweek*, July 22, 1946, p. 28.

"Displaced Persons." *Commonweal* 43 (March 1, 1946): pp. 502–4.

Döblin, Alfred. "Germany Is No More. Life among the Ruins." *Commentary* 2, no. 3 (September 1946): pp. 227–32.

Ehrenfreund, Norbert. "Constab Seizes 46 in Dawn Raid on DP Camp." *Stars and Stripes*, April 26, 1947, pp. 1, 12.

"Festung Berchtesgaden?" *Weltwoche*, February 2, 1945.

Flemming, Joe. "Anti-Semitism Still Exists in Zone, Survey Shows." *Stars and Stripes*, May 5, 1947, p. 7.

Flowerman, Samuel H., and Marie Jahoda. "Polls on Anti-Semitism: How Much Do They Tell Us?" *Commentary* 1, no. 6 (April 1946): pp. 82–86.

"4 SA Officers to Go on Trial Tomorrow." *Stars and Stripes*, April 7, 1947, p. 4.

"German Girls: U.S. Army Boycott Fails to Stop GIs from Fraternizing with Them." *Life*, July 23, 1945, pp. 35–37.

"Germany: Chaos and Comforts." *Time*, April 16, 1945, p. 38.

"The G.I. and VD." *Newsweek*, September 2, 1946, p. 50.

Gray, J. Glenn. "Munich University: Class of '50. A Case Study in German Re-Education." *Commentary* 5, no. 5 (May 1948): pp. 440–48.

Gringauz, Samuel. "Jewish Destiny as the DP's See It." *Commentary* 4, no. 6 (December 1947): pp. 501–9.

———. "Our New German Policy and the DP's: Why Immediate Resettlement Is Imperative." *Commentary* 5, no. 6 (June 1948): pp. 508–14.

Gruson, Sydney. "U.S. Fears Uprising of Young Germans." *New York Times*, March 23, 1946, p. 4.

———. "Polish Refugee Slain during Raid on Camp by 200 German Police." *New York Times*, March 30, 1946.

BIBLIOGRAPHY

———. "1,000 Nazis Seized by Allies as First Major Attempt to Revive Party Is Crushed." *New York Times,* March 31, 1946.

Gurfein, M. I., and Morris Janowitz. "Trends in Wehrmacht Morale." *Public Opinion Quarterly* 10 (1946): pp. 78–84.

Harrison, Earl G. "The Last Hundred Thousand." *Survey Graphic* 34 (December 1945): pp. 470–72.

Headen, T. P. "What Shall He Tell the Germans?" *Army Information Digest* 1 (July 1946): pp. 17–20.

Heym, Stefan. "But the Hitler Legend Isn't Dead." *New York Times Magazine,* January 20, 1946, p. 8.

Hill, Gladwin. "Big Job for U.S. in Reich." *New York Times,* April 29, 1945.

———. "Displaced Groups Put under Guard." *New York Times,* November 27, 1945.

Hulen, Bertram D. "President Orders Eisenhower to End New Abuse of Jews." *New York Times,* September 30, 1945.

Hyman, Abraham S. "Displaced Persons." *American Jewish Yearbook* 49 (1949): pp. 455–73.

"Invitation to a Voyage." *Commonweal* 42 (October 12, 1945): p. 612.

Janowitz, Morris. "German Reactions to Nazi Atrocities." *American Journal of Sociology* 52, no. 2 (September 1946): pp. 141–46.

"Jews in U.S. Camps Held Ill-Treated." *New York Times,* November 22, 1945.

Johnston, Richard J. H. "7th Army Expects Last Big Battle." *New York Times,* April 15, 1945.

Jordy, William H. "Germans and the Occupation." *Commonweal* 43 (March 8, 1946): pp. 521–24.

Kirkpatrick, Clifford. "Reactions of Educated Germans to Defeat." *American Journal of Sociology* 54 (1948/1949): pp. 36–47.

Knauth, Percy. "The German People." *Life,* May 7, 1945, p. 69.

———. "Fraternization: The Word Takes on a Brand-New Meaning in Germany." *Life,* July 2, 1945, p. 26.

Lessner, Erwin. "Hitler's Final V Weapon." *Collier's,* January 27, 1945, pp. 14, 47–48.

"Letter from Germany." *Commonweal* 42 (April 13, 1945): pp. 645–46.

Long, Tania. "Spawn of the Nazi Code." *New York Times Magazine,* November 25, 1945, pp. 8, 32.

———. "They Long for a New Fuehrer." *New York Times Magazine,* December 9, 1945, pp. 8, 44.

———. "Troops in Bavaria Back Fraternizing." *New York Times,* January 27, 1946.

———. "Munich University Hotbed of Nazism." *New York Times,* April 23, 1946.

Lubell, Samuel. "The Second Exodus of the Jews." *Saturday Evening Post* 219 (October 5, 1946): p. 16.

MacCormac, John. "Wandering Hordes in Reich Alarming." *New York Times,* April 7, 1945.

BIBLIOGRAPHY

Mayo, George E. "A Corporal in Germany." *Army Information Digest* 2 (March 1947): pp. 6–10.

Middleton, Drew. "Nazi Die-Hards Man Their 'National Redoubt.'" *New York Times,* April 8, 1945.

———. "3rd Army 15 Miles from Austrian Line." *New York Times,* April 26, 1945.

———. "Dark German Outlook Encourages Resistance." *New York Times,* January 20, 1946.

Morgan, Edward P. "They Seek a Promised Land." *Collier's,* May 4, 1946, p. 67.

Moskowitz, Moses. "The Germans and the Jews: Postwar Report. The Enigma of German Irresponsibility." *Commentary* 2, no. 1 (July 1946): pp. 7–14.

"Nazi Officers Caught in Underground Plot." *Stars and Stripes,* March 29, 1947, p. 4.

"Nazis See Project for Mass Murder." *New York Times,* February 14, 1945.

"Nazi Underground in Action, Foe Says." *New York Times,* April 2, 1945.

Neumann, Franz. "Re-Educating the Germans. The Dilemma of Reconstruction." *Commentary* 3, no. 6 (June 1947): pp. 517–25.

O'Donnell, James P. "Do the Fraüleins Change Our Joe?" *Newsweek* 26 (December 24, 1945): pp. 50–52.

"Officials, Jews Term Munich Row 'Closed.'" *Stars and Stripes,* May 2, 1947, p. 4.

"One Killed in Clash Near Refugee Camp." *New York Times,* July 26, 1946.

Pinson, Koppel S. "Jewish Life in Liberated Germany: A Study of the Jewish DP's." *Jewish Social Studies* 9, no. 1 (1947): pp. 101–26.

"Poison Bread Fells 1,900 German Captives in U.S. Army Prison Camp Near Nuremberg." *New York Times,* April 20, 1946.

"Poison Found in Reich Bakery." *St. Louis Post Dispatch,* April 28, 1946.

"Poison Plot to Kill 15,000 Nazi Prisoners Bared in Nuernberg; 2,283 Made Ill." *St. Louis Post Dispatch,* April 22, 1946.

"Poison Plot Toll of Nazis at 2,283." *New York Times,* April 23, 1946.

"Pravda Says Nazis Dig in for New War." *New York Times,* February 27, 1945.

"The Prospect for Germany." *Commonweal* 43 (January 25, 1946): pp. 371–72.

Reed, Ernest. "DP Train Raid Nets $500,000 Illegal Cargo." *Stars and Stripes,* May 6, 1947, p. 4.

Riess, Curt. "Will Goebbels Win His Goetterdaemmerung?" *New York Times Magazine,* February 25, 1945, pp. 8, 35–36.

———. "Planned Chaos—The Nazi Goal." *New York Times Magazine,* April 22, 1945, pp. 10–11, 39.

Rogers, Robert R. "Four SA Men to Face Trial for Nazi Plot." *Stars and Stripes,* March 27, 1947, pp. 1, 12.

Schiff, Victor. "Last Fortress of the Nazis." *New York Times Magazine,* February 11, 1945, pp. 9, 46–47.

Schmidt, Dana Adams. "Jews Embittered by Life in Germany." *New York Times,* July 30, 1946.

BIBLIOGRAPHY

"7 Germans Sentenced in Resistance Moves." *Stars and Stripes,* April 26, 1947, p. 4.

Srole, Leo. "Why the DP's Can't Wait: Proposing an International Plan of Rescue." *Commentary* 3, no. 1 (January 1947): pp. 13–24.

"SS Remnants Warn German Women: Bavaria Underground Placards Threaten Reprisals for Any Fraternizing with the Yanks." *New York Times,* September 30, 1945.

Steinhoff, A. "Jugend hinter Gittern." *Der Regenbogen* 2, nos. 11–12 (1947).

Steinmeier, D. "The Constabulary Moves Fast." *Army Information Digest* 2, no. 11 (November 1947): pp. 7–16.

"Tide of 'DP's' Ebbs." *New York Times,* August 30, 1945, p. 10.

"To Tell or Not to Tell Is Query of Worried Home-Bound GI's." *Stars and Stripes,* June 28, 1946.

"Troopers Subdue Polish DP Riot in Altstadt Camp." *Stars and Stripes,* May 12, 1947, p. 4.

U.S. Army War Department General Staff, G-2. "The Problem of Displaced Persons in Europe." *Intelligence Review* 10 (April 18, 1946): pp. 27–33.

———. "Occupational Problems in Germany and Austria." *Intelligence Review* 30 (September 5, 1946): pp. 40–48.

———. "The Displaced Persons Problem in Germany and Austria." *Intelligence Review* 43 (December 5, 1946): pp. 32–38.

———. "German Attitudes toward the Occupation." *Intelligence Review* 74 (July 17, 1947): pp. 28–36.

"U.S. Survey Discloses Returning German Soldiers' Views." *New York Times,* August 23, 1945.

"Victory: Germany." *Commonweal* 42 (June 29, 1945): pp. 259–61.

Vosser, Harry. "Hitler's Hideaway." *New York Times Magazine,* November 12, 1944, p. 36.

"Yank-Fraulein Romances Seen Ruining Occupation." *Stars and Stripes,* June 24, 1946.

Army Talks.

Commonweal.

Fränkische Landeszeitung (Ansbach).

Fränkische Landeszeitung (Neustadt).

Fränkische Tagespost.

Jüdischen Rundschau.

Life.

Neue Zeitung.

Newsweek.

New York Times.

Nürnberger Nachrichten.

Stars and Stripes (European Edition).

St. Louis Post-Dispatch.

Süddeutsche Zeitung.
Time.
Völkischer Beobachter.
Windsheimer Lager-Bulletin.
Windsheimer Zeitung.

DIARIES, MEMOIRS, LETTERS, AND DOCUMENT COLLECTIONS

Absolon, Rudolf, ed. *Das Wehrmachtsstrafrecht im 2. Weltkrieg. Sammlung der grundlegenden Gesetze, Verordnungen und Erlasse.* Kornelimünster: Bundesarchiv, Abt. Zentralnachweisstelle, 1958.

Andreas-Friedrich, Ruth. *Battleground Berlin: Diaries, 1945–1948.* Translated by Anna Boerresen. New York: Paragon House Publishers, 1990.

Arrington, Grady P. *Infantryman at the Front.* New York: Vantage Press, 1959.

Atwell, Lester. *Private.* New York: Simon and Schuster, 1958.

Bach, Julian, Jr. *America's Germany: An Account of the Occupation.* New York: Random House, 1946.

Barden, Judy. "Candy Bar Romance—Women of Germany." In Arthur Settel, ed., *This Is Germany.* 1950. Reprint, Freeport, N.Y.: Books for Libraries Press, 1971, pp. 161–76.

Böll, Heinrich. *The Bread of Those Early Years.* Translated by Leila Vennewitz. Evanston: Northwestern Univ. Press, 1994.

———. *The Silent Angel.* Translated by Breon Mitchell. New York: St. Martin's Press, 1994.

Borsdorff, Ulrich, and Lutz Niethammer, eds. *Zwischen Befreiung und Besatzung. Analysen des US-Geheimdienstes über Positionen und Strukturen deutscher Politik 1945.* Wuppertal: Peter Hammer Verlag, 1976.

Bourke-White, Margaret. *"Dear Fatherland, Rest Quietly": A Report on the Collapse of Hitler's "Thousand Years."* New York: Simon and Schuster, 1946.

———. *Portrait of Myself.* New York: Simon and Schuster, 1963.

Boyd, W. Y. *The Gentle Infantryman.* Los Angeles: Burning Gate Press, 1985.

Boyle, Kay. *The Smoking Mountain: Stories of Germany during the Occupation.* New York: Alfred A. Knopf, 1952.

Bradley, Omar N. *A Soldier's Story.* New York: Holt, Rinehart, and Winston, 1951.

Breloer, Heinrich. *Geheime Welten. Deutsche Tagebücher aus den Jahren 1939 bis 1947.* Frankfurt: Eichborn, 1999.

Butcher, Harry C. *My Three Years with Eisenhower: The Personal Diary of Captain Harry C. Butcher, U.S.N.R., Naval Aide to General Eisenhower, 1942–1945.* New York: Simon and Schuster, 1946.

BIBLIOGRAPHY

Chandler, Alfred D., Jr., ed. *The Papers of Dwight David Eisenhower. The War Years: IV.* Baltimore: Johns Hopkins Univ. Press, 1970.

Christen, Peter. *From Military Government to State Department. How a German Employee Sees the Work of US Military Government and the State Department in a Small Bavarian Town, Its Success and Its Handicaps.* Translated by Charlotte Golke. Erding/Munich: A.P. Wagner, 1950.

Clay, Lucius D. *Decision in Germany.* Garden City, N.Y.: Doubleday, 1950.

Cohen, Henry. "The Anguish of the Holocaust Survivors." Public Lecture, April 13, 1996. http://www.remember.org.witness/cohen.html, pp. 1–6.

Crum, Bartley C. *Behind the Silken Curtain. A Personal Account of Anglo-American Diplomacy in Palestine and the Middle East.* New York: Simon and Schuster, 1947.

Dagerman, Stig. *Deutscher Herbst: Reiseschilderung.* Frankfurt: Suhrkamp, 1987.

Davis, David Brion. "World War II and Memory." *Journal of American History* 77, no. 2 (September 1990): pp. 580–87.

Dorn, Walter L. *Inspektionsreisen in der US-Zone: Notizen, Denkschriften und Erinnerungen aus dem Nachlaß.* Edited and translated by Lutz Niethammer. Stuttgart: Deutsche Verlagsanstalt, 1973.

Easton, Robert. *Love and War: Pearl Harbor through V-J Day. World War II Letters and Later Reflections by Robert and Jane Easton.* Norman: Univ. of Oklahoma Press, 1991.

Eisenhower, Dwight D. *Crusade in Europe.* New York: Doubleday, 1948.

Enzensberger, Hans Magnus, ed. *Europa in Ruinen: Augenzeugenberichte aus den Jahren 1944–1948.* Munich: Deutsche Taschenbuch Verlag, 1995.

Freytag von Loringhoven, Hanns. *Das letzte Aufgebot des Teufels. Dramatischer Einsatz des Volkssturmbataillons 7/108 Franken.* Nuremberg: im Selbstverlag (Druckhaus Nürnberg), 1965.

Fritz, Georg. *Das Jahr 1945. Ein deutscher Patriot zwischen Zusammenbruch und Neubeginn.* Berg: Druffel Verlag, 1995.

Fry, James C. *Combat Soldier.* Washington, D.C.: National, 1968.

Gelin, Joseph. *Nürnberg, 1943–1945: Erlebnisse eines französischen Arbeiterpriesters.* Bamberg: Bayerische Verlags-Anstalt, 1995.

Giles, Henry E. *The G.I. Journal of Sergeant Giles.* Compiled and edited by Janet Holt Giles. Boston: Houghton Mifflin, 1965.

Glaser, Daniel. "The Sentiments of American Soldiers Abroad toward Europeans." *American Journal of Sociology* 51, no. 5 (March 1946): pp. 433–38.

Glaser, Hermann. *1945: Ein Lesebuch.* Frankfurt: Fischer Taschenbuch Verlag, 1995.

Goebbels, Joseph. *Tagebücher 1945: Die letzten Aufzeichnungen.* Hamburg: Hoffmann und Campe, 1977.

Gollancz, Victor. *Leaving Them to Their Fate: The Ethics of Starvation.* London: Victor Gollancz, 1946.

———. *In Darkest Germany.* London: Victor Gollancz, 1947.

BIBLIOGRAPHY

Gray, J. Glenn. *The Warriors: Reflections on Men in Battle.* New York: Harper and Row, 1959.

Gustafson, Walter. *My Time in the Army: The Diary of a World War II Soldier.* Chicago: Adams, 1968.

Habe, Hans. *Aftermath.* New York: Viking Press, 1947.

————. *Off Limits.* Translated by Ewald Osers. New York, 1956.

Harmatz, Joseph. *From the Wings.* Lewes, Sussex, England: Book Guild, 1998.

Harmon, Major General E. N. *Combat Commander: Autobiography of a Soldier.* With Milton MacKaye and William Ross MacKaye. Englewood Cliffs, N.J.: Prentice-Hall, 1970.

Hasenclever, Walter. *Ihr werdet Deutschland nicht wiedererkennen: Erinnerungen.* Berlin: Kiepenheuer und Witsch, 1975.

Helton, Carl, and Marvin Drum. "Company A, 17th Armored Infantry Battalion." http://www.acu.edu/academics/history12ad/17aibx/.

Herz, Ulrich, ed. "Windsheim im Frühjahr 1945." Bad Windsheim: Steller-Gymnasium, 1995.

————. "Und das Leben geht weiter: Windsheim, 1945–1949." Bad Windsheim: Steller-Gymnasium, 1996.

Heymont, Irving. *Among the Survivors of the Holocaust, 1945: The Landsberg DP Camp Letters of Major Irving Heymont, United States Army.* 1982. Reprint, Cincinnati: Hebrew Union College Press, 1992.

Hilliard, Robert L. *Surviving the Americans. The Continued Struggle of the Jews after Liberation: A Memoir.* New York: Seven Stories Press, 1996.

Hirschmann, Ira A. *The Embers Still Burn.* New York: Simon and Schuster, 1949.

"History of the 495th Armored Field Artillery Battalion, 12th Armored Division." http://www.acu.edu/academics/history/12ad/495afax/howlong.htm.

"History of the 17th Armored Infantry Battalion, 12th Armored Division." http://www.acu.edu/academics/history/12ad/17aibx/hist17.htm;

Holzträger, Hans. *Die Wehrertüchtigungslager der Hitler-Jugend, 1942–1945: Ein Dokumentarbericht.* Ippesheim: Verlag des Arbeitskreises für Geschichte und Kultur der deutschen Siedlungsgebiete im Südosten Europas e.V., 1991.

Huebner, Klaus H. *Long Walk through War: A Combat Doctor's Diary.* College Station: Texas A & M Univ. Press, 1987.

Hulme, Kathryn. *The Wild Place.* Boston: Little, Brown, 1953.

Hutler, Albert A. *Agony of Survival.* Macomb, Ill.: Glenbridge Publishing, 1989.

Hutton, Bud, and Andy Rooney. *Conquerors' Peace: Report to the American Stockholders.* New York: Doubleday, 1947.

Institut für Besatzungsfragen. *Das DP-Problem. Eine Studie über die ausländischen Flüchtlinge in Deutschland.* Tübingen: Mohr, 1950.

Jenkins, Reuben E. "The Battle of the German National Redoubt—Planning Phase." *Military Review* 26, no. 9 (December 1946): pp. 3–8.

————. "The Battle of the German National Redoubt—Operational Phase." *Military Review* 26, no. 10 (January 1947): pp. 16–26.

BIBLIOGRAPHY

Jering, Karl. *Überleben und Neubeginn. Tagebuchaufzeichnungen eines Deutschen 1945–1946*. Munich: Günter Olzog Verlag, 1979.

Jünger, Ernst. *Strahlungen II: Das zweite Pariser Tagebuch; Kirchhorster Blätter; Die Hütte im Weinberg*. Munich: Deutscher Taschenbuch Verlag, 1988.

Kardorff, Ursula von. *Berliner Aufzeichnungen, 1942–1945*, 2nd ed. Munich: Deutscher Taschenbuch Verlag, 1976.

Kästner, Erich. *Notabene '45: Ein Tagebuch*. Frankfurt: Fischer Bücherei, 1961.

Kirkpatrick, Clifford. "Reactions of Educated Germans to Defeat." *American Journal of Sociology* 54, no. 1 (July 1948): pp. 36–47.

Klemperer, Victor. *I Will Bear Witness: A Diary of the Nazi Years*. Vol. 2, *1942–1945*. Translated by Martin Chalmers. New York: Random House, 1999.

Knauth, Percy. *Germany in Defeat*. New York: Alfred A. Knopf, 1945.

Köhler, Heinrich. *Lebenserinnerungen des Politikers und Staatsmannes, 1878–1949*. Edited by Josef Becker. Stuttgart: Kohlhammer, 1964.

Kolbenhoff, Walter. *Von unserem Fleisch und Blut*. Munich: Nymphenburg, 1947.

Kovner, Abba. "The Mission of the Survivors." In Yisrael Gutman and Livia Rotkirchen, eds. *The Catastrophe of European Jewry: Antecedents, History, Reflections*. Jerusalem: Yad Vashem, 1976, pp. 671–83.

Krause, Walter C. *So I Was a Sergeant: Memoirs of an Occupation Soldier*. Hicksville, N.Y.: Exposition Press, 1978.

Kriegl, Hermann. *Sinnlos in den Krieg gejagt: Das Schicksal von Reserve-Offiziers-Bewerbern 1945. Zeitzeugen und Dokumente*. Diessen: Grafische Kunstanstalt und Verlag Jos. C. Huber, 1995.

Krüss, James. *Coming Home from the War. An Idyll*. Translated by Edelgard von Heydekampf Bruehl. New York: Doubleday, 1965.

Kuby, Erich. *Das Ende des Schreckens: Januar bis Mai 1945*. Munich: Deutscher Taschenbuch Verlag, 1986.

Leinbaugh, Harold P., and John D. Campbell. *The Men of Company K: The Autobiography of a World War II Rifle Company*. New York: William Morrow, 1985.

Lucas, James. *Experiences of War: The Third Reich*. London: Arms and Armour Press, 1990.

Lyons, Carl J. "Personal Account, Company A, 17th Armored Infantry Battalion, 12th Armored Division." http://www.acu.edu/academics/history/12ad/17aibx/lyons6.htm.

MacDonald, Charles. *Company Commander*. Washington, D.C.: Infantry Journal Press, 1947.

Maier, Reinhold. *Ende und Wende: Das Schwäbische Schicksal, 1944–1946. Briefe und Tagebuchaufzeichnungen*. Stuttgart: Rainer Wunderlich Verlag, 1948.

Malzahn, Manfred. *Germany, 1945–1949: A Sourcebook*. London: Routledge, 1991.

Mann, Thomas. *Doctor Faustus. The Life of the German Composer Adrian Leverkühn as Told by a Friend*. Translated by John E. Woods. New York: Vintage Books, 1997.

BIBLIOGRAPHY

Manuel, Frank E. *Scenes from the End: The Last Days of World War II in Europe.* South Royalton, Vt.: Steerforth Press, 2000.

Merritt, Anna, and Richard Merritt, eds. *Public Opinion in Occupied Germany: The OMGUS Surveys, 1945–1949.* Urbana: Univ. of Illinois Press, 1970.

Mosley, Leonard. *Report from Germany.* London: Victor Gollancz, 1945.

Mossak, Erhard, ed. *Die letzten Tage von Nürnberg.* Nuremberg: Noris Verlag, 1952.

Muhlen, Norbert. "Americans and American Occupation in German Eyes." *Annals of the American Academy of Political and Social Science* 295 (September 1954): pp. 52–61.

Müller, Rolf-Dieter, and Gerd R. Ueberschär, eds. *Kriegsende 1945: Die Zerstörung des Deutschen Reiches.* Frankfurt: Fischer Taschenbuch Verlag, 1994.

Murphy, Audie. *To Hell and Back.* New York: Henry Holt, 1949.

Noelle, Elisabeth, and Erich Peter Neumann. *Jahrbuch der Öffentlichen Meinung 1947–1955.* Allensbach am Bodensee: Verlag für Demoskopie, 1956.

Nürnberger Erinnerungen 4. Nuremberg: A. Hoffmann, 1991.

Ostermann, Rainer, ed. *Kriegsende in der Oberpfalz: Ein historisches Tagebuch.* Regensburg: Buchverlage der Mittelbayerischen Zeitung, 1995.

Padover, Saul. *Experiment in Germany: The Story of an American Intelligence Officer.* New York: Duell, Sloan, Pearce, 1946.

Petersen, Neal H., ed. *From Hitler's Doorstep: The Wartime Intelligence Reports of Allen Dulles, 1942–1945.* University Park: Pennsylvania State Univ. Press, 1996.

Phibbs, Brendan. *The Other Side of Time: A Combat Surgeon in World War II.* Boston: Little, Brown, 1987.

Pollack, James Kerr. *Besatzung und Staatsaufbau nach 1945: Occupation Diary and Private Correspondence, 1945–1948.* Edited by Ingrid Krüger-Bulcke. Munich: R. Oldenbourg Verlag, 1994.

Posener, Julius. *In Deutschland 1945–1946.* Jerusalem: Siedler, 1947.

Randall, Howard M. *Dirt and Doughfeet: Combat Experiences of a Rifle-Platoon Leader.* New York: Exposition Press, 1955.

Richert, Theodor Georg. "Neuhof an der Zenn im April 1945." *Fürther Heimatblätter* 17, no. 5 (1967): pp. 160–67.

Rodnick, David. *Postwar Germans: An Anthropologist's Account.* New Haven: Yale Univ. Press, 1948.

Rose, Arno. *Werwolf 1944–1945: Eine Dokumentation.* Stuttgart: Motorbuch Verlag, 1980.

Rossmeissl, Dieter, ed. *Demokratie von außen. Amerikanische Militärregierung in Nürnberg, 1945–1949.* Munich: Deutscher Taschenbuch Verlag, 1988.

Ruhl, Klaus-Jörg. *Unsere verlorenen Jahre: Frauenalltag in Kriegs-und Nachkriegszeit 1939–1949 in Berichten, Dokumenten und Bildern.* Darmstadt: Luchterhand, 1985.

Salomon, Ernst von. *Der Fragebogen.* Hamburg: Rowohlt, 1961.

BIBLIOGRAPHY

Scherpe, Klaus R. *In Deutschland unterwegs. Reportagen, Skizzen, Berichte, 1945–1948.* Stuttgart: Philipp Reclam jun., 1982.

Schminck-Gustavus, Christoph U., ed. *Hungern für Hitler: Erinnerungen polnischer Zwangsarbeiter im deutschen Reich, 1940–1945.* Reinbek bei Hamburg: Rohwohlt Taschenbuch Verlag, 1984.

Schröder, Michael. *Bayern 1945: Demokratischer Neubeginn. Interviews mit Augenzeugen.* Munich: Süddeutscher Verlag, 1985.

Seewald, Peter. "'Grüß Gott, ihr seid frei.' Passau 1945." In Wolfgang Malanowski, ed., *1945. Deutschland in der Stunde Null.* Reinbek bei Hamburg: Rowohlt Taschenbuch Verlag, 1985, pp. 95–119.

Shochet, Simon. *Feldafing.* Vancouver: November House, 1983.

Speier, Hans. *From the Ashes of Disgrace: A Journal from Germany, 1945–1955.* Amherst: Univ. of Massachusetts Press, 1981.

Spender, Stephen. *European Witness.* London: Hamish Hamilton, 1946.

Standifer, Leon. *Not in Vain: A Rifleman Remembers World War II.* Baton Rouge: Louisiana State Univ. Press, 1992.

———. *Binding Up the Wounds: An American Soldier in Occupied Germany, 1945–1946.* Baton Rouge: Louisiana State Univ. Press, 1997.

Stolper, Gustav. *German Realities.* New York: Reynal and Hitchcock, 1948.

Strong, Kenneth. *Intelligence at the Top: The Recollections of an Intelligence Officer.* London: Cassell, 1968.

"Tagebuch einer Zwanzigjährigen." In Erich Kuby, *Das Ende des Schreckens, Januar bis Mai 1945.* Munich: Deutscher Taschenbuch Verlag, 1986, pp. 156–64.

Tapert, Annette, ed. *Lines of Battle: Letters from American Servicemen, 1941–1945.* New York: Pocket Books, 1987.

Terkel, Studs. *"The Good War": An Oral History of World War II.* New York: Pantheon Books, 1984.

Testaments to the Holocaust. Series Three: *The Henriques Archive from the Wiener Library, London.* Woodbridge, Conn.: Primary Source Microfilm, 2000.

Thurnwald, Hilde. *Gegenwartsprobleme Berliner Familien: Eine Soziologische Untersuchung an 498 Familien.* Berlin: Weidmann, 1948.

Toole, John H. *Battle Diary.* Missoula, Mont.: Vigilante Press, 1978.

Tumey, Ben. *G.I.'s View of World War II: The Diary of a Combat Private.* Hicksville, N.Y.: Exposition Press, 1959.

Vornberger, Albrecht, ed. "Keiner wußte, was geschah—Windsheim in der Nazi-Zeit." Ansbach: DGB-Bildungswerk Westmittelfranken, n.d.

Weibel-Altmeyer, Heinz. *Alpenfestung: Ein Dokumentarbericht.* Vienna: Cura Verlag, 1966.

Wellershof, Dieter. *Der Ernstfall: Innenansichten des Krieges.* Cologne: Kiepenheuer und Witsch, 1995.

White, William L. *Report on the Germans.* New York: Harcourt Brace, 1947.

Wind, Max, and Helmut Günther, eds. *Kriegstagebuch. 17. SS-Panzer-Grenadier-Di-*

BIBLIOGRAPHY

vision "Götz von Berlichingen": 30. Oktober 1943 bis 6. Mai 1945. Munich: Schild Verlag, 1993.

Winkel, Udo. *Nürnberg, 1945–1949: Quellen zur Nachkriegsgeschichte.* Nuremberg: Stadtarchiv, 1989.

Wysling, Hans, ed. *Letters of Heinrich and Thomas Mann, 1900–1949.* Translated by Don Reneau, with Additional Translations by Richard and Clara Winston. Berkeley: Univ. of California Press, 1998.

Zink, Harold. *American Military Government in Germany.* New York: Macmillan, 1947.

Zolling, Peter. "Was machen wir am Tag nach unserem Sieg? Freiburg 1945." In Wolfgang Malanowski, ed., *1945. Deutschland in der Stunde Null.* Reinbek bei Hamburg: Rowohlt Taschenbuch Verlag, 1985, pp. 120–38.

SECONDARY SOURCES

Ambrose, Stephen. *Eisenhower and Berlin, 1945.* New York: Norton, 1967.

———. *The Supreme Commander.* New York: Doubleday, 1970.

———. *Eisenhower.* Vol. 1, *Soldier, General of the Army, President-Elect, 1890–1954.* New York: Simon and Schuster, 1983.

———. *Band of Brothers: E Company, 506th Regiment, 101st Airborne from Normandy to Hitler's Eagle's Nest.* New York: Simon and Schuster, 1992.

Barnouw, Dagmar. *Germany 1945: Views of War and Violence.* Bloomington: Indiana Univ. Press, 1996.

Bar-Zohar, Michael. *The Avengers.* Translated by Len Ortzen. New York: Hawthorn Books, 1969.

Bauer, Yehuda. *Out of the Ashes: The Impact of American Jews on Post-Holocaust European Jewry.* Oxford: Oxford Univ. Press, 1989.

Bechdolf, Ute. "Den Siegern gehört die Beute. Vergewaltigungen beim Einmarsch der Franzosen im Landkreis Tübingen." *Geschichtswerktatt* 16 (1988): pp. 31–36.

Beck, Earl R. *Under the Bombs: The German Home Front, 1942–1945.* Lexington: Univ. Press of Kentucky, 1986.

Becker, Wolfgang. "Zahnersatz gegen Kochplatte. Der Schwarze Markt im Nachkriegsdeutschland." In Spiegel Special, *Die Deutschen nach der Stunde Null, 1945–1948* 4 (1995): pp. 96–101.

Bedessem, Edward N. *Central Europe Campaign: 22 March–11 May 1945.* Washington, D.C.: U.S. Army Center of Military History, 1992.

Bennett, Ralph. *Ultra in the West.* New York: Charles Scribner's Sons, 1979.

Benz, Wolfgang. *Süddeutschland in der Weimarer Republik. Ein Beitrag zur deutschen Innenpolitik 1918–1923.* Berlin: Duncker und Humblot, 1970.

———. *Neuanfang in Bayern, 1945–1949: Politik und Gesellschaft in der Nachkriegszeit.* Munich: C.H. Beck, 1988.

BIBLIOGRAPHY

―――, ed. *Die Vertreibung der Deutschen aus dem Osten. Ursachen, Ereignisse, Folgen.* Frankfurt: Fischer Taschenbuch Verlag, 1985.

Bergen, Doris. "Death Throes and Killing Frenzies: A Response to Hans Mommsen's 'The Dissolution of the Third Reich: Crisis Management and Collapse, 1943–1945.'" *Bulletin of the German Historical Institute* (Washington, D.C.) 27 (fall 2000): pp. 25–37.

Biddiscombe, Perry. *Werwolf! The History of the National Socialist Guerrilla Movement, 1944–1946.* Toronto: Univ. of Toronto Press, 1998.

―――. "'The Enemy of Our Enemy': A View of the *Edelweiss Piraten* from the British and American Archives." *Journal of Contemporary History* 30 (1995): pp. 37–63.

―――. "Dangerous Liaisons: The Anti-Fraternization Movement in the U.S. Occupation Zones of Germany and Austria, 1945–1948." *Journal of Social History* 34 (spring 2001): pp. 611–47.

Blessing, Werner K. "'Deutschland in Not, wir im Glauben...' Kirche und Kirchenvolk in einer katholischen Region, 1933–1949." In Martin Broszat, Klaus-Dietmar Henke, and Hans Woller, eds. *Von Stalingrad zur Währungsreform. Zur Sozialgeschichte des Umbruchs in Deutschland.* Munich: R. Oldenbourg, 1988, pp. 3–111.

Blumenstock, Friedrich. *Der Einmarsch der Amerikaner und Franzosen im Nördlichen Württemberg im April 1945.* Stuttgart: W. Kohlhammer Verlag, 1957.

Bosl, Karl. "Franken in Bayern, Bayern und Franken. 150 Jahre Zugehörigkeit zu Bayern." *Schönere Heimat* 23 (1964): pp. 206.

Botting, Douglas. *From the Ruins of the Reich: Germany, 1945–1949.* New York: Crown, 1985.

Botzenhart-Viehe, Verena. "The German Reaction to the American Occupation, 1944–1947." Ph.D. diss., University of California–Santa Barbara, 1980.

Boyes, Roger. "Jewish Partisans Investigated over SS Poison Plot." *Times* (London), February 3, 2000.

Brenner, Michael. *Nach dem Holocaust. Juden in Deutschland, 1945–1950.* Munich: C.H. Beck, 1995.

Broszat, Martin, and Elke Fröhlich, eds. *Bayern in der NS-Zeit.* Vol. 2, *Herrschaft und Gesellschaft in Konflikt: Teil A.* Munich: R. Oldenbourg Verlag, 1979.

Broszat, Martin, and Elke Fröhlich, eds. *Bayern in der NS-Zeit.* Vol. 6, *Die Herausforderung des Einzelnen. Geschichte über Widerstand und Verfolgung.* Munich: R. Oldenbourg Verlag, 1983.

Broszat, Martin, Elke Fröhlich, and Anton Grossmann, eds. *Bayern in der NS-Zeit.* Vol. 3, *Herrschaft und Gesellschaft in Konflikt: Teil B.* Munich: R. Oldenbourg Verlag, 1981.

Broszat, Martin, Elke Fröhlich, and Falk Wiesemann, eds. *Bayern in der NS-Zeit.* Vol. 1, *Soziale Lage und politisches Verhalten der Bevölkerung im Spiegel vertraulicher Berichte.* Munich: R. Oldenbourg Verlag, 1977.

BIBLIOGRAPHY

Browder, Dewey A. *Americans in Post–World War II Germany: Teachers, Tinkers, Neighbors, and Nuisances.* Lewiston, Maine: Edwin Mellen Press, 1998.

Brückner, Joachim. *Kriegsende in Bayern 1945. Der Wehrkreis VII und die Kämpfe zwischen Donau und Alpen.* Freiburg: Verlag Rombach, 1987.

Brumlik, Micha, ed. *Jüdisches Leben in Deutschland seit 1945.* Frankfurt: Jüdische Verlag bei Athenäum, 1988.

Burgauer, Erica. *Zwischen Erinnerung und Verdrängung: Juden in Deutschland nach 1945.* Hamburg: Rowohlt, 1993.

Burianek, Otto R. "From Liberator to Guardian: The U.S. Army and Displaced Persons in Munich, 1945." Ph.D. diss., Emory University, 1992.

Cambel, A. B. *Applied Chaos Theory: A Paradigm for Complexity.* San Diego: Academic Press, 1993.

Campbell, Joan. *Joy in Work, German Work: The National Debate, 1800–1945.* Princeton: Princeton Univ. Press, 1989.

Chamberlain, Brewster. "Todesmühlen. Ein früher Versuch zur Massen 'Umerziehung' im besetzten Deutschland, 1945–1946." *Vierteljahrshefte für Zeitgeschichte* 29 (1981): pp. 420–36.

Churchill, Winston. *The Second World War.* Vol. 6, *Triumph and Tragedy.* Boston: Houghton Mifflin, 1953.

Cohen, Rich. "A Final Mission." *Newsweek,* September 11, 2000, pp. 70–74.

———. *The Avengers.* New York: Alfred A. Knopf, 2000.

Conner, Ian. "The Churches and the Refugee Problem in Bavaria, 1945–1949." *Journal of Contemporary History* 20, no. 3 (July 1985): pp. 399–421.

Craig, Gordon. *The Germans.* New York: G.P. Putnam's Sons, 1982.

Cramer, Friedrich. *Chaos and Order: The Complex Structure of Living Systems.* Translated by David I. Loewus. New York: VCH Publishers, 1993.

Culbert, David. "American Film Policy in the Re-education of Germany after 1945." In Nicholas Pronay and Keith Wilson, eds., *The Political Re-education of Germany and Her Allies after World War II.* London: Croom Helm, 1985, pp. 175–85.

Czarnowski, Gabriele. "Zwischen Germanisierung und Vernichtung: Verbotene polnisch-deutsche Liebesbeziehungen und die Re-Konstruktion des Volkskörpers im Zweiten Weltkrieg." In Helgard Kramer, ed. *Die Gegenwart der NS-Vergangenheit.* Berlin: Philo, 2000, pp. 295–303.

D'Addario, Ray. *Nürnberg damals—Heute.* Nuremberg: Verlag Nürnberg Presse, 1970.

Dahl, Walther. *Rammjäger. Das letzte Aufgebot.* Heusenstamm bei Offenbach: Orion-Heimreiter Verlag, 1961.

Dastrup, Boyd L. *Crusade in Nuremberg: Military Occupation, 1945–1949.* Westport, Conn.: Greenwood Press, 1985.

Davis, Douglas. "Survivor Reveals 1945 Plan to Kill Six Million Germans." *Jewish Bulletin,* March 27, 1998.

BIBLIOGRAPHY

Davis, Franklin, Jr. *Came as a Conqueror: The United States Army's Occupation of Germany, 1945–1949.* New York: Macmillan, 1967.

de Mildt, Dirk. *In the Name of the People: Perpetrators of Genocide in the Reflection of Their Post-War Prosecution in West Germany. The "Euthanasia" and "Aktion Reinhard" Trial Cases.* The Hague, London, and Boston: Martinus Nijhoff Publishers, 1996.

D'Este, Carlo. *Eisenhower: A Soldier's Life.* New York: Henry Holt, 2002.

Dinnerstein, Leonard. "The U.S. Army and the Jews: Policies toward the Displaced Persons after World War II." *American Jewish History* 8, no. 3 (1979): pp. 353–66.

———. "German Attitudes toward the Jewish Displaced Persons (1945–50)." In Hans L. Trefousse, ed., *Germany and America: Essays on Problems of International Relations and Immigration.* New York: Brooklyn College Press, 1980, pp. 241–47.

———. *America and the Survivors of the Holocaust: The Evolution of a United States Displaced Persons Policy, 1945–1950.* New York: Columbia Univ. Press, 1982.

Domentat, Tamara. *"'Hallo Fräulein.' Deutsche Frauen und amerikanische Soldaten.* Berlin: Aufbau-Verlag, 1998.

Doubler, Michael D. *Closing with the Enemy: How GIs Fought the War in Europe, 1944–1945.* Lawrence: Univ. Press of Kansas, 1994.

Drasdo, Louise. "Keinen Dank für Veronika Dankeschön." *Sozial extra* 4 (1986): p. 36.

Dünninger, Josef. "Franken und Bayern. Die Begegnung zweier Stämme im neuen Staatsverband." *Schönere Heimat* 23 (1964).

Eder, Angelika. "Jüdische Displaced Persons im deutschen Alltag: Eine Regionalstudie, 1945–1950." *Fritz Bauer Jahrbuch* (1997): pp. 163–87.

———. *Flüchtige Heimat: Jüdische Displaced Persons in Landsberg am Lech, 1945 bis 1950.* Munich: Uni-Dr., 1998.

Elkins, Michael. *Forged in Fury.* New York: Ballantine Books, 1971.

Erker, Paul. "Revolution des Dorfes? Ländliche Bevölkerung zwischen Flüchtlingszustrom und landwirtschaftlichem Strukturwandel." In Martin Broszat, Klaus-Dietmar Henke, and Hans Woller, eds. *Von Stalingrad zur Währungsreform. Zur Sozialgeschichte des Umbruchs in Deutschland.* Munich: R. Oldenbourg, 1988, pp. 367–425.

Estermann, Alfred. *Bad Windsheim: Geschichte und Gegenwart einer fränkischen Stadt.* Bad Windsheim: Verlagsdruckerei Heinrich Delp, 1989.

Fait, Barbara. "Die Kreisleiter der NSDAP—nach 1945." In Martin Broszat, Klaus-Dietmar Henke, and Hans Woller, eds. *Von Stalingrad zur Währungsreform. Zur Sozialgeschichte des Umbruchs in Deutschland.* Munich: R. Oldenbourg, 1988, pp. 213–47.

Fäßler, Peter. "1945 im deutschen Südwesten: Formen der friedlichen Übergabe." *Sozialwissenschaftliche Informationen* 24, no. 2 (1995): pp. 131–39.

BIBLIOGRAPHY

Fenske, Hans. *Konservativismus und Rechtsradikalismus in Bayern nach 1918*. Berlin/ Zurich: Gehlen, 1969.

Franck, Dieter. *Jahre unseres Lebens 1945–1949*. Munich: Piper, 1980.

Franz, Günther. *Der deutsche Bauernkrieg*. Darmstadt: Wiss. Buchges, 1977.

Franz, Werner. "Die Geschichte des Marktes Ippesheim." http://www.nea-online.de/ gemeinden/ippesheim/history/geschichte2.html.

Frei, Norbert, and Sybille Steinbacher, ed. *Beschweigen und Bekennen. Die deutsche Nachkriegsgesellschaft und der Holocaust*. Göttingen: Wallstein Verlag, 2001.

Freier, Elisabeth, and Annette Kuhn, eds. *"Das Schicksal Deutschlands liegt in der Hand seiner Frauen": Frauen in der deutschen Nachkriegsgeschichte*. Düsseldorf: Schwann Verlag, 1984.

Fritzsch, Robert. *Nürnberg im Krieg: Im Dritten Reich 1939–1945*. Düsseldorf: Droste Verlag, 1984.

Fröhlich, Elke. "Stimmung und Verhalten der Bevölkerung unter den Bedingungen des Krieges." In Martin Broszat, Elke Fröhlich, and Falk Wiesemann, eds. *Bayern in der NS-Zeit*. Vol. 1, *Soziale Lage und politisches Verhalten der Bevölkerung im Spiegel vertraulicher Berichte*. Munich: R. Oldenbourg Verlag, 1977, pp. 571–688.

———. "Ein junger Märtyrer." In Martin Broszat and Elke Fröhlich, eds., *Bayern in der NS-Zeit*. Vol. 6, *Die Herausforderung des Einzelnen. Geschichten über Widerstand und Verfolgung*. Munich: R. Oldenbourg Verlag, 1983, pp. 228–57.

"50 Jahre Polizei in Mittelfranken." http://www.polizei.bayern.de/ppmfr/wir/ hist.htm.

Gaines, Edward. "From Bayreuth to Nuremberg: Richard Wagner and the German National Socialist *Weltanschauung*." *USM History Review*. http:// usmcug.usm.maine.edu/~history/review/RevEssay10.htm.

Geis, Jael. "'Ja, man muß seinen Feinden verzeihen, aber nicht früher, als bis sie gehenkt werden.' Gedanken zur Rache für die Vernichtung der europäischen Juden im unmittelbaren Nachkriegsdeutschland." In *Menora: Jahrbuch für deutsch-jüdische Geschichte*. Munich: Piper Verlag, 1998, 9:pp. 155–80.

Gellately, Robert. *The Gestapo and German Society: Enforcing Racial Policy, 1933– 1945*. Oxford: Clarendon Press, 1990.

———. *Backing Hitler: Consent and Coercion in Nazi Germany*. Oxford: Oxford Univ. Press, 2001.

Giles, Geoffrey, ed. *Stunde Null: The End and the Beginning Fifty Years Ago* (Occasional Paper No. 20). Washington, D.C.: German Historical Institute, 1997.

Gimbel, John. *A German Community under American Occupation: Marburg, 1945– 1952*. Stanford: Stanford Univ. Press, 1961.

Glaser, Hermann. *Rubble Years: The Cultural Roots of Postwar Germany, 1945–1948*. New York: Paragon House, 1986.

Goedde, Petra. "From Villains to Victims: Fraternization and the Feminization of Germany, 1945–1947." *Diplomatic History* 23, no. 1 (1999): pp. 1–20.

BIBLIOGRAPHY

————. *GIs and Germans: Culture, Gender, and Foreign Relations, 1945–1949*. New Haven: Yale Univ. Press, 2003.

Golücke, Friedhelm. "Das Kriegsende in Franken. Ein Überblick über die militärischen Ereignisse im März und April 1945." *Mainfränkisches Jahrbuch für Geschichte und Kunst* 28 (1976): pp. 103–22.

Gordon, Harold. *Hitler and the Beer Hall Putsch*. Princeton: Princeton Univ. Press, 1972.

Goschler, Constantin. "The Attitude towards Jews in Bavaria after the Second World War." *Leo Baeck Institute Yearbook* 36 (1991): pp. 443–58.

Gräter, Carlheinz. *Der Bauernkrieg in Franken*. Würzburg: Stürtz Verlag, 1975.

————. "Der Königshofer Turmberg im Bauernkrieg." *Badische Heimat* 78 (1998): pp. 233–38.

Grossmann, Anton. "Fremd- und Zwangsarbeiter in Bayern, 1939–1945." In Klaus J. Bade, ed. *Auswanderer—Wanderarbeiter—Gastarbeiter. Bevölkerung, Arbeitsmarkt und Wanderung in Deutschland seit der Mitte des 19. Jahrhunderts*. Ostfildern: Scripta Mercaturme Verlag, 1984, pp. 584–619.

Grossmann, Atina. "Eine Frage des Schweigens? Die Vergewaltigung deutscher Frauen durch Besatzungssoldaten." *Sozialwissenschaftliche Informationen* 24, no. 2 (1995): pp. 109–19.

————. "Trauma, Memory, and Motherhood: Germans and Jewish Displaced Persons in Post-Nazi Germany, 1945–1949." *Archiv für Sozialgeschichte* 38 (1998): pp. 215–39.

————. "Victims, Villains, and Survivors: Gendered Perceptions and Self-Perceptions of Jewish Displaced Persons in Occupied Postwar Germany." *Journal of the History of Sexuality* 11, nos. 1–2 (January/April 2002): pp. 291–318.

Günther, Helmut. *Die Sturmflut und das Ende. Geschichte der 17. SS-Pz.Gren.Division "Götz von Berlichingen."* Vol. 3, *Mit dem Rücken zur Wand*. Munich: Schild Verlag, 1991.

Habermann, Willi, ed. *Der Bauernkrieg in Taubergrund*. Bad Mergentheim: Volkshochschule, 1975.

Hagen, Walter. *Unternehmen Bernhard. Ein historischer Tatsachenbericht über die größte Geldfälschungsaktion aller Zeiten*. Wels: Verlag Welsermühl, 1955.

Hallig, Christian. *Festung Alpen—Hitlers letzter Wahn*. Freiburg: Herder Taschenbuch Verlag, 1989.

Hamann, Brigitte. *Hitler's Vienna: A Dictator's Apprenticeship*. New York: Oxford Univ. Press, 1999.

Hambrecht, Rainer. *Der Aufstieg der NSDAP in Mittel- und Oberfranken 1925–1933*. Nuremberg: Schriftenreihe des Stadtarchivs Nürnberg, 1976.

————. "Geschichte im 20. Jahrhundert: Die Bezirksämter Neustadt an der Aisch, Scheinfeld, und Uffenheim 1919–1972." In Landkreis Neustadt an der Aisch-Bad Windsheim, ed., *Heimatbuch für der Landkreis Neustadt an der Aisch-Bad Windsheim*. Neustadt an der Aisch: Landkreis Neustadt an der Aisch-Bad Windsheim, 1982, pp. 380–418.

BIBLIOGRAPHY

Harrer, Peter. *Wahrhafte und gründliche Beschreibung des Bauernkriegs.* Kaiserslautern, 1937.

Haupt, Werner. *Das Ende im Westen 1945.* Dorheim: Podzun, 1972.

Heineman, Elizabeth. "The Hour of the Woman: Memories of Germany's 'Crisis Years' and West German National Identity." *American Historical Review* 101, no. 2 (April 1996): pp. 354–95.

———. *What Difference Does a Husband Make? Women and Marital Status in Nazi and Postwar Germany.* Berkeley: Univ. of California Press, 1999.

Heinzle, Joachim, and Anneliese Waldschmidt, eds. *Die Nibelungen. Ein deutscher Wahn, ein deutscher Alptraum. Studien und Dokumente zur Rezeption des Nibelungenstoffs im 19. und 20. Jahrhundert.* Frankfurt: Suhrkamp Verlag, 1991.

Henke, Klaus-Dietmar. *Die amerikanische Besetzung Deutschlands.* Munich: R. Oldenbourg Verlag, 1995.

Herbert, Ulrich. *Fremdarbeiter: Politik und Praxis des 'Ausländer-Einsatzes' in der Kriegswirtschaft des Dritten Reiches.* Bonn: J.H.W. Dietz Nachf., 1985.

———. *Geschichte der Ausländerbeschäftigung in Deutschland 1880 bis 1980. Saisonarbeiter, Zwangsarbeiter, Gastarbeiter.* Bonn: J.H.W. Dietz Nachf., 1986.

———. *A History of Foreign Labor in Germany, 1880–1980: Seasonal Workers, Forced Laborers, Guest Workers.* Translated by William Templer. Ann Arbor: Univ. of Michigan Press, 1990.

Hillel, Marc. *Die Invasion der Be-Freier. Die GIs in Europa, 1942–1947.* Translated by Michele Schönfeldt. Hamburg: Ernst Kabel Verlag, 1981.

Hillmann, Jörg, and John Zimmermann, eds. *Kriegsende 1945 in Deutschland.* Munich: R. Oldenbourg Verlag, 2002.

Hinsley, F. Harry. *British Intelligence in the Second World War.* New York: Cambridge Univ. Press, 1988.

Hitchens, Christopher. "The Wartime Toll on Germany." *Atlantic Monthly,* January/February 2003, pp. 182–89.

Hoettl, Wilhelm. *Hitler's Paper Weapon.* London: Rupert Hart-Davis, 1955.

Hofmann, Hanns Hubert. "Ländliches Judentum in Franken." *Tribüne. Zeitschrift zum Verständnis des Judentums* 7 (1968): pp. 2894–2900.

Höhn, Maria. "Frau im Haus und Girl im Spiegel: Discourse on Women in the Interregnum Period of 1945–1949 and the Question of German Identity." *Central European History* 26 (1993): pp. 57–90.

———. "Stunde Null der Frauen? Renegotiating Women's Place in Postwar West Germany." In Geoffrey Giles, ed. *Stunde Null: The End and the Beginning Fifty Years Ago* (Occasional Paper No. 20). Washington, D.C.: German Historical Institute, 1997, pp. 75–88.

Hyman, Abraham S. *The Undefeated.* Jerusalem: Geffen Publishing House, 1993.

Jacobmeyer, Wolfgang. "Polnische Juden in der amerikanischen Besatzungszone Deutschlands, 1946–1947." *Vierteljahrshefte für Zeitgeschichte* 25 (1977): pp. 120–36.

BIBLIOGRAPHY

———. "Jüdische Überlebende als 'Displaced Persons.' Untersuchungen zur Besatzungspolitik in den deutschen Westzonen und zur Zuwanderung osteuropäischer Juden 1945–1947." *Geschichte und Gesellschaft* 9 (1983): pp. 421–52.

———. *Vom Zwangsarbeiter zum Heimatlosen Ausländer. Die Displaced Persons in Westdeutschland 1945–1951*. Göttingen: Vandenhoeck und Ruprecht, 1985.

Jahnke, Karl Heinz. *Hitlers letztes Aufgebot: Deutsche Jugend im sechsten Kriegsjahr, 1944–1945*. Essen: Klartext Verlag, 1993.

Jenk, Gabriele. *Steine gegen Brot. Trümmerfrauen schildern den Wiederaufbau in der Nachkriegzeit*. Bergisch-Gladbach: Bastei Lübbe, 1988.

Kantara, John. "Der Krieg war aus, Dov Shenkal und seine Freunde hatten nur ein Ziel: Vergeltung für den Massenmord an den Juden." *Die Zeit* 50 (1997).

Kellert, Stephen. *In the Wake of Chaos: Unpredictable Order in Synamical Systems*. Chicago: Univ. of Chicago Press, 1993.

Kennett, Lee. *G.I.: The American Soldier in World War II*. New York: Warner Books, 1987.

Kershaw, Ian. "Antisemitismus und Volksmeinung. Reaktionen auf die Judenverfolgung." In Martin Broszat and Elke Fröhlich, eds. *Bayern in der NS-Zeit*. Vol. 2, *Herrschaft und Gesellschaft in Konflikt: Teil A*. Munich: R. Oldenbourg Verlag, 1979, pp. 281–348.

———. *Popular Opinion and Political Dissent in the Third Reich: Bavaria, 1933–1945*. Oxford: Clarendon Press, 1983.

———. "German Popular Opinion and the 'Jewish Question,' 1939–1943: Some Further Reflections." In Arnold Pauker, ed. *Die Juden im Nationalsozialistischen Deutschland*. Tübingen: J.C.B. Mohr, 1986, pp. 365–86.

———. *The Führer Myth: Image and Reality in the Third Reich*. Oxford: Oxford Univ. Press, 1987.

Kirkpatrick, Lyman B., Jr. *Captains without Eyes*. Boulder, Colo.: Westview Press, 1987.

Kissel, Hans. *Der deutsche Volkssturm, 1944–1945: Eine territoriale Miliz im Rahmen der Landesverteidigung*. Frankfurt: Mittler, 1962.

Klee, Katja. *Im "Luftschutzkeller des Reiches." Evakuierte in Bayern, 1939–1953*. Munich: R. Oldenbourg Verlag, 1999.

Koch, Christian, Rainer Büschel, and Uli Kuhnle. *Trümmerjahre: Nürnberg, 1945–1955*. Munich: Hugendubel, 1989.

Koch, Thilo. *Fünf Jahre der Entscheidung. Deutschland nach dem Kriege, 1945–1949*. Frankfurt: Akademische Verlagsgesellschaft Athenaion, 1969.

Königsseder, Angelika, and Juliane Wetzel. *Lebensmut im Wartesaal. Die jüdischen DPs (Displaced Persons) im Nachkriegsdeutschland*. Frankfurt: Fischer Taschenbuch Verlag, 1994.

Korte, Jeff. "Eisenhower, Berlin, and the National Redoubt." *Gateway: An Academic Journal on the Web*. Issue #6, http://grad.usask.ca/gateway, pp. 1–32.

BIBLIOGRAPHY

Krauss, Marita. "'Vee GAYT ess ee-nen.' Lebenssplitter aus dem Umgang mit Besatzern." In Friedrich Prinz and Marita Krauss, eds., *Trümmerleben*. Munich: Deutscher Taschenbuch Verlag, 1985, pp. 177–215.

Kroener, Bernhard, Rolf-Dieter Müller, and Hans Umbreit, eds. *Das Deutsche Reich und der Zweite Weltkrieg*. Vol. 5, *Organisation und Mobilisierung des deutschen Machtbereichs. Kriegsverwaltung, Wirtschaft und personelle Resourcen, 1942–1945*. Stuttgart: Deutsche Verlags-Anstalt, 1988.

Krüger, Peter. "Etzels Halle und Stalingrad: Die Rede Görings vom 30. 1. 1943." In Heinzle and Waldschmidt, eds., *Die Nibelungen*, pp. 153–69.

Kugelmann, Cilly. "Identität und Ideologie der Displaced Persons: Zwei historische Texte aus den DP-Lagern." *Babylon* 5 (1989): pp. 65–72.

Kulischer, Eugene M. *Europe on the Move*. New York: Columbia Univ. Press, 1948.

Kundrus, Birthe. "Forbidden Company: Romantic Relationships between Germans and Foreigners, 1939 to 1945." *Journal of the History of Sexuality* 11, nos. 1–2 (January/April 2002): pp. 201–22.

Kunze, Karl. *Kriegsende in Franken und der Kampf um Nürnberg im April 1945*. Nuremberg: Selbstverlag des Vereins für Geschichte der Stadt Nürnberg, 1995.

Latour, C. F., and Thilo Vogelsang. *Okkupation und Wiederaufbau. Die Tätigkeit der Militärregierung in der amerikanischen Besatzungszone Deutschlands, 1944–1947*. Stuttgart: Deutsche Verlags-Anstalt, 1973.

Leder, Harald. "Americans and German Youth in Nuremberg, 1945–1956: A Study in Politics and Culture." Ph.D. diss., Louisiana State University, 1977.

———. "Changing People's Minds? American Reorientation in Germany after World War II." http://home.t-online.de/home/RIJONUE/leder.htm.

Lehmann, Albrecht. *Im Fremden ungewollt zuhaus. Flüchtlinge und Vertriebene in Westdeutschland, 1945–1990*. Munich: C.H. Beck, 1991.

Lenman, Robin. "Julius Streicher and the Origins of the NSDAP in Nuremberg, 1918–1923." In Anthony Nicholls and Erich Matthias, eds. *German Democracy and the Triumph of Hitler*. New York: St. Martin's Press, 1971, pp. 129–59.

Libby, Brian A. "The United States Constabulary in Germany." *Indiana Military History Journal* 13, no. 3 (October 1988): pp. 4–13.

Linderman, Gerald F. *The World within War: America's Combat Experience in World War II*. Cambridge: Harvard Univ. Press, 1997.

Lohalm, Uwe. *Völkischer Radikalismus. Die Geschichte des Deutschvölkischen Schutz- und Trutzbundes 1919–1923*. Hamburg: Leibniz Verlag, 1970.

Löns, Hermann. *Der Wehrwolf*. Düsseldorf: Diederichs, 1958.

Lowenstein, Steven M. "The Struggle for Survival of Rural Jews in Germany, 1933–1938: The Case of Bezirksamt Weissenberg, Mittelfranken." In Arnold Pauker, ed. *Die Juden im Nationalsozialistischen Deutschland*. Tübingen: J.C.B. Mohr, 1986, pp. 115–24.

BIBLIOGRAPHY

MacDonald, Charles B. *The Last Offensive*. Washington, D.C.: Office of the Chief of Military History, U.S. Army, 1973.

Malanowski, Wolfgang, ed. *1945—Deutschland in der Stunde Null*. Reinbek bei Hamburg: Rowohlt Taschenbuch Verlag, 1985.

Mammach, Klaus. *Der Volkssturm: Bestandteil des totalen Kriegseinsatz der deutschen Bevölkerung, 1944–1945*. Berlin: Akademie Verlag, 1981.

Mankowitz, Zeev W. *Life between Memory and Hope: The Survivors of the Holocaust in Occupied Germany*. Cambridge: Cambridge Univ. Press, 2002.

Maser, Werner. *Die Frühgeschichte der NSDAP. Hitlers Weg bis 1924*. Frankfurt: Athenäum, 1965.

Medoff, Rafael. "The Response of Orthodox Jewry in the United States to the Holocaust: The Activities of the Vaad ha-Hatzala Rescue Committee, 1939–1945." *Holocaust and Genocide Studies* 15, no. 2 (2001): pp. 353–57.

Meek, Marvin L. "Ultra and the Myth of the German 'National Redoubt.'" M.A. thesis, U.S. Army Command and General Staff College, 1999.

Merritt, Richard L., and Bruce A. Williams. *Democracy Imposed: U.S. Occupation Policy and the German Public, 1945–1949*. New Haven: Yale Univ. Press, 1995.

Merry, Uri. *Coping with Uncertainty: Insights from the New Sciences of Chaos, Self-Organization and Complexity*. Westport, Conn.: Praeger Publishers, 1995.

Messerschmidt, Manfred. "Deutsche Militärgerichtsbarkeit im Zweiten Weltkrieg." In Hans-Jochen Vogel, Helmut Simon, Adalbert Podlech, eds. *Die Freiheit des Andern*. Baden-Baden: Nomos Verlagsgesellschaft, 1981, pp. 111–42.

———. "Die Wehrmacht in der Endphase. Realität und Perzeption." In *Aus Politik und Zeitgeschichte (Das Parlament)*, B 32–33 (1989), pp. 33–46.

Messerschmidt, Manfred, and Fritz Wüllner. *Die Wehrmachtjustiz im Dienste des Nationalsozialismus. Zerstörung eine Legende*. Baden-Baden: Nomos Verlagsgesellschaft, 1987.

Meyer, Sibylle, and Eva Schulze. *Von Liebe sprach damals keiner: Familienalltag in der Nachkriegszeit*. Munich: C.H. Beck, 1985.

Minott, Rodney. *The Fortress That Never Was: The Myth of Hitler's Bavarian Stronghold*. New York: Holt, Rinehart, and Winston, 1964.

Mommsen, Hans. "The Dissolution of the Third Reich: Crisis Management and Collapse, 1943–1945." *Bulletin of the German Historical Institute* 27 (fall 2000): pp. 9–23.

Müller, Rolf-Dieter, Gerd Ueberschär, and Wolfram Wette, eds. *Wer zurückweicht wird Erschossen. Kriegsalltag und Kriegsende in Südwestdeutschland, 1944–1945*. Freiburg: Dreisam Verlag, 1985.

Münkler, Herfried. *Machtzerfall. Die letzten Tage des Dritten Reiches dargestellt am Beispiel der hessischen Kreisstadt Friedberg*. Berlin: Siedler Verlag, 1985.

———. "Das Nibelungenschicksal und die deutsche Nation. Zur Funktion von Mythen in der Politik." *Forschung Frankfurt: Wissenschaftsmagazin der Johann Wolfgang Goethe-Universität Frankfurt* 1, no. 1 (1989): pp. 4–11.

BIBLIOGRAPHY

Naimark, Norman. *The Russians in Germany: A History of the Soviet Zone of Occupation, 1945–1949.* Cambridge: Harvard Univ. Press, 1995.

Naumann, Klaus. *Der Krieg als Text. Das Jahr 1945 im kulturellen Gedächtnis der Presse.* Hamburg: Hamburger Edition, 1998.

Niedhart, Gottfried, and Dieter Riesenberger, eds. *Lernen aus dem Krieg? Deutsche Nachkriegszeiten 1918 und 1945.* Munich: C.H. Beck, 1992.

Niethammer, Lutz. "Amerikanische Besatzung und bayerische Politik, 1945." *Vierteljahrshefte für Zeitgeschichte* 15 (1967): pp. 155–210.

———. *Die Mitläufer-Fabrik. Die Entnazifizierung am Beispiel Bayerns.* 1972. Reprint, Berlin/Bonn: J.H.W. Dietz Nachf., 1982.

"The Nibelungenlied." Online Medieval and Classical Library Release #31. University of California-Berkeley. http://sunsite.berkeley.edu/OMACL/Nibelungenlied.

Ophir, Baruch Z., and Falk Wiesemann. *Die jüdische Gemeinden in Bayern.* Munich: R. Oldenbourg, 1979.

"Ortsteil Abtsgreuth Geschichte: Nachkriegszeit und Gegenwart." http:www.muenchsteinach.de/abtsgreuth/geschichte/histabti.htm.

Overmans, Rüdiger. *Deutsche militärische Verluste im Zweiten Weltkrieg.* Munich: R. Oldenbourg Verlag, 1999.

Peterson, Edward N. *The American Occupation of Germany: Retreat to Victory.* Detroit: Wayne State Univ. Press, 1977.

———. *The Many Faces of Defeat: The German People's Experience in 1945.* New York: Peter Lang, 1990.

Petree, Judy. "History of Chaos Theory." www.wfu.edu/~petrejh4/HISTORYchaos.htm.

———. "Complexity: Self-Organization in Chaos." www.wfu.edu/~petrejh4/selforg.htm.

Piekalkiewicz, Janusz. *Spione, Agenten, Soldaten: Geheime Kommandos im Zweiten Weltkrieg.* Munich: Herbig, 1969.

Pohl, Dieter. *Von der "Judenpolitik" zum Judenmord. Der Distrikt Lublin des Generalgouvernements, 1939–1944.* Frankfurt: Peter Lang, 1993.

———. *Nationalsozialistische Judenverfolgung in Ostgalizien, 1941–1944. Organisation und Durchführung eines staatlichen Massenverbrechens.* Munich: R. Oldenbourg, 1996.

Pommerin, Reiner, ed. *The American Impact on Postwar Germany.* Providence, R.I.: Berghahn Books, 1994.

Pridham, Geoffrey. *Hitler's Rise to Power: The Nazi Movement in Bavaria, 1923–1933.* New York: Harper Torchbooks, 1973.

Prigogine, Ilya, and Gregoire Nicolis. *Exploring Complexity: An Introduction.* New York: W.H. Freeman, 1998.

Prigogine, Ilya, and Isabele Stengers. *Order Out of Chaos: Man's New Dialogue with Nature.* New York: Bantam Books, 1984.

Prinz, Friedrich, ed. *Trümmerzeit in München: Kultur und Gesellschaft einer Deutschen Großstadt im Aufbruch, 1945–1949.* Munich: C.H. Beck, 1984.

BIBLIOGRAPHY

Prinz, Friedrich, and Marita Krauss, eds. *Trümmerleben: Texte, Dokumente, Bilder aus den Münchner Nachkriegsjahren.* Munich: Deutscher Taschenbuch Verlag, 1985.

Pronay, Michael, and Keith Wilson, eds. *The Political Re-education of Germany and Her Allies after World War II.* Totowa, N.J.: Barnes and Noble, 1985.

Proudfoot, Malcolm J. *European Refugees, 1939–1952.* Evanston: Northwestern Univ. Press, 1956.

Riehl, Wilhelm Heinrich. *Die deutsche Arbeit.* Stuttgart: J.G. Cotta'scher Verlag, 1861.

Rosenberg, Emily. "'Foreign Affairs' after World War II: Connecting Sexual and International Politics." *Diplomatic History* 18 (winter 1994): pp. 59–70.

Rosensaft, Menachem Z. *Life Reborn: Jewish Displaced Persons, 1945–1951. Conference Proceedings.* Washington, D.C.: U.S. Holocaust Memorial Museum, 2000.

Rückert, Christoph. *Ipsheim: Die Chronik eines fränkischen Dorfes.* Ipsheim: Marktgemeinde Ipsheim, 1989.

Ruffner, Kevin Conley. "The Black Market in Postwar Berlin: Colonel Miller and an Army Scandal." *Prologue: Quarterly of the National Archives and Records Administration* 34, no. 3 (fall 2002): pp. 171–83.

Ruhl, Klaus-Jörg. *Die Besatzer und die Deutschen: Amerikanische Zone, 1945–1948.* Düsseldorf: Droste Verlag, 1980.

———, ed. *Unsere verlorene Jahre: Frauenalltag und Nachkriegszeit, 1939–1949.* Darmstadt: Luchterhand, 1985.

———, ed. *Frauen in der Nachkriegszeit, 1945–1963.* Munich: Deutscher Taschenbuch Verlag, 1988.

Rupieper, Hermann-Josef. "Bringing Democracy to the Frauleins: Frauen als Zielgruppe der amerikanischen Demokratisierungspolitik in Deutschland, 1945–1952." *Geschichte und Gesellschaft* 17 (1991): pp. 61–91.

———. *Die Wurzeln der westdeutschen Nachkriegsdemokratie: Der amerikanische Beitrag, 1945–1952.* Opladen: Westdeutscher Verlag, 1993.

Russell, John. *No Triumphant Procession: The Forgotten Battles of April 1945.* London: Arms and Armour Press, 1994.

Ryan, Cornelius. *The Last Battle.* New York: Pocket Books, 1966.

Sanden, Erika. *Das Kriegsgefangenlager Langwasser als Forschungsobjekt.* Nuremberg: Beiträge zur politischen Bildung 3, 1986.

Sander, Helke, and Barbara Johr, eds. *BeFreier und Befreite: Krieg, Vergewaltigungen, Kinder.* Frankfurt: Fischer, 1995.

Sayer, Ian, and Douglas Botting. *America's Secret Army. The Untold Story of the Counter Intelligence Corps.* New York: Franklin Watts, 1989.

Schardt, Angelika. "'Der Rest der Geretteten.' Jüdische Überlebende im DP-Lager Föhrenwald 1945–1947." In Wolfgang Benz, ed., *Dachauer Hefte 8: Überleben und Spätfolgen.* Munich: Deutscher Taschenbuch Verlag, 1996, pp. 53–68.

Schick, Christa. "Die Internierungslager." In Martin Broszat, Klaus-Dietmar Henke, and Hans Woller, eds. *Von Stalingrad zur Währungsreform. Zur Sozialgeschichte des Umbruchs in Deutschland.* Munich: R. Oldenbourg, 1988, pp. 301–25.

Schilling, Donald G. "Politics in a New Key: The Late Nineteenth-Century Transformation of Politics in Northern Bavaria." *German Studies Review* 17, no. 1 (February 1994): pp. 33–57.

Schlememer, Thomas. "Der Amerikaner in Bayern: Militärregierung und Demokratisierung nach 1945." In Heinrich Oberreuter, ed. *Freundliche Feinde? Die Alliierten und die Demokratiegründung in Deutschland.* Munich: Olzog, 1996, pp. 67–100.

Schmidt-Harzbach, Ingrid. "Eine Woche im April: Berlin 1945, Vergewaltigung als Massenschicksal." In Helke Sander and Barbara Johr, eds. *BeFreier und Befreite: Krieg, Vergewaltigungen, Kinder.* Munich: Kunstmann, 1992.

Schmitt, Peter. "Selbstjustiz wird nach über 50 Jahren verfolgt." *Süddeutsche Zeitung,* September 22, 1999.

———. "Jüdische Rächer lösen Kontroverse aus." *Süddeutsche Zeitung,* November 3, 2000.

Schörken, Rolf. *Jugend 1945. Politisches Denken und Lebensgeschichte.* Frankfurt: Fischer Taschenbuch Verlag, 1995.

Schramm, Wilhelm von. *Geheimdienst im Zweiten Weltkrieg. Organisationen, Methoden, Erfolge.* Munich: Langen, 1979.

Schrijvers, Peter. *The Crash of Ruin: American Combat Soldiers in Europe during World War II.* New York: New York Univ. Press, 1998.

Schwarz, Klaus-Dieter. *Weltkrieg und Revolution in Nürnberg.* Stuttgart: Klett, 1971.

Schwarz, Leo W. "The DP's: Fiction and Fact." *American Zionist* 43, no. 15 (June 1953): pp. 16–19.

———. *The Redeemers: A Saga of the Years 1945–1952.* New York: Farrar, Straus and Young, 1953.

See, Klaus von. "Das Nibelungenlied—ein Nationalepos?." In Joachim Heinzle and Annelise Waldschmidt, eds., *Die Nibelungen. Ein deutscher Wahn, Ein deutscher Alptraum.* Frankfurt: Suhrkamp, 1991, pp. 43–57.

Segev, Tom. *The Seventh Million. The Israelis and the Holocaust.* Translated by Haim Watzman. New York: Hill and Wang, 1993.

Seidler, Franz W. *Deutscher Volkssturm: Das letzte Aufgebot, 1944–1945.* Munich: F.A. Herbig Verlagsbuchhandlung, 1989.

———. *Phantom Alpenfestung? Die geheimen Baupläne der Organisation Todt.* Berchtesgaden: Verlag Plenk, 2000.

Seiler, Signe. *Die GIs: Amerikanische Soldaten in Deutschland.* Reinbek bei Hamburg: Rowohlt, 1985.

"17. SS-Panzer Grenadier Division 'Götz von Berlichingen.'" http://home.swipnet.se/normandy/gerob/pzdiv/17sspgdiv.html.

"The 17th SS-Panzer-Grenadier Division." http://www.100thww2.org/gerunit2/17.html.

BIBLIOGRAPHY

Shepardson, Donald E. "The Fall of Berlin and the Rise of a Myth." *Journal of Military History* 62, no. 1 (January 1998): pp. 135–53.

Shukert, Elfrieda Bethiaume, and Barbara Smith Scibetta. *War Brides of World War II*. New York: Penguin, 1988.

Sonderdruck der *Nürnberger Nachrichten. Trümmerjahre 1945–1950*. Nuremberg: Nürnberger Nachrichten, 1985.

Spiegel Special. *Die Deutschen nach der Stunde Null, 1945–1948*, vol. 4. Hamburg: Spiegel-Verlag Rudolf Augstein, 1995.

———. *Die Flucht der Deutschen. Die Spiegel-Serie über Vertreibung aus dem Osten*. Hamburg: Spiegel-Verlag Rudolf Augstein, 2002.

Spiwoks, Erich, and Hans Stöber. *Endkampf zwischen Mosel und Inn: XIII. SS-Armeekorps*. Osnabrück: Munin Verlag, 1976.

Steffens, Gerd. "Die praktische Widerlegung des Rassismus: Verbotene Liebe und ihre Verfolgung." In Fred Dorn and Klaus Heuer, eds. *"Ich war immer gut zu meiner Russin." Zur Struktur und Praxis des Zwangsarbeitersystems im Zweiten Weltkrieg in der Region Südhessen*. Pfaffenweiler: Centaurus, 1991, pp. 185–200.

Steinbach, Peter, and Johannes Tuchel, eds. *Widerstand gegen den Nationalsozialismus*. Bonn: Bundeszentrale für politische Bildung, 1994.

Steinert, Marlis G. *Hitler's War and the Germans: Public Mood and Attitude during the Second World War*. Edited and translated by Thomas E. J. de Witt. Athens, Ohio: Ohio Univ. Press, 1977.

Steinmetz, Horst, and Helmut Hofmann. "Das Juden Progrom vom November 1938." *Windsheimer Zeitung*, November 9, 1988.

Stephenson, Jill. "Triangle: Foreign Workers, German Civilians, and the Nazi Regime. War and Society in Württemberg, 1939–1945." *German Studies Review* 15, no. 2 (May 1992): pp. 339–59.

———. "'Emancipation' and Its Problems: War and Society in Württemberg, 1939–1945." *European History Quarterly* 17, no. 2 (July 1987): pp. 345–65.

Stöber, Hans. *Die eiserne Faust. Bildband und Chronik der 17. SS-Panzergrenadier-Division "Götz von Berlichingen."* Neckargemünd: Vowinckel, 1966.

———. *Die Sturmflut und das Ende. Geschichte der 17. SS-Pz.Gren.Division "Götz von Berlichingen."* Osnabrück: Munin Verlag, 1976.

Stöber, Hans, and Helmut Günther. *Die Sturmflut und das Ende. Geschichte der 17. SS-Pz.Gren.Division "Götz von Berlichingen."* Vol. 3, *Mit dem Rücken zur Wand*. Munich: Schild Verlag, 1991.

Stouffer, Samuel, et al. *The American Soldier*. Vol. 2, *Combat and Its Aftermath*. Princeton: Princeton Univ. Press, 1949.

Strecker, Gabriele. *Überleben ist nicht genug: Frauen 1945–1950*. Freiburg im Breisgau, 1981.

Ströbel, Otto. *Die Männer von Brettheim*, 2nd ed. Kirchberg an der Jagst: Wettin Verlag, 1988.

BIBLIOGRAPHY

Stuhlpfarrer, Karl. *Die Operationszonen "Alpenvorland" und "Adriatisches Küstenland"* *1943–1945.* Publikationen des österreichischen Instituts für Zeitgeschichte und des Instituts für Zeitgeschichte der Universität Wien, vol. 7. Vienna: Hollinek, 1969.

Supp, Barbara. "Trümmerfrauen: Protokoll eines gescheiterten Aufbruchs." In Spiegel Special, *Die Deutschen nach der Stunde Null, 1945–1948* 4 (1995): pp. 84–89.

Tauber, Kurt P. *Beyond Eagle and Swastika: German Nationalism since 1945.* Middletown, Conn.: Wesleyan Univ. Press, 1967.

Tessin, Georg. *Verbände und Truppen der deutschen Wehrmacht und Waffen-SS.* 4 vols. Frankfurt: E.S. Mittler und Sohn, 1965–1980.

Tobias, Jim. *Der Kibbuz auf dem Streicher-Hof. Die vergessene Geschichte der jüdischen Kollektivfarmen, 1945–1948.* Nuremberg: Dahlinger und Fuchs, 1997.

———. "Die Juden hatten ein Recht, sich zu rächen." *Aufbau: deutsch-jüdische Zeitung,* October 1, 1999.

———. "Rache macht schlechte Politik." *Aufbau: deutsch-jüdische Zeitung,* May 4, 2000.

———. *Vorübergehende Heimat im Land der Täter—Jüdische DP Camps in Franken von 1945–1949.* Nuremberg: Antogo Verlag, 2002.

Tobias, Jim, and Peter Zinke, *Nakam. Jüdische Rache an NS-Tätern.* Hamburg: Konkret Literatur Verlag, 2000.

Troll, Hildebrand. "Aktionen zur Kriegsbeendigung im Frühjahr 1945." In Martin Broszat, Elke Fröhlich, and Anton Großmann, eds., *Bayern in der NS-Zeit.* Vol. 4, *Herrschaft und Gesellschaft im Konflikt,* Part C. Munich: R. Oldenbourg Verlag, 1981, pp. 645–89.

Veeh, Helmut. *Die Kriegsfurie über Franken 1945 und das Ende in den Alpen,* 3rd ed. Bad Windsheim: Verlagsdrückerei Heinrich Delp, 1998.

Vernant, Jacques. *The Refugee in the Post-War World.* New Haven: Yale Univ. Press, 1953.

Vorländer, Herwart. "NS-Volkswohlfahrt und Winterhilfswerk des deutschen Volkes." *Vierteljahrshefte für Zeitgeschichte* 34, no. 3 (July 1986): pp. 341–80.

———. *Die NSV: Darstellung und Dokumentation einer Nationalsozialistischen Organisation.* Boppard: Boldt, 1988.

"Vorschriften sind Vorschriften." *taz,* February 2, 2000.

Waite, Robert G. L. *Vanguard of Nazism: The Free Corps Movement in Postwar Germany, 1918–1923.* New York: Norton, 1952.

Waldrop, Mitchell. *Complexity: The Emerging Science at the Edge of Order and Chaos.* New York: Simon and Schuster, 1992.

Watt, Roderick. *"Wehrwolf* or *Werwolf?* Literature, Legend, or Lexical Error into Nazi Propaganda?" *Modern Language Review* 87, no. 4 (October 1992): pp. 879–95.

Wetzel, Juliane. *Jüdisches Leben in München, 1945–1951: Durchgangsstation oder Wiederaufbau?* Munich: Kommisions-Verlag Uni-Druck, 1987.

———. "'Mir szeinen doh.' München und Umgebung als Zuflucht von Überlebenden

BIBLIOGRAPHY

des Holocaust, 1945–1948." In Martin Broszat, Klaus-Dietmar Henke, and Hans Woller, eds. *Von Stalingrad zur Währungsreform. Zur Sozialgeschichte des Umbruchs in Deutschland.* Munich: R. Oldenbourg, 1988, pp. 327–64.

———. "'Displaced Persons.' Ein vergessenes Kapitel der deutschen Nachkriegsgeschichte." *Aus Politik und Zeitgeschichte (Das Parlament),* B 7-8/95, pp. 34–39.

Wiesemann, Falk. "Judenverfolgung und nichtjüdische Bevölkerung, 1933–1944." In Martin Broszat, Elke Fröhlich, and Falk Wiesemann, eds. *Bayern in der NS-Zeit.* Vol. 1, *Soziale Lage und politisches Verhalten der Bevölkerung im Spiegel vertraulicher Berichte.* Munich: R. Oldenbourg Verlag, 1977, pp. 427–86.

Wilhelm, Hans-Heinrich. *Rassenpolitik und Kriegsführung. Sicherheitspolizei und Wehrmacht in Polen und in der Sowjetunion, 1939–1942.* Passau: Wissenschaftsverlag Richard Rothe, 1991.

Willenbacher, Barbara. "Zerrüttung und Bewährung der Nachkriegs-Familie." In Martin Broszat, Klaus-Dietmar Henke, and Hans Woller, eds. *Von Stalingrad zur Währungsreform. Zur Sozialgeschichte des Umbruchs in Deutschland.* Munich: R. Oldenbourg, 1988, pp. 595–618.

Willoughby, John. "The Sexual Behavior of American G.I.'s during the Early Years of the Occupation of Germany." *Journal of Military History* 62 (January 1998): pp. 155–74.

———. *Remaking the Conquering Heroes: The Postwar American Occupation of Germany.* New York: Palgrave, 2001.

Wohlfahrt, Jürgen. "Die Bauernkriegs-Schlacht von Königshofen. Ein Versuch, Einige Historische Rätsel zu Lösen." *Hierzuland* 19, no. 1 (1995): pp. 18–31.

Wolfrum, Edgar. "Widerstand in den letzten Kriegsmonaten." In P. Steinbach and J. Tuchel, eds. *Widerstand gegen den Nationalsozialismus.* Bonn: Bundeszentrale für politische Bildung, 1994, pp. 537–52.

Woller, Hans. "Zur Demokratiebereitschaft in der Provinz des Amerikanischen Besatzungsgebiets." *Vierteljahrshefte für Zeitgeschichte* 31 (1983): pp. 335–64.

———. "Die Militärregierung vor Ort—Einfluß und Grenzen amerikanischer Politik während der Besatzungszeit." In Dieter Galinski and Wolf Schmidt, eds. *Jugendliche erforschen die Nachkriegszeit. Materialen zum Schülerbewerb Deutsche Geschichte 1984/85.* Hamburg: Körber-Stiftung, 1984.

———. *Gesellschaft und Politik in der amerikanischen Besatzungszone. Die Region Ansbach und Fürth.* Munich: R. Oldenbourg Verlag, 1986.

Wright, Burton. *Army of Despair: The German Volkssturm, 1944–1945.* Ann Arbor: Univ. of Michigan Press, 1983.

Wüllner, Fritz. *Die NS-Militärjustiz und das Elend der Geschichtsschreibung: Ein grundlegender Forschungsbericht.* Baden-Baden: Nomos Verlag, 1991.

Wunderlich, Werner. "'Ein Hauptbuch bey der Erziehung der deutschen Jugend . . .' Zur pädagogischen Indienstnahme des *Nibelungenliedes* für Schule und Unterricht im 19. und 20. Jahrhundert." In Joachim Heinzle and Anneliese

BIBLIOGRAPHY

Waldschmidt, eds., *Die Nibelungen. Ein deutscher Wahn, Ein deutscher Alptraum. Studien und Dokumente zur Rezeption des Niebelungstoffs im 19. und 20. Jahrhundert.* Frankfurt: Suhrkamp Verlag, 1991, pp. 119–34.

Wyman, Mark. *DP's: Europe's Displaced Persons, 1945–1951.* Ithaca: Cornell Univ. Press, 1989.

Yelton, David K. "'Ein Volk Steht Auf.' The German Volkssturm and Nazi Strategy, 1944–1945." *Journal of Military History* 64, no. 4 (October 2000): pp. 1061–83.

———. *Hitler's Volkssturm. The Nazi Militia and the Fall of Germany, 1944–1945.* Lawrence: Univ. Press of Kansas, 2002.

Ziemke, Earl F. *The U.S. Army in the Occupation of Germany, 1944–1946.* Washington, D.C.: Center for Military History, U.S. Army, 1975.

Zimmermann, Wilhelm. *Der grosse deutsche Bauernkrieg,* 6th ed. Berlin: Verl. d. Europ. Buch, 1980.

Zink, Harold. *The United States in Germany, 1944–1955.* Princeton, N.J.: Van Nostrand, 1957.

Zofka, Zdenek. "Wahlen in Bayern 1848–1994." *Der Staatsbürger* 11 (November 11, 1994): pp. 5–11.

Zühl, Antje. "Zum Verhältnis der deutschen Landbevölkerung gegenüber Zwangsarbeitern und Kriegsgefangenen." In Werner Röhr, Dietrich Eichhltz, Gerhart Hass, and Wolfgang Wippermann, eds. *Faschismus und Rassismus. Kontroversen um Ideologie und Opfer.* Berlin: Akad. Verlag, 1992, pp. 342–52.

Zurwehme, Martin. "'. . . aber die Treue ist gehalten bis in den Tod.' Der Nibelungenmythos im 19. und 20. Jahrhundert." *Geschichte lernen* 52 (1996): pp. 34–41.

INDEX

INDEX

INDEX

Germany: anger at requisition of homes, 48, 199, 236–37, 240, 244; attitudes of American soldiers toward, 46–56, 73–75, 199–201, 229; attitudes toward American occupation, 209–22; attitudes toward American soldiers, 46–48, 57–60, 207–8; attitudes toward displaced persons, 223–35, 255; attitudes toward foreign workers, 223–27; attitudes toward Jews, 237–38, 240–41, 255; denazification in, 200–203, 219–20; feminization of, 207–8, 213–15; material conditions in, 1, 31, 33, 196, 229–35, 237–38; morale in, xiv–xv, 33–37, 39–46, 49, 60, 70–71, 91, 103, 114, 117, 120, 122–23, 128, 130, 137, 141–43, 150–51, 153–54, 157–58, 169, 270–72; opposition to fraternization, 209–18; postwar anti-Semitism, 240–41; postwar desecrations of Jewish cemeteries, 28, 240; postwar sense of shame, 267–69; victim self-image of, 62, 65–66, 116, 164, 195–96

Gestapo, 9, 83, 157, 220, 226; continued activities at war's end, 140–48, 177, 271; and execution of foreign workers, 97, 225–27; German fear of, 48, 83, 157; and reports concerning national redoubt, 15–17; and *Weibersturm* of Windsheim, 145–49

G-2 (Intelligence section, U.S. Army), 15–17, 114, 203, 250

GIs: African Americans, 80, 92, 108, 180, 182, 206, 209, 217–18, 221; anti-Semitism among, 239, 242–43, 245, 252–53; attitudes toward displaced persons, 223–24, 227–30, 233–34; attitudes toward Germans, 44, 46–56, 199–201, 229; attitudes toward German soldiers, 73–75, 88–89, 92; attitude toward other nations, 55–56; and black market activity, 206, 234–35; and concentration camps, 50–55, 236, 272; and fraternization, 53–54, 200–201, 206–12, 214–18, 242, 272–73; German view of, 46–48, 57–60, 207–8;

and German youth, 200–203, 216–20; racial tension among, 216–17; relations with Jewish Displaced Persons, 235–36, 238–39, 241–43, 245–55, 273

Goebbels, Joseph: and Alpenfestung, 6–7, 9; at Burg Hoheneck, 163; and military situation in the west, 32–34, 40, 43, 60, 116–17; propaganda of, 44–45, 62–63; reaction to German civilian surrender in the west, 49, 60; and *Werwolf* program, xi–xii, 67, 196–99

Goering, Hermann, 66–67, 165
Gollachostheim, 119, 126–27
Gollach River, 103, 110–11, 113
Gollhofen, 96, 103–5, 119, 230
Gontard, Hans, 5–6
Gooch, Robert, 249–50
Gottfried, Georg, 126–28
Gottschalk (*Sturmbannführer,* Brettheim), 133–37
Götz, Ludwig, 167–68
Götz von Berlichingen, 68. *See also* SS, Seventeenth SS Panzergrenadier Division
Gray, J. Glenn, 56
Graydon, Charles, 179
Great Britain, 62–63
Grenzschutz Nordbayern, 25
Grimm, Hans, 202
Grinberg, Zalman, 255
Großhabersdorf, 162, 170
Großharbach, 96, 110
Grünsfeld, 76, 84
guerrilla warfare, 1–2, 5, 7, 9–10, 13, 18, 20, 67, 198, 202, 206–7, 221, 223, 272
Günzburg, 162, 181, 187

Haganah, 259–60, 265
Haislip, Wade, 174
Hanselmann, Friedrich, 132–37
Harmatz, Joseph, 256, 258, 260–64
Harrison, Earl G., 228, 236
Harrison, Eugene, 17
Harrison Report, 236
Hausamann, Hans, 3–4
Heckfeld, 75–77, 79
Heckfelder Wald, 75, 79

INDEX

376

INDEX

INDEX

INDEX

INDEX

INDEX

INDEX